Using
Active
Server Pages™

Special Edition

que®

Special Edition

Using

Using
Active
Server Pages™

Scot Johnson, Keith Ballinger,
Davis Chapman, et al.

que®

Special Edition Using Active Server Pages

Library of Congress Catalog No.: 97-69808

ISBN: 0-7897-1389-6

02 01 00   6 5

Interpretation of the printing code: the rightmost double-digit number is the year of the book's printing; the rightmost single-digit number, the number of the book's printing. For example, a printing code of 97-1 shows that the first printing of the book occurred in 1997.

Screen reproductions in this book were created using Collage Plus from Inner Media, Inc., Hollis, NH.

Contents at a Glance

Table of Contents

Credits

PRESIDENT
Richard Swadley

SENIOR VICE PRESIDENT/PUBLISHING
Don Fowley

GENERAL MANAGER
Joe Muldoon

MANAGER OF PUBLISHING OPERATIONS
Linda H. Buehler

EXECUTIVE EDITOR
Brad Jones

EDITORIAL SERVICES DIRECTOR
Carla Hall

MANAGING EDITOR
Jodi Jensen

ACQUISITIONS MANAGER
Cheryl D. Willoughby

ACQUISITIONS EDITOR
Kelly Marshall

PRODUCT DIRECTOR
Al Valvano

PRODUCTION EDITOR
Heather Kaufman Urschel

COORDINATOR OF EDITORIAL SERVICES
Charlotte Clapp

WEBMASTER
Thomas H. Bennett

PRODUCT MARKETING MANAGER
Kourtnaye Sturgeon

TECHNICAL EDITOR
Ramesh Chandak

SOFTWARE SPECIALIST
Brandon K. Penticuff

ACQUISITIONS COORDINATOR
Carmen Krikorian

SOFTWARE RELATIONS MANAGER
Susan D. Gallagher

SOFTWARE COORDINATOR
Andrea Duvall

EDITORIAL ASSISTANT
Jennifer L. Chisholm

BOOK DESIGNER
Ruth Harvey

COVER DESIGNER
Sandra Schroeder

PRODUCTION TEAM
Elizabeth Deeter
Shawn Ring

INDEXER
Christine Nelson

Composed in *Century Old Style* and *ITC Franklin Gothic* by Que Corporation.

To my family, for remembering to slide food under the door, and to Isaiah, the best 13-year-old Internet developer I know!

To my friends, who refused to believe my existence was more than bits and bytes.

And to all the other stones that have been overturned in my life to make me the person I am today. Scot Johnson

To my lovely wife, Lara, for believing in me. Keith Ballinger

To my son Jacob, who makes it all worth it. Steven Potts

About the Authors

Scot Johnson (yes, only one "t") (**sjohnson@i3solutions.com**) can often be found standing on a soap box preaching how Internet technologies can play a critical role in current business and communication environments. In his experience, Scot architects, develops, and manages the transition of traditional desktop and mainframe applications to the Web. Scot has written articles for various trade magazines and has been published in *Visual InterDev Unleashed*. In his free time, Scot enjoys the sweet sounds of a Fender Stratocastor, dry martinis, fine cigars, and, of course, a medium-rare steak.

Keith Ballinger is a partner with Vision Information Services, a company focused on Web development and creating tools for Web developers. Keith currently spends much of his time at client sites helping them to create the new generation of Web-based applications. When he's not working, Keith enjoys spending time with his wife and friends. He also sings and plays guitar in the Portland, Oregon-based band, Conduit.

Davis Chapman first began programming computers while working on his Master's Degree in Music Composition. Writing applications for computer music, he discovered that he enjoyed designing and developing computer software. It wasn't long before he came to the realization that he stood a much better chance of eating if he stuck with his newfound skill and demoted his hard-earned status as a "starving artist" to a part-time hobby. Since that time, Davis has focused on the art of software design and development, with a strong emphasis on the practical application of client/server technology. Davis was the lead author for Que's *Building Internet Applications with Delphi 2* and *Web Development with Visual Basic 5*, as well as a contributing author on Que's *Running a Perfect Web Site, Second Edition*, and *Platinum Edition Using Visual Basic 5*. He has been with the Dallas, Texas-based consulting firm B.R. Blackmarr & Associates for the past seven years, and can be reached at **davischa@onramp.net**.

Steven Potts is an Atlanta-based consultant specializing in Windows programming and Internet software development. He has coauthored over a dozen books on a variety of computing topics, including Visual C++, Visual Basic, and Active Server Pages.

Acknowledgments

I would like to thank Corey Burnett for ensuring that I wasn't writing technical jargon only to myself. I would also like to thank the incredible staffs at Automated Concepts, Inc., Financial Dynamics, Inc., and InterSoft Inc., for unsurpassed technical expertise, support, and inspiration. *Scot Johnson*

Thanks to everyone at Que, especially Kelly and Heather: You both have been great! I also couldn't have done this without all the great support my family, friends, and business partners have given me. Also, a special thanks to John Richardson for showing me how a real engineer works and so much else. *Keith Ballinger*

Tell Us What You Think!

As the reader of this book, you are our most important critic and commentator. We value your opinion and want to know what we're doing right, what we could do better, what areas you'd like to see us publish in, and any other words of wisdom you're willing to pass our way.

As the Executive Editor for the Programming team at Macmillan Computer Publishing, I welcome your comments. You can fax, email, or write me directly to let me know what you did or didn't like about this book—as well as what we can do to make our books stronger.

Please note that I cannot help you with technical problems related to the topic of this book, and that, due to the high volume of mail I receive, I might not be able to reply to every message.

When you write, please be sure to include this book's title and authors, as well as your name and phone or fax number. I will carefully review your comments and share them with the authors and editors who worked on the book.

Fax: 317-817-7070

Email: `adv_prog@mcp.com`

Mail: Brad Jones
        Executive Editor
        Macmillan Computer Publishing
        201 W.103rd Street
        Indianapolis, IN 46290 USA

Introduction

What do we really know about the Internet? The Internet is an unregulated band of computers that continuously share information. This information may contain fundamental truths, profound thoughts and visions, or integrated deceit and outright lies. How many people are under the impression that because they found information on the Web, that the information is absolute truth?

The only thing that can definitely be said about the Internet is that it is a network of computers that provides a vast distribution medium to a countless number of people. However, tapping into this vast resource base is only as effective as the communication mechanism between you and your target audience and the ability of the audience to receive and process the information. Speakers and television screens are useless without a transmitter to translate and receive radio and television signals. Likewise, the multitudes of thin-client browsers are rendered useless without an effective, application-oriented Web server. ■

The Purpose of This Book

With the integration of the Microsoft Internet Information Server 4.0, the Microsoft Transaction Server, and Active Server Pages, the power of distributing worthwhile applications over the Web is a reality, which leads to the vision of this book. This book is solely dedicated to demonstrating the powerful functionality of Active Server Pages to deliver real-world applications over the Web.

In order to fully understand Web application development, you first have to recognize that this environment is not the traditional development environment you are used to. Even though the phrase "it's just HTML," echoed from many IS managers' offices, many of the inherent development issues taken for granted in traditional application development are not available in the stateless world of HTTP. In addition, applications have become more content-centric rather than process-centric. The new development team now includes content creators, graphic artists, and network engineers, as well as traditional application developers, database programmers, and project managers.

Active Server Pages provide a powerful interface to develop programming logic that can be used to implement and distribute your information through applications across the Web. The book provides a systematic, hands-on approach to decrease the Web-based learning curve to implement Active Server Page technology.

Who Should Use This Book

This book is targeted for the existing application developer that has some experience developing client/server applications, yet provides a basic foundation for newer developers. Remember, the goal of this book is to provide a knowledge transfer mechanism that enables application developers to transition their existing experience developing applications into building robust, scalable, Web-based applications using Active Server Pages. At the same time, this book provides the foundation to help push beginning- and junior–level application developers into the more advanced developer roles.

This book does not require developers to have experience developing applications with Active Server Pages. This book is intended to leverage developers with some Microsoft Visual Basic skills and database development skills and apply that knowledge to Web application development. However, to help those with less experience in Web development and Visual Basic to quickly come up to speed in developing Web-based applications, Parts I and II of the book are designed to give an architecture perspective and a primer of VBScript. This primer is intended not to teach every detail of VBScript, but is designed to show developers the needed programming functionality to rapidly produce ASP applications.

How the Book Is Organized

This book is organized in a manner that demonstrates what it takes to build, develop, and deliver Web-based applications. As you might expect, it starts with the basics and proceeds to the more advanced topics. This organization goal is intended to create an environment that provides a smooth transition from the highly defined application development tools available today to the much broader development environment that forms Web-based programming.

This book is separated into six parts, each part building off the preceding to demonstrate the technical evolution of Active Server Pages. Each part of the book ends with an example chapter that demonstrates the use of the various objects and tools covered in the preceding chapters. Even though the content of each part may be technically different, all of the examples focus on using Active Server scripts to build enterprise Web-based applications.

- Part I   Introduction to Active Server Pages
- Part II   VBScript: The Foundation of Active Server Pages
- Part III   Active Server Objects: The Essential Building Blocks
- Part IV   Active Server Components
- Part V   Database Management with Active Server Pages
- Part VI   Active Server Pages and the Enterprise Solution
- Appendixes

Part I   Introduction to Active Server Pages

Part I focuses on introducing the high-level, conceptual layers needed to understand Web-based application development. This part of the book describes the differences between static and dynamic Web sites and how delivering Web-enabled applications requires a host of integrated systems working together.

Part II   VBScript: The Foundation of Active Server Pages

Part II introduces the primary scripting language driving Active Server Pages functionality. VBScript provides the interpretation or processing layer between the requesting browser and server-side data storage units. Active Server Pages use VBScript to convert coded processing logic into native HTML. The pure HTML output is then accessible to any HTML-compatible browser type.

Part III   Active Server Objects: The Essential Building Blocks

Part III demonstrates the core functionality of Active Server Pages. Active Server Pages are comprised of six programmable objects that are used to manipulate, manage, and control the various aspects of Web processing. This part focuses on identifying the scope and composition of Active Server Pages applications and how each object can be utilized in delivering your Web-based applications.

Part IV   Active Server Components

Part IV discovers how components can be used to implement additional functionality on your Web site and Web server applications. These components can be used to perform application functionality that might not be made available through native VBScript. Furthermore, these components provide the basic links to tap into other information stores accessible to the Web servers. This part of the book closes with the creation of a sample Web site that uses most of the installed Internet Information Server components.

Part V   Database Management with Active Server Pages

Part V focuses on using the ActiveX Data Object to provide a rich set of database functionality. Active Serve Pages can use the Active Data Object to insert, update, and delete information from any ODBC-compliant database. This section wraps up by adding database functionality to an online catalog Web site.

Part VI   Active Server Pages and the Enterprise Solution

Part VI demonstrates how Active Server Pages technology is used within a variety of Web-based systems to help build, manage, and distribute your Web applications. This part of the book demonstrates using the Microsoft Transaction Server to maximize resource and database connection-polling features, how to use the Visual InterDev ASP development tool, and how to manage your site with the Internet Information Server 4.0. Further, this part of the book explains the role of the Microsoft Message Queue Server and how to build intranet/extranet capabilities for your sites and applications. This part of the book ends with converting the sample Web online catalog registration system into a distributed n-tier application database-driven application.

Conventions Used in This Book

Que has over a decade of experience developing and publishing the most successful computer books available. With that experience, we've learned what special features help readers the most. Look for these special features throughout the book to enhance your learning experience.

The following font conventions are used in this book to help make reading it easier:

- *Italic type* is used to introduce new terms.
- Screen messages, code listings, and command samples appear in `monospace type`.
- Shortcut keys are denoted with underscores.

 Tips present advice on a quick or often overlooked procedure. These include shortcuts.

CAUTION

Cautions warn you about potential problems that may cause unexpected results or mistakes to avoid.

N O T E Notes present interesting or useful information that isn't necessarily essential to the discussion. A note provides additional information that may help you avoid problems or offers advice that relates to the topic. ▨

This is an exciting time to be an application developer. The new Web-based application development paradigm presents exciting challenges in the world of application development. As we begin to see how the Web is slowly being integrated in many aspects of our lives, this book is intended to make designing, developing, and deploying ASP applications a reality.

Introduction to Active Server Pages

Getting Started with Web Enabling: Creating Dynamic Applications with Active Server Pages

The goal of this chapter is to provide the basic framework and architectural concepts needed to Web-enable your applications. To accomplish this, I will identify and discuss the ever-growing number of Web technologies that collectively are needed to build and deliver your Web-based systems. The secondary goal of this chapter is to help define the impact of COM technology on Web development, the application developer, training and delivery requirements, and infrastructure costs.

First and foremost, I want to clearly define what the term *Active Server Pages* means to Web-based application development. Active Server Pages is a new technology from Microsoft that provides the capability for the Web server to process application logic and then deliver standard HTML to the client browser. The results can then be delivered to a variety of client-side Web technologies, such as standard HTML, ActiveX, Java, browser plug-ins, and DHTML. Although fairly straightforward, this simple concept has great ramifications in shifting traditional applications to the Web. The first direct

Static Content versus Dynamic Content

Learn the differences between static content and dynamic content.

The Changing Internet Application Architecture

Learn how all the different pieces of the extended Internet architecture fit together to deliver Web-based applications.

The Dynamic Content Revolution

Learn how dynamic content applications have evolved over time, and how COM has formed the foundation of dynamic content.

Active Server Pages and the ActiveX Platform

Discover how Active Server Pages and the ActiveX platform are used to extend Web server functionality and the benefits Active Server Pages bring to Web-enabling your applications.

result of using Active Server Pages is that only HTML is sent to the client's browser. ASPs do not automatically send ActiveX controls to the browser. By default, ASPs send only ASCII text to the browser. This lets any browser types running on any operating systems to access the applications and workflow logic embedded in the ASP scripts.

Active Server Pages give you the ability to deliver more than just HTML. ASP enables you to deliver HTML, client-side scripting, Web controls, and server-side processing and connectivity features. ASP scripts can deliver client-side scripts, such as VBScript and JavaScript, to be executed on the client's browser. In addition, ASP can also deliver a wide range of Web functionality by acting as a transfer vehicle for ActiveX controls, Java applets, and other Web components. In addition, ASPs not only produce dynamic HTML depending on the client request, but also provide the capability to tap into existing systems, such as databases, document retrieval services, mail servers, groupware servers, and other COM-based information servers. ASPs now act as an HTML interpreter that was once only accessible through native interfaces, such a Microsoft Exchange client, Lotus Notes client, or a customized Visual Basic application. With the wide range of functionality, Active Server Pages and the Internet Information Server act as a medium for porting existing applications to—and building new applications for—the Web. ■

Static versus Dynamic Content

The World Wide Web has progressed from Web pages that couldn't support images to a global network capable of supporting full-scale applications. This transition is made possible through changing static information into dynamic, database-driven applications using logic executed on the Web server.

Static Content

The World Wide Web was initially created to share textual documents around the world. These textual documents were static documents that served primarily as online reference materials. The term *static* is used to refer to these documents because the requesting user had no ability to interact with the content delivered from the Web server. These documents were converted from their original source type into *Hypertext Markup Language* (HTML). Once in HTML format, the document could be delivered from a Web server to any Web browser using the *Hypertext Transfer Protocol* (HTTP). This static approach to creating and reading Web pages and Web content is still used in many sites today to display personal information, corporate profiles, or online reference material that does not frequently change (see Figure 1.1).

Dynamic HTML Content

The billboard approach, or the posting of static information on the Web, suited the needs for general information dissemination. However, the Web user community started to require greater functionality from this vast information medium called the Internet. This need for advanced functionality using dynamic content eventually grew into the need to develop and deploy entire applications that used the World Wide Web as a global network. The term *dynamic* describes the process of creating HTML content depending on the information that is sent or submitted to the Web server. The Web server would process the information and convert the output into HTML. The resultant HTML, tailored for the specific user input and application settings, is then delivered to the browser. Figure 1.2 shows an example of dynamic content at the Federal Express Web site. The FedEx tracking site uses information entered by the user to track the location of a package. If you know the Airbill tracking number, country destination, and ship date, the Web application searches the FedEx tracking information storage system and returns the location of the package.

Part
I

Ch
1

FIG. 1.1

Traditional corporate Web sites are often examples of static content.

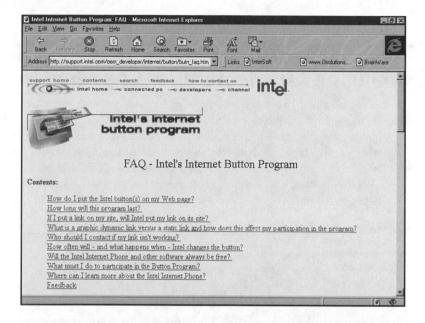

FIG. 1.2

Dynamic HTML enables the HTML content to change depending on the information submitted by the user.

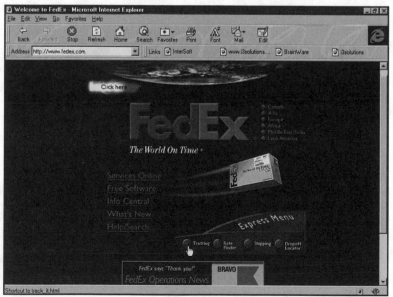

Initially, sites would process small pieces of information, such as accepting user information from a customer feedback page. This information could be stored in text files, converted to an e-mail message, or displayed back to the requesting user for verification. But eventually, these smaller modules gained more flexibility by performing calculations and reading and writing to databases until Web-based applications began to emerge. Soon, as the benefits of developing and deploying applications over the World Wide Web became apparent, the conversion of standard desktop applications into a Web-based format had begun.

Designing and Deploying Web-Enabled Applications: A Changing Architecture for Changing Needs

Developing Web-based applications relies on many network and application components working together to deliver information to the requesting client. In the once simple world of HTTP, Web browsers extracted information from Web servers, as shown in Figure 1.3. This Web-based architecture relied on existing network infrastructure and the TCP/IP protocol stack to broadcast, carry, route, and assemble in-transit data. TCP/IP is not exclusively used with the World Wide Web; it is also used in other services such as Gopher, File Transfer Protocol (FTP), and Telnet.

FIG. 1.3

The simple data-sharing architecture that formed the premise of the World Wide Web.

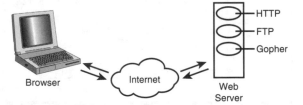

However, after some standardization of HTML languages, image specifications, and protocol stacks, the world slowly began to see the Internet for what it is: a global network of computers. This band of network computers is owned by a combination of public and private localized networks. These networks consist of private and public organizations and government organizations that pay and maintain these backbones.

Although there is not a centralized organization unit for controlling the Internet itself, there are several organizations that propose standards and guidelines on how the Internet should be used. For example, the Internet Activities Board (IAB) is responsible for reviewing Internet networking issues, such as architecture and TCP/IP and domain name issues. The World Wide Web Consortium (W3C) suggests guidelines and standardization for the World Wide Web.

With so many forces influencing how the Internet behaves and operates, utilizing this global network in the same way you use your own private network presents many challenges. To transform the global network into a reliable application platform, the original architecture of the Web must be enhanced to meet many needs that we take for granted when developing traditional applications. The enhanced architecture to develop and deploy your Web-enabled applications can be seen in Figure 1.4.

FIG. 1.4
The evolution of Web architecture to support the basic needs of a Web-enabled application.

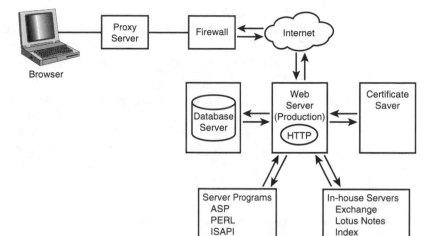

As you can see, not only is there a dramatic shift in the number of components now needed to create, develop, and deploy applications, but there is also a fundamental shift in the method for developing applications. For the past several years, the shift to client/server architecture has crept into IT shops around the world. The client/server world relies on the processing power found on the client machine to off load server requests and processing loads.

However, the benefits of distributing the processing onto the client in traditional client/server applications are quickly overshadowed by the amount of manpower needed to deploy and update applications. As you saw in Figure 1.4, the Web-based architecture represents a shift back to the server-centric deployment model. This model enables a centralized deployment and distribution mechanism without relying on individual client configurations. Furthermore, the server-centric model also enables a central connection point to external resources, such as in-house data stores like Microsoft Exchange, Lotus Notes, or your own custom-built proprietary data systems. Let's take a closer look at the different components needed in the new Web architecture paradigm.

The Web Browser

The Web browser provides a graphical, text-based terminal interface to the Web server. This terminal approach provides an interface between the user and the Web server. The Web browser is responsible for translating HTML sent by the Web server into a graphical user interface within the browser.

The choice of Web browser is often directly related to the needs of the targeted user. For example, if one design goal of your Web application is to reach the largest user group, your application should rely only on HTML standards, which can be used to deliver information to all browsers. However, if your targeted user group is somewhat more defined, you can design your solutions to take advantage of the special characteristics of the planned user community. For example, if you need to build an intranet application in which all desktops are running

Windows 95 and NT operating systems, you can use ActiveX controls that run in Internet Explorer. If your application assumes the use of Internet Explore 3.0 or Netscape Navigator 3.0 and up, an HTML-only or HTML and Java applet application can be deployed. In most situations, you will find that defining your targeted user community will dictate the look and feel of your applications and Web browser.

The Web browser can also use client-side *scripting* to perform tasks and operations within the browser. Scripting languages such as JavaScript, JScript, and VBScript are used to reduce server processing and network bandwidth by performing actions such as field validation or calculations within the requesting browser. For example, you can create a mini-online help system by displaying a help message when the user moves the mouse over a hyperlink.

The Web Server

The Web server has several responsibilities that all center around delivering HTML to the requesting client browser. The traditional billboard or information-sharing approach, which initially created the need for the World Wide Web, quickly demanded more functionality from the user community. The Web servers were soon able to process executable scripts that gave needed functionality and connectivity to other systems, as you saw in Figure 1.2. The capability to process and establish these connections to other server-side components is made possible through program execution on the server from various executable sources. Some of these sources include the Common Gateway Interface (CGI), ISAPI, PERL, REXX, Java, VBScript, and JScript. All of these processes are aimed at developing application logic that is processed on the server. The server-side scripts, either acting as stand-alone applications or embedded in Active Server Pages, can be used to transform the Web server into a gateway that exposes information stored in other servers. In particular, the Internet Information Server can access information from database servers, mail and news servers, or any other COM-based server, such as Lotus Notes or Microsoft Exchange.

The HTTP-TCP/IP Connection

One of the most amazing features of the Internet is that all the Internet technologies are based on sending and receiving simple ASCII text. The ASCII text is transferred via *TCP/IP*. TCP/IP is responsible for wrapping or packaging data into smaller packages and sending the information across the network. These smaller packages each have a destination address that is used to route and re-route the packages. Therefore, packets can take a variety of approaches to reaching the destination depending on network loads. When the data packets are received at the destination, the data is re-assembled back into a complete document. TCP/IP also performs error checking to ensure that no data packets were lost in transit. TCP itself is a connection-based protocol, which is responsible for establishing a communication session between a client and server.

The HTTP service runs as an application on the Web server, and is responsible for managing the Hypertext Transfer Protocol. HTTP is a client/server protocol that accepts requests and delivers requests via HTML. However, unlike most traditional client/server applications such as FTP and Gopher, once HTTP delivers the information to the requesting client, the connection or persistence is released. This feature was built into the original design of HTTP. HTTP was designed to accept and handle large numbers of client requests. To maximize the number of potential clients, HTTP typically releases the connection after the information is delivered by the server to minimize the number of busy or concurrent connections.

Services such as FTP and Gopher, however, keep the connection between the client and server open until the session is terminated. If a user has an open connection to the server but is not transmitting any data, the connection is still kept open, possibly preventing other users from connecting to the server. Fortunately, the inherent drawbacks of the connectionless HTTP protocol can be avoided (depending on the client configuration) by using the HTTP KeepAlive request.

The HTTP KeepAlive request maintains a TCP connection between the client and server (if both the server and client's browser are configured to use this feature). The importance of the KeepAlive function arises when you need to ensure that information delivered from the server is completely transmitted to the requesting browser. When the client receives the complete data stream, a trigger indicating a completed transmission is returned to the server. The HTTP KeepAlive also enables multiple requests over one connection. Because every item on a Web page generates individual server requests, the KeepAlive session will increase performance by using one concurrent connection to the HTTP server instead of having to spend resources making separate connections.

By itself, the HTTP service is incapable of directly interfacing with the network interface to exchange data. The Web server relies on Windows Sockets and the Transportation Layer and Internet Protocol (IP) to provide the communication layer between the HTTP service and the network interface, as shown in Figure 1.5.

FIG. 1.5
The Internet Service Suite relies on Windows Sockets to translate data from the network interface to the HTTP, FTP, and Gopher service layers.

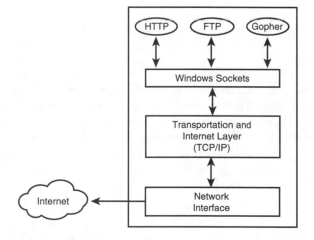

The Database Server

The database server plays a vital role in Internet application development. The database server can be used to store, search, and retrieve information that is stored in a database. This same database that distributes information to Web users can also be accessed and maintained from within your corporate walls. For example, a database can be used for an online class registration system where users can search the database for classes they are interested in and register for classes via the Web. The administration department can then access this same information to process the new class registration from either a traditional application built with a tool such as Visual Basic, C++, Delphi, or PowerBuilder, or it can access the information via a browser interface.

When using the HTTP server as a connection utility to database servers, there is a slight shift in architecture that differs from traditional application development. For example, suppose you are creating an online classified section for your local newspaper and you want to create a search mechanism that searches for all vehicles of a particular type. From an architecture perspective, this application will have three components: the requesting browser, the Web server, and the database server (see Figure 1.6). The browser is responsible for submitting query requests and displaying the results from the database. The Web server is responsible for accepting the query from the browser, creating a connection to the database, querying the database, formatting the results into HTML, and delivering the HTML to the requesting browser. The database server is responsible for accepting requests from the Web server and delivering results back to the Web server.

FIG. 1.6
When accessing database information from a Web browser, the Web server acts as the client to the database server.

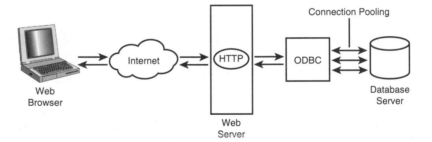

Notice that a database connection is not made directly from the browser to the database server. Instead, the database connection is established only between the Web server and the database server. As a result, the Web server—not the Web browser—acts as the client to the database server. This point is particularly important when you create and administer permissions to your database server. The Internet Information Server automatically creates an NT user account named *IUSR_computername* to accept anonymous requests from browsers. In order for you to create a connection from the Web server to the database server, the *IUSR_computername* user account must have permissions on the database server.

Proxy Servers

Proxy servers are designed to mimic the functionality of the browser cache, but instead of being applied at the browser level, they are applied at the network level. This temporary cache stores Web page information when a user first downloads it. This information can then be accessed by additional users from the proxy server, instead of users retrieving information from the site itself.

Although proxy servers increase the apparent speed of the Internet connection, they can cause problems when developing applications for the Web. For example, because the proxy server is designed to act as a replacement for the Web server, how do you ensure that the user is receiving the results from the Web server and not the proxy server cache? Furthermore, not all proxy servers support the different security authentication methods, such as NT Challenge/ Response (NTLM) password authentication.

Firewalls

A *firewall* is a combination of hardware and/or software that is designed to keep private networks secure. Although firewalls are intended to keep internal networks free from hackers, often these same firewalls prevent you from delivering applications to your users. For example, depending on the security permissions assigned by the firewall administrators, firewalls can prevent cookies, ActiveX controls, and Java applets from reaching the requesting browser. If users of your Web-based applications are reporting irregular behavior, remember to check possible firewall and proxy server limitations.

Certificate Servers

As the popularity of the Internet explodes, people are finding new ways to exploit this global network of computers. Companies are using the Internet as an extension of their own private networks by offering access to internal information for their employees or customers through the public Internet. This capability to access private intranet information via an Internet connection is often referred to as an *extranet*, which requires explicit security configuration and management.

However, protecting the private network is only half the security concern. Protective measures must also be in place to ensure user security and privacy rights. For example, what assurance does a user have that the online catalog site he is about to place a credit card order with is really the company the site portrays it to be? Unfortunately, this is one of the largest disadvantages of having an unregulated global network with no central administration unit. Anybody can place information on the Web, with no preventative measures to ensure that this information is accurate or true.

The *certificate server* was developed to help ensure data integrity for your Web sites or applications. Data integrity is composed of two parts. The first part, client and server authentication, is often overlooked. On the public Internet, third-party vendors offer authentication services to verify the identity and validity of the Web server and Web browser. However, if you are building an application for your intranet or extranet, you do not have to rely on these external sources for authentication. The certificate server helps to ease this burden of proof for client and server authentication by enabling you to issue digital certificates. These digital certificates can then be administered and managed by the certificate server to regulate entrance to a particular site or application.

After user and server identification has been properly established, the second part of maintaining data integrity over the Internet is to ensure data protection while information is being transferred from the Web server to the client browser. The certificate server uses the digital certificates with client and server encryption schemes, such as Secure Socket Layers (SSL) and Private Communication Technology (PCT) protocols, to ensure data integrity.

External Servers

One of the most exciting aspects of moving to a server-centric application deployment model is the capability to use the HTTP server as a gateway to other application servers. These other application servers can consist of pre-built application-based software, such as Microsoft Exchange, the Index Server, or the News Server. However, you are not limited to these canned applications. You can build your own application server to meet your specific application needs. This flexible method for extending the reach of your Web server into other applications presents exciting opportunities for Web-based application development. Now these servers, which were once accessible only via a proprietary client interface, can be accessed by any browser anywhere in the world.

The Evolution of Active Server Pages

The concept of processing application logic on the Web server and connecting to external servers from the Web server is not a new idea specific to Active Server Pages. The capability to create dynamic HTML by sending information to an executable file existed before the emergence of Active Server Pages through the Common Gateway Interface.

Common Gateway Interface

The *Common Gateway Interface* (CGI) was one of the first methods used to create dynamic HTML. CGI enables direct communications between the HTTP server and executable scripts. Programming in CGI provided a standard communication and processing mechanism between the requesting client browser, the gateway program, and the HTTP server. The CGI programs help create a standard interface with the HTTP server to eliminate having to learn the specifics of Hypertext Transfer Protocol.

CGI programs are usually written in a scripting language such as the Practical Extraction and Report Language (PERL). The early PERL scripts were created to run in UNIX because the early HTTP servers only existed on the UNIX platform. However, with the emergence of HTTP servers for NT, the Internet Information Server supports PERL 5.0 scripts. To initiate a CGI executable, simply reference the name of the executable script and pass any required parameters as shown below:

```
<A Href = "/myCGIscripts/CalcInterest.exe?Principal=300000"> Calculate Interest
using CGI</A>
```

In this example, the script named `CalcInterest.exe` is created and passed an argument named `Principal` with the value of `300000`.

When a PERL script is called on the Web server, the Web server treats the PERL script as a separate executable. This executable program is not limited to just one script; it can consist of multiple scripts running on separate machines. However, because the hosting server treats CGI applications as separate executables, a new process is created for each instance in which the CGI application is called. Creating new processes on the server is a very expensive resource task and can cause significant resource drain and performance issues, especially when considering scalability issues as your Web sites and applications grow. Furthermore, CGI applications suffer from the inability to share information across applications. This is because each new CGI process is created within its own memory space and cannot dynamically share information with other memory spaces of other instantiated CGI programs.

Internet Server Application Programming Interface

The *Internet Server Application Programming Interface* (*ISAPI*) builds on the lessons learned from the shortcomings found in CGI applications. ISAPI shares the same functional aspects of CGI programming but differs from traditional CGI programming in the way the script is executed. ISAPI relies on loading scripts into the HTTP server's memory space to reduce the resource drain required to create a new process, as shown in Figure 1.7. The significance of using a shared memory space is that all the resources made available to the HTTP service are now made available to the ISAPI applications.

FIG. 1.7
ISAPI applications are loaded in the same memory space as the HTTP server.

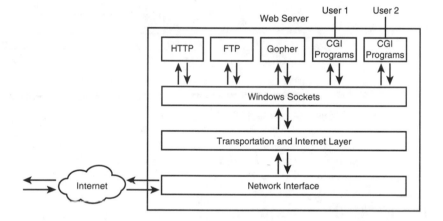

However, as in most situations, often the greatest strength of a product is also its greatest weakness. Careful and thorough coding and testing must be used when creating an ISAPI application. Because the ISAPI application shares the same memory space as the HTTP server, if the ISAPI application crashes, you can also bring down the HTTP server. If the ISAPI application terminates without cleaning up the corrupted memory space, runaway processes or memory leaks could result.

ISAPI is implemented in one of two ways: either as an ISAPI application or as an ISAPI filter. *ISAPI applications* are used to encapsulate the functionality found in traditional desktop applications, but now load that logic into the Web-based arena. To reference an ISAPI application, use the same methodology used to reference the CGI executable by calling the ISAPI DLL and passing the appropriate filters, as shown in the following code:

```
<A Href = "/myCGIscripts/CalcInterest.DLL?Principal=300000"> Calculate Interest
using ISAPI</A>
```

ISAPI filters are used to process information being sent to the HTTP server and post-process the HTTP server responses. The filter acts as an analytical tool to monitor information being sent to and being generated from the HTTP server and acts as another layer protecting the HTTP server from the network layer (see Figure 1.8).

FIG. 1.8

ISAPI filters wrap the HTTP server with conditioners for pre- and post-processing capabilities.

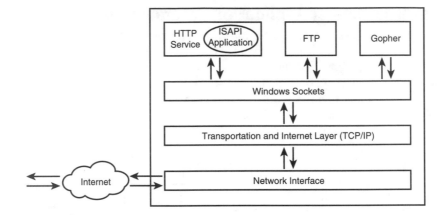

This inline filtering capability can provide extensive functionality to your Web server. For example, you can use ISAPI filters to provide public or customizable encryption, authentication, and compression schemes. Furthermore, you can use ISAPI filters to initiate authentication methods, create advance-logging features, or scan incoming requests to thwart possible security attacks. With the Internet Information Server 4.0, ISAPI applications and filters can be applied not only globally across the entire server, but also to specific applications residing on the server.

The HTML Object Model

Up to this point, I have focused largely on the various servers and server components needed to create dynamic content. However, to fully consider the entire Internet architecture, you also have to consider how the browser translates and organizes the HTML sent to it from the Web server.

Just as programming languages adhere to a defined specification identifying the structure of the language, each Web browser follows its own internal model or blueprint that defines how the browser operates. The *object model* usually represents a hierarchical organization chart that identifies the different relationships between objects and collections for the particular browser system. For example, Figure 1.9 illustrates the Internet Explorer object model.

In most situations when you design Web-enabled applications, you only have to consider the specific browser's object model when you develop client-side scripts. These scripts, interpreted within the browser, provide advanced functionality not found in native HTML. Client-side scripting languages, such as JavaScript, VBScript, and JScript, are used to manipulate the content delivered by the server. The scripts manage the content by manipulating the object model of the browser. Typically, this involves controlling the object model as a response to a particular user event. This client-side programming functionality can be as complex as you need it to be. For example, the HTML object model is used when the user navigates to a different frame page, as shown in the following example:

```
<A Href = "/frames/readme.htm" TARGET = "frmain">Terms and Conditions</A>
```

FIG. 1.9
Browser object models define how the browser controls and organizes the HTML delivered by the Web server.

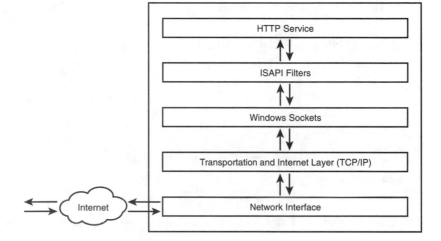

When user clicks the `Terms and Conditions` link, the HTML model is responsible for displaying the `readme.html` in the frame window named `frmain`. The client-side scripts work the object model to manipulate the information. The HTML object model can be used to read and extract information from or about a page. For example, the HTML object model exposes the hierarchical navigation to determine how many frames are located on a page, as shown in the following code:

```
Window.Document.Frames.Count
```

Furthermore, client-side scripting can be used manipulate the HTML objects on a page. For example, the following code illustrates a JavaScript function, named `SetValue`, which is used to set the value of a check box named `chkReturnEmail`:

```
<SCRIPT LANGUAGE = "JavaScript">
    Function SetValue(){
        If (Document.FrmData.ChkReturnEmail.Checked){
            Document.FrmData.ChkReturnEmail.Value = "True"
        }
        Else{
            Document.FrmData.ChkReturnEmail.Value = "False"
        }
    }
</SCRIPT>
```

This script uses the HTML object model to determine whether a check box named `chkReturnEmail` is selected. The HTML object model is used to set the hierarchical relationship between objects on the page. For example, an HTML check box named `chkReturnEmail` is located on a HTML form named `frmData`. The `JavaScript` function uses the HTML hierarchy to check if check box is selected. If the check box is selected, the script function sets the value of the check box to `True`. This value would then be sent to the Web server when the page is submitted.

Keep in mind that the object models for different browsers differ slightly. As a result, your Web-based applications should be thoroughly tested to ensure compatibility across browsers and client-side scripting engines.

Dynamic HTML Object Model

As the evolution of HTML continues, the Dynamic HTML object model expands the functionality found in the standard HTML object model. The Dynamic HTML object model now enables almost complete control over all aspects of Web pages by expanding properties of the document object, as shown in Figure 1.10.

FIG. 1.10
The new Dynamic HTML object model enables greater control of pages.

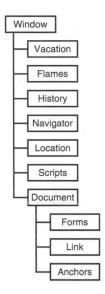

This new and improved object model embraces using stylesheets, content positioning, and downloadable fonts to control the look and feel of your sites and applications. Stylesheets enable Web page authors to control the visual characteristics of their sites from a single template. The visual style components for an entire site, such as alignment and font attributes, can be managed from a single template file. New content-positioning features eliminate the limitations of positioning items that existed in standard HTML. In standard HTML, you could not layer items, such as text or images, on top of each other. Dynamic HTML gives you the capability to layer items on an Web page. In addition, Dynamic HTML also enables the capability to download fonts that are required for the design or display effect for your site. Downloadable fonts eliminate the dependence of having to rely on fonts that have been previously installed on the client's machine.

Dynamic HTML is intended to give greater flexibility in programming functionality and controlling and regulating how the site is displayed. In order to use these new features of Dynamic HTML, a Dynamic HTML-compatible browser is required. Internet Explorer 4.0 and Netscape Communicator 4.0 browsers support the Dynamic HTML standard. However, regardless of what client interprets it, the HTML is still delivered from functionality to process application logic on the Web server.

Active Server Pages and The Active Server Model: A COM-Based Evolution

Active, active, active. Everything released from Microsoft has the tag "Active" attached to it: Active Server Pages, Active servers, ActiveX controls, the ActiveX framework, ActiveX Control Pad, and Active scripting. The goal for this section is to define the implications that the "Active" tag carries and what it means for applications that you want to port to the Web.

The Active revolution can trace its origins back to the development of the *Common Object Model* (*COM*). COM was a standard developed by Microsoft to create a standard communication mechanism between components. This binary standard would enable non-vendor specific components to interface with each other. When components had a communication standard, cross-vendor components should share their property methods and events with other components. This process of activating another component's properties, methods, and events is known as *OLE automation*.

An example of OLE automation is the capability to embed an Excel spreadsheet in a Word document. However, the OLE automation offers great flexibility in application development. You can create your own OLE servers in COM-based tools that expose their methods to calling programs. These OLE servers can be interfaced from native Win32 clients, such as Visual Basic, Delphi, and PowerBuilder applications, or from middle-tier components, such as the Web server. OLE automation servers can be created as stand-alone executables (.exe) or they can exist as process Dynamic Link Libraries. As stand-alone executables, the OLE servers perform in a similar manner to CGI scripts, where the application is created as a new process in its own memory space. You can also compile your OLE server as a DLL to create ISAPI application and filters.

The reach of COM automation originally enabled OLE controls, or OCX controls, to decrease development time by adding extra functionality to the native application development environment, such as Visual Basic or Delphi. These controls represent pre-canned functionality that would otherwise have to be coded by hand. For example, a grid OCX control could be added to a Visual Basic form to retrieve, filter, and display information from a database into a grid layout. This drag-and-drop database functionality would have taken a considerable amount of time if that functionality had to be coded by hand. These OLE controls have been recompiled and optimized as ActiveX controls to add that same functionality to Web pages.

Distributed COM (*DCOM*) is a Microsoft standard that enables COM objects to communicate across machine boundaries regardless of network configurations. This distributed component communication mechanism is the foundation that provides the Internet Information Server and

Active Server Pages the flexibility to communicate with other COM-based systems. For example, this functionality enables you to expose database information from any ODBC-compliant data source, access mainframe data via the SNA server, and extract information from COM-based servers, such as Lotus Notes, Exchange, or your own customized server.

Active Server Pages represent the capability to process application logic on the Web server. The ASP scripting engine can process any script-compliant language, such as VBScript and JScript. These script-compliant languages are referred to as ActiveX scripts because they can be processed on the Web server. The ActiveX scripting engine is actually a COM component itself.

Furthermore, the ActiveX scripting engine can also process requests made by non-ActiveX scripting languages, such as PERL, LISP, and REXX scripts. The process that makes this possible is using COM to provide an OLE wrapper around these scripts. This wrapper acts as an interpreter between the non-ActiveX scripts and the ActiveX scripting language.

Furthermore, ActiveX documents refer to the same process of converting OLE controls to ActiveX controls, but instead of being applied at the individual component level, COM technology is applied at the application level. ActiveX documents refer to the capability to load entire applications as a COM object within the Internet Explorer.

As you can see, COM provides ASPs with great functionality to access various information stores on the server side and deliver that information—as HTML—to the client. However, the flexibility is not necessarily guaranteed when delivering solutions via client-side ActiveX controls or ActiveX documents. Keep in mind that in order to load the ActiveX controls or ActiveX documents, the requesting browser must be COM compatible, meaning the ActiveX controls and documents must be compatible with both the browser and the browser's operating system. Using client-side ActiveX controls may not be the best solution to reach the maximum of users on the Internet, but they do provide great value for intranet/extranet applications. Intranet/extranet applications are unique because, in most situations, the user group's development platform is standardized and well defined. This standardization enables you to tailor your solutions to the user group's profile instead of trying to deliver a solution to the lowest common denominator.

The Composition of Active Server Pages

As you can see, most of the Internet Information Server's expanded connectivity features are a result of the processing of logic in Active Server Pages. Active Server Pages are text-based files comprised of a combination of HTML tags and Active Server scripts. The Active Server scripts, whether written in VBScript, JScript, or your own script-compliant language, are interpreted by the Active Server engine. The Active Server scripts usually contain variables, operators, and statements to control the application logic processed by the server. For more detailed information about the specifics of an ASP application, please refer to Chapter 10, "The Composition of an Active Server Application."

ASP Delimiters   Active Server scripts are distinguished on the page from HTML tags (> and < symbols) and normal content by using the <% and %> delimiters. The delimiters can either be grouped to contain multiple lines of script code or can be embedded within HTML tags. For example, the following example demonstrates assembling a group of VBScript Active Server scripts into a subroutine:

```
<%
Sub CalcNewBalanceRef(ByRef Balance)
    Balance = FormatCurrency(Balance+Balance*22.5/100/12)    '=== Calculate
Balance
    Response.Write Balance                                   '=== Write balance
to page
End Sub
%>
```

Alternatively, you can integrate HTML tags with Active Server tags, as shown below:

```
<%@ LANGUAGE="VBSCRIPT" %>
<HTML>
<BODY><Title>Date Printed: <% = Now %> </Title>         <!--Prints Current Time
and Date
<% If Session("NewUser") Then %>                         <!--Checks if this is a
new user
    <P>Welcome to the online reservation system</P>     <!--Prints generic
message
<% Else %>                                              <!--User is
registered
    <P>Welcome back, <% Session("UserName") %>! </P>    <!--Creates custom
message
<% End If>
</BODY>
</HTML>
```

This example uses several inline delimiters to create dynamic content when a user enters the page. Inline delimiters are used write the current system time to the HTML title tag. The Active Server script then checks session variables to determine whether the user is a new user or if he has been to the site before. If the user is a new user, a generic Welcome message is displayed. However, if the user has been to the site before, a customized message displaying the user name is shown on the page.

Setting the ASP Scripting Language   There are two different ways to set the scripting language that will process the ActiveX scripting logic. The first method is to rely on the default scripting language of the Internet Information Server, VBScript. However, relying on the default scripting language is not always a good practice. As Web sites and applications grow, you may have to move your application to other servers where the default scripting language is not the same as the one you delivered your scripts in. To prevent errors because of an incorrect scripting language trying to interpret your scripts, use the LANGUAGE attribute to explicitly define the proper scripting interpreter, as shown here:

```
<%@ LANGUAGE="VBSCRIPT" %>
```

If JScript was the desired scripting language, use JScript with the LANGUAGE tag, as shown here:

```
<%@ LANGUAGE = JScript %>
```

Alternatively, server-side scripting can be implemented outside the Active Server delimiters by using the <SCRIPT> tag and the RUNAT attribute. For example, the following code creates a function called dbNull that is used to eliminate NULLs when writing information from a database.

```
<SCRIPT RUNAT=Server LANGUAGE="VBScript">
<!--
Function dbNull(vDBText)
    Dim Ret                      '=== Initializes variable
    If IsNull(vDBText) Then      '=== Test Null condition
        Ret = ""                 '=== set variable to zero-length string
    Else
        Ret = Trim(vDBText)      '=== Trim and blank spaces
    End If
    dbNull = Ret                 '=== Return result back to function
End Function
-->
</SCRIPT>
```

Keep in mind that an Active Server Page does not have to contain any HTML to use the Active Server Page functionality. For example, the following code sample automatically routes the requesting browser to another page at /newlocation/default.asp:

```
<% Response.Redirect "/newlocation/default.asp"    '=== Routes browsers to new
location %>
```

Automatically routing users to a new page location (if your site/application has moved or has changed filenames) is a common technique.

You can build from this concept and create Active Server Pages that do not display any ML content but are just used to process application logic and workflow. For example, in the following script, if a new user enters a site, he is automatically routed to the Registar.asp. If the user is not a new member, he sees the Member.asp.

```
<%
If Session("NewUser") Then            '=== Check to see if the user is a new user
Response.Redirect "/Register.asp"     '=== Automatically directs to register site
Else
Response.Redirect "/Member.asp"       '=== Directs user to the members site
End If
%>
```

Variables, Operators, and Statements   In order to process application logic and workflow, each scripting language has its own specific syntax that is used to define and set variables, use operators for comparing items, and use statements to help define and organize the code.

Active Server Components and Objects   The scripting variables, operators, and statements can be used to tap into special Active Server tools that add programming functionality to the ActiveX Server. These tools consist of Active Server objects and Active Server components. Active Server objects are built-in objects that collectively represent the functionality of the ActiveX Server. Six individual objects are used to dissect the different roles and responsibilities of the server into manageable and programmable aspects. For example, the `Request` object is responsible for retrieving or accepting information from the browser. Another Active Server object, the `Response` object, is responsible for sending information to the client. The `Session` object is responsible for managing information for a specific user session. The `Server` object is responsible for the administrative functionality of the server. The `Application` object is used to manage all information in the ASP application. The `ObjectContext` object is used manage transaction processing for components managed by the Microsoft Transaction Server. The objects will be covered in greater detail in Part III, "Active Server Objects: The Essential Building Blocks."

Active Server components run on the server to provide extra functionality that extends the reach of the Active Server Page beyond the Web server. For example, you can use Active Server components to create a database connection; create, send, and manage e-mail; determine the requesting browser type; and much more. Furthermore, you are not limited to only the components that ship with the Internet Information Server; you can build and distribute your own components. For more information on the components that ship with the IIS 4.0, see Chapter 17, "Implementing Existing Server-Side Components." For more information on building your own components, please see Chapter 18, "Creating Your Own Active Server Components." Chapter 28, "Working with the Microsoft Transaction Server," illustrates how to use the Transaction Server to manage your components.

Server Side Includes   Your Active Server Pages can also use *Server Side Includes* (SSI). SSI enables you to insert information from a text file into your Active Server Pages before the page is interpreted. Server Side Includes are very useful for adding information that is common across multiple pages, such as header, toolbar, or footer information. For example, includes are used to display footer information such as copyright information or contact information. Furthermore, Server Side Includes are particularly useful as you start developing vast libraries of scripting functions that can easily be inserted into your Active Server Pages.

From Here...

In this chapter, I have covered the basic principles needed to Web-enable your site or application. Having an overview of the ever-expanding Web architecture is critical when considering building and deploying secure, robust, and scalable Internet-based solutions. This chapter has discussed the migration from static to dynamic content, as well as shown how the evolution of COM has transformed OLE and OCX technology from client-side ActiveX controls to extending this functionality at the server level.

Active Server Pages provide the ability to process server-side logic and can also deliver rich client-side functionality by delivering HTML, client-side JavaScript, JScript, or VBScript, Java Applets, ActiveX controls, and other Web components. In addition, ASP scripts do not necessarily have to display content to the browser but can also be used to process and control logic and workflow on the server.

At this point, you have seen the general architecture needed to develop and deploy Web-based applications. Chapter 2 will expand on this role to identify the tools needed to make the rollout of your Web applications possible. After that, Part II of the book will demonstrate using VBScript to perform the server-side processing of ASP. Parts III and IV will cover the details of ASP objects and components. Part V will demonstrate how to tap into database functionality using Active Server Pages. Part VI will cover how ASP integrates with other existing systems, such as the Microsoft Transaction Server, the Microsoft Messaging Queue, and the Internet Information Server.

For additional information, please see the following chapters:

- Chapter 4, "Working with Operators," demonstrates how to use variables to start building ActiveX scripts.
- Chapter 10, "The Composition of an Active Server Application," will illustrate the different pieces of an ASP application.
- Chapters 17 and 18, "Implementing Existing Server-Side Components" and "Creating Your Own Active Server Components," will teach you how to use server-side VBScript to provide connections to pre-built and customizable servers.
- Chapter 21, "Working with ADO's `Connection` Object," describes how to establish a database connection.
- Chapter 31, "Using Internet Information Server 4.0 to Manage Your Web Applications," demonstrates how to use the various features of the Internet Information Server to help manage your sites and applications.
- Chapter 32, "Putting It All Together: Creating an N-Tier Online Catalog Application," demonstrates how to build ActiveX components to create an n-tier distributed application for the Amazing DataWidget WareHouse Catalog.

CHAPTER 2

Developing and Deploying Active Server Page Applications

Now that the various components that comprise dynamic Web-enabled applications have been identified in Chapter 1, this chapter is dedicated to discussing how ASP technologies are used to create, develop, manage, and deploy your sites and applications. Active Server Pages use the Internet Information Server as a gateway to communicate with other systems, such as SNA, mail, and database servers. This chapter introduces you to the various ASP tools needed to move from theory into the tangible programmatic tools to meet your specific business needs: The Microsoft Management Console, which is used to administer your applications; Visual InterDev, which provides an integrated development environment for creating Active Server Pages; FrontPage, which is used as a graphical user interface tool to add content and create templates that can be manipulated by your Active Server Pages; and the Script Wizard and Script Debugger, which can be used to create and debug client and server scripts. ■

Active Server Pages and Component Architecture

Discover how Active Server Pages, component architecture, and the Transaction Server all work together to build scalable, distributed, Web-based applications.

The Internet Information Server

Learn how the advances in Internet Information Server help manage Active Server Page sites and applications.

Active Server Tools

Discover the variety of tools you can use to create, develop, and deploy Active Server Pages and Active Server scripts.

Tying It Together

Learn how Active Server Pages can be used with your current information system to deliver information to any HTML-compliant browser.

Planning Active Server Web Sites and Applications

Successfully developing and deploying dynamic Web sites and applications depends on the strength and flexibility of your Web server to deliver content via server-side scripting. These two areas have been the focus of Microsoft's Internet vision with its release of the Internet Information Server 4.0 (IIS 4.0 or just IIS). Internet Information Server 4.0 provides a transactional-based Web server that is tightly integrated with the NT operating system. The advances in IIS 4.0 provide advantages that can be separated into two camps: improvement in HTTP-related service areas and the additional functionality in the managing and developing application functionality. The advancements in the HTTP services area enable Internet Information Server to manage multiple Web sites, tailor site- or application-specific settings, and enable HTTP 1.1 support. Advances made in the application development side include transactional-based applications, process isolations, SSL support, Active Data Object (ADO), and new development tools.

The remainder of this chapter will focus on how to take advantage of all the features of Active Server Pages and Internet Information Server. Using IIS and ASP, you can build dynamic, secure, transactional-based applications by following these basic ASP guidelines:

1. Create Active Server Pages to provide a browser-independent transportation vehicle for embedded workflow, business logic, and transaction processing.
2. Create COM-based components to process core application logic within the Microsoft Transaction Server.
3. Configure the IIS site using the Microsoft Management Console to provide application-specific settings, such as Secure Socket Layer, client authentication, or process isolation.

Why Use Components?

In Chapter 1, I briefly mentioned that you can use server-side components to add functionality to your Web server applications. The value of this concept should not be underestimated. *Component architecture* is a direct result of the ideals driving Object Oriented Programming (OOP). OOP focuses on developing a series of reusable components that collectively can be used to minimize application development time and distribution problems while capitalizing on the benefits of code reuse. By separating an application into smaller, self-contained modules, individual components can be created, tested, and implemented more quickly without worrying how it is going to effect the rest of the application. In addition, applications can be developed faster because as your library of components grows, entire applications will simply become a collection of components.

Component architecture also enables applications to be easily updated and quickly re-deployed because only individual modules have to recompiled and tested. This is unlike traditional application development, in which the entire application would have to be recompiled, re-tested and re-deployed. This new architecture model is shown in Figure 2.1.

FIG. 2.1

Component-based architecture separates complex applications into smaller, more manageable parts.

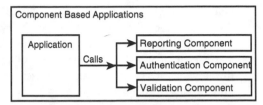

One of the greatest advantages of using component architecture is *scalability*. In traditional application development, the entire application is embedded within one executable file. If an application exhausts system resources of the host machine, the entire application would have to be moved onto a more powerful machine. Component architecture enables you to distribute individual components onto other systems to meet processing needs. This component distribution process not only enables you to plan for scaling and load balancing concerns, but also enables you to maximize your existing investment in hardware.

For example, assume that you build a component that performs a search against a database. This database searching component can be called from a native Win32 client, such as a Visual Basic or Delphi application, and from a HTTP request initiated by any Web browser, as shown in Figure 2.2.

FIG. 2.2

COM components enable any Web client access to the same information and application logic as native Windows applications.

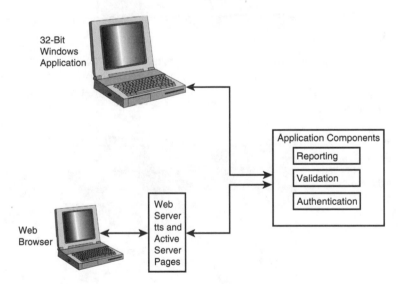

In theory, component architecture brings many benefits to application development, but how can you transform this theory into tangible benefits to your application or organization? COM-based components can be built using tools from most software vendors today, including Microsoft, Borland, Powersoft/Sybase, Oracle, IBM, and Micro Focus. COM objects can be compiled as in-process dynamic link libraries or stand-alone executables. (The details of how to create a COM component are discussed in Chapter 18, "Creating Your Own Active Server Components.")

Once the COM object is created, the object has to be registered. If the object is to be run on the local system, the REGSVR32.EXE server registration utility should be used to register the component. If you are installing the component to run on the remote system, use the DCOMCNFG.EXE utility. The DCOMCNFG utility, as shown in Figure 2.3, enables you to configure the component's properties and permissions. Both of these utilities can be found in the Windows System directory.

FIG. 2.3

The DCOMCNFG utility enables remote components to be configured on remote machines.

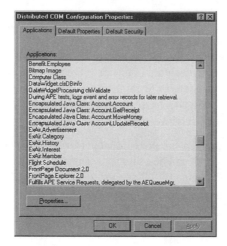

Alternatively, you can install and manage your components by using the Microsoft Transaction Server, as shown in Figure 2.4. The Transaction Server provides complete component management ranging from resource and pooling management to transaction process and monitoring capability.

FIG. 2.4

The Transaction Server manages components and gives the capability to accept or reject changes made by components.

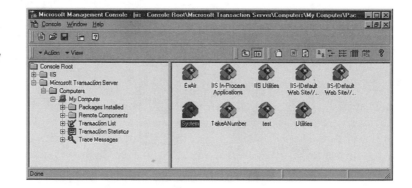

Why Use Transactions?

Transactions take the functionality found in individual components and create a logical unit of work from a specific series of component interactions. The capability to automatically roll back the changes made by the components is particularly useful in application development. For example, consider a simple game between two rival teams. As the two teams play, penalties and goals are tracked. If one team scores a goal, that goal is only valid if the scoring team did not also cause a penalty. If the scoring team was responsible for the penalty, the results of the play are nullified and the score is rolled back to the previous score. If no infractions occur, the score is counted and play continues. The Transaction Server acts as the referee who initiates the start of the game. When play starts, the Transaction Server issues a `BeginTrans` command. The `BeginTrans` command marks a checkpoint where violations will cause game play to be returned back to. If a goal is scored and the scoring team did not cause a penalty, the Transaction Server issues a `CommitTrans` statement to count the goal. However, if the scoring team was guilty of creating the violation, the Transaction Server issues a `RollbackTrans` to void the goal and restart play at the last valid `BeginTrans` statement.

This same methodology can be applied to using components that perform your own unique business rules. For example, consider a situation in which a sales ordering system checks and holds an item in inventory until the credit card payment process has been successfully completed. You can use your favorite COM development tool to build two components. The first component reserves an item from the inventory database. The second component processes the credit card order. You can use transaction processing to abort the reservation of the item if the credit card is rejected. If the credit card order is successfully processed, the transaction, or in this case the reservation, can be accepted and the changes permanently made to the inventory.

The capability to manage the logical grouping of work by one or more components is handled by the Transaction Server. The Transaction Server, as you saw in Figure 2.4, is responsible for managing component transactions as well as component resource and management issues. The Transaction Server utilizes *Just in Time* (*JIT*) activation to optimize system resources consumed by components. The Transaction Server only activates a reference to a component when it is needed before creating a new object, but it also enables the object reference to exist when the object is not in use or is deactivated. In addition, now the Transaction Server eliminates the need to code component security, threading, process handling, and concurrency issues into your components. This integrated component management reduces development cost while providing a scalable environment for your components. For more information about the details of the Microsoft Transaction Server, see Chapter 28 "Working with the Microsoft Transaction Server."

One of the exciting new features of IIS is that transaction processing is built directly into Active Server Pages. Now you can call the transaction `SetAbort` or `SetComplete` methods directly within an Active Server Page to provide rollback or acceptance of changes made by components. In previous version of IIS, transaction processes were only available within the component itself, meaning the success or failure logic was built into the component, not the calling Active Server Page. However, now transactions can be controlled from the Active Server Page. For the details of Active Server Page transaction processing, see Chapter 12, "Controlling the Server with the `Server` Object and Using Transaction Processing with the `ObjectContext` Object."

Creating Active Server Pages

After the various components have been built for your site, the next step is to create the Active Server Pages that you will use to process application logic on the Web server. Active Server Pages are simply text files, just like HTML files. You can create Active Server Pages in an ANSCI editor, such as Notepad or VI. However, you can also use Microsoft Visual InterDev to create and manage your Web-based applications. In conjunction with Visual InterDev, you can use any HTML graphical user interface, such as FrontPage, to help generate the HTML. Instead of writing HTML by hand, you can use the generated HTML as a template that can be manipulated by your Active Server code. For more information on using Visual InterDev, please refer to Chapter 27, "Visual InterDev: The Active Server Pages Integrated Development Environment."

Visual InterDev

Microsoft's Visual InterDev is a development environment in which you can create, edit, deploy, and manage Active Server Pages. Visual InterDev combines a rich set of database connectivity tools, wizards, and design-time controls to increase the functionality and decrease the development time to build Active Server Applications. The Visual InterDev Development Environment can be seen in Figure 2.5.

FIG. 2.5

Visual InterDev provides an integrated development environment for Active Server Page scripts and applications.

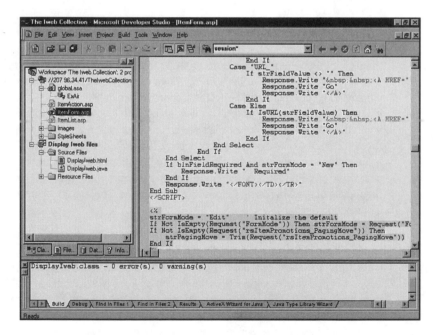

The functionality of Visual InterDev can be categorized into four sections:

- File and source code management
- Database connectivity and live design-time access

- Active Server Page functionality
- Client-side functionality

For more information about Visual InterDev, please see Chapter 27.

FrontPage

FrontPage and other GUI HTML tools add value to creating Active Server Pages by adding the visual components that are missing from Visual InterDev. At the time this book went to press, Visual InterDev does not perform visual drag-and-drop placement and does not provide easy access to the control's properties, events, and methods directly onto Active Server Pages. Developers have grown accustomed to this capability that is found in tools such as Visual Basic or HAHTSite from HAHT software. Visual InterDev does enable you to launch HTML GUI creation tools, such as FrontPage, to generate the visual aspects of a Web page. The page can then be used as stand-alone HTML page to host static content or can be used to generate a skeleton or template page to properly place and control dynamic content from ASP scripts, as shown in Figure 2.6.

Part

I

Ch

2

FIG. 2.6

Use the visual aspects of GUI HTML editors to control page layout.

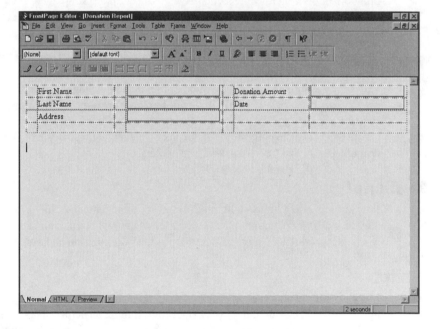

This technique of using GUI tools to quickly generate HTML can save a lot of time and frustration spent on getting complicated HTML page layout properly adjusted. After the page is created, you can edit the HTML source code to create the dynamic content on the page while relying on the HTML tags to quickly generate the look and feel of the page.

ActiveX Scripting Languages: Linking It All Together

Using Visual InterDev is a good environment for generating Active Server scripts, but eventually you will have to get down to the details of script code. Active Server Pages are the combination of ActiveX scripting and HTML tags. The processing of server-side scripts is what gives Internet Information Server its application-based functionality. The script processing also enables Internet Information Server to act as an interpreter between remotely distributed browsers and proprietary in-house systems. The Internet Information Server comes with scripting engines to process VBScript and JScript. The default scripting engine for the Internet Information Server is VBScript.

Keep in mind that scripting languages are not fully functional programming languages like C or C++. Scripting languages are interpreted, not compiled, and they cannot be used to create stand-alone applications. These scripting languages rely on a host to interpret the code. Although you might consider this a weakness, this dependence on host-based processing enables the scripts to be portable to a variety of environments. This flexibility is what enables these scripting languages to be interpreted on both the Web clients and Web servers. Although the functionality is generally the same between the scripting languages, deciding what scripting language to use is a function of leveraging your existing language skill set in client- and server-side processing and delivering that functionality to the largest user base.

VBScript

VBScript was initially created by Microsoft to be a lightweight scripting language to interpret user events triggered within the Internet Explorer browser. VBScript is actually created from Visual Basic for Applications (VBA), a pure subset of Visual Basic. VBScript can be used to create references to control HTML intrinsic objects, ActiveX (formally known as OLE) automation objects, ActiveX controls, and Java applets.

JavaScript

JavaScript is also a lightweight, interpreted scripting language that provides the same functionality as its VBScript counterpart. The syntax of the JavaScript language is similar to C. JavaScript is a product of Netscape Communications Corporation and Sun Microsystems, Inc.

JScript

JScript is Microsoft's version of JavaScript, and it was designed to lend OLE-based functionality found within VBScript to the JavaScript programming structure. This is not to imply one scripting language is stronger or weaker than the other; each scripting language has its own strengths and weakness. The trick is to determine which scripting language best meets your application and targeted users needs.

N O T E Even though JScript is a modeled after JavaScript, there are incompatibilities between the two object models. These slight differences could generate runtime scripting errors. To prevent errors, remember to thoroughly test your scripts before deploying your applications. ■

The JScript and JavaScript object models are similar, but variations between the models exist. As a result, the slight varieties can generate runtime errors when executing your JavaScript.

Scripting Tools

Because of their portability, scripting languages are finding their way into more and more applications. For example, VBScript, once limited to existing only in Internet Explorer browser clients, not only provides the core scripting functionality driving Active Server Pages but is now being integrated into Microsoft Office applications, such as Microsoft Outlook. With the rising importance being placed on scripting languages, script development environments are beginning to emerge.

Part

I

Ch

2

Microsoft Script Wizard and the Script Debugger

Microsoft currently uses two separate tools to handle creating and debugging scripts. Someday you can expect these two tools to be merged into one interface, but at the time of this writing, the Script Wizard and Script Debugger are located as separate tools. The Script Wizard provides a tree view-based navigation methodology to create, edit, and delete scripts on a page. The Script Wizard, as shown in Figure 2.7, scans the current page for programmable objects, and lists the associated properties, methods, and events for each object, which enables you to associate client actions with a Web-based event. For example, you can determine when the user clicks a button to display an alert window.

FIG. 2.7
The Script Wizard enables you to associate and code client- and server-side scripts.

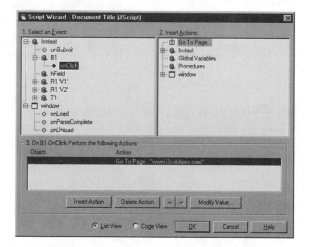

The Script Wizard can be found in both FrontPage and Visual InterDev. However, there are definite areas where this interface can be improved. For example, the Script Wizard does not provide a what-you-see-is-what-you-get (WYSIWYG) environment to easily set the properties and associate events.

The Microsoft Script Debugger provides debugging capabilities for both client- and server-side VBScript and JScript. The Script Debugger is similar to the debugging environment found in Visual Basic (see Figure 2.8). This environment enables you to set breakpoints, retrieve and assign property and object values, and provide different stepping mechanisms to systematically debug your scripts. For a closer view at the Script Debugger, see Chapter 9, "Using the Script Debugger."

FIG. 2.8
The Script Debugger provides client and server debugging features for VBScript and JScript.

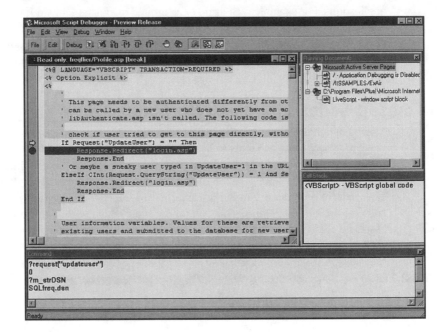

Visual JavaScript

Visual JavaScript is Netscape's JavaScript development environment, as shown in Figure 2.9. Visual JavaScript has a GUI interface that provides HTML creation and editing functionality, drag-and-drop graphical representation of code items on an HTML page, a one button deployment mechanism, and an inline debugger.

The Visual JavaScript utilities are server-side JavaScript and JavaScript components that supply application logic processing and database functionality. These JavaScript components rely on Common Object Request Broker Architecture (CORBA) and Internet Inter-Orb Protocol (IIOP) combination standard.

For more information about the Visual JavaScript tools, visit Netscape at **http://www.netscape.com**.

FIG. 2.9
Visual JavaScript from Netscape is a complete JavaScript client- and server-side scripting development environment.

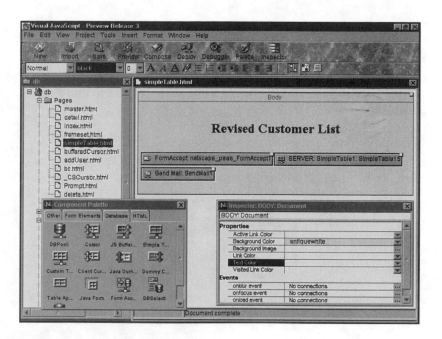

The Internet Information Server

The Internet Information Server 4.0 is the foundation you need to deliver and configure your Active Server applications, and it provides a rich set of HTTP features, including the extensive site and server management features found in the Microsoft Management Console (MMC). IIS 4.0 also provides Secure Socket Layer 3.0 and client authentication to help ensure that your content is delivered solely to its intended audience. In addition, the IIS supports HTTP 1.1 standards, which give the latest functionality of the Hypertext Transfer Protocol and server-side Java.

The Microsoft Management Console

IIS 3.0 uses the Internet Service Manager to administer the Internet-based services such as HTTP, FTP, and Gopher servers. However, with the release of Internet Information Server 4.0, the Internet Service Manager has been converted into a generic networking interface called the Microsoft Management Console (MMC).

The MMC is now a centralized networking administration tool that not only manages the Internet-based services, such as the HTTP, FTP, and Gopher services, but also can be used to manage network services and other BackOffice products, such as SMTP and News services, as shown in Figure 2.10.

Within the Internet Information Server 4.0, you can configure multiple Web sites/applications from within the Microsoft Management Console. Furthermore, the MMC enables each site to have its own unique application settings. For example, Figure 2.11 demonstrates implementing an encryption ISAPI filter that will only be applied to that specific site or application instead of all the sites on the HTTP server.

FIG. 2.10

Networking interfaces are now managed through the Microsoft Management Console.

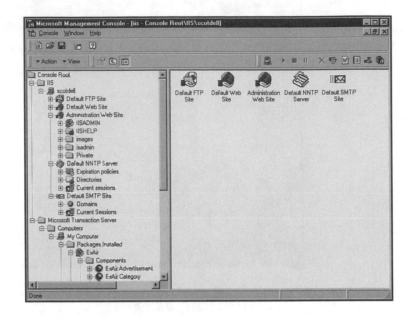

FIG. 2.11

IIS 4.0 enables to you manage multiple Web sites, each with their own application settings.

This feature is particularly useful when you consider the administration costs needed to manage large-scale intranets. Now you can use the MMC to create local Web site administrators or *operators*, as shown in Figure 2.12.

These operators can now control the specifics of their sites without having to bother the server administrator. The assigned Web operators can remotely manage the site/application through an HTML version of the Internet Service Manager, as shown in Figure 2.13.

FIG. 2.12
IIS 4.0 reduces webmaster administration by allowing local operators to administer their own sites based on NT user security accounts.

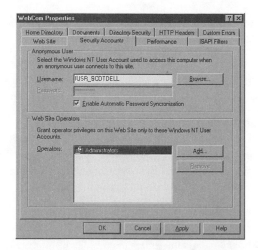

FIG. 2.13
The MMC can transfer administration tasks to local site operators.

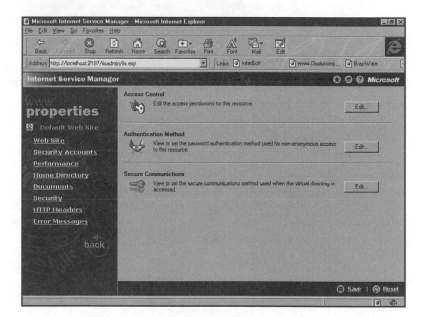

For more information on the MMC, please see Chapter 31, "Using Internet Information Server 4.0 to Manage Your Web Applications."

Secure Socket Layer 3.0 and Client Authentication

The need to safely deliver information between the Web client and server is paramount when developing Web-enabled applications. To that end, Internet Information Server 4.0 supports Secure Socket Layer 3.0, which provides a secure channel between the browser and the server.

In conjunction with SSL 3.0, the Internet Information Server also provides its own certificate server. Now you can issue your own certificates to provide client authentication for your Active Server Pages and ISAPI applications.

HTTP 1.1 Support

The Internet Information Server also supports the new HTTP 1.1 specifications. The HTTP 1.1 standard provides many advantages over HTTP 1.0. However, in order to utilize these new improvements, both the requesting browser client and Web server must be HTTP 1.1 compliant. For more information about detecting the browser type and version of browsers visiting your site or application, please refer to the Browser Capabilities Component discussion in Chapter 17, "Implementing Existing Server-Side Components."

HTTP 1.1 has four new features that help the Web server deliver and manage content. The first two features, persistent connections and pipelining, change the fundamental communication mechanisms between the Web client and Web server. In traditional HTTP 1.0, when a browser requests a page from the Web server, a connection to the Web server is established via TCP. Then the Web server would accept the request, process the request, and respond to the request usually by delivering information to the user. After the information was delivered to the requesting client, the connection between the Web client and server was released. The overhead associated with creating and releasing connections requires a significant amount of server resources. The real problem was that a connection is made and released for every item in an HTML page. For example, if an HTML page contains six images, a minimum of seven individual connections (including the initial request for the page) are requested, established, and released from the server. Multiply the amount of requests per page times the amount of hits that your site receives, and the resource load can be easily visualized. Further notice that only one request per connection was allowed.

HTTP 1.1 helps resolve the need to establish multiple connections, which are limited to only one request per connection, by using *persistent connections* and *pipelining*. Persistent connections enable the established communication channel between the browser and the server to be kept open for a set period of time, instead of closing after the server issues its first response. Pipelining adds to this persistent connection functionality by enabling multiple requests to be transmitted over the same connection before receiving any responses from the host.

HTTP 1.1 also supports the HTTP PUT and HTTP DELETE commands to help publish and manage files via HTTP. The HTTP PUT command enables information to be uploaded to a server. As a complement to this feature, the HTTP DELETE command provides the capability to remove content from the Web server.

The Internet Information Server accepts header information from a requesting browser that identifies the HT TP level of the requesting client. If the browser is HTTP 1.1-compliant, the server responds by sending an HTTP 1.1 response. If the browser is 1.0-compliant, the Web server uses HTTP 1.0 to respond to the client.

Server-Side Java

IIS 4.0 provides an updated Java Virtual Machine that was initially shipped in IIS 3.0. The Java Virtual Machine is responsible for interpreting the Java pseudo code. The communication between the Java Virtual Machine (VM) and Internet Information Server is made possible via DCOM. Remember, DCOM was designed to provide a communication specification that enables component communication regardless of networking protocol or machine boundaries. DCOM is also the communication vehicle that enables any ActiveX components, whether executed on the browser's client or Web server, to communicate.

Extending Active Server Pages into Your Existing Network

At this point, I have covered the complete spectrum of architecture considerations and application development tools. However, I want to emphasize the benefits of implementing an Active Server Page architecture. Consider the typical network scheme illustrated in Figure 2.14.

FIG. 2.14
Applying Active Server-based component architecture to your network schema.

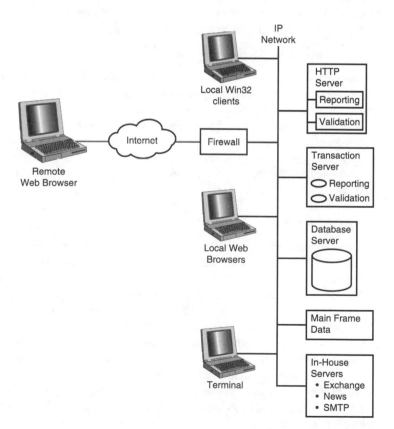

The IP-based network running a variety of mainframe terminals and workstations running on Windows 3.1, Window 95, and NT provides access to database servers and host-based information stored within a mainframe. In this network architecture, there are various ways that clients can access information. The following situations are used to demonstrate the different types of data access architecture and how Active Server Pages can be implemented to access the same information on any Web browser.

Terminal Access

Host-based systems are information systems in which the application logic and information storage is stored within a remote hosting environment. This type of system removes all processing responsibility from the client and uses the client simply as a display mechanism. In Figure 2.14, the terminal gains access to the host application by establishing a session to a mainframe of the network. The mainframe provides all the processing of application workflow and delivers that information to the terminal.

Client/Server

In the traditional client/server world, the processing power of the application is distributed between the client's machine and the server machine. The client, typically a Windows-based application, will request information from a database server. After the data is received, this information can be processed on the client's machine. The server plays a split role in this environment. Typically, the database server is used to store information and also shares some of the processing power by using applying logic embedded in triggers and stored procedures. The client/server configuration starts with replacing the dumb terminal with a machine capable of localized information storage and processing power. The installed applications on this machine are responsible for controlling the user workflow. The application can also make calls directly to server to retrieve information. The server receives, processes, and returns the information to the calling client. The client application can use the information within the application to complete its desired task.

N-Tier Client/Server

The n-tier client/server model expands on the traditional client/server model by introducing a middle tier. This middle tier, often called the *business tier*, houses the business rules of the application. This business rule tier moves some of the processing logic contained in the client application and the database server into third, or middle, tier. The shift of the business rules into this middle tier enables the application logic to be separated into smaller components. These components can then be managed by the Transaction Server to increase reliability, programmability, and scalability of the application. In addition, centralized updates to the application can be made at the middle tier to reduce deployment costs to remote clients. As you can see in Figure 2.14, the Win32 client application would call a component that is managed by the Transaction Server. This component would then complete its intended purpose. In this situation, the component retrieves information from the database and returns the result back to the calling Win32 application.

Web Access

The Web browser architecture blends the basic functionality of the terminal emulator and client/server architecture together to access in-house information stores. The Web browser is the equivalent of a graphical terminal emulator that uses the HTTP server as a connection point to the network. Once it is connected to the network, the Web server acts as a client to other servers on the network. (This situation is also demonstrated in Figure 2.14, where the Web client is connected to an HTTP server.) Once connected to the HTTP server via Intranet or Internet access, the HTTP server is responsible for processing application workflow issues, making connections to servers, and translating the information in HTML. This processing power is implemented using Active Server Pages. For example, the HTTP server delivers a page to the client's browser requesting information that will be used for a database lookup. If the user enters the appropriate information in the required fields, the Active Server Page can extract the information and establish a connection to the database server. The database server can then process and deliver the information back to the Web server. The Web server and Active Server Pages then format the information and deliver it back to the browser.

N-Tier Web Access

Web-based systems merge the terminal emulator and client/server architecture schemas to provide a flexible application architecture. This architecture can also enjoy the benefits of component architecture by enabling Web clients and native Win32 clients to access COM-based components. The components, managed by the Transaction Server, do not care what systems are activating them (security permission dependent, of course). Therefore, the Web server and the Win32 client application receive the same treatment and functionality from the middle tier component layer.

For example, assume that a component was created to be responsible for running a specific database report. This database report component can be called by both an Active Server Page via the HTTP server or from a 32-bit Windows application to retrieve the same report information.

This type of approach brings real benefits to delivering information solutions. In most situations, you will need to implement this component-based approach to meet the advanced functionality needs of the in-house application administration staff and provide access to the same information to any Web browser in the world.

From Here...

In this chapter, you have learned how to apply the Web-based architecture to your existing architecture and what tools are needed to deploy Web-based systems. The convergence of application architecture and application development tools center around delivering functionality via the Internet Information Server and Active Server Pages. Together, the stage is set to provide an exciting time in application development, where the shift to component-based architecture with thin-client browsing capabilities will reap tangible benefits for your application or organizational needs.

The Internet Information Server shares half the responsibility by:

- Processing Active Server scripts, CGI, WinCGI, and the Java Virtual Machine on the server.
- Managing multiple Web sites and applications within the same server.
- Supporting Secure Socket Layer 3.0 client authentication, integrated Certificate Server, and HTTP 1.1 standards.
- Supporting process isolation and component load and unloading capability to eliminate having to stop and restart the entire Web site.

Active Server Pages, on the other hand, extend the functionality of the IIS Web server by:

- Utilizing transactional-based scripts for thread and process management of components.
- Providing server-side script debugging capabilities.
- Running each application within its own process to minimize HTTP service failures.
- Accessing database connectivity through the ActiveX Data object to any ODBC-compliant database.

Internet Information Server and Active Server Pages use the scripting languages that are the glue that hold everything together. Whether the scripts are processed at the Web server or within the browser, scripts provide the valuable interactions between Web objects, such as HTML, ActiveX, or Java-based objects.

At this point, you should be ready to get into the details of Active Server Pages. Looking forward, the rest of the book focuses on implementing Active Sever pages separating the ASP functionality into five modules:

- Part II, "VBScript: The Foundation of Active Server Pages," focuses on learning how VBScript is used to power the application logic driving your Web-based applications.
- Part III, "Active Server Objects: The Essential Building Blocks," illustrates the six built-in objects that collectively form the foundation to ASP applications.
- Part IV, "Active Server Components," guides you through the installable components the ship with the Internet Information Server.
- Part V, "Database Management with Active Server Pages," provides a foundation on how to access your database via Active Server Pages.
- Part VI, "Active Server Pages and the Enterprise Solution," walks you through how to tap into the functionality of other systems through Active Server Pages.

VBScript: The Foundation of Active Server Pages

CHAPTER 3

VBScript Programming Basics: Variables and Scope

The core functionality of Active Server Pages is centered on the server-side processing of application logic on the Web server. Active Server Pages process script-compliant languages to provide a tight integration of accessing server-side data components with application logic to deliver standard HTML to any browser. This powerful combination is made possible through the execution of scripting languages processed using Microsoft Internet Information Server. VBScript, one of many possible server–side scripting languages, provides the communication mechanism essential to interfacing with COM-based servers, such as Microsoft Exchange Server, Microsoft Index Server, Database Servers, or Lotus Notes Domino Servers.

Furthermore, Active Server Pages and VBScript enable you to access your own customized ActiveX servers that are compiled as in-process Dynamic Link Libraries (DLLs). These ActiveX servers are installed as components (formally known as OLE servers) to meet your specific application needs. These ActiveX components can be written with various tools such as Visual C++, Visual

Introducing VBScript

Learn how VBScript provides the foundation of Active Server Pages and why it is essential for Web-enabling your applications.

Scripting the Web Client and Web Server with VBScript

VBScript is the glue that holds Web browser and Web server components together. Learn how VBScript provides the interaction between ActiveX controls and the HTML object model on the Web browser and how VBScript provides processing power and communication links between the Web server and various server-side objects.

VBScript Datatypes

Master how VBScript stores variable information and how the various subtypes and conversion functions are used to harness the flexibility of the *Variant* datatype.

Variable Declaration

Discover how to declare variables, and identify scope issues within VBScript to run on Active Server Pages or the Web client.

Basic, and Delphi to include such functionality as database access, internal messaging, and workflow systems. This extension of your existing network and application servers is solidly integrated within the Web server through the server-side processing of VBScript. VBScript acts as translator to provide the seamless extension of your existing network and application infrastructure to any Web client. ■

What Is VBScript?

VBScript is a lightweight scripting language that provides programming functionality based on the Visual Basic programming language. VBScript is natively executed on the Internet Explorer browser and can be executed in other browsers through plug-in technologies. VBScript is also the default scripting language of the Internet Information Server 3.0 and later. The use of scripting languages, such as VBScript and its JScript counterpart, is particularly interesting because the script source code is actually embedded as text within the Web page. This capability to deliver text-based programmatic functionality is vastly different from traditional applications in which client functionality requires executing compiled source code.

As Microsoft Office became the office automation industry standard, VBA and VB became an integral part of every Microsoft Office product. The VBScript language is derived from the Visual Basic for Applications and Visual Basic programming languages. VBA was originally created to supply non-programmers, such as managers or sales personnel, with the ability to add programming functionality into their office documents without learning the specifics of a programming language. VBA was then developed to provide the capability to add programming logic into all office products. At the same time, the emergence of browser-based technology also shared the need for a lightweight programming interface. VBScript was created to meet these needs.

Because of its VBA/VB-based background, VBScript enjoys a large developer base, allowing users to be well-positioned to create intelligent Web pages by adding script to be executed on the Web client or used to create the actual HTML page sent to the browser. The script-embedded pages are loaded in the client's browser and used to execute logic to based on a user's actions. These scripted Web pages can now take advantage of functionality not found in native HTML by enabling VBScript to manage and manipulate the HTML object model.

Traditionally, scripting languages perform programming tasks on the Web browser. Client-side scripting adds value by embedding script processing in the Web page itself. For example, client-side tasks can include field validation, client-side image mapping, data manipulation, and user dialog boxes. Client-side scripting also plays a vital role in offloading processing power from the Web server and reducing the amount of network traffic by eliminating the amount of round-trip requests to the server. For example, you can use client-side scripting to ensure that the user has entered only numbers and prompt the user for correct information without requiring any processing from the Web server.

This transferring of responsibility is critical to maximize Web server performance, especially in server-centric Web-based applications. The server-centric view merges client/server and host-based architecture to enable a centralized deployment mechanism that takes advantage of processing power on the requesting client. When you consider that your Internet applications can have potentially thousands of concurrent connections, distributing processing can significantly reduce the Web server workload.

Scripting can also be used for more than the client-side validation of HTML intrinsic objects, such as single and multiline text boxes, option buttons, check boxes, and drop-down lists. Developers can use VBScript to attach, control, and manipulate ActiveX controls and Java applets within Web pages. Because VBScript is a subset of VBA, many Microsoft Office products use native VBScript code directly in Office forms. This tight integration of VBScript into the BackOffice suite enables you to minimize code development as applications are ported to the Web.

Until now, VBScript was a useful, lightweight scripting language that could manipulate, control, and process objects in an HTML Web page. However, VBScript could only process ActiveX controls, Java applets, and scripting logic on the Microsoft Internet Explorer. With the release of IIS 3.0 and Active Server Pages, VBScript has now extended its reach into the Web server. VBScript now provides unlimited programming flexibility at the Web-server level without relying on a specific browser type. The server-side processing of VBScript within Active Server Pages allows for the dynamic HTML creation needed to customize, create, and deliver user-defined Web pages. It is important to note that the Web pages that are delivered by Active Server Pages are pure HTML and contain nothing proprietary to Microsoft's Internet Explorer. This ability is needed to deliver basic application features we take for granted in traditional application development. The flexibility to respond to user-defined requests is essential for creating applications. Creating customized HTML pages is made possible through Active Server scripting and the combination of server-side scripting and Active Server Pages. Furthermore, this server-side programming does not rely on a server proprietary development tool that you have to train or find from a limited developer base. Now the same Visual Basic programming skills can be directly applicable to programming on the Web server.

VBScript's History

VBScript was initially developed to extend client-side HTML functionality based on an event-driven programming model. VBScript 1.0 was initially released as a part of the Internet Explorer 2.0 browser, and provided a large amount of programming flexibility found in its native VBA and Visual Basic programming models. The largest difference between VBScript and Visual Basic is that VBScript prevents any file access. This is because one of VBScript's primary design objectives was to provide a safe scripting language that would prevent malicious intent from harming underlying browser subsystems. With the release of the Internet Information Server 3.0 and Active Server Pages, VBScript can now also be executed on the Web server.

VBScript 2.0 expands programming flexibility found in the initial release of VBScript by allowing two main programming features. The first expanded flexibility of VBScript 2.0 is the capability to connect to ActiveX (OLE) automation servers from the Web server level. This connection feature provides the interface to database servers, application servers, and a multitude of Active Server components. All these connections will be discussed in Parts II, III, and IV.

> **N O T E**   Remember: Using the ActiveX Server, a.k.a. IIS 3.0, does not limit your user base to only
> ActiveX-compliant browsers. The ActiveX Server uses server-side scripting to provide
> transparent data flow from proprietary server-side systems to any browser. ▪

Extending Functionality on the Web Client and Web Server

As the advantages of thin-client architecture continued to gain momentum, the need to provide programming capabilities at the Web server became increasingly clear if delivering applications over the Web were to become a reality. With Microsoft's introduction of the Active Platform, VBScript was transformed from a limited Internet Explorer user base to providing vast programming extensibility on the server.

Communication Between Objects and Events

Web developers can use VBScript to add application logic to native HTML that would traditionally require server-side processing. VBScript enables the management of application workflow and object management based on manipulating the HTML object model. An *object model* represents a hierarchical blueprint of all objects, methods, events, and operators that exist for a given language. The HTML object model is what makes the interaction between all objects on an HTML page possible within the browser.

Manipulating Client-Side ActiveX Controls   VBScript can manipulate the HTML object model to act as the communication mechanism that enables objects, such as intrinsic HTML controls, ActiveX controls, and Java applets, to interact and communicate with each other. This interaction is important because it allows the different objects to share their respective properties, events, and methods. In Figure 3.1, for example, an HTML button initiates a VBScript subroutine that processes the value of a radio button group and displays the result to the user. Listing 3.1 shows the source code used to build this example.

FIG. 3.1
VBScript provides interaction between HTML, ActiveX, and Java objects in the browser.

Listing 3.1 *3_EXT_FUNCT_CLIENTCONTROLS.ASP*—Using VBScript to manipulate HTML controls.

```
<HTML>
<HEAD>
<TITLE>Client Controls</TITLE>
</HEAD>
<body bgcolor="#FFFFFF">
<SCRIPT language="VBScript"><!--
Sub checkradio()
for i=0 to 2
        if document.frmbrowser.r1.item(i).checked then
                MsgBox "You have selected " &
document.frmbrowser.r1.item(i).value
        End if
next
end sub
--></SCRIPT>
<form method="POST" name="frmbrowser" onsubmit>
    <div align="center"><center><table border="1" cellspacing="1"
    width="40%" bordercolor="#808080">
        <TR>
            <TD width="100%"><table border="0" cellpadding="2"
            width="100%">
                <TR>
                    <TD align="center" colspan="2" width="100%"
                    bgcolor="#000080"><font color="#FFFFFF"
                    face="Arial Rounded MT Bold"><strong>What is
                    your favorite browser?</strong></font></TD>
                </TR>
                <TR>
                    <TD align="right"><input type="radio" checked
                    name="r1" value="Internet Explorer"></TD>
                    <TD>Internet Explorer </TD>
                </TR>
                <TR>
                    <TD align="right"><input type="radio"
                    name="r1" value="Netscape"></TD>
                    <TD>Netscape Navigator </TD>
                </TR>
                <TR>
                    <TD align="right"><input type="radio"
                    name="r1" value="Mosaic"></TD>
                    <td>Mosaic </TD>
                </TR>
                <TR>
                    <TD align="center" colspan="2" width="100%"><input
                    type="button" name="Your Choice"
                    value="Make Choice" language="VBScript"
                    onclick="call checkradio()"></TD>
                </TR>
            </TABLE>
            </TD>
        </TR>
```

continues

Part

II

Ch

3

Listing 3.1 Continued

```
        </TABLE>
        </center></div>
    </form>
    </body>
    </HTML>
```

You can further extend client-side scripting by using VBScript to communicate with ActiveX controls that have been downloaded and registered on the client's machine. For example, Figure 3.2 demonstrates an HTML button that uses VBScript to acquire the date selected from an ActiveX Calendar Control.

FIG. 3.2
VBScript extracts information from ActiveX controls on the browser.

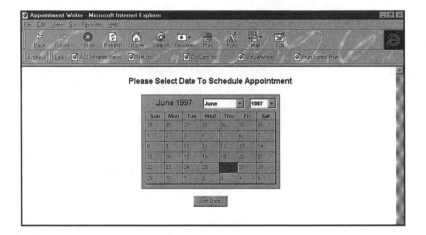

Manipulating Server-Side ActiveX Controls VBScript's communication functionality isn't just limited to client-side controls; it also applies to the Web server components as well. The same interaction that existed between the client-side HTML buttons and VBScript's searching event and the ActiveX control in the preceding examples also applies to VBScript and non-visual Active Server Page components. Figure 3.3 illustrates server-side VBScript scripting accessing the Active Server Page Browser Component. The Browser Component, as discussed in Chapter 17, "Implementing Existing Server-Side Components," is used by the Internet Information Server to determine what type of browser is requesting information from the Web page.

Listing 3.2 shows the VBScript source code that creates an instance of the Active Server Page Browser Component on the Web server and then displays the browser's properties on the HTML page.

FIG. 3.3
VBScript is used on the Web server to control an Active Server Page Browser Component to identify the requesting browser type.

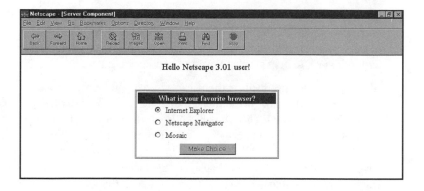

Listing 3.2   *EXT_FUNCT_WEBSERVER.ASP*—Controlling ASP components and displaying the results to the browser.

```
<%@ language="VBScript" %>
<HTML>
<head>
<TITLE>Server Component</title>
</head>
<body bgcolor="#FFFFFF">
<center>
<%  Set bc = Server.CreateObject("MSWC.BrowserType") %>
<p><font size="4">
Hello <%= bc.browser  %> <%= " " &bc.version  %> user!
</font></p>
</center>
</BODY>
</HTML>
```

Part
II

Ch
3

Differences Between VBA, VB, and VBScript

If you have coding experience in Visual Basic or VBA, you're probably interested in learning about the differences between the environments. The most dramatic difference is the development environment. As with initial releases of HTML, VBScript, JScript, and JavaScript, all the code had to be written by hand in an ASCII-based text editor. This was intentionally done to enable any text editor anywhere in the world to be capable of creating HTML tags. However, the release of visual design tools, such as the ActiveX Control Pad, FrontPage98, Visual InterDev, and the Script Wizard, enables you to create and manage HTML and HTML objects in a GUI-like environment.

I use the term "GUI-like" because these emerging environments will need to mature several versions before they achieve the functionality found in GUI application development tools today. In addition, the current tool set is a variety of single-point products that are independent of one another, making development, testing, and deployment cumbersome. For example, prior to the ActiveX Control Pad, manipulating ActiveX controls was an extremely cumbersome process available only via a text editor. However, the ActiveX Control Pad provides a visual environment similar to Visual Basic, and enables ActiveX controls to be visually placed and the objects' properties manipulated. The ActiveX Control Pad used another Microsoft product, the Script Wizard, to help develop VBScript and JavaScript code.

Although the two products by themselves have good merit, using the two in conjunction proved to be awkward. For example, traditional Visual Basic will expose a control's default event when you double-click the object. However, if you double-click an object in the ActiveX Control Pad, its properties are displayed. In order to place code in that event, such as a button's OnClick event, the Script Wizard would have to be started first. Then the specific object would have to be selected from a list displaying all objects on the page. Afterward, the specific event would have to be selected in order to place code in that event.

The Script Wizard, as seen in Figure 3.4, is a step in the right direction, but there's still room for improvement in both the design-time and runtime components. For example, the Script Wizard can create VBScript but there are no built-in debugging features. Traditionally, to test your scripts, you have to exit the Script Wizard, save the new script, and refresh your browser to see if it performs as needed.

FIG. 3.4
The Script Wizard provides a GUI-like VBScript and JavaScript development interface.

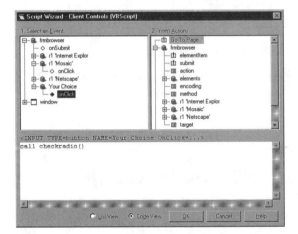

To further add to the scripting frustration, the Script Wizard lacks many of the features that developers have grown accustomed to over the years. The largest of the missing components is the lack of a runtime debugger directly within the Script Wizard. Microsoft has released a beta of the Script Debugger for Internet Explorer that provides inline-debugging capabilities. The Script Debugger, as demonstrated in Chapter 9, "Using the Script Debugger," enables you to debug client- and server-side scripts by using breakpoints, step-through, colored syntax, and a debug window to check variables or initiate new code. But, again, this acts as a separate product. The Script Debugger can be downloaded from the Microsoft at **http://www.microsoft.com/workshop/prog/scriptie/**.

Server- and Client-Side Syntax

You probably noticed in Listings 3.1 and 3.2 that the VBScript client-side syntax varies from the VBScript server-side code. The browser-based VBScript code is neatly contained inside the <SCRIPT></SCRIPT> HTML tags, whereas the VBScript server code is dispersed throughout the Active Server Page using the <% %> tags. However, you can also use the <SCRIPT> tag to run VBScript at the server by specifying the RUNAT.

The Web Browser Client Syntax   The <SCRIPT> tag enables various scripting engines, such as VBScript, JavaScript, or even your own scripting language, to process the embedded HTML code. You can embed scripting languages into HTML by using the following syntax:

```
<SCRIPT LANGUAGE=scripting language>
```

where *scripting language* is any ActiveX scripting language.

Each scripting language—VBScript, JScript, and JavaScript—has a defined object model. The specific differences between the three standard scripting languages is beyond the scope of this chapter, but can be investigated further in Que's *Special Edition Using JavaScript, Special Edition Using JScript*, and *Special Edition Using VBScript*.

For example, the following code demonstrates using client-side VBScript to write text to a Web page. The example uses the OnLoad event of the page to trigger the LoopWrite subroutine.

```
<SCRIPT LANGUAGE="VBScript">
<!--
Sub LoopWrite()
  Dim I
  I = 1
  Do While I  < 8
    Document.Write "<p> <font size =" & i & ">" & " Welcome"
    I = I + 1
  Loop
End sub
-->
</SCRIPT>

<HEAD>
<TITLE>The Do While Loop</title>
</HEAD>
<BODY bgcolor="#FFFFFF" onload = LoopWrite()>
</BODY>
</HTML>
```

Placement of *<SCRIPT>* Tags   When an HTML page contains scripting information, the Web browser parses and compiles the Web page as the browser receives the information from the Web server. Scripts are instantiated in the order that they appear in the HTML. However, problems arise in the browser world because Internet Explorer supports both JavaScript and VBScript. Consequently, each scripting language requires its own separate interpreter to provide communication between the browser and the embedded script. Because each scripting language is unique, a scripting error will occur if the default JavaScript interpreter is initiated and realizes that it's trying to interpret VBScript code.

> **CAUTION**
>
> In previous versions of Internet Explorer, if a block of <FORM> code is placed ahead of a block of <SCRIPT> code, an `Object doesn't support the property or method` error may result.

To prevent errors from occurring, make sure any <SCRIPT> tag is placed before (remember from top down) an object event. To avoid this problem, all <SCRIPT> tags should be defined within the <HEAD>...</HEAD> tags. Using the <HEAD> location ensures any script code that may be called by a form element has already been loaded and compiled by the proper scripting interpreter.

IIS 3.0 Server Syntax   VBScript is the default scripting language of the Active Server. As mentioned previously, server-side VBScript uses the <%...%> and the <SCRIPT></SCRIPT> tag delimiters within Active Server Pages. With the exception of Input and MsgBox, the Active Server processes any valid VBScript code within these delimiters. Because the Active Server Pages are processed at the server, these traditional user interface dialog boxes are ignored. Furthermore, you're not limited to using VBScript as your Active Server scripting engine. Notice the syntax similarities between client and server scripting language selection:

```
<%@ LANGUAGE = Scripting Language %>
```

where *Scripting Language* is any ActiveX scripting language.

You can also use the <SCRIPT> tags to process script at the server. This syntax is similar to the client-side scripting, but the RUNAT tag specifies the location to process this script.

```
<SCRIPT Language = "VBScript" Runat ="Server">
Function ConvertNull(varTemp)
    If IsNull(varTemp) Then
        ConvertNull=""
    Else
        ConvertNull = Trim(vartemp)
    End If
End Function
</SCRIPT>
```

This code example is called to convert values extracted from a database into empty strings or the database value.

Security

VBScript was initially designed to be a safe, interpreted language to be executed on the Internet Explorer browser. Designed to minimize possible security violations to the client's file and subsystems, VBScript prevents any file input/output and prevents access to the client's operating system. To further prevent destructive intentions, VBScript uses only one datatype, Variant.

Internet Explorer Browser Security   The Internet Explorer browser has additional security features built into the administrative functions of the browser. I will not cover all the security configuration issues that are available in the Internet Explorer browser, but I will highlight the topics that relate to VBScript. The Security tab of the View | Options menu in Internet Explorer enables the browser to control whether ActiveX controls, plug-ins, ActiveX scripts, Java, and Active content can be used in the browser. In the example demonstrating the use of VBScript to control a client-side ActiveX control, if the Safety Level of the browser were set to High, then unsafe objects would not be loaded on the browser, as shown in Figure 3.5.

FIG. 3.5
Internet Explorer enables three levels of security for Active content.

After the security settings are set, Internet Explorer manages the browser security concerns. For example, if your security settings are set on high, Internet Explorer warns you of the potential conflicts and will not display a potentially dangerous control, as shown in Figure 3.6.

FIG. 3.6
The Internet Explorer prevents unsafe objects from being loaded onto the browser.

 Using VBScript to reference an unsafe ActiveX control while security is set to High in Internet Explorer could cause an `Object required` error. To resolve the problem, change the security settings to Medium and accept all the warnings.

Server Security   Server-side scripting security is based on the NT File System (NTFS) architecture and the Internet Information Server. NTFS is responsible for access control to your site by enabling the administrator to set the individual user permissions for the site. These permission settings not only dictate who has access to files on Web server, but also enable you to provide different access levels to the files. For example, everybody can have read access to files in a directory, but only the administrator can write files into that directory. To help monitor these security settings, NTFS enables you to provide auditing capacities to monitor the file-level security settings. This automatic security record-keeping is essential for tracking possible security infractions on your system.

The Internet Information Server provides various client authentication methods to verify the identity of the requesting user. In addition, protecting the data while in transit is made possible through Secure Sockets Layer (SSL). SSL is responsible for encrypting the data as it is transferred between the client and Web server. The Internet Information Server also provides the capability to limit the execute permissions on each Web site.

VBScript Variable Datatypes

The use of programming variables is the basis of any programming language. A *variable* acts as a temporary storage location for your application to access and manipulate data. Variables are identified by a name and contain information stored in memory as a value.

Variant

While Visual Basic supports many datatypes, VBScript only supports one datatype, Variant. This datatype is unique because it represents all the datatypes found native in Visual Basic, such as Integer, String, Double, and Currency. The Variant datatype's power is that the characteristics of the variable change depending on what type of information it stores. However, this automatic conversion capability is countered by the performance loss needed to identify the variable type.

Subtypes

The Variant datatype consists of smaller units called *subtypes*. Subtypes identify how the data is stored within the Variant. They're centered on the String, Numeric, Byte, Boolean, Date, Empty, Null, Error, and Object datatypes (see Table 3.1). The specialized subtypes exist to provide optimized functions for extended functionality of the specific datatype, as well as small, lightweight functions optimized for speed.

Table 3.1 The VBScript 2.0 Subtypes

Category	Description
Empty	Value is 0 for numeric variables or a zero-length string ("") for string variables.
Null	Variant intentionally contains no valid data.
Boolean	True or False.
Byte	Integer in the range 0 to 255.
Integer	Integer in the range -32,768 to 32,767.

Category	Description
Currency	-922,337,203,685,477.5808 to 922,337,203,685,477.5807.
Long	Integer in the range -2,147,483,648 to 2,147,483,647.
Single	Single-precision, floating-point number in the range -3.402823E38 to -1.401298E-45 for negative values; 1.401298E-45 to 3.402823E38 for positive values.
Double	Double-precision, floating-point number in the range -1.79769313486232E308 to -4.94065645841247E-324 for negative values; 4.94065645841247E-324 to 1.79769313486232E308 for positive values.
Date (Time)	Number that represents a date between January 1, 100 to December 31, 9999.
String	Variable-length string that can be up to approximately 2 billion characters in length.
Object	Object.
Error	Error number.

As mentioned previously, the subtypes of Variant provide for a wide range of conversion functions used to manipulate the subtypes, such as date/time values, string expressions, and currency values, as shown in Table 3.2.

Table 3.2   Conversion Functions in VBScript 2.0

Category	Converts to
CByte	Byte
CCur	Currency
CDate	Date
CDbl	Double
CInt	Integer
CLng	Long
CSng	Single
CStr	String

For more information about the details of the conversion functions, please see Chapter 7, "Datatype Conversion Features."

Part
II

Ch

3

Identifying the Datatype

With the various subtypes available, at some point it might be necessary to determine what variable subtype you're dealing with. The VarType function returns a numeric value that identifies the subtype. Table 3.3 displays the results of the VarType function.

Table 3.3 Identifying the Datatype

Subtype	Return Value
Empty	0
Null	1
Integer	2
Long	3
Single	4
Double	5
Currency	6
Date (Time)	7
String	8
Automation Object	9
Error	10
Boolean	11
Variant	12
Non-Automation Object	13
Byte	17
Array	8192

Using Variables

Now that the different characteristics of the Variant datatype and the conversion functions have been briefly covered, the length of time that the variable is available is critical in application development. This section will discuss scope or lifetime of variables in memory, how to create a variable, and the limitations and restrictions of using VBScript variables.

Variable Scope

Variables in VBScript can exist at two levels or scopes: either at the *script* or *procedure* levels. The term *scope* refers to the amount of time that the variables can be referenced in memory.

The amount of time, often referred to as the *variable lifetime*, depends on the level at which the variables are declared.

- *Script-level* code is contained outside all `Function` or `Sub` modules.
- *Procedure-level* code is contained within a `Function` or `Sub` module.

Procedure-level code is a subset of script-level code. Therefore, any variable declaration made inside one function or subroutine can't be referenced in a separate script or subroutine. To share variables across procedures, you have to use a script-level variable. (Script-level variables are the equivalent of global variables in Visual Basic.) For example, the code in Listing 3.3 demonstrates scoping issues with script and procedure-level variables.

Listing 3.3   *SCOPE_AND_LIFETIME.ASP*—Using scope to determine a variable's lifetime.

```
<SCRIPT language="VBScript">
<!--
Dim vTotalDays      <!-- Script Level Variable: Longer Scope  -->
VtotalDays = Request.QueryString("Days")
Sub GetVehicleInfo(vDays)
        Dim vSubTotal     <!-- Procedure Level Variable: Limited Scope   -->
        if Len(Trim(frmGetData.txtVehicleType.value)) = 0 then
                vMsgStr = "Please Select A Vehicle"
                vVehicleInfo = ""
                vBillRate = 0
        Else
                vMsgStr = ""
                vVehicleInfo = frmGetUserInfo.value
                vBillRate = RS("Rate")
        End if
        VSubTotal = (vBillRate*vTotalDays)
        MsgBox "Your Total is " & vSubTotal
End Sub
Sub SaveInfo()
        RS("SubTotal")= vSubTotal      <!-- Out of Scope: Stores a Null -->
        RS("TotalDays")= vTotalDays      <!-- In Scope:  Stores the Value -->
End Sub
-->
</SCRIPT>
```

This example illustrates how variable scoping issues can cause logical errors in your application. The two VBScript functions are used to help calculate and save a subtotal for a car reservation system. The subroutine `GetVehicleInfo` is used to calculate the subtotal of the rented vehicle and display a message box to the user. The `SaveInfo` function is used to write the subtotal and the total amount of days the vehicle was used into a database. After running the script, the developer noticed that the vehicle subtotal was not being saved to the database. The root of this problem arises from the improper use of variable scoping. The variable `vTotalDays` is properly stored because it is declared as a script level variable and can be accessed by any subroutine in the script. However, the variable `vSubtotal` was not declared as a procedure-level

Part
II

Ch
3

variable and cannot be shared among procedures. Even though the vSubtotal variable is created and calculated in the GetVehicleInfo subroutine, it cannot be seen in the SaveInfo subroutine. As a result, when the subtotal is stored into the database, a NULL value is stored.

Declaring Variables

As previously mentioned, variables contain two characteristics: a name and a value. Variables can be created either *explicitly* by declaring a variable name, or *implicitly* by simply referring to a variable name. Explicit declaration refers to the process of creating or instantiating a variable by directly calling the variable name with either the Dim, Public, or Private keywords. The Dim, Public, and Private keywords are used to define the length of time the variable can be referenced in the application. Implicit declaration refers to the process of creating a variable on-the-fly by referring to the variable name. In both cases, when a variable is declared or initialized, the default value of the variable depends on the assumed datatype. A numeric variable is initialized to 0, whereas a string variable is initialized to a zero-length string ("").

Dim The Dim statement is used to explicitly declare a variable. You will notice that in VBScript, as in Visual Basic, you do not have to declare a variable as a specific datatype. This change in syntax is a result of the existence of only one datatype—Variant. Dim's syntax is as follows:

```
Dim varname[([subscripts])]
```

where *varname* is the name of the variable and *subscripts* represents the number of declared dimensions.

The Dim statement can also be used to store information in arrays. An array is treated as one variable, but it is used to contain a collection of similar information. This collection is accessed by iterating through the array starting at the lower bound of zero. Arrays can also be multidimensional, allowing up to 60 dimensions. For example, the following code creates a static array with 21 sequential indexes or storage locations that represents the items ordered from an online shopping catalog. Because arrays are zero-based, 21 sublocations of the variable ItemsOrdered are actually stored. The second and third lines of code populate the first and second indexes in the array with a value from a text box on the Order Form page.

```
Dim ItemsOrdered(20)
ItemsOrdered (0) = frmOrderForm.TxtOrderItemNum.Value
ItemsOrdered (1) = frmOrderForm. TxtOrderItemNum.Value
```

ReDim The ReDim function is used when manipulating dynamic arrays. Arrays can exist in two forms: static or dynamic. A *static array* sets the number of indexes when the array is declared. The previous example demonstrated the use of a static array. *Dynamic arrays* allow the number of indexes to vary at runtime. Dynamic arrays are created by using empty parentheses () when initially declaring the variable.

Working with dynamic arrays is a little more difficult than working with static arrays. Dynamic arrays are used when the allocation of storage space is necessary, allowing you to add memory space to your array. To accomplish this, use the ReDim command to properly allocate memory space. The ReDim command is used to redefine the array size to be larger or smaller as needed. If you want to increase the size of the array and keep its contents, use the Preserve keyword. For example, the following code creates a dynamic array call RentedVehicles and resizes the array to six elements. The last line of code expands the number of elements in the array to 11, while also preserving any data in the first six elements.

```
Dim RentedVehicles()
ReDim RentedVehicles(5)
RentedVehicles(0) = frmOrderForm.TxtSelectedVehicle.Value
ReDim Preserve RentedVehicles(10)
```

 You first must ReDim a dynamic array before you can assign values to it.

Public   The Public declaration keyword is new to VBScript 2.0. Public is implemented at script level to declare public variables that have scope throughout the existence of the processing of the page. The Public declaration can also include static and dynamic array declaration. The Public syntax is as follows:

```
Public varname[([subscripts])]
```

where *varname* is the name of the variable and *subscripts* represents the number of declared dimensions.

Private   The Private statement, also new to VBScript 2.0, is the opposite of the Public statement. Private variables are available only to the script level in which they are declared and can be used with static and dynamic array processing. Private's syntax is as follows:

```
Private varname[([subscripts])]
```

where *varname* is the name of the variable and *subscripts* represents the number of declared dimensions.

Table 3.4 illustrates identifying variable scope by the declaration type.

Table 3.4   Determining Variable Scoping with Declarations in VBScript

Declaration	Script Scope
Dim	Script level, procedure level
ReDim	Procedure level, procedure level
Public	Script level
Private	Script level

TIP When a variable is first declared, the default value of the variable depends on the assumed datatype. A numeric variable is initialized to 0, whereas a string variable is initialized to a zero-length string (" ").

Option Explicit   The `Option Explicit` statement is used to prevent variables from being implicitly created within VBScript. To use the `Option Explicit` statement, use the following syntax:

```
Option Explicit
```

The `Option Explicit` statement must be declared before any script is processed by the scripting engine.

The code in Listing 3.3 demonstrated the difference between script- and procedure-level processing. The variable `VtotalDays` was explicitly declared using the `Dim` keyword, whereas the variables `vMsgStr`, `vVehicleInfo`, and `vBillRate` were implicitly declared by simply referencing the variable name.

Declaration Limitations

Even though VBScript is a text-based system, the VBScript interpreter follows its own defined programming model. The programming model defines a blueprint of conventions that the VBScript language needs to follow to operate. The rules are usually manifest in syntax, operators, and naming conventions. Variable names in VBScript also follow a standard convention. The following is a list of VBScript naming conventions.

- Variables cannot contain an embedded period.
- Variables must be fewer than 255 characters.
- Variable must be unique in the scope.
- Variables must begin with an alphabetic character.
- VBScript must have fewer than 127 procedure-level variables instantiated.
- VBScript must have fewer than 127 script-level variables instantiated.

TIP A multidimensional, multi-indexed array is viewed as only one variable in VBScript.

From Here...

Variable declaration, datatypes, and scoping issues form the foundation of the VBScript programming language. To use this knowledge, you next have to look at what types of operations you can perform on variables. The following chapters provide this information:

- Chapter 4, "Working with Operators," demonstrates how to use variables to start building to ActiveX scripts.
- Chapter 7, "Datatype Conversion Features," illustrates the subtype conversion features available to manipulate your datatypes.

- Chapter 20, "Database Access with ADO," guides you through an overview of accessing and managing your database connections.
- Chapter 21, "Working with ADO's `Connection` Object," describes how to establish a database connection.
- Chapter 23, "Working with ADO's `Recordset` Object," teaches you how to use database cursors and manipulate the resultant database query information.

Working with Operators

VBScript provides a variety of programming operators to help manipulate variables in your Active Server Pages. Most programming languages break down their object models into logical groups based on functionality. The ability to manipulate objects and variables form the foundation of workflow control in an application. This chapter discusses the use of arithmetic, comparison, logical, and concatenation operators in VBScript 2.0 and explains how VBScript prioritizes these operators. ■

Arithmetic Operators

Learn how to use the arithmetic operators to manipulate your numeric variables and mathematical functions.

Comparison Operators

Examine the comparison operators needed to compare and contrast variables, datatypes, and objects.

Logical Operators

Discover how logical operators extend the comparison operators' functionality by applying comparison operators to Boolean expressions.

Concatenation Operators

Learn how to properly use the numeric and string concatenation operators without having to experience the programming troubles from automatic datatype conversion.

Order of Operations

Guard against programming logic errors in your ActiveX scripting by learning how VBScript systematically processes operators.

Arithmetic Operators

The VBScript arithmetic operators perform various mathematical calculations. Most of the arithmetic operators have the following syntax:

```
myResult = myExp1 Operator myExp2
```

where *myExp1* and *myExp2* are numeric expressions and *Operator* is a mathematical operator.

The arithmetic operators supported by VBScript are listed in Table 4.1.

Table 4.1   Arithmetic Operators

Operator	Symbol	Description
Addition	+	Sums two numbers.
Subtraction	-	Finds the difference between two numbers or sets the negative value of a number.
Multiplication	*	Multiplies two numbers.
Division	/	Divides two numbers.
Integer Division	\	Divides two numbers and returns an integer result.
Exponentiation	^	Raises a number to the power of an exponent.

Addition

The addition operator (+) is used to sum numeric expressions. It can also be used to append or concatenate strings together, so great care must be used with the addition operator. The syntax for the addition operator is:

```
myResult = myExp1 + myExp2
```

where *myExp1* and *myExp2* can be variables of any subtype. Remember, there is only one datatype in VBScript: Variant. Adding two variables may produce unexpected results because of the Variant's capability to change subtypes automatically based on the variable's datatype. To prevent unexpected results, consider the following operation rules for the addition operator, as shown in Table 4.2.

Table 4.2   Rules of Addition Operator

If expressions are...	Then operator will...
Both Numeric	Add
Both Strings	Concatenate
String and Numeric	Add

Consider a situation where the addition of two numbers is required. The following code with variables `myVar1` and `myVar2` (both of `Variant` datatype) illustrates the unexpected results that may occur when using the addition operator.

```
<%
myVar1 = 30: myVar2 = "5"
myResults1 = myVar1 + myVar2      '=== Returns 35
myResults2 = myVar2 + myVar2      '=== Returns "55"
myResults3 = myVar2 + myVar1      '=== Returns 35
myResults4 = myVar1 + myVar1      '=== Returns 60
%>
```

You can see from this example that, without a proper understanding of the `Variant` datatype and the behavior of the addition operator, a VBScript programmer could become frustrated quickly with unexpected results! In the above example, the variables are first created and initialized. Both of these variables are of the `Variant` datatype. However, VBScript has already assigned an automatic subtype to each. The variable `myVar1` is of subtype `Integer` because it was assigned an integer value. The variable `myVar2` is of subtype `String` because it was assigned a string value. Then, in the third line of code, `myVar1` and `myVar2` are added together. Following the rules in Table 4.2, adding a string value and a numeric value together results in the two values being summed. In this situation VBScript automatically converts `myVar2` to a numeric value and adds it to `myVar1`, and then assigns the sum to `myResults1`. The next line of code concatenates the two string variables to produce the literal string `"55"` for the result. The fifth line of code produces the same results as the third line. VBScript converts `myVar2` to a numeric value and adds it to `myVar1`. The last line simply adds two numeric values together.

To help prevent some of these datatype issues, VBScript offers conversion functions to explicitly convert a variable to a desired subtype. The `CStr` function converts a variable to a `String` subtype and the `CInt` function converts a variable to an `Integer` subtype. The conversion functions will be discussed in greater depth in Chapter 7, "Datatype Conversion Features," and are demonstrated in the following script:

```
<%
dim myVar1, myVar2, myResults
myVar1=5: myVar2=10
myResults = CStr(myVar1) + CStr(myVar2)      '=== Returns "510"
myResults = CStr(myVar1) + CInt(myVar2)      '=== Returns 15
myResults = CInt(myVar1) + CStr(myVar2)      '=== Returns 15
%>
```

Remember, in order to protect yourself from potential programming errors, always be sure to use the conversion functions to ensure your addition operator performs as expected with the proper datatypes.

TIP To prevent unexpected string concatenation when using the addition operator, use conversion functions to ensure proper data subtypes.

Subtraction

The subtraction (-) operator is used to determine the difference between two numbers or is used to negate a positive number. The dual functionality of the subtraction operator requires two different syntaxes. To determine the difference between numbers, use the following syntax:

```
myResult = number1 - number2
```

where *number1* and *number2* are numeric subtypes.

To provide the unary negation, or the negative value of an expression, use the following syntax:

```
myResult = -(expression)
```

where *expression* is a numeric subtype.

The subtraction operator is often referred to as the negation operator because is negates a positive number. If the result of the negation operator is empty, the result is treated by other numeric expressions as if it were zero (0).

Multiplication

The multiplication operator (*) is used to return the results of two numbers multiplied together. The multiplication operator uses the following syntax:

```
myResult = number1 * number2
```

where *number1* and *number2* are numeric subtypes. If either *number1* or *number2* is NULL, the data subtype of the result variable will be NULL. If *number1* or *number2* is Empty, the value of the empty variable will be converted to zero.

Division

The division operator (/) is used to divide one numeric expression into another numeric expression. The syntax for the division operator is:

```
myResult = number1 / number2
```

where *number1* and *number2* are numeric expressions and *myResult* returns a floating-point datatype.

The rules for the multiplication operator also apply to the division operator. If either *number1* or *number2* is NULL, the resulting data subtype is NULL. If either numeric expression is Empty, that numeric expression is treated as a zero.

Exponentiation

The exponential operator (^) is used to raise a number to the power of an exponent. The exponential operation is performed using the following syntax:

```
myResult = number ^ exponent
```

where *number* and *exponent* are any numeric value.

Keep in mind that *number* can be negative only if *exponent* is an integer value. Also, if the *number* or *exponent* variables are NULL, then the resulting data subtype will also be NULL.

Integer Division Operator

The integer division operator (\) is used similarly to the division operator (/) but is specifically designed to return an integer result. The integer division operator uses the following syntax:

```
myResult = number1 \ number2
```

where *number1* and *number2* are numeric expressions that are rounded to either a Byte, Integer, or Long subtype before the division. Furthermore, if either numeric expression is NULL, the result is NULL; and if either expression is Empty, the numeric expression is treated as a zero.

 TIP Use the TypeName function to determine the subtype of a variable.

For example, consider the following script:

```
<%
myExp1 = NULL                          '=== Assigns a NULL
myExp2 = 2000.86                       '=== Assigns a Value
myResult = myExp1 \ myExp2             '=== Performs Integer Division but is
➥assigned a NULL value
Response.Write myResult &"<BR>"        '=== Write nothing to page
%>
```

This script would not return any values because the NULL value assigned to the variable myExp1 produces a NULL result. This assignment of NULL often occurs when extracting information from a database. To prevent the cascading of the NULL datatype, use the VarType character as shown below:

```
<%@ LANGUAGE="VBSCRIPT" %>

<SCRIPT LANGUAGE = "VBScript" RUNAT = SERVER>
Function TrimNulls(vValue)
   Select Case TypeName(vValue)
     Case "Null"
           ret = 0
     Case Else
           ret = vValue
   End Select
TrimNulls = ret
End Function
</SCRIPT>

<HTML>
<HEAD>
<BODY>
myExp1 = NULL                                         '=== Assigns NULL
myExp2 = 2000.86                                      '=== Assign value
myResult = TrimNulls(myExp1) \ TrimNulls(myExp2)      '=== Trims out the NULL
➥values
```

```
Response.Write "myExp1: " &TypeName(myExp1) &"<BR>"      '=== Displays NULL
Response.Write "myExp2: " &TypeName(myExp2) &"<BR>"      '=== Displays Double
Response.Write "myResult: " &TypeName(myResult) &"<BR>"  '=== Displays Long
Response.Write myResult &"<BR><HR>"                      '=== Returns 0
</BODY>
</HTML>
```

In the code example, the function `TrimNulls` was used to place `NULL` values with `0` values. As a result, the ASP script returns a `0` for the variable `myResults`.

Modulus Operator

The modulus operator (`MOD`) is used to return only the remainder when two numbers are divided. The modulus operator uses the following syntax:

```
myResult = number1 MOD number2
```

where *number1* and *number2* can be any numeric expression. The `MOD` operator divides *number1* by *number2* to return only the remainder portion of the result. For example, the expression `E = 21 Mod 8.37` returns the value `5` of a type `Long`. Using the regular division operator on the expression `F = 21 / 8.37` returns `2.5089605734767` of type `Double`.

In addition to supporting basic mathematical functionality, VBScript also supports several trigonometric and logarithmic functions. Table 4.3 lists these mathematical functions.

Table 4.3   Mathematical Functions Supported in VBScript

Function	Description
Sin	Determines the sine of an angle.
Cos	Determines the cosine of an angle.
Tan	Determines the tangent of an angle.
ATan	Determines the arctangent of a number.
Exp	Determines the base of natural logarithms raised to a power.
Sqr	Determines the square root of a number.
Log	Determines the natural logarithm of a number.

The extended mathematical functions use the following syntax:

```
myResult = Function (expression)
```

For example, to find the cosine of a 30-degree angle, the following code would be used:

```
<% MyAngle = Cos(30) %>
```

Comparison Operators

Comparison operators analyze the relationship between expressions. Remember that expressions can be any combination of keywords, operators, variables, or constants that form a string, number, or object. VBScript uses different comparison operator syntax when comparing expressions and when comparing objects. If you are comparing expressions, the following syntax is used:

```
myResult = myExp1 (operator) myExp2
```

where *myExp1* and *myExp2* contain any legal expression, and the comparison operator represents a symbol that defines a relationship between the two expressions. The comparison operators used in VBScript are illustrated in Table 4.4.

Table 4.4   Comparison Operators

Operator	Symbol	Description
Equality	=	Is equal to
Inequality	<>	Is not equal to
Greater Than	>	Is greater than
Lesser Than	<	Is less than
Greater Than or Equal To	>=	Is greater than or equal to
Less Than or Equal To	<=	Is less than or equal to
Object Equivalence	IS	Object comparison

Comparison operators give you the ability to determine the relationship between two expressions. Traditionally, developers expect these comparisons to evaluate to either True or False. But it is important to consider a third possibility: NULL. If either expression in the comparison is a NULL datatype, the comparison will return a NULL value. This is important to keep in mind when designing application logic. Programmers should design an application flow that responds to the possibilities of a comparison evaluating to True, False, or NULL. Table 4.5 represents the control logic for the traditional comparison operators, excluding the IS comparison operator.

Table 4.5   The Comparison Operator Results

Operator	Returns True if	Returns False if	Returns NULL if
<	myExp1 < myExp2	myExp1 >= myExp2	myExp1 or myExp2 = NULL
<=	myExp1 <= myExp2	myExp1 > myExp2	myExp1 or myExp2 = NULL
>	myExp1 > myExp2	myExp1 <= myExp2	myExp1 or myExp2 = NULL

continues

Part

II

Ch

4

Table 4.5   Continued

Operator	Returns True if	Returns False if	Returns NULL if
>=	myExp1 >= myExp2	myExp1 < myExp2	myExp1 or myExp2 = NULL
=	myExp1 = myExp2	myExp1 <> myExp2	myExp1 or myExp2 = NULL
<>	myExp1 <> myExp2	myExp1 = myExp2	myExp1 or myExp2 = NULL

Comparison operators act like arithmetic operators in that they also change behavior based on the datatypes of the operands. You can help prevent unexpected results by identifying the datatype by using the TypeName function or by using string conversion utilities, such as CStr and CLng. (These formatting and conversion functions are discussed in further detail in Chapter 7.) For example, if the variable vNumber = 11\3 (the integer division function), then TypeName(vNumber) returns Integer.

Use Table 4.6 to serve as a guideline of expected logic performed based on operand subtype.

Table 4.6   Evaluating Expressions Using VBScript Comparison Logic

Expression	Performed logic
If both are numeric	Numeric comparison.
If both are strings	Perform a string comparison.
If one expression is numeric and the other is a string	The numeric expression is less than the string expression.
One expression is Empty and the other is numeric	Perform a numeric comparison, using 0 as the Empty expression.
One expression is Empty and the other is a string	Perform a string comparison, using a zero-length string ("") as the Empty expression.
Both expressions are Empty	The expressions are equal.

The second type of comparison operator is the object comparison operator. The IS operator is used to compare object references. If you are comparing objects, the following syntax is used:

```
myResult = object1 IS object2
```

where object1 and object2 represent objects and the use of the keyword IS determines a relationship between objects.

When comparing objects, there is no NULL possibility. The relationship is either True or False. If the objects are the same, then the IS function returns True. If the objects are not the same, the function returns False.

Equality Comparison

The equality operator is the most commonly used comparison operator. The equality comparison is used to determine whether a condition is equal to a value, and in most situations, provides the coding logic to react to a decision. An example of an equality comparison would be a test to determine the color of a shirt. This test would be implemented by comparing the value of the variable myShirt to determine whether the color of a shirt was blue. To perform the equality comparison, use the following syntax:

```
Expression = Condition
```

where *Expression* and *Condition* are any valid VBScript expression. To test whether the color of the shirt is Blue, you would then use the equality (=) comparison operator in any type of decision-making process:

```
<% If myShirt = "Blue" Then %>    '=== If then loop with equality comparison
operator
```

or

```
<% Do While myShirt = "Blue" %>    '=== Do while loop with comparison operator
```

What's interesting about the equality comparison is that the comparison can be made either implicitly or explicitly. An implicit equality comparison is used to evaluate whether a specific expression is True or is often used to determine if larger categories of values are True. For example, you may not be interested in testing for a specific time value, but you might want to know whether the current variable actually contains a date value, as shown in the following script:

```
<%
timeStamp = Now
If IsDate(timeStamp) Then
    Response.Write "The time is " & timeStamp
End If
%>
```

Part

II

Ch

4

The script accomplishes this by using the IsDate function to test whether the VBScript variable timeStamp contains a date value. Because the NOW function returns the existing system's time and date, the ISDATE function in the first line would return True. In this situation, after successfully testing the IsDate function, the next line of script writes the current date and time to the page.

An explicit equality comparison verifies that an evaluated expression and a variable's value are equal. For example, the following example is used to see what fruit is on sale today and set the prices accordingly. If the variable vFruit ="Apple", then the following comparison would fail.

```
<%
If vFruit = "banana" Then        '=== Does 'Apple' = 'Banana', no
    vStr = "Sale Today"          '=== If true then set additional variable
    vPrice = vSalePercent * vProductCost
Else                             '=== Comparison is not equal, so this is
```

```
➥executed
     vStr = "Special Today"
     vPrice = vSpecialPercent * vProductCost
End If
%>
```

Inequality Comparison

The inequality operator (<>) provides the opposite functionality of the equality comparison, ensuring that an evaluated statement is *not* equal to a variable's value. This type of comparison is often used when you need to test for a range of values instead of a specific value. For example, if you need to test for all color shirts not equal to 'Blue', then use the inequality operator to search for all values not equal to 'Blue'. This inequality comparison is demonstrated in the following example:

```
<%
If myShirt <> 'Blue' Then
     MsgStr = "You look better in blue"         '=== This line is not executed
End If
%>
```

Greater Than Comparison

The greater than (>) comparison determines whether one expression is larger than another expression. For example, if the variable vAcctBalance ="200", the following logic would fail and the value of vChargePercent would be equal to 0.25636.

```
<%
If vAcctBalance > "500" Then
     vChargePercent = 0.23953
Else
     vChargePercent = 0.25636
End If
%>
```

Less Than Comparison

The less than (<) comparison operator, opposite in functionality to the greater than operator, determines whether the expression on the left side of the operator is smaller or less than the expression on the right side. For example, the following comparison will return True if the current value of the vGasTank variable is "4.5".

```
<%
If vGagTank < 6.5 Then
     vMsg = "Better get gas soon!"
End If
%>
```

Object Comparison

Object comparison (IS) operator can only be used to compare object types and cannot compare other objects properties. The following example demonstrates how the IS operator is used to compare objects. The Set statement is first used to create replica objects, MySecondObject and MyThirdObject, from the object MyObject. Next, the Set statement is used to create another object, YourSecondObject, from the object YourObject.

```
<%
Dim MyObject, MySecondObject, MyThirdObject, YourObject, YourSecondObject,
➥MyResult
Set MySecondObject = MyObject                    '=== Assign object references.
Set MyThirdObject = MyObject
Set YourSecondObject = YourObject
MyResult = MySecondObject IS MyThirdObject       '=== Returns True.
MyResult = YourSecondObject IS MyThirdObject     '=== Returns False.
%>
```

Remember that the Set command is used to declare and reference objects. The Dim command is used to declare and reference variables.

Logical Operators

Logical operators help to expand the functionality found in comparison operators by using a different evaluation approach. The logical operator focuses on the Boolean method of determining whether a process returns True or False (see Table 4.7).

Table 4.7   Logical Operators

Operator	Symbol	Description
Conjunction	AND	Performs a logical conjunction.
Negation	NOT	Performs logical negation.
Disjunction	OR	Performs a logical disjunction.
Exclusion	XOR	Performs a logical exclusion.
Equivalence	EQV	Performs a logical equivalence.
Implication	IMP	Performs a logical implication.

The VBScript operators work behind the scenes performing a *bitwise* comparison of bits that represent numeric expressions. Comparing the two expressions is simply a straightforward comparison of bits (either a 0 [zero] or 1 [one]), as demonstrated in Table 4.8. It's important to note that these logical operators operate on Boolean expressions. Therefore, in evaluating the expression myVarB = Not (yourVarA), where yourVarA = 'Valid', the NOT operator would return a 'Type mismatch' error.

Part

II

Ch

4

Table 4.8 Bitwise Comparison: The Foundation of Logical Operators

Bit Expression1	Bit Expression2	Result
0	0	0
0	1	1
1	0	1
1	1	1

Negation (*NOT*)

The negation comparison (NOT) is used to perform logical negation on an expression. This logical comparison is similar to the negatory comparison operator. The NOT operator uses the following syntax:

```
myResult = Not myExpression
```

where *myExpression* is any expression. The NOT operator actually performs its operations by inverting the bit value of the variable. Therefore, if the variable *myExpression* is equal to True, the result of the negation operator would be False. The negation operator is used to return one of three results: True, False, or NULL, as shown in Table 4.9.

Table 4.9 The Results of the Negation (*NOT*) Operator

Expression	Result
True	False
False	True
NULL	NULL

Remember that a NULL value represents a variable that contains no valid data. Consequently, any operator that performs a function on this variable will reproduce a corresponding NULL result. Therefore, it is very important to declare your datatypes within your Active scripts. Also, keep in mind that an empty string ("") is not equivalent to a NULL string, as seen in the code listing below.

```
<%
MyVar = ""
myResult = IsNull(MyVar)      '=== Returns False.
%>

<%
MyVar = NULL
MyResult = IsNull(MyVar)      '=== Returns True.
%>
```

A NULL string is a Variant datatype that contains no valid data, whereas an Empty string is a Variant datatype that contains data, but of length zero. An Empty string is most often the result of an un-initialized or unassigned variable.

Conjunction (*AND*)

The logical conjunction (AND) is used to group two or more comparisons together and evaluate the group of comparisons together as one comparison. The AND conjunction requires that all comparisons in the group evaluate to True for the conjunction to evaluate to True. If any one comparison evaluates to False, then the conjunction evaluates to False. For example, the code listed below will fail because myVarA is less than myVarC.

```
<%
Dim myVarA, myVarB, myVarC
myVarA = 40
myVarB = 25
myVarC = 55
If (myVarA > myVarB) AND (myVarA > myVarC) Then
      '=== This statement will not be executed
End If
%>
```

The previous example demonstrates that both expressions, (myVarA > myVarB) and (myVarA > myVarC) must evaluate to True. However, even though the first expression is True, the AND operator fails because the second expression returns False. The behavior of the logical AND operator can be seen in Table 4.10.

Table 4.10   The Logical *AND* Operation Conditions and Results

Expression1	*Expression2*	**Result**
True	True	True
True	False	False
True	NULL	NULL
False	True	False
False	False	False
False	NULL	False
NULL	True	NULL
NULL	False	False
NULL	NULL	NULL

Disjunction (*OR*)

The logical disjunction (OR) operator is used to test whether any of a series of expressions evaluates to True. The OR operator requires the following syntax:

```
myResult = expression1 OR expression2
```

where *expression1* or *expression2* is any valid VBScript expression.

The OR operator provides different programming flexibility than the logical AND operator. The OR operator will evaluate to True if any of the comparisons evaluate to True, whereas the AND operator will evaluate to True only if all the comparisons evaluate to True.

```
<%
Dim A, B, C, D, MyResult
A = 100: B = 80: C = 60: D = Null      '=== Initialize variables.
MyResult = A > B Or B > C              '=== Returns True.
MyResult = B > A Or B > C              '=== Returns True.
MyResult = A > B Or B > D              '=== Returns True.
MyResult = B > D Or B > A              '=== Returns Null.
%>
```

Table 4.11 provides the conditions and results of the OR logical operator.

Table 4.11   The Logical *OR* Conditions and Results

Expression1	*Expression2*	**Results**
True	True	True
True	False	True
True	NULL	True
False	True	True
False	False	False
False	NULL	NULL
NULL	True	True
NULL	False	NULL
NULL	NULL	NULL

Exclusion (*XOR*)

The exclusion operator (XOR) is used to test whether two expressions differ in results. The exclusionary operator requires the following syntax:

```
myResult = expression1 XOR expression2
```

where *expression1* and *expression2* are valid VBScript expressions. The best way to see how the exclusionary operator works is demonstrated in the following example. The first and third exclusionary comparisons return a False value because both expressions individually return the same value. Essentially, the XOR operator is testing whether the two expressions return different values. The second exclusionary comparison returns a True value because the two individual comparisons returned different values, one True and the other False.

```
<%
Dim A, B, C, D, MyResult
A = 100: B = 80: C = 60: D = Null      '=== Initialize variables.
MyResult = A > B XOR B > C             '=== Returns False.
MyResult = B > A XOR B > C             '=== Returns True.
MyResult = B > A XOR C > B             '=== Returns False.
MyResult = B > D XOR A > B             '=== Returns NULL.
%>
```

A more complete display of the XOR results, depending on the expressions, is illustrated in Table 4.12.

Table 4.12 The *XOR* Logical Operator Conditions and Results

Expression1	Expression2	Results
True	True	False
True	False	True
False	True	True
False	False	False

Equivalence (*EQV*)

The equivalence operator (EQV) is used to perform a logical equivalence of two expressions. The equivalence operator requires the following syntax:

```
myResult = expression1 EQV expression2
```

The equivalence operator is use to determine whether the two expressions produce similar results. For example, consider the following script:

```
<%
Dim A, B, C, D, MyResult
A = 100: B = 80: C = 60: D = Null      '=== Initialize variables.
MyResult = A > B EQV B > C             '=== Returns True.
MyResult = B > A EQV B > C             '=== Returns False.
MyResult = A > B EQV B > D             '=== Returns NULL.
%>
```

The evaluation of the first EQV expression in the statement A > B EQV B > C will return True because both expressions produce similar results. The second EQV expression, B > A EQV B > C, returns False because the two expressions produce dissimilar results. The third expression returns NULL, illustrating the cascading effect of using NULL and VBScript operators. The EQV logical operator results are demonstrated in Table 4.13.

Table 4.13   The EQV Logical Operator Conditions and Results

Expression1	Expression2	Results
True	True	False
True	False	True
False	True	True
False	False	False

Concatenation Operators

There are two operators in VBScript that are used to link or join strings together (see Table 4.14). The ampersand (&) operator is the true concatenation operator. The addition (+) operator can also be used to join strings. However, the addition operator, as described above, is primarily designed for adding numeric datatypes and can result in unpredictable results depending on the variable datatype.

Table 4.14   Concatenation Operators

Operator	Symbol	Description
String Concatenation	&	Used to concatenate strings.
String and Numeric Operations	+	Used for string concatenation and numeric addition.

& Operator

The ampersand (&)operator is used to concatenate or join strings expressions together. The & operator requires the following syntax:

```
myResult = expression1 & expression2
```

where *expression1* and *expression2* are valid VBScript string expressions. A common use of the ampersand operator is to collect information from different objects associated with Web pages and construct a resulting string. This resulting string is often used to construct URLs with user-defined variables or to create SQL strings for database access. For example, the following code uses the concatenation operator to construct a string that will be used to access product information from a database.

```
<%
Dim sqlStr
sqlStr = "SELECT * "
sqlStr = sqlStr & "FROM Products"     '=== Generates the string "SELECT * FROM
➥Products"
%>
```

You can also use this operator to create a string that uses values pulled from any object within the script's scope. For example, the following code takes the value in a textbox named txtFirstName on a form named frmLogin and concatenates it with the text "Hello" to create a string that holds "Hello" and the user name.

```
<%
Dim MyStr
MyStr = "Hello" & Trim(frmLogin.txtFirstName.value)     '=== Returns "Hello "
➥and user name.
%>
```

The ampersand operator also has special rules regarding data subtypes. If the concatenated expression is not a string, it will be converted to a String subtype. If either of the expressions is a NULL, then the resulting concatenated string is a zero-length string (""). However, if both expressions are NULL, the ampersand returns a NULL value.

+ Operator

The addition (+) operator can also be used to append strings, but using this operator for string manipulation is not recommended because the + operator performs two functions: the addition of numeric values and the concatenating of string values. The ambiguity occurs when the + operator is functioning on expressions of different subtypes. The addition operator requires the following operator syntax:

```
myResult = expression1 + expression2
```

where *expression1* and *expression2* are valid VBScript expressions.

If both expressions are numeric, the + operator will execute its numeric summarization features. If both expressions are strings, the + operator will concatenate the strings. If one expression is a Numeric and the other expression is a String subtype, then the + operator will add them together.

```
<%
dim vVar, vStr
vVar = 30: vStr = "5"
myResults = vVar + vVar     '=== Returns 60
myResults = vStr + vStr     '=== Returns 55
myResults = vStr + vVar     '=== Returns 35
%>
```

Operator Precedence

Operator precedence is used to describe the order in which different operators are evaluated in a combination of keywords, operators, and variables. VBScript is similar to Visual Basic in terms of the order in which VBScript systematically processes expressions.

Expressions are evaluated based on the category of the operator, as shown in the following list. Arithmetic operators are processed first, followed by the comparison operators, and then logical operators are evaluated last.

1. Arithmetic operators
2. Comparison operators
3. Logical operators

 TIP   Concatenation are evaluated after the arithmetic operators and before the comparison operators.

The precedence of arithmetic and logical operators within their own operator group is defined in Table 4.15. The arithmetic operators are executed first from the exponential operator to the subtraction operator. The logical operators' execution priorities range from the logical negation operator to the logical implication operator.

Table 4.15   The Arithmetic and Logical Operators' Execution Hierarchy from Highest to Lowest

Description	Symbol	Description	Symbol
Exponential	^	Negation	NOT
Unary Negation	-	Conjunction	AND
Multiplication	*	Disjunction	OR
Division	/	Exclusion	XOR
Integer Division	\	Equivalence	EQV
Modulus Arithmetic	MOD	Implication	IMP
Addition	+		
Subtraction	-		

Unlike the hierarchical execution approach of the arithmetic and logical operators, the comparison operators all share the same level of importance. The comparison operators are executed in order of appearance from left to right. A similar left-to-right rule also applies to situations where multiplication and division operators or addition and subtraction operators occur together.

To add programming control to the use of operators, the use of parentheses overrides the default operator precedence described above. All operations within parentheses take precedence over operations outside parentheses and nested parentheses. However, all operations within parentheses follow the default operator precedence. For example, consider the following script:

```
<%
Response.Write (5 + 10 * 20 - 5) &"<BR>"        Returns 200
Response.Write (5 + 10 * (20 - 5)) &"<BR>"      Returns 155
%>
```

The first line of the preceding script first performs the multiplication of 10 * 20. Then the addition operator adds 5 to the total and the subtraction operator subtracts 5 to return 200 as the result. However, the second line of code first executes the expression in the parentheses (20-5). Afterward, that result is multiplied by 10 and then 5 is added to the result to return 155.

From Here...

In this chapter, you have learned the various operators that provide the different types of comparison logic in VBScript. The arithmetic operators are used to manipulate your numeric expressions and mathematical functions. The comparison operators compare and contrast variables, datatypes, and objects. VBScript uses logical operators to apply comparison operators to Boolean expressions and concatenation operators to append strings expressions. Finally, you saw that VBScript also has a defined order of operations that dictates in what order operators will be processed.

At this point, you are ready to learn how VBScript uses these operators with decision operators to help control program and application workflow in your ASP scripts.

- Chapter 5, "Controlling Program Flow with VBScript," demonstrates how to use logical and looping operators to build your applications.
- Chapter 6, "Working with Functions, Subroutines, and Dialog Boxes," illustrates event-driven programming through the use of reusable code modules.
- Chapter 7, "Datatype Conversion Features," describes the datatype conversion functions in VBScript that ensure proper application execution.
- Chapter 8, "Putting It All Together with VBScript," demonstrates how to use VBScript to perform calculations and display the results using Active Server Pages, and illustrates how to use client-side validation on the Internet Explorer browser.
- Chapter 9, " Using the Script Debugger," describes how to use the Microsoft Script Debugger to provide inline-debugging capabilities for your client- and server-side scripts.

Part
II

Ch
4

Controlling Program Flow with VBScript

Now that the basics of VBScript variables and operators have been covered, this chapter will cover how to control program execution flow in VBScript. In Chapter 3, you learned how to store and retrieve values from variables. Chapter 4 illustrated how to use operators to compare, evaluate, and manipulate variables. The next step is to investigate the various control structures in VBScript that are used to create the fundamental logic driving your application. This program execution control comes in two forms: decision structures and looping structures. *Decision structures* execute conditional statements and, as a result of a test, decision branches of the appropriate result statements. *Looping structures* cyclically process a section of code until the conditional statement is satisfied. ■

Making a Decision

Learn what types of programmatic control mechanisms exist for controlling application workflow in VBScript and how to implement the conditional logic in your application.

Using Looping Logic

Discover the different looping structures available in VBScript and how they are used to repeat a process until a condition is met.

Stopping the Process Flow

Investigate how to programmatically interrupt your script execution using the *Exit* statement and how to handle error trapping in VBScript.

Error Trapping

Learn how to use VBScript's *Err* object to handle runtime errors and error trapping in your ASP and client-side scripts.

Using Decision Structures

Making a decision in VBScript is possible through three basic decision structures: If...Then, If...Then...Else, and Select Case decision trees. These structures test conditions and perform actions depending on the logic contained in the code. In most situations, the decision statements are largely responsible for making decisions that drive the business rules for your applications. The If...Then statement is used to test a condition and execute a block of code if the condition is valid. The If...Then...Else statement performs the same functionality as the If...Then statement, but it gives you the option of executing a second block of code if the condition is not satisfied. Finally, the Select Case statement enables you to test for multiple conditions rather than limit yourself to simple true/false situations. The Select Case statement lets you test for multiple conditions and execute blocks of code based on the value of an expression.

The *If...Then* Condition

The most commonly used decision-based control structure in VBScript is the If...Then statement. The If...Then statement is used to test a Boolean (True or False) condition and execute script based on the results. If the evaluated condition is True, the immediate script following the Then statement is executed. The If...Then statement uses the following syntax:

```
IF condition THEN
     statement
End If
```

where condition is an evaluated expression and statement represents a block of code that is executed if condition is True. Once the statement is finished processing or the condition is returned False, program execution is returned to the code line immediately following the End If statement.

The condition must be an expression that can be evaluated as either True or False. The resultant True or False transcription enables the scripting logic to present a straightforward approach to controlling logic and program workflow. For example, the following situation determines whether the conditional statement of myVar > 50 is True. If so, the condition returns True and the string message is assigned. However, if myVar is less or equal to 50, the expression evaluates to False and programmatic control skips to the next statement after the End If statement.

```
<%
Dim myVar
myVar = 100                                 '=== Initialize variables
if (myVar > 50) Then                        '=== Condition evaluates True
     strMsgStr = "Do you want to play again?" '=== Executed line
End if
%>
```

Besides testing the Boolean result of a comparison operator as described above, you can also test an expression that directly returns True or False. For example, consider the following situation that demonstrates using the IsDate function to execute a multi-line script block that writes the number of days left until the year 2000. If the variable myDate is not a valid date, such as "00/00/1999", the resultant statements are not executed. For more information about the VBScript's evaluation functions, please see Chapter 7, "Datatype Conversion Features."

```
<%
dim myDate
myDate = now                                                '=== Initialize
➥to today's date
If IsDate(myDate) Then                                      '=== Is myDate
➥a Date Sub Type
    Dim myDays
    myDays = DateDiff("d",myDate,"1/1/2000")                '=== Find days
➥until year 2000
    Response.Write myDays &" days left until the year 2000!"  '=== write
➥results to page
End if
%>
```

You can also expand the testing conditions of the If...Then statements to contain other If...Then statements. *Nesting* conditional statements is accomplished by placing one If...Then statement in the result block of another If...Then statement. Nesting conditional statements enables you to incorporate multiple dependent conditions in your code. For example, the following code uses nested conditions to remind you to check your credit card balance on New Years day in the year 2000. The second nested loop executes if you set the variable myDate to any valid date greater than or equal to "1/1/2000".

```
<%
myDate = now                                          '=== Initialize to today's
➥date
if IsDate(myDate) then                                '=== Is it a valid date?

    If (DateDiff("d","1/1/2000",myDate) >= 0) then    '=== Is the current date
➥past 1/1/2000?
        Response.Write "Have you checked you credit card balance today?"
    End if

End if
%>
```

This previous example first ensures that the variable myDate is an actual date. If the variable is a date, then the second conditional If...Then statement is used to only write the warning message if the date is 1/1/2000.

This single result approach of the If...Then statement to applying application logic has limited use. In most situations, you often need to implement an either/or approach to application workflow. This branching capability is demonstrated with the If...Then...Else statement.

The *If...Then...Else* Statement

The If...Then...Else statement expands the traditional If...Then statement by adding a failure condition using the Else statement. This Else condition enables the decision logic to present a failure option within the original If condition. This internal routing separates scripting code that would otherwise have to be placed in a second If...Then statement. The If...Then...Else statement requires the following syntax:

```
If condition Then
    statements
```

Part

II

Ch

5

```
Else
    elsestatements
End if
```

where *condition* is a Boolean expression or function, *statements* is the code that is executed if the condition statement evaluates to True, and *elsestatements* is the code that is executed if the *condition* evaluates to False.

The If...Then...Else presents two different directions the application logic can follow. First, you can combine the previous illustrated nested If...Then examples into one conditional If...Then...Else condition. For example, the following example uses the If...Then...Else statement to determine the amount of days between the current date and the year 2000. If there are still days left before the year 2000, the script will present a friendly reminder showing the amount of days left until the year 2000. Once the year 2000 arrives, the script will remind the user to check his credit card balance.

```
<%
dim myDays
myDays = DateDiff("d", Now, "1/1/2000")              '=== Find amount of days until
year 2000
If myDays > 0 Then                                   '=== Still time left
    Response.Write myDays &" days left until the year 2000!"
Else                                                 '=== Gulp!
    Response.Write "Have you checked you credit card balance today?"
End if
%>
```

Notice that the creation of the variable myDays is not necessary for the conditional statement. The statement If (DateDiff("d", Now, "1/1/2000") > 0) then could replace the statement if myDays > 0. However, because you want to use the results of the DateDiff function later in the code block, fewer resources are consumed by storing the variable once instead of requiring additional processor cycles to recalculate the DateDiff function for the display message.

You can further expand the If...Then...Else functionality to enable multiple test conditions by adding the ElseIf statement. Use the following syntax to provide multiple test condition:

```
If condition Then
    statements
ElseIf condition-n Then
    elseifstatements
Else
    elsestatements
End If
```

Now you can test conditional statements for more than two conditions at a time. For example, the following code illustrates assigning the tax form helper documentation according to the number of exemptions an employee selects.

```
<%
Dim myExemptions, myTaxHelperID              '=== Initialize variable
myExemptions = 2                             '=== Set variable
If myExemptions = 0 Then
    myTaxHelperID = "Publication 1678"
```

```
ElseIf myExemptions = 1 then
    myTaxHelperID = "Publication 1713"
ElseIf myExemptions = 2 then              '=== This row selected
    myTaxHelperID = "Publication 1779"
Else
    myTaxHelperID = "Publication 1648"
End if
Response.Write myTaxHelperID              '=== Write to page the selected result
%>
```

In the previous example, the code evaluated in the ElseIf condition evaluates until the condition returns True. When the condition returns True, the code following the Then statement is executed. If the ElseIf condition evaluates to False, then the next conditional statement is evaluated. For example, in this situation, the first two Else conditions are evaluated to be False. However, the third condition returns True and the resultant Then conditional block is executed. In this example, the variable myTaxHelperID is set to "Publication 1779". If none of the conditions in the entire If...Then...Else blocks evaluate to True and an Else condition exists, the Else statement will be executed. The Else statement acts as the default code block for the entire If...Then...Else block. If the Else statement does not exist, then no code is executed.

 TIP Always include an Else statement to act as the default statement in case no conditions evaluate to True. This will minimize potential shortcomings in programming logic when all the evaluation conditions fail.

The value of the Else condition should not be underestimated; it plays a critical role in determining workflow. For example, the following code sets the variable myExemptions by accepting a value from a hyperlink using the Active Server Page Response object. This code segment is responsible for evaluating the input and setting the Web page to redirect the browser. For example, in the previous code example, the variable myExemptions was set to 2. In this case, this code would set the variable myTaxHelperID equal to Publication 1779. Then the variable gotoURL would create the string 'Publication 1779.asp' and automatically direct the user to that page, assuming it exists.

Part

II

Ch

5

```
<%
Dim myExemptions, myTaxHelperID                   '=== Initialize variable
myExemptions = Response. QueryString("taxExemption")   '=== Retrieve value from
➥the URL string
If myExemptions = 0 Then
    myTaxHelperID = "Publication 1678"
ElseIf myExemptions = 1 then
    myTaxHelperID = "Publication 1713"
ElseIf myExemptions = 2 then
    myTaxHelperID = "Publication 1779"
Else
    myTaxHelperID = "Retry"
End if
Dim gotoURL                                       '=== Initiate variable
gotoURL = myTaxHelperID &".asp"                   '=== Create the page
➥location to browse
```

```
Response.Redirect gotoURL                          '=== Send user to
➥correct page
%>
```

If the calling page sends in a value of null or a zero-length string for the 'taxExemption variable', the Else condition would be evaluated to create a retry.asp page. This page would give the user another chance to select from the list of correct forms. However, it you elected not to use the Else condition, the variable myTaxHelperID would never be set. Consequently, an HTTP error would result trying to redirect the browser to a page named '.asp'. For more information about the Response object, see Chapter 14, "Speaking to the Web Client: The Response Collection."

Although the use of nested ElseIf statements enables the selection of one execution block from multiple execution blocks, doing so requires that many separate conditions be evaluated. The Select Case statement has been designed to provide a more effective mechanism for accomplishing this.

The *Select Case* Statement

The Select Case statement is designed to improve the efficiency of code that needs to accomplish extended If...Then...ElseIf statements. The Select Case statement is used to select a code block by evaluating the test condition once and then comparing the result with multiple conditions. The If...Then...Else statements, on the other hand, require conditional testing for every conditional statement. The syntax of the Select Case statement is

```
Select Case testexpression
    Case expressionlist
        statements . . .
    Case Else expressionlist
        elsestatements
End Select
```

where testexpression is any numeric or string expression and expressionlist is one or more of the possible matching expressions.

The logical sequence of the Select Case statement is similar to the If...Then...Else statements where both conditions enable the case for a failure condition. The Else clause in the Select Case statement is used when the conditional statement does not match any expression in the expression list. For example, the previous If...Then...ElseIf example can be rewritten into a Select Case statement.

```
<%
Dim myExemptions, myTaxHelperID              '=== Initialize variables
myExemptions = 2                             '=== Set variable
Select Case myExemptions                     '=== Evaluate condition
    Case 0
        myTaxHelperID = "Publication 1678"
    Case 1
        myTaxHelperID = "Publication 1713"
    Case 2
        myTaxHelperID = "Publication 1779"   '=== Evaluates line
    Case Else
        myTaxHelperID = "Publication 1648"
```

```
End Select
Response.Write myTaxHelperID                         '=== Write results
%>
```

Likewise, you can convert the If...Then...Else example into a Select Case statement to minimize processing power required to route the browser to the appropriate page depending on the input.

```
<%
Dim myExemptions, myTaxHelperID                          '=== Initialize variable
myExemptions = Response. QueryString("taxExemption")     '=== Retrieve value from
➥the URL string
Select Case myExemptions                                 '=== Evaluate condition
     Case 0
          myTaxHelperID = "Publication 1678"
     Case 1
          myTaxHelperID = "Publication 1713"
     Case 2
          myTaxHelperID = "Publication 1779"
     Case Else
          myTaxHelperID = "Retry"
End Select
Dim gotoURL                                              '=== Initiate variable
gotoURL = myTaxHelperID &".asp"                          '=== Create the page
➥location to browse
Response.Redirect gotoURL                                '=== Send user to correct
➥page
%>
```

By using the Select Case features, you can turn this decision operator into a very robust tool in developing your applications. For example, the Select Case statement can be used to implement a client-side validation method to ensure that data is entered correctly on a form.

```
Function FieldValidate()
Dim ret
Title = "Validation Errors"
Select Case True
     Case ((Len(Document.frmOrder.txtFirstName.value)) < 1)
          MsgBox "Please enter your first name", 48 ,title

     Case ((Len(Document.frmOrder.txtLastName.value)) < 1)
          MsgBox "Please enter your last name", 48, title

     Case ((Len(Document.frmOrder.Txtamount.value)) < 1)
          MsgBox "Please enter an amount greater than zero", 48, title
     Case ((Len(Document.frmOrder.Txtwidgetname.value)) < 1)
          MsgBox "Please enter a Widget Name", 48, Title
     Case else
          FieldValidate = True
End Select
End Function
```

In this example, the Select Case statement searches through the case criteria looking for the first expression that returns True. Each condition is used to identify a required field. For example, Figure 5.1 demonstrates a form that requires values in all text box fields.

FIG. 5.1
The Data Widgets
Incorporated HTML order
form requires values in
all text boxes.

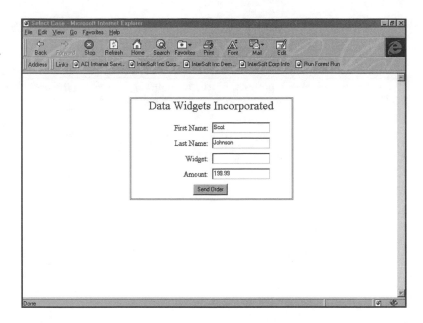

The Select Case statement is used in this example to determine whether one of the required fields on the form is blank. The Select Case will test each expression to evaluate to True. When a True statement is found, a message box is displayed to alert the user of the required field.

For more information about using user dialog boxes such as the message box, please see Chapter 6, "Working with Functions, Subroutines, and Dialog Boxes."

Implementing Looping Logic

Looping structures in VBScript provide the capability to cyclically repeat code. The repeating process can occur a set number of times or until a condition is met. VBScript provides four looping structures to help control your application's programming logic: the For...Next, Do...Loop, While...Wend, and the For Each...Next loops.

The *For...Next* Statement

The For...Next loop repeats a section of code a specific number of times. This is particularly useful if you know the number of cycles or iterations required. The syntax for the For...Next loop is the following:

```
For counter = start To end Step stepsize
     statements
     Exit For
     statements
Next
```

where *counter* is a numeric variable that maintains the current iteration number, and *start* and *end* provide the starting and ending counter positions.

> **CAUTION**
>
> Notice that the `Next` operator does not require the `counter` variable as in Visual Basic. If you add the `counter` variable, VBScript will generate an `Expected end of statement` runtime error.

The `For...Next` loop also enables you to specify the step size between iterations. The step size is added to the counter to determine the value of the next counter. In addition, the step size can also be positive or negative. A positive step size will iterate from the starting position and finish when the counter is greater than or equal to the end counter. The following example uses a `For...Next` loop with a counter set to start at 65 and end at 122 to print every third ANSI character value.

```
<%
Dim myCounter
%>
<%
For myCounter = 65 to 122 step 3
     Response.Write chr(myCounter)        '=== Writes 'A D G J M P S V Y etc...
Next
%>
```

If the step size is negative, it also starts at the beginning position and adds the negative step size to the position to determine the next counter value. For the negative step size, the `For...Next` loop will end when the counter is less than or equal to the ending value. The following example cycles through a negative step size to display the lowercase values of the alphabet.

```
<%
For myCounter = 122 to 97 step -1
     Response.Write chr(myCounter)        '=== Displays results:
zyxwvutsrqponmlkjihgfedcba
Next
%>
```

Keep in mind that the `Next` operator in VBScript differs from `Next` operator in native Visual Basic. Native Visual Basic requires a certain counter variable to be specified in the `Next` statement. However, VBScript does not require the counter variable. In the `Next` operator, a statement automatically increments the counter variable designated in the `For` statement. If you add the counter variable, VBScript will generate an `Expected end of statement` runtime error. Furthermore, if you nest `For...Next` loops, VBScript prevents naming the counter variables the same name. For example, the following code generates the VBScript runtime error `Invalid 'For' loop control variable`.

```
<%
Dim myCounter                            '=== Initiates Variable
For myCounter =1 to 3                     '=== Starts first FOR loop
     For myCounter = 1 to 10              '=== Generate Run Time Error
          If (myCounter = 4) Then
               Exit For
```

```
        Else
                Response.Write chr((100+ myCounter))
        End If
    Next
Response.Write myCounter
Next
%>
```

You can also use this For...Next logic to step from a collection of the same objects on the Web client. For example, Figure 5.2 illustrates VBScript that enables you to select your favorite browser type.

FIG. 5.2

Client-side example of using a *For...Next* loop to cycle through controls on HTML page.

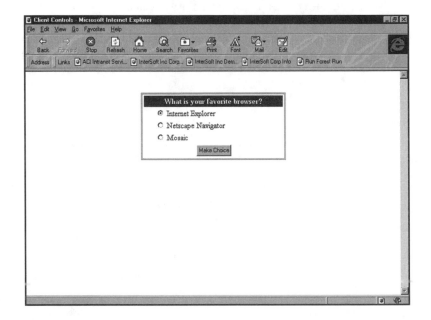

The For...Next loop can now be applied to cycle through the controls and display what button was displayed by the browser:

```
<SCRIPT LANGUAGE="VBScript">
<!--
Sub checkradio()
For I = 0 to 2
    If document.frmbrowser.r1.item(i).checked then
        MsgBox "You have selected " & document.frmbrowser.r1.item(i).value
    End if
Next
End Sub
-->
</SCRIPT>
```

When the Make Choice button is pressed, the previous code is executed to loop through the radio box searching for the selected item. After the radio box that is checked is found, a message box is displayed with the result.

The *Do...Loop* Statement

The `Do...Loop` is also used to execute cyclical code, but unlike the `For...Next` loop, it continues to perform an operation indefinitely until a condition is met. The `Do...Loop` offers two conditional operators to evaluate the conditions: the `While` and `Until` operators. Both operators continue processing until the evaluated function returns `True`.

The `Do...While/Until` loops can be implemented in two variations:

```
Do {While ¦ Until} condition
     statements
     Exit Do
     statements
Loop
```

Or alternatively:

```
Do
     Statements
     Exit Do
     statements
Loop {While ¦ Until} condition
```

The difference between the two syntaxes is the location of the conditional statement. In the first syntax structure, the conditional statement is located in the same execution line as the `Do` key word. In the second `Do...Loop` syntax, the conditional statement is located at the end of the loop code. This change in location gives programmers the flexibility to test the validity of the condition first and then process the code block, or to process the code block first and then evaluate the condition. The following example demonstrates the use of the `Do...Loop`:

```
<%
Dim myCounter, myMaxValue
myMaxValue = 100
Do While myCounter < myMaxValue        '=== Inner loop.
     myCounter = myCounter + 1          '=== Increment Counter.
     If myCounter = 50 Then             '=== Test condition
          Exit Do                       '=== Exit loop.
     End If
Loop
%>
```

The `Do...Loop` can also contain other nested `Do...Loops`. The following example cycles through the first six months of the year and then cycles through the number of days in each month. (This example uses some functions that have not been covered yet, but will be covered in upcoming chapters.)

```
<%
Dim myMonthCount, myTotalMonths, myYear
myMonthCount = 1: myTotalMonths = 6: myYear = 1997        '=== Initialize
➥variables
Do While myMonthCount <= myTotalMonths                    '=== Start outer
➥month loop
     Dim myFirstDate, mySecondDate, iDayCount
     Response.Write MonthName(myMonthCount)               '=== Write month
     myFirstDate = (myMonthCount &"/01/" &myYear)         '=== Sets first
➥month
```

```
        mySecondDate = (myMonthCount+1 &"/01/" &myYear)        '=== Sets second
➥month
    myDayCount = DateDiff("d", myFirstDate, mySecondDate)+1  '=== determines
➥days per month
    iDayCount = 1                                           '=== Initialize
➥counter
        Do While iDayCount < myDayCount                    '=== Inner day
➥counter
            Response.Write " " &iDayCount                  '=== Write results
            iDayCount = iDayCount + 1                       '=== Iterate day
        Loop                                               '=== Inner loop
Response.Write "<BR>"                                       '=== Start new line
➥on new month
myMonthCount = myMonthCount + 1                             '=== Iterate to a
➥new month
Loop                                                        '=== Outer loop
%>
```

This example demonstrates using multiple `Do...Loops` to cycle through a six-month period of time and write the amount of days in each month to the Web page. Two loops are needed for this function: one to cycle through the amount of months, the other loop is needed to cycle through the amount of days in each month. This dual looping approach is commonly used when dealing with groups of similar objects. For example, nested `Do` loops would be needed to display all credit card transactions for all users on a corporate charge card.

The *While...Wend* Statement

Another looping operator that is similar in behavior to the `Do...Loop` is the `While...Wend` statement. The `While...Wend` loop repeats an operation while a condition is `True`. The `While...Wend` statement uses the following syntax:

```
While condition
    statements
Wend
```

where *condition* is a numeric or string expression that can be evaluated to `True` or `False`, and *statements* represents a code block that is executed when the condition evaluates to `True`.

When the `While` condition is `True`, all statements are processed until the `Wend` statement is reached. At that point, the program control is shifted back to the `While` condition and the condition is evaluated again. The cycle continues until the condition returns `False`. At that point, the statement following the `Wend` statement is executed. For instance, the following example uses the `While...Wend` statement to increment the counter variable by one when the value of the counter is less than 100. When the value of the `While` condition returns `False`, the loop is exited and a string message `100 counters were set` is written to the page.

```
<%
Dim myCounter
myCounter = 0                        '=== Initialize variable.
While myCounter < 100                '=== Evaluate the condition.
    myCounter = myCounter + 1         '=== Increment Counter.
Wend                                 '=== End While loop when myCounter > 99.
Response.Write myCounter &"counters were set"     '=== Write counter to page
%>
```

NOTE   Remember, when evaluating condition statements in VBScript, if a condition is Null, the
condition returns a False. ■

The *For Each...Next* Statement

The For Each...Next loop is a new feature in VBScript 2.0. The For Each...Next loop repeats
a group of statements for each element in a collection or array. What this means is that you can
cycle through a group of objects, such as text boxes or database fields, and manipulate the
properties of those objects. A *collection* acts as a storage unit that contains a set of similar
objects. The collection is stored as an array that has a sequential index that identifies the individual storage units, called *elements*. Because the objects are similar, they have the same properties and can be accessed by code.

This idea of a collection can best be illustrated by comparing collections to an apartment building. The apartment building serves as a large storage unit that contains the individual apartments. This group of apartments shares common characteristics, such as having an apartment
number and number of bathrooms. If you want to determine the total number of kitchens that
exist in the entire apartment complex, you would use the following statement to examine the
AppartmentComplex collection:

```
For Each Apartment in AppartmentComplex
     Total = Total + Appartment.kitchens
Next
```

In a code-specific situation, most of your Active Server Page objects use collections to house
information about the object. For example, you can display all the values stored in a cookie file
by using the Request object's Cookie collection, as demonstrated below.

```
<%
For Each key in Request.Cookies("mycookie")
%>
<%= cookie %> (<%= key %>) = <%= Request.Cookies(cookie)(key)%>
<%
Next
%>
```

This example would write all the values stored in the cookie named "mycookie". For more
information about cookies and the Request object, see Chapter 15, "Retrieving User Information: The Request Object."

Interrupting the Program Flow

You have seen the implementation of decision-based and iterative logic. VBScript also gives you
the ability to explicitly change the navigational flow of your application by using the Exit statement. The Exit statement provides the functionality to jump out of the current script block
back into the host script code. The On Error statement helps control program execution when
a runtime error occurs.

Part

II

Ch

5

The *Exit* Statement

In some situations, you need to be able to stop the current executing logic found in a code procedure. This often happens when a condition is met and additional code processing is unnecessary. The Exit statement permits this change in programmatic flow from a Do...Loop, For...Next, function, or subroutine to the calling script block. Exit uses the following syntax:

```
Exit ProcedureCall
```

where *ProcedureCall* can be the Do, For, Sub, or Function keywords.

Here's how to control the program flow inside a For...Next loop: In order to exit a For...Next loop, the Exit statement can be placed anywhere inside the calling For...Next loop. Recall the For...Next syntax:

```
For counter = start To end [Step stepsize]
    statements
    Exit For
    statements
Next
```

When the Exit For statement is encountered in the code, VBScript transfers control to the statement after the calling Next statement. Therefore, if you have nested For...Next loops, as shown in the example below, the program control will jump out of the embedded For K loop back into the For J loop.

```
For J = 1 To 10
    Private myLastRecord
        For K = 1 To 10
            If IsNull(myArray(K)) then      '=== Tests for Null Values
                Exit For                     '=== Exits out of For K loop
            Else
                myLastRecord = myarray(k)
            End if
        Next                                 '=== Next I loop
        Response.Write myLastRecord          '=== On the Exit event, program
➥returns here
    Next                                     '=== Next j
```

The Exit For statement can also be applied to exiting the For Each...Next loop.

The same exiting process that exists for the For...Next loop can be applied to the Do...While loop. Recall the Do...While loop syntax:

```
Do {While ¦ Until} condition
    statements      Exit Do
    statements
Loop
```

The following example expands on the counter loop illustrated in the previous example by allowing a flag to be set by the inner Do loop to stop the execution of the outer loop. Also, notice that the inner loop uses the Do...While loop and the outer loop uses a Do...Until loop.

```
<%
Dim myCheck, myCounter
myCheck = True: myCounter = 0            '=== Initialize variables.
Do                                       '=== Create outer do loop.
     Do While myCounter < 100            '=== Inner loop.
          myCounter = myCounter + 1      '=== Increment Counter.
          If myCounter = 50 Then         '=== If condition is True.
               myCheck = False           '=== Set value of flag to False.
               Exit Do                   '=== Exit inner loop.
          End If
     Loop
Loop Until myCheck = False               '=== Exit outer loop immediately.
%>
```

The Exit statement can also be used to return application flow to the host script that called a function or subroutine. The Exit function and Exit Sub statements return control to the statement following the calling statement.

```
Function mySearch(mySearchVar)
     ' VBScript statement                     '=== Sample code
     If StrFound = False Then          '=== Checks a variable
          mySearch = False             '=== Sets the return value of function
          Exit Function                '=== Exit the function
     End If
     ' More statements        '=== Sample code
End Function
```

The *On Error* Statement

The On Error statement is not actually used to interrupt program flow but to react to program interruptions as a result of runtime errors. The On Error statement gives you a limited amount of error-handling control and uses the following syntax:

```
On Error Resume Next
```

There are no options available with the On Error statement. The On Error statement simply enables VBScript runtime error handling. Without the On Error statement, if a runtime error occurs, the application stops and the error message is displayed to the user. In most situations, a runtime error is caused by trying to complete an invalid operation. However, the On Error Resume Next statement continues to process the application by returning control to the statement immediately after the statement where the error was generated.

The following example illustrates using an On Error Resume Next statement. The improper use of the Month function will produce a Type Mismatch error and would consequently close the script, if the On Error was not included.

```
<%
On Error Resume Next             '=== Turns on Error Handling at this point
Dim myMonth, myMessageStr
myMonth = Month("Scot")          '=== Type Mismatch error is generated
Response.Write myMonth           '=== Application Focus is returned here
%>
```

In this example, the program control is returned to the line following the misuse of the Month function. Because the variable myMonth was not set, nothing is written to the page.

Remember that VBScript, unlike its parent Visual Basic, does not support the GoTo option. The GoTo functionality gave you the ability to write error-handling packages that could be referenced when an error occurred. The GoTo feature has been omitted from VBScript. With only inline error handling available in VBScript, trapping your errors becomes more cumbersome than in Visual Basic. For more information on the Error object, please see the next section.

Error Trapping with the *Err* Object

The basis of VBScript error handling is made possible by using the Err object. The Err object is created when a runtime error occurs. The Err object is used to store information about the error and expose its different methods. The syntax for the Err object is:

```
Err[.{property ¦ method}]
```

where *property* is the Err object properties listed in Table 5.1 and the *method* is the Err object methods listed in Table 5.2. In VBScript code, the On Error statement is used to enable error handling. However, the only error response that exists is to use the Resume Next statement. The Resume Next statement is used to respond to an error condition by enabling the program to continue execution with the next statement after the one that produced the error. Therefore, to enable error handling in VBScript, use the following line of code:

```
<% On Error Resume Next %>
```

The On Error statement used by VBScript enables limited functionality when compared to its native Visual Basic development counterpart. If no error handling is activated, any runtime error that is generated at the server will be fatal, resulting in the immediate termination of the script. However, if error handling is activated and you, for example, misspell a function, the application continues by executing the next line in the code.

Remember that because ASP code is compiled from the top of the page to the bottom of the page, the placement of the tags is important. Error trapping on the page can only begin after the On Error Resume Next statement. Any runtime error that occurs before the On Error Resume Next statement will cause a fatal error and shutdown of the script. This is demonstrated in the following example where the On Error Resume Next statement is located in the middle of the script. The improper use of the Month function produces a Type Mismatch error and consequently closes the script.

```
<%
Dim myMonth, myMessageStr
myMonth = Month("Scot")                '=== Type Mismatch error is generated

On Error Resume Next                   '=== Turns on Error Handling at this point
Response.Write myMonth                 '=== Application Focus is returned here
%>
```

Therefore, in most situations when error handling is going to be implemented, it is best to place the On Error Resume Next statement at the very beginning of the page.

N O T E Error handling begins after the `On Error Resume Next` statement in the script. Any runtime errors generated before the error handling declaration will produce a fatal runtime error. ■

Remember: Error handling returns the application focus back to the line immediately following the statement that generated the error. This return functionality is important to consider when using subroutines and functions. For example, Listing 5.1 calls subroutines to perform a task. However, code within the subroutine improperly declares the VBScript `Round` function and produces a runtime error. Because error handling is initiated at the script level, the program execution is returned to the following statement in the script-level code, not to the next line within the `GenerateError` subroutine procedure.

Listing 5.1   Example of error trapping code.

```
<% On Error Resume Next %>
<%
'=============================== Begin Sub Module ===============================
Sub GenerateError()
        myVar = Round("myNumber",5)          '=== Incorrect use of Round Function
        Response.Write Err.Description       '=== This line is not executed
End Sub
'=============================== Close Sub Module ===============================
%>

<Center>Using the Error Statements</center><BR>
<%
Response.Write "Executed First Line <BR>"    '=== Writes 'Executed First Line'
➥to page
call GenerateError()                         '=== Error is generated here
Response.Write "Executed Third Line <BR>"     '=== Program control is returned
here
%>
```

The error handling also has the capability to provide localized error trapping at the procedure level. Listing 5.2 limits error handling only to code within the `GenerateError` function. This example checks the return result of the function to determine whether an error was generated within that function. If an error was generated (the result of `GenerateError = True`) the error message is written to the page. If the `GenerateError` function returns `False`, a return message stating that the transaction was successful is written to the page.

Listing 5.2   More error trapping code.

```
<%
'================================= Begin Function Module =====================
Function GenerateError()
On Error Resume Next                     '=== Enable error trapping in function
```

continues

Listing 5.2 Continued

```
only
        myVar = Round("myNumber",5)                     '=== Generate error
        If Err then
                GenerateError = True
        Else
                GenerateError = False
        End if
End Function
'================================= Close Function Module =====================
%>

<% '================================= Begin Script ==========================
%>
<center>Using the Error Statements </center><BR>
<%
if GenerateError() then                                 '=== Check results of
➥Function: Returns True
        Response.Write "Warning: The Following Error Has Occurred: <BR>"
        Response.Write Err.Description & "<BR>"          '=== Write the description
of the error
Else                                                    '=== No errors
        Response.Write "Data Transfer Successful<BR>"
End if
%>
<% '================================= End Script ============================
%>
```

Notice that even though the Err object was created in the GenerateError function, the Err object has page-level scope and can be referenced anywhere on the page. However, if faulty code generates a runtime error outside the GenerateError function, the server will process the script up to the point where the error was generated and create a fatal error, as shown in the following example.

```
<%
'================================= Begin Function Module ======================
Function GenerateError()
On Error Resume Next
        myVar = Round("myNumber",5)           '=== Generate an error trying to round a
        ➥string
        If Err then
                GenerateError = True
        Else
                GenerateError = False
        End if
End Function
'================================= Close Function Module ======================
%>

<% '================================= Begin Script ==========================
%>
<center>Using the Error Statements </center><BR>
<%
```

```
if GenerateError() then                          '=== Check results of
➥Function: Returns True
    Response.Write "Warning: The Following Error Has Occurred: <BR>"
    Response.Write Err.Description & "<BR>"       '=== Write the description of
➥the error
Else                                             '=== No errors, proceed
    Response.Write "Data Transfer Successful<BR>"
    myVar = Round("myNumber",5)                  '=== Generate fatal error and
➥terminate script
End if
%>
<% '=================================== End Script ===============================
%>
```

In the previous example, the `GenerateError` function will generate an error trying to round a string. However, because error trapping is enabled for the function, the script continue process when program control is returned to the calling script. However, program execution will terminate when a runtime error is generated at script level.

Also, keep in mind that if a property of the `Err` object is referenced before the `Err` object is actually created, no runtime errors are produced when the properties are referenced. The following example demonstrates referencing properties of the `Err` object without the explicit creation of an `Err` object.

```
<%
If Not(Err) then                                 '=== If no
➥Error Objects exist
    Response.Write "Error Number: " &Err.Number &"<BR>"     '=== Returns 0
    Response.Write "Error Description: " &Err.Description    '=== Return
➥zero length string
    myErrorType = Vartype(Err.Number)            '=== Returns
➥Long
    myErrorType = Vartype(Err.Description)        '=== Returns
➥String
End If

%>
```

The *Err* Object's Properties

Active Server Pages uses the error handling found in VBScript to process and manage runtime errors. VBScript handles error trapping with the `Err` object. The `Err` object has several properties and two methods. The `Err` object's properties are listed in Table 5.1.

Table 5.1 *Err* Object Properties

Property	Description
Description	Returns a descriptive string associated with an error.
HelpContext	Returns a context ID for a topic in a help file.

continues

Part

II

Ch

5

Table 5.1 Continued

Property	Description
HelpFile	Returns a fully qualified path to a help file.
Number	Returns a numeric value specifying an error (default property).
Source	Returns the name of the object or application that originally generated the error.

The Err object's Description, Number, and Source properties are used to provide more information about the runtime error. The Description property explains the VBScript error that has occurred. The Number property returns the VBScript-specific error number. This property is useful because you can retrieve the specific error number and tailor your application accordingly. The Source property returns the application or instantiated object that generated the runtime error.

The Source property is also important because now you can provide a customized error and help response system. Although an application error lowers productivity and irritates users, a customized error and help response system enables a smooth transition from an instantaneous runtime crash to a customized help-based solution. This help-based solution system can not only change the user's perception of your application, but can also help the user by providing additional debugging information.

You can use the properties of the Err object to access more information from the VBScript help file and also reference your own help files from your own custom created application. The Err object's HelpFile and HelpContext properties provide the pointers to the help files. The HelpFile property sets the path to the help file and the HelpContext identifies the context ID used to display the help topic content.

Using the *Err* Object Methods

The Err object also provides methods to control the Err object. The Err object's methods, as shown in Table 5.2, can be used to generate a runtime error or reset the Err object's properties using the Clear method.

Table 5.2 The *Err* Object's Methods

Method	Description
Raise	Generates a runtime error.
Clear	Clears all property settings of the Err object.

The Err object has two methods that enable you to control the Err object. The Raise method enables you to generate a runtime error, which is particularly useful in debugging your applications. The Raise method requires the following syntax:

```
object.Raise(number, source, description, helpfile, helpContext)
```

where *object* is the Err object, *number* is a long integer subtype used to uniquely identify the number, *source* is a string used to describe the application or object that generated the error, *description* is used to explain the raised error, *helpfile* is the fully qualified path to the help file, and *HelpContext* is the pointer to the specific content topic.

```
<%
Err.Raise 6, "You just simulated an 'overflow' error! "        '=== Generate an
➥Err Object
Err.Clear                                                       '=== Clear the Err
%>
```

You have to watch when you are controlling the programmatic workflow in your application that you don't inadvertently reset your Err object. The Err.Clear method is automatically executed whenever an On Error Resume Next, an Exit Sub, or Exit Function statement is called.

From Here...

This chapter covered how VBScript controls the programmatic application flow. VBScript controls the process flow by using decision-based logic and looping logic. Decision logic is based on the If...Then, If...Then...Else, and Select Case statements. These statements are used to evaluate conditions and make a decision based on the expression returned from the conditional statement. VBScript uses looping logic to repeat a block of code until a condition evaluates to True. VBScript uses the For...Next, Do...Loop, While...Wend, and the For Each...Next statements to complete the cyclical processing. In addition, VBScript also provides a mechanism to stop the current processing flow by using the Exit statement. Finally, the Err object was illustrated to examine how to handle error trapping with VBScript.

For related information, please see the following chapters:

- Chapter 6, "Working with Functions, Subroutines, and Dialog Boxes," illustrates event-driven programming through the use of reusable code modules.

- Chapter 7, "Datatype Conversion Features," features the data type conversion functions in VBScript to ensure proper application execution.

- Chapter 13, "Managing the User Session: The Session Object," demonstrates how to track user-specific information through your Web application.

- Chapter 14, "Speaking to the Web Client: The Response Collection," describes how to transfer the server-side information to the Web client using the Response collection.

- Chapter 19, "Putting It All Together: Creating an Online Registration System," illustrates how to use the different ActiveX components that ship with the Internet Information Server to create a Web site for the Amazing DataWidget WareHouse online catalog.

Part

II

Ch

5

Working with Functions, Subroutines, and Dialog Boxes

VBScript was initially developed by Microsoft to provide event-driven programming functionality to Web pages for users of the Internet Explorer browser. *Event-driven programming* is the process of executing code that depends on the actions that occur in an application. This customized programming approach is different from the traditional model of procedural programming, in which an application was designed to complete a specific objective. The traditional procedural approach relies on the application to execute code, whereas event-driven code relies on user input to execute code. This chapter will cover how VBScript uses procedures to create smaller modules of code that are executed by a user's actions. In addition, the Message and Inbox dialog boxes will demonstrate how to provide user interaction on the Web client. ■

Introduction to Event-Driven Programming

This section provides an overview of event-driven programming and how it applies to VBScript.

Using Procedure Modules

Learn how to utilize functions and subroutines to build re-useable code and provide logical application flow using procedures.

Client-Side Dialog Boxes

Discover how to utilize client-side dialog boxes to display and retrieve information from the user.

Introducing Event-Driven Programming

In most event-driven application development environments, such as Visual Basic or Visual C++, objects have specific events or actions that can be controlled or monitored. These actions, such as clicking a button, can then be used to determine the code that is to execute next. Figure 6.1 demonstrates an example of event-driven programming. This example shows how VBScript displays different pop-up menu boxes depending on the button that is pushed. If the button labeled "Say Hello" is pushed, the OnClick event of the pressed button is executed. If script code exists to be executed on the OnClick event, then that code would be executed. In this situation, a message box with "Hello" is displayed. However, if the second button labeled "Say Goodbye" is pushed, the OnClick event of the button labeled "Say Goodbye" is processed.

FIG. 6.1

Event-driven programming reacts to user events.

As mentioned in Chapter 3, VBScript code is actually text that is embedded as a scripting language within the HTML page. The embedded code exists within the HTML page, and the SCRIPT tag tells the browser what language is being used. The HTML syntax for the SCRIPT tag is the following:

```
<SCRIPT LANGUAGE='scripting language'>
Script Application logic here
</SCRIPT>
```

where 'scripting language' is any script-compliant language.

The language tag is used to determine the interpreter that processes the script. The HTML-embedded script is actually interpreted as the page is initially loaded into the browser. The preloading process enables objects to be verified as secure or unsecure before they are loaded into the browser, as mentioned in Chapter 3.

Once the text has been loaded into the browser, HTML intrinsic objects are instantiated by the browser. The term *instantiated* simply means that the browser has created the object and reserved a named memory space where the object can be referenced. These instantiated objects have a scope equal to the length of time that the page is loaded in memory of the browser. For example, the following code creates an HTML button named btnHello.

```
<INPUT TYPE=BUTTON VALUE="Say Hello" NAME="btnHello">
```

Once an object is instantiated, embedded script languages can access the object's properties, methods, and events. Most event-driven programming languages access an object's events, properties, or methods by using the following syntax:

```
Object.[Events, Properties, Methods]
```

Utilizing, managing, and coordinating an object's events, properties, and methods form the basis of event-driven programming. By separating the characteristics of an object into these three categories, the script language can trap or react to an object's properties, methods, and especially its events.

An *event* is a predefined action of an object. VBScript can then react to the object's action by executing a code module that is associated with that event. For example, the intrinsic HTML button has an OnClick event. This OnClick event is triggered when the button is pressed. These predefined events are usually named by concatenating the name of the object with an underscore and the name of the event: *name_event*. Therefore, when the HTML button is clicked, the browser interprets an event named btnHello_OnClick. In this situation, you place code in this event procedure to display a message to the user via a message box. The following code illustrates utilizing the OnClick event of a button.

```
<SCRIPT LANGUAGE="VBScript">
    Sub BtnHello_OnClick
        MsgBox "Hello!", 0, "VBScript Demo"
    End Sub
</SCRIPT>
```

Even though trapping an object's events and executing code are the foundations of event-driven programming, being able to access an object's properties and methods is also important. An object's property is used to describe a characteristic of that object. For example, the HTML button described above has a Name property set to 'btnHello' and Value property set to 'Say Hello'. You can display the name of a control by accessing its Name property. Most objects have a minimum of two properties: a Name property and a Value property. The following example demonstrates how to display information that has been entered into a text field when the OnClick event of a button is executed:

```
<SCRIPT LANGUAGE="VBScript">
<!--
Sub btnDisplayText()
msg = frmtest.txtInformation.value
call window.alert(msg)
End Sub
-->
</SCRIPT>
```

You can further manipulate the object via its methods. A method call is used to cause an action to occur on a particular object. For instance, in the previous example, the window.alert(msg) statement executes the pop-up dialog box from the window object.

Part
II

Ch
6

Using Procedures: Subroutines and Functions

Now that the basics of event-driven code have been discussed, it is time to investigate how VBScript stores the code that is executed on an object's events. One of the greatest benefits of event-driven programming is the capability to store code that is bundled together in script procedures. These procedures can be used on both client and server-side scripts and they provide the most flexible way to re-use code and provide a clear and logical workflow.

Procedures in VBScript are either subroutines or functions. *Functions* are procedures that return a value to the calling code module. *Subroutines* are procedures that do not return a specific value; they simply execute code. Subroutines are used to act as a self-contained section of code used to process information. Functions provide interaction with the calling script code by not only processing logic, but also providing results back to the script.

General Procedure Rules

Although subroutines and functions differ in terms of returning values back to the calling script, they share many common rules. Most of the similar rules for procedures are found in the declaration, variable use, and naming conventions.

Procedure Declaration   Because functions and subroutines are specific categories of script procedures, the two share many of the same rules and logic. VBScript calls for both functions and subroutines to use the following syntax:

```
Public ¦ Private procedure name arglist
     statements
     Exit Procedure
     statements
End Sub
```

where *procedure* identifies a function or subroutine, *name* identifies the procedure name, and *statements* contains the code to be executed when the procedure is referenced. The name of the procedure must follow the same naming rules that are applicable to variables:

- Procedure names must begin with an alphabetic character.
- They can't contain an embedded period or type-declaration character.
- Procedure names must be unique within the same scope.
- They cannot be longer than 255 characters.

The subprocedure has two optional arguments—the Public/Private declaration and the argument list.

Public Versus Private Declarations   Procedures, similar to variables, can be made public or private within a page (either HTML or ASP). By declaring a procedure as private, you limit the accessibility of that procedure to only those scripts where the procedure is declared. When a procedure is declared as public, any script within that page can reference the procedure. If no explicit declaration of public or private is made, the procedure is assumed to be a public procedure.

N O T E Variables declared in procedures have scope only within that procedure and are not preserved when the application control is passed between procedures. ■

Argument Lists The second optional argument is the *argument list*. The argument list declares the variables defined by the procedure that are assigned by the calling code. Placing a variable in the argument list is the equivalent of implicitly declaring a variable within a procedure. If you try to re-declare the variable using a `Dim` or equivalent statement, you will generate a `'Named Redefined'` error.

When the calling code calls the procedure, the variables in the argument list are first implicitly instantiated. Then the calling values are transferred to the new localized variable located in the procedure's argument list. Creating your own localized variables enables you to create a descriptive naming convention that facilitates easy code re-use and logical operation. The following example demonstrates how procedures use their own localized variable names.

```
<%
Sub CheckUserId(UserAction, UserIssue)      '=== Begin Subroutine
    Dim IdValid                             '=== Create local variable
    IdValid=(UserAction &" " &UserIssue)    '=== Uses Local Sub values
    Response.Write "<BR>" &IdValid          '=== Writes "Scan P34—Table" to page
    Response.Write "<BR>" &MyClientAction   '=== Writes "Scan" from calling code
End Sub                                     '=== End Subroutine
%>

<%
...
Dim myClientAction, myClientIssue
myClientAction="Scan": myClientIssue="P34—Table"   '=== Initialize Variables
Call CheckUserId(myClientAction, myClientIssue)     '=== Calling VBScript code
Response.Write "<BR>" &Idvalid                       '=== Writes a blank line
Response.Write "<BR>" &UserAction                    '=== Writes a blank line

...
%>
```

The client code calls a subroutine called `CheckUserId` and supplies two variables named `myClientAction` and `myClientIssue`. The values of these variables are then transferred to the local subroutine variables named `UserAction` and `UserIssue`. The subroutine creates these procedural scope variables and writes the strings `'Scan'` and `'P34-Table'` to the HTML page. After the last statement of the subroutine is executed, program control is returned to the line immediately after the calling of the subroutine. At this point, the application tries to write the subroutine's local variable, `'IdValid'`, and the subroutine's declaration variable, `UserAction`, to the page. However, because those variables have a scope limited to that subroutine, no values are actually written to the page.

Subroutines and functions do not require an argument list. An argument list simply acts as a mechanism to transfer data from the calling client code into the host-based procedure. However, if multiple variables exist, they must be separated by a comma. Furthermore, unless public variables are created outside procedures, variables processed by the procedure must enter through the argument list. The values of a local argument list are not preserved from procedure to procedure.

The arglist argument has the following syntax and parts:

```
ByVal ¦ ByRef varname( )
```

where *ByVal* declares that the variable is passed by value, *ByRef* declares that the variable is passed by reference, and *varname* is the name of the argument variable.

Why is this important? Passing a variable by reference allows the variable's value to be permanently changed within the procedure. Variables passed by value allow a temporary copy of the variable to be made within the procedure. This temporary variable can be manipulated at will by the procedure level script. However, when the program execution is returned to the calling code, the temporary copy of the variable is destroyed and the original value is restored.

In most situations, you don't expect a procedure to permanently modify its arguments. Careful attention must be given when passing arguments ByRef or ByVal to prevent the corruption of your data. For example, assume that you are writing code that is used to manipulate account balance information.

```
<%
sub CalcNewBalanceVal(ByRef Balance)
    Balance=(FormatCurrency(Balance+Balance*22.5/100/12))
End sub

sub StoreBalance(AcctNumber, AcctBalance)
    Response.Write "<BR> Your Balance is " &AcctBalance
End sub


dim myAcctBalance
myAcctBalance = 3250
Call CalcNewBalanceVal(myAcctBalance)
...
[some time later in code]
...
Call StoreBalance(myAcctNumber,myAcctBalance)          '=== Stores $3250.00
%>
```

In this example, you use two subroutines to assist your calculations. One procedure calculates a balance and the other stores the information. The first procedure demonstrates using the ByVal function to pass the Balance variable into the subroutine for processing. Afterward, this value is called by the Store Balance procedure to store the value of Balance into a database with the value of $3250.

However, passing the value by reference can cause a variable to retain its changed value elsewhere in code:

```
<%Sub CalcNewBalanceRef(ByRef Balance)
  Balance=(FormatCurrency(Balance+Balance*22.5/100/12))
End sub

sub StoreBalance(AcctNumber, AcctBalance)
    Response.Write "<BR> Your Balance is " &AcctBalance
End sub

dim myAcctBalance
myAcctBalance = 3250
Call CalcNewBalanceRef(myAcctBalance)
Call StoreBalance(myAcctNumber,myAcctBalance)      '=== Stores $3310.94
%>
```

Notice what happens when the Balance variable is passed by reference in the CalcNewBalanceRef subroutine. The variable Balance maintains its new value even after the programming focus has returned to the calling script. When that variable is later called to be stored, the incorrect value is used because the variable value is permanently changed.

Nesting Procedures   If you want to permanently change the value of variable, the proper way to accomplish this is to use a function that returns a value to a variable, which ensures a clear way to track and manage variables in your code.

Further, similar to the logical operators discussed in Chapter 5, procedures (both subroutines and functions) can be nested within each other. In the example above, if storing the new balance information always occurs after the calculation of the new balance, you might want to consider calling the StoreBalance routine from inside the CalcNewBalanceRoutine. The following code list demonstrates the capability to nest procedures:

```
<%
Sub CalcNewBalanceRef(ByRef Balance)
    Balance=(FormatCurrency(Balance+Balance*22.5/100/12))
    Call StoreBalance(Balance)
End Sub

Sub StoreBalance(AcctBalance)
    Response.Write "<BR> Your Balance is " &AcctBalance
End Sub
%>

<%
Dim myAcctBalance
myAcctBalance = 3250
Call CalcNewBalanceRef(myAcctBalance)
%>
```

As you can see, the nesting of procedures makes the calling client code much easier to read. However, this recursion technique can lead to problems if it is not properly managed. Problems arise because procedures can endlessly call themselves until stack overflow occurs.

Part

II

Ch

6

Exit Statements   If you need to exit a procedure before the End Sub or End Function statements, use the Exit statement. The Exit statement is used to immediately exit from a subroutine or function procedure, and it is typically used when a condition is met and does not require additional code processing within the procedure. The program execution continues with the statement following the statement that called the subroutine. Furthermore, you are not limited to just one Exit statement in your procedure. Multiple exit conditions can exist anywhere in the procedure. However, in most situations, you might want to create smaller subroutines and functions to further compartmentalize programming flexibility. Using smaller procedure modules in lieu of multiple Exit statements helps prevent unstructured logic errors and erratic application flow.

Subroutines

In the previous section, the general topics governing the rules of using procedures (subroutines and functions) were discussed. In general, most rules apply to both subroutines and functions, but some individual differences exist. Remember that subroutines are used to store a collection of code that is used to perform a commonly used task. Subroutines require the following syntax:

```
Public ¦ Private Sub name (arglist)
     statements
     Exit Sub
     statements
End Sub
```

Subroutines are called or executed in one of two ways. The first method explicitly calls the subroutines using the Call statement. Call adheres to the following syntax:

```
Call subname argumentlist
```

where *subname* is the subroutine name.

The *argumentlist* is an optional value that is used to reference the variables, if any, that are needed by the subroutine. If you use the Call statement to declare your subroutine and the subroutine uses variables, the variables must be enclosed in parentheses.

The second manner of calling the subroutine is to implicitly call the subroutine. This type of activation takes place by simply referencing the name of the subroutine and its arguments. If arguments are required, parentheses are not required in the calling code. For instance, notice how the example below activates the same subroutine using the explicit Call statement and the implicit execution by using the WriteInfoMsg subroutine name:

```
<%
Sub WriteInfoMsg(StrTitle, MsgType)
    Response.Write "<BR>" &MsgType &StrTitle &"<BR>"
End Sub
%>
```

```
<%
Dim StrCompany
StrCompany = "BrainWare Inc"
WriteInfoMsg StrCompany, "Welcome to "              '=== Implicit subroutine
↪call
Call WriteInfoMsg(StrCompany, "Thanks for visiting ") '=== Explicit Subroutine
↪Call
%>
```

 TIP Use parentheses when using the `Call` statement to explicitly execute a subroutine with arguments. No parentheses are required when implicitly executing a subroutine.

Functions

Functions, on the other hand, are used to accept arguments, process these arguments, and return the results to the calling code. The `Function` statement has the following syntax:

```
Public ¦ Private Function name (arglist)
    statements
    name = expression
    Exit Function
    statements
    name = expression
End Function
```

The foundation of the `Function` procedure is built on the grouped processing functionality found in the subroutine procedure. The `Function` procedure is a separate procedure that accepts arguments to perform a series of code statements and returns the results of the processed code statements directly to the client code. The only way to accomplish this return of processed information using `Subroutines` is to manipulate a variable that has global scope inside the procedure. The `Function` procedure enables you to immediately have access to the manipulated data. This instantaneous return of processed data is performed the same way as other native VBScript function, such as `Sqr`, `Cos`, or `Chr`.

For instance, the following example uses a `Function` to return the calculated balance:

```
<%
Function CalcNewBalance(Balance)
    Balance=(FormatCurrency(Balance+Balance*22.5/100/12))
    CalcNewBalance = Balance
End Function

Dim myOldAcctBalance, myNewAcctBalance
myOldAcctBalance = 3250
myNewAcctBalance = CalcNewBalance(myOldAcctBalance)
Response.Write "<BR> Your Balance is " & myNewAcctBalance
%>
```

In this example, the `CalcNewBalance` function returns the new calculated balance, which is assigned to the variable `myNewAcctBalance`.

Part

II

Ch

6

Using Dialog Boxes to Interact with Users

Dialog boxes are used to present information to and request information from the user within the client's browser. These pre-built, modal dialog boxes are only instantiated on the Web client to perform client-side interaction. Active Server Pages, because they are executed on the server, have no need for pop-up dialog boxes to occur on the server. If you try to use a server-side dialog box, you will generate a `Permission Denied` error. However, you can use return values from the dialog boxes to solicit information from the user and transfer that data to your Active Server Page. The message dialog box is used to present a message box to the user and trap the results. The input box is used to gather textual information from the user.

Message Box

The message box is used to present warnings, errors, alerts, or information to the user. In addition, the message box gives you the flexibility to determine what button the user has selected. These available options enable you to control programming workflow depending on which buttons were pressed. To use the message box, use the following syntax:

`MsgBox(prompt, buttons, title, helpfile, context)`

where

- *prompt* is the required message string
- *buttons* are the available message box buttons
- *title* is the text that appears in the title bar of the message box
- *helpfile* is the name of the helpfile used to provide contextual help
- *context* is the numerical identifier used to display the topic information from the Helpfile

The message box has several optional parameters that enable you to create appropriate prompting mechanisms needed for your applications. The capability to customize the functionality of the message box dialog occurs through the *button* option of the message box. The *button* option enables you to control three visual components of the message box:

- The type of buttons
- The icon style of the button
- The default button

VBScript's message box provides six different prompting mechanisms to display information, warnings, or confirmations to the user. The default prompt is the standard OK dialog box. To change which buttons are displayed on the message box, use the constants listed in Table 6.1.

Table 6.1   Message Box Buttons

Constant	Value	Description
vbOKOnly	0	Display OK button only. (Default.)
vbOKCancel	1	Display OK and Cancel buttons.
vbAbortRetryIgnore	2	Display Abort, Retry, and Ignore buttons.
vbYesNoCancel	3	Display Yes, No, and Cancel buttons.
vbYesNo	4	Display Yes and No buttons.
vbRetryCancel	5	Display Retry and Cancel buttons.

The default message box is simply used to present a message to the user and present only the OK button on the message box, as seen in Figure 6.2.

FIG. 6.2

Use the default VBScript message box when you want the user to acknowledge a request.

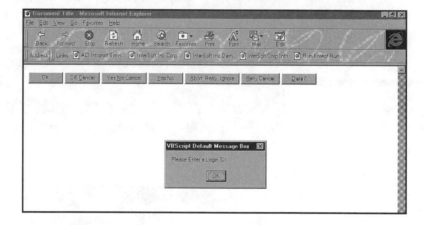

The vbOKOnly message box is generated by the following code:

```
Sub loadOK()
    dim strMsg, iButton, strTitle, index
    strMsg = "Please Enter a Login ID!"        '=== set message string
    iButton = 0                                '=== default: vbOkOnly
    strTitle = "VBScript Default Message Box"  '=== set title bat text
    index = MsgBox(strMsg, iButton, strTitle)  '=== trap the results
End sub
```

In most decision-making applications, you have to prompt the user with one of two options, either Continue or Stop the process or Continue, Stop, or Cancel the process. For example, Figure 6.3 illustrates the use of the button constant vbYesNoCancel to present the user the Yes, No, and Cancel buttons on the message box.

FIG. 6.3
Use VBScript's dialog
constants to display the
Yes, No, and Cancel
dialog box.

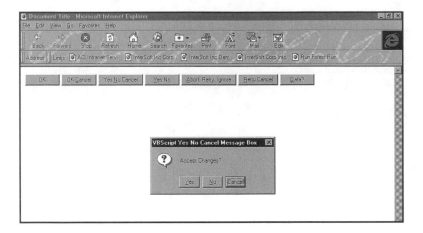

The button options also allow you to control the displayed icon in the message box. This ability
to choose the icon gives you the opportunity to express the tone of the message. For example,
Figure 6.4 illustrates displaying the Critical Message icon.

FIG. 6.4
Dialog boxes can
display different icons to
express the tone of
message.

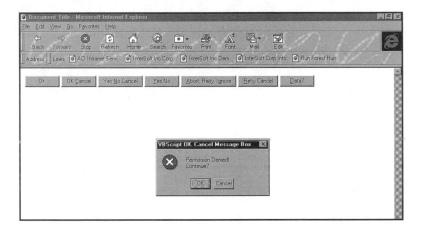

Notice the use of the carriage return and line feed characters in the following code, which
drives Figure 6.4. The carriage return, chr(13), and line feed, chr(10), characters are used to
help control how the information is displayed in the message box.

```
Sub loadOKCancel()
    dim strMsg, iButton, strTitle, index
    strMsg = "Permission Denied!" &(Chr(13) & Chr(10)) & "Continue?"      '=== Set
➥the message string
    iButton = vbOkCancel + vbCritical              '=== OK and Cancel, critical icon
    strTitle = "VBScript OK Cancel Message Box" '=== Set the title bar text
    index = MsgBox(strMsg, iButton, strTitle)   '=== Trap the results
End Sub
```

VBScript supports four different icons that can be displayed in dialog boxes. The available
constants and values are listed in Table 6.2.

Table 6.2   The Dialog Boxes Icons

Constant	Value	Description	Icon
vbCritical	16	Displays Critical Message icon.	⊗
vbQuestion	32	Displays Warning Query icon.	?
vbExclamation	48	Displays Warning Message icon.	⚠
vbInformation	64	Displays Information Message icon.	ⓘ

The third option the button tag controls is the selection of the default button on the messaging window. The default button is used to automatically set the focus on a specific button. Because the application focus is set onto a button, code behind the default button is executed when the user hits the Enter key. For example, Figure 6.5 depicts setting the default button to the Retry button of an Abort, Retry, or Ignore dialog box.

FIG. 6.5
Use the button property to set the default button option of the dialog box.

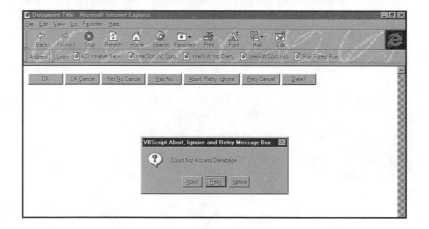

The capability to set the default focus to a particular button is based on the keywords listed in Table 6.3.

Table 6.3   The Default Button Options in VBScript's Dialog Boxes

Constant	Value	Description
vbDefaultButton1	0	First button is default.
vbDefaultButton2	256	Second button is default.

continues

Table 6.3	Continued	
Constant	**Value**	**Description**
vbDefaultButton3	512	Third button is default.
vbDefaultButton4	768	Fourth button is default.

The code behind Figure 6.5 is a combination of all the available functions of the button option. This code, shown below, is using both the VBScript dialog constants as well as the constants' values. The three-option dialog that generates the Abort, Ignore, and Retry option buttons are created using the constant vbAbortRetryIgnor or its value 2. The value 32, or the constant vbQuestion, displays the question mark icon. The constant vbDefaultButton2 or its value of 256 sets focus to the second button on the dialog window.

```
Sub loadAbortRetryIgnor()
    dim strMsg, iButton, strTitle, index
    strMsg = "Could Not Access Database"         '=== Set the message string
    'iButton = vbAbortRetryIgnore +vbQuestion +vbDefaultButton2    '=== Using
➥Constants
    iButton = 2 + 32 + 256                        '=== Using values
    strTitle = "VBScript Abort, Ignore and Retry Message Box"    '=== Set the
➥title bar text
    index = MsgBox(strMsg, iButton, strTitle)    '=== Trap the results
End sub
```

After the user has selected from an available action, the core functionality of the message box is to retrieve the options that the user has selected. To obtain the results the user has selected from the dialog, keep in mind that the dialog boxes act as a prepackaged function within VBScript. To determine the option that the user has selected, simply assign the results of the dialog box to a variable, as shown below. Notice that this same assignment methodology is used to retrieve results from a function.

```
index = MsgBox(strMsg, iButton, strTitle)
```

Once this value is determined, use the Message Box result constant, listed in Table 6.4, to determine the results.

Table 6.4	Message Box Result Constants	
Constant	**Value**	**Description**
VbOK	1	OK
VbCancel	2	Cancel
VbAbort	3	Abort
VbRetry	4	Retry
VbIgnore	5	Ignore
VbYes	6	Yes
VbNo	7	No

Input Box

Unlike the limited button set returned by the message box, the input box is designed to accept textual input from the user. The input box dialog displays a prompt for the user to enter data and click a button, and returns the text entered into the text box when the user selects the OK button. The InputBox uses the following syntax:

InputBox(prompt[, *title*], *default*, *xpos*, *ypos*, *helpfile*, *context*)

where

■ *prompt* is the required string expression used to display a question to the user

■ *title* is the text to appear in the title bar of the input window

■ *default* is the default text that will appear in the text box

■ *xpos* and *ypos* represent the position on the screen where the box is displayed

■ *helpfile* refers to the name of the help file for the application

■ *context* refers to the numeric ID needed to retrieve context information

N O T E When both the helpfile and context options are used, a Help button is automatically added to the dialog box. ■

The InputBox dialog returns values in two situations: when the user presses OK or when the user selects the Cancel button. When the user clicks OK or presses Enter, the InputBox function returns whatever is in the text box. If the user clicks Cancel, the function returns a zero-length string (""). The following code sample illustrates how to display the input dialog box shown in Figure 6.6.

```
Sub LoadInputBox()
    dim Index, strMsg, strTitle, strDefualt
    strMsg = "Welcome to BrainWare International!"
    strMsg = strMsg &(Chr(13) & Chr(10))
    strMsg = strMsg &(Chr(13) & Chr(10))
    strMsg = strMsg &"Where did you hear about this site?"
    strTitle = "Request Information"
    strDefault = "AltaVista Search Engine"
    Index = InputBox(strMsg, strTitle, strDefault)
End Sub
```

FIG. 6.6

Use the InputBox to collect textual data from the user.

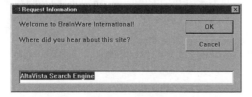

This code uses the variable strMsg and the concatenation operator to sequentially build the prompt string. The text that appears at the top of the InputBox is set by the strTitle variable and the strDefault variable is used to initially populate the text box.

From Here...

In this chapter, you have learned how VBScript uses procedures to help create logical blocks of code. These logical units of code can be used to modulize your application into smaller pieces of code, which enables you to reuse the same code procedures in multiple places in script, as well as make your code easier to follow and debug.

Functions are used to process information and return the results back to the calling script. Subroutines are used to process a block of code without returning information to the script. The Function and Subroutine procedures can accept values to be processed within the code module. These arguments can be passed into the procedures by either ByRef or ByVal. The ByVal declaration passes the variable by its value, whereas ByRef declares that the variable is passed by reference. Keep in mind that passing variables by reference will cause the variable's value to permanently change beyond the scope of the procedure. Whereas, using the ByVal declaration limits the scope of the changed variable value to the procedure.

This chapter also identified VBScript's dialog box functions. The message box is used to display information to the user and require the user to respond. The message box can use a variety of constants to customize the display mechanism presented to the user. The Input box is also a VBScript function that is used to solicit information from the user.

At this point, you should be well poised to start using the multitude of built-in VBScript functions that are used to manipulate the Variant subtypes. After that, the Microsoft Script Debugger will be demonstrated to illustrate how to use inline debugging capabilities for your client- and server-side scripts.

- Chapter 7, "Datatype Conversion Features," illustrates the subtype conversion functions.
- Chapter 8, "Putting It All Together with VBScript," solidifies Part I by demonstrating VBScript running on the Web client and IIS server.
- Chapter 10, "The Composition of an Active Server Application," lays the foundation for building the Active Server Pages application.
- Chapter 15, "Retrieving User Information: The Request Object," demonstrates how to implement Active Server Pages and VBScript to retrieve information from the user.

Datatype Conversion Features

Identifying the *Variant* Sub Datatype

Learn how to prevent unexpected logical and programmatic errors by identifying the sub datatypes.

Converting the Datatype

Utilize subtype conversion features to force the generic *Variant* datatype to specific sub datatypes.

Using Formatting Functions

Discover how to utilize the VBScript 2.0 formatting features to take advantage of built-in date/time, currency, percent, and number formatting displays.

In the previous three chapters, the various effects from the Variant datatypes were discussed. With operators that change behavior as the sub datatype changes for a variable, VBScript has various sub datatype identification tools to maximize and convert the specific sub datatypes. Furthermore, VBScript 2.0 ships with formatting functions to help control how date/time, currency, percent, and numbers are displayed. Together, these features combine to identify, manage, and display variable information. ■

Identifying the Datatype

VBScript uses identification functions to determine a specific sub datatype. The identifier functions return a Boolean value indicating whether the given datatype is determined. This Boolean value can be used to provide the logical decision-making points in your application.

The *IsArray* Function

The IsArray function is used to determine whether a Variant is an array. An *array* is a series of variables that are stored as one variable, with each variable uniquely identified by an index number. The value of the variable can be determined by referencing the index number. The IsArray function requires the following syntax:

```
IsArray(myVarName)
```

where *myVarName* is any valid variable name.

The IsArray function returns True if the expression is an array and False if the expression is not an array. The following example illustrates the successful results of the IsArray function.

```
<%
Dim myRray(), myArrayResult           '=== Declares dynamic array
Redim myRray(1)                       '=== Re declares the array (needed to
➥populate w/data)
myRray(0)="myData"                    '=== Loads first element
MyArrayResult = IsArray(myRray)       '=== Returns True
%>
```

Arrays are particularly useful because they can be treated as a variable. This variable can be passed from page to page to act as an individual storage unit to house data. The following example illustrates testing for arrays using the IsArray function.

```
<%
Dim myArray, myResult
myArray = Array(ID, Password, Permissions)      '=== Loads Array with the new
➥Array function
myResult = IsArray(myArray)                      '=== Returns True
myResult = IsArray(myResult)                     '=== Returns False
%>
```

In this example, the new VBScript 2.0 IsArray function is used to create an array and store the array as a Variant variable. The first use of the IsArray function returns a True value because the variable myArray is actually storing an array. However, the second result returns False because the variable myResults is a Boolean value.

The *IsDate* Function

The IsDate function examines an expression and determines whether the expression can be converted into a date. The expression can already be a date expression or can be a string expression that can be interpreted by the Variant datatype as a date expression. The IsDate uses the following syntax:

```
IsDate(myExpression)
```

The IsDate function returns True if the expression can be converted to a date and False if the expression is unable to convert the expression. For example, the following demonstrate the results of IsDate function and various date formats.

```
<%
dim myDateLong, myDateLiteral, myDateShort, myResults

myDateLong = "APRIL 30, 1971"
myDateLiteral = #4/30/71#
myDateShort = "APR 30, 71"
myDateDash = "04-30-71"
myBadDate = "Not a Date"

myResults = IsDate(myDateLong)          '=== Returns True.
myResults = IsDate(myDateLiteral)       '=== Returns True.
myResults = IsDate(myDateShort)         '=== Returns True.
myResults = IsDate(myDateDash)          '=== Returns True.
myResults = IsDate(myBadDate)           '=== Returns False.
%>
```

The *IsEmpty* Function

The IsEmpty function is used to determine whether a value has been assigned since the variable was created. When a variable is first created, it is assigned a special value called the Empty value. This Empty value is different from a zero length string ("") or a NULL value. The Empty value is determined by using the IsEmpty function with the following syntax:

IsEmpty(*myExpression*)

where *myExpression* is a valid expression.

The IsEmpty expression returns True when the expression is an Empty value. Not only can an expression exist as an Empty value before it is assigned, but a variable can also be explicitly set to Empty. For example, in the following code sample, the value of myUserId is declared and tested for the Empty value.

```
<%
Dim myUserId

If IsEmpty(myUserId) Then                '=== Returns True, value still unassigned
    MyUserID = "Administrator"           '=== Sets the value
    Response.Write MyUserId              '=== Displays the value to page
End if

If Not IsEmpty(myUserID) Then
    myUserID = Empty                     '=== Sets to Empty Data Type
    Response.Write (IsEmpty(MyUserId))   '=== Returns True
End If
%>
```

The *IsNull* Function

One of the biggest sources of confusion over datatypes comes from the lack of understanding of the NULL value. The NULL value, like the Empty value, is treated as a special type of value in the datatypes. The NULL datatype represents the anti-datatype, meaning it represents an expression that does not contain an existing datatype. As mentioned previously, the NULL is not the same as the Empty or zero length strings. The IsNull function returns a Boolean value indicating whether the evaluated expression contains a NULL value. The IsNull function requires the following syntax:

IsNull(*myExpression*)

where *myExpression* is a valid expression.

The IsNull function returns True if the expression contains a NULL. If the expression contains any other datatype, the IsNull function returns False.

The IsNull function is important for evaluating an expression because of the unique behaviors of the NULL datatype. The NULL datatype, when used with any expression or any operator, replicates itself to produce a NULL value. The following example illustrates three results of the IsNull function.

```
<%
Dim myNullVar, MyNullResults
MyNullResults = IsNull(myNullVar)        '=== Returns False, variable is empty

myNullVar = ""
MyNullResults= IsNull(myNullVar)         '=== Returns False, variable is zero length

myNullVar = Null
MyNullResults = IsNull(myNullVar)        '=== Returns True, variable is Null
%>
```

If you are testing for NULL, you must use the IsNull function. The IsNull function is necessary because of the residual effects of NULL. Any existence of NULL in an expression or operator will transform the expression to NULL itself. Therefore, if any comparison operator is used to test for NULL, the entire expression itself becomes NULL, resulting in the perpetual failure of the expression. This perpetual failure is seen in the following example in which an expression is tested to see if the variable is equal and then not equal to NULL.

```
<%
Dim MyNullVar
myNullVar = Null                                     '=== Set variable to Null

If myNullVar = Null Then                             '=== Test for Null using an
➥operator
     response.write "Never Will Occur" & "<BR>"      '=== This will never execute
Else
     response.write "Equal to Null Comparison Failed" & "<BR>"
End If

If myNullVar <> Null Then                                '=== Test for Not
➥Null condition
     Response.Write "Never Will Happen Either" & "<BR>"      '=== This will never
➥execute
Else
     Response.Write "Not Equal to Null Comparison Failed" & "<BR>"
End if
%>
```

The *IsNumeric* Function

The IsNumeric function determines whether an expression can be evaluated as a number. You will notice that the IsNumeric function has similar functionality to the IsDate function by evaluating the possibility of converting a specific datatype. The IsNumeric function uses the following syntax:

```
IsNumeric(myExpression)
```

where *myExpression* is a valid expression.

The IsNumeric function returns True if the entire expression can be converted to a numeric expression. If the expression contains any other datatypes, the IsNumeric expression returns False, as shown in the following example:

```
<%
Dim myNumericVar, myNumResults

myNumericVar = "53"
myNumResults = IsNumeric(myNumericVar)        '=== Returns True.

myNumericVar = "459.95"
myNumResults = IsNumeric(myNumericVar)        '=== Returns True.

myNumericVar = "45 Help"
myNumResults = IsNumeric(myNumericVar)        '=== Returns False.

myNumericVar = "$45.65"
myNumResults = IsNumeric(myNumericVar)        '=== Returns True.

myNumericVar = "April 30, 1971"
myNumResults = IsNumeric(myNumericVar)        '=== Returns False.
%>
```

The *IsObject* Function

The IsObject function indicates whether or not a variable is an ActiveX object, and requires the following syntax:

```
IsObject(myexpression)
```

where *myExpression* is a valid ActiveX automation object. An ActiveX automation object is an object that exposes its own properties and methods through COM interfaces.

The IsObject returns True if the expression is evaluated as an object. If the expression represents any other datatype, the IsObject function returns False. For example, the following code example returns True:

```
<%
Set bc = Server.CreateObject("MSWC.BrowserType")
Response.Write IsObject(bc)  & "<BR>"
%>
```

The *VarType* Function

The core functionality of the IS datatype identifiers is powered by the VarType function. The VarType function presents the subtype category of a variable by using the following syntax:

```
VarType(varname)
```

where *varname* is any variable name. Unlike the other identifier functions, the VarType function returns the VBScript constants that are used to identify the datatype. For instance, in the following example the result of the VarType function indicates that the tested variable is an ActiveX object type.

```
<%
dim myVarType                                  '=== Declare variables
Set bc = Server.CreateObject("MSWC.BrowserType")   '=== Create Browser sniffer
myVarType = VarType(bc)                         '=== Returns a 9, vbObject
%>
```

The complete listing of variable types is presented in Table 7.1.

Table 7.1 Identify the Sub Datatype with the *VarType* Function

Constant	Value	Description
vbEmpty	0	Uninitialized (default)
vbNull	1	Contains no valid data
vbInteger	2	Integer
vbLong	3	Long
vbSingle	4	Single
vbDouble	5	Double
vbCurrency	6	Currency
vbDate	7	Date
vbString	8	String
vbObject	9	Object
vbError	10	Error
vbBoolean	11	Boolean
vbVariant	12	Variant (used only for arrays of variants)
vbDataObject	13	Data access
vbDecimal	14	Decimal
vbByte	17	Byte
vbArray	8192	Array

The Formatting Functions

One of the major stumbling blocks that developers encounter when learning VBScript is the lack of formatting functions that are inherent to programming languages like Visual Basic. However, VBScript 2.0 has introduced new formatting strings to aid in the conversion and manipulation of currency, data and time values, numbers, and percent values. These formatting functions are based on the number, currency, time, and date settings found in the Regional Settings of the Control Panel. Figure 7.1 illustrates the options available in the Regional Settings component of the Control Panel. Keep in mind that Regional Settings are only specific to the machine the VBScript code is being executed on. For example, if you are using a formatting function on an Active Server Page, the Regional Settings on the Web server will be used to dictate formatting. Whereas, if you are using client-side VBScript to display the current time and date, the local Web browser's Regional Settings would be applied.

FIG. 7.1
Configure the Regional Settings within the Control Panel.

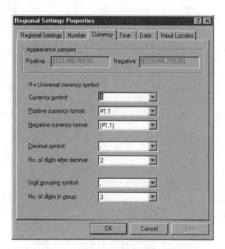

The *FormatDateTime* Function

The FormatDateTime function enables you to present a date expression in five convenient common date/time formats. The formats, as listed in Table 7.2, present the dates in a general format, a long and short date format, and a long and short time format.

Table 7.2   Date Format Constants

Constant	Value	Description
VbGeneralDate	0	Displays a date or time.
VbLongDate	1	Displays the long date format.
VbShortDate	2	Displays the short date format.
VbLongTime	3	Displays a long time format.
VbShortTime	4	Displays a short time format.

Part
II

Ch
7

Using these settings, you can dictate how date and time information will be manipulated. This formatting feature is often used when cleaning data for database storage or is used to present date and time information to the user without a large amount of hand coding.

The FormatDateTime function returns the formatted date or time value by using the following syntax:

```
FormatDateTime(Date[,NamedFormat])
```

where *Date* is a date expression and *NamedFormat* is the VBScript constant that determines the presentation display format. For example, the variable myDate is set to the current date and time of the system using the Now function. However, you can extract and display the date and time components of the time in long or short formats, as shown in the following code:

```
<%
dim myDate, myFormatDate                            '=== Variable declaration
myDate = cdate(Now)                                 '=== Initiates Variables
myFormatDate = FormatDateTime(myDate,vbGeneralDate) '=== Produces 6/20/97
➡7:51:21 PM
myFormatDate = FormatDateTime (myDate,vbLongDate)   '=== Produces Friday,
                                                         June 20, 1997
myFormatDate = FormatDateTime (myDate,vbShortDate)  '=== Produces 6/20/97
myFormatDate = FormatDateTime (myDate,vbLongTime)   '=== Produces 7:51:21 PM
myFormatDate = FormatDateTime (myDate,vbShortTime)  '=== Produces 19:51
%>
```

The *FormatCurrency* Function

The FormatCurrency function focuses on returning a formatted currency value. The currency symbols are based on the selected number, currency, time, and date settings used in the Regional Settings within the Control Panel. The FormatCurrency function returns the currency format using the following syntax:

```
FormatCurrency(Expression[,NumDigitsAfterDecimal [,IncludeLeadingDigit
[,UseParensForNegativeNumbers [,GroupDigits]]]])
```

where *expression* is the required numeric expression to be formatted. As you can see, the FormatCurrency has several options. The NumDigitsAfterDecimal option indicates the optional number of digits to display to the right of the decimal point. The IncludeLeadingDigit is the optional constant used to determine whether or not to include the leading zero. The UseParensForNegativeNumbers enables parentheses to be displayed in place of the negative sign to represent numbers less that zero. The GroupDigits gives the capability to follow the group delimiter options specified in the Currency tab of the Control Panel.

The last three options, IncludeLeadingDigit, UseParensForNegativeNumbers, and GroupDigits are *Tristate constants*. The Tristate constants provide the flexibility to use a constant that has three positions or values. These display values are usually dictated by the Regional Settings of the Control Panel. The *Tristate* constants are defined in Table 7.3.

Table 7.3 The *FormatCurrency* Tristate Constants

Constant	Value	Description
TristateTrue	-1	Option is True.
TristateFalse	0	Option is False.
TristateUseDefault	-2	Use the settings from the computer's Regional Settings.

For the FormatCurrency function, the specific Regional Settings are located in the Currency and Number tabs.

For example, the following code demonstrates the FormatCurrency features:

```
<%
dim myCurrencyValue, myInterestValue, myFormatCurrency, myTotal

myCurrencyValue = 16299.98: myInterestValue = 0.21     '=== Initialize Variable
myTotal = myCurrencyValue + (myCurrencyValue*myInterestValue)
myInterestLost = myCurrencyValue - myTotal

myFormatCurrency =FormatCurrency(myCurrencyValue)          '=== Displays $16,299.98
myFormatCurrency =FormatCurrency(myTotal, 4)              '=== Displays $19,722.9758
myFormatCurrency =FormatCurrency(myInterestLost, TristateFalse, 0, TristateTrue)
'=== Displays -$3,423
myFormatCurrency =FormatCurrency(myInterestLost, TristateTrue, 0, -1)
'=== Displays ($3,423)
%>
```

The *FormatPercent* Function

The FormatPercent function returns the formatted percent value of an expression. The FormatPercent function accomplishes this by multiplying the value by 100 and concatenating the percent (%) character onto the results. The FormatPercent function uses the following syntax:

```
FormatPercent(Expression[,NumDigitsAfterDecimal [,IncludeLeadingDigit
[,UseParensForNegativeNumbers [,GroupDigits]]]])
```

where *Expression* is the required expression to be formatted. The remaining options, NumDigitsAfterDecimal, IncludeLeadingDigit, UseParensForNegativeNumbers, and GroupDigits, are the same options available in the FormatCurrency function. However, in this situation, the default system settings are located in the Number tab of the Regional Settings in the Control Panel.

The following code demonstrates examples that utilize the different FormatPercent options.

```
<%
Dim myInterestRate, myFormatPercent
myInterestRate = 0.2159                          '=== Initialize Interest Rate
```

```
myFormatPercent = FormatPercent(myInterestRate)       '=== Returns 21.59%
myFormatPercent = FormatPercent(myInterestRate, 1)    '=== Returns 21.6%
myFormatPercent = FormatPercent(-myInterestRate,TristateTrue, 0, -1)
➥'=== Returns (22%)
myFormatPercent = FormatPercent(myInterestRate/100, , -1, TristateTrue)
➥'=== Returns 0.22%
%>
```

The *FormatNumber* Function

The FormatNumber function enables the customized display of a numeric expression. Following in the tradition of the other formatting functions, the FormatNumber uses the following syntax:

```
FormatNumber(Expression[,NumDigitsAfterDecimal [,IncludeLeadingDigit
[,UseParensForNegativeNumbers [,GroupDigits]]]])
```

where *Expression* is the required numeric expression to be formatted. The available options and Tristate constants are also the same as the FormatCurrency and FormatDateTime functions.

```
<%
Dim myNumber, myFormatNumber
myNumber = 22/7                                          '===
➥Initialize variables
myFormatNumber = FormatNumber(myNumber)                  '=== Results
➥in 3.14
myFormatNumber = FormatNumber(myNumber, 8)               '=== Results
➥in 3.14285714
myFormatNumber = FormatNumber(-myNumber, 1, 0, -1)       '=== Results
➥in (3.1)
myFormatNumber = FormatNumber(3-myNumber, 3, -1, TristateFalse  '=== Results
➥in -0.143
%>
```

Datatype Conversions

Throughout the investigation of the various operators and functions in VBScript, the potential hazards of the automatic conversion of the Variant datatypes abound. To prevent un-intentional errors from occurring, VBScript provides conversion utilities to tighten the control on the sub datatypes. Furthermore, as Active Server Pages begin to distribute applications worldwide, issues such as regional formatting become a concern. The conversion functions were designed with this in mind. Most of the conversion functions recognize regional currency and formatting issues and can seamlessly interact with different display settings without changing the underlying datatypes.

VBScript provides nine conversion functions to help reduce the chance of runtime or logic-based errors. The conversion functions and descriptions are listed in Table 7.4.

Table 7.4 Sub Datatype Conversion Functions

Function	Return Type	Data Range
CBool	Boolean	True or False
CByte	Byte	0 to 255
CCur	Currency	-922,337,203,685,477.5808 to 922,337,203,685,477.5807
CDate	Date	Any valid date expression
CDbl	Double	-1.79769313486232E308 to -4.94065645841247E-324 for negative values; 4.94065645841247E-324 to 1.79769313486232E308 for positive values
CInt	Integer	-32,768 to 32,767; fractions are rounded
CLng	Long	-2,147,483,648 to 2,147,483,647; fractions are rounded
CSng	Single	-3.402823E38 to -1.401298E-45 for negative values; 1.401298E-45 to 3.402823E38 for positive values
CStr	String	Returns string values, except Null

When using the conversion functions, the data ranges are important to keep in mind. If you try to use a function to evaluate an expression that is not in the targeted conversion group, a runtime error will occur.

Cbool Function

The CBool function converts an expression into a subtype of Boolean. The CBool function accomplishes this by using the following syntax:

CBool(*expression*)

The Boolean conversion process will convert any numeric expression to either True or False. Any other expressions will produce a Type Mismatch error. For example, the following code uses the CBool function to convert an expression into Boolean subtype.

```
<%
Dim myBoolValue1, myBoolValue2, myBoolResult, myDataType
myBoolValue1 = 100: myBoolValue2 = 99.5          '=== Initialize variables.
myBoolResult = CBool(myBoolValue1 = myBoolValue2)   '=== Returns a Boolean of
➥False
myDataType = VarType(myBoolResult)               '=== Identifies Boolean
                                                     subtype

myBoolValue1 = 100: myBoolValue2 = 100           '=== Reset Values
myBoolResult = CBool(myBoolValue1 = myBoolValue2)   '=== Returns a Boolean of
➥True

myBoolValue1 = 100                               '=== Resets Value
myBoolResult = CBool(myBoolValue1)               '=== Returns a Boolean of
➥False
%>
```

Part

II

Ch

7

Notice in the first two examples, the Boolean results of the expression `myBoolValue1 = myBoolValue2` were successful in returning `Boolean` values. In the first situation, the expression returned `False` because the numeric values were not the same. However, in the second situation, the `CBool` function returned `True` because the variables were equal. In the third situation, the `CBool` function returns `False` because even though the variable exists, the expression of the single variable by itself does not return a value. Keep in mind that the Boolean conversion process can only evaluate numeric expressions. In the following code example, the Boolean conversion process produces runtime errors when trying to evaluate string values.

```
<%
myBoolValue1 = "Foo"                    '=== Set Value to string Foo
myBoolResult= CBool(myBoolValue1)       '=== Results in Type Mismatch Error

myBoolValue1 = ""                       '=== Reset Value
myBoolResult= CBool(myBoolValue1)       '=== Results in Type Mismatch Error
%>
```

CByte Function

The `CByte` function converts an expression into a subtype of type `Byte`. The `CByte` function requires the following syntax:

`CByte(expression)`

The following example illustrates using the `CByte` conversion function:

```
<%
Dim myByteValue, myDataType
myByteValue = 99.987654                 '=== myByteValue is a Double.
myDataType = CByte(myByteValue)         '=== Returns 100
%>
```

NOTE Before using the conversion functions, remember to check the range of the input expression to prevent conversion errors. ■

CCur Function

The `CCur` function is used to convert ordinary variant expressions into the currency subtype. The `CCur` function uses the following syntax to return conversion results.

`CCur(expression)`

The currency conversion function is important when considering your potential global user base. The currency conversion functions recognize the different currency formatting issues, such as various separator symbols, different thousand separators, and other currency display options.

```
<%
Dim myCurrValue, myDataType            '=== Initialize Values
myCurrValue = 16299.214588             '=== Sets myCurrValue is a Double.
                       myDataType = CCur(MyCurrValue * 2)'=== Returns
                                                              32598.4292
%>
```

The currency conversion function converts the value 32598.429176 to 32598.4292.

CDate Function

The CDate function is used to merge a variant variable into a date subtype. The CDate function requires the following syntax:

```
CDate(date)
```

where *date* is a valid date expression. The IsDate function mentioned in the beginning of this chapter is used to determine whether an expression can be converted into a date subtype. The CDate function is actually the function that does the conversion into the date subtype.

One advantage that the CDate function has at its disposal is the capability to recognize date and time literals. Date literals are comprised of a defined set of characters surround by pound (#) signs. The defined character set is defined in the Regional Settings of the Control Panel. You can use the CDate function to display localized regional formats when building multi-region applications.

```
<%
Dim myDateValue, myTimeValue, myDataType
myDateValue = "February 12, 1969"          '=== Initialize date.
myDataType = CDate(myDateValue)            '=== Convert to Date 2/12/69

myTimeValue = "4:35:47 PM"                 '=== Initial time.
myDataType = CDate(myTimeValue)            '=== Convert to Date 4:35:47 PM.
%>
```

N O T E Use date literals, such as #4/30/1997# and #12:30:00 PM#, to ensure that your date and time strings are portable across multiple regions. ■

CDbl, CInt, CLng, CSng

The CDbl, CInt, CLng, and CSng conversion functions are all used to provide conversion between the number datatypes. The CDbl function is used to convert variables to double precision subtypes. The CInt function is used to transform variables into single precision subtypes. The CLng function is used to convert variables into Long subtypes. The CSng function is used to convert an expression into a single-precision sub datatype. These numeric conversion functions use the following syntax:

```
nConversionFunctions(expression)
```

where *nConversionFunctions* is the CDbl, CInt, CLng, or CSng conversion names and *expression* is the evaluated expression in any valid expression.

The following example illustrates the conversion of a double-precision sub datatype to a single-precision and Integer datatype.

Part
II
Ch
7

```
<%
Dim myFirstValue, mySecondValue, myDataType, myValue
myFirstValue = 157.3585705: mySecondValue = 194.6465794      '=== Initializes
➥variables
myDataType = VarType(myFirstValue)                           '=== Returns a Double
myDataType = VarType(mySecondValue)                          '=== Returns a Double
myValue = CSng(myFirstValue)                                 '=== Converts to
➥Single 157.3586
myValue = CSng(mySecondValue)                                '=== Converts to
➥Single 194.6466
myValue = CInt(mySecondValue)                                '=== Converts to
➥Integer 195
%>
```

> **N O T E**   When using the CInt and CLng functions, remember that these functions always round to
> the nearest even number, therefore 2.5 rounds to 2, and 3.5 rounds to 4. ■

CStr Function

The CStr function is used to convert an expression into a string subtype. The CStr function
uses the following syntax:

CStr(*expression*)

where *expression* is a valid expression. The result of the CStr function always returns a string
subtype, with the exception of when the expression contains a NULL value. Table 7.5 illustrates
the results of the CStr function when a variety of subtypes compose the expression.

Table 7.5   The *CStr* Return Values

If CStr(expression)	CStr **Returns**
Boolean	A string containing True or False
Date	A string containing a date in the short-date format
Empty	A zero-length string ("")
Error	A string containing the word Error followed by the error number
Numeric	A string containing the number
Null	A runtime error

The following example uses the VarType function to determine the subtypes.

```
<%
Dim myValue, myDataType
myValue = 16299.99                        '=== Initialize variable
myDataType = VarType(myValue)             '=== Initially a Double
myValue  = CStr(myValue)                  '=== Converts to String
myDataType =VarType(myValue)              '=== Results in a String
```

```
myValue  = CStr(Now)              '=== Convert a Date to String, produces
➡6/21/97 12:39:05 AM
myDataType =VarType(myValue)       '=== Results in a String
%>
```

From Here...

From this chapter, you learned that the VBScript datatype identification and conversion functions are used to explicitly convert Variant sub datatypes. In addition, VBScript 2.0 has introduced four new formatting functions that are used to easily format date/time, currency, percent, and numeric values. These new functions eliminate the need to build VBScript formatting code from scratch into your scripts.

For related information, please see the following chapters:

- Chapter 10, "The Composition of an Active Server Application," will illustrate the different pieces of an ASP application.

- Chapter 12, "Controlling the Server with the Server Object and Using Transaction Processing with the ObjectContext Object," demonstrates how the Server Object controls and manages the ASP applications.

- Chapters 17 and 18, "Implementing Existing Server-Side Components" and "Creating Your Own Active Server Components," will teach how to use server-side VBScript to provide connections to pre-built and customizable servers.

- Chapter 20, "Database Access with ADO," provides a firsthand approach on using VBScript to manipulate your databases.

- Chapter 31, "Using Internet Information Server 4.0 to Manage Your Web Applications," demonstrates how to use the various features of the Internet Information Server to help manage your sites and applications.

- Chapter 32, "Putting It All Together: Creating an N-Tier Online Catalog Application," demonstrates how to build ActiveX components to create an n-tier distributed application for the Amazing DataWidget WareHouse Catalog.

Part

II

Ch

7

Putting It All Together with VBScript

This chapter demonstrates how to use VBScript to build a miniature application that uses client- and server-side processing scripting to calculate the aerodynamic drag for a vehicle over a range of speeds. This application uses server-side ASP scripts to perform to the core processing of the engineering calculations, which can be processed by any browser. Once the functionality of the VBScript programming logic has been demonstrated, VBScript will also be used on the client to ensure that the required HTML fields are properly filled in by the user. ■

Create Active Server Scripts with VBScript

Learn how to implement VBScript within your Active Server Pages to create application and processing logic that runs on the Web server.

Create Client-Side VBScript

Utilize client-side scripts to process application logic that will be executed within the Internet Explorer browser to perform client-side validation.

Create Browser-Specific Code

Discover how to use Active Server Pages to identify the requesting browser and tailor the client-side scripting to the specific browser type.

Application Overview

One of the largest benefits of using ASP on the server is that any browser can have access to the application logic embedded on the Web server. To illustrate that fact, this application will demonstrate a sample application that performs aerodynamic drag calculations. These calculations are performed by executing ASP scripts on the Internet Information Server from any HTML-compliant browser.

Figure 8.1 demonstrates the interface to enter information on the vehicle specification page in Internet Explorer.

FIG. 8.1

Using Internet Explorer to gather vehicle specifications.

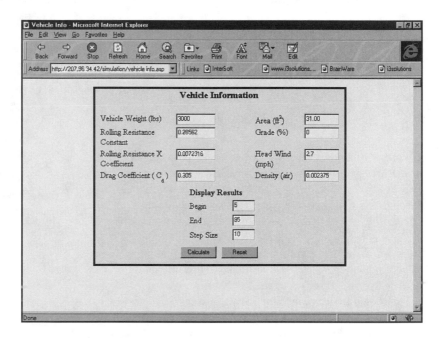

The advantage of using an HTML-based system is that you are not constrained to one specific browser type; you can gather the same information from other browsers. For example, Figure 8.2 illustrates using Netscape Navigator to enter vehicle information.

After the user enters the vehicle information, the ActiveX scripting engine on the Internet Information Server processes the calculations. In this situation, the ActiveX scripting engine will process VBScript to perform the calculations, but the calculations can be written in JScript, PERL, REXX, or any other script-compliant engine. After the drag values have been calculated, the results are delivered from the Internet Information Server to the browser as HTML (see Figure 8.3).

The key point to remember here is that only HTML is delivered to the browser. The processing of VBScript occurs only on the server. Processing VBScript on the server does not limit the access to ActiveX-compatible browsers or operating systems. Figure 8.4 illustrates the complete results being delivered to Netscape Navigator (with no ActiveX plug-in installed—there are no cards up my sleeves!).

FIG. 8.2

Any HTML-compliant browser can be used to access the application.

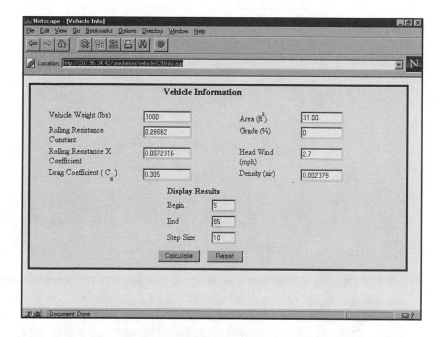

FIG. 8.3

After processing, the results of the server-side calculations are delivered to the browser.

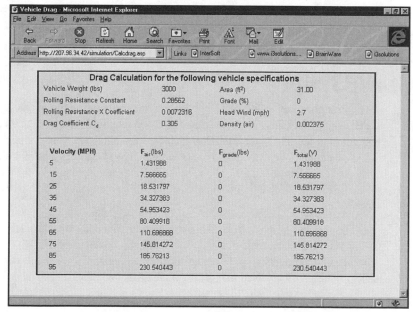

FIG. 8.4
Processing VBScript on the server does not limit application access to a browser-specific delivery mechanism.

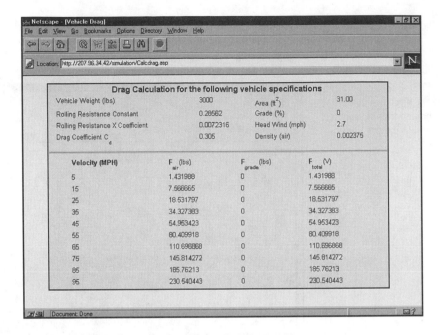

You will build this mini-application in three phases. The first phase demonstrates how to use server-side VBScript to create the basic functionality of the Active Server application. Second, you will add client-side VBScript and JavaScript to perform client-side validations. Finally, you will return to the server-side VBScript to maximize the flexibility and power of the server-side scripts.

Creating Server-Side Active Server Scripts with VBScript

The first phase of building this application demonstrates some of the features of server-side VBScript processing. The mini-application will use Active Server Pages to run a fuel economy simulation model for vehicles. Specifically, this application demonstrates the relation of drag or air resistance to velocity. This chapter will not cover the specifics of the engineering formulas used to calculate this information, but will focus on how to use VBScript 2.0 within Active Server Pages. Keep in mind that this application serves as a template that can contain any type of application logic.

As you saw in Figures 8.1 and 8.3, two pages are used in the application. The first page is a simple forms-based page that collects information from the user. This page passes information to the second page via the Internet Information Server. The second page is the page that actually contains the application logic for the calculations, and it is also responsible for displaying the calculation results to the requesting browser.

To start building this application, you can use your favorite method of creating and managing Active Server applications. You can use the Internet Service Manager in IIS 3.0 to create a new virtual directory to house your pages. Alternatively, if you are using IIS 4.0, you can use the Microsoft Management Console to create a new Web site or virtual directory. (If you need more information on configuring your Web site with the MMC, please see Chapter 31, "Using Internet Information Server 4.0 to Manage Your Web Applications.")

As far as Active Server Page development tools, choose your favorite ASP development environment. If you like, you can use your favorite ASCII editor to create and edit your Active Server Pages. Alternatively, FrontPage enables you to create Active Server Pages and server-side scripting, and Visual InterDev provides the most functionality tailored toward application developers. Regardless of the development environment you choose, the functionality of Active Server Pages remains the same.

Creating the Visual InterDev Project

Visual InterDev will be used in this chapter for this VBScript simulation project. After creating a new Web project on the Web server, create two Active Server Pages that will act as the input page and the results page. To create new Active Server Page files within Visual InterDev, select New from the File menu. Next, choose Active Server Page from the File tab, and name the first ASP file `Vehicle Info` and the second ASP file `CalcDrag`. Visual InterDev will create Active Server Pages based on the default ASP template. For more information on using Visual InterDev, please see Chapter 27, "Visual InterDev: The Active Server Pages Integrated Development Environment."

When you create the new files in Visual InterDev, the files are automatically opened in the Visual InterDev editor. This editor serves as your primary development environment.

Creating a Static Page   The first page, `Vehicleinfo.htm`, does not require any server-side processing when the page is delivered to the browser. It is simply used to collect information from the user. With the Active Server Page revolution, you may be tempted to convert all of your HTML files to ASP files. However, this is not recommended. When Internet Information Server processes files with an .ASP extension, it uses the Active Server scripting engine to interpret the page—even if no Active Server script is embedded on the page. This relatively small amount of processing power can be significantly amplified depending on your Web site's size and load.

 T I P   Resist the temptation to convert all HTML files to ASP files. To prevent the unnecessary use of processing power, only convert the HTML files that require script processing.

To create this page, you can code the HTML by hand or use any GUI HTML creation tool, such as FrontPage or HotMeTal. You can activate any external tool from within Visual InterDev by right-clicking the file you want to open. When you choose the Open With option, a pop-up dialog displays the configured tools for this file type (see Figure 8.5).

FIG. 8.5

With Visual InterDev, you can use external tools to create and edit files.

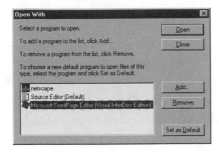

This example will use Visual InterDev FrontPage to create the template page. The FrontPage version that ships with Visual InterDev is a scaled-down version of the full Microsoft FrontPage product that enables basic Web creation and script wizard interface, but does not include items such as the various wizards and clipart libraries that are available in the full product. If you do not have FrontPage for Visual InterDev configured, select the Add button to add the new editor. The FrontPage editor that ships with Visual InterDev is usually located at `/devestudio/VintDev/ISFP/Bin/isfp.exe`.

After the Visual InterDev FrontPage editor is open, create the Web page that will collect the user information. This page consists of several nested tables, text boxes, and Submit and Reset buttons. The nested tables are used to control positioning of objects on a Web page. Figure 8.6 illustrates using tables with the border property set to zero.

FIG. 8.6

Use invisible nested tables to control page layout.

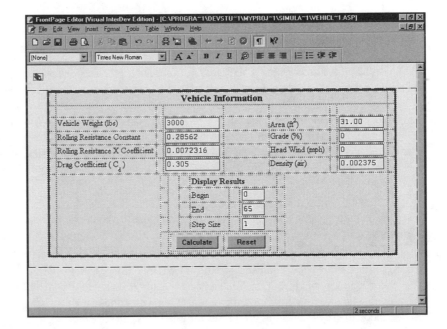

Text boxes are used to enable the user to enter information into the page. The HTML Submit and Cancel buttons are used to control the processing of the form objects on a page. The Submit button posts or sends the information to the designated page on the Web server. The specific page is set within the form `Action` event. For example, the following code will send the information entered on a form to the `calcdrag.asp` page.

```
<FORM ACTION="Calcdrag.asp" METHOD="POST" NAME="frmInfo">
```

The Cancel button is used to reset all HTML objects to their initial values.

Take time to name all your HTML objects on the page using a standard naming convention. There are several naming conventions available, just be sure to pick a method and stick to it. Standardizing your code will benefit you in the long run by creating code that is easier to read and reducing errors due to misspellings and bad references.

For example, name the HTML forms with the `frm` prefix to help you visually identify an object's type. If the form is used to collect information about the user's vehicle, name the form `frmVehicleleInfo`. You name the objects in FrontPage by double-clicking the object or right-clicking and selecting the appropriate Properties tag. Standardizing the names of your objects is important because it will also help to prevent errors. For example, if you name a text box `txtVehicleWeight`, take care to remember the capitalization scheme you have chosen. VBScript, which is case insensitive, can reference an object using any combination of upper- and lowercase letters. However, JavaScript is case sensitive. Therefore, if you try to reference the text box `txtVehicleWeight` as `txtvehicleweight` within JavaScript, an error will occur.

Creating the Dynamic Template   After you create the information collection page, save the application. Now it is time to start creating the core VBScript programming functionality that performs the vehicle calculations in Active Server Pages. The role of the second page is to accept the vehicle information passed to it, process it, and display the results. The second page will act as a template to host whatever information is processed by the ASP script. For example, the physical HTML page should have the same format regardless of the range of valid vehicle weights or speed ranges to be calculated.

Using FrontPage to Create a Template   In most situations, developers can perform data collection, manipulation, and retrieval with relative ease, but displaying this information is often the tedious part. This is particularly true with Web deployment and the joys of learning HTML. To help take away some of the pains of developing HTML, use the same HTML GUI tools that you used to create the static page to create the template to display the dynamic information.

In this example, you want to return the information entered about the test vehicle specifications at the top of the page. After creating the header, you need to create a template that will be repeated for every record displayed. To do that, create an HTML table with two rows under the header information. The first row is used as the table header describing the columns. The second row represents the row that will be repeated within the VBScript looping code to display the results, as shown in Figure 8.7.

After saving and closing the page, you are now ready to start creating the core server-side VBScript.

FIG. 8.7
Use GUI HTML editors to
quickly create HTML
templates to write your
ASP data into.

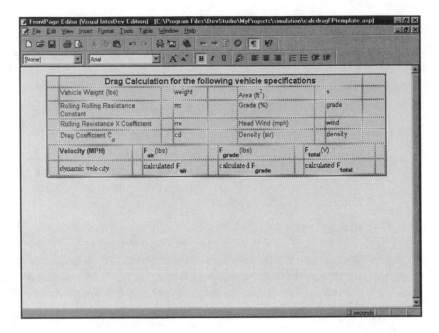

Building Data Retrieval and Display

To help further define how to code this mini-application, you should review the workflow process. The first phase obtains the information that is passed to the page and displays the values in the header. The second phase takes the information and processes it according to the given engineering equations and writes the output to the page.

VBScript Declarations The first line of the Active Server Page should contain *process directives* that are used to help the Active Server scripting engine process that Active Server Page. For instance, to set the default scripting engine required to process the script contained in the <% and %> tags, use the LANGUAGE directive:

```
<%@ LANGUAGE = VBScript %>
```

This tag should be placed within the ASP file when the file is initially created via Visual InterDev. If the tag has been deleted, add it to the first line of text.

Remember that the process directive must be on the first line of the ASP, and you must include a space between the @ and the LANGUAGE tag. You can also set other characteristics of the page within the process directive. The process directive enables you to use the CODEPAGE keyword to work with multilingual sites, the LCID to set the locale identifier, the TRANSACTION keyword to enable transaction processing, and ENABLESESSIONSTATE to track user sessions. These directives are covered in greater detail in Chapter 10, "The Composition of an Active Server Application."

After setting the default scripting language for the page, insert the VBScript Option Explicit statement. The Option Explicit statement forces all variables to be explicitly declared by using the Dim, ReDim, Public, or Private keywords.

The Option Explicit tag must be declared before any header information is sent to the browser. Failure to initiate this will generate an Expected statement error, as shown in Figure 8.8.

FIG. 8.8
Failing to define the Option Explicit statement before sending information to the browser will generate an error.

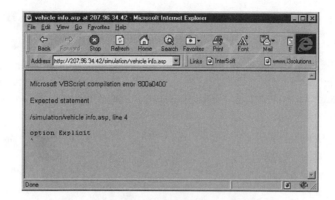

Placing the Option Explicit statement after any HTML tag, as shown below, generates this error:

```
<%@ LANGUAGE="VBSCRIPT" %>
<!DOCTYPE HTML PUBLIC "-//IETF//DTD HTML//EN">        <!--Output is sent to computer
➡→
<% Option Explicit %>                                 <!--Generate error →
<HTML>
```

To correct this, simply place the Option Explicit tag after the LANGUAGE directive:

```
<%@ LANGUAGE="VBSCRIPT" %>
<% Option Explicit %>                                 <!--Sets Option Explicit →
<!DOCTYPE HTML PUBLIC "-//IETF//DTD HTML//EN">        <!--Output is sent to computer
➡→
<HTML>
```

Next, create variables to store the input from the user so that you can manipulate the values in the engineering formulas. You can accomplish this by using the Dim keyword and the variable name. For example, the following code declares variables that represent the input items from the user:

```
<%      '=== User Variables
    Dim Weight        '=== Vehicle Weight
    Dim RRConst       '=== Rolling Resistance Constant
    Dim RRXcoef       '=== Rolling existence Coefficient
    Dim Grade         '=== Grade
    Dim Cd            '=== Coefficient of Drag
    Dim Sarea         '=== Frontal Surface Area
    Dim Headwind      '=== Headwind
    Dim Density       '=== Density of medium
    Dim StepSize      '=== Display Increment
    Dim VelBegin      '=== Begin Display at this velocity
    Dim VelEnd        '=== Close Display at this velocity
%>
```

Comments are used after each declaration statement to help identify the purpose of each variable. However, to improve performance, the multiple variable declarations can all occur on one line:

```
<%
Dim Weight, RRConst, RRXcoef, Grade, Cd, Sarea, Headwind, Density, StepSize,
VelBegin, VelEnd
➡%>
```

The improvements come not from the reduced number of comments on a page, but from the number of times VBScript has to process each line. By collecting the multiple declaration statements within one statement, VBScript only has to parse the line one time. If declare statements are made on individual lines, VBScript must parse each line separately.

Retrieving User information   Now that you have created variables on the server to hold the user information, you are going to use an Active Server object to help retrieve information from the requesting Web page. The Request object is used to extract values from items contained on an HTML form. Because you have to use this information to process logic on the page, assign these values to the variables declared in the previous section.

To obtain the values the users entered in a text box on a form, use the text box name within the Request object, as shown in Listing 8.1.

Listing 8.1   Gathering information from the HTML form.

```
<%
    Weight = Request.Form("txtweight")
    RRConst = Request.Form("txtrrconstant")
    RRXcoef = Request.Form("txtxcoef")
    Grade = Request.Form("txtgrade")
    Cd = Request.Form("txtcd")
    Sarea = Request.Form("txtarea")
    Headwind = Request.Form("txtheadwind")
    Density = Request.Form("txtdensity")
    StepSize = Request.Form("txtstepsize")
    VelBegin = Request.Form("txtbegin")
    VelEnd = Request.Form("txtend")
%>
```

For more information on the Request object, see Chapter 15, "Retrieving User Information: The Request Object."

Writing the Information to the Page   Now that you have the information in memory on the page, you can create the page header, which returns the information the user entered for the calculations. To accomplish this, you have to write the variable information to the page. Active Server script uses two different ways to write information to a page: the Response.Write method or its shorthand notation of <% =%>.

To write these values in the appropriate location on the template page that was created in FrontPage, you should mix HTML tags with Active Server tags. Find the location where you need to write information on the page with the Visual InterDev editor. In this case, look for the location of the string (weight). This string was added to the page to serve as a placeholder when you created the page in FrontPage. When you have found this string in the Visual InterDev editor, replace it with the Active Server tags to write the variable weight to the page. Specifically, you are looking for the following HTML:

```
<td valign="top"> (Weight) <td>     <! -- Original HTML from FrontPage →
```

The string (Weight) must be replaced with the Response tag, as shown in the following code:

```
<td valign="top"> <% Response.Write weight %> </td>
```

Continue replacing the placeholders that were created in FrontPage with the appropriate Response.Write tags. If you save and reopen the calcdrag.asp page in FrontPage, FrontPage interprets the Active Server script as script, as shown in Figure 8.9.

FIG. 8.9
FrontPage uses a script icon to represent the Active Server script.

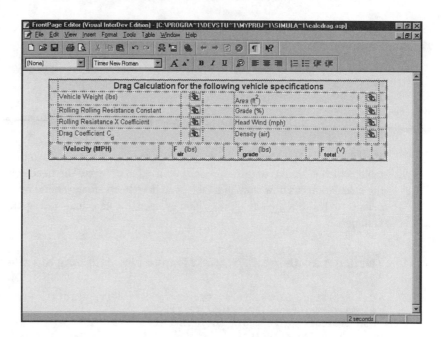

Processing the Logic

Now that you know how to integrate Active Server script within HTML, you will use VBScript to perform calculations and use looping logic to complete a task a certain number of times.

VBScript has a variety of built-in mathematical functions to help perform the various calculations. For example, the drag force due to air resistance is expressed by the following equation:

```
Fdrag = 0.5 * Density * ((Velocity + Headwind)^2)*(88/60)^2 * Cd * Sarea
```

As you can see from this equation, VBScript handles addition, multiplication, division, and exponential arithmetic statements. Furthermore, you can tap into the trigonometric functions. The following example illustrates using the arctangent function to calculate the slope:

```
slope = atn(Grade/100)*(180/(22/7))
```

Because you want to perform the drag calculations over a range of velocities, you need to implement looping logic. This looping logic will repeat a section of code either until a condition is met or for a specific number of times. In this situation, you will implement a For...Next loop to repeat the drag calculation for a specific number of times. Usually you implement a For...Next loop from 1 to an upper limit with a step size of 1. However, in this situation, you have asked the user to specify the start and end positions and at what increments to perform the calculations. You can implement this conditional logic to calculate the drag force for multiple velocities starting at velBegin and ending at velEnd with an increment size of stepsize:

```
<%
Dim iVelocity
For iVelocity = velbegin to velend step stepsize
    Velocity = iVelocity
    Fdrag = 0.5 * Density * ((Velocity + Headwind)^2)*(88/60)^2 * Cd * Sarea
Next
%>
```

This iterative looping procedure enables the application to calculate and show the drag values from 5 to 95 mph at every 10 mph.

Now that the calculations are done, you need to write these values to the results template table, which is similar to the approach you used to generate the header information. To write the calculations as new rows in a table, you have to create new table rows (<TR>) and table cells (<TD>) within the For...Next loop by using the Response.Write method, as shown in Listing 8.2.

Listing 8.2   Using a *For...Next* loop to calculate drag at various speeds.

```
<%
Dim Frolling, Slope, Velocity, Fdrag, iVelocity, Ftotal, Fgrade
Slope = atn(Grade/100)*(180/(22/7))
For iVelocity = velbegin to velend step stepsize
    Velocity = iVelocity
    Response.Write "<TR>"
    Response.Write "<TD width='18'> </TD>"
    Response.Write "<TD valign='top'><font face='arial' size='2'
color=#000080>" &Velocity "</font></TD>"
    Response.Write "<TD width='2'> </TD>"
    Fdrag = 0.5 * Density * ((Velocity + Headwind)^2)*(88/60)^2 * Cd * Sarea
    Response.Write "<TD valign='top'><font face='arial' size='2'
color=#000080>" &Round(Fdrag,6) &"</font></TD>"
    Fgrade = Weight*Sin(slope * (22/7)/180)
    Response.Write "<TD valign='top'><font face='arial' size='2'
color=#000080>" &Round(Fgrade,6) &"</font></TD>"
    Response.Write "<TD width='2'> </TD>"
    Ftotal = Fdrag+Frolling+Fgrade
    Response.Write "<TD valign='top'><font face='arial' size='2'
```

```
color=#000080>" &Round(Ftotal,6) &"</font></TD>"
      Response.Write "<TD width='6'> </TD>"
      Response.Write "</TR>"
Next
   %>
```

Notice the use of batch processing of server scripting instead of mixing HTML tags and Active Server script delimiters. This helps increase the performance by reducing the need to switch back and forth between processing server script and HTML tags.

This looping logic also incorporates the use of a VBScript formatting feature. The Round function is used to round a number to a specific number of decimal places. In this situation, round all calculated values to six decimal places.

Minor Error Trapping

Finally, you want to include some server-side validation before you try to process the calculations. Even though the server is not the optimal location to validate input, this preliminary example is used to demonstrate that it is possible. The best place to perform the validation is within the client browser's environment. The advantage of processing information on the client is that it reduces the server load and network traffic. However, for the purposes of the VBScript server examples, the application will display an error page if the user does not properly enter certain values.

To accomplish this simple validation and display technique, server-side script will determine whether the values of the weight and surface area variables are greater than zero. To check the value of both the variables, use the conditional If...Then statement with the OR comparison operator. The If...Then statement is used to test a specific condition and take action depending on the result. The conditional operator OR is used to test whether either condition evaluates to True. Together, these can be implemented to ensure that the variables Weight and Sarea are both greater than or equal to zero.

```
<%
If Weight <= 0 Or Sarea <= 0 Then
     Response.Redirect "Error.asp"
End If
%>
```

In this situation, if either the Weight is negative (less than or equal to zero) or the Sarea is negative, the user is automatically routed to an error page. It is true that there are various error navigation methods you can implement. However, for this example, I want to simply demonstrate how to implement VBScript on the server without going into too much complexity.

Creating Client-Side VBScript

As I mentioned earlier, the server is not the ideal place to validate user input. To reduce server load and network traffic, client-side scripting should be implemented. This section will demonstrate how to build both VBScript and JavaScript client-side validation scripts. The JavaScript functions are included because other browsers do not interpret VBScript, although it is supported on the IIS Web server and on the Internet Explorer browser. Loading VBScript-based client-side scripting in other browsers will generate scripting runtime errors, as shown in Figure 8.10.

FIG. 8.10
VBScript client-side
script will generate
errors on non VBScript-
compliant browsers.

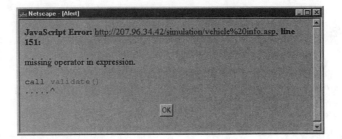

The simplest validation to deploy on the client is to test the values of the text boxes. Because the purpose of this application is to perform calculations, you must trap for blanks, zero values, and non-numeric values to ensure proper arithmetic operations.

To build this validation method, you are going to create a subroutine that is responsible for validating field values. This subroutine will first check to see if the values of the fields are valid. If all the fields pass the inspection, the form is submitted to the server for processing. If a field contains an invalid number, an error message will prompt the user about the incorrect entry and set the focus to the troubled field.

Restructuring the HTML

The first step needed to build this functionality is to add the validation subroutine. The validation subroutine will check certain HTML fields for proper values before the user tries to perform the calculations. The validation routine is actually triggered with the Click event of the Calculate button. If the validation passes, the form data will be passed onto the calculation page. If the validation fails, the user is prompted and control is returned back to the browser. If the validation passes, the information is sent to the Web server for processing. However, to build this functionality, you have to change the Submit button into a regular HTML button because the Submit button will always execute the Submit event of the form. By converting the Submit button into a normal button, the Submit event of the form can be controlled via scripting. To change the Submit button to a normal button, either double-click the Submit button within FrontPage to change its property or find the following line of code in the HTML file:

```
<INPUT LANGUAGE="VBScript" TYPE=submit VALUE="Calculate" NAME="btncalcclient">
```

Change the TYPE from Submit to Button, and add the Onclick event to reference a subroutine called validate, as shown below:

```
<INPUT LANGUAGE = "VBScript" TYPE = button VALUE = "Calculate" ONCLICK = "call
validate()"
 NAME = "btncalcclient">
```

Notice that if the button type is left as a Submit button with the Onclick event, as shown below, the form will be sent to the Web server for processing even if the validation subroutine fails.

```
<INPUT LANGUAGE="VBScript" TYPE=SUBMIT VALUE="Calculate" ONCLICK="Call
➥Validate()"
NAME="btncalcclient">
```

Building the Validation Subroutine

Now you are ready to build the validation subroutine. Because you are checking multiple text box values on the form, you might be inclined to develop a series of nested If...Then...Else loops. This brute-force method requires every if condition to perform a comparison operation to determine whether the condition is met. A more efficient way to complete this task is to implement the Select Case statement. The Select Case statement enables the condition statement to be evaluated only one time and picks the execution option that matches the results. Listing 8.3 demonstrates using the Select Case statement to find all conditions that return True. If an expression returns True, an error has been found and the return value of the Select Case statement is set to False. After exiting the Select Case statement, the ret value is examined to determine if all the values tested in the Select Case statement are valid. If so, the form is submitted to the Web server by calling the Submit event of the form.

Listing 8.3   Using the *Select Case* statement to perform client-side validation.

```
<SCRIPT LANGUAGE="VBScript">
<!--
Sub Validate()
 Select Case True              '=== Test all conditions that return True
   Case frminfo.txtweight.value <= 0
     Ret = False
     Msgbox "Weight must be greater than zero"
     Call frminfo.txtweight.focus()
   Case frminfo.txtarea.value <= 0
     Ret = False
     Msgbox "Frontal surface area must be greater than zero", 16
     Call frminfo.txtarea.focus
   Case frminfo.txtbegin.value < 0
     Ret = False
     Msgbox "Beginning time value must be greater than zero", 32
     Call frminfo.txtbegin.focus()
   Case frminfo.txtdensity.value <= 0
     Msgbox "Density must be greater than zero", 48
     Ret = False
     Call frminfo.txtdensity.focus()
   Case Else
     Ret = True
 End Select
 If Ret Then                    '=== Did validation pass?
    frminfo.submit               '=== If so, submit the form
 End if
End sub
-->
</SCRIPT>
```

Part

II

Ch

8

If the subroutine finds an invalid value, the user is prompted with the appropriate warning, as shown in Figure 8.11.

FIG. 8.11
Client-side scripting reduces server load and network traffic by executing within the browser environment.

You can expand the functionality of the Validate subroutine to be as complex as needed. For example, you can tap in to the built-in VBScript variable functions to test whether a field is empty or whether the value is a numeric value, as shown in Listing 8.4.

Listing 8.4   Using VBScript functions to perform client-side validation.

```
<%
Select Case True
    Case Not IsEmpty(frminfo.txtdensity.value)
        Ret = False
        Msgbox "Please enter a density value"
        Call frminfo.txtdensity.focus()
    Case Not IsNumeric(frminfo.txtweight.value), frminfo.txtweight.value<=0
        Ret = False
        Msgbox "Incorrect data for weight"
        Call frminfo.txtweight.focus()
    Case Else
        Ret = True
End Select
If Ret Then                          '=== Did validation pass?
    frminfo.submit                   '=== If so, submit the form
End if

End Select
%>
```

Testing for a VBScript-Compliant Browser

To prevent VBScript client-side coding from being delivered to a non-VBScript–compliant browser, Web server variables can be used to determine information about the requesting client. The Web server can extract information about the requesting client from variables passed to the server from the client's HTTP header request (see Listing 8.5).

Listing 8.5   Using HTTP header information to detect the browser type.

```
<%
If Instr(Request.ServerVariables("HTTP_USER_AGENT"),"MSIE") Then
        '=== This is an IE browser
        '=== Put client-side VBScript functions here
```

```
Else
            '=== This is not an IE browser. Is it a Netscape Browser?
    If Instr(Request.ServerVariables("HTTP_USER_AGENT"),"Mozilla") Then
            '=== Netscape Browser
            '=== Put JavaScript Functions here
        End If
End If
%>
```

This server-side VBScript uses the `InStr` function to search for a string within another string. The line of VBScript looks for the string `MS IE` within the `HTTP_USER_AGENT` server variable. If the string is found, the requesting browser is Internet Explorer. If the browser is not Internet Explorer, the same test can be applied to determine if the user has a Netscape browser.

Using this capability to determine the browser type, you can customize your script to deliver VBScript only to Internet Explorer browser. However, this might not always be the best approach to solving your client-side scripting needs and depends on the target user base of your application. If you are building applications specifically for Internet Explorer, a VBScript environment can help you leverage your in-house Visual Basic skills. If you are building applications for an HTML 3.0 environment, there is no need to build two different client-scripting versions because both Internet Explorer and Netscape Navigator support JavaScript. If you are building applications to run at a lower compliance level, such as in text-based browsers, validation on the server is your only option.

You can also use the Browser Capability Component to detect the specific browser type and the available features of the specific browser. The Browser Capability Component is one of the various installable components that ship with the Internet Information Server. The Browser Capability Component uses the `HTTP_USER_AGENT` server variable to look up the capabilities of the different browser types in an INI file. For a more detailed discussion of the Browser Capability Component, see Chapter 17, "Implementing Existing Server-Side Components."

From Here...

In this chapter, you discovered how to use VBScript to implement execution logic to run on the ActiveX Server and within the Internet Explorer browser. VBScript provides an excellent development tool that enables you to test variable datatypes and control program flow by using operators and conditional statements for both server-side and client-side processing. In addition, the need to offload processing power onto the browser client helps to reduce the processing requirement of the server and reduce network bandwidth.

For related information, please see the following chapters:

- Chapter 10, "The Composition of an Active Server Application," will illustrate how six built-in ASP objects collectively form an ASP application.

- Chapter 12, "Controlling the Server with the `Server` Object and Using Transaction Processing with the `ObjectContext` Object," demonstrates how the `Server` object controls and manages ASP applications.

- Chapter 18, "Creating Your Own Active Server Components," will teach how to create your own ActiveX components to meet the needs of your applications.

- Chapter 16, "Putting It All Together: Building an Online Catalog," demonstrates how to use the existing components, including the Browser Capability Component, that ship with IIS 4.0.

- Chapter 20, "Database Access with ADO," provides a firsthand approach on using VBScript to manipulate your databases.

Using the Script Debugger

The Microsoft Script Debugger 1.0 finally provides an in-line debugging tool that has been missing from the family of scripting programming tools. This logical extension is necessary to start transforming scripting languages into more mature development environments. The Script Debugger provides a debugging capability for VBScript and JScript, and can also be used to debug Java programs. This flexibility enables the Scripting Debugger to control, trap, and change variables in both server-side and client-side scripts. Server-side scripts embedded in Active Server Pages are trapped and processed on the Internet Information Server before the results are sent to the requesting browser. Client-side scripts are embedded within the HTML on the browser client. ∎

Using the Script Debugger

Learn how the Script Debugger can be activated to process server–side ASP scripts and client-side VBScript and JScript.

Trapping and Debugging Scripts

Discover how to set breakpoints to systematically step through the code to check and verify the script's variable values and properties.

Identifying Errors

The Script Debugger helps minimize the runtime errors, syntax errors, and logical errors that might plague your scripting applications.

Using the Script Debugger

The Script Debugger is installed on the client's machine to perform server- and client-side debugging capabilities with the Internet Explorer browser. The Script Debugger built into the Internet Explorer 4.0 can be started as a stand-alone application or can be activated in programmatic ways. Figure 9.1 displays a client machine debugging a server-side ASP script.

FIG. 9.1
The Script Debugger debugs client and server VBScript, JScript, and Java programs.

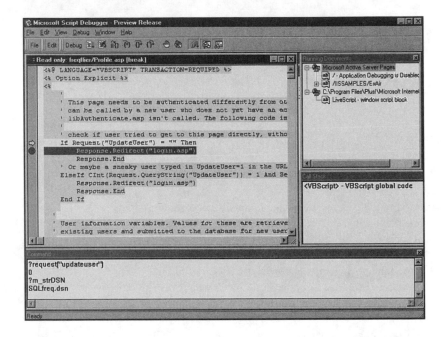

The focus of this book has been primarily on Active Server Pages running on the Internet Information Server, but the Script Debugger can also debug client-side scripts. To debug server-side scripts, the debugging property must be activated for the ASP application. The Internet Information Server 4.0 enables you to control the ASP application settings using the Microsoft Management Console, as shown in Figure 9.2.

To debug Java applications, the Microsoft Script Debugger can only be used with the Microsoft Java Virtual Machine (VM) version 2174 or later. The ActiveX-enabled Java VM is shipped with the Internet Explorer 4.0 and the Internet Information Server 2.0. To enable Java debugging in the Microsoft Script Debugger, select the option to enable Java debugging from the Options, View menu. Then select the root path for the Java source files in the Source Path location.

FIG. 9.2

Activate server-side ASP script debugging from the Microsoft Management Console.

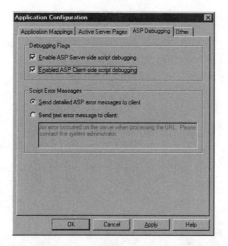

To activate script debugging capabilities for server-side scripts, right-click the ASP application within the Microsoft Management Console and select Property. Then click the Configuration button in the Application Settings section of the Virtual Directory tab. If only the Create button is available from the Application Settings section, create an ASP application by clicking the Create button. Clicking the Configuration button exposes the various properties of the ASP application, such as ASP application caching and programmatic settings. For more information on using the MMC to configure your ASP applications, please see Chapter 31, "Using Internet Information Server 4.0 to Manage Your Web Applications."

After Script Debugger permissions have been set on the Server, the Script Debugger can be activated manually or automatically when server-side errors occur. The Script Debugger processes the error via a dialog box, as shown in Figure 9.3.

The Script Debugger can also be activated programmatically from within HTML. To activate the Script Debugger from VBScript, use the Stop keyword; if you are using JScript, use the keyword Debugger. When the Internet Information Server processes the Stop or Debugger request, the Script Debugger is started and program control is returned to the current line (see Figure 9.4).

The Script Debugger can also be automatically activated when viewing the client source code on the Internet Explorer browser. After the Script Debugger has been installed, select Source from the View menu within the Internet Explorer browser.

FIG. 9.3
The Script Debugger automatically detects ASP scripting errors and directs you to the scripting error.

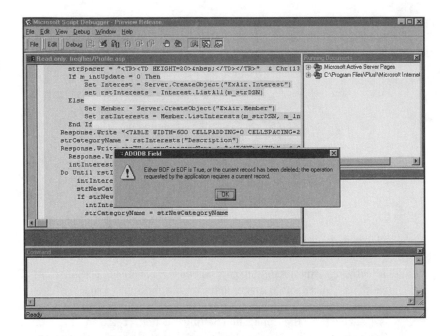

FIG. 9.4
The Script Debugger can be programmatically activated from within the script.

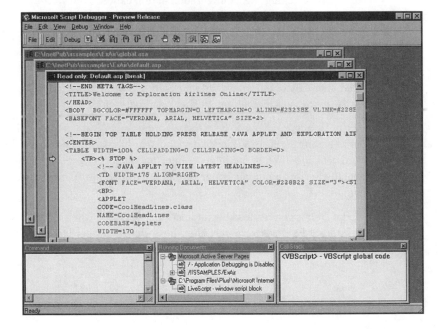

Managing the Script Components

The Script Debugger consists of four windows, as shown in Figure 9.5. This group of windows enables you to manage and view the script source code, control the script workflow, and determine and set variable and property values for your client and server scripting needs. The four windows that make up the scripting wizard are the Script window, the Command window, the Running Documents window, and the Call Stack window (see Table 9.1).

FIG. 9.5

The Script Debugger mimics the functionality and look and feel of Visual Basic to provide script debugging.

Script window—

Running Documents window—

Call Stack window—

Command window—

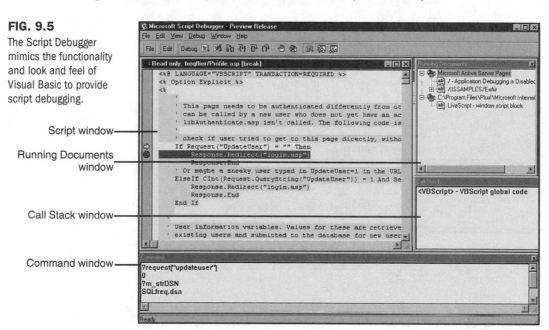

Part

II

Ch

9

Table 9.1   The Script Debugger Windows

Window Name	Purpose
Script window	Displays the script source code.
Command window	Sets and retrieves variable and property values.
Running Documents window	Manages the files that can be debugged.
Call Stack window	Traces the procedures and functions within the script.

The Script window is primarily responsible for displaying the source code. The Script window uses syntax coloration, images, and highlighting to indicate scripting syntax, breakpoints, and the current line the script is processing. The Command window is used to set and retrieve object values within the executing script page. The Running Documents window manages multiple script windows in a hierarchical tree-view format. The Call Stack window is used to manage and track procedure calls between subroutines and procedures within a page.

Keep in mind that the scripts displayed in the Script Debugger are activated on a read-only basis. In order to manipulate the script code, a new script document must be created from within the Script Debugger and saved to the appropriate location. Once the new document is created, you can copy the script code into the new document and have complete control to manipulate that document as needed within the Script Debugger.

N O T E The source code in the Script window is read only. In order to have full read-write permissions to a file, create a new script code from within the scripting wizard and copy the script code into the new file for testing, editing, and debugging purposes. ▪

The Script Debugger has a toolbar that provides shortcuts to a variety of debugging features. Table 9.2 illustrates the toolbar icons with a brief description.

Table 9.2 The Scripting Debugger Debug Toolbar

Icon	Description
	Starts or continues execution of the current script.
	Stops debugging the current script.
	Breaks into Debugger at the next statement.
	Step into next statement.
	Step over next statement.
	Step out of current execution function.
	Insert or remove breakpoint at the current line.
	Clear all breakpoints.
	Display the Running Documents window.
	Display the Command Input/Output window.
	Display the current Calling Stack window.

Of all the different ways to start the Script Debugger, the easiest method is to use the Running Documents window. The Running Documents window contains a list of pages that have been loaded into the browser for ASP applications that have server-side scripting capabilities turned on. You can use this listing to open documents in the Script window to start debugging by double-clicking the page. After the page is loaded, you can set breakpoints within your script to help control where the Debugger will stop processing the script. To start debugging, simply reload or refresh the page in the browser. Alternately, you can also directly start debugging a page by right-clicking the document in the Running Document window and selecting the Break At Next Statement option, as shown in Figure 9.6.

FIG. 9.6
Use the Running Documents window to start the debugging process.

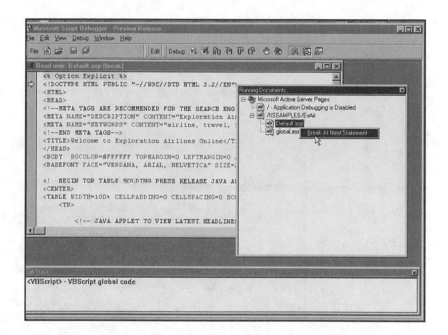

Although selecting this action does not immediately bring up the script code in the Script window, when the page is refreshed in the browser, the code debugger "breaks" in to the normal execution and starts stepping through the first line of script in the Script Debugger environment. This debugging technique is what is displayed in Figure 9.6.

Controlling Script Flow

The majority of script debugging effort involves setting breakpoints in the code to temporarily pause the script processing. This temporary suspension of processing enables you to check and verify the values of properties or variables at that point in the script. Controlling the application flow and monitoring application objects is accomplished through the use of breakpoints, stepping mechanisms, and the Call Stack window.

Breakpoints and code stepping mechanisms provide the foundation of the Script Debugger. *Breakpoints* are used to set locations within scripts where the execution of the script is temporarily stopped and program control is transferred to the Script Debugger. After the Script Debugger has control of the script, different step mechanisms and program windows are used to incrementally process the remaining script and to set and retrieve values. To set a breakpoint, place your cursor on the line of code where you want the breakpoint to occur and click the SetBreakpoint icon (refer to Table 9.2). The breakpoint is symbolized by the red highlighting of the script line of code and the stop-sign shaped icon to the left of the Script window, as shown in Figure 9.7.

FIG. 9.7
Use breakpoints to transfer program execution from the processing client to the Script Debugger.

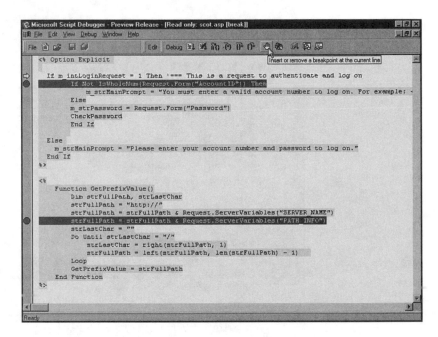

The yellow arrow, shown at the left side of the screen in Figure 9.7, indicates the line the Script Debugger is waiting to execute.

Notice that breakpoints can only be set on lines of code where code execution occurs. For example, a breakpoint cannot be set on the first line of code in Figure 9.7, the <% Option Explicit %>, or on lines where variables are declared using the Dim keyword. Furthermore, breakpoints only apply to the first statement in a line of code. For example, in VBScript, multiple statements can be embedded on one line of code using the colon (:) as a separator (see Figure 9.8).

In Figure 9.8, a breakpoint is placed on a code line that contains multiple statements separated by colons (:). If the single step method is chosen, only the first statement on that line is executed, as you can see by viewing the values of the variables in the Command window in the bottom of Figure 9.8. The value of variable vWarningStr is assigned User Profile, but the remaining variable assignments for the variables vServerLoc and vProfile are unassigned.

FIG. 9.8
Breakpoints only apply to the first statement in a line of code.

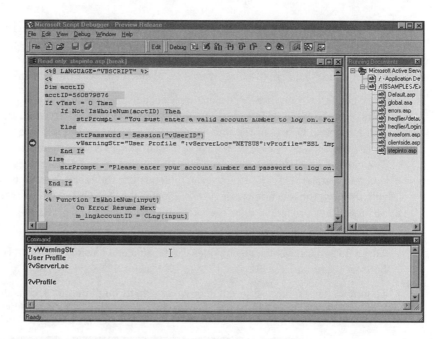

After program control is transferred to the Script Debugger, the Command window can be used to set and retrieve information from within the script. (The Command window is similar to the Debug window found in Visual Basic.) For example, Figure 9.1 is using the Command window to determine the value of the `Request(UpdateUser)` object using VBScript syntax. Notice that you are not limited to extracting only ASP components, you can access any object or variable on that page. The Command window will accept any script command supported by the scripting language that is interpreting the current page. To determine any property on a page using VBScript, use a question mark (?) followed by the object, or use the `Debug.Write` method followed by the object name. For example, to determine the document title, use the following syntax:

```
? Document.Title
```

Alternatively, you can use the `Write` method to display a procedure level variable named `iCounter`:

```
Debug.Write iCounter
```

If you want to determine a variable or property value using JScript, simply type in the variable name in the Command window.

You can also assign variables from within the Command window using the same naming rules that apply for your scripting language. For example, to assign the variable `iCounter` the value of 3 in VBScript, the following line of code would be entered into the Command window:

```
Icounter = 3
```

When the Script Debugger reaches a breakpoint, all data transfer to the requesting client is stopped and is explicitly controlled by the Script Debugger. This means that if a breakpoint is located in the middle of a Web page, HTML is delivered to the browser up until the breakpoint is processed. The Script Debugger now regulates the flow of the remaining data.

The Script Debugger has three stepping mechanisms to control how to execute selected portions of the script: Step Into Next Statement, Step Over Next Statement, and Step Out of Current Execution Function. The Step Into Next Statement is used to process the next line of script. The Step Over Next Statement is used to skip over calls to functions and subroutines. The current procedure is still executed, but the current line pointer does not enter the called procedure statement. This enables you to determine the result of a function without having to step through the function's code details. Finally, the Step Out statement enables the remaining script within a procedure to be executed and debugging control returned to the line preceding the calling procedure.

These different navigation techniques can be applied by using the Script Debugger toolbar buttons shown in Table 9.2.

To fully understand the different debugging step-through methods, consider the ASP debugging session shown in Figure 9.9.

FIG. 9.9

The Script Debugger offers different methods to step through the scripting code.

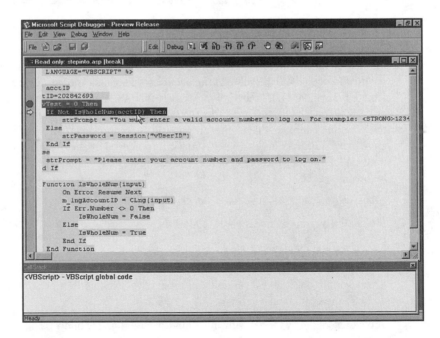

If the Step Into Next Statement method is used, the Script Debugger would start to evaluate the IsWholeNum function. As the Script Debugger starts to evaluate the function, the program control is evaluating the first line of the IsWholeNum function, as shown in Figure 9.10. Notice that the Call Stack window identifies that the IsWholeNum procedure is being called.

FIG. 9.10

The Step Into Next statement method sequentially processes script one line at a time.

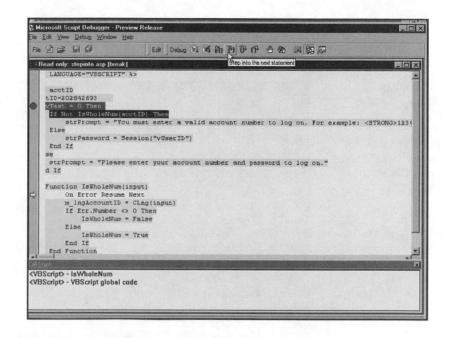

Consequently, if the Step Out method is selected from the toolbar, the Script Debugger would process the remaining script within the function and return control to the *next* line following the calling parent function, as shown in Figure 9.11.

FIG. 9.11

The Step Out method finishes processing the function and returns control to the statement after the parent calling function.

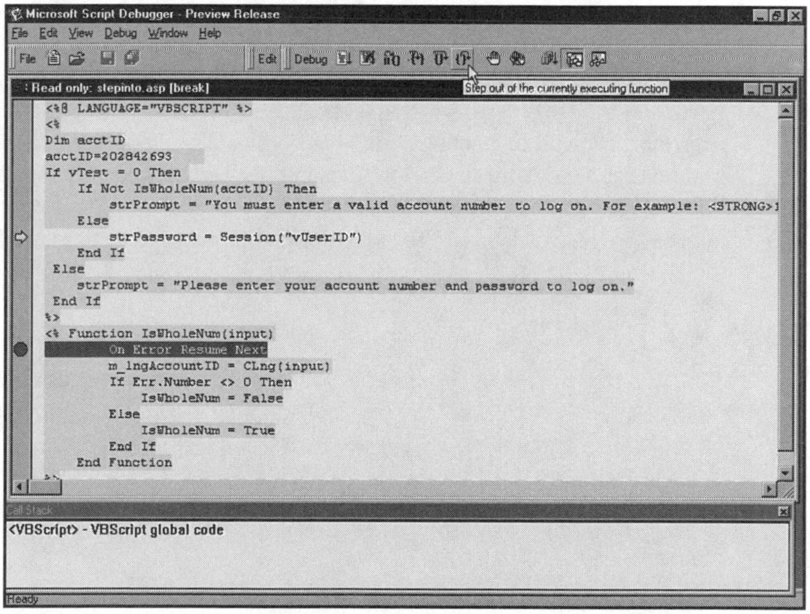

If the Step Over Next Statement stepping method is initially selected from the starting point displayed in Figure 9.10, the function is calculated and the Script Debugger returns programmatic control to the appropriate If...Then condition, as shown in Figure 9.12.

FIG. 9.12

The Step Over Next statement enables you to see the results of a function or subroutine without having to step through the procedure itself.

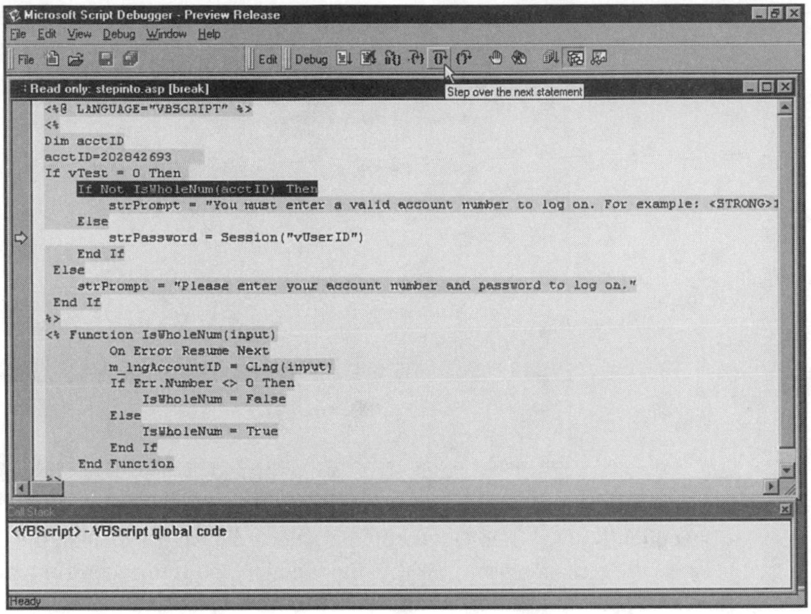

The Call Stack window is used to track the script procedures and events that have been loaded. The Call Stack contents are arranged historically with the most recent scripts located at the top of the list (refer to Figure 9.11). This window is particularly useful when you need to trace a series of nested procedures within an application. It enables you to quickly navigate from procedure to procedure without having to incrementally follow every line of executing code. Keep in mind that the Call Stack window does not display the values of variables within the procedure, just the name of the currently executing procedure. If you want to retrieve and set variable and property values for the current procedure, use the Command window.

Types of Errors

Unfortunately, the Script Debugger is still incapable of helping application developers create bug free code. Regardless of the result of scripting errors, the Script Debugger helps minimize the debugging runtime errors, syntax errors, and logical errors.

Runtime Errors

Runtime errors are a result of trying to process a line of code that is impossible to complete or are the result of using incorrect script syntax. In most situations, runtime errors are inadvertently overlooked as a result of not considering all the possible situations for a conditional statement. For example, consider the following statement:

```
Fuel_Economy = (Miles_Traveled) / (Gallons_Used)
```

In most situations, this calculation would successfully return the calculated fuel economy of a vehicle. However, what happens if the variable `Gallons_Used` is zero? The resulting division by zero is an invalid operation and would generate a runtime error (see Figure 9.13).

FIG. 9.13
Runtime errors are the result of trying to execute code that is impossible to process.

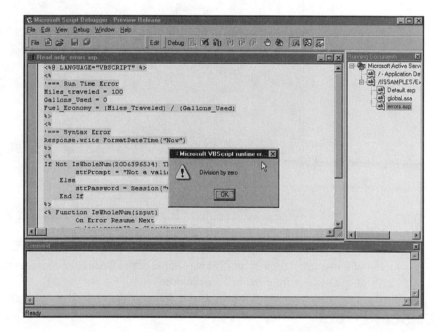

To prevent most runtime errors from occurring, familiarize yourself with the situations where these errors might occur. Then you can trap or construct code to prevent these runtime errors from occurring. For instance, in the previous example to determine fuel economy, first ensure that the variable `Gallons_used` is a non-zero, real number before you try the division operation.

Syntax Errors

Syntax errors are a direct result of the improper use of the language's object model. Each language has a specific set of explicit instructions that are needed for the compiler to process the embedded application logic. If the script syntax is incorrect, the compiler does not know how to process the request and will generate a runtime error. For example, consider the following faulty statement:

```
Response.Write FormatDateTime("Now")
```

When the script engine processes this request, the FormatDateTime function is expecting a date/time variable subtype. However, in this situation, the application developer inadvertently put quotes around the Now keyword. As a result of trying to process a string datatype, the FormatDateTime function will generate an error, as shown in Figure 9.14.

FIG. 9.14
Syntax errors are generated when the compiler attempts to compile improper code statements.

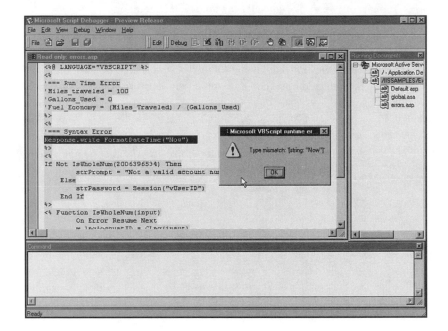

The Script Debugger currently does not scan your scripts for incorrect script syntax to warn you of potential runtime errors. However, the Script Debugger does identify the specific line of script code where the runtime error occurs.

Logical Errors

Logical errors are often the most frustrating errors to trap. Logical errors are the direct result of code not executing as the application developer *intended*. The dilemma of developing code is that the compiler does exactly what the code tells it to do, nothing more, nothing less. If there is a gap between how the application is *intended* to behave and how it *actually* behaves, logical errors will result. There are no bullet-proof methods to prevent logical errors from occurring; only testing, analysis, and experience can prevent faulty application logic.

From Here...

This chapter showed that the Script Debugger is a valuable resource in testing and debugging your server- and client-side scripts. Thin-client development tools are slowly maturing into the ranks the other traditional client-server integrated development environments have enjoyed for years. The Script Debugger provides inline debugging capabilities for VBScript, JScript and Java. The Script Debugger mimics the debugging functionality found in Visual Basic, which enables:

- Color syntax highlighting to identify code modules via the Script windows.
- Setting and removing multiple breakpoints within a page.
- Step Into, Step Over, and Step Out of navigation methods.
- Direct retrieval and setting of variable and property values via the Command window.
- Easy page and procedural navigation with the Running Document and Call Stack windows.
- Chapter 10, "The Composition of an Active Server Application," will illustrate the various components of an ASP application.
- Chapter 13, "Managing the User Session: The Session Object," illustrates the nuances of tracking a user through an ASP application.
- Chapter 15, "Retrieving User Information: The Request Object," demonstrates how to collect information from the user using forms, hidden fields, and cookies.
- Chapter 16, "Putting It All Together: Building an Online Catalog," demonstrates how to use the existing components, including the Browser Capabilities Component, that ship with IIS 4.0.
- Chapters 17 and 18, "Implementing Existing Server-Side Components," and "Creating Your Own Active Server Components," will teach you how to use server-side VBScript to provide connection to pre-built and customizable servers.
- Chapter 20, "Database Access with ADO," provides a firsthand approach to using VBScript to manipulate your databases.

Part

II

Ch

9

Active Server Objects: The Essential Building Blocks

10

The Composition of an Active Server Application

This chapter provides an overview of how the various systems that form the present-day Web enterprise are identified and encapsulated into separate, manageable Active Server objects. These various objects each have their specific functionality but collectively interact to form the foundation of Active Server Pages. ■

The Active Server Page Application Blueprint

Discover the text-based files, directories, and virtual directories and scripting languages that interact to form Active Server Page applications.

The Application Manager: The *GLOBAL.ASA* file

Learn about the importance of the *GLOBAL.ASA* file and how it manages the *Application* and *Session* objects and in what situations is it activated.

Understanding ASP Scoping issues

Discover how the ASP objects use four different scoping and lifetime issues and in what situations should they be applied.

The Fundamental ASP Server Objects

Introduce yourself to the six ASP objects that drive the functionality of delivering ASP applications.

Debugging Active Server Pages

Although no built-in debugger exists for ASP, learn how to use the *Err* object, the Registry settings, and the *FileSystem* object to assist in the debugging process.

The Components of an Active Server Page Application

An Active Server Page application is comprised of various items that together form the ASP application. The collection consists of various text-based files, Server objects and components, and ActiveX Server scripting, as shown in Figure 10.1.

FIG. 10.1
The eclectic collection that forms Active Server applications.

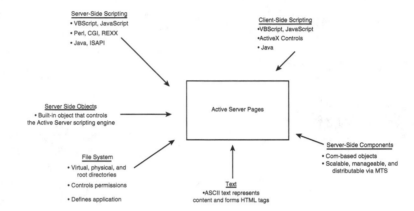

Text Files

Active Server Page applications are really a collection of text files that are interpreted by the Internet Information Server. These ASP scripts are composed of HTML tags, Active Scripting code (using languages such as JScript and VBScript), and standard text, as shown in Listing 10.1.

Listing 10.1   An ASP file uses HTML tags, ASP scripts, and standard text.

```
<HTML>                                      '=== Traditional HTML Tags
<HEAD>                                       '=== Standard HTML
<TITLE>
Welcome                                      '=== Standard Text
</TITLE>
</HEAD>
<BODY>
<%                                           '=== Active Server Script
Sub WriteWelcomeMessage ()
      Dim myGreeting
      If Time >=#12:00:00 AM# And Time < #12:00:00 PM# Then
            myGreeting = "Good Morning!"
      Else
            myGreeting = "Hello!"
      End If
      Response.Write mygreeting
End Sub
%>
```

```
<% Call WriteWelcomeMessage %>              '=== Executing the Active Server
subroutine
</BODY>
</HTML>
```

Traditional HTML files consist of only HTML tags for page layout and standard text to display text. The HTML tags are used to create and display the content in the Web page. The difference between the HTML and ASP files is that ASP files simply expand the role of HTML tags by adding scripting processing tags to control the HTML tags.

Keep in mind that pages with just HTML are a subset of ASP pages. This means that any traditional HTML-compliant Web page is already an Active Server Page, with one exception: the file extension. To convert your existing HTML pages to Active Server Pages, simply rename the HTM or HTML file with an ASP file extension. The Internet Information Server will see the file extension and automatically interpret the ASP file.

N O T E The ActiveX scripting engine will process all pages with an .ASP file extension. Therefore, to maximize server performance, only convert HTM or HTML files to ASP files when scripting functionality is needed for the page. Otherwise, unnecessary resources will be consumed when processing the ASP file for namesake only. ■

Furthermore, the ASP and the IIS Web server do not have support issues with HTML versions you want to process and deliver to your sites and applications. Because the server doesn't view the actual HTML embedded in the ASP files, the delivered HTML version is limited only by the HTML/browser level of your targeted user base. You can create your Active Server scripts to sense what type of browser is visiting your site and send the appropriate HTML version according to requesting browser's capabilities. Chapters 12, "Controlling the Server with the `Server` Object and Using Transaction Processing with the `ObjectContext` Object," and 17, "Implementing Existing Server-Side Components," illustrate how to use the HTTP server variable and the Browser Capabilities Component to determine the type of browser visiting your site.

Physical, Root, and Virtual Directories

Your ASP application is simply a collection of text files located in a directory or its subdirectories residing on the Web server. The base directory for your ASP application is referred to as a *virtual root*. The virtual root is what is referenced by the Web server as the container that holds all the files needed for the ASP application. Virtual directories are also used by the IIS Web server as file containers. Virtual directories help prevent you from having to know the exact file paths of files and to prevent users from obtaining more information about the Web server's underlying sub-systems.

An example of a virtual root is VBScript in the URL **www.microsoft.com/VBScript**. The VBScript virtual directory is use by the Internet Information Server to map this virtual path to a physical directory location. The virtual directory settings are managed by the Internet Service Manager. The Internet Service Manager manages the physical drive mappings with virtual roots, permissions, and logging. Figure 10.2 illustrates the role of physical and virtual directory structures.

FIG. 10.2
Internet Service
Manager regulates the
relationship between
virtual and physical
directory settings.

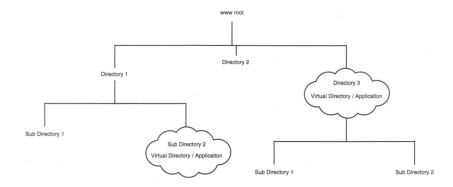

ASP Scripting Languages and HTML

The heart of Active Server Pages programming is the processing of server-side scripts. Server-side scripting provides the capability to manipulate variables and application flow through procedure-based coding, connect to a variety of external sources to retrieve information, and control output to the Web browser. Part II of this book covered the foundations of VBScript, the default scripting language of the Internet Information Server. However, you can also use JScript, REXX, PERL, or any other script-compliant language that can be processed by the server. The scripting language, now processed by both the Web server and Web client, acts as an interpreter to execute the text-based Internet protocol. To set the scripting language for an Active Server Page, use the LANGUAGE directive:

```
<%@ LANGUAGE = ScriptingLanguage RUNAT = Location %>
```

where ScriptingLanguage is the primary scripting language for that page and Location is the location of script interpretation.

An ASP directive tells the IIS Web server how to interpret the individual ASP file. The LANGUAGE directive is used to set the proper interpreter for your *primary* scripting language for the page. It is important to note that ASP pages can use a variety of scripting languages throughout your ASP application that are different from the primary scripting language. Active Server applications can be comprised of pages written for several scripting languages. To use VBScript as the primary scripting language for a given ASP page, use the LANGUAGE directive in the first line of the Active Server Page.

```
<%@ LANGUAGE = "VBScript" RUNAT = "Server"%>
```

CAUTION
If no space is placed between the directive symbol (@) and the LANGUAGE attribute, the server will generate a 'Missing Language attribute' error.

The LANGUAGE directive is just one of the directives available when using ASP. The various ASP directives will be covered in greater depth later in this chapter.

Remember, the primary scripting language determines the language that will be used to process the Active Server script contained within the <% %> delimiters on your pages. If you want to change the default scripting language for your Web server, you have to change the DefualtScriptLanguage key within the Registry in IIS 3.0 or use the Microsoft Management Console in II 4.0, as shown in Figure 10.3. For more information on using the MMC to configure the IIS 4.0 and Active Server settings, please see Chapter 31, "Using Internet Information Server 4.0 to Manage Your Web Applications."

FIG. 10.3
The Microsoft Management Console regulates the HTTP and ASP settings for IIS 4.0.

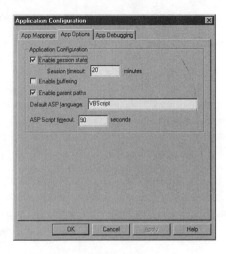

By default, VBScript is the default scripting language when you install IIS. Therefore, explicitly setting the primary scripting language on each page in your application prevents errors that might otherwise occur if the host Web server has a different default scripting language defined. In other words, don't assume that every Internet Information Server uses VBScript as its default scripting language.

The <% %> tags enable the Internet Information Server to differentiate between HTML and Active Script functions located between the Active Server delimiters. The Active Server delimiters can be placed either inline or within delimited code blocks. The following example demonstrates combining HTML and inline Active Server script to write the name of the user to the page and the estimated shipping date.

```
<Center>Thank you, <% Response.Write Session("UserName") %>, for your
order.</Center><Br>
<Center>Your order should arrive by <% Response.Write FormatDateTime(Now + 7,
vbShortDate) %></Center>
```

The first line of the previous code example tells the Internet Information Server to write a value to a page by using the <% %> tags. In this example, the username has been stored in a session variable named "UserName". Therefore, the expression <% Response.Write Session("UserName") %> will write the username onto the Web page. The second line of code uses VBScript functions, covered in Part II, "VBScript: The Foundation of Active Server Pages," to add a week to the current date. After the estimated shipping date is determined, the Response object is used to write the shipping date onto the Web page.

Listing 10.2 demonstrates a code block that is used to contain a subroutine called `GenerateMsg`.

> **Listing 10.2   Using delimiters to execute blocks of code.**
>
> ```
> <%@ LANGUAGE="VBSCRIPT"%>
>
> <%
> '============== Begin Subroutine Modules ==============
> Sub GenerateMsg()
> Response.Write "You have mail!"              '=== Writes message to page
> End Sub
> '================ End Subroutine Modules ==============
> %>
>
> <HTML>
> <BODY>
> <%
> Call GenerateMsg()      '=== Call the subroutine GenerateMsg
> %>
> </BODY>
> </HTML>
> ```

Remember, the `<% %>` tags are used to indicate Active Server scripts. The Active Server script can use any script-compliant language (such as VBScript, JScript, PERL, or REXX) within these tags to manipulate variables, process logic, and make database connections.

The Active Server Page Project File: *GLOBAL.ASA*

As you start building ASP applications, the `GLOBAL.ASA` file will play a central role in managing them. The .ASA file extension is an acronym for Active Server Applications. The `GLOBAL.ASA` file enables the management of two critical objects used to track state information in an ASP application. The advent of Active Server Pages gives developers the ability to track user information from page to page within a Web-based application. Remember, the Hypertext Transfer Protocol (HTTP) is a connectionless or stateless protocol. Users connect to a Web server, request a page, receive a page, and then disconnect. In the past, there was no way to track a user's activity as he jumped from page to page. ASP helps to bring state and session tracking to the Web for cookie-compliant browsers and networks. For more information about tracking state, see Chapter 13, "Managing the User Session: The `Session` Object."

This tracking capability is essential to implement any Web-based workflow application. When an application is first started, the `GLOBAL.ASA` file is loaded into memory. This file is used to track application events and individual user events, variables, and objects. The `GLOBAL.ASA` file is an optional file located in the root directory of any ASP application. An example of a `GLOBAL.ASA` file is shown in the following code.

```
<SCRIPT LANGUAGE="VBScript" RUNAT="Server">
'====================== Session and Application Procedures =====================
Sub Session_OnStart               '=== Session Level events and object placed here
End Sub

Sub Session_OnEnd                 '=== Close session event code is placed here
End Sub

Sub Application_OnStart           '=== Application level variables used here
End Sub

Sub Application_OnEnd             '=== Close any application objects here
End Sub
'==============================================================================

'====================== Session and Application Events =========================
Session_OnStart                   '=== Runs the first time a user runs any page in
your application
Session_OnEnd                     '=== Runs when a user's session times out or
quits your application
Application_OnStart               '=== Runs once when the first page of your
application is run
                                  '=== for the first time by any user
Application_OnEnd                 '=== Runs once when the Web server shuts down
'==============================================================================
</SCRIPT>
```

 TIP In previous versions of Active Server Pages, the GLOBAL.ASA file was named GLOBAL.ASP.

The GLOBAL.ASA file tracks the OnStart and OnEnd events of the Application and Session objects, as demonstrated in Figure 10.4. The Application_OnStart and Application_OnEnd are used to monitor all Application objects that are available to all users within the ASP application. For more information on the Application object, please see Chapter 11, "Controlling the Application: The Application Object."

The Session_OnStart and Session_OnEnd events are used to manage the Session objects. The Session objects are used to track individual user information. However, unlike the Application object, the Session object cannot share information between other user sessions; it can only be used to pass information from page to page. It is also important to point out that you cannot declare a variable outside a <SCRIPT> tag within the GLOBAL.ASA file. Trying to use any text outside the <SCRIPT> tag, with the exception of the <OBJECT> tag, will generate a runtime error. The specific details of the Session object will be fully discussed in Chapter 13.

Part
III

Ch
10

FIG. 10.4
The GLOBAL.ASA
file manages
Application and
Session objects.

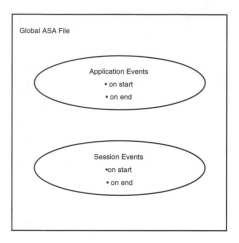

Global ASA File

Application Events
• on start
• on end

Session Events
•on start
• on end

Tracking Application Events

In most traditional application environments, a user must take some action to launch an application. Usually a command is issued from the keyboard or a command button is pressed in a graphical environment. As application development swings back to the server-centric deployment model, the start of an application is not necessarily connected to a specific user action. For example, assume a proposal letter generation system is installed on a user's desktop. When the user needs to generate a new proposal letter, the application is started, the user uses the application, and when finished, the user shuts down the application and exits the system. In a server-centric world, such as database servers or Web server environments, these application services may already be running when the user decides to access them. The user can use the application and, when he is finished, leave the application, yet the application process is not terminated on the server. This separation between application services and user services is the underlying function of the GLOBAL.ASA file.

The GLOBAL.ASA file is an optional file that is used to manage the Application object. The Application object has two events: the Application_OnStart event and the Application_OnEnd event. The Application_OnStart event is triggered the first time any page in application is called. The Application_OnEnd event occurs when an application is closed down. The Application shutdown event occurs when the Internet Information Server needs to recompile and reload the GLOBAL.ASA file back into memory. The Application object also lets you lock and unlock Application object properties to ensure that values don't inadvertently get changed. The Application object will be discussed in much greater detail in Chapter 11.

The GLOBAL.ASA file is an optional file that does not have to be used when creating ASP applications. If the file exists, the Application and Session events can be processed accordingly. If the GLOBAL.ASA file does not exist, the corresponding events are not processed and the Application and Session events cannot be trapped.

Tracking Session Events

The Session object is used to track and manage individual user sessions in an application. The Session object has two events: the Session_OnStart event and the Session_OnEnd event. Session_OnStart is triggered when a new user enters the application. When the Session_OnStart event is triggered, a unique ID is assigned to the user and is used to monitor the user within the ASP application. However, the Session_OnEnd event is not so well defined. The Session_OnEnd event usually occurs when a timeout value has expired on the Web server or the session is explicitly ended in code.

Tracking and monitoring an individual user session is one of the biggest challenges in building ASP applications because the Web uses the Hypertext Transfer Protocol (HTTP). The HTTP protocol is described as *stateless* because it is used to initiate a request from an HTTP client and deliver the response from the server. After the request has been fulfilled, the connection between the client and server is eliminated. Although this model may be ideally suited for simple request processing systems, the lack of client/server concurrency plagues application development via HTTP.

Unlike the application events, objects and variables that are activated in the session event are localized only to that user session and cannot be referenced by another user session. But the user session information can be passed from page to page within the application. If variables need to be shared across individual sessions, the application-level object would have to be used.

Activating the *GLOBAL.ASA* File

The GLOBAL.ASA file is primarily accessed based on session-level events, and is called in three situations:

- When the Application OnStart or OnEnd event is triggered.
- When a Session_OnStart or Session_OnEnd event is triggered.
- When a reference is made to an object that has to be instantiated in the GLOBAL.ASA file.

If the GLOBAL.ASA file is used, it is implicitly called in one of three ways. First, assuming that the ASP application is not currently running, a request is made from a Web browser to the Internet Information Server for an ASP page. The Internet Information Server in turn looks for the requested ASP page in a virtual directory. The Web server associates the virtual directory representing an ASP application, and searches for an existing Application object created from the requested ASP application. If no Application objects exist, the Web server tries to locate the GLOBAL.ASA file in the application's root directory. If the GLOBAL.ASA file is found, the Application_OnStart and Session_OnStart events are sequentially triggered to create an Application and Session object. After the Session object is created, the user is assigned unique session identification.

The second situation in which the GLOBAL.ASA file is used is when a new user accesses an already running application and the user does not have an application session identifier.

As mentioned above, when a user makes a call to an ASP application, a unique session ID is generated to identify and track the user. If no session identification is defined for the current application, the GLOBAL.ASA file is used to generate the unique ID on the Session_OnStart event.

The third situation in which the GLOBAL.ASA file is activated is when a calling Active Server Page references an object declared in the GLOBAL.ASA file. You can create an application- or session-level object by using the <OBJECT> tag in the GLOBAL.ASA file, as shown below. It is important to point out that the <OBJECT> tags must be placed outside the <SCRIPT> tags to prevent errors from occurring.

```
<SCRIPT LANGUAGE="VBScript" RUNAT="Server">

'===================== Session and Application Procedures =====================
Sub Session_OnStart          '=== Session Level events and object placed here
End Sub

Sub Application_OnStart      '=== Application Level events and object placed here
End Sub
'=============================================================================

Session_OnStart
'=== Session_OnEnd
'=== Application_OnStart
'=== Application_OnEnd
'=============================================================================

</SCRIPT>

<OBJECT RUNAT=Server SCOPE=Application ID=MyDBConnection
PROGID="ADODB.Connection">
</OBJECT>
```

In the preceding example, even though the global or application-level database connection is declared in the GLOBAL.ASA file, the object itself is not created until it is referenced. This late binding feature helps to conserve resources by creating the objects only when they are needed. For example, the ActiveX Data Object (ADO) declared in the GLOBAL.ASA file in the previous example can be referenced by calling any of its methods from any ASP within the application.

```
<% Response.Write MyDBConnection.Open("myDSNConnection") %>
```

The details of using the ADO and other objects that ship with the Internet Information Server will be covered in greater depth in Part IV, "Active Server Components."

N O T E To prevent runtime errors, the <OBJECT> tag used to declare application-level objects must be outside the <SCRIPT> tags in the GLOBAL.ASA file. ▪

Upon finding the GLOBAL.ASA file and determining that the Application object does not exist for that project, the Application_OnStart event is executed. After the Application_OnStart event is complete, the Session_OnStart event is triggered because this is a new user to the application.

Therefore, the order of execution in which an ASP application performs is as follows:

1. GLOBAL.ASA
2. Application_OnStart
3. Session_OnStart
4. Session_OnEnd
5. Application_OnEnd

One of the most common misconceptions about the GLOBAL.ASA file is that it can be used as a library for commonly used functions and subroutine procedures. The GLOBAL.ASA file can only be used to create references to objects and trap the start and ending events of the Application and Session objects. The best way to share code modules across Active Server Pages is to use *Server Side Includes* (SSI). SSI provides a convenient means to extract data (functions, subroutines, and so on) from a source file and place it into an Active Server Page.

Part III

Ch 10

One of the drawbacks of the stateless request process using HTTP is that once the GLOBAL.ASA file is loaded into memory for a user session, any consequential change to the GLOBAL.ASA file is not implemented until the user starts a new user session. If you decide to make changes to the GLOBAL.ASA file, IIS will start the process to reset the application. First, the HTTP service stops accepting any new requests for pages and continues to process any requests that are waiting in the queue. After the HTTP service is finished with the requests, the Internet Information Server closes all sessions by executing the Session_OnEnd event. After the Session_OnEnd event is finished, IIS closes the application by executing the Application_OnEnd event. At this point, the GLOBAL.ASA file is recompiled and reloaded into memory. However, during that time, any additional HTTP requests made to the Web server will generate an error message stating "The request cannot be processed while the application is being restarted." or "Create object failed". After the recompiled GLOBAL.ASA file is reloaded, new users will be able to access the changed file.

Understanding Scoping Issues in Active Server Applications

As you discovered in Part II of this book, variables in VBScript have a defined lifetime or scope. Often these scoping issues are related to how you declare the variable or at what level you declare the variable. A similar situation exists when using variables in ASP applications.

GLOBAL.ASA Scoping Level

If it is used, the GLOBAL.ASA file represents the highest level available to set application- and session-level variables. A variable's scope depends on where the variable is declared. However, just because you don't declare a variable within the application and session OnStart events does not mean you can't create application- and session-level variables later in your ASP application.

> **N O T E** Any text not included within the <SCRIPT> tags in the GLOBAL.ASA file will produce a syntax error. ■

The GLOBAL.ASA file can use multiple <SCRIPT> tags and multiple supported scripting languages. However, all text in the GLOBAL.ASA file must be contained within the <SCRIPT> tags. The following two code examples demonstrate using VBScript and JScript in the GLOBAL.ASA file.

```
<SCRIPT LANGUAGE = "VBScript" RUNAT = "Server">
Sub Session_OnStart
     '== Data Connection Variable
     Session("ConnectionString") = "DSN=CWI"
     Session("ConnectionTimeout") = 15
     Session("CommandTimeout") = 30
     Session("RuntimeUserName") = ""
     Session("RuntimePassword") = ""
End Sub
</SCRIPT>
```

This can also be illustrated using JScript within the GLOBAL.ASA file:

```
<SCRIPT LANGUAGE = "JScript" RUNAT = "Server">
Function Session_OnStart() {
     //== Data Connection Variables
     Session("ConnectionString") = " DSN = CWI"
     Session("ConnectionTimeout") = 15
     Session("CommandTimeout") = 30
     Session("RuntimeUserName") = ""
     Session("RuntimePassword") = ""
}
</SCRIPT>
```

These examples are both triggered when a new Session object has been created. When the Session_OnStart event is processed, as shown in the preceding ASP scripts, session variables are set to help open database connections as the user walks through the application.

Application-Level Scope

In Active Server Pages, a global variable is now referred to as an application-level variable. Application-level variables are global in the sense that they are accessible across multiple user sessions. To declare an application-level variable that can be shared across the entire application with multiple users, you use the Application_OnStart event.

Application-level variables often include commonly referenced items that are needed throughout your application. For example, suppose your ASP application includes a drop-down box whose values are drawn from a database. It is more efficient to make the database query one time and store the values in an application-level variable than it is to query the database for every user. The application-level variable can then be referenced by individual user sessions to minimize database input/output. However, if the values in the drop-down box change frequently, the application-level variable might not contain the correct data because the application variable is only refreshed when the ASP application is restarted.

Chapter 11 illustrates several examples that demonstrate how to use application variables. The following code example illustrates loading database connection variables as application variables.

```
<SCRIPT LANGUAGE = "VBScript" RUNAT = "Server">
Sub Application_OnStart
    '== Data Connection Variable
    Application ("ConnectionString") = "DSN = CWI"
    Application ("ConnectionTimeout") = 15
    Application ("CommandTimeout") = 30
    Application ("RuntimeUserName") = ""
    Application ("RuntimePassword") = ""
End Sub
</SCRIPT>
```

Once this script is loaded in the GLOBAL.ASA file, all users of the ASP application can reference these variables whenever a database connection is needed.

Session-Level Scope

If you need to create user-level variables, you can declare the variables in the Session_OnStart event in the GLOBAL.ASA file. This is commonly done when a database connection is needed in the application. The actual database connection, in most situations, should not be made in the Session_OnStart event because you want to utilize the database connection, thread, and resource pooling available with ODBC 3.0 and the Microsoft Transaction Server.

 TIP To increase your ASP application performance, establish and release database connections as needed to utilize ODBC 3.0's database connection, threading, and pooling features.

Chapter 16, "Putting It All Together: Building an Online Catalog," demonstrates using application- and session-level variables to create the Amazing DataWidgets WareHouse.

Procedure-Level Scope

Procedure-level variables are those variables that are declared and used on individual ASP pages. These variables are subject to the limitations defined by the scripting language responsible for processing the ASP. Variables in VBScript can exist at two levels: either at the *script* or *procedure* levels. (Refer to Chapter 3 for a detailed discussion of variable scoping.)

Part
III

Ch
10

Unlike the objects declared in the GLOBAL.ASA file, the Application_OnStart, Application_OnEnd, Session_OnStart, and Session_OnEnd events cannot be called from any ASP within the application. If you try to call those events, the ASP page thinks that you are trying to reference an undefined procedure call on the current page and generates an error.

The Fundamental Active Server Page Objects

Active Server Pages derive their rich functionality from the use of six inherent objects that do have to be instantiated. These objects have their own predefined functionality and their own respective properties, methods, and events. These objects form the foundation of Active Server Pages development and consequently have their own chapters dedicated to fully describe them.

The *Application* Object

The Application object is used to manage all information in the ASP application. The information can be accessed and passed between different users in the application. Because multiple people can try to simultaneously change application variables, the Application object enables locking and unlocking of its variables. When a variable is locked, other users cannot modify the properties of an Application object. The Application object is covered in more detail in Chapter 11, "Controlling the Application: The Application Object."

The *Server* Object

The Server object is responsible for the administrative functionality of the server. One of the most exciting aspects of the Server object is the capability to create an instance of a server via its CreateObject method. This capability to tap into existing ActiveX servers transforms the Web server from a simple file manager into a data translator. The MapPath method of the Server object maps a physical or virtual path to a directory on the server. The ScriptTimeOut property determines the amount of time a script can run before the script process is terminated. The HTMLEncode methods enables HTML encoding of a string. A complete listing of all the properties, methods, and events for the Server object can found in Chapter 12.

The *ObjectContext* Object

The ObjectContext object is used by ASP to control transaction processing using the Microsoft Transaction Server (MTS). This direct processing within the MTS environment enables Active Server Pages to explicitly control, commit, and rollback features of objects managed by MTS. For more details on the ObjectContext object, please see Chapter 12.

The *Session* Object

The Session object is responsible for managing information for a specific user session. These variables are not accessible by other user sessions, but they can be passed from page to page within the ASP application. The SessionID property uniquely identifies the particular user session. The Timeout property sets the time in minutes that the SessionID is valid. Once the SessionID is invalid, the application destroys the user's variables and the user must enter the application from the beginning. If the Timeout property is not reached, executing the Abandon method will destroy the specific user session. Details of the Session object can be found in Chapter 13.

The *Response* Object

The Response object is responsible for sending output from the server to the requesting client. The three most common Response object methods are the Write, Redirect, and Response methods. The Response object uses the Write method to send HTTP output to the browser. The Redirect method provides the capability to redirect the client browser to a different URL. The Response object enables a Cookie collection to set cookie values on the client's browser. More details on the Response object can be found in Chapter 14, "Speaking to the Web Client: The Response Collection."

Part
III

Ch
10

The *Request* Object

The Request object is primarily responsible for retrieving information from the client browser, and it uses five collections to provide for communication between the client browser and Web server. (A *collection* is commonly referred to as a grouping of common objects.) The ClientCertificate collection retrieves certification fields from Web browsers. The Cookies collection enables the server to collect information from client-side cookies. The Form collection retrieves values posted by a client form. Finally, the QueryString collection enables values to be parsed from the HTTP URL string. The Request object can also retrieve server environmental variables. To learn more about the Request object, see Chapter 15, "Retrieving User Information: The Request Object."

Debugging Active Server Pages

Although Active Server Page technology is rapidly changing the way applications are being deployed, the debugging of Active Server Pages is still an area that needs to be improved. The role of debugging is primarily the role of the ASP scripting language itself. If the host scripting language supports error handling, processing, and debugging, errors generally fall into two categories. The first role is the capability of Active Server Pages to handle error trapping when scripts are processed on the Web server. VBScript provides a limited runtime error object that provides some runtime error processing.

The second debugging role is providing real-time debugging capabilities that enable the Active Server Page code to be tested at design time. This type of debugging is the responsibility of the integrated development environment (IDE) tool used to create the application. Currently the most common tools used to create Active Server Pages are text editors, such as Notepad, or development environments such as Microsoft Visual InterDev. Inline debugging is obviously not available in simple editors or even Visual InterDev. However, the Microsoft Script Debugger provides inline debugging capabilities for VBScript, JScript, and Java applications. For more information on using the Script Debugger, please see Chapter 9, "Using the Script Debugger."

Trapping Errors with the *Err* Object

Active Server Pages use the error handling found in VBScript to process and manage runtime errors. VBScript handles error trapping with the Err object. The Err object has several properties and two methods. The Err object's properties and methods can be accessed using the following syntax:

```
Err[.{property | method}]
```

where Err is the generated error object. The Err object's properties provide information about the error object. These properties are listed in Table 10.1.

Table 10.1   The *Err* Object's Properties

Property	Description
Description	Sets or returns the referenced error description.
Number	Sets or returns the number value of the error.
Source	Sets or returns the Application object that generated the error.
HelpFile	Sets or returns the fully qualified path to the help file.
HelpContext	Sets or returns the topic ID with the help file.

The Err object also provides methods that control it. The Err object's methods, as shown in Table 10.2, can be used to generate a runtime error or reset the Err object's properties.

Table 10.2   The *Err* Object's Methods

Method	Description
Raise	Generates a runtime error.
Clear	Resets all object properties.

In VBScript code, the On Error statement is used to enable error handling. The Resume Next statement is used to respond to an error condition by enabling the program to continue execution with the next statement after the one that produced the error. Therefore, to enable error handling in VBScript, use the following line of code:

```
<% On Error Resume Next %>
```

If no error handling is activated, any runtime error that is generated at the server will result in the immediate termination of the script. However, if error handling is activated, the application continues by executing the next line in the code.

```
<%
On Error Resume Next                    '=== Turns on Error Handling
Dim myMonth
myMonth = FormatDate(Now)               '=== Spelling Error produces error
Response.Write myMonth                   '=== Application Focus is returned here
%>
```

In this example, a blank string is written to the page because the VBScript does not have a built-in function named FormatDate. When the Err object is created because of the improper spelling of the FormatDateTime function, the script is not immediately terminated and processing continued throughout the ASP. In this example, a blank line is written to the page. For detailed information about error trapping in VBScript, please refer to Chapter 5, "Controlling Program Flow with VBScript."

Trapping Errors with the Web Server Log File

You can also utilize two Registry Settings, the ScriptErrorsSentToBrowser and the ScriptErrorMessage, to help control and manage primitive error trapping in Active Server Pages. The ScriptErrorsSentToBrowser Registry Setting is used to determine whether the specific error information will be written to the Web server log file and to the requesting browser. The ScriptErrorsSentToBrowser enables you to trap and log useful debugging, such as the filename, error line numbers, and description messages. If ScriptErrorsSentToBrowser is disabled, the string in the ScriptErrorMessage is displayed to the browser. The ScriptErrorMessage contains either the default error message or it can be customized to meet your needs. The default message is An error occurred on the server when processing the URL. Please contact the system administrator.

Trapping Errors by Writing Text Files

Another primitive method you can use to debug your ASP applications is to create your own log file using the VBScript FileSystem object. The FileSystem object enables you to read and write to text files on the Web server. Using this object, you can create a log file that can be viewed for bugging purposes, as shown in the following code:

```
<%
DebugFileName = Server.MapPath ("/myApp") + "\debuglog.txt"
Set FileObject = Server.CreateObject("Scripting.FileSystemObject")
Set FileOut= FileObject.OpenTextFile(DebugFileName, 8, True)
%>
```

Part
III

Ch
10

This example first uses the Server.MapPath method to create the physical path setting to the debuglog.txt file. The FileSystemObject is used to return a TextStream object to read and write to a customized debugging text file. The FileObject.OpenTextFile method is used to read from or append to the file. In this example, any new information will be appended to the text file and a new text file will be created if the existing file cannot be found.

This is particularly useful in the OnStart or OnEnd events of the Application and Session objects in the GLOBAL.ASA file, where certain objects cannot be referenced in different events. For example, you can write variable values to a text file on the Application_OnEnd event to check the values of the variable and to verify that the Application_OnEnd event was actually called.

You can also use the text file error-trapping approach to determine the variables or execution points in an ASP, which is accomplished by writing values at different points in the ASP. For example, the following example demonstrates writing a debug file to track the application workflow.

```
<%
DebugFileName = Server.MapPath ("/myApp") + "\debuglog.txt"
Set FileObject = Server.CreateObject("Scripting.FileSystemObject")
Set FileOut= FileObject.OpenTextFile(DebugFileName, 8, True)

FileOut.WriteLine("Function PadStr Initiated")       '=== Writes Initiated string
to LogFile
newValue = PadStr(myString, 5)                        '=== Calls Function
FileOut.WriteLine("Function PadStr Completed")        '=== Writes Complete string to
➥LogFile
%>
```

In this situation, the string Function PadStr Initiated is written to the debugging file using the WriteLine method. Then the custom-created PadStr function is called. If the PadStr is successful, the TextStream object writes the string Function PadStr Completed to the debug file.

Integrating the debugging technique throughout your ASP would lead to a debug file from which you could follow the process that leads to the error. The following debug file illustrates the user and ASP events:

```
'=== Debug.Txt: Generate 11/23/97 10:32 AM
Welcome Page Initiated
  Function LoadCookieValues Initiated
  Function LoadCookieValues Completed
Welcome Page Completed
Login Page Initiated
  Function dbLogin initiated
```

Reviewing the debug log shown above, the Welcome page was successfully loaded, but the problem appears to be somewhere after the function dbLogin is called.

Although not as robust as traditional debuggers, this textual debugging feature can be very useful especially when dealing with debugging from an offsite or remote location. For example, if an application encounters an error, you can have the application variables trigger a miniature debugging system. This system can track application variables and user events to a text file for record keeping and debugging. This process of tracking the issues that lead up to the error will help to systematically reproduce the error and reduce debugging time.

Controlling Access to the Site

Controlling who has access to your site and application information is critical when building Web-based applications. Specifically, for many intranet sites are adding extranet capabilities, restricting access to your site is critical to maintain control over sensitive information. This control can be established in two ways for your ASP Web sites and applications: at the Web server level and at the file level. Regardless of the different level of security you choose to implement, setting up Web security requires close communication between Web site administrators and network administrators.

Part
III

Ch
10

Web Server Packet Filtering

The first layer of control is through TCP/IP packet filtering at the Web server level. The Web server can accept or reject requests based on where the request is being generated. To grant or deny access to your Web server, open the Property settings for the site. To regulate access using the Microsoft Management Console, use the Directory Security tab, as shown in Figure 10.5.

FIG. 10.5

The Directory Security tab of the MMC enables TCP/IP filtering at the Web server level.

If you are using Internet Information Server 3.0, the TCP/IP packet filter is located in the Internet Information Service Manager on the Advanced tab, as shown in Figure 10.6.

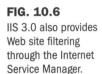

FIG. 10.6

IIS 3.0 also provides Web site filtering through the Internet Service Manager.

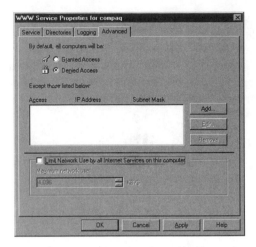

Both the MMC and the Internet Service Manager grant and restrict access based on individual computer IP addresses, a group of computers using an IP and submask, or entire domains of computers.

File Level Access Control

The second control layer to regulate the permission of the site is to manage the permission at the file level. Typically, when you set up the Internet Information Server, the username IUSR_machinename is created to represent the Internet guest account. When an anonymous user requests pages from your public site, NT uses this security setting to access the requested files. Therefore, to restrict access to only authorized users or groups, use the NT file permission to administer user rights. To view the security rights of files on the Web server, right-click the file or directory and select the Property item. The Security tab is used to manage the different levels of access on the file or directory.

Clicking the Permission button displays who has rights to the file or directory and what level of access they have. For example, Figure 10.7 illustrates that the Internet guest account has permissions to this file. If you double-click the user account, the detailed permissions of the file can be viewed.

FIG. 10.7

Access permissions can be assigned by using the File Permissions dialog box.

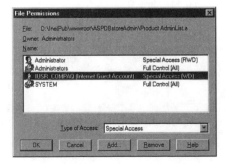

To prevent anonymous users from accessing this file, remove the anonymous guest account and assign the desired user or group permissions. Now that the Internet guest account has been removed, when the Internet Information server tries to access this file, the user will be prompted for proper NT identification. This technique enables only user with valid NT user accounts to access this site. Now, when any page on the Web site is requested, the user is prompted with an authorization dialog box, as shown in Figure 10.8.

FIG. 10.8
Remove anonymous access permissions to prompt user for valid NT user accounts.

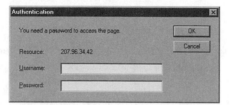

Keep in mind that the username and password are being passed in non-encrypted form from the Web browser to the Web server. A potential hacker could intercept the packet and retrieve the NT username and password. To prevent this situation from occurring, only transmit usernames and passwords over a Secure Socket Layer or other encrypted channels.

Configuring Active Server Pages

Active Server Pages require configuration at two levels. For IIS 3.0, the Registry provides a storage location needed for the Web service configurations. In IIS 4.0, the Metabase is used to store information about the IIS Web server. The Metabase is a hierarchical database that expands the functionality of the Registry by allowing properties to be set at the computer, Web site, virtual directory, directory, and file levels.

The second location where Active Servers Pages are configured is at the file level. Usually, a Web server interface tool, such as the Internet Service Manager, performs the file level configuration automatically for you. These custom interfaces provide a way to configure the security permissions that are needed to view, read, and execute your Web subsystems without using traditional administration tools.

The Metabase

The Metabase is a hierarchical database used to store configuration information about the IIS 4.0 server. The easiest way to configure the metabase is through the Internet Service Manager. The metabase ASP settings can be found by selecting the App Options property sheet on the Home Directory property sheet, and then clicking the Configuration button.

The Metabase is used to store all configuration issues about the IIS 4.0 Web server. Table 10.3 illustrates the related metabase tags for Active Server Pages.

Table 10.3   The Metabase Tags

Name	Description
AspBufferingOn	Controls whether Active Server Pages buffers output to a browser. If set to True (that is, set to 1), HTTP headers can be sent to the browser from anywhere within a script.
AspLogErrorRequests	Sets whether the Web server writes unsuccessful client requests to the Windows NT event log file. The value 1 turns error logging on, and 0 turns it off.
AspScriptErrorSentToBrowser	Determines whether the Web server writes the filename, error and line numbers, and description to the client browser and to the Windows NT event log.
AspScriptErrorMessage	Sets the error message that appears in a client browser if detailed ASP error messages are disabled.
AspScriptFileCacheSize	Sets the amount of memory in bytes to allocate for the caching of precompiled script files. A setting of 0 indicates that no script files will be cached. A value of -1 indicates that all script files will be cached.
AspScriptEngineCacheMax	Sets the value for the maximum number of ActiveX language engines that Active Server Pages keep cached in memory.
AspScriptTimeout	Sets the length of time Active Server Pages will allow a script to run before terminating the script and recording the event to the event log.
AspSessionTimeout	Sets the default amount of time a Session object should be maintained after the last request associated with the Session object is made.
AspEnableParentPaths	Sets the flag to control whether Active Server Pages can enable paths relative to the current directory using the .. operator.
AspAllowSessionState	Sets the flag controls to determine whether Active Server Pages can maintain session state in the ASP applications. If disabled, the ASPSessionID cookie will not be sent to clients and any attempts to store anything in the session or to use Session_OnStart or Session_OnEnd will generate an error.
AspScriptLanguage	Sets the primary scripting language for all Active Server Page applications.
AspExceptionCatchEnable	Used to set controls flag to monitor exception catching from components. If enabled, Active Server Pages will catch exceptions that are thrown by components.

Name	Description
AppAllowDebugging	Sets whether or not Active Server Page debugging is enabled.
AppAllowClientDebug	Determines whether or not Active Server Pages client-side debugging is enabled.
ScriptMaps	Used to set what applications will interpret the script filename extensions.
CGITimeout	Sets the maximum time in seconds the WWW service will wait for a response from CGI scripts.
CacheISAPI	Used to indicate whether ISAPI DLLs are loaded and cached if the DLLs are unloaded after they are run.

The Registry Settings

In Windows-based operating systems, the Registry contains important information that can help you optimize your Active Server Pages. These Active Server settings are used to control the interaction between the Internet Information Server HTTP service and the Active Server Page interpreter engine. From an organizational aspect, the Active Server Pages process is a sub-category of the Web server service. Naturally, the Active Server process running as a standalone process would be worthless if it were unable to accept and deliver HTTP requests to the client.

The Registry itself represents a hierarchical database used to store system-level information. This system database contains critical information about configuration issues within Windows 95 and Windows NT environments. The Registry acts as the central repository for your system settings, and manages settings from one location across different applications. The Registry also prevents user and application settings from being disbursed in various directories in various files on the system. Specifically, the centralized storage location prevents configuration files from being loaded in various .INI, .BAT, .SYS, and other files.

The database is typically managed through native Windows controls, such as the components found in the Control Panel. Because the database is central to maintaining your operating system, improper settings made in the Registry can cause catastrophic operating system failure.

The Registry is best viewed and configured with a graphical Registry navigation tool, such as the Registry Editor. The Registry Editor is executed by running REGEDIT.EXE from the command line.

The Registry Editor provides a convenient hierarchical viewing mechanism. The Active Server Pages Registry settings are found in the following file path:

```
HKEY_LOCAL_MACHINE\SYSTEM
\CurrentControlSet
 \Services
  \W3SVC
   \ASP
    \Parameters
```

The Registry settings, as shown in Table 10.4, contain many settings that are central to administrating the Active Server Pages. For example, you can use the Registry settings to change the default scripting language of the Active Server, which is VBScript. As mentioned earlier in the chapter, unless otherwise specified by the <% *LANGUAGE* %> on a page, the default scripting language is responsible for processing the script contained within the <% %> tags. To change the default scripting language of the machine, change the date value of the DefaultScriptLanguage Registry setting. For example, if the default scripting is JScript, you can convert the default scripting language to VBScript by changing the DefaultScriptLanguage Registry name to VBScript.

Unless otherwise stated, most changes require the Web server to be restarted for changes to take effect.

Table 10.4   Active Server Pages Registry Settings

Name	Description
AllowSessionState	Sets whether Active Server Pages can make session state in applications. If the session state is not allowed, the ASPSessionID cookie will not be sent to clients that access the Web site. Consequently, if code existed in the GLOBAL.ASA file, within the Session_OnStart or Session_OnEnd events, an error will be generated.
BufferingOn	Sets whether Active Server Pages buffers output to a browser. If BufferingOn is activated, all output is completely collected in memory before being sent to the browser.
DefaultScriptLanguage	Sets the primary scripting language for all Active Server Pages applications on the server. To override this setting on a page basis, use the <%@ LANGUAGE = ScriptingLanguage %> on the first line of an Active Server Page.
EnableParentPaths	Sets whether Active Server Pages can enable browser navigation from the current directory. If so, the browser is able to navigate up the directory tree using the parent directory operator (..).
LogErrorRequests	Sets whether the Web server can write unsuccessful client requests to the Windows NT event log file.
MemFreeFactor	Sets the maximum length of the free memory as a percentage of the used memory list.

Name	Description
MinUsedBlocks	Sets the minimum length of the used memory list before elements can be freed.
NumInitialThreads	Sets the number of worker threads that Active Server Pages creates when it is started.
ProcessorThreadMax	Sets the maximum number of worker threads to create per processor. According to documentation, it is not recommended to create more than 20 threads per processor.
RequestQueueMax	Sets the maximum number of ASP requests to keep in the queue for each thread. Once the maximum requests have been made, the server returns a ServerTooBusy message to the browser.
ScriptEngineCacheMax	Sets maximum number of ActiveX language engines that Active Server Pages will keep cached in memory.
ScriptErrorMessage	Sets the error message that appears on a browser if ScriptErrorsSentToBrowser.
ScriptErrorsSentToBrowser	Sets whether the Web server writes debugging specifics, such as the filename, error and line number, and error descriptions to the browser in addition to the log.
ScriptFileCacheSize	Sets the amount of memory in bytes to allocate for the caching of precompiled script files, which improves the performance of Active Server Pages.
ScriptFileCacheTTL	Sets the amount of time that script files will remain in the memory cache before being phased out if there have been no references to those scripts.
ScriptTimeout	Sets the length of time Active Server Pages will allow a script to run to completion. This can be overridden in a script by calling the Server.ScriptTimeout method.
SessionTimeout	Sets the default amount of time a Session object should be maintained after the last request associated with the object is made. This can be overridden in a script by using the Session.Timeout method call.
StartConnectionPool	Sets whether ODBC connection pooling is turned on (default) or off.
ThreadCreationThreshold	Sets the number of requests that can be maintained in the common queue to process Active Server Pages. If requests exceed this number, a new thread is created in the thread pool but is always less than the amount specified in the ProcessorThreadMax amount field.

Part

III

Ch

10

Web Server Interface Utilities

An ASP application consists of a group of ASP files collected in a virtual directory. The permissions on this virtual or application directory regulate the rights and permissions of the ASP application. Most Web servers provide an interface that enables you to configure and administer the Web server. Usually this interface is provided in two forms, through a native client utility and through an HTML interface. Regardless of the method used to administer the Web service, the settings needed for ASP applications are the same. In order for the Web server to process the ASP files, the permission on the files must have read and execute permissions set. Assuming that IIS and Active Server Pages have been properly installed, setting these permissions is most easily done via the Internet Service Manager. To configure the permissions on a directory via the Internet Service Manager, select a directory from the Virtual Directory tab, as shown in Figure 10.9.

FIG. 10.9
Configuring directory permissions to control the ASP execution permissions.

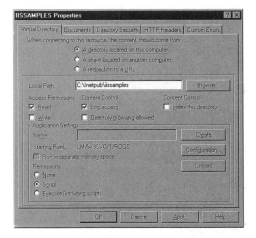

After selecting the appropriate directory, set the read and execution check boxes to enable all files in that directory to be read and executed by the Web server. If you were using the HTTP service to simply deliver ordinary HTML files with no embedded scripting, the files in that directory would only need to have read access. If just read permission is set when using ASP files, the Active Server scripts would be displayed on the requesting client's browser, as shown in Figure 10.10. The script is shown because the Web server is simply transferring all the text in the page to the browser without executing it.

However, if you have a directory that contains all your Perl scripts for a Web application, the directory permissions would have to be set to execute in order for the files to process. If just execute permission is set for the directory that contains static content, the Web server will only display the text on the requesting page. All links that require the server to read any other type of information will display as broken links.

Typically, if you use graphical user interface (GUI) tools such as Visual InterDev or FrontPage to create ASP applications, the read and execute permissions for the virtual directory of the Web would be set.

FIG. 10.10
Active Server script is displayed as text if the execute permission is not set for the directory.

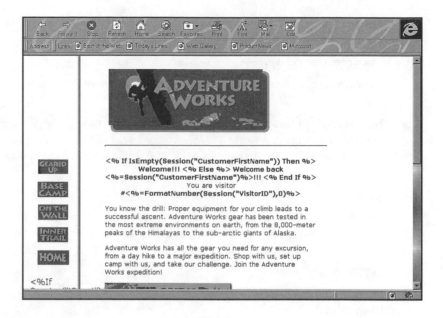

For a more detailed discussion on administering your site, Chapter 31 provides an overview of how to manage your sites using the Internet Services Manager.

Using ASP Directives

Active Server Pages have the capability to override page-level settings that have been stored in the Metabase or Registry settings. Directives are used by ASPs to let the IIS know how to process the individual ASP files. IIS 4.0 uses five directives to control page-level processing, as shown in Table 10.5.

Table 10.5   IIS 4.0 ASP Directives

Directive	Description
@CodePage	Sets the code page of an ASP script.
@EnableSessionState	Sets whether or not session information is stored.
@Language	Sets the primary scripting language of the ASP file.
@LCID	Sets the local identifier for the ASP file.
@Transaction	Indicates whether ASP scripts should be processed as a transaction.

The ASP directives must be located on the first line of the ASP file. The syntax for the processing directives is

```
<%@DirectiveName=Value%>
```

where `DirectiveName` is a valid processing directive and `Value` is a value assigned to the directive.

The @CodePage Directive   The `@CODEPAGE` directive is used to set the code page for an ASP file. The code page represents a unique character set used to define a specific language and localized region. To set the code page for an ASP file, use the following syntax on the first line of ASP script:

```
<%@CODEPAGE=codepage%>
```

where `codepage` is a valid code page. The `@CodePage` directive can be superceded by the `Session.CodePage` property. For example, the following code is used to change the code page used to display Japanese Kanji:

```
<%@CODEPAGE = 932%>
```

For more information on the code page, code page values, and the `Session` object, please see Chapter 13.

The @EnableSessionState Directive   The `@EnableSessionState` processing directive is used to control whether session tracking is applied to the ASP file. The `@EnableSessionState` directive enables session tracking to be turned on or off. To use this page-level feature, use the following syntax:

```
<%@EnableSessionSstate=True¦False %>
```

For example, to disable session tracking information on a specific ASP file and consequently decrease the processing time, the following code would be used:

```
<%@EnableSessionsState = False %>
```

This feature is beneficial when processing functionality is required in ASP scripts but tracking the user information is not necessary. If monitoring user information via the `Session` object is not necessary, the scripting engine processing load can be reduced.

The @Language Directive   The `@Language` directive is used to set the primary scripting language for the ASP file. The primary scripting language is responsible for processing all script between the `<% %>` delimiters. To set the primary scripting language for a page, use the following syntax on the first line of the ASP file:

```
<%@Language=scriptengine %>
```

where `scriptengine` is a valid script engine on the server. IIS 4.0 ships with the `VBScript` and `JScript` scripting engines. Therefore, the following code example sets the primary scripting engine to `VBScript`:

```
<%@Language = VBScript %>
```

The @*LCID* Directive   The @LCID processing directive is responsible for setting the local identifier for an ASP file. The local identifier uses standard international numeric abbreviations to specify local date, currency, and time formats. To use the LCID directive, use the following syntax on the first line of the ASP file:

```
<%@LCID=localeidentifier %>
```

where LCID is the valid local identifier. This directive is particularly useful for sites that must support multiple languages. For example, to set the local identifier to use the French local identifier, use the following code:

```
<%@LCID= 1036 %>
```

As with the @CodePage directive, the @LCID directive can be overwritten by the Session.LCID property.

The @*Transaction* Directive   The transaction-processing directive is used to enable the IIS Web server to treat the ASP script as a transaction monitored by the Microsoft Transaction Server (MTS). To use the @Transaction directive on an ASP file, use the following syntax:

```
<%@TRANSACTION=value %>
```

where value is the level of transaction support. The MTS transactions can have four levels of support, as shown in Table 10.6.

Table 10.6   ASP Transactional Support in the Microsoft Transaction Server

Value	Description
Required	Script initiates a transaction.
Required_New	Script initiates a transaction.
Supported	Script will not initiate a transaction.
Not_Supported	Script will not initiate a transaction.

Notice in Table 10.6 that although four values of transactional support are given, the transactional ASP script processing is either initiated or not initiated. However, you can use these transactional support values to add functionality to components managed by the MTS. For more information on managing components from ASP scripts, please see Chapter 12.

To enable transactional ASP processing, use the following syntax on the first line of the ASP file:

```
<%@Transaction = Required %>
```

As with other directive, the @Transaction directive is only supported while the current page is processed and is terminated after the page is finished processing. For more information on using the Microsoft Transaction Server, please see Chapter 28, "Working with the Microsoft Transaction Server."

Handling Known Active Server Page Issues

As Active Server technology continues to grow, different versions of the Active Server Pages exist. As in any emerging technology, known development issues arise that can cause potential damage to your Web applications. Table 10.7 categorizes the different ASP versions and builds to help identify what version of Active Server Pages you are running.

Table 10.7   ASP Version Information

ASP Version	ASP Build	ASP DLL Version	ASP DLL Date
1.0	1.12.09	1.12.06	12/6/96
1.0A	1.13.31	1.13.09	1/31/97
1.0B	1.15.14	1.15.14	3/14/97

There have been two significant issues discovered with Active Server Pages. The first temporary setback was that the script code of the ASP could be viewed in the client browser by placing a period (.) at the end of a URL. This viewing privilege opened huge security concerns by exposing the source code driving ASP applications, Internet Database Connector (IDC) applications, and Common Gateway Interface (CGI) applications. A hotfix to NT 4.0 SP2 has been posted at the Microsoft FTP site at:

```
FTP://ftp.microsoft.com/bussys/winnt/winnt-public/fixes/usa/nt40/hotfixes-
postsp2/iis-fix/readme.1st
```

To obtain additional information about this problem, see article Q163485 of the Microsoft Knowledge Base on the Microsoft support Web site.

The second issue regarding Active Server Pages is the existence of a memory leak for systems that have upgraded to ASP version 1.0B. The rate of the memory leak is proportional to how heavy the site is accessed. The memory leak can be demonstrated by using the NT Performance Monitor to track the Active Server Page object. The NT Performance Monitor provides a data collection mechanism to generate data for graph and charts for NT server objects. A hotfix to NT 4.0 SP3 is also available at:

```
FTP://ftp.microsoft.com/bussys/winnt/winnt-public/fixes/usa/nt40/hotfixes-
postsp3/asp-fix/readme.1st
```

Note that this hotfix should only be applied to systems that have upgraded to 1.0B. For systems that have not upgraded, the 1.0 and 1.0A version will not apply this hotfix. For more information on this problem, see article Q150934 in the Microsoft Knowledge Base.

Most of the ASP updates are included in the NT service packs, but are not necessarily automatically installed to update the Active Server Pages when the service packs are installed. For example, NT 4.0 Service Pack 3 includes a separate standalone setup executable for ASP 1.0B that is not installed automatically when you apply the NT Service Pack.

From Here...

As you can see, an Active Server Page application consists of many files, directories and virtual directories, and six built-in ASP objects. The Metabase and Registry settings are used to store the IIS Web server configuration for your static and dynamic HTML needs. At this point, with the lofty application architecture in place, the specifics of Active Server Page objects can be discovered. The following chapters will provide a detailed approach on how to use the specific ASP objects and how they all tie in together to deliver Web applications to any HTML-compliant browser.

- Chapter 13, "Managing the User Session: The Session Object," illustrates the nuances of tracking a user through an ASP application.

- Chapter 15, "Retrieving User Information: The Request Object," demonstrates how to collect information from the user using forms, hidden fields, and cookies.

- Chapter 16, "Putting It All Together: Building an Online Catalog," demonstrates how to use the ActiveX components that ship with IIS 4.0.

- Chapter 17, "Implementing Existing Server-Side Components," illustrates how to use the various components that ship with IIS and Active Server Pages in your applications.

- Chapter 18, "Creating Your Own Active Server Components," provides a walk-through to the tools and examples on how to create tailored functionality via custom components.

Controlling the Application: The *Application* Object

Active Server Pages has six built-in objects for programmers to use. The Application object is used to control and manage all items that are available to all users of an Active Server application. The Application items can be variables needed for all users in the application, or they can be instantiated objects that provide special server-side functionality. This chapter will demonstrate what the Application object represents, how to trap its events, and how to use its properties and methods to manage an ASP application. ■

Trapping Application Events

Discover how the *Application* object is used to manage Active Server Page applications and how to use the beginning and ending events to initiate and close your ASP applications.

Controlling Application Variables

Examine how to use the *Lock* and UnLock application methods to prevent multiple users from simultaneously changing application variables.

Using Application-Level Components

Understand how to create components at the application level that are accessible to all users and learn how to use application-level static and dynamic arrays.

Implementing Application Collections

Learn how to use the *Application* object's *Contents* and *Static* collections to help manage application-level variables and objects.

Trapping Application Events

The `Application` object is a single object that is created to represent an instance of an ASP application. From the previous chapter, you learned that an Active Server application is actually a collection of ASP files. These files are housed in directories and subdirectories that comprise virtual directories on the Web server. When *any* ASP file is requested from a virtual Active Server directory, the `Application` object is instantiated to start, manage, and share information throughout the entire ASP application. Information can then be shared to all users in the application. As you can see, this process of starting an application is different from the traditional application startup mechanisms. Most applications are started by calling a single executable file. However, with Active Server Pages, the application is started by calling any .ASP file in the virtual directory. The `Application` object is the fundamental object that is used to start and manage ASP applications. The `Application` object is a single object that can be accessed by any user of that application. The individual users, represented by `Session` objects, can read and update the `Application` object as needed. The `Session` objects can use the `Request` and `Response` objects to communicate information to the browser. Figure 11.1 represents the relationship of the `Application` object and the `Session`, `Request`, and `Response` objects.

FIG. 11.1

The Application object represents an instance of an ASP application that can be accessed by any user.

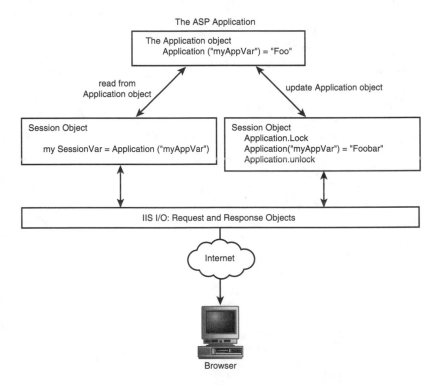

IIS uses the `Application` object not only to share information among all users in the application, but also to manage application processes and resources. IIS 4.0 enables you to run entire ASP applications within their own process space to protect against a catastrophic failure of an application from bringing down the entire the entire HTTP server. Furthermore, the process isolation enables you to wrap transaction processing directly in Active Server Pages. For more information on configuring the ASP application, refer to Chapter 10, "The Composition of an Active Server Application."

The `Application` object, as well as the other Active Server objects, follows the familiar `object.method` syntax:

`Application.method`

where `Application` is the Active Server Application object.

The `Application` object has two events: `Application_OnStart` and `Application_OnEnd`. The `Application` object is created by the Active Server to represent a physical start up of an Active Server application. Once the `Application` object is started, all subsequent users can reference its objects and variables.

The `Application_OnStart` and `Application_OnEnd` events are good examples of event-driven programming. Most of the examples discussed in Chapter 6, "Working with Functions, Subroutines, and Dialog Boxes," demonstrate client-side, event-driven examples, such as trapping the `Click` event of an HTML button. The `Application` events are good examples of server-side, event-driven programming. The server-side scripting of the `Application` object is controlled in the `GLOBAL.ASA` file. The `GLOBAL.ASA` file is responsible for trapping the start and end events of the `Application` and `Session` objects. These events use the similar syntax of `object.event` that is found in the client-side examples but are not necessarily required to use the `Application` and `Session` objects.

The `Application_OnStart` and `Application_OnEnd` events, shown in Table 11.1, are used in the `GLOBAL.ASA` file to initiate code when either of these events is triggered.

Table 11.1 The *Application* Object's Events

Event	Description
`Application_OnStart`	Initiated when the ASP application is first started.
`Application_OnEnd`	Initiated when the ASP application is terminated.

The server-side scripting of the `Application` object is controlled in the `GLOBAL.ASA` file. The `GLOBAL.ASA` file is responsible for trapping the start and end events of the `Application` and `Session` objects. The individual application events are found in the `GLOBAL.ASA` file and are executed in a similar manner to any subroutine or function. As seen in Chapter 6, subroutines and functions are executed by calling the procedure name. For example, the following `GLOBAL.ASA` file only initiates the `Application_OnStart` event. The `Application OnEnd` event will not be executed because it is commented out. For more information on the `GLOBAL.ASA` file, please see Chapter 10.

```
<SCRIPT LANGUAGE="VBScript" RUNAT = "Server">
```

Part

III

Ch

11

```
Sub Application_OnStart            '=== Defines Application Object's OnStart Event
        Application("strMessage") = "Welcome to Active Server Pages"
End Sub

Application _OnStart               '=== Call this procedure
' Application_OnEnd                '=== Ignored, commented out

</SCRIPT>
```

TIP The Application_OnStart and Application_OnEnd events are not necessarily required to use the Application object.

Declaring Application-Level Variables

As seen in Part II, "VBScript: The Foundation of Active Server Pages," the proper use of variables forms the foundation of any programming model. The same is true when dealing with Active Server objects. Variable declaration in the Application object is a topic that has some interesting characteristics that need to be properly understood when building Active Server Page applications.

Application object-level variables are accessible by all users of an application and share information common to all users. Application-level variables can be defined as needed in any ASP file, not just in the Application_OnStart and Application_OnEnd events of the GLOBAL.ASA file. This means application variables can be also be created in the Session events and during page-level script processing. Keep in mind, from the previous chapter that an ASP application is the collection of Active Server Pages contained in a virtual directory on the Web server. Multiple users can be navigating through a variety of different pages but all have access to a common set of data. The Application object acts as the manager for this library of shared information.

Variables have two levels of scope in Active Server Pages: page-level variables and object-level variables. The page-level variables are defined by a scripting language within the ASP scripts. The page-level scripting only has scope as that page is being processed. Once the page is finished processing, the page-level variables are destroyed and the resources released. Part II of this book focused on using VBScript to create, process, and manage page-level variables.

The second type of variable is the object variable. Object-level variables transcend page-level variables because the scope of object variables extends beyond page-level variable processing. Object-level variables exist in two forms: at the session level and at the application level. Session-level variables are used to pass variables from page to page for a specific user and application-level variables are used to share common information between all users. These application and session variables are global to all page-level variables on Active Server Pages.

Application- and session-level variables are declared by simply using the desired variable name with the appropriate object-level reference. To declare a variable, use the following syntax:

ObjectLevel(*varName*)

where *ObjectLevel* is the Application or Session object and *varName* is the name of the variable.

For example, to declare an application-level variable named myAppWelcomeStr that can be accessible to all users, use the following line of code in either the GLOBAL.ASA file or in any ASP file:

```
Application("myAppWelcomeStr") = "Welcome To ASPTraining Center Online"
```

Notice the difference between this type of implicit declaration at the object level and how variables are declared at the script level. The script-level variables in VBScript can be declared explicitly using the Dim keyword or can be implicitly declared by assigning a variable to a variable name. Listing 11.1 uses the combination of declaring an application-level object in the GLOBAL.ASA file to set the welcome message for the application and then uses page-level scripting to write the message to the page.

Listing 11.1   Declaring an application-level object to set a welcome message for all users in the application.

```
'============= The Global.ASA File Begin ===========
<SCRIPT LANGUAGE="VBScript" RUNAT="Server">
Sub Application_OnStart
    Application("myWelcomeStr") = "Welcome to ASP International"
    Application("myTitle")= " ASP International Corporate Home "End Sub

</SCRIPT>
'============= The Global.ASA File End ===============



'============= A Requesting ASP Page ================
<%@ LANGUAGE="VBSCRIPT" %>

<HTML>
<HEAD>
<TITLE><% =Application("myTitle")%></TITLE>
</HEAD>
<BODY>

<Center><B>
<% = Application("myWelcomeStr")                    '=== Writes variable on page
Â%>
<% Application("myAppConnectStr") = "DBconnect"      '=== Creates an applica-
tion Âlevel variable
</B></Center>

</BODY>
</HTML>
'===================== ASP End ============================
```

Part

III

Ch

11

Notice how this code also uses the application variable myTitle to set the values used in the HTML title bar. In addition, this example also writes the string 'DBconnect' to the application variable named myAppConnectStr.

> **CAUTION**
>
> Take care to ensure proper spelling with application- and session-level variables. The lack of the Option Explicit functionality found at the script level may lead to incorrect variable assignments or zero length string retrievals.

Although you can use page-level and object-level variables in Active Server Pages, they are not exclusive to themselves. You can utilize both types of variables at different scoping levels as needed within any ASP. In addition, you can utilize VBScript variables and control logic in the GLOBAL.ASA events to process your application logic. For example, the following script builds a counter that tracks the amount of users entering a site using the application- and session-level objects.

```
<SCRIPT LANGUAGE="VBScript" RUNAT="Server">
Sub Application_OnStart                       '=== Sets an Application variable
     Application("counter")="1"
End Sub
</SCRIPT>

<SCRIPT LANGUAGE="VBScript" RUNAT="Server">
Sub Session_OnStart                           '=== Using the Session Level
➥event
     dim userCounter
     userCounter =Application("counter")
     userCounter = Counter + 13
     Application("Counter")= userCounter       '=== Update the Application
➥variable

End Sub
</SCRIPT>
```

In this example the Application_OnStart event is used to initiate the counter variable to 1 when the ASP application is created. As new users enter the site, the Session_OnStart event uses VBScript to increment the counter. For more information on the Session object and its events, please see Chapter 13, "Managing the User Session: The Session Object."

Notice that the scripting variables declared in the Application_OnStart event are not themselves perceived as application-level variables by other ASP files in the application. For example, if you try to reference the *userCounter* script variables declared in the Session_OnStart event, the return of the variable would be a zero length string.

 TIP   Script-level variables used in the GLOBAL.ASA application and session events are not accessible from other ASPs.

The same programming functionality can be created in the Application_OnEnd event. The Application_OnEnd event will not usually contain information critical to a specific Web user. Most of the processing contained in the Application_OnEnd event will pertain more to administration functions, such as writing to a log file when the Web server is being shut down.

In the previous sections, I have used the `Application_OnStart` and `Application_OnEnd` events to illustrate how application-level variables are used. Now let's take a closer look at details of each `Application` event.

Application_OnStart Event

To start using the `OnStart` event of the `Application` object, the appropriate script tags must be defined in the `GLOBAL.ASA` file. The `Application_OnStart` event requires the following syntax:

```
<SCRIPT LANGUAGE=ScriptLanguage RUNAT=Server>
Sub Application_OnStart
. . . '=== Your application initialization code here
End Sub

</SCRIPT>
```

The `Application_OnStart` event is executed before any user or session event is triggered. Any attempts to call a `Session`, `Response`, or `Request` object will generate a fatal runtime error because these objects have not been created at this point. However, you can reference the `Server` object. The `Server` object is used to help provide HTTP administration features. The `Server` object is looked at more closely in Chapter 12, "Controlling the Server with the `Server` Object and Using Transaction Processing with the `ObjectContext` Object."

> **CAUTION**
>
> Referencing the `Session`, `Request`, and `Response` objects in the `Application_OnStart` event will create a runtime error. These objects cannot be called because they have not been instantiated at this point.

Part

III

Ch

11

Application_OnEnd Event

The `Application_OnEnd` event requires the following syntax within the `GLOBAL.ASA` file similar to the `Application_OnStart` event:

```
<SCRIPT LANGUAGE=ScriptLanguage RUNAT=Server>
Sub Application_OnEnd
    '=== Your Script Here
End Sub

</SCRIPT>
```

The `Application_OnEnd` event occurs when the Web server terminates the `Application` object. Shutting down the Web server can occur in two situations. The first situation is the obvious closing down of the HTTP service via termination of the process or via the Microsoft Management Console or the Internet Service Manager. The second situation automatically occurs when the `GLOBAL.ASA` file needs to be recompiled and reloaded into memory. This situation occurs when changes have to be made and saved to the `GLOBAL.ASA` file. When the `Application` object detects that the `GLOBAL.ASA` file has changed, the `Application` object starts to shut down the HTTP service. When the `Application` object initiates the shutdown process, the HTTP service refuses any additional browser requests while the new `GLOBAL.ASA` file is being loaded into memory.

As in the `Application_OnStart` event, any references to the `Session`, `Request`, or `Response` objects will generate an error. The `Session`, `Request`, and `Response` objects are closed before the `Application_OnEnd` event, so trying to reference a closed object will generate an error.

Controlling Application-Level Variables with Methods

The capability to create or change application-level variables on any page of the ASP application by any or all users creates the need to control and regulate variable access. The `Application` object has two methods designed to control variable access, the `Lock` and `UnLock` methods (see Table 11.2). These methods help to prevent simultaneous multiple users from changing application-level variables.

Table 11.2   The *Application* Object's Methods

Name	Description
Lock	Prevents other users from changing `Application` object properties.
UnLock	Enables other users to modify the `Application` object's properties.

The application methods require the following syntax and can be referenced from any point within the application:

`Application.Method`

where `Application` is the `Application` object and `Method` is the `Lock` or `UnLock` method.

Lock Method

The goal of the `Lock` method is to tightly control `Application` object's properties by preventing concurrent users from modifying the same application-level variables at the same time. The `Lock` method gives a single user session the sole administration rights to an application variable or variables. The individual user retains control of the `Application` object until the `Application.UnLock` method is declared. The `Lock` method is implemented using the following syntax:

`Application.Lock`

To prevent users from simultaneously changing the same `Application` object properties, use the `Lock` and `UnLock` methods in conjunction. For example, suppose that you build an intranet application to help disperse information about the status of current project. To prevent two managers from simultaneously trying to change the due date of a project, use the `Lock` method to freeze only the `Application` object properties to one user session.

```
<%
Application.Lock
Application("vDueDate") = Request.Form("txtDueDate")
```

```
Application.UnLock
%>
This application was processed on
<%= FormatDateTime(Application("vDueDate"), vbShortDate) %>.
```

Keep in mind that the Lock and UnLock methods do not keep track of the permissions of users to change these variables. The specific user permissions are the responsibility of the Active Server Page code to monitor using the Session object.

UnLock Method

To release control of the locked application variables, the Application.UnLock method is used. The Application.UnLock method does not have to be explicitly called to release control of the application variables. The Application.UnLock method is implicitly called in two situations. The first situation is when the processing of a page is complete and the UnLock method has not been called. Although the Application object is available to all users and all page-level scripts, the Application OnStart and OnEnd events must occur on the same script page. If not, the OnEnd event is automatically triggered to release the Application object's control. The following code illustrates using the Lock and UnLock methods to set a database connection string and UnLock method.

```
<%
Application.Lock                                 '=== Prevent other users
➥from simultaneously modifying values
Application ("DataWidget_ConnectionString") = "DSN=datawidgets;DriverId=25;FIL=MS
Access;MaxBufferSize=512;PageTimeout=5;"
Application ("DataWidget_ConnectionTimeout") = 15
Application ("DataWidget_CommandTimeout") = 30
Application ("DataWidget_RuntimeUserName") = ""
Application ("DataWidget_RuntimePassword") = ""
Application.UnLock                               '=== Explicitly declared
%>

This application uses the
<%= Application(" DataWidget_ConnectionString ") %> Database Connection.
```

If the UnLock method was not explicitly declared, the Web server would automatically release control of the Application object from the specific user session when the page was finished processing.

The second situation where UnLock is called is when the script processing for a page times out. The Web server monitors the amount of time allocated to resource processing. The process of terminating a request due to exceeding the amount of time allotted for processing is referred to as *timing out*. Specifically, the server monitors the amount of time the specific user session is inactive and the amount of time spent processing the script embedded on the current page. When a user becomes inactive by not making any requests in a specified amount of time, the resources assigned to the individual Session object are freed, as demonstrated in Chapter 13. Likewise, if the processing of an ASP file exceeds a given amount of time to finish processing, the page processing is aborted. A Timeout error is usually an indication that it was a large processing request, a connection could not be established, or something is wrong with the current process. The server uses the Registry settings to store the timeout values and various other values critical for the Active Server Pages to function properly. The page-level timeout value is stored in the ScriptTimeOut of the ASP Registry settings or in the IIS MetaDatabase. The default page-level script timeout value is 90 seconds.

Using Components at the Application Level

Variable manipulation at the application level is only half of the benefit of using the Application object. The second benefit of using the Application object is the capability to connect to ActiveX objects that have application-level scope. ActiveX objects enable you to connect into registered server-side automation object, such as e-mail, workflow, and database systems. For example, you can use a single database connection for an entire application by creating the database connection as an application-level object.

Instantiating Application-Level Objects

Application-level objects have many of the same characteristics that are common to application-level variables. However, you are not limited to only using variables at the application level, you can also create automation objects that have application-level scope. This enables you to create a global instance of the object and enable multiple user sessions to have access to the Application object.

Object declarations can have three different scoping levels. The first two scoping levels, the application- and session-level objects, can only be created in the GLOBAL.ASA file. You can create a reference to an automation object by embedding the unique class identifier either by the ProgID or the ClassID within the object tag. The ProgID represents the registered name of the object. The ClassID refers to the registered class number of the object. To create a server-side object, use the following syntax:

```
<OBJECT RUNAT = Server SCOPE = Scope ID = Identifier PROGID = "progID"¦CLASSID
="ClassID">
</OBJECT>
```

where *Scope* identifies the object's lifetime and *ID* identifies the object's instantiated name. The scope of the object can either be "Application" to specify an application-level object scope, "Session" to specify a session-level object, or "Page" or left blank to specify a page-level object. Using the existing objects that ship with the Active Server will be covered in greater detail in Chapter 17, "Implementing Existing Server-Side Components."

```
<OBJECT RUNAT = Server SCOPE = Scope ID = Identifier PROGID = "progID"¦CLASSID
="ClassID">
```

To create an application-level object, two steps are necessary. The first is to specify the scope of the object to "Application". The second step is to embed the <OBJECT> tag in the GLOBAL.ASA file. The <OBJECT> tag must be placed *outside* the <SCRIPT> and </SCRIPT> tags used to define the GLOBAL.ASA file. If an <OBJECT> tag or any other tag is found between the <SCRIPT> tags, the script interpreter will try to process the <OBJECT> tags and consequently generate an error. This <SCRIPT> and <OBJECT> tag layout is illustrated in the following code:

```
<SCRIPT LANGUAGE="VBScript" RUNAT="Server">
Sub Application_OnStart
        '=== Application Level events and object placed here
End Sub

Application_OnStart
</SCRIPT>

<OBJECT RUNAT = Server SCOPE = Application
ID = MyAdrot PROGID = "MSWC.AdRotator">
</OBJECT>

<OBJECT RUNAT=Server SCOPE=Application ID=MyDataConn
PROGID="RemoteConn.DataConn">
</OBJECT>
```

In the preceding example, two components are declared to have application scope in the GLOBAL.ASA file. The first object, the AdRotator Component, is a component that ships with the Internet Information Server that rotates advertising banners on Web pages. This component is covered in more detail in Chapter 17. The second component is a custom created component that is used to ensure that a data connection exists between two remote offices. The ID descriptor of the Object tag specifies the name of the Application object that will be referenced by calling ASP code. This example uses the registered name to specify the type of identifier needed to instantiate this object on the Web server. For more information on the specifics of using objects in Active Server Pages, please see Chapter 10.

The application-level object can now be accessed from any ASP in the application by using the ID name of the object. The following example displays a new banner on the page by calling the GetAdvertisement method of the AdRotator Component and checking the existence of a live connection between remote offices by using the CheckDataConnection method of the MyDataConn component. This capability to call the Application object from any page prevents the server from having to create a new instance of the component on every page where the component's functionality is needed.

```
<%
Dim ScheduleFilePath, adrot
ScheduleFilePath="datawidgetswarehouse.txt"
Response.Write adrot.GetAdvertisement(ScheduleFilePath)

bConnectionResult = MyDataConn.CheckDataConnection("Dallas")
If bConnectionResult then
     ret = MyDataConn.TransferData('Inventory')
Else
     ret = MyDataConn.CheckDataConnection("Reston")
End If
%>
```

Part
III

Ch
11

Then, using VBScript's `If...Then` logic, if the connection is valid, the `TransferData` method of the `MyDataConn` method is executed to transfer inventory information to the Dallas office. To learn more about creating your own Active components, please see Chapter 18, "Creating Your Own Active Server Components."

Using Arrays at the Application Level

Another useful application-level variable is the array. Arrays provide a centralized location to help organize and contain variables that are logically grouped. Arrays can be created at either the application, session, or page levels. Arrays are useful because they can be passed between pages as variables provided that they are declared as an application- or session-level variable.

Using application-level arrays is a more efficient way to provide information to an entire application. Application arrays are best used to contain commonly accessed groups of information that would usually require constant interaction or external calls. For example, if you are designing a training registration scheduling service and need to display the list of training classes offered, an application-level array would be a good way of storing this information and making it available to all pages in your ASP application. Because this is static information, populating an array once from a database conserves resources and processing power and saves you from having to make a database call for every request. The following code populates the array in the `Application_OnStart` event of the `GLOBAL.ASA` file.

Listing 11.2   Populating an application-level array.

```
<SCRIPT LANGUAGE="VBScript" RUNAT="Server">

Sub Application_OnStart
    Dim aMyAppTraining(4)                            '=== Creates a
➥fixed size array
    aMyAppTraining (1)="Using Active Server Pages"   '=== Starts
➥assigning array
    aMyAppTraining (2)="Internet Architecture: The Basics"
    aMyAppTraining (3)="Content Management"
    aMyAppTraining (4)="Internet Application WorkFlow"
     Application("aTraining")= aMyAppTraining        '=== Assigns
➥Application variable
End Sub

Sub Session_OnStart
End Sub

Sub Session_OnEnd
End Sub

Sub Application_OnEnd
End Sub


</SCRIPT>
```

The Dim statement in this example declares a static length array, in this situation of size 4. (Remember that arrays are now one-based instead of the traditional 0-based arrays.) The aMyAppTraining array is then populated with the available training classes. After the array is loaded with information, an application-level variable named aTraining is created and loaded with the new populated training array.

After this array is loaded as an application variable, the array can be referenced and manipulated from any ASP page. To retrieve a local reference to the training class array, simply create a reference to the array by referring to the application variable where it was stored.

```
<%
Dim aLocalTrainingArray
aLocalTrainingArray = Application("aTraining")
%>
```

At this point, the variable aLocalTrainingArray is only a local array. Therefore, any changes to this array will exist only within this page. For example, you can overwrite the local array values by reassigning a local array element. However, that change, as well as the local reference to the array, will be destroyed after the page is finished processing.

```
aLocalTrainingArray (4)="My New Class"
```

Once this is accomplished, the array can be processed as any other local array. For example, to determine how many elements exist in the array, use the VBScript Ubound function. The following code populates the variable iClass with the total amount of classes available.

```
<%
iClass= Ubound(aLocalTrainingArray)
%>
```

The number of classes in the array will then be used to cycle through the array and write to the page. To cycle through the array, a For...Next loop is used to iterate through each array item. Once the new item is reached, the array value is written to the page using the Response object and the array index.

```
<%
For i = 1 to iClass
     Response.Write(aLocalTrainingArray (i) & "<BR>")
Next
%>
```

Notice that the For...Next loop could have used the following syntax to produce the same results.

```
<%
For i = 1 to Ubound(aLocalTrainingArray)
     Response.Write(aLocalTrainingArray (i) & "<BR>")
Next
%>
```

However, as the development application model moves back toward the server-centric environment, optimizing your code to be efficient is very important. Using the preceding code listing requires the upper bound of the array to be calculated every time to loop iterates. A better use of processing power would only calculate the upper bound of the array once and then use that variable in the For...Next loop.

The application-level arrays should only be used with information that is basically static. However, you can also use dynamic arrays in the Application and Session objects. For example, a dynamic training class array could have been declared using the following code:

```
Sub Application_OnStart
        Dim aMyAppTraining()                              '=== Creates a dynamic
➥array
        Redim aMyAppTraining (4)                          '=== Allocates temporary
➥storage space
        aMyAppTraining (1) = "Using Active Server Pages"
        aMyAppTraining (2) = "Internet Architecture: The Basics"
        aMyAppTraining (3) = "Content Management"
        aMyAppTraining (4) = "Internet Application WorkFlow"
        Application("aTraining") = aMyAppTraining         '=== Assigns Application
➥variable
End Sub
```

The following code listing puts the GLOBAL.ASA file and the calling ASP code together in one reference point:

```
===================================    The Global.ASA File =====================
<SCRIPT LANGUAGE="VBScript" RUNAT="Server">

Sub Application_OnStart
    Dim aMyAppTraining(4)                                 '=== Creates a fixed size
array
    aMyAppTraining (1)="Using Active Server Pages"
    aMyAppTraining (2)="Internet Basics"
    aMyAppTraining (3)="Content Management"
    aMyAppTraining (4)="Internet Application WorkFlow"
    Application("aTraining")= aMyAppTraining              '=== Loads local
array into Application object

    Application("LastDisplayedOn") = Now                  '=== Sets an Application
variable
End Sub

</SCRIPT>
===================================    The Calling ASP code ==================
<%@ LANGUAGE="VBSCRIPT" %>
<html>

<head>
<title>Reading the Application Array                      </title>
</head>

<body bgcolor="#FFFFFF">

<p><font face = "Arial"><b>Ask about special group rates for the
following classes:</b><br>
<%
```

```
if IsArray(Application("aTraining")) then
aLocalTrainingArray = Application("aTraining")
iClass = UBound(aLocalTrainingArray)
For i = 1 to iClass
      Response.Write(aLocalTrainingArray(i) & "<BR>")
Next
else
      Response.Write ("Bad array")
End if
%>
</font></p>
<BR>Last viewed somewhere at: <% Response.Write Application("LastDisplayedOn") %>
<%
Application.Lock
Application("LastDisplayedOn") = Now
Application.UnLock
%>
</body>
</html>
```

The previous code listing loads the training class array into memory and displays the results on a Web page. The GLOBAL.ASA file also sets an application array LastDisplayedOn, which is updated every time a user browses this site, by using the Lock and UnLock methods. Figure 11.2 demonstrates the results of this code listing.

FIG. 11.2
The Application object stores the array of classes in memory, which enables any client to access the information.

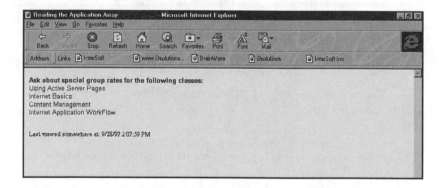

Remember in the above example that the application array is only loaded on the Application_OnStart event. If the information changes more frequently than the Application_OnStart event, you may want to consider another object variable that is more closely related to the needed frequency period.

You can also populate your application-level arrays from a database. The Amazing DataWidget Web Site demonstrates this technique as shown in Chapter 32, "Putting It All Together: Creating an N-Tier Online Catalog Application." This example chapter combines using the Application and Session objects to load, create, and manipulate static arrays and database-driven arrays to create an online catalog system.

Part
III

Ch
11

The *Application* Collection

The Application object, like all the ASP objects, uses collections to help manage all objects that have been given application scope. The Application object uses two collections, as shown in Table 11.3.

Table 11.3   The *Application* Object's Collections

Name	Description
Contents	Identifies Application object declared without the <OBJECT> tag.
StaticObjects	Identifies Application object declared with the <OBJECT> tag.

The *Contents* Collection

The Contents collection is used to contain all items that have been created during a session that have not been declared with the <OBJECT> tag. The Contents collection requires the following syntax:

```
Session.Contents(Key)
```

where Key is the name of the property to retrieve. The Contents collection manages all application-level variables declared through a user session across all pages. For example, in the following code listing, application variables have been declared in the GLOBAL.ASA file.

```
Application("aTraining")= aLocalTrainingArray       '=== Application object
Application("LastDisplayedOn")
```

The Contents collection can then reference these variables by using the required syntax, as shown below:

```
<%
Response.Write(Application.Contents("aTraining"))
Response.Write(Application.Contents("LastDisplayedOn"))
%>
```

A more useful approach to using collections is to iterate through the collection to obtain a list of all application-level variables. You can loop through the collection to determine whether a variable has been declared using a For...Next loop. For example, the following code demonstrates how to loop through all the Application.Contents objects:

```
<%
  For Each Key in Application.Contents
      Response.Write Key & "<BR>"
  Next %>
%>
```

This code will iterate through the current Contents items to display the following list:

```
ATRAINING
LASTDISPLAYEDON
```

The *StaticObject* Collection

The StaticObject collection is similar to the Contents collection, but StaticObject is used to manage all session-level objects that have been declared with the <OBJECT> tag. The StaticObject collection uses the following syntax:

```
Application.StaticObjects(Key)
```

where *Key* is the property to retrieve.

The StaticObject collection can also be used to reference an application variable or multiple application variables. For example, consider the following GLOBAL.ASA file, which declares ADO and Ad Rotator application objects and loads an application-level array:

```
<SCRIPT LANGUAGE="VBScript" RUNAT="Server">

Sub Application_OnStart
    Dim aMyAppTraining (4)                      '=== Creates a fixed size array
    aMyAppTraining (1)="Using Active Server Pages"
    aMyAppTraining (2)="Internet Basics"
    aMyAppTraining (3)="Content Management"
    aMyAppTraining (4)="Internet Application WorkFlow"
    Application("aTraining")= aMyAppTraining             '=== Loads Applica-
➥tion array variable

    Application("LastDisplayedOn")=Now          '=== Create Application variable
End Sub

</SCRIPT>


===============    Create Application Level Database Connection   ===============
<OBJECT
RUNAT = Server
SCOPE = Application
ID = MyDBConnection
PROGID = "ADODB.Connection">
</OBJECT>


===============    Create Application Level Advertisement Rotator   =============
<OBJECT
RUNAT = Server
SCOPE = Application
ID = MyAdrot
PROGID = "MSWC.AdRotator">
</OBJECT>
```

To list all items in the StaticObject collection, use the For...Next loop to step through the <OBJECT> collection, as shown below:

```
<%
For Each Key In Application.StaticObjects
    Response.Write(Key & "<BR>")
Next
%>
```

Part

III

Ch

11

This iterative process will write the names of the Application objects, shown below, to the page:

```
MyAd
MyConnection
```

From Here...

At this point, you can see that the Application object provides a manageable means to distribute information to all users in the ASP application. The Application object also provides variable management by using the Lock and UnLock methods. This chapter also demonstrated how to use the OnStart and OnEnd events to initialize and close your application.

The following chapters focus on using the Application object and VBScript knowledge to demonstrate how to use the remaining ASP objects to create your Web applications. The next four chapters are each dedicated to learning how to fully exploit the Session, Request, Response, and Server objects.

- Chapter 12, "Controlling the Server with the Server Object and Using Transaction Processing with the ObjectContext Object," discusses how the Active Server encapsulates the HTTP service to control administrative function on the Web server.

- Chapter 13, "Managing the User Session: The Session Object," illustrates the nuances of tracking a user through an ASP application.

- Chapter 14, "Speaking to the Web Client: The Response Collection," explains how the Response object communicates with the requesting Web client.

- Chapter 15, "Retrieving User Information: The Request Object," describes how to gather information from the user using forms, hidden fields, and cookies.

- Chapter 17, "Implementing Existing Server-Side Components," illustrates how to use the various components that ship with IIS and Active Server Pages to provide rich functionality to your applications.

- Chapter 26, "Putting It All Together: Creating a Dynamic Database Application," illustrates how to use the Application object to store information extracted from a database to provide database interaction for the Amazing DataWidget WareHouse.

- Chapter 32, "Putting It All Together: Creating an N-Tier Online Catalog Application," demonstrates how to build ActiveX components to create n-tier distributed applications for the Amazing DataWidget WareHouse Catalog.

Controlling the Server with the *Server* Object and Using Transaction Processing with the *ObjectContext* Object

Expanding the Server

Exploit one of the most exciting features of ASP and IIS by using the *CreateObject* method to add external functionality to your HTML pages.

Using Encoding Techniques and Directory Utilities

Learn how to use URL and HTML encoding techniques to control the text-based HTML output from the HTTP server and implement the *MapPath* method to manipulate files on your Web server for Server-Side Includes (SSI) or text-based capabilities.

Regulating Server Properties

Learn how to control the amount of processing time allowed for Active Server Page scripts.

The Server object is an ASP object that is used to control administrative features of the IIS Web server and actions that deal with HTTP service. The Server object provides the capability to create instances of Component Object Model (COM) based components on the server. This presents exciting possibilities to use the IIS Web server as a translator between external clients and internal systems. This capability to provide access to numerous internal systems through ASP with additional server-side directives, such as file mappings and encoding techniques, presents unlimited possibilities for your ASP applications. ■

Controlling the *Server* Object Using Methods

The Server object is one of the six built-in objects that are provided with Active Server Pages and IIS 4.0. The Server object represents a programmable interface to the HTTP service that provides a mechanism to administer and control the Web server that is traditionally found only through the proprietary HTTP server native interfaces. The Server object is used to expose the properties and methods of the HTTP server. Although the capability to control the HTTP functions is a valuable resource, one of the most exciting and most powerful components of the IIS server is its capability to create instances of the components on the server.

The Server object is referenced using the following syntax:

`Server.Method/Property`

where Server is the Active Server object.

The Server object uses four methods to control various aspects of the Web server, as shown in Table 12.1.

Table 12.1   The *Server* Object's Methods

Method	Description
CreateObject	Creates a Server instance of an object.
MapPath	Translates the Web server's virtual path settings to the physical path on the server.
HTMLEncode	Utilizes HTML encoding to deliver text to browser.
URLEncode	Utilizes URL encoding techniques.

The CreateObject method enables the Web server to create instances of components running on the server. This capability to create links to other systems or embedded application logic gives tremendous programming functionality to the Web server. The MapPath method is used to map the virtual settings of the Web server to physical path settings. The Server object can also provide encoding techniques, using the HTMLEncode and the URLEncode methods, to ensure that information is properly transferred between the Web server and the requesting client.

Expanding the Web Server with the *CreateObject* Method

Perhaps one of the most exciting features of Active Server Pages is the capability to create an instance of an ActiveX object. This capability to tap into ActiveX objects provides a virtually endless number of ways to deliver information to any Web client that were once only available to proprietary client software or dedicated network connections. The Server object acts as a translator between the in-house data and information stores and virtually any Web browser.

The capability of the Web server to provide a bridge between remote users and centralized network stores is made possible by the CreateObject method. The CreateObject method creates a connection to an instance of an ActiveX object. This connection mechanism is based on the Common Object Model (COM). COM provides the standard for objects to communicate with one another. An *ActiveX Automation Server* refers to the capability for one COM object to interact or activate another object's properties, methods, and events. The IIS `Server` object uses this communication mechanism to create a new instance of an ActiveX object using the `CreateObject` method. The `CreateObject` method uses the following syntax:

```
Server.CreateObject(progID)
```

where *progID* is the class or type of object to be instantiated. The `progID` also requires the following special format:

```
appname.objecttype
```

where *appname* is the application name hosting the object, and *objecttype* is the class or type of the object to create. All COM-based objects are required to have one class type per application name.

The `CreateObject` method provides the foundation for accessing ActiveX components. The Active Server ships with five components that can be used immediately: Database Object, Ad Rotator, Browser Component, Content Streaming Component, and the Server-Side Includes (SSI) Component. These components will be fully discussed in Chapter 17, "Implementing Existing Server-Side Components." However, as an example here, the following code demonstrates using the `CreateObject` method to create an instance of the Browser Component. The Browser Component is used to determine what type of browser is requesting pages from a Web site. Some sites might be specially designed to maximize the capabilities of a specific browser type. Determining the requesting browser type has traditionally been accomplished using client-side JavaScript, but now it can be accomplished using the Browser Component.

```
Set BrowserType = Server.CreateObject("MSWC.BrowserType")
```

Notice the use of the `Set` keyword in the preceding code snippet. The `Set` keyword is required because the `CreateObject` function returns a pointer to the created object. To use the methods and properties of the object, simply reference the object in any ASP file. For example, to determine whether the requesting browser is ActiveX compatible, use the Boolean `ActiveX Controls` property of the Browser Component. In this situation, if the client is capable of using client-side ActiveX controls, the function `LoadActiveXControls` is initiated. If the requesting browser does not support ActiveX controls, the `LoadHTMLOnly` procedure is called.

```
<%
If BrowserType.ActiveXControls Then
    Call LoadActiveXControls()
Else
    Call LoadHTMLOnlyVersion()
End if
%>
```

You can also access the object's built-in methods. For example, the Ad Rotator Component that ships with IIS and Active Server Pages uses a method called `GetAdvertisement`. The `GetAdvertisement` method is responsible for retrieving information from a scheduling file that is used to display images on the Web page and route the user to the appropriate page. In this example, the `GetAdvertisement` method is used to retrieve sale price information from a file located in the `salesprices` virtual directory in a file called `specials.txt`. Remember that the virtual directory acts as a container for your ASP applications and is used as an alias to hide the physical directory structure of your Web server. For more information on virtual directories, please see Chapter 10, "The Composition of an Active Server Application."

```
<%= ad.GetAdvertisement("/saleprices/specials.txt") %>
```

The `CreateObject` method only creates objects that have page-level application scope. This limited scope object is unlike the objects that were created in the `GLOBAL.ASA` that could either have application- or session-level scope. Because the local objects only have page-level scope, the objects are destroyed when the page is finished processing. If you need to access the same component multiple times, in most situations you would benefit from using an application- or session-level object. Creating an object once reduces the overhead required to constantly create and destroy the object. If you have further questions about using application-level variables, objects, or arrays, see Chapter 11, "Controlling the Application: The `Application` Object," for more information.

Managing Server Information with *MapPath*

The `Server` object uses the `MapPath` method to track and manage path information on the server. The path information acts as a translator between the virtual or relative directories of the Web server to the physical directories on the server. The `MapPath` method requires the following syntax:

```
Server.MapPath(path)
```

where `Server` is the Active Server object and *path* is a physical or virtual directory.

The `MapPath` method is primarily used to help manage the underlying file system of the Web server. It is particularly useful when you consider that the Internet itself is based on a text-based delivery system that passes files from location to location. Organizing the massive number of files is not an easy task, and gathering and organizing the files into various directories will help you in terms of structure and sanity. However, programming the ASP to find files in various physical and virtual directories is often a daunting task. To eliminate broken links and missing files, the `MapPath` method helps with ASP file management.

In most situations, you will use the `MapPath` method and other `server` variables to provide virtual path information needed for hyperlinks or `Include` statements. But before the combination of the `MapPath` method and the different `server` variables is discussed, let's investigate the details of the `Path` statement.

The `MapPath` method provides the link between the virtual paths and the physical paths on the Web server through the `Path` statement. The `Path` statement represents the directory structure, whether the file structure is virtual or physical, that you want to specify. There are two basic rules to remember with the `Path` arguments.

- `Path` arguments that start with a backslash (\) or a forward slash (/) are used to represent virtual directories.
- `Path` arguments that do not start with the backslash or forward slash represent relative directories.

The `Path` statement is used to give a directory location relative to either the virtual directory or physical directory. The `Path` statement uses the backslash (\) and forward slash (/) to tell the `Server` object to use virtual directories. For example, to map a path to the `scripts` virtual directory, use the following statement:

```
<% = Server.MapPath("\Scripts")%>          '=== Returns 'C:\InetPub\Scripts'
```

The previous code example demonstrates the role of the `MapPath` to associate the virtual directory managed by the Web server with the physical directory structure managed by the operating system. In this situation, the `MapPath` statement explicitly defines the physical location `C:\InetPub\Scripts` from the virtual directory `\Scripts`. When the forward slash is used in the `Path` argument, the server processes the request in the same manner, treating it as a virtual directory.

```
<% = Server.MapPath("/Scripts")%>     '=== Returns 'C:\InetPub\Script'
```

Furthermore, if just the backslash or the forward slash were used in the `MapPath` method, the root directory of the Web server would be returned:

```
<% = Server.MapPath("/")%>      '===Returns 'C:\InetPub\wwwroot'
<% = Server.MapPath("\")%>      '===Returns 'C:\InetPub\wwwroot'
```

The `MapPath` statement is also used to manipulate relative paths by excluding the forward or backslash characters. For example, if just the word "scripts" is represented as the `Path` argument, the server would return results of apparent creation of a directory from where the ASP file was executed. In the following situation, the ASP file was run in the `Sales` directory.

```
<% = Server.MapPath("Scripts")%>     '=== Returns
➥'C:\InetPub\wwwroot\Sales\Scripts'
```

The reason the word *apparent* is used to describe the return result of the previous listed `MapPath` statement is because the `MapPath` statement does not create a non-existent directory or return an error if the directory does not exist. The `MapPath` statement simply finds the current execution directory and adds the `Path` value to it.

If the `Path` argument is excluded or contains a zero-length string, the `MapPath` method returns an error:

```
<% = Server.MapPath( )%>          '=== Returns a Wrong number of arguments Error
<% = Server.MapPath("")%>         '=== Returns a missing path error
```

You are prevented from directly mapping to another machine via the UNC, machine name, or IP address. If you need to map a drive to another machine, use the Internet Information Manager to manipulate virtual directories.

```
<% Response.Write Server.MapPath("\\207.96.34.41\Scripts")%>     '=== Returns an
➥'Invalid Path Character' error
```

In most situations, you will want to use the combination of the virtual directory and a filename to point to a given source document, such as a text file or HTML file. These files can include HTML files, images, or text files. For example, the following path generator produces a reference to a file called `myNewLeads.txt` in the `mySalesCalls` virtual directory.

```
<% Response.Write Server.MapPath("\mySalesCalls\myNewLeads.txt")%>
```

Part

III

Ch

12

Not only can you use the MapPath method to reference files, but you can also use it to generate paths to a Server-Side Include. The following example uses the MapPath statement to set the complete path location to retrieve information from an include file.

```
<% Response.Write Server.MapPath("/mySalesApp/FooterInfo.inc")%>
```

However, you do not have to use a fully qualified path with the MapPath method. The following example uses the MapPath method to manage the server-side path needed to create an HTML anchor link.

```
<a href = "<%= Server.MapPath("Sales")%>\Orders\OrderForm.htm" target = "frMain">
'=== Returns 'a href = "C:\InetPub\wwwroot\Sales\Orders\OrderForm.htm" target =
"frMain"'
```

This MapPath method is often used in conjunction with server variables to assign relative and virtual directory settings. One particular server variable is the PATH_INFO variable. The PATH_INFO variable returns the virtual directory path information and the page that is being called. For example, the following code extracts the path and page information from the current executing page using the Request.ServerVariables variables.

```
<% = Request.ServerVariables("PATH_INFO")%> '=== Returns '/Sales/mySales.ASP'
```

In the above situation, an ASP file named mySales.asp is executed from the Sales virtual directory. (The Request object will be covered in much greater length in Chapter 15, "Retrieving User Information: The Request Object.") You can also combine the MapPath method with the Request.ServerVariable information to meet your needs. The following example uses both the Server and Request objects to produce the full path of the calling ASP file:

```
<% = Server.MapPath(Request.ServerVariables("PATH_INFO"))%>      '=== Returns
'C:\InetPub\wwwroot\Sales\mySales.ASP'
```

Using the Server Encoding Methods

All Web technology is based on the transfer of simple text across the Internet or an intranet via the TCP/IP protocol and the translation of that text into content within the Web browser. The Web content and the information being displayed is controlled and manipulated by HTML tags. These layout tags help arrange the content on the page. Because the browser only interprets text, embedded non-ANSI characters get misinterpreted as text or simply are not available from the keyboard. As a result of this difficulty in translating text into browser characters, the Web server or browser often tries to process or write non-desired text. To prevent this confusion from occurring, encoding methods use *escape codes* to explicitly tell the client what to display by using a combination of the % character and the associated ASCII hexadecimal code or reserved code. This is particularly important when dealing with blank spaces, accented characters, punctuation, and non-ASCII characters. For example, notice the OnClick event of the following button. When the button is pressed, the browser navigates to another Web location. Because single quotes are needed to embed the desired site location, the reserved characters '&quot' are used to ensure that the embedded quotes are not misinterpreted on some clients.

```
<html>
<HEAD>
<title>Embedded Reserved Characters</title>
</HEAD>
<BODY>
    <FORM METHOD="POST">
        <INPUT LANGUAGE="VBScript"
                TYPE=button
                VALUE=" Login "
                ONCLICK="Window.location.href =
&quot;www.myWebApplication.com&quot;"
            NAME="btnLogin"
        >
    </FORM>
</BODY>
</html>
```

You can see the possible errors that may arise, particularly with ASP, due to the extensive use of the <, >, and % characters. To help prevent the misinterpretation of characters, encoding techniques—at both the HTML and URL levels—help to explicitly control characters on HTML pages and within the URL.

Using the *URLEncode* Method

The URLEncode method of the Server object is centered on delivering explicit information from the Web server to the client via the URL. Using the URL is one of the traditional ways to pass information from a Web client to the Web server. This transferring of information via the URL is usually accomplished using hyperlinks and forms. In both situations, information is passed to a file on the Web server, which processes information contained in the URL.

However, as mentioned previously, only ASCII-based characters can be sent via HTTP. If characters such as blanks and punctuation are passed, erratic and unpredictable results will occur. To ensure that all the characters entered by the user are properly passed to the server, the characters must be scanned to make sure that only known characters are being sent. For example, to use the URL encoding methods, use the following syntax:

```
Server.URLEncode(string)
```

where Server is the Server object and *string* is the string to apply the URL encoding rules.

The server-side processing uses the filename in the URL to process information that precedes the question mark (?) using the following syntax:

```
http://www.myApplication.com/processdata.asp?FieldName1=
➡FieldValue1&FieldName2=FieldValue2
```

The previous code example illustrates the calling of a file processdata.asp on the Web server www.myApplication.com to process information in the URL fields named FieldName1 and FieldName2. The file processdata.asp extracts the data from the named fields for its internal processing. In this situation, this processing file is an Active Server Page, however, this processing can also call executable or Common Gateway Interface scripts to process information.

Part
III

Ch
12

The processing of information via the URL is based on the simple field/value motif, where fields are assigned a value and are passed as a string set through the URL, as shown in the following snippet:

```
Fieldname = Fieldvalue
```

If multiple field values are used, the ampersand (&) character acts as the AND operator to concatenate the field values together.

The only problem with passing data via the URL occurs when you pass certain characters, such as blanks or formatting characters. For example, if `Fieldvalue1` contained a space, as in the name "Data Widgets Inc.," the processing page would only accept the "Data" section of the value, because the HTTP text stream has been interrupted by a non-ASCII character and it stops processing the assignment of that value. To enable a continuous text stream of information to the browser, the plus character (+) is used to replace the blank spaces. There are several other instances where the passed data must be modified to transfer data. However, the URLEncode method makes data transfer via the URL much easier. The URLEncode method performs the following processes to the data:

- Spaces are transformed into plus (+) symbols.
- Fields are left unencoded.
- An unencoded equal sign assigns an unencoded field name with the data value.
- Non-ASCII characters are transformed into escape codes.

One of the most common places where URL encoding is implemented is in link navigation or forms-based processing. Link navigation is often used to list information, and it provides drill-down capabilities on each link. This type of situation is most often implemented in database parent–child relationships, where information such as customer names is displayed in a list. If you click the customer name in the list, the customer name is passed via the URL to find the customer details, such as shipping and contact information. The URLEncode method automatically applies the encoding rules to ensure that information is properly passed in the URL.

For example, suppose you want to pass the string `"Dave's #1 Fan"` via the URL. You can see two potential problems with the string: the existence of formatting characters and blank spaces. To successfully pass this entire string to a calling page when the user clicks a hyperlink, apply the URLEncode method as shown in the following code:

```
<a href="urlencodeServer.asp?txtInput=<% =Server.URLEncode("Dave's #1 Fan")
➥%>">Send info via a link</a>
```

The URLEncode method converts the string `"Dave's #1 Fan"` into HTML source code that the Web browser interprets to be the following:

```
<a href="urlencodeServer.asp?txtInput=Dave%27s+%231+Fan">Send info via a link</a>
```

Now, to complete the cycle, the requesting page can accept the entire string `"Dave's #1 Fan,"` formatting characters and blank spaces, into the field named `txtInput`.

Using the *HTMLEncode* Method

The HTMLEncode method is used by the server to explicitly define the characters to be displayed to a page. This method plays an important role in ensuring that information is properly displayed on the Web page. To use the HTMLEncode feature, use the following syntax:

```
Server.HTMLEncode(string)
```

where Server is the Server object and *string* is the string to encode.

The HTMLEncode method is important to ensure that the proper characters are displayed on the page and not processed by the server. For example, if you are preparing an online class on Active Server Pages and need to display HTML and ASP syntax on your pages, the HTMLEncode feature would be helpful to present the code instead of executing the code. If you want to display the syntax for creating an HTML table that was 100-percent wide, you would want to display, but not execute, the <Table Width = 100%> syntax. To accomplish this, use the HTMLEncode method as seen below:

```
<% =Server.HTMLEncode("<Table Width='100%'>") %>
```

If you view the source code at the browser, you will notice that the previous code was interpreted as the following:

```
&lt;Table Width='100%'&gt;
```

The same process is directly applicable to ASP syntax. For example, if you want to display the syntax for the Session.Abandon method and you write the correct syntax—<% Session.Abandon %>—on the ASP source page, when the page executes your Session object will be destroyed. Using the HTMLEncode method ensures that escape sequences are properly inserted for any character that might be misinterpreted as execution characters.

```
<%= Server.HTMLEncode("<% Session.Abandon % >") %>
```

The Server.HTMLEncode method translated the greater than and less than (> and <) symbols into &lt and &gt characters.

```
&lt;% Session.Abandon % &gt;
```

This encoding technique is more suitable when applied to ensure the proper data transfer of information from the Web server to the browser, particularly when you are writing information from a database. For example, you can use the same encoding technique to retrieve values from a database RecordSet object. In the following situation, the HTMLEncode method is applied to write the "CompanyName" field to the ASP page.

```
<%Response.Write Server.HTMLEncode(rs.Fields("CompanyName").Value)%>
```

The *Server* Object Properties

The Server object has only one property, as shown in Table 12.2. The ScriptTimeout is used to set the amount of time the Server will process the ASP script before terminating the request.

Part

III

Ch

12

Table 12.2   The *Server* Object's Property

Method	Description
ScriptTimeout	Sets or retrieves the maximum amount of seconds the server will process the ASP.

The ScriptTimeout property is a property of the Server object that prevents a process from running endlessly. Without a limitation to control how long a process is allowed to stay alive, run-away threads can consume large amounts of system resources and leave the requesting browser waiting endlessly for a response. A ScriptTimeout event indicates that something has gone wrong within the ASP code or something has gone wrong with an external call to an instantiated object.

In either case, the Server object relies on the ScriptTimeout property to prevent the situation from happening. The ScriptTimeout property sets the timeout values at both the server level and the page level. The default script timeout value for all Active Server Pages is stored in the ScriptTimeout Registry in IIS 3.0 or the Metabase in IIS 4.0. The default timeout value for script processing is 90 seconds. If a ScriptTimeout event occurs, a Timeout event is written to the event log of the Web server.

The script timeout setting can also be controlled on the individual ASP. This page-level control is used to override the default timeout value indicated in the Registry. Just as the default scripting language can be overridden at the page level, the same capability exists for the timeout value. The ScriptTimeout value requires the following syntax:

```
Server.ScriptTimeout = Seconds
```

where *Seconds* indicates the number of seconds allotted for page-level scripting to process.

After this amount of time has been reached, the Server object stops processing the script and writes an event to the event log. To determine the timeout value for your server, use the following code:

```
<% Response.Write Server.ScriptTimeout %>
```

If the default settings are still in place, the code should return 90.

For example, the following code overrides the default timeout value by setting the page-level timeout to 20 seconds and generating an infinite loop to trigger the ASP Timeout event.

```
<%
Server.ScriptTimeout = 20
dim iCount
iCount = 0

Do While iCount < 10
     If iCount = 9 Then
         iCount = 1
     End If
     iCount = iCount +1
Loop
%>
```

After the script times out, an `ASP 0113 Script Timed Out` error displays the following message to the user:

```
error 'ASP 0113'
```

```
Script timed out
```

```
/TimeOutExample.asp
```

```
The maximum amount of time for a script to execute was exceeded. You can change
this limit by specifying a new value for the property Server.ScriptTimeOut or by
changing the value for ScriptTimeout in the registry.
```

At the same time, the Web server log file also records and describes the error:

```
207.96.34.41, -, 7/3/97, 21:58:52, W3SVC, [Server Info] /TimeOutExample.asp,
¦ASP¦-¦ASP 0113¦Script timed out
```

The location of your Web server log can be found on the Logging tab of the Internet Server Manager. The logs can be written to a text file or written to an ODBC-compliant database.

Using the *ObjectContext* Object for ASP Transaction Processing

With the Internet Information Server 4.0, Active Server Pages have a direct interface to controlling components in the Microsoft Transaction Server. This interface is made possible through the `ObjectContext` object. The `ObjectContext` is used to help manage and define the conditions of an instantiated object managed by the Microsoft Transaction Server (MTS). These conditions are used to help identify properties of the object, such as what process created the object or when is the unit of work complete. The context properties are used by the Microsoft Transaction Server (MTS) to allocate resources to the instantiated object. To support transaction processing in your ASP, both of the components managed by MTS and the ASP must be properly configured.

Configuring the MTS components

The MTS manages components by setting four transaction properties, as shown in Table 12.3. These properties enable you to configure different levels of transaction support.

Part

III

Ch

12

Table 12.3   The MTS Component Properties

Property	Description
`Requires a transaction`	Sets the component object to execute within the scope of the transaction.
`Requires a new transaction`	Sets the component object to execute only within its own transaction.

continues

Table 12.3 Continued	
Property	**Description**
Support transactions	Sets the component object to execute within the scope of the client's transactions.
Does not support transactions	Sets the object, does not run within a transaction.

In order to use transaction-level processing, the Components property must be set to either Requires a transaction, Requires a new transaction, or Support transactions. For more details on how to create your own customized components, please see Chapter 18, "Creating Your Own Active Server Components." For more information on setting up and configuring MTS to manage your components, please see Chapter 28, "Working with the Microsoft Transaction Server."

Setting Up ASP to Support Transactions

Active Server Pages use the Transaction directive to initiate page-level transactional processing. When the scripting engine processes this directive, the Active Server Page is executed as a transaction on the Transaction Server. To initiate your page as a transaction, use the following directive syntax in the first line of your ASP:

```
<%@ Transaction = Required %>
```

This interaction between the Web server and the MTS enables direct commit and rollback of an MTS object directly from an Active Server Page. Now your application logic can be consolidated in an Active Server Page, while core-processing functionality is left to the MTS components.

N O T E A transaction cannot occur over multiple Active Server Pages; as a result, MTS components should not be stored in Application or Session objects. ■

Controlling Success and Failure with Methods

The ObjectContext is used to identify when that object transaction is complete. In addition, you can control the object's completed task by immediately accepting its results, temporarily delaying the results, or completely rejecting the object's work. This capability to control whether or not the object's work is accepted is made possible through the SetComplete and SetAbort methods, as shown in Table 12.4.

Table 12.4 The *ObjectContext* Methods	
Method	**Description**
SetComplete	Sets the work of an object as a success and permanently accepts the changes to the resource.

Method	Description
SetAbort	Sets the work of an object as a failure and returns the resource to it original state, neglecting any changes made to the resource.

The *SetComplete* Method

The SetComplete method is used to commit an MTS object's transaction as a success. The changes made by the object method on a resource are permanently committed. To accept changes made by object, use the following syntax:

```
ObjectContext.SetComplete
```

For example, assume that an MTS object is used to transfer funds from a credit table into a debit table, as portrayed in the following example:

```
<%@Transaction = Required
Set AccountTransfer = Server.CreateObject("myCompany.AccountProcessing")
If AccountTransfer.MoveFunds("Credit", "Debit", "300000") then
    '=== Transfer of funds was successful
    ObjectContext.SetComplete
Else
    '=== Failure, Send transaction fee for wasting packets
    ObjectContext.SetAbort
End if
%>
```

In this example, if the transfer of $300,000 is successful from the Credit account to the Debit account, the SetComplete method finalizes this transfer of funds. However, if the funds were not available, the transaction is rolled back to its original state.

After the SetComplete method is executed, the OnTransctionCommit event, if available, is processed on the script. If the subroutine is not available, the Active Server Page continues processing the script.

The *SetAbort* Method

The SetAbort Method is used to roll back changes as a result of an object method. When the SetAbort method is called, the object rejects the completed work and returns the transaction back to its original state. To reject changes made by the MTS object, use the following syntax:

```
ObjectContext.SetAbort
```

The previous example demonstrated the use of the SetAbort method to roll back transactions made by an MTS object.

After the SetAbort method is executed, the OnTransactionAbort event, if available, is processed on the script. If the subroutine is not available, the Active Server Page continues processing the script.

Trapping the *ObjectContext*'s Events

The ObjectContext has two events that are triggered after the ObjectContext's methods are executed, as seen in Table 12.5. The OnTransactionCommit event is triggered after the SetComplete method. The OnTransactionAbort event is triggered after the SetAbort method is called.

Table 12.5 The *ObjectContext*'s Events

Event	Description
OnTransactionCommit	Event triggered after the ObjectContext.SetComplete method is executed.
OnTransactionAbort	Event triggered after the ObjectContext.SetAbort method is executed.

OnTransactionCommit Event

The ObjectContext object SetComplete method triggers the OnTransactionCommit event. When the SetComplete method is processed, the script will process the OnTransactionCommit subroutine. The simplest example using the OnTransactionCommit event is demonstrated below:

```
<%@TRANSACTION = Required %>
<%
Sub OnTransactionCommit()
    Dim strMessage
    strMessage ="This was generated by executing the SetComplete method "
    strMessage = strMessage & "to trigger the OnTransactionCommit event"
    Response.Write strMessage
End Sub
%>
<HTML>
<HEAD>
<TITLE>Set Complete</TITLE>
</HEAD>
<BODY>

<%
ObjectContext.SetComplete
%>

</BODY>
</HTML>
```

The example initiates transaction processing using the TRANSACTION = Required directive and executes the SetComplete method to trigger the OnTransactionCommit() event. In this example, the OnTransactionCommit subroutine writes the following text to the page:

```
This text message was generated by executing the SetComplete method to trigger
the OnTransactionCommit event
```

Of course, you are not limited to just writing messages to the page. For example, the following example uses a custom-created ActiveX control to transfer account data.

```
<%@TRANSACTION = Required LANGUAGE="VBScript"
Sub OnTransactionCommit()
    Response.Redirect "CreateVirutalReceipt.ASP"
End Sub
Sub OnTransactionAbort()
    Response.Redirect "InsufficientFunds.ASP"
End Sub

Set AccountTransfer = Server.CreateObject("myCompany.AccountProcessing")
If AccountTransfer.MoveFunds("Credit", "Debit", "300000") Then
    '=== Transfer of funds was successful
    ObjectContext.SetComplete
End if
%>
```

In this code example, if funds were properly transmitted, the `ObjectContext.SetComplete` method triggers the `OnTransactionCommit()` event of the code to route the user to an ASP page called `CreateVirutalReceipt.ASP`.

OnTransactionAbort Event

Similar to its counterpart, the `OnTransactionAbort` event is triggered when the `ObjectContext` object `SetAbort` method is executed. When the `SetAbort` method is processed, the script will process the `OnTransactionCommit` event. To illustrate using the `OnTransactionAbort()` event, consider the following example:

```
<%@TRANSACTION = Required %>
<%
Sub OnTransactionAbort()
    Dim strMessage
    strMessage ="This text message was generated by executing the SetAbort
    ➥method "
    strMessage = strMessage & "to trigger the OnTransactionAbort event"
    Response.Write strMessage
End Sub
%>
<HTML>
<HEAD>
<TITLE>Set Abort</TITLE>
</HEAD>
<BODY>

<%
ObjectContext.SetAbort
%>

</BODY>
</HTML>
```

The example initiates transaction processing using the TRANSACTION = Required directive and executes the SetAbort method to trigger the OnTransactionAbort() event. In this example, the OnTransactionAbort subroutine writes the following text to the page:

This text message was generated by executing the SetAbort method to trigger the OnTransactionAbort event

Just as you saw in the OnTransactionCommit event, you can expand the role of your ActiveX components to now handle success and failures for transferring account information. The following example demonstrates using both the OnTransactionAbort() and OnTransactionCommit() events.

```
<%@Transaction = Required LANGUAGE="VBScript"
Sub OnTransactionCommit()
    Response.Redirect "CreateVirutalReceipt.ASP"
End Sub
Sub OnTransactionAbort()
    Response.Redirect "InsufficientFunds.ASP"
End Sub

Set AccountTransfer = Server.CreateObject("myCompany.AccountProcessing")
If AccountTransfer.MoveFunds("Credit", "Debit", "300000") then
    '=== Transfer of funds was successful
    ObjectContext.SetComplete
Else
    '=== Failure, Send transaction fee for wasting packets
    ObjectContext.SetAbort
End if
%>
```

The previous code example fails to properly transfer account information, the ObjectContext.SetAbort methods explicitly rolls back the transaction and executes the OnTransactionAbort() subroutine.

From Here...

In this chapter, we have covered the ASP Server object, which is used to control objects on the Web server. The CreateObject method provides capabilities to instantiate objects on the Web server to add functionality to Active Server Pages. These components, such as the Browser Capability Component and the Database Access Component, are discussed in further detail in Chapter 17, "Implementing Existing Server-Side Components." The MapPath method is used to provide an interface between the virtual and physical directory paths mappings. The Server object also uses encoding techniques to ensure that information from the Web server is properly transferred between the client and server.

For related information, please see the following chapters:

- Chapter 13, "Managing the User Session: The Session Object," illustrates the nuances of tracking a user through an ASP application.
- Chapter 15, "Retrieving User Information: The Request Object," depicts how to gather information from the user using forms, hidden fields, and cookies.

- Chapter 17, "Implementing Existing Server-Side Components," discusses the various components that ship with IIS and Active Server Pages.

- Chapter 18, "Creating Your Own Active Server Components," walks you through the tools and examples on how to create tailored functionality via custom-created components.

- Chapter 19, "Putting It All Together: Creating an Online Registration System," illustrates how to implement the different ActiveX components that ship with the Internet Information Server to create a Web site for the Amazing DataWidgets WareHouse online catalog.

Part

III

Ch

12

Managing the User Session: The *Session* Object

One of the biggest shortcomings of deploying applications over the Web is the inability to track application workflow. The connectionless protocol, HTTP 1.0, is used only to quickly send and receive ASCII-based information. Consequently, Web-based applications can rely either on continuously updating an application tracking database on the Web server or writing excessive amounts of information to client-side cookies. With the rollout of Active Server Pages, a server-side Session object combines the functionality of both of these user-tracking methods. The Session object gives cookie-based browsers a method to track user-specific information across different Active Server Pages. The user-specific information can be stored and accessed from any page in the ASP application by the individual user. This tracking mechanism stores an equivalent session fingerprint in a client-side cookie that is used to reference the actual data stored in memory on the Web server. The data, accessible to the user through the entire application, is accessible only to the specific user that created the information. This chapter discusses how to implement the different aspects of the Session object, as well as how to track user state information on browsers or networks that do not support cookies. ∎

Tracking User Workflow with Session Variables

Discover how session variables are used to store information that can be accessed from any page in your application.

Implementing the *Session* Object's Variables, Properties, and Events

Learn the specifics of the *Session* object and how to use its properties to manage the user session, and use the *OnStart* and *OnEnd* events to initialize ASP code when a new user enters your application.

Managing User Resources on the Server

Learn how to set session resources needed to control processing and resources on the Internet Information Server.

Using Session-Level Components

Discover how to use session-level objects to refer to an instantiated component across different Web pages that are limited only to a specific user.

Understanding the Session Collection

Learn how to use the *Session* collection to help manage session-level objects within your ASP application.

Using Session Variables to Track User Workflow

The Session object tries to overcome the shortcomings of developing workflow applications over a stateless protocol. By their very nature, the Web server and HTTP are used only to transfer and process discrete requests for information. Once the request is processed and the information delivered, the connection between the client and server is released. Although this "accept and release" policy provides great scalability for delivering information to a large number of requests, it presents a fatal flaw in the application development arena. The Session object provides the capability to track user information throughout an ASP application. The tracking functionality is largely based on setting a unique user ID when the Web client first enters the ASP application. That ID is then transferred back and forth between the Web client and the Web server during additional requests to monitor and track the specific user information. The stored session information is unique to the specific user and cannot be shared or accessed between the requesting users. If information needs to be shared between different users, that information should be assigned to an Application object. For more information on using the Application object, please see Chapter 11, "Controlling the Application: The Application Object."

Identifying the User

The capability to uniquely identify a user and track the user location in a Web application has been a sore spot for Web application developers. Excruciating tricks and workarounds were implemented in the past to try to overcome Web process management and browser-based navigation techniques. Even though there have been great advances in Web application development tools, the same processes of passing values through URLs, hidden fields, cookies, or databases still prevail in today's Web development environment.

The unique identification of the user and tracking user information based on a unique ID is the foundation of the ASP Session object. The Session object presents many benefits that help decrease the amount of development time required to build Web-based applications for cookie-compliant browsers. The Session object, like the Application object, enables developers to trap when the user enters and leaves an application. The Session object is created when a new user enters the ASP application. A new user is a user that does not have a Session object currently created for him.

The Session object acts as a subset of the Application object. In Chapter 11, you saw that the Application object is responsible for managing information and resources that are needed in an ASP application. As a result, when the ASP application is shut down the dependent Session object is also destroyed.

The Session object is based on using cookies to store and transfer a unique user ID between the browser client and the Web server. A *cookie* is a text file used by the Web browser to store information. This unique ID, the SessionID, is used to create and reference server-side objects specific to a particular user. If cookies are not permitted on the client browser, because of firewall issues, browser incompatibility, or desktop/network security concerns, the Session object is rendered useless. If cookies are not permitted, ASP applications can still be developed and deployed. However, most of the state tracking will have to be done through more cumbersome methods, such as using HTML hidden fields and passing information via the URL.

When a user enters the application, the ASP Server object first checks to see if the requesting user has a valid SessionID. If the SessionID is found in the requesting HTTP header, the user is identified as an active user and is able to continue in the application. The term "active" user is used to describe a user that has not left the application, either by logging out of the application or triggering a Session Timeout or Abandon method.

If a valid SessionID is not found in the HTTP header, the Server object generates a unique identifier and sends it to the browser to be stored in a temporary cookie. This identifier is needed to create a unique Server object that represents that specific user session. The purpose of the identifier is to generate an exclusive identification to tie the actions of the browser client to corresponding objects on the Web server. After the SessionID is assigned, the browser passes a unique token to identify itself and its associated server-side variables. For more information on the Server object, please see Chapter 12, "Controlling the Server with the Server Object and Using Transaction Processing with the ObjectContext Object."

> **CAUTION**
>
> Session objects are only supported on Web browsers and networks that support cookies.

The Problem with Cookies

In a cookie-friendly world, the Session object greatly helps manage tracking user state in an ASP application. However, when dealing with non-cookie–compliant browsers or networks, it is not possible to track user information via the Session object. Typically this capability to uniquely identify a user is of importance when the possibility of client impersonation might occur. This counterfeiting of a user can occur in two situations. The first is if the SessionID is captured while the data is in transit between the client and server. The second possible security violation occurs when the cookie file itself is copied from the user machine to another machine. With a valid SessionID, a potential hacker could temporarily clone himself as a valid user.

To prevent these possible security infractions, three levels of security must be addressed: access to the Web server, in-transit data security, and user verification.

N O T E To prevent security lapses:

- Use SSL to encrypt in-transit data.

- Control access and permissions using NTFS on the Web server.

- Issue digital certificates to ensure user authentication. ■

Part

III

Ch

13

Secure socket layers (SSLs) can be implemented to ensure data integrity when the information is being passed between the Web server and browser client. SSL encrypts the in-transit data between the Web server and client to prevent the packets from being easily interpreted for valuable information.

Server-side security can also be implemented by using the Windows NT File System (NTFS) security. NTFS enables you to implement security on the Web server by using user or group permissions. Furthermore, SSL client certificate authentication can be used to make the requesting client prove its identity using a *client certificate*. Once the client is proved to be trusted, a digital identification is assigned to the user. Therefore, you can require the digital certificate before allowing clients access to your application. For more information on setting security access and settings for your Web applications, see Chapter 31, "Using the Internet Information Server 4.0 to Manage Your Web Applications."

In addition to having to having to worry about firewall and network security considerations, the individual browser has the capability to accept or reject cookie information.

Active Server Pages also enable you to read and write information to a cookie file. For more information on how to use cookies to store information on the client's browser, please see Chapter 14, "Speaking to the Web Client: The Response Collection." To extract information from the client's browser, see Chapter 15, "Retrieving User Information: The Request Object."

Implementing Session Variables and Properties

The Session object is responsible for managing user information. To start tracking and manipulating user workflow, you can start using the Session object's methods and properties using the following syntax:

Session.*property*|*method*

Where Session is the Session object. The Session object has four properties, as listed in Table 13.1.

Table 13.1   The *Session* Object's Properties

Property	Description
SessionID	Returns the unique user session identifier.
TimeOut	Returns or sets the user timeout value in minutes.
CodePage	Sets the language attribute for the deployed pages.
LCID	Sets the local identifier used to set local date, currency, and time formats.

Declaring Session Variables

Session variables are declared in a manner similar to declaring application variables. To create or reference a session variable, use the `Session` object and name of the variable with the following syntax:

```
Session(varName)
```

where *varName* is the name of the session-level variable. Remember that session-level variables are only available to the user session that created the object and cannot be shared among separate user sessions.

If you want to create a session-level variable, simply assign a value to a session variable name. There is no declaration statement that exists for the session- or application-level variables. Therefore, you do not have to use the `Dim`, `Redim`, `Public`, `Private`, or `Const` declared statements that are found in VBScript to explicitly create variables. For example, to create a new session variable called `SalesUserName` and assign a value of `Wynn` to that variable, use the following code:

```
<%
    Session("SalesUserName") = "Wynn"      '=== Creates and assigns session variable
    Session("SalesToDate") = 24
%>
```

This same syntax that is used to create a session variable is also used to reference an existing variable name. For example, to change the session variable `SalesUserName` value to `Lois`, use the same syntax.

```
<%
    Session("SalesUserName") = "Lois"      '=== Reassigns value of session variable
    Session("SalesToDate") = 28
%>
```

Because the session variables are only available to the specific user session, no `Lock` and `Unlock` methods are needed to prevent simultaneous updates to the same variable. However, great care should be taken to ensure the correct spelling of session- and application-level variables. If a session or application variable is misspelled, a new variable with that misspelling is created.

One of the most common uses of the `Session` object is to set database connection properties. The database connection properties are recommended to be made at the session level to allow you to tap into the new features of ODBC 3.5 and component management using Microsoft Transaction Server. The `Session_OnStart` event of the `GLOBAL.ASA` file is a convenient location to store all the variables needed to connect to the database, as shown in the following code:

```
Sub Session_OnStart
     Session("ConnectionString") = "DSN = myIntraNet"
     Session("ConnectionTimeout") = 15
     Session("CommandTimeout") = 30
     Session("RuntimeUserName") = ""
     Session("RuntimePassword") = ""
End Sub
```

Part

III

Ch

13

Notice in the previous code that the actual database connection is not established in the Session_OnStart event. Instead, the connection should be opened and closed only as needed in the ASP code on the individual ASP pages. The reason for this "connect only as needed" policy is to enable ODBC 3.5 and the Transaction Server to manage your database connection and pooling capabilities. Opening the database connection only when you need to gives you more scalability in terms of overall connection resources.

This approach is fundamentally different from the traditional database connection environment where connecting to and disconnecting from a database required significant resources. Even if ODBC 3.5 is not used, dedicating a database connection from the time a user enters the application is not the most efficient database management technique. For example, how are you to know that the requesting client will use the dedicated database connection? How do you prevent running out of database connections? Connecting and optimizing your database connection will be discussed in Chapter 28, "Working with the Microsoft Transaction Server." In addition, Chapter 32, "Putting It All Together: Creating an N-Tier Online Catalog Application," will demonstrate building ActiveX database components that use the Transaction Server to manage database connections.

The *SessionID* Property

The Session object uses a SessionID to keep track of user information from page to page within the ASP application. The Web server generates the SessionID when a new session is started. The SessionID is available using the following syntax:

```
Session.SessionID
```

where Session is the Session object.

A new session is started if no existing Session objects exist for the requesting user. Only one Session object exists per user per Application object. To display the SessionID, use the SessionID property as illustrated below:

```
<% = Session.SessionID %>
```

or

```
<% Response.Write(Session.SessionID) %>
```

For example, the following script displays the user's SessionID:

```
Your SessionID is: <% Response.Write(Session.SessionID) %>
```

This script would return the following results with the individual user's ID:

```
Your SessionID is 24214
```

The *Timeout* Property

The Timeout property sets or returns the amount of time, in minutes, that the Session object can remain inactive before the user's Session object resources are released. This property is necessary because the stateless HTTP protocol prevents the application from knowing whether the user has actually finished the application or has simply left the application and navigated to another site. The Session object tries to overcome this lack of a persistent connection by using the `Timeout` property. To prevent an unlimited number of `Session` objects from being created on the server, the `Timeout` property helps to conserve server resources by destroying unattended user sessions. To set the `Timeout` property, use the following syntax:

```
Session.Timeout [ = nMinutes]
```

where `Session` is the `Session` object and *nMinutes* is the timeout value specified in minutes.

To display the default `Session.Timeout` value for your Web server, use the following code:

```
<% = Session.Timeout %>
```

Unless otherwise stated, IIS 3.0 uses the Registry to regulate the session timeout value. IIS 4.0 stores all configuration information in a new storage location called the *Metabase*. To set the `Timeout` value in the Metabase, use the Property tab of the specified Web site in the Microsoft Management Console.

The default value of the `SessionTimeOut` Registry setting is 20 minutes. After the specified amount of time has passed and no activity has occurred with the `Session` object, the server will destroy and release all resources related to that session.

To temporarily override the `Timeout` setting, you can specify a new timeout value by assigning a value to the `Timeout` property directly in the ASP file. This capability to set the individual timeout values was important in the IIS 3.0 world when individual Web applications could not have their own unique settings. IIS 3.0 only enables settings to be applied at the HTTP server level, not at the individual application levels. Therefore multiple applications running from the same HTTP server all had to use the same application settings. However, with IIS 4.0, individual applications can have their own unique settings. In any case, the `Timeout` value enables the developer to specify the appropriate timeout value without relying on the Web site administrator to make the change. The following example sets a new Session `Timeout` value of five minutes:

```
<% Session.Timeout = 5 %>
```

The reason the word "temporary" is used to describe the change in the `Session.Timeout` property is because when a new `Session` object is created, the `Session` object pulls the default session timeout value from the Registry. Therefore, unless reassigned either in the `Session_OnStart` or at the page level, the new `Session` object uses the timeout value specified in the Registry.

To illustrate this point, the following code writes the current session timeout value and current `SessionID` value to a page. Then the ASP changes the `Session.Timeout` property from the default value to one minute.

```
<%
Response.Write "Existing Session ID: " &Session.SessionID & "<BR>"
                          '=== Writes SessionID
Response.Write "Existing Session Timeout: " &Session.Timeout & "<BR>"
                          '=== Writes TimeOut value
Session.Timeout = 1                  '=== Sets New Timeout value to 1 minute
Response.Write "New Session Timeout: " &Session.Timeout & "<BR>"
                          '=== Writes the new TimeOut value
%>
```

Part
III

Ch
13

The previous code returns the following results:

```
Existing Session ID: 35441
Existing Session Timeout: 20
New Session Timeout: 1
```

After this code is executed the first time, the `Session Timeout` value is set to one minute. If the code is executed again after one minute, a new `SessionID` will be written to the page and the default session timeout value will be assigned.

To further illustrate the destruction of the `Session` object and its resources, the previous code is modified to include a session variable named `myUserName`.

```
<%
Response.Write(Session("myUserName")) & "<BR>"          '=== Writes blank first time
➥page is called
Response.Write(Session.SessionID) & "<BR>"              '=== Writes the SessionID
Response.Write(Session.Timeout) & "<BR>"                '=== Writes the default
➥timeout value
Session("myUserName") = "FlintStone"                    '=== Assigns value to variable
Session.Timeout = 1                                      '=== Re-assign new timeout
➥value
%>
```

The first time the code is processed, the session variable `myUserName` has no value and consequently returns a zero length string. After writing the `SessionID` and timeout values to the page, the session variable `myUserName` is assigned the value FlintStone. If the page is refreshed or called again within one minute, the first line of code now writes `FlintStone` to the page. The remaining code writes the same `SessionID` and the newly assigned timeout value to the page. However, if the page is refreshed after the allotted timeout value of one minute, the old `Session` object is destroyed and replaced by a new `Session` object. The results now write a zero length string for the session variable `myUserName`, a new `SessionID`, and the default timeout value. These various effects of destroying the `Session` object can be seen in Table 13.2.

Table 13.2   Result from the *Session.Timeout* Sample Code

ASP Code	Initial Execution	Refresh Before Timeout	Refresh After Timeout
Session("myUserName")	-	FlintStone	-
Session.SessionID	13530	13530	16384
Session.Timeout	20	1	20

The *LCID* Property

The `LCID` property is used to set the local identifier properties for an ASP. The local identifier is used to control the display formatting that is specific to a localized location or region. The `LCID` property requires the following syntax:

```
Session.LCID(=LCID)
```

where LCID is the valid local identifier. For example, to set the local identifier to use the French local identifier, use the following code:

```
<%
Session.LCID = 1036
%>
```

The LCID is a standard abbreviation that identifies localized formatting issues, such as time, date, and currency formats. If you want to take advantage of different regional settings to display formatted information, you would have to change the regional settings on the Web server itself. For example, if the Regional Settings for the Web server are set to French (Luxembourg), the assigned time, date, and currency formatting issues would look like the following script:

```
<%
Dim amtDue
amtDue = 30
Response.Write("The amt Due was printed on " &FormatDateTime(Now) &"<BR>")
Response.Write("Your total amount is " &FormatCurrency(amtDue)&"<BR>")
%>
```

This script would produce the following result:

```
The amt Due was printed on 30/09/97 13:43:55
Your total amount is 30,00 F
```

However, instead of limiting the Web server to displaying information to only one language type, the LCID property enables you to set this LCID for the ASP file. For example, the following ASP uses the French LCID to display information in the stand French LCID without changing the display format for the entire Web server.

```
<%
Session.LCID =1036
Dim amide
amide = 30
Response.Write("The was printed on " &FormatDateTime(Now) &"<BR>")
Response.Write("Your total amount is " &FormatCurrency(amtDue)&"<BR>")
%>
```

The previous example writes the current date, time, and currency values to the page using the French regional setting. For example, the French date formatting is used to display the current date and time, 30/09/97 13:43:55. If the regional settings were set on English (United States), and the Session.LCID setting were removed, the previous code example would produce and format results specific to that region, as follows:

```
The was printed on 9/30/97 1:54:03 PM
Your total amount is $30.00
```

Keep in mind that you can also set the LCID using the LCID directive. The syntax for the LCID directive is the following:

```
<%@ LCID =  a local identifier %>
```

For more information on using directives, please see Chapter 10, "The Composition of an Active Server Application."

Part
III

Ch

13

The *CodePage* Property

Active Server Pages also provide additional support for multi-lingual sites by supporting multiple character maps. A specific language's character map consists of that language's letters, numerals, and punctuation characters. The `CodePage` property of the `Session` object is used to assign the specific character map for an ASP. To implement the `CodePage` feature, use the following syntax:

```
Session.CodePage = CodePage
```

where `CodePage` is a valid code page for the scripting engine. For example, to set the `CodePage` property to Japanese, use the Japanese `CodePage` setting:

```
<% Session.CodePage = 950 %>
```

Similar to the `LCID`, `CodePage` can also be set using the `CodePage` directive with the following syntax:

```
<%@ CodePage = valid code page %>
```

For more information on using directives, please see Chapter 10.

Trapping Session Events

The `Session` object uses two events, shown in Table 13.3, to symbolize when a user enters and exits the ASP application: the `Session_OnStart` and `Session_OnEnd` events. A new `Session` object is created by the Active Server to represent when a new user has started to use the ASP application. After the `Session` object is started, information pertaining to that user's session can be stored on the Web server.

Table 13.3 The *Session* Object's Events

Event	Description
Session_OnStart	Triggered when a new user enters an ASP application.
Session_OnEnd	Initiated when the ASP `Session` object is terminated.

Session_OnStart

The `Session` object, like the `Application` object, uses two events in the `GLOBAL.ASA` file to execute code on the session starting and ending events. The code contained in these events is processed before the requested page is processed. The biggest difference between the two objects is scope. The `Application` object is used to share information that is global to all users in the ASP application, whereas the `Session` object is used to store and track information specific to the individual user. Also, remember that the `GLOBAL.ASA` file is an optional file that does not have to be used in order to create `Session` and `Application` objects. The `GLOBAL.ASA` simply represents a central location to help administer application- and session-level objects and events.

To execute code at the start of a new Session object, you must use the GLOBAL.ASA file. The Session_OnStart event requires a layout similar to the following GLOBAL.ASA syntax:

```
<SCRIPT LANGUAGE = ScriptLanguage RUNAT = Server>
Sub Session_OnStart
     '=== The Code to be executed when a new user enters the app
End Sub

</SCRIPT>
```

The Session_OnStart is often used to set properties that will be used throughout the user's stay in the application. One of the most common uses of the Session_OnStart event is to define settings for the user session. For example, in most applications, you need to define constants that are used in the application. You can set these constants by placing the variable declarations in the Session_OnStart event, as shown below:

```
Sub Session_OnStart
     const MaxOrders = 25
     const MaxRequests = 10
     const MaxAmount = 15
End Sub
```

Session events can reference any other ASP object in the OnStart and OnEnd events. The following example demonstrates the Session_OnStart event's capability to access application-level variables to create a counter to track the amount of users who browse the application. Further examples in this section will demonstrate using other objects, such as the Response object, in the Session_OnStart event.

```
Sub Session_OnStart
     Application.Lock
     Application("iUserCounter")= application("iUserCounter") + 1
     Application.UnLock
End Sub
```

Because the Session_OnStart event starts when a user initiates a user session, this is often the position where you will want to read cookie information from the client machine. Cookie information is often used to provide a temporary storage location to store user-specific information, such as a customized display or available options within an ASP application. For example, you may want to determine the last time that a user entered an application so you can display any new information or news. This process of retrieving information from a cookie is made possible by using the Cookie collection of the Response and Request ASP objects. The Response object is responsible for writing information to the client browser and the Request object is responsible for retrieving information from the browser. Chapters 14 and 15 focus on the details of client interaction in more detail. For example, the following code extracts the user's favorite search engine from a cookie file:

```
Sub Session_OnStart
     SearchEngine = Request.Cookies("SearchEngine")
End Sub
```

Part
III

Ch
13

Furthermore, you can utilize the `Session_OnStart` event to force the user into a particular page when they enter an application. This is a very important feature when you consider the potential workflow nightmares that browser bookmarks present to developers. Bookmarks are dangerous to application workflow because they provide a manner to bypass required steps to reach a certain point in the application. This is important not only for fulfilling process requirements, but also in terms of possibly bypassing application security. In most situations, you want to limit who can access your ASP application as well as control the rights and permissions of the user within the application. Using the `Session_OnStart` event prevents a user from entering an application via a bookmark or from entering a specific URL address. Because the `Session_OnStart` event is executed every time a new user enters the application, you can force the user to always enter a logon page to enter the application. The routing of the user to the logon page is accomplished by using the `Redirect` method of the `Response` object. The `Response` object is covered in much greater detail in Chapter 14. The following example forces a user into a login screen regardless of where he tries to enter an application:

```
<SCRIPT LANGUAGE="VBScript" RUNAT="Server">

Sub Session_OnStart
     dim startPage
     startPage = "Login.asp"
     Response.Redirect(startPage)
End Sub

Session_OnStart

</SCRIPT>
```

The previous example uses the `Response` object to force the user to the `Login.asp` page every time he enters the application.

Session_OnEnd

The `Session_OnEnd` event, also located in the optional `GLOBAL.ASA` file, is triggered when the current `Session` object is closed. The `Session_OnEnd` event requires the following syntax:

```
<SCRIPT LANGUAGE=ScriptLanguage RUNAT=Server>

Sub Session_OnEnd
     '=== Closing code here
End Sub

Session_OnEnd

</SCRIPT>
```

where *ScriptLanguage* is any script-compliant language.

The `Session_OnEnd` event is triggered when the `Session` object is abandoned or times out. During this pre-shutdown of the `Session` object, all interaction with the client browser is prohibited. When the `Session_OnEnd` event is triggered, all new HTTP requests are terminated while the existing requests in the queue are processed. Any ASP code requests to the Response or Request objects in the Session_OnEnd event will generate an error. References to all objects internal to the Web server, such as the Server, Application, or Session objects, are still valid. However, references to the Server.MapPath method would cause a 'type mismatch' error to occur. The valid object calls for the Session_OnEnd events are illustrated in Table 13.4.

Table 13.4 *Session_OnEnd* Object Calls

Valid Objects	Invalid Object Calls
Server	Request
Session	Response
Application	

Controlling User Session Resources

The Session object uses ASP settings to help regulate the amount of resources consumed by a specific user's session. If session information is being stored, calling the Abandon method destroys the session resources.

The *Abandon* Method

The Abandon method is used to destroy and release the resources consumed by Session objects. The Abandon method can be implicitly or explicitly called. The implicit execution of the Abandon method is automatically called when the Session.Timeout value is exceeded. The explicit destruction of the Session object is called using the following syntax:

Session.Abandon

where *Session* is the current Session object.

In most situations, the Abandon method is executed implicitly when the Session.Timeout value is passed. Usually the timeout value passes after the user has finished using the application and has navigated to another Web application. The Web application has no way to determine whether the user is simply inactive, is finished with the application, or has browsed to another site.

The Session.Abandon method has some special scoping characteristics that need to be addressed. First, when the Session.Abandon method is called, the Web server continues to process the remaining ASP code on the page. This is unlike the Server.Timeout event and the Response.Redirect methods, in which code execution on that page is instantly terminated. The following code demonstrates how the ASP continues to write the welcome message to the page after the Abandon method is called.

```
<%
Response.Write(Session.SessionID) &"<BR>"          '=== Writes ID to page
Session("myUserName")="Rubble"                     '=== Assigns value to variable
Response.Write(Session("MyUserName")) &"<BR>"      '=== Write variable
Session.Abandon                                    '=== Call to abandon current
                                                         session
Response.Write("Welcome to BrainWare International") &"<BR>"     '=== Writes
➥message
%>
```

This previous example writes the SessionID and variable name Rubble to the page and then executes the Abandon method. At this point, the processing of the script does terminate, but it does write the string "Welcome to BrainWare International" to the page.

Keep in mind that this capability to continue processing ASP script varies from object to object. For example, consider the Server object. If the Server.Timeout is exceeded, as shown in the following example, the script processing is instantly terminated and scripting control is released from the current page. For more information about the Server.Timeout property, see Chapter 12.

```
<%

dim iCount
iCount = 0

DO WHILE iCount < 10            '=== Start of infinite loop
     IF iCount = 9 THEN
              iCount = 1
     END IF
     iCount = iCount +1
LOOP

Response.Write(Server.ScriptTimeOut)      '=== Never is executed because script
➥timesout
%>
```

The second Session object scoping issue to remember is that all of a Session object's properties that were created before the Session.Abandon method call are now destroyed . The Abandon method destroys all the properties of the Session object without actually destroying the Session object itself. For example, if you try to reference a session variable that existed before the Session object was abandoned, no values will be returned from the Session object:

```
<%
Session("myUserName")="Rubble"                     '=== Sets Session variable
Response.Write(Session("MyUserName")) &"<BR>"      '=== Writes variable to page
Session.Abandon                                    '=== Destroys pointers to
➥properties
Response.Write(Session("MyUserName")) &"<BR>"      '=== Writes a zero length string
%>
```

Third, because the Session object itself is not yet destroyed, the Session object can be used to temporarily store user properties. Only after the page has completely finished processing is the current Session object placed in the queue for destruction. For example, the following code calls the `Session.Abandon` method, but still uses the `Session` object to create another session variable before the `Session` object is destroyed.

```
<%
Response.Write(Session.SessionID) &"<BR>"              '=== Writes 94734 to page
Session("myUserName")="Rubble"                         '=== Assigns session value
Response.Write(Session("MyUserName")) &"<BR>"          '=== Writes 'Rubble' to page
Session.Abandon                                        '=== Calls the abandon method
Session("myUserName")="FlintStone"                     '=== Assigns session variable
Response.Write(Session("MyUserName")) &"<BR>"          '=== Writes 'FlintStone' to page
Session("myBossName")="Slate"                          '=== Creates new Session variable
Response.Write(Session("myBossName")) &"<BR>"          '=== Writes 'Slate' to page
Response.Write(Session.SessionID) &"<BR>"              '=== Writes 94734 to page, same
➥as above
%>
```

When the `Session.Abandon` method is called, the closing of the `Session` object triggers the `Session_OnEnd` event in the `GLOBAL.ASA` file.

Configuring the *Session* Object

As previously mentioned, IIS 4.0 relies on the Metabase to store configuration settings for the Web server, and the Microsoft Management Console (MMC) is used to configure the Metabase, whereas IIS 3.0 uses the Registry as its primary configuration information store. The `AllowSessionState` Registry value is used to indicate whether Active Server Pages should track user state information. If `AllowSessionState` is set to 1, session information will be recorded. As a result, any code in the `Session_OnStart` and `Session_OnEnd` events will be initiated, as well as writing the `SessionID` to a client-side cookie. If the `AllowSessionState` Registry setting is set to 0, the `Session` object is not created to monitor user workflow information. Consequently, the Web server will not send cookie information to the client and any reference to a `Session` object, including the actual `Session_OnStart` and `Session_OnEnd` events, will generate an error. If you are now using the `Session` object, turning the session information off can improve performance as a result of eliminating the need to process additional HTTP header requests, to allocate and de-allocate memory space, and to send and receive cookie information.

Using Session-Level Objects

The `Session` object can also be used to create references to other instantiated objects, which are then available throughout the user's specific session. However, because individual objects must be created on the Web server for every `Session` object, the threading model of the component must be considered to avoid locking out any users.

Instantiating Session-Level Objects

As with page- and application-level objects, objects can be instantiated at the session level. Creating an object with session-level scope enables that object to be referred to during the lifetime of that user session. Session-level objects give you the ability to share information

Part
III

Ch
13

particular to a user from page to page within an application. The instantiated session-level object is destroyed whenever the user Session object is destroyed. In order for reallocation of session resources to occur, the Session.Abandon method must be called or the Session.Timeout value must be exceeded.

You can create a reference to an automation object by embedding the unique class identifier either by the ProgID or the ClassID within the object tag. The ProgID represents the registered name of the object. The ClassID refers to the registered class number of the object. To create a server-side object, use the following syntax:

```
<OBJECT RUNAT = Server SCOPE = Scope ID = Identifier PROGID = "progID"¦CLASSID
="ClassID">
</OBJECT>
```

Instantiating Session-Level Objects

One consideration when using components is the component threading model. The *component threading model* dictates how components will run on the server. A single-threaded component prevents multiple users from initiating requests on the same component. This single-serve approach prevents information from being mixed across multiple users. However, this presents a large obstacle when implementing Web-centric solutions. For applications with a large number of users, a single instance component can cause significant delays while the users are sequentially given access to the component. Keep in mind that the threading is relative to the processor, not the specific user of application sessions. Therefore, managing your component's threading models will play a critical role in the performance of your site. For this reason, only objects that use the apartment and free threading models can be stored within session variables.

N O T E Only session-level objects that are free threading and apartment threaded can be stored in Session variables. ■

For more information on component threading issues, please see Chapter 18, "Creating Your Own Active Server Components."

Storing Arrays in the *Session* Object

One of the most common uses of Session object is to store a session array that contains information about the user's progress in an application. As you saw in Chapter 10, the Application object is used to store an array of training classes that is loaded into memory when an ASP application begins. Using the Application array is suitable when the required information does not change often. However, in general, your applications will contain a wide variety of dynamic information that depends on interaction with individual users.

Implementing a session array is done in the same manner as declaring a session variable. For example, a local array called myArray is added to a session variable named mySessionArray in the following example:

```
<% Session("mySessionArray") = MyArray %>
```

If a session variable named mySessionArray does not exist, the session variable is created. If a variable of that name already exists, the existing data is overwritten by the assignment of the array.

To create a session-based array, the first step is to create a page-level array in VBScript using the Dim keyword. The following example demonstrates creating a local array, assigns values to the array, and then transfers the local array into a session variable.

```
<%
Dim aLocalTraining(4)                           '=== Creates a fixed size array
    aLocalTraining (1)="Using Active Server Pages"
    aLocalTraining (2)="Internet Basics"
    aLocalTraining (3)="Content Management"
    aLocalTraining (4)="Internet Application WorkFlow"
Session("aTraining")= aLocalTraining            '=== Assigns local array in the
                                                    Session object

%>
```

Now the user can access this information from any other page by referring to the session variable aTraining.

```
<%
If IsArray(Session("aTraining")) then           '=== Validates array
     dim aTraining, iclass
     aTraining =  Session("aTraining")           '=== Creates local array
     iClass = Ubound(aTraining)                   '=== Finds upper limit for array
     For i = 1 to iClass                          '=== Loop through results
            Response.Write(aTraining(i) & "<BR>")      '=== Write array to page
     Next
Else
     Response.Write ("Error in processing array")
End If
%>
```

You can also utilize the Session_OnStart event in the GLOBAL.ASA file to populate a session-level array. The same approach is used to create, fill, and transfer the local page array to the session variable. The following example uses a session-level array to hold user information. In this situation, information about the requesting client is stored when the user first enters the application.

```
<SCRIPT LANGUAGE="VBScript" RUNAT="Server">


Sub Session_OnStart
     Dim myUserInfoArray (4)       '=== Creates a fixed size array
     myUserInfoArray (1) = "myScreenResolution"        '=== Assigns text to first
➥element
     myUserInfoArray (2) = "myBrowserType"             '=== Assigns text to second
➥element
     myUserInfoArray (3) = "myOperatingSystem"         '=== Assigns text to third
➥element
     Session("myUserInfoArray ") = myUserInfoArray
End Sub
```

```
Sub Session_OnEnd
End Sub

</SCRIPT>
```

To use this information, create a local instance of an array and assign the session array to the local array. For example, to automatically route the user to pages designed for a specific resolution, the second element of the session array `myUserInfoArray` is used to check the user resolution set in the `Session_OnStart` event.

```
<%@ LANGUAGE="VBSCRIPT" %>
<%
dim aUserInfo
aUserInfo = session("myUserInfoArray")            '=== Create Local Array
Select Case aUserInfo(2)                           '=== Check value
     Case "800x600"
            Response.redirect "/VGA/Intro.asp"     '=== Redirect to this page
     Case else
            Response.redirect "/LowRes/Intro.asp"
End Select
%>
```

Notice how this ASP script is a non-visual Web page that simply processes information. This technique can be used throughout your applications to provide processing logic without having to embed all your code in pages that are displayed to the browser.

This concept of using session arrays to store a collection of user information is used extensively in the online catalog examples illustrated in Chapters 16, "Putting It All Together: Building an Online Catalog," 19, "Putting It All Together: Creating an Online Registration System," and 26, "Putting It All Together: Creating a Dynamic Database Application." These chapters demonstrate using application and session arrays to display information throughout a site and keep track of what the user has ordered.

Managing Session Variables Using Collections

The `Session` object also utilizes collections to help manage session-level variables. Session-level variables can be categorized into two classes based on how the variable is declared, as shown in Table 13.5. Variables can be declared with or without the <OBJECT> tag. If the session-level object is declared as an object using the <OBJECT> tag, the object is managed by the `StaticObject` collection. If the variable is not declared using the <OBJECT> tag, the session-level variable is managed by the `Contents` collection.

Table 13.5 The *Session* Collection

Name	Description
Contents	Contains all session-level variables that have not been created with the <OBJECT> tag.
StaticObject	Contains all session-level objects declared with the <OBJECT> tag.

The *Contents* Collection

The Contents collection contains all items that have been created during a session and that have not been declared with the <OBJECT> tag. The Contents collection requires the following syntax:

```
Session.Contents( Key )
```

where *Key* is the name of the property to retrieve. The Contents collection manages all session-level variables declared through a user session across all pages. For example, assume that the following session-level variables have been declared in separate ASP.

```
<% Session("myAcctNum") = "IR-404-3305-S" %>      '=== Declared in one ASP
<% Session("myDepVersion") = "50-TT-50" %>        '=== Declared in another ASP
```

The Contents collection can then reference these variables by using the required syntax, as shown below:

```
<%
Response.Write(Session.Contents("myAcctNum"))
Response.Write(Session.Contents("myDepVersion"))
%>
```

Furthermore, you can iterate through the collection to obtain a list of all session-level variables by using a For...Next loop:

```
<%
For Each Key In Session.Contents
      Response.Write(Key & "<BR>")
Next
%>
```

The *StaticObject* Collection

The StaticObject collection is similar to the Contents collection, but it is used to manage all session-level objects that have been declared with the <OBJECT> tag. The StaticObject collection uses the following syntax:

```
Session.StaticObjects( Key )
```

where *Key* is the property to retrieve. The StaticObject collection can also be used to reference a single session variable or multiple session variables. For example, consider the following GLOBAL.ASA file that declares an ADO and an Ad Rotator Session object as well as loads a session-level array:

```
<SCRIPT LANGUAGE="VBScript" RUNAT="Server">

Sub Session_OnStart
      Dim aTraining(4)        '=== Creates a fixed size array
      aTraining(1)="Using Active Server Pages"
      aTraining(2)="Internet Basics"
      aTraining(3)="Content Management"
      aTraining(4)="Internet Application WorkFlow"
      Session("aTraining")=aTraining
End Sub
```

Part
III

Ch
13

```
Session_OnStart
</SCRIPT>
<OBJECT RUNAT = Server SCOPE = Session ID = MyConnection PROGID =
➥"ADODB.Connection">
</OBJECT>
<OBJECT RUNAT = Server SCOPE = Session ID = MyAd PROGID = "MSWC.AdRotator">
</OBJECT>
```

To list all items in the StaticObject collection, use the For...Next loop to step through the
<OBJECT> collection:

```
<%
For Each Key In Session.StaticObjects
      Response.Write(Key & "<BR>")
Next
%>
```

This iterative process will write the names of the Session objects, shown below, to the page:

```
MyAd
MyConnection
```

From Here...

In this chapter, the versatility of the Session object is demonstrated to track user-specific
information for cookie-based browsers. Your ASP applications can still be written if cookies are
not supported on the browser's clients, however, the Session object will be rendered useless.
However, in situations where cookies are supported, the Session object can be used to store a
variety of user-specific information using variables, arrays, and even ActiveX components. The
Session object uses the Session.Timeout and Session.Abandon properties and methods to
help manage resources on the server.

For related information, please see the following chapters:

- Chapter 15, "Retrieving User Information: The Request Object," depicts how to gather
  information using forms, hidden fields, and cookies.

- Chapter 17, "Implementing Existing Server-Side Components," demonstrates how to use
  the various components that ship with IIS Active Server Pages.

- Chapter 18, "Creating Your Own Active Server Components," walks you through
  the tools and examples on how to create tailored functionality via custom-created
  components.

Speaking to the Web Client: The *Response* Collection

Controlling how information is distributed from the Web server to the requesting browser forms half of the foundation needed to deliver Active Server applications. The Active Server uses a built-in object called the Response object to control and manage the data sent to the browser. The Response object is responsible for controlling the delivery of data, writing HTTP header information, writing text, HTML, scripting variables, and non-textual information, and controlling cookies on the client browser.

The Response object is separated into three sections that are used to properly display information between the client and server. The Cookies collection provides a valuable resource in administering and controlling client-side cookies. The Cookies collection enables you to create, control, and manipulate information stored in cookies. The Response object's properties enable you to set many of the physical properties of pages, such as the lifetime of the page in the client's cache. The Response object's methods are used to explicitly control the flow of information from the server to the browser, and enable you to buffer pages on the server, write textual, non-textual, and HTML information to pages, and write information to the Web server log files. ∎

Utilizing the *Response Cookies* Collection

Discover how to create client-side cookies to store user or application information, control the lifetime of the cached cookie, and manipulate data within the cookie.

Using the *Response* Object's Properties

Learn how to control the data properties of information delivered to the browser by regulating how information is sent to the browser, controlling the lifetime of the page on the client's browser, and other page management essentials.

Controlling the *Response* Object Using Methods

Tap into the power of the *Response* object by learning how to control the information flow from the server to the browser by using buffering, logging, and Web page redirection capabilities.

The *Response* Collection

The Response object, in addition to the other built-in Active Server Page objects, uses collections to help group common indexes. A *collection* represents a logical storage unit that helps manage information. The Response object only uses one collection, the Cookies collection. The Cookies collection manages and controls both cookie files and the data stored within the cookies. This temporary storage location is used in a variety of ways in Web application development. One of the most common uses of cookies is to store the last visited Web page in an application or site and the last time and date a particular page or Web site was accessed. This same concept of tracking user activity throughout a site can be applied to the application workflow process. Cookies provided a mechanism to track a user's location within the application.

The Cookies collection enables single or multiple variables to be stored and manipulated in temporary text files on the client's browser. To write variables to cookies, use the Response object in conjunction with the Cookies collection. The Cookies collection requires the following syntax:

```
Response.Cookies(Cookie)[(key)¦.attribute] = value
```

where Response is the built-in Response object, *Cookie* is the name of the cookie file, *key* identifies a dictionary element, *attribute* is a specific characteristic of the cookie, and *value* is the value being assigned to the cookie.

To assign a value to a cookie, use the Cookies collection syntax as described above. For example, to create a cookie named myLowFatCookie and assign it a value of A banana, use the following syntax:

```
<% Response.Cookies("myLowFatCookie") = "A Banana" %>
```

Notice that you do not have to manually trap and replace non-ANSI characters when extracting or writing the information to the cookie. The encoding process is built into the Response and Request Cookies collections. As a result, the encoding process automatically filters out any non-ANSCI characters. In the previous example, the HTTP header string that is sent from the Web server converts the string A Banana to A+Banana. For more information about URL and HTML encoding methods, see Chapter 12, "Controlling the Server with the Server Object and Using Transaction Processing with the ObjectContext Object."

Keep in mind that you cannot write information to a cookie file after HTTP header information has been sent to the requesting browser. In other words, you cannot send cookie information after to the browser after any HTML tags are sent to the browser without generating an error. For example, to successfully write the cookie information to a browser, you must follow the code syntax like this:

```
<%@ LANGUAGE="VBSCRIPT" %>
<% Response.Cookies("myLowFatCookie") = "A Banana" %>
<HTML>
<HEAD>
<TITLE>Write a simple cookie</TITLE>
</HEAD>
<BODY>
```

```
A cookie was just written to your system.
</BODY>
</HTML>
```

However, if you try to write data to the cookie after the Web server has delivered any HTML, a `Header` error will occur. The following script indicates the improper placement of the `Response.Cookies` placement in the ASP script:

```
<%@ LANGUAGE="VBSCRIPT" %>
<HTML>
<HEAD>
<TITLE>Write a simple cookie</TITLE>
</HEAD>
<BODY>
<% Response.Cookies("myLowFatCookie") = "A Banana" %>
A cookie was just written to your system.
</BODY>
</HTML>
```

This improper placement of the `Cookies` collection will generate the following error:

```
Response object error 'ASP 0156'
Header Error
/DemoCookie/writecookievalues.asp, line 7
The HTTP headers are already written to the client browser. Any HTTP header
modifications must be made before writing page content.
```

To correct this error, place the `Response.Cookies` attribute before the `<HTML>` tag.

Writing information to cookies is worthless if the information is never extracted again. To extract the data from the cookie, the `Request` object's `Cookie` collection is used. For example, to retrieve the data from the newly written `myLowFatCookie`, use the following code:

```
<% Response.Write(Request.Cookies("myLowFatCookie")) %>
```

In this situation, the text `A Banana` is extracted from the `myLowFatCookie` cookie file. To find out more about the details of retrieving information from the browser, see Chapter 15, "Retrieving User Information: The `Request` Object."

Notice that the cookie acts as a single storage unit for information. If you write additional information to the cookie, all previously held information in the cookie is overwritten. For example, if you assign the value `An Apple` to `myLowFatCookie`, the previously held value of `A Banana` is overwritten.

```
<% Response.Cookies("myLowFatCookie") = "An Apple"        '=== Over writes
➥previous value %>
```

In most situations, if your application implements cookies, you will want to use this temporary storage location to house multiple values. These multiple values can be accessed using keys. *Keys* enable the conversion of a single unit storage location into smaller, identifiable units within an object. This key approach is similar to the concept of using indexes to identify subunits within an array.

Part
III

Ch
14

To store multiple variables within the same cookie, use the `key` attribute of the `Cookies` collection. The following example creates three keys: `Breakfast`, `Lunch`, and `Dinner`, and assigns the corresponding `Banana`, `Apple`, and `Orange` values.

```
<%
Response.Cookies("myLowFatCookie")("Breakfast") = "Banana"
Response.Cookies("myLowFatCookie")("Lunch") = "Apple"
Response.Cookies("myLowFatCookie")("Dinner") = "Orange"
%>
```

Remember: If the cookie is assigned a new value, the key values are destroyed. If you re-assign the `Dinner` key to `Orange`, as shown in the following code example, the previously assigned key values, `Breakfast`, `Lunch`, and `Dinner`, would be destroyed.

```
<% Response.Cookies("myLowFatCookie")("Dinner") = "Orange" %>
```

The `Cookies` collection also uses attributes to help manage cookies on the browser. Table 14.1 displays the cookie attributes that can be set by the `Response` collection.

Table 14.1   The Attributes of the *Response Cookies* Collection

Name	Description
Expires	Sets the date when the cookie will expire.
Domain	Specifies cookie delivery to only members specified by this domain.
Path	Determines the delivery path information.
Secure	Specifies whether the cookie is secure.
HasKeys	Returns whether the cookies contain multiple values.

The *Expires* Attribute

To create a cookie that exists until a specific date, use the `Expires` attribute. The following code demonstrates setting the lifetime of a cookie to exist until December 30, 1999.

```
<%
Response.Cookies("myLowFatCookie")("Breakfast") = "Banana"
Response.Cookies("myLowFatCookie")("Lunch") = "StrawBerry"
Response.Cookies("myLowFatCookie")("Dinner") = "Orange"
Response.Cookies("myLowFatCookie").Expires = "December 30, 1999"
%>
```

One of the easiest ways to verify the cookie expiration date is to turn on the cookie warning within your browser. After this warning is activated, the browser will display the contents and expiration date of the cookie trying to be sent to your browser. You can explicitly control whether or not to accept the cookie. If you choose to accept the cookie, that cookie, the data within it, and the cookie attributes are written to your browser. If you do not choose to accept the cookie, no information is written to the browser. In Figure 14.1, the contents of the cookie and the expiration date of `December 30, 1999` are displayed as a result of activating the Cookie warning indicator in Internet Explorer.

FIG. 14.1
Displaying the cookie data and expiration date using the browser Cookie warning flag in IE 4.0.

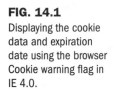

The ability of the user to reject cookies demonstrates another shortcoming with relying on cookies for Web application development. The ability of the user to reject information that your application may deem necessary presents a drawback in controlling and monitoring user state information.

When using the attributes of the Response Cookies collection, make the effort to ensure that valid data is being used. For example, if an incorrect date were entered for the cookie expiration date, a Response runtime error would occur. For example, if an expiration date of December 32, 1999 were used for myLowFatCookie, the Response object would generate a runtime error:

```
<% Response.Cookies("myLowFatCookie").Expires = "December 32, 1999"  '=== Run
➥time error %>
```

If no expiration date is assigned to the cookie, the cookie will expire at the end of the user's session. For more information about using the Session object, please see Chapter 13, "Managing the User Session: The Session Object."

The *Domain* Attribute

The Response object also enables you to limit the distribution of cookie files to specific domains. The Domain attribute of the Cookie collection is used to identify what domains cookies will be issued to. For example, to only distribute cookies to the domain MyCompany.Com, use the following code:

```
<%
Response.Cookies("myLowFatCookie")("Breakfast") = "Another Banana"
Response.Cookies("myLowFatCookie")("Lunch") = "One StrawBerry"
Response.Cookies("myLowFatCookie")("Dinner") = "A Orange"
Response.Cookies("myLowFatCookie").Expires = "December 30, 1999"
Response.Cookies("myLowFatCookie").Domain = "MyCompany.Com"
%>
```

Part
III

Ch
14

The *Path* Attribute

The Path attribute extends the Domain attribute by specifying a path location in the domain that cookies will be sent to. For example, instead of issuing cookies to all requests in the MyCompany domain, the requests can be limited to requests from the Diet virtual directory:

```
<%
Response.Cookies("myLowFatCookie")("Breakfast") = "Another Banana"
Response.Cookies("myLowFatCookie")("Lunch") = "One StrawBerry"
Response.Cookies("myLowFatCookie")("Dinner") = "A Orange"
Response.Cookies("myLowFatCookie").Expires = "December 30, 1999"
Response.Cookies("myLowFatCookie").Domain = "MyCompany.Com"
Response.Cookies("myLowFatCookie").Path = "/Diet"
%>
```

The *Secure* Attribute

The Secure attribute of the Cookies collection is used to set whether or not the cookie is delivered over a secure channel. The Secure attribute accepts a Boolean value of True if False. For example, to deliver our myLowFatCookie over a secure channel, set the Secure attribute to True, as shown below:

```
<%
Response.Cookies("myLowFatCookie")("Breakfast") = "Another Banana"
Response.Cookies("myLowFatCookie")("Lunch") = "One StrawBerry"
Response.Cookies("myLowFatCookie")("Dinner") = "A Orange"
Response.Cookies("myLowFatCookie").Expires = "December 30, 1999"
Response.Cookies("myLowFatCookie").Domain = "MyCompany.Com"
Response.Cookies("myLowFatCookie").Path = "/Diet"
Response.Cookies("myLowFatCookie").Secure = True
%>
```

If a secure channel is not detected in the HTTP header, the cookie information will not be sent.

The *HasKeys* Attribute

The HasKeys attribute is used to determine whether multiple values are stored within the cookie. A *key* is the term used to identify the variable name within a collection. One of the best ways to prevent keys from being overwritten within cookies is to use the HasKeys attribute of the Cookies collection. The HasKeys attribute can be used as an indicator to determine whether a cookie has keys:

```
<%= Response.Cookies("myLowFatCookie").HasKeys %>
```

Remember that you can utilize the looping functionality found in the For...Each...Next loop to search for existing key values from a cookie or reset all keys to a value. The following example determines whether the cookie contains multiple values and the reads from the cookie and lists all the stored values:

```
<%
    For Each key in Request.Cookies("myLowFatCookie")
        Response.Write Request.Cookies("myLowFatCookie")(key) &"<BR>"
    Next
%>
```

Notice that to run the previous example, you can also utilize the For...Each...Next to resets all the keys in the cookie to the string "Empty Value".

```
<%
For Each key in Response.Cookies("myLowFatCookie")
    Response.Cookies("myLowFatCookie")(key) = "Empty Value"
Next
%>
```

Again, the cookie warning indicator in IE3.0 displays that the key values have been all updated to "Empty Value" in the requested cookie, as shown in Figure 14.2.

FIG. 14.2
Use keys to reset values in cookies to prevent destroying other cookie keys.

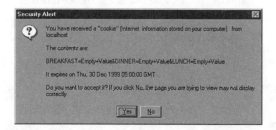

Notice that the word *key* in the For Each...Next is not a keyword but is used to represent an element or variable in a valid object collection. The previous example can be re-written using a non-descriptive variable name to accomplish the same looping functionality.

```
<%
For Each FatCell in Request.Cookies("myLowFatCookie")
    Response.Write Request.Cookies("myLowFatCookie")( FatCell) &"<BR>"
 Next
%>
```

Using the *Response* Object's Properties

The Response object has various properties that are used to set the characteristics of information delivered by the server. These characteristics are used between the browser and the server to provide a communication mechanism between the information provider and information consumer. Using the properties of the Response object controls this "hand-shake" capability between the browser's client and Web server. Table 14.2 illustrates the Response object's properties.

Table 14.2 The *Response* Properties

Property Name	Description
Buffer	Sets whether or not page output is buffered.
CacheControl	Enables dynamic output of ASP to be cached by proxy servers.

Part

III

Ch

14

continues

Table 14.2 Continued	
Property Name	**Description**
CharSet	Appends the name of the character set to the content-type header.
Expires	Sets the amount of time in which the page cached on the browser expires.
ExpiresAbsolute	Sets the date and time in which a page cached on a browser expires.
IsClientConnected	Determines whether the browser has disconnected from the server.
Status	Indicates the status line returned by the server.
PICS	Adds the value of a PICS label to the pics-label field of the response header.

The *Buffer* Property

The Buffer property is used to control when information is sent to the requesting browser. The Web server can either stream information to the user as the server is processing the script, or it can wait to release all the data after the entire script is finished processing. The Buffering property enables you to process information on the server before sending any HTTP Header information to the browser. To utilize this preprocessing approach, the Response buffering requires the following syntax:

```
Response.Buffer [= flag]
```

where Response is the Response object and *flag* can be set to either True or False (see Table 14.3).

Table 14.3 The Buffering Flags	
Flag	**Description**
True	Server buffering is cached until the entire ASP page has completed processing or the Flush or End methods have been called.
False	Server buffering is disabled, enabling output to be streamed to the browser as it is processed.

The Buffer property is used to override the BufferingOn Registry setting at the ASP level. For example, to ensure that buffering is disabled on an ASP even if server buffering is enabled in the Registry, the following ASP code can be used:

```
<% Response.Buffer = False %>
```

If the buffering flag is set to True, the Web server output is cached until all the ASP code has finished processing or the Flush or End Response methods have been called. If buffering is set to False, server buffering is disabled and information is sent to the browser as the server processes it.

Enabling buffering on the Web server increases server performance because the server does not have to continuously create and release HTTP connection resources for every item delivered by the ASP. Although this streamlining approach can enhance server performance, care must be taken to not alienate the user by not displaying any output. The user may assume that the Web site is down or is slow because no information is being presented to the browser.

Keep in mind that the Buffering property only refers to controlling the release point where information is sent to the requesting browser and does not influence the Session object or any HTTP Keep-Alive request. Also, enabling buffering presents a presentation delay to the users. Consequently, your application or network may appear to be slow or congested.

Buffer activating code should be placed within the first lines of code on the page. Because buffering cannot be set after output is sent to the browser, the Buffer tag must be placed before any text is streamed to the client. Trying to change the buffering characteristics after data has been sent to the client will produce a runtime error. For example, the following code will generate a runtime error because information is already being streamed to the client.

```
<%@ LANGUAGE="VBSCRIPT" %>
<% Session("UserName") = "Harvey West" %>
<HTML>
<HEAD>
<TITLE>Response Error</TITLE>
</HEAD>
<BODY>

Hello <% = Session("UserName") %>
<% Response.Buffer = True           '=== Produces runtime error %>
</BODY>
</HTML>
```

As a result of the incorrect placement of the Buffer property, the following error is produced:

```
Response object error 'ASP 0156'
Header Error
/Demo/bufferingerror.asp, line 10
The HTTP headers are already written to the client browser. Any HTTP header
modifications must be made before writing page content
```

To correct this code, place the buffering tag after the LANGUAGE directive:

```
<%@ LANGUAGE="VBSCRIPT" %>
<% Session("UserName")="Harvey West" %>
<HTML>
<HEAD>
<TITLE>Response Error</TITLE>
</HEAD>
<BODY>
```

Part

III

Ch

14

```
Hello <% = Session("UserName") %>
<% Response.Buffer = True              '=== Produces runtime error %>
</BODY>
</HTML>
```

The buffering property is very useful in situations where information must be processed before sending any HTTP header information to the requesting browser. This is particularly useful considering that the HTTP header information can only be sent to the requesting browser once. As you have seen with different ASP objects, such as the `Cookies.HasKeys` property and the `Response.Redirect` method, trying to re-send any HTTP header information after the initial HTTP header information has already been sent will generate a runtime error. The `Response.Buffer` property is useful to prevent these errors. For example, consider the previous `Cookie` collection example where all the values are stored in a cookie. To determine whether the cookie contained multiple values, the `HasKeys` property must be used before sending any HTML to the browser to prevent an error. To accomplish this in one seamless step, enable buffering to allow the `HasKeys` property to be utilized after HTML is called in the ASP, as shown below:

```
<%@ LANGUAGE="VBSCRIPT" %>
<% Response.Buffer = True %>
<HTML>
<HEAD>
<TITLE>Read Cookies information and Buffer Output</TITLE>
</HEAD>
<BODY>
<%
If  Response.Cookies("myLowFatCookie").HasKeys Then            '=== Would have
➥normally generated an error
    For Each key in Request.Cookies("myLowFatCookie")
        Response.Write Request.Cookies("myLowFatCookie")(key) &"<BR>"
    Next
End If
%>
</BODY>
</HTML>
```

The *CacheControl* Property

The `Response` object uses the `CacheControl` property to enable a proxy server to cache output from Active Server Pages. The `CacheControl` requires the following syntax:

```
Response.CacheControl [= Cache Control Header ]
```

where *Cache Control Header* can be `True` or `False`. If the *Cache Control Header* is set to `False`, the `Cache Control` header is considered private, meaning the results of the ASP page will pass through a proxy server without caching the individual users request. To enable caching of ASPs on the proxy server, set the *Cache Control Header* to `True`. Now the proxy server will cache the ASP output and consider the results as public to all users requesting that page:

```
Response.CacheControl = True
```

The *CharSet* Property

The ContentType, another property of the Response object, is used to regulate how a requesting browser displays the textual information that is deliverer from the Web server. The CharSet property of the Response object is used to set the character set of the ContentType that is displayed on the requesting browser. The CharSet property controls the ContentType header information by using the following syntax:

```
Response.Charset(CharSetName)
```

where *CharSetName* is the character set designated for a particular page. For example, to change the character set for a page to ISO-LATIN-1, use the following example:

```
<% Response.Charset("ISO-LATIN-1") %>
```

The content-header delivered from the Web server would be:

```
content-type:text/html; charset = ISO-LATIN-1
```

Notice that, if the Response.Charset property is not specified, the CharSet label is not added to the content-header string. Furthermore, the CharSet property does not check to validate if the CharSet name is a valid standard.

Setting the CharSet value is often done using the META HTML tags. For example, consider the default META tag that uses the International Organization for Standards (ISO) 8859-1 standard:

```
<META HTTP-EQUIV = "Content-Type" content = "text/html; charset=iso-8859-1">
```

If an ASP were written in Japanese, you would use the following CharSet:

```
<META HTTP-EQUIV = "Content-Type" CONTENT = "text/html; charset=shift_jis">
```

However, now you can set the character set using the ASP Response.CharSet property. Table 14.4 is a list of valid character set tags and associated code page values.

Table 14.4 Valid Character Set Values and *CodePage* Values

CharSet Tag	*CodePage*
us-ascii	1252
iso8859-1	1252
ascii	1252
iso_8859-1	1252
iso-8859-1	1252
ANSI_X3.4-1968	1252
iso-ir-6	1252
ANSI_X3.4-1986	1252

continues

Part

III

Ch

14

Table 14.4   Continued

CharSet Tag	*CodePage*
ISO_646.irv:1991	1252
ISO646-US	1252
Us	1252
IBM367	1252
cp367	1252
csASCII	1252
latin1	1252
iso_8859-1:1987	1252
iso-ir-100	1252
ibm819	1252
cp819	1252
Windows-1252	1252
iso8859-2	28592
iso-8859-2	28592
iso_8859-2	28592
latin2	28592
iso_8859-2:1987	28592
iso-ir-101	28592
l2	28592
csISOLatin2	28592
windows-1250	1250
x-cp1250	1250
windows-1251	1251
x-cp1251	1251
windows-1253	1253
windows-1254	1254
shift_jis	932
shift-jis	932
x-sjis	932

CharSet Tag	*CodePage*
ms_Kanji	932
csShiftJIS	932
Extended_UNIX_Code_Packed_Format_for_Japanese	932
csEUCPkdFmtJapanese	932
x-euc-jp	932
x-euc	932
csISO2022JP	932
iso-2022-jp	932
windows-1257	1257
big5	950
csbig5	950
x-x-big5	950
GB_2312-80	936
iso-ir-58	936
chinese	936
csISO58GB231280	936
csGB2312	936
gb2312	936
csKOI8R	20866
koi8-r	20866
ks_c_5601	949
ks_c_5601-1987	949
korean	949
csKSC56011987	949
euc-kr	949
ISO_8859-8:1988	1255
iso-ir-138	1255
ISO_8859-8	1255
ISO-8859-8	1255

continues

Table 14.4 Continued	
CharSet Tag	**CodePage**
Hebrew	1255
CsISOLatinHebrew	1255
Windows-1256	1256
Windows-874	874
Windows-1258	1258

The *ContentType* Property

The ContentType property enables you to specifically control the HTTP content-type that is sent to the browser. The content-type is used by the browser to interpret the information sent from the server. The browser uses the content-type information to determine how it should interpret the information, such as treat the information as text, HTML, or as an image file. The ContentType functionality is implemented using the following syntax:

```
Response.ContentType [= ContentTypeID ]
```

where *ContextTypeID* is the browser-specific MIME content-type.

The content-type is formatted into two sections, a general content category and a sub-content category, as seen in the following syntax:

"General Category/Sub Category"

For example, the following list displays some common content-types:

text/HTML
image/GIF
image/JPEG

Content-types are stored within the browser and usually are associated with file extensions and helper applications. *Helper applications* are programs that are automatically started when the file type is sent to the browser.

Notice that the browser controls the content-types on the client machine. If the client has an associated content-type configured on the client and you specify a specific content-type, the setting on the browser will be interpreted by the client. Remember that you can specific the content-type of an item, but the client's browser is ultimately in control of how the information is interpreted and displayed.

The *Expires* Property

The Response.Expires property is an interesting feature that enables you to specify the amount of time in minutes before the page is expired from the browser cache. The Expire property uses the following syntax:

```
Response.Expires [= number]
```

where *number* is the number of minutes the page will remain active in the cache.

After this time expires, the browser will be forced to retrieve information from the hosting site. If the client requests the same page before the expiration timeout value, the page will be retrieved from the client cache. For example, to force new requests for a page from the Web server, set the Expire property to 0, as seen in the following example:

```
<% Response.Expires = 0 %>
```

However, if you are designing your site for proper scalability and load considerations, this constant requesting to the Web server might not be optimal. Not all situations require constant data retrieval mechanisms back to the Web server. For example, consider sale items in an online catalog. This information would contain product descriptions, images of the products, and sale price information. If this was mostly static information displayed on commonly referenced pages, multiple requests to the Web server would be redundant and a waste of processing power and bandwidth.

Remember that the Response.Expires property controls the expiration time for a delivered page in the browser and the previously discussed Cookies.Expires attribute controls the lifetime of a cookie file. However, although you can programmatically control the page settings, you should not rely on this information to be present in the cache. The cache settings in the browser override the page programmatic settings. For example, if the client's browser does not cache Web pages, setting an expiration time for an ASP is useless.

The *ExpiresAbsolute* Property

The ExpiresAbsolute is an expansion of the Expire property. The ExpiresAbsolute property enables you to specify the exact time and date a page will expire in the browser's cache. The ExpiresAbsolute property requires the following syntax:

```
Response.ExpiresAbsolute [= [date] [time]]
```

where *date* is the date on which the page will expire, and *time* indicates the time the page will expire. However, notice the expiration date and time is converted to Greenwich Mean Time.

To enable the page to expire on December 31, 1999 at 11:59:59 PM GMT, the following syntax should be used:

```
<% Response.ExpiresAbsolute = #Dec 31,1999 23:55:59 # %>
```

If you try to set the page ExpiresAbsolute property to a time in the past, the current date and time stamp will be used as the expiration date and time values for the page.

The *PICS* Property

The Recreational Software Advisory Council on the Internet (RSACi) is a nonprofit organization that provides an advisory council and rating system for software games and Web sites. This rating system sets a standard for monitoring levels of sex, nudity, violence, and offensive language. RSACi works with the Platform for Internet Content Selection (PICS) to provide a standard rating system to indicate labeling information for Internet-based content.

Part
III

Ch
14

ON THE WEB

For more information on these rating systems, visit the RSACi Web site at **www.rsac.org** or the PICS
site at **www.w3.org**.

The PICS property of the Response object enables you to control rating values to the PICS-label
field in the response header. This functionality can be controlled by using the following syntax:

```
Response.PICS(Picslabel)
```

where *PicsLabel* is the formatted PICS label.

To implement the PICS Response property, the following example adds the required PICS
rating labels to the response header field:

```
<% Response.PICS("(PICS-1.1 <http://www.rsac.org/ratingv01.html> labels on " &
➥chr(34) & "1997.01.05T08:15-0500" & chr(34) & " until" & chr(34) &
➥"1999.12.31T23:59-0000" & chr(34) & " ratings (v 0 s 0 l 0 n 0))") %>
```

The delivered header information is sent to the requesting client to enable client-side rating
systems to help control content. If content advising has been enabled on the client's browser,
the browser will determine whether the delivered ratings are acceptable according to the rating guidelines set on the client's browser. Figure 14.3 illustrates setting the ratings on the
Internet Explorer 4.0 browser.

FIG. 14.3

You can set ratings for
your site with this dialog
box.

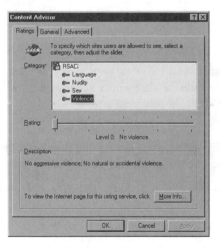

The previous Response.PICS code example would deliver the following HTML to the client's
rating systems.

```
pics-label:(PICS-1.1 <http://www.rsac.org/ratingv01.html> labels on
➥"1997.01.05T08:15-0500" until "1999.12.31T23:59-0000" ratings (v 0 s 0 l 0 n 0))
```

The *Status* Property

The Response object uses the Status property to control the status line returned by the Web server. The status line is used to determine the results of the Web server request and is specified by HTTP specifications. To implement this functionality, use the following syntax:

```
Response.Status = StatusDescription
```

where *StatusDescription* is the status code and status code description. The following is a list of common HTTP status lines that can be returned by the Web server.

- 400 Bad Request
- 410 Unauthorized - Login Failed
- 404 Not Found
- 406 Not Acceptable
- 412 Precondition Failed
- 414 Request-URL Too Long
- 500 Internal Server Error
- 501 Not Implemented
- 502 Bad Gateway

One of the most common uses of the Status property is to force authenticate the requesting user. For example, to force user validation for a page, use the following code to prompt the user for a username and password:

```
<% Response.Status = "401 Unauthorized" %>
```

When this page is requested, the username and password window is displayed to solicit login information from the user, as shown in Figure 14.4.

FIG. 14.4

Use the Status property to authenticate user access to pages.

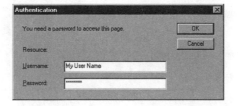

The username and password can then be examined to determine whether access is available to the requested pages. However, keep in mind that the username and password are being sent to the server in clear text. This unsecure communication mechanism provides the potential for malicious individuals to obtain critical information by filtering or examining the IP packets. To guard against this potential security pitfall, only transmit critical information across a Secure Socket Layer (SSL) connection.

Part
III

Ch
14

The *IsClientConnected* Property

The IsClientConnected property is used to expand the capability of the Session object to track the user. The IsClientConnected tracks whether the requesting browser has disconnected from the server since the last time the server issued a Response.Write command. The IsClientConnected property requires the following syntax:

```
Response.IsClientConnected()
```

The IsClientConnected property provides an extension of the Session.Timeout capability by enabling the requesting browser to exceed the session timeout variable without losing server connection, and is often implemented before processing script. The following example tests the Response object to see whether the connection is valid before calling a function to transfer data.

```
If Response.IsClientConnected Then
        vTransfer = TranferInfo("AcctRetail", "AcctWholeSale")
Else
        VTransfer = ReConnect("UserName", "Department")
End If
```

If the user is still connected to the Web server, a script function called TransferInfo begins transferring information from the "AcctRetail" department to the "AcctWholeSale" department. If the connection is not valid, the user tries to reestablish the connection.

Sending Output to the Browser: The *Response* Methods

The Response methods are used to explicitly control information flow from the server to the browser. The Response methods are used to control not only the textual information that is displayed in textual or HTML format, but also HTTP header information, non-textual content such as binary images, and Web server log files. In addition, the Response methods control server buffering and page redirection issues. Table 14.5 lists the available Response methods.

Table 14.5 The *Response* Methods

Method Name	Description
Write	Writes a string to the current HTTP output.
BinaryWrite	Writes information to the current HTTP output without any character conversion.
Clear	Erases any buffered HTML output.
End	Stops the Web server from processing the script and returns the current result.
Flush	Bypasses buffering and sends output immediately to client.
Redirect	Attempts to automatically route the browser to a URL.

Method Name	Description
AddHeader	Writes a string to the HTML header.
AppendToLog	Writes a string to the end of the Web server log entry.

The *Write* Method

The `Write` method of the `Response` object is used to send output to the browser. The `Write` method requires the following syntax:

```
Response.Write variant
```

where `variant` is any `variant` datatype supported by the Visual Basic scripting engine. For example, to display the time a page was requested by using the `Write` method, use the following example:

```
<% Response.Write now %>
```

The `Write` method is then used to write the value to the requesting page:

```
12/23/97 11:48:38 PM
```

Textual content can also be added to the `Write` method by constructing an argument using concatenation strings. For example, the following example adds a descriptive message to the VBScript `Now` function.

```
<% Response.Write "Hello, at the tone, the time will be: " &now %>
```

This code example produces the following output on any requesting browser:

```
Hello, at the tone, the time will be: 1/13/98 10:38:47 PM
```

The `Write` method can also use arguments to hold information in the ASP, instead of directly embedding functions in the `Write` method. The parentheses are optional, but help to provide a clear logical grouping for the input arguments, as shown in Listing 14.1.

Listing 14.1   Using the *Write* method to display the time.

```
<%@ LANGUAGE="VBSCRIPT" %>

<HTML>
<HEAD>
<TITLE>The Time</TITLE>
</HEAD>
<BODY>

<%
dim myTimeStamp, myMsgStr
myTimeStamp = Now
myMsgStr = "Hello, at the tone, the time will be: "
myMsgStr = myMsgStr & myTimeStamp
```

Part

III

Ch

14

continues

Listing 14.1   Continued

```
Response.Write(myMsgStr)            '=== Notice the user of parenthesis
%>

</BODY>
</HTML>
```

This example creates a variant `myTimeStamp` and assigns the system time and date stamp to it. Then the `Write` method is used to write the same information to the requesting page as in the previous example. For more information about the concatenation operators in VBScript, please refer to Chapter 4, "Working with Operators."

Just like any other server-side script, you can integrate HTML and scripting tags together. For example, to expand on the previous example, the HTML text, "Your virtual receipt, printed on: " can be added to the ASP:

```
<%
dim myTimeStamp
myTimeStamp = Now
%>
Your virtual receipt, printed on: <% Response.Write(myTimeStamp) %>
```

The code produces the following output:

```
Your virtual receipt, printed on: 11/23/97 11:48:38 PM
```

Finally, you can directly embed HTML tags within the `Write` method. The same concatenation technique is used to add HTML tags to the variant string. For example, to center the previous time message on the browser page, add the HTML tags as shown in Listing 14.2.

Listing 14.2   Printing a virtual time stamp.

```
<%@ LANGUAGE="VBSCRIPT" %>

<HTML>
<HEAD>
<TITLE>The Time</TITLE>
</HEAD>
<BODY>

<%
dim myTimeStamp, myMsgStr
myTimeStamp = Now
myMsgStr = "Your virtual receipt, printed on: "
myMsgStr = myMsgStr & myTimeStamp
myMsgStr = "<CENTER>" & myMsgStr & "</CENTER>"
Response.Write(myMsgStr)
%>
</BODY>
</HTML>
```

This example displays a message centered on the HTML page. Furthermore, you are not limited to passing the HTML tags embedded in the argument. Just as the argument was constructed within the Write method, as previously shown with text and the Now function, the same approach can be applied to HTML tag:

```
<%
dim myMsgStr
myMsgStr = myMsgStr & Now
myMsgStr = "<CENTER>" & myMsgStr & "</CENTER>"
Response.Write(myMsgStr & "<BR>")
%>
```

This example adds an HTML break to the centered message by concatenating the HTML break tag <BR> directly into the Write method. The break tag creates a hard return on the page.

As seen throughout this book, two different syntaxes are used to write information to a page: the <% and %> scripting tags and now the Response.Write method. The Response.Write method is actually what is called when you implement the shorthand notation to write to an ASP page using the <% and %> delimiters. But remember, the shorthand notation of the Response.Write method is intended only to be used for inline script processing, not within blocks of code. Inline processing occurs when HTML text is integrated with ASP code, as seen in the following example:

```
"Hello, at the tone, the time will be: " <% = now %> <BR>
```

Furthermore, there are some unique behaviors that are associated with using the two display methods. The first peculiar behavior of the <% %> tag is that this feature cannot be used within procedures, that is, subroutines and functions, in your ASP. To write to a page from within a procedure, the Response.Write method must be used.

```
<%
Sub WriteData(myArgument)
        Response.Write(myArgument)       '=== Write the argument to page
        = myArgument                     '=== Generates runtime error
End Sub
%>
```

The runtime error is produced because VBScript is trying to associate a value to a variable when it sees the equal sign. If you really must use the shorthand Write delimiter within a procedure, you can accomplish this by splitting the procedure with script delimiters:

```
<%
Sub WriteData(myArgument)
        Response.Write(myArgument &"<BR>")
        %>
        <% = myArgument %>
        <%
        Response.Write(myArgument &"<BR>")
End Sub
%>
```

Part

III

Ch

14

However, you can see that this is not encouraged because the additional delimiters break up the logical grouping of the procedure and make the procedure hard to follow and read.

The second interesting point about displaying information occurs with the `Response.Write` method. Because the ASP scripting engine uses the `<%` and `%>` delimiters to indicate the beginning and ending of script tags, care must be taken not to cause the scripting engine to close a script tag as it is processing the script. This premature termination of the script engine often occurs in two situations. The first situation is when trying to write HTML tags that use the percent (`%`) sign. For example, if you are trying to display the actual HTML tags needed to create a table using the `Write` method, as seen in the following, a runtime error would result:

```
<% Response.Write "<TABLE Border = 1 WIDTH = 100%>" %>
```

In this situation, the Active Server scripting engine interprets the `%>` tags needed to close the `Table Width` tag as the ending of a script tag and stops processing the tag. The script would start processing and displaying a table, but would produce the following error:

```
Microsoft VBScript compilation error '800a0409'
Undetermined string constant
Response.Write "
```

The second most common situation where the script is prematurely terminated is where the syntax for ASP code is trying to be displayed. For example, if you are trying to display the syntax for the `Response.Write` method on an HTML page, the following line of code produces the same `'Undetermined string constant'` runtime error shown in the previous example:

```
<% Response.Write("Syntax: <% Response.Write Variant %> ") %>    <!-- Run Time
➥Error -- >
```

To keep these errors from occurring, escape characters must be generated to ensure the Web server properly receives the correct information from the Active Server engine. Escape characters can either be implemented by hand or automatically processed by using the `Server` object encoding methods. To implement the proper escape characters by hand, the closing script tag `%>` should be replaced with `%\>`. Proper solutions to both problems are illustrated in the following example:

```
<%
Response.Write "<TABLE  Border = 1 WIDTH = 100%\>"
Response.Write (Server.HTMLEncode("Syntax: <% Response.Write Variant %\>"))
%>
```

For more information on the different encoding mechanisms, please see Chapter 12.

N O T E When using the `Response.Write` method, the `variant` datatype to be delivered to the client cannot contain the string `%>`. This string is interpreted by the VBScript engine as an end script delimiter. Instead, use the string `%\>` to write the close script delimiter tag. ■

The `Write` method uses the `variant` datatype to send information to the browser. The `Variant` datatype, although the most versatile of datatypes, does have it limitations. The `Variant` datatype itself can only contain 1,022 bytes of information. If you try to use a variable that is larger than 1,022 bytes, a runtime error will occur.

The *AddHeader* Method

The AddHeader method enables you to add customized header information to the existing HTTP header. The HTTP header information is the communication mechanism between every request between the browser and the client. The header information is processed before any output to the browser is displayed. To use the AddHeader method, use the following syntax:

```
Response.AddHeader name, value
```

where *name* is the name of the new header variable and *value* is the value assigned to the new header variable.

The AddHeader method must be called before any content is sent to the browser. Failure to do so will generate a runtime error because the HTTP protocol first sends header information to the browser. After the header information is sent to the browser, the content is sent to the browser. Content information is sent when any HTML or Response.Write method is called. For example, you can use the preprocessing approach to identify a customized data encryption technique before data is returned back to the user:

```
<% Response.AddHeader "DB-Encrypt", "128-Bit" %>
```

In this situation, a custom header variable named "DB-Encrypt" is assigned a value of "128-Bit" and is delivered to the browser.

The *AppendToLog* Method

The AppendToLog method of the Response object enables you to append information directly to the Web server log file. This limited reporting feature is often used for error trapping and limited reporting features. To use the Web server log functionality, use the following syntax:

```
Response.AppendToLog string
```

where Response is the built in Response object and *string* is an 80-byte character string.

One of the most common implementations of this method is to use the AppendToLog method as a logging device or remote debugging tool. For example, you may want to track how many times a custom ActiveX server component is accessed, but embedded scripting logic does not always activate the component every time the page is accessed. Therefore, to track how many times that component is called, the log file can be used to store that information.

```
<%
Response.AppendToLog "Billing Server Activated"
Call LoadBillingServer("myMachineName")
Response.AppendToLog "Billing Server Terminated"
%>
```

This code writes the following information to the Web server's log file:

```
127.0.0.1, -, 11/24/97, 13:57:00, W3SVC1, SCOTDELL, 127.0.0.1, 161342, 485, 228,
➥200, 0, GET, /Logappend.asp, Billing Server Activated,
127.0.0.1, -, 11/24/97, 13:58:00, W3SVC1, SCOTDELL, 127.0.0.1, 161342, 485, 228,
➥200, 0, GET, /Logappend.asp, Billing Server Terminated,
```

Part

III

Ch

14

Because the Internet Information Server log file is comma-delimited, avoid using commas in the data string. The log file can then be exported to a variety of data sources, and customized reporting can enable you to monitor the activity of your sites and applications. To get the most from your Web server, use this logging capability with the NT Performance Monitor to get an accurate representation of your site's activity and resource management. For more information on monitoring the IIS performance, please see Chapter 31, "Using Internet Information Server 4.0 to Manage Your Web Applications." For an in-depth discussion on using the NT Performance Monitor, please see *Special Edition Using Windows NT Server*, Second Edition (0-7897-1388-8).

The *BinaryWrite* Method

The BinaryWrite method enables direct non-formatted output to be displayed to the requesting browser. This direct output is useful when displaying non-string information, such as various image formats. To use the BinaryWrite method, use the following syntax:

```
Response.BinaryWrite data
```

where *data* is information that will be sent to the browser without any character conversion.

An example of using the BinaryWrite method is to display images on a Web page in thumbnail format. Assuming that an ActiveX component that converts a full-size JPEG image into a thumbnail format is installed on the server, the BinaryWrite method can be called to display the image.

```
<%
Dim mySessionObj
set mySessionObj = Server.CreateObject(myActiveX.ThumbNailComposer)
myThumbNail = mySessionObj.MakeThumbNail("Corporate Logo")
Response.BinaryWrite myThumbNail
%>
```

This example instantiates the ThumbNailComposer component and calls the MakeThumbNail method of that object. This method converts the full-size image, named "Corporate Logo", into a thumbnail image and stores that image temporarily in the myThumbNail image. Next, the BinaryWrite method is used to display this binary image to the requesting page.

The *Clear* Method

The Clear method is used to erase any HTML that has been buffered on the server. The buffer content is stored on the server by setting the Response.Buffer property to True. To destroy the temporary storage location, the Clear property uses the following syntax:

```
Response.Clear
```

where Response is the built-in Response object and Clear is the Clear method. To clear any HTML output that has been buffered, use the following line of code:

```
<% Response.Clear %>
```

There are two interesting points about the Clear method. The first point is that the Clear method only clears the HTML output from the server and does not clear the HTML header output. When the Response.Clear method is called, the header output is still sent to the browser, but only the content is destroyed. The second point is that the Clear method only is applicable if the buffer object has been created or turned on. If the Clear method is called and buffering is not enabled, the following runtime error will occur:

```
Response object error 'ASP 0159'

Buffering Off

Buffering must be on
```

To prevent this error from occurring, you can trap for the buffer property, as demonstrated in Listing 14.3.

Listing 14.3   Using the *Clear* method to destroy buffered content.

```
<%@ LANGUAGE="VBSCRIPT" %>
<% Response.Buffer = True %>
<HTML>
<BODY>
<%

Response.Write "This example demonstrates using buffered output that is never
➥displayed to the requesting user. The Clear method destroys the cached
➥content"
%>
</BODY>
</HTML>
If Response.Buffer Then            '=== Checks if Buffering is enabled
      Response.Clear               '=== Clears the cached buffer and does not
➥display anything to the user
End If
%>
```

This example prevents a buffering runtime error from occurring if buffering was not activated. By trapping the Buffer property using the if Response.Buffer then code, the buffer can be properly cleared using the Response.Clear method.

The *End* Method

The End method also is used to manage the buffered server output. The End method returns the current buffered output up to the point where the End method is called. To use the End method, use the following syntax:

```
Response.End
```

where Response is the built-in Response object and End activates the End method. To present the buffered output to the browser up until the point where the End method is called, use the following code:

```
<% Response.End %>
```

The Response.End method is treated by the Active Server engine in a similar way to how the Response.Redirect method is used. When the End method is called, the Active Server engine terminates the processing of any remaining ASP scripts and sends the current output to the client. Any remaining script is not processed, as shown in Listing 14.4.

Listing 14.4   Terminating script output using the *End* method.

```
<%@ LANGUAGE="VBSCRIPT" %>
<HTML>
<BODY>
<%
Response.Write "This information is processed and sent to the browser"
Response.End
Response.Write "But this information is never displayed"..
%>
</BODY>
</HTML>
```

The previous example uses the End method to display the welcome message and terminate processing any remaining script. If you do not want display any information to the browser, you can also combine the End and Clear methods, as shown in the following example:

```
<%
If CheckDataError("StationID") Then
        If Response.Buffer Then          '=== Checks if Buffering is enabled
                Response.Clear            '=== Clears the cached buffer
                Response.End              '=== Display nothing to browser
        End if
End If
%>
```

The script example checks to see if the function CheckDataError returns an error message. If an error is found, that is CheckDataError returns True, the Response buffer is cleared and terminated using the End method. Because the Clear method is called immediately before the End method, the End method sends no data to the client.

The *Flush* Method

The Flush method is used by the Response object to immediately send any buffered output to the browser. The syntax for the Flush method is as follows:

```
Response.Flush
```

where Response is the built-in Response object and Flush calls the Flush method. The Flush method can only be used if buffering has been activated. The following code uses the Flush method to write the buffered output to the browser:

```
<% Response.Flush %>
```

The Flush method also requires that buffering be set to True before activating the Flush method. Failure to set the buffering property properly will result in a runtime error. To prevent the HTTP header runtime error from occurring and to allow the script to continue processing throughout the page, use the following code:

```
<%
If CheckDataError("StationID") Then
      If Response.Buffer hen              '=== Checks if Buffering is enabled
             Response.Write (ErrorMsg)    '=== Displays the error message
             Response.Flush               '=== Clears the cached buffer but
➥allow script to process
      End If
      Call WriteLogFile("myLogFile")      '=== Record activity to log file
End If
%>
```

The previous example builds on the functionality used in the Clear and End methods, except in this situation the Flush method is used to display the resultant error message and enable the script to continue processing on the server. In this situation, after the error is returned to the browser, a procedure named WriteLogFile records the success or failure of the event.

The *Redirect* Method

The Redirect method is another useful method of the Response object. The Redirect method is used to route the browser to another Web page. The Redirect method is implemented by using the following syntax:

Response.Redirect *URL*

where Response is the built-in Response object and *URL* is the Uniform Resource Locator that indicates where the browser is routed. The Redirect method must be called before any HTML is delivered to the browser. Failure to call the Redirect method before any HTML is sent to the browser will generate the following header error message:

```
Response object error 'ASP 0156'
Header Error
/YourASPFile.asp, line X
The HTTP headers are already written to the client browser. Any HTTP header
modifications must be made before writing page content
```

When the Response.Redirect method is called from an ASP, the browser is automatically redirected to the new URL location. The Redirect method can be used to ensure that a user who has your site bookmarked gets automatically routed to your new pages. This traditionally occurs if a particular page is bookmarked and you change the name of the page. For example, assume your corporate information Web page was just converted to an ASP to add functionality to that page. The previous page, named CorpInfo.htm, is now renamed CorpInfo.ASP. However, if browsers have your page bookmarked, the requesting browsers will receive an HTTP Object Not Found error. To prevent this from occurring, the Response.Redirect method can be used within the CorpInfo.htm file:

```
<%
Response.Redirect "CorpInfo.ASP"
%>
```

This example now automatically routes the browser to the new and improved CorpInfo.ASP page. Notice that once the server processes the Redirect command, the browser is automatically

Part
III

Ch
14

routed to the new URL without processing script that is contained after the `Redirect` method, as shown below:

```
<%
Response.Redirect "CorpInfo.ASP"        '=== Redirects browser to new page
Dim myVar                               '=== This script is never processed
myVar = "Foo"
%>
```

In this example, the server never processes the script following the `Redirect` method, which declares and sets the variable `myVar`. This script is ignored and the server immediately starts parsing the `CorpInfo.ASP` page.

The `Redirect` method is most useful to help process and route non-visual code pages. These non-visual code pages contain logic that is used to determine workflow through an application. A good example of this routing feature is seen as the main page to many sites to help personalize or tailor a site for a user preference. This non-visual page often checks the requestor's browser type, screen resolution, and for the existence of a cookie that stores user information.

```
<%
If Instr(Request.ServerVariables("HTTP_USER_AGENT"),"MSIE") Then
        Response.Redirect "LoadActiveXSite.asp"            '=== Load ActiveX site
     Else
Response.Redirect "LoadHTMLSite.asp"                       '=== Load the HTML based site
End If
%>
```

In the previous example, the browser type is determined by using the `Request` object. Once the browser type is determined, the user is automatically routed to pages that are optimized for the specific browser. In this instance, if the browser is Internet Explorer, the user is transferred to an ActiveX-based Web site. If the browser is any other browser, the HTML-based pages are loaded.

You can also use the `Redirect` method within the `GLOBAL.ASA` event to ensure that all cookie-compliant users are routed to a specific page when they enter an ASP application. For example, the following code illustrates routing all uses to the `Login.ASP` page on the `Session_OnStart` event.

```
<SCRIPT RUNAT=Server Language = VBScript>
Sub Session_OnStart
     Response.Redirect("Login.ASP")
End Sub
</SCRIPT>
```

For more information on the `GLOBAL.ASA` file, please refer to Chapter 10, "The Composition of an Active Server Page Application." The `Session` object is covered in more detail in Chapter 13, "Managing the User Session: The `Session` Object."

The interesting point about this decision or routing process is that this automatic routing can be applied to a variety of validation and workflow processes, or can be used to simply to access a commonly referred library of ASP code. Chapter 32 demonstrates using several non-visual ASP code pages to process application logic for a Web-based catalog system.

From Here...

In this chapter, you learned how the Response object plays a critical role in delivering a wide range of information to the browser. The Response object uses the Cookies collection to manage writing information to cookies to requesting browsers. The Cookies collection use various attributes that enable multiple values to be stored within a single cookie, explicit control over how long a cookie will live on the browser, control over which domain and virtual directories will cookies be issued, and whether or not to pass cookie information over secure or non-secure channels. In addition, the Response object uses its various properties to determine how information is sent to the browser, the length of time the delivered page will exist in the client's cache, and server-side buffering capabilities. Finally, the Response methods control writing information to the HTTP header string and the delivered HTML page, the capability to write to the Web server log files, control when information is released, and automatic routing capabilities.

Please see the following chapters for related information:

- Chapter 15, "Retrieving User Information: The Request Object," discusses how to gather information from the user using forms, hidden fields, and Cookies.

- Chapter 17, "Implementing Existing Server-Side Components," demonstrates how to use the various components that ship with IIS Active Server Pages.

- Chapter 18, "Creating Your Own Active Server Components," walks you through the tools and examples on how to create tailored functionality via custom created components.

- Chapter 19, "Putting It All Together: Creating an Online Registration System," illustrates how to implement the different ActiveX components that ship with the Internet Information Server to create a Web site for the Amazing Data Widgets Warehouse online catalog.

Retrieving User Information: The *Request* Object

The Request object is responsible for retrieving information from the Web browser. The Request object is filled with various types of collections, properties, and methods that provide many ways to retrieve information from the user. The Request object processes traditional Web-based forms and provides a greater flexibility for gleaning information from the user. This chapter will demonstrate how to use the Request object to retrieve information from the browser. ■

Extracting Data Using the *Form* and *QueryString* Collections

Discover how the *Form* and *QueryString* collections are used to gather and process information from the browser.

Using the *Certificate* Collection

Discover how to use the *Certificate* collection to ensure client verification through certificate authentication.

Retrieving *Cookie Information* and Using the *Server* Collections

Use the *Cookie* collection to manage and store client-side cookies, and use the *Server* collection to use server and client variables to tailor your application base.

Understanding the *Request* Object

On the Web, extracting information from users via traditional forms processing provides basic data-collection functionality. Data entered using input fields is submitted to an executable process, typically through Common Gateway Interface, on the Web server. This process, which usually runs as an out-of-process thread, receives and manipulates the user input. Most of these processes convert form data into automated e-mail that is sent to a person to process, write to a text file, or manipulate a database.

The transfer of information from the client to the Web server is accomplished by using variable names and associated values embedded in the URL. Typically, the information is sent to the Web server using a Post method. The Post method transfers the data from the client to the Web server. The Post method is determined by the ACTION event of the HTML form. The ACTION event is triggered when the form is activated by a SUBMIT event, as seen in the following HTML:

```
<FORM Name = "frmLogin" ACTION = "ValidateLogin.ASP" METHOD = "POST">
```

When the previous example is submitted, the information on the form named "frmLogin" is posted or sent to the ASP file "ValidateLogin" for processing. The Submit event of the form is usually triggered by a client event, such as clicking on a button or image. The following HTML creates a Submit button with a caption displaying "Login".

```
<INPUT TYPE = "SUBMIT" VALUE = "Login">
```

Keep in mind that you can also trigger the Submit event of the form by executing the Form.Submit event. For example, the following JavaScript function is executed on the client's browser to submit a form only if the username and password fields have been completed.

```
function chklogin(form)
{
    if (form.txtusername.value == ""){
        alert("Please Enter a User Name");
        setfocususername(form);}
    else{
        if (form.txtpassword.value == ""){
            alert("Please Enter a Password");
            setfocuspassword(form);}
        else{
            form.submit();
        }
    }
}
```

The capability to accept information from the browser has expanded from simple URL variable manipulation. In order to develop and deploy your application over the Web, you also need the ability to accept information from forms, accept and reject digital certificates to identify users, and read cookie information from the requesting browser.

The Request object was initially created to help control and manipulate the data flowing into the Web server as a result of the Post method. The Request object uses collections, properties, and methods to retrieve information from the user. To use the Request object, use the following syntax:

```
Request[collection¦property¦method](variable)
```

where Request is the Request object, *collection* is the available collection, *property* is the Request properties, *method* is the Request methods, and *variable* is a Request variable.

For example, to reference a Request variable named OpenDatabase, simply reference the variable name, as shown in the following example.

```
<% = Request("OpenDatabase") %>
```

Now, lets take a closer look at the Request object's collections and methods.

Accepting User Information Using the *Request* Collections

The Request object uses separate objects that can be grouped together and referred to by code as a single unit. This grouping of common objects is referred to as a *collection*. The Request object uses five collections, listed in Table 15.1, to interface with the calling client.

Table 15.1   The *Request* Collection

Collection Name	Description
ClientCertificate	Retrieves the certification fields issued by the Web browser.
Cookies	Retrieves the values of cookies sent in an HTTP request.
Form	Retrieves the values of form elements posted to the HTTP request.
QueryString	Retrieves the values of the variables in the HTTP query string.
ServerVariables	Retrieves the values of predetermined environment variables.

The ClientCertificate is used to help verify that information is coming from a trusted client. The digital identification is maintained by a third party to help verify not only that users are who they say they are, but that the server is properly represented by the appropriate hosting facility. The Cookie collection is used to access information temporarily stored in text files on the client's machine. The Form collection is used to directly access information from specific field values on an HTML form. The QueryString collection is used to help manipulate variables that are passed through the URL. The ServerVariable collection is used to identify the requesting browser's environment.

If a Request variable is not found, ████
tions for the first instance of ████
lections in the followin ████

1. QuerySt ████
2. F ████

████ var ████

If multiple insta ████ one collection, the first insta ████ located
will be used.

To minimize the poss ████ of accessing an incorrect variable, you should refrain from giving two
variables in different collections the same name.

The *ClientCertificate* Collection

The Request object's ClientCertificate collection is used to provide proper security identification across unsecured environments. Controlling and monitoring your information in this environment consist of regulating the aspects of information dissemination. The first area, *privacy*, is used to prevent unwanted parties from viewing information that has been intercepted in transit. Using encryption techniques such as Secure Socket Layers helps to ensure that your data will remain intact as it crosses unsecured environments. The second security area is *authentication*. Now that the information can safely pass between points, it is necessary to verify that the users are who they say they are.

To deal with these security concerns, the ClientCertficate collection helps ease the burden of developing digitally secure applications. Specifically, the ClientCertificate collection is used to retrieve certification fields issued by the Web browser. The ClientCertificate is used when the requesting Web browser uses the SSL3.0/PCT1 protocol to create a secure connection to the Web server. If the client requests a secure connection, the browser sends the certification fields to the server. In turn, the server retrieves the certification information via the ClientCertificate collection.

The certification process is not a built-in component of Active Server Pages. However, IIS 4.0 ships with a Certificate Server to help create trusted user communities. To learn more about how to configure your Web server to request client certificates, see the documentation provided with the Certificate Server. To use Certificate Server values, use the following syntax:

```
Request.ClientCertificate( Key[SubField] )
```

where *Key* is the name of the certification field and *SubField* is the individual field located within the certification field. Table 15.2 lists the various certificate fields available.

Table 15.2 The *ClientCertificate* Certification Fields

Key	Description
Subject	Returns a list of subfield values that contain information about the subject of the certificate.
Issuer	Contains a list of subfield values containing information about the issuer of the certificate.
ValidForm	Returns when the certificate becomes valid.
ValidUntil	Specifies when the certificate expires.
SerialNumber	Returns the certification serial number as an ASCII representation of hexadecimal bytes.
Certificate	Returns the binary stream of the entire certificate content in ASN.1 format.

The use of subfields enables specific information to be retrieved from the Subject and Issuer Key fields, as mentioned above. Table 15.3 presents the available subfields for the ClientCertificate collection.

Table 15.3 The *ClientCertificate* Collection Subfields

Value	Description
C	Specifies the name of the country of origin.
O	Specifies the company or organization name.
OU	Specifies the name of the organizational unit.
CN	Specifies the common name of the user.
L	Specifies a locality.
S	Specifies a state or province.
T	Specifies the title of the person or organization.
GN	Specifies a given name.
I	Specifies a set of initials.

If no certificate is sent, the ClientCertificate collection returns EMPTY.

Retrieving Cookie Information Using the *Cookies* Collection

The Cookies collection is used by the Request object to retrieve values stored in text files on the client's machine. The Cookies collection requires the following syntax:

```
Request.Cookies(cookie)[(key)¦.attribute]
```

used to determine whether the cookie has multiple values in a dictionary format. A Dictionary object is a term that is used to describe a set of stored data items, usually in a Key/Value format.

If the HasKeys property returns True, then multiple keys exist within the cookie. To test for multiple keys in a cookie named myLowFatCookie, use the following code:

```
<%= Request.Cookies("myLowFatCookie ").HasKeys %>
```

The "myLowFatCookie" cookie is the one created in Chapter 14, "Speaking to the Web Client: The Response Collection." To create this cookie with key values, use the following code:

```
<%
Response.Cookies("myLowFatCookie")("Breakfast") = "Banana"
Response.Cookies("myLowFatCookie")("Lunch") = "Apple"
Response.Cookies("myLowFatCookie")("Dinner") = "Orange"
%>
```

In most situations, you want to make decisions based on the value of the HasKeys property. This is done by using the results of the HasKeys property in a conditional statement, such as an If...Then loop, as displayed in the following example:

```
<%
If Request.Cookies("myLowFatCookie").HasKeys then
        Response.Write("You have Keys!")
else
        Response.Write("No Keys Found")
End if
%>
```

Now that the cookie is determined to have multiple key fields, the keys can be extracted and assigned to variables to be manipulated by the ASP script. The testing and extracting of cookie values to server-side variables is demonstrated in the following example:

```
<%
If Request.Cookies("myLowFatCookie").HasKeys then
        vBreakfastMenu = Request.Cookies("myLowFatCookie")("Breakfast")
vLunchMenu = Request.Cookies("myLowFatCookie")("Lunch")
vDinnerMenu = Request.Cookies("myLowFatCookie")("Dinner")
else
        vMsgStr = "No Message"
End if
%>
```

This example extracts and assigns vBreakfastMenu the value of Banana, vLunchMenu the value of Apple, and vDinnerMenu is assigned the value of Orange, from the myLowFatCookie created in the previous code example.

You can also utilize the collections to cycle through all keys within a collection. The capability to cycle through the keys is made possible by using a For...Next loop. The following example writes the key names and the associated values to the Web page:

```
<%
If Request.Cookies("myLowFatCookie").HasKeys then
        For Each key in Request.Cookies("myLowFatCookie")
                Response.Write(key &": ")
                Response.Write(Request.Cookies("myLowFatCookie")(key) &"<BR>")
        Next
else
        Response.Write("No Keys Found")
End if
%>
```

This example writes the following output to the Web page:

```
LUNCH: Strawberry
DINNER: Orange
BREAKFAST: Banana
```

This same concept of manipulating the keys in the Cookies collection can also be applied to cycling through multiple cookies in the Cookies collection, as shown in the following example:

```
<%
For Each cookie in Request.Cookies
        Response.Write(cookie & " = " & Request.Cookies(cookie))
Next
%>
```

The *Form* Collection

The Request object Form collection helps to facilitate data retrieval from HTML forms. The Form collection captures the value from an HTML form that submits information via the HTTP Post method. The Forms collection requires the following syntax:

```
Request.Form(parameter)[(index)¦.Count]
```

where *parameter* is the name of the Form collection, *index* is the specific form element, and *Count* identifies the number of elements that exist on a form. For example, to obtain a value entered in a text field named txtUserFirstName from a form, use the Form collection to reference the field name, as shown in the following code:

```
Hello <%= Request.Form("txtUserFirstName") %>
```

The form used for this example is shown in Figure 15.1.

As you can see in Figure 15.1, the previous code example writes Brian to the Web page. Keep in mind that hidden fields can also be referenced via the Forms collection. Hidden fields are often used as a temporary memory location on the Web page. This temporary memory location gives some flexibility in storing and keeping track of user information.

The Form collection itself actually contains all the Form objects and their values from the posted information. For example, the following line of code displays the entire Form object from the posted information:

```
<% Response.Write (Request.Form)    '=== Displays the entire form object %>
```

This Request.Form returns the entire Form collection to the page, as displayed in the next line of code:

```
FormfrmHidden = lowRes & txtUserFirstName = Brian & txtUserForm = Dawson &
txtUserForm = 23-DD & txtUserForm = Arizona & btnProfile = Add + Profile
```

When a particular field or parameter is referenced, the Request object parses the Form Collection and returns the value. For example, the following scripts take the user name and password to create a SQL string:

```
<%
dim vUserName, SQLstr
vUserName = Request.Form("txtUserFirstName") & " " &
Request.Form("txtUserLastName")
SQLstr = "SELECT Accntnum FROM Activity WHERE "
SQLstr = SQLstr & "UserAcct = '" & vUserName & "'"
%>
```

The generated SQL string from the Form collection would be the following:

```
SELECT Accntnum FROM Activity WHERE UserAcct = 'Brian Dawson'
```

One of the most powerful utilities of the Form collection is the capability to iterate though the collection. The iteration approach that enables you to cycle through the collection is implemented by using the For...Next loop. For example, to iterate through the Form collection and display each field name and corresponding value, each item in the Form collection is read, as shown in the following example:

```
<%
For Each x In Request.Form
      Response.Write(x & " = " & Request.Form(x) & "<BR>")
Next
%>
```

This iterative parsing of the Form collection produces the following output:

```
BTNPROFILE = Add Profile
TXTUSERMACHINENAME = Arizona
TXTUSERID = 22-DD
TXTUSERLASTNAME = Dawson
TXTUSERFIRSTNAME = Brian
FRMHIDDEN = LowRes
```

Furthermore, the same approach can be applied to iterating through a form element that has multiple values. To determine if a form element has multiple values, the Count property of the Form collection is used, as seen in the following example:

```
<% vCount = Request.Form("myHTMLElement").Count %>
```

If the Count property returns 0, the element is not found. If the Count property returns a value greater than 1, the form element has multiple values. These multiple elements can then be referred to by their index. For example, Figure 15.2 illustrates three radio boxes that enable the user to vote for his favorite browser. The radio buttons are all named the same to create a control array named rdoBrowser.

FIG. 15.2

Use the Form collection to cycle though a control array to determine the user input.

Determining which button the user has selected within the control array without the use of collections can be a tedious task. However, using collections helps eliminate unnecessary coding and enables iteration through all the items in the Form collection. Once the selected value is located, the value of the selected radio button can be used for coding purposes. The following code cycles through the control array determines the value that is selected, and displays the value of the radio box.

```
<%
For Each item In Request.Form("rdoBrowser")
     Response.Write item & "<BR>"
Next
%>
```

The previous code finds that the selected value of the radio box of the Internet Explorer radio box is selected and passes the embedded value of IE to the Web page. This iteration technique can also apply to multi-selected items. For example, if the Internet Explorer and Netscape Navigator radio boxes were selected, the information stored in the HTML values for the radio boxes would return InternetExplorer and NetscapeNavigator would be written to the ASP page.

The *QueryString* Collection

The QueryString collection is used by the Request object to extract variables from the HTTP query string. The query string is textual content that occurs after the question mark character (?) in the URL string. For example, the following URL points to the www.planet.locator.com domain and executes the checkplanet.asp script. This script accepts the query string of planet = Jupiter for processing by the page:

```
HTTP://www.planet.locator.com/scripts/checkplanet.asp?planet=Jupiter
```

string, *index* is the element index, and *Count* specifies the number of variables in the query string.

To reference the variable name using the Request object, call the sent variable name. For example, to write to a variable named myPlanet from a QueryString variable named planet, use the following syntax:

```
<% myPlanet = Request.QueryString("planet") %>
```

If the URL http://www.planet.locator.com/scripts/checkplanet.asp?planet=Jupiter were submitted to the server, the text Jupiter would be assigned to the variable. In most situations, you will use these variables to drive workflow issues, such as constructing queries to guide information on the resultant pages. For example, the following syntax creates a SQL statement from input of the user that is used to find all information about the planet Jupiter.

```
<%
Dim strSQL                                    '=== Initiates variable
strSQL = "Select * From tbPlanet "           '=== Creates SQL string
strSQL = strSQL & "where fldPlanet = "
strSQL = strSQL & Request.QueryString("planet")
%>
```

When this section of script is finished executing, the SQL string variable strSQL returns Select * From tbPlanet where fldPlanet = Jupiter. Notice that the QueryString collection is not the only means to extract the information from the URL. You can also use the Request object and directly reference the planet variable name using the following code:

```
<% Request("planet") %>
```

Therefore, the same SQL string can be generated using the previous Request object syntax:

```
<%
Dim strSQL                                    '=== Initiates variable
strSQL = "Select * From tbPlanet "           '=== Creates SQL string
strSQL = strSQL & "where fldPlanet = "
strSQL = strSQL & Request ("planet")
%>
```

Just as I introduced keys and indexes in the Cookies and Forms collections, the QueryString collection also utilizes this functionality. The Request.QueryString(*parameter*).Count property can be used to determine if a parameter has multiple values. Table 15.4 discusses the return results of the Count property.

Table 15.4   The *QueryString* Collection *Count* Property

Return	Description
0	Parameter not found.
1	A single parameter is found; multiple values do not exist.
>1	Multiple values for the parameter exist.

If the Count property returns a 0, the QueryString parameter does not exist. If the Count property returns a 1, only a single instance of that parameter exists. If any other result is returned, multiple values for the parameter exist. To access a parameter with multiple values, the index value must be used.

Consider the following URL link that contains today's sale items:

```
<a href
="querystringresults.asp?SaleItem=Dry+Cigars&SaleItem=Pink+Socks&SaleItem=
➥Narrow+Ties">Today's Sale Items</a><BR>
```

This link refers to an ASP named querystringresults.asp on the server. If the requested page were scanning the Request object for a variable named DiscountedItem, no results would be found because the parameter DiscountedItem does not appear in the QueryString.

You use the Count property to help manage and control the content on the page. For example, you do not want your pages to be dependent on specific information being passed to the page; you want to design very flexible pages that enable the content to fit into a template. If you want to design a page to display specialty items, such as sales, discounted items, or new items, several approaches can be taken. The simplest approach is to design a single page for each type of specialty item. However, this requires three pages to be created and maintained, and the calling links to these pages have to be updated. A more efficient manner in terms of design and maintenance is to create one page that changes depending on the input. This is best implemented by using the Count property. The following code checks to determine whether the variable is passed to the page and if it is passed to the page, displays the data:

```
<%
if Request.QueryString("DiscountItem").Count then
Response.Write(Request.QueryString("DiscountItem"))
End if
%>
```

If the previous sale item URL were passed to the Request object, the Discount Count property would return False and no unnecessary discounted items would be displayed on the page. However, to display the SaleItem information, the previous example can be expanded as follows:

```
<%
if Request.QueryString("DiscountItem").Count then
Response.Write(Request.QueryString("DiscountItem"))
Elseif Request.QueryString("SaleItem").Count then
     Response.Write(Request.QueryString("SaleItem"))
End if
%>
```

```
Dry Cigars, Pink Socks, Narrow Ties
```

Now the parameter array items can be accessed in two different ways. The first is to use the Count property to iterate through the index. This approach is shown in the following example:

```
<%
Dim vCount
vCount = Request.QueryString("SaleItem").Count
For I = 1 To vCount
     Response.Write Request.QueryString("SaleItem")(I) & "<BR>"
Next
%>
```

This code determines the number of items in the index and cycles through the items in the collection to write the values to the page.

The second method to obtain all the values from the QueryString collection is to use a For...Next loop to identify each unit in the collection. This same method demonstrated in the Cookies and Form collection processing can be applied to the QueryString collection, as shown below:

```
<%
For Each item In Request.QueryString("SaleItem")
     Response.Write item & "<BR>"
Next
%>
```

Now the previous page display example can be expanded to handle multiple input types and display all information passed to the page, as shown below.

```
<%
'=== Display Discount Items ===
If Request.QueryString("DiscountItem").Count Then          '=== Checks to see
➥item exists
     Dim vCount
     vCount = Request.QueryString("DiscountItem").Count        '=== Sets item
➥count
     For I = 1 To vCount
          Response.Write Request.QueryString("DiscountItem")(I) & "<BR>"
     Next
End If

'=== Display Sale Items ===
If Request.QueryString("SaleItem").Count Then              '=== Checks to see
➥item exists
   For Each item In Request.QueryString("SaleItem")
       Response.Write item & "<BR>"
   Next
End if
%>
```

Notice how the two different uses of the For loops are used to iterate through the QueryString collection. The first loop that displays the discounted items uses the Count property to step through the QueryString index. The second loop is responsible for iterating through the SaleItem collection using the For Each statement.

The *ServerVariables* Collection

The ServerVariables collection is used to obtain server environmental variables. However, these server variables are not specific to the server and can obtain information from the requesting client. To use these features, the ServerVariables collection requires the following syntax:

```
Request.ServerVariables (ServerVariable)
```

where *ServerVariable* is name of the server variable. Table 15.5 displays a list of common server variables.

Table 15.5   The Server Environmental Variables

Variable Name	Description
*ALL_HTTP	Displays all HTTP headers sent by the client.
*ALL_RAW	Retrieves all headers as they are sent by the client.
*APPL_MD_PATH	Retrieves the metabase path for the ISAPI DLL.
*APPL_PHYSICAL_PATH	Retrieves the physical path corresponding to the Metabase.
AUTH_TYPE	Displays the authentication method used by the server.
*AUTH_USER	Retrieves the authenticated user name in raw format.
AUTH_PASSWORD	Displays the value entered in the client's authentication dialog using basic authentication security.
*CERT_COOKIE	Returns the Unique ID for client certificate.
*CERT_FLAGS	Displays whether the client certificate is valid.
*CERT_ISSUER	Displays issuer field of the client certificate.
CERT_KEYSIZE	Returns the number of bits in Secure Sockets Layer connection key size.
*CERT_SERIALNUMBER	Displays the client certificate serial number field.
*CERT_SERVER_ISSUER	Displays the of the server certificate issuer field.
*CERT_SERVER_SUBJECT	Displays the server certificate subject field.
*CERT_SUBJECT	Displays the client certificate subject field.
CONTENT_LENGTH	Returns the length of the content.

continues

CONTENT_TYPE	Returns the data type of the content
GATEWAY_INTERFACE	Returns the version of the CGI specifications used on the server.
HTTP_<HeaderName>	Returns the information in the *HeaderName*.
*HTTPS	Returns whether or not the request came in through secure channel (SSL).
*HTTPS_KEYSIZE	Returns the number of bits in Secure Sockets Layer connection key size.
*HTTPS_SECRETKEYSIZE	Returns the number of bits in server certificate private key.
*HTTPS_SERVER_ISSUER	Returns the server certificate issuer field.
*HTTPS_SERVER_SUBJECT	Displays the server certificate subject field.
*INSTANCE_ID	Returns the ID for the IIS instance.
*INSTANCE_META_PATH	Returns the Metabase path for the instance of IIS that responds to the request.
LOGON_USER	Displays the NT login account the request is made from.
PATH_INFO	Displays the server path information.
PATH_TRANSLATED	Returns the translated version of the PATH_INFO.
QUERY_STRING	Returns the query string in the URL.
REMOTE_ADDR	Displays the IP address of the requesting machine.
REMOTE_HOST	Displays the name of the requesting host.
REQUEST_METHOD	Returns the method that initiated the request.
SCRIPT_NAME	Displays the virtual path to the executing script.
SERVER_NAME	Returns the server's host name, DNS alias, or IP address.
SERVER_PORT	Returns the server port number the request is made on.
SERVER_PORT_SECURE	Returns a 1 if request is made on a secure port, 0 if unsecured.
SERVER_PROTOCOL	Returns the name and version of the requesting protocol.
SERVER_SOFTWARE	Returns the name and version of HTTP server.
URL	Returns the base portion of the URL.

(indicates the new IIS 4.0 server variables.)*

The following examples are some of the possible results of scaning various server variables.

```
REQUEST_METHOD GET SCRIPT_NAME /demo/servervariables.asp
SERVER_NAME 207.96.34.07
SERVER_PORT 80
SERVER_PORT_SECURE 0
SERVER_PROTOCOL HTTP/1.1
SERVER_SOFTWARE Microsoft-IIS/4.0
URL /Demo/servervariables.asp
HTTP_ACCEPT application/vnd.ms-excel, application/vnd.ms-powerpoint, image/gif,
image/x-xbitmap, image/jpeg, image/pjpeg, application/msword, */*
HTTP_ACCEPT_LANGUAGE en-us
HTTP_CONNECTION Keep-Alive
HTTP_HOST 207.96.34.41
HTTP_USER_AGENT Mozilla/4.0 (compatible; MSIE 4.0; Windows NT)
HTTP_ACCEPT_ENCODING gzip, deflate
```

Listing 15.1 demonstrates the capability to display all the items in the ServerVariables collection and their respective values.

Listing 15.1   Use the *ServerVariable* collection to display information about the Web server and the requesting client.

```
<TABLE border = "1">
<% For Each name In Request.ServerVariables %>
<TR>
    <TD> <%= name %> </TD>
    <TD>  <%= Request.ServerVariables(name) %> </TD>
</TR>
<% Next %>
</TABLE>
```

One of the most useful capabilities of the ServerVariable collection is the capability to solicit environmental information from the requesting browser. To obtain the requesting browser's environmental information, capitalize on the HTTP_<HeaderName> component of the server variables. The HTTP_<HeaderName> variables can contain a wide variety of information about the browser client. For example, if an Internet Explorer 3.0 browser makes a request to the IIS, the browser sends a variety of information, such as the screen resolution, operating system, processor type, and more:

```
HTTP_ACCEPT
HTTP_ACCEPT_LANGUAGE
HTTP_CONNECTION
HTTP_HOST
HTTP_USER_AGENT
HTTP_PRAGMA
HTTP_COOKIE
HTTP_UA_PIXELS
HTTP_UA_COLOR
HTTP_UA_OS
HTTP_UA_CPU
```

now not consistent between browsers. For example, a Netscape Navigator 3.0 browser would only send the following variables:

```
HTTP_ACCEPT
HTTP_CONNECTION
HTTP_HOST
HTTP_USER_AGENT
```

From these headers, various information about the browser can be determined. In fact, the Browser Capability Component uses the HTTP header information to help identify characteristics of the browser. For more information about this component, please see Chapter 17, "Implementing Existing Server-Side Components."

With this information available, you can help control and customize your application based on the user environment. The significance here is that you do not need to rely on the user to correctly fill out a preference list or worry about storing this information in cookies. For example, you can customize the layout of your site or application depending on the requesting browser type. Although this browser identification capability is available as an ASP component, you can extract the information directly from the header using the HTTP_USER_AGENT server variable without creating an instance of the Browser Capability Component:

```
<%
if Instr(Request.ServerVariables("HTTP_USER_AGENT"),"MSIE") then
        '=== IE specific tags
Elseif Instr(Request.ServerVariables("HTTP_USER_AGENT"),"Mozilla") then
        '=== Netscape tags are placed here
end if
%>
```

This example combines the use of server variables with the VBScript InStr function. The InStr function is used to search for a string within another string. For example, the first line of code uses the InStr function to search the USER_AGENT header string for the substring MSIE. If that string is found, the requesting browser is Internet Explorer and can utilize functionality specific to that browser. You can further refine your application by examining the display and operating system variables. The following information is a result of trapping the HTTP_<Header> information for a client browser:

```
HTTP_UA_PIXELS 800x600
HTTP_UA_COLOR color8
HTTP_UA_OS Windows NT
HTTP_UA_CPU x86
```

Finally, The HTTP_<Header> is expandable to accept customized header information. To accept a customized header, simply append the header name onto the HTTP_ string. For example, if the browser sends a header named myHeader to the server, the Request object can process the value assigned to that header by using the following syntax:

```
<% vMyHeader = Request.ServerVariables("HTTP_myHeader") %>
```

The *Request* Properties and Methods

Now that the different Response collections have been covered, the Request object has one property and one method. The TotalBytes property dictates the total amount of bytes sent in the request. The BinaryRead method is used to accept and store data sent from a browser.

The *TotalBytes* Property

The TotalBytes property is used to return the number of bytes sent by a browser. To transfer this information to the server, the client uses the Post method to send form information in the HTML body tags. The TotalBytes property requires the following syntax:

```
Request.TotalBytes
```

To use the total number of bytes, assign the output of the Request object to a variable, as shown below:

```
<% myByteCount = Request.TotalBytes %>
```

This byte information is determined by examining the length of the Form collection. For example, if the User Profile form displayed in Figure 15.1 is posted to the server, the value of the TotalBytes equals 128. The length of the Form object is also 128.

The *BinaryRead* Method

The BinaryRead method is used to read binary information that is sent to the server from a Post request. To use the BinaryRead method, use the following syntax:

```
myBinArray = Request.BinaryRead(count)
```

where count is the number of bytes to place into an array named myBinArray. To perform a binary read from information submitted on a form, use the following example:

```
<%
Dim binread
binread = Request.BinaryRead(Request.TotalBytes)
%>
```

Notice that you cannot call or reference any item in the Form collection once the BinaryRead method has been called. For example, if the following code is executed, a runtime error will occur:

```
<%
vCache = Len(Request.Form)
Dim binread
binread = Request.BinaryRead(Request.TotalBytes)
%>
```

Executing the code will generate the following error:

```
Request object error 'ASP 0206'
```

```
Cannot call BinaryRead
```

```
Cannot call BinaryRead after using Request.Form collection.
```

From Here...

From this chapter, you can see that the real power of the Request object lies within the five collections listed below. The collections can be utilized to extract information from locations on the browser.

The Form collection helps you obtain information from the information submitted to the server.

The Cookies collection is used to help control and manage not only information stored within the client-side cookies, but also the properties of the cookies.

The QueryString is used to extract information passed in the URL.

The ServerVariables are used to determine both server and browser environmental conditions.

The ClientCertificates are used to ensure the identity of the requesting browser.

Now that retrieving information using the Request object has been covered, the next step is to discover how to use ActiveX components to extend the Web server's functionality. These ActiveX components can exist from components that are shipped with the Internet Information Server or can be created using your own ActiveX development tools. To learn about related topics, please see the following chapters:

■ Chapter 17, "Implementing Existing Server-Side Components," demonstrates how to use the various components that ship with IIS Active Server Pages.

■ Chapter 18, "Creating Your Own Active Server Components," walks you through the tools and examples on how to create tailored functionality via custom-created components.

■ Chapter 20, "Database Access with ADO," demonstrates how to use database information to build the Amazing Data Widget Warehouse Catalog.

■ Chapter 31, "Using Internet Information Server 4.0 to Manage Your Web Applications," demonstrates how to use the various features of the Internet Information Server to help manage your sites and applications.

Putting It All Together: Building an Online Catalog

Using Application and Session Arrays

Learn how to use application- and session-level variables and arrays to create power programming tools.

Controlling the Interface

Implement the *Request* and *Response* objects to control the interaction between the browser and the Web server.

Managing the Server

Discover how to use the *Server* object to control server-side tasks and how non-visible ASPs act as non-compiled programming libraries.

This chapter will demonstrate how to use the different Active Server objects to collectively form a simple online catalog system. The Amazing DataWidgets WareHouse company uses the various Active Server Page objects to provide a simple online catalog system that enables users to browse catalog listings and select items to order and then process the order. For demonstration purposes for this part of the book, this example excludes any database manipulation that might detract from the focus on the Active Server objects. Instead, this chapter focuses on demonstrating the functionality of each Active Server object to provide the framework that is needed to add more advanced functionality in later chapters. ■

The ASP Online Catalog Application: An Overview

The Amazing DataWidgets WareHouse Online catalog provides online users the opportunity to visit a Web site and order from DataWidgets' growing online catalog. Once the user has entered the online software catalog, the catalog application will display and list the three products available for sale, as shown in Figure 16.1.

FIG. 16.1
The Active Server Pages objects are used to collect, process, and return information to the user.

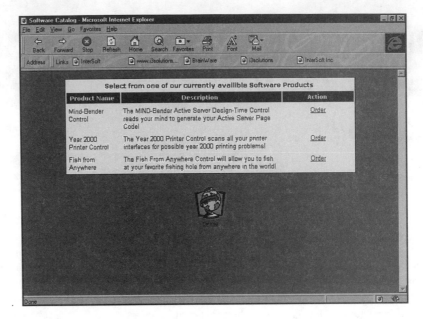

From these items, the shopper can select items to place into his electronic shopping basket. The shopping basket is used to display what items the user has selected to purchase. The user can select just one item to purchase or he can continue shopping for other items. The Active Server Pages remember and keep track of what items are placed in the shopping basket specific to each individual user session, as shown in Figure 16.2.

After the user is ready to purchase the items he selected in his virtual shopping session, the application asks the user for shipping information. After the shipping information is gathered, the order is processed and a summary page is returned to the user, as shown in Figure 16.3.

To deliver this function, the Active Server Pages use five of the six Active Server objects: the Application object, the Session object, the Response object, the Server object, and the Request object. The rest of this chapter takes a closer look at how each object was used in the application.

FIG. 16.2
The shopping basket is an example of tracking the specific actions of an individual user session.

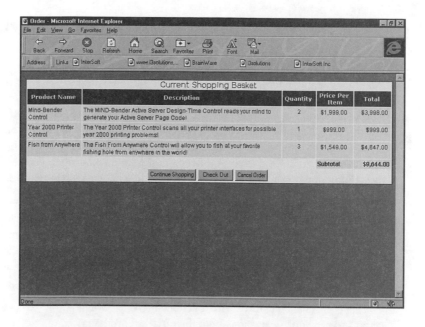

FIG. 16.3
The Active Server objects process the user's order request and shipping information and return a summary page.

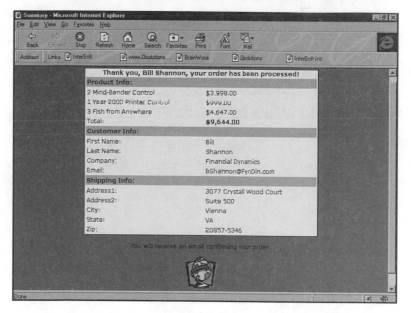

Pre-Loading Application Variables Using the *GLOBAL.ASA*

The first stage in building the Amazing DataWidgets WareHouse is to make the catalog data accessible to the user. Effective communication of information to your browser is a combination of determining the right data access methods and how to best use the information retrieved. The Amazing DataWidgets WareHouse Catalog site, like most online catalog service sites, does not require constant interaction with the database because the schedule information is somewhat static. Of course, you need greater interaction when you register to information pertaining to that site, but the catalog or schedule information is relatively constant.

Knowing this information about the site's content and wanting to achieve the greatest performance by reducing server input/output, the software catalog section is loaded as an application-level variable. As you saw in Chapter 11, "Controlling the Application: The Application Object," application-level variables are accessible across all users of the site. Because multiple users have access to this information, the Lock and UnLock methods are used to control updates to all application variables.

Because the catalog can be formed in logical groups, you are going to use application-level arrays to provide information about the different products and to track how many of the products the user wants to purchase. In addition, you are going to utilize the application-level arrays for preloading other information on the Web server. For example, the Amazing DataWidgets WareHouse also has an online computer hardware catalog. Therefore, to provide a system that can easily be expanded into other catalog areas, you are going to create a master array called aCatalog to list the current catalog services.

Creating Application-Level Variables and Arrays

Although an application-level variable can be created anywhere in the application, the logical choice is to load the variable when the application starts up in the Application_OnStart event of the GLOBAL.ASA file. For example, consider that the Amazing Web site is going to contain two catalogs within the same site. The catalogs are contained in the aCatalog array within the Application_OnStart event, as shown in GLOBAL.ASA file in Listing 16.1.

Listing 16.1   Loading application-level arrays in the *GLOBAL.ASA* file.

```
<SCRIPT LANGUAGE="VBScript" RUNAT="Server">

Sub Application_OnStart
    Dim aCatalog(2,2)
    aCatalog(1,1)="Software Components"
    aCatalog(1,2)="SoftwareCatalog.asp"
    aCatalog(2,1)="Hardware Components"
    aCatalog(2,2)="HardwareCatalog.asp"
Application("aCatalog")=aCatalog
```

```
Application_OnStart

</SCRIPT>
```

In this example, a two-dimensional array is created that stores the catalog name and the catalog starting page. When the ActiveX Server processes this page, the `Application_OnStart` event will trigger the `Sub Application_OnStart` event. When this event is triggered, the `Dim aCatalog(2,2)` statement creates and allocates a local space for a two-by-two memory space. You will increase the performance of your site by eliminating the `REDIM` statement throughout your site. `REDIM`, although important for dynamically allocating array space, requires extensive resource to dynamically create, reduce, and resize arrays. By explicitly controlling the size of the array, you do not have to use resources to resize the array. This local array can then be converted into an application-level object by using the application keyword name, as shown below:

```
Application("aCatalog") = aCatalog
```

This array can be processed from anywhere in the Active Server scripts. Likewise, you can take the same approach to load the individual software components into an application-level variable. In particular, you are going to load three components into an array, and each component will have four properties that you will store in the array. To accomplish this, you need to declare a three-by-four array: the first element will store the name of the component; the second element will store the description of the element; and the third element will store the unit price per component. The first item is a placeholder for how many items are ordered. The creating and setting of the `aSoftware` array is shown in Listing 16.2.

Listing 16.2   Loading the online catalog in the *GLOBAL.ASA* file.

```
<SCRIPT LANGUAGE="VBScript" RUNAT="Server">

Sub Application_OnStart
    Application("iTimeOut") = 30

'=== Load the two available catalogs
    Dim aCatalog(2,2)
    aCatalog(1,1)="Software Components"
    aCatalog(1,2)="SoftwareCatalog.asp"
    aCatalog(2,1)="Hardware Components"
    aCatalog(2,2)="HardwareCatalog.asp"
    Application("aCatalog")=aCatalog

'=== Load the currently available products
    Dim aSoftware (3,4)
    aSoftware(1,1)="Mind-Bender Control"
    aSoftware(1,2)="The MIND-Bender Active Server Design-Time Control reads
➡your mind to generate your Active Server Page Code!"
    aSoftware(1,3)= "1999"
    aSoftware(1,4)= "0"
```

continues

Listing 16.2 Continued

```
        aSoftware(2,1)="Year 2000 Printer Control"
        aSoftware(2,2)="The Year 2000 Printer Control scans all your printer
➡interfaces for possible year 2000 printing problems!"
        aSoftware(2,3)="999"
        aSoftware(2,4)="0"

        aSoftware(3,1)="Fish from Anywhere"
        aSoftware(3,2)="The Fish From Anywhere Control will allow you to fish at
➡your favorite fishing hole from anywhere in the world!"
        aSoftware(3,3)="1549"
        aSoftware(3,4)="0"
Application("aSoftware")=aSoftware

End Sub

Application_OnStart

</SCRIPT>
```

This example uses the GLOBAL.ASA file to load the available products for the online catalog application. The GLOBAL.ASA file was used to stay within bounds of the ASP objects covered in this part of the book. Part V of this book, "Database Management with Active Server Pages," will cover the details of how to connect your Active Server Pages to database. Chapter 26, "Putting It All Together: Creating a Dynamic Database Application," will demonstrate how the ActiveX Data Object is used to drive the Amazing DataWidget's WareHouse online catalogs. Furthermore, Chapter 32, "Putting It All Together: Creating an N-Tier Online Catalog Application," demonstrates how to build your own database components and manage them with the Microsoft Transaction Server.

Creating the User's Shopping Basket Using Session-Level Arrays and Variables

Now that the application-level variables are taken care of, you need to create session-level variables to track the activities of individual user sessions. This capability to track individual user settings is made possible using the Session object. The Session object is covered in greater detail in Chapter 13, "Managing the User Session: The Session Object." The Session object is necessary to create individual shopping baskets to keep track what items the user wants to buy. To use this approach you will use the Session_OnStart event to create an individual copy of the software array stored in the Application object to represent a list of available products, as shown below:

```
Sub Session_OnStart
    Dim usershoppingbasket
    usershoppingbasket = Application("aSoftware")
    session("basket") = usershoppingbasket
End Sub
```

In this case, when a new user enters the application, the `Session_OnStart` event creates a session array named `basket`. This user-specific array can be manipulated at the session level without having to worry about inadvertently changing the application-level variables. Keep in mind that the `Session` object is only created on browsers and networks that support cookies.

Creating and Managing Active Server Pages and Workflow

At this point, all the data for the application has been loaded into memory. The main screen of the Amazing DataWidgets WareHouse site uses the application-level array named `aCatalog` to list the currently available catalog for online viewing, as shown in Figure 16.4.

FIG. 16.4

The main catalog page uses the application-level catalog array to display a list of available catalogs.

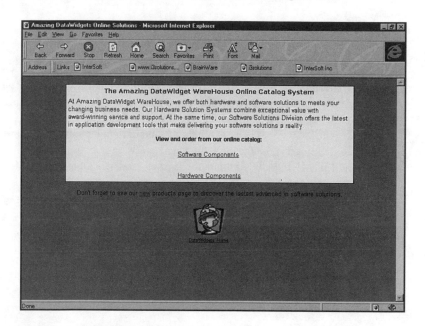

Accessing Application-Level Arrays

To use the application-level array at the page level, create a page variable using the `Dim` statement. To copy the application-level variable onto the page, simply set the new variables you create equal to the desired application-level variable, as shown in the following line of code:

```
Dim aLocalCatalog
aLocalCatalog = Application("aCatalog")
```

Now that a local version of the array has been created, use a `For...Next` loop to write the names of the catalogs and the appropriate `HREF` locations to the Web page, as shown in Listing 16.3.

Listing 16.3   Writing the information to the Web page.

```
<TR>
<TD>
<%
Dim aLocalCatalog, iCount
aLocalCatalog = Application("aCatalog")                '=== Create local copy of
➥array
If IsArray(aLocalCatalog) Then                         '=== Test to see if it is
➥an array
   For iCount = 1 to Ubound(aLocalCatalog,1)
Response.Write("<P><Font Face = 'Arial'><A Href ='"  &aLocalCatalog(iCount,2)
&"'> " &aLocalCatalog(iCount,1) & "</A></Font></P><BR>")
   Next
End If
%>
</TD>
</TR>
```

In this example, after the local variable is created, the IsArray function verifies that the newly assigned variable is, in fact, an array. If the variable is an array, the ASP will start iterating through the different catalogs. The For...Next loop uses the Ubound function to determine the upper element count of the array. In the example syntax, the statement Ubound(aLocalCatalog,1) determines the amount of elements in the first dimension of the aLocalCatalog array. Notice how the Response.Write statement is a mix of Active Server script and HTML tags. When this loop is processed, the following HTML is produced.

```
<TR><TD>
<P><Font Face = 'Arial'><A Href='SoftwareCatalog.asp'> Software Components</A></
Font></P><BR>
<P><Font Face ='Arial'><A Href='HardwareCatalog.asp'> Hardware Components</A></
Font></P><BR>
</TD></TR>
```

This same logic is applied to displaying the list of available software components on the Software Catalog page. Listing 16.4 demonstrates how to write the available ActiveX components that are for sale using an HTML table.

Listing 16.4   Writing the product list to the Web page.

```
<TR>
<TD colspan="3">
<%
Dim aSoftwareCatalog, iCompTitle, iComrDesc
aSoftwareCatalog = Application("aSoftware")
If IsArray(aSoftwareCatalog) Then
   For iCompTitle = 1 to Ubound(aSoftwareCatalog,1)
      Response.Write "<TR>"
```

```
        For iComrDesc = 1 to 2
            Response.Write("<TD Valign='top'><Font Face='Arial'>"
&aSoftwareCatalog(iCompTitle,iComrDesc))
            Response.Write("</Font></TD>")
        Next
        Response.Write("<TD valign='top' width='25%' align='center'><font
Face='Arial'><a href='additem.asp?product=" &Server.HTMLEncode(aSoftwareCatalog
(iCompTitle,1))& "'>Order</A></Font></TD></TR>")
    Next
End If
%>
</TD>
</TR>
```

When the ASP is interpreted, the following HTML is generated by the Internet Information Server to produce the component software catalog listing.

```
<TR>
<TD colspan="3">
<TR>
    <TD valign='top'><font Face='Arial'>Mind-Bender Control</font></TD>
    <TD valign='top'><font Face='Arial'>The MIND-Bender Active Server Design-Time
Control reads your mind to generate your Active Server Page Code!</font></TD>
    <TD valign='top' width='25%' align='center'><font Face='Arial'><a
href='additem.asp?product=Mind%2DBender+Control'>Order</a></font></TD>
</TR>
<TR>
    <TD valign='top'><font Face='Arial'>Year 2000 Printer Control</font></TD><TD
valign='top'><font Face='Arial'>The Year 2000 Printer Control scans all your
printer interfaces for possible year 2000 printing problems!</font></TD>
    <TD valign='top' width='25%' align='center'><font Face='Arial'><a
href='additem.asp?product=Year+2000+Printer+Control'>Order</a></font></TD>
</TR>
<TR>
    <TD valign='top'><font Face='Arial'>Fish from Anywhere</font></TD>
    <TD valign='top'><font Face='Arial'>The Fish From Anywhere Control will allow
you to fish at your favorite fishing hole from anywhere in the world!</font></TD>
    <TD valign='top' width='25%' align='center'><font Face='Arial'><a
href='additem.asp?product=Fish+from+Anywhere'>Order</a></font></TD>
</TR>
</TD>
</TR>
```

This is the HTML that displays the product listing seen Figure 16.2. Note that because only HTML was generated by the ASP code list, the catalog results can be displayed in both the Internet Explorer browser and the Netscape Navigator 3.0 browser, as shown in Figure 16.5.

FIG. 16.5

The software component catalog listing as seen with Netscape Navigator.

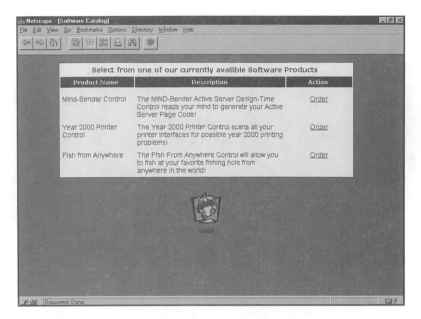

Using the *Server* Object's Encoding Techniques

Writing the available products names, descriptions, and HREF locations to the Web page was made possible using the Server object's URLEncode method. The Server.URLEncode method is used to apply URL encoding rules to the desired string. URL encoding is used to translate non-ANSI characters into escape characters that can be properly transported over HTTP. The URL encoding techniques translate spaces into plus signs (+) and use the ampersand (&) to concatenate variables together. This is an important step to include when writing information to an HTML page. For example, the Server.URLEncode method was used in the following code listing to generate the HREF links:

```
Response.Write("<TD valign='top' width='25%' align='center'><Font Face='Arial'><A
Href='additem.asp?product=" &Server.HTMLEncode(aSoftwareCatalog(iCompTitle,1))&
"'>Order</A></Font></TD></TR>")
```

This code example, extracted from Listing 16.4, would generate the following hyperlink:

```
<A Href='additem.asp?product=Fish+from+Anywhere'>Order</A>
```

When this link is activated, only the entire string Fish from Anywhere is assigned to the variable product. If the Server.URLEncode method were not applied, the following HTML would be produced:

```
<A Href='additem.asp?product=Fish from Anywhere'>Order</A>
```

If this hyperlink is selected, only the string Fish would be assigned to the product variable.

For more information on the Server object, see Chapter 12, "Controlling the Server with the Server Object and Using Transaction Processing with the ObjectContext Object."

Using ASPs as Non-Visual Code Libraries

If you noticed from the previous HTML output, all the hyperlinks for the catalog listings point to the same Additem.Asp file. The Additem.Asp is a non-visual ASP that accepts variables and performs an action depending on the value of the variable passed to it. This method enables you to treat Active Server Pages as code libraries to process application logic and workflow.

Using non-visual ASP files is important to prevent unnecessary application logic from being repeated if the user decides to refresh the browser display. For example, when the user had ordered a catalog item, the user's shopping basket needs to be updated with the selected item. Traditionally, you may put the update functionality in the calling page that is used to display the order shopping basket items. However, if the user refreshes the browser while on the shopping basket page, the page will add another item to the shopping cart. By using non-visible Active Server Pages, you can prevent this type of behavior from occurring. For instance, consider the situation where the user clicks the hyperlink to order a software component. The Additem.Asp file, as seen in Listing 16.5, processes the request and adds the appropriate item to the shopping basket array.

Part
III
Ch
16

Listing 16.5 Using non-visual ASP to perform application and workflow processing.

```
<%@ LANGUAGE="VBSCRIPT" %>
<%
Dim product, iproducts
product = Request.QueryString("product")
Dim aLocalbasket
If InStr(product, "Mind") Then                 '=== Search for Mind-Bender
    aLocalbasket =Session("basket")
    aLocalbasket(1,4)=aLocalbasket(1,4) + 1   '=== Adds counter to Mind Bender
    Session("basket")=aLocalbasket
Elseif InStr(product, "Year") Then
    aLocalbasket =Session("basket")
    aLocalBasket(2,4)=aLocalBasket(2,4) + 1   '=== Adds counter to Year 2000
    Session("basket")=aLocalbasket
Elseif InStr(product, "Fish") Then
    aLocalbasket =Session("basket")
    aLocalBasket(3,4)=aLocalBasket(3,4) + 1
    Session("basket")=aLocalbasket
Else
    Response.Redirect "Error.Asp"             '=== Route user to Error page
End If
Response.Redirect "Order.Asp"                 '=== Route to the order display
page
%>
```

This code illustrates how to use the Request object to extract information from variables embedded in the URL string. The Request object, as discussed in Chapter 15, "Retrieving User Information: The Request Object," is responsible for retrieving information from the user. After the product variable is extracted using the QueryString property, it is compared to existing products using the VBScript InStr function, which returns True if the string is found and returns False if the string could not be found in the argument.

After an existing product is found, the user's shopping basket, which is located in Session('Basket') variable, is copied to a page-level variable. Now the local page array can be manipulated as needed. In this situation, you are updating the fourth array element, which is used to store the amount of items ordered of the product name in the first array element. After the local array has been updated, it is reassigned back to the session level, where other Active Server Pages can access it. After the user's shopping basket has been updated, the Response.Redirect method routes the browser to the Order.Asp page. The Response object is responsible for sending output to the browser. The Redirect method is used to push the browser to another page. For more information regarding the Response object, see Chapter 14, "Speaking to the Web Client: The Response Collection."

You can see the powerful effect that non-visual Active Server Pages and the Response.Redirect method can add to the programming functionality of your Active Server Page applications. This functionality enables you to gain some control over the nuances of using the browser's refresh button. Because the update shopping basket functionality is not attached to a specific visual Active Server Page, the use of the browser's navigation buttons is eliminated from processing application logic. For example, the SoftwareCatalog.asp is only responsible for displaying available software items. The Order.Asp page is only used to display information in the user's shopping basket. Therefore, using the browser's navigate forward, back, and refresh buttons between these pages will not corrupt the workflow of the application.

The Order.Asp file follows the same coding style of the CatalogSoftware.Asp page. The Order.Asp page is used to display the currently selected items in the user's shopping basket and enable the user to continue shopping, pay for the order, or cancel the order. The user's selections are sent to the same ASP file for processing.

Examining the Shopping Basket

To find out whether the user placed any items placed in his shopping basket, his shopping basket is searched for all items that have an item count greater than zero. If the item count is greater than zero, the total is calculated by multiplying the unit count by the unit price, as shown in Listing 16.6.

Listing 16.6 Examining and displaying the user's shopping basket.

```
<%
Dim iCounter, itemsordered, aBasket, name, description, unitprice, amtordered,
subtotal
ABasket = Session("basket")
For iCounter = 1 to ubound(aBasket,1)          '=== Iterate through user basket
   Itemsordered = aBasket(iCounter,4)          '=== Find if any items are ordered
   If itemsordered > 0 Then                     '=== If any items are ordered
        name = aBasket(iCounter,1)             '=== Name of item
        description = aBasket(iCounter,2)       '=== Description of item
```

```
        unitprice = aBasket(iCounter,3)              '=== Unit Price
        subtotal = FormatCurrency(subtotal+unitprice*itemsordered)      '===
Calculate subtotal
%>
  <TR>
  <TD Width="15%" Bgcolor="#F7EFDE" valign="top"><Font Size="2" Face="Arial"><%
Response.Write name      %></Font></TD>
  <TD width="50%" bgcolor="#F7EFDE" valign="top"><Font Size="2" Face="Arial"><%
Response.Write description   %></font></TD>
  <TD Align="center" bgcolor="#F7EFDE" valign="top"><font size="2"
Face="Arial"><% Response.Write itemsordered %></font></TD>
  <TD align="center" width="10%" bgcolor="#F7EFDE" Valign="top"><Font
size="2"face="Arial">
  <% Response.Write FormatCurrency(unitprice) %></font></TD>
  <TD align="right" width="10%" bgcolor="#F7EFDE" Valign="top"><Font size="2"
face="Arial">
  <% Response.Write FormatCurrency(unitprice*itemsordered) %></Font></TD>
  </TR>
<%
  End If
Next
%>
```

This ASP code is used to display what items the user has ordered, as shown in Figure 16.6. Notice the use of the VBScript FormatCurrency function. The FormatCurrency function is used to return a formatted currency expression. The returned value uses the currency symbols that are defined in the system control panel. These formatting features can be covered in greater depth in Chapter 7, "Datatype Conversion Features."

FIG. 16.6

The user-specific shopping basket is maintained by an array variable stored by the Session object.

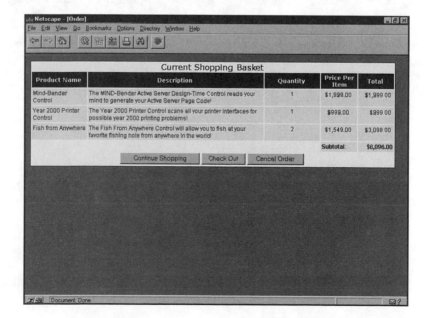

Using the *Request* Object in a Multi-Button Form

After the user views the contents of his shopping basket, he has the option to continue shopping, cancel the order, or proceed with the order. To make this functionality possible, the same approach you used to pass arguments via the QueryString in the hyperlinks to a non-visual code page is used. Listing 16.7 illustrates using three submit buttons on the bottom of the order form to call the GoTo.Asp file.

Listing 16.7   Posting multiple values using the same HTML form.

```
<FORM NAME="frmbutton" Action="GoTo.ASP?" Method="Post">
<TR>
<TD align="center" colspan="5" width="100%">
<INPUT TYPE="submit" NAME="btngoto" VALUE="Continue Shopping">
<INPUT TYPE="submit" NAME="btngoto" VALUE="Check Out">
<INPUT TYPE="submit" NAME="btngoto" VALUE="Cancel Order">
</TD>
</TR>
</FORM>
```

When any of the navigation buttons are pressed, as shown in Figure 16.6, the button's value is submitted to the GoTo.ASP file. The ASP then processes the value by using the Request object to determine what button is pressed and using the Select Case statement to decide what action to take (see Listing 16.8).

Listing 16.8   Accepting and processing multiple values from an HTML form.

```
<%@ LANGUAGE="VBSCRIPT" %>
<% OPTION EXPLICIT
Dim gotopage
Select Case Request("btngoto")
  Case "Continue Shopping"
    gotopage="softwarecatalog.asp"
  Case "Cancel Order"
    Session.Abandon
    gotopage="softwarecatalog.asp"
  Case "Check Out"
    gotopage="customer.asp"
  Case Else
    gotopage="softwarecatalog.asp"
  End Select
Response.Redirect gotopage
%>
```

In this code, the browser is redirected to the software catalog page if the user decides to shop for more items. If the user decides to pay for the items in the shopping cart, the browser is routed to the customer information page. If the user decides to cancel his order, the

Session.Abandon method is called and the user is routed to return shopping at the software catalog page. The Session.Abandon method destroys all Session objects for that user session, effectively erasing all information about that session. The Session objects are destroyed after the page is finished processing. However, because the user is routed to another page within the web, a new Session object is created and the user is treated as if they entered the site for the first time.

If the user decides to cancel the order, the Session.Abandon method destroys that user's Session object. As a result, all information about the user is destroyed. For example, if the same user decides to cancel the order, the Session.Abandon method purges the order items. When the user orders a new item, the item is placed in the shopping basket, as shown in Figure 16.7.

FIG. 16.7

The Session.
Abandon method
destroys all settings for
the specific user and
creates an empty
shopping basket for
new items.

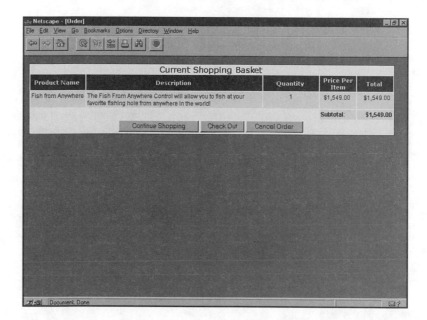

Extracting Information Using the *Request* Object

If the user is ready to "check out," the browser is directed to the customer page. The customer page enables the user to enter user profile and shipping information. After the user has correctly entered the required information, the information is posted to the SaveUser.ASP page. This non-visual ASP is used to read the values entered in the form and create session variables. Typically, and as shown in later chapters, this would be the location of rules-based, server-side processing such as address verification, credit card validation, or inventory processing. In Listing 16.9, the SaveUser.Asp file creates session variables by extracting values from HTML form fields.

Listing 16.9   Extracting information from an HTML form and storing the user information.

```
<%@ LANGUAGE="VBSCRIPT" %>
<%
Server.ScriptTimeout = Application("iTimeOut")
Session("UserFirstName")=Request.Form("txtfirstname")
Session("UserLastName")=Request.Form("txtlastname")
Session("UserCompany")=Request.Form("txtCompany")
Session("Useremail")=Request.Form("txtemail")
Session("UserAddress1")=Request.Form("txtaddress1")
Session("UserAddress2")=Request.Form("txtaddress2")
Session("UserCity")=Request.Form("txtcity")
Session("UserState")=Request.Form("txtstate")
Session("UserPostal")=Request.Form("txtpostal")
Session("UserCountry")=Request.Form("txtcountry")
Response.Redirect "summary.asp"
%>
```

In previous examples, the Request object was used to extract variables from the URL QueryString and to determine the value of a button when it was pushed. The same concept is used to gather HTML form data using the Request object. The Request.Form property identifies the name of the individual HTML form element to retrieve the information from. Keep in mind that the Request object does not extract information directly from the HTML form, but parses the information sent to the Web server via an HTTP Post. After the processing is complete, the browser is shifted to the summary page.

The summary page, as shown in Figure 16.3, is used as a virtual receipt to confirm to the user the amount of items ordered, the total cost, and to whom and where the items are being sent. The exact same logic that is applied to display the items in the shopping cart is used to display information in the summary page; the only difference is the HTML formatting.

From Here...

In this chapter, you have seen the integration of Active Server Pages built-in objects used to build this simple online ordering system. This application demonstrated how to extract information from hyperlinks and forms. The Application object is used to pre-load data that can be accessed from any user within the site. For information that is relatively static, pre-loading this information once can save a considerable amount of resources from retrieving the same information on a frequent basis. The Session object provides the core functionality of the online ordering system by enabling a user-specific virtual shopping basket. The shopping basket consists of transferring and maintaining application-, session-, and page-level arrays and variables. The Server object is used to apply encoding techniques to string information, reset the information about the current user, and set the ScriptTimeOut value for pages. The Response object is used to control output sent to the browser by writing information to the ASP with the Write method. The Response object also plays an important role by using the Redirect method to route the user to the desired page. The Request Object is used for retrieving information from the user. For related information, see the following chapters:

- Chapter 18, "Creating Your Own Active Server Components," walks you through the tools and examples on how to create tailored functionality via custom created components.
- Chapter 20, "Database Access with ADO," teaches you how to use the Data Access Component to connect to any ODBC-compliant database.
- Chapter 26, "Putting It All Together: Creating a Dynamic Database Application," illustrates how to use the `Application` object to store information extracted from a database to provide database interaction for the Amazing DataWidget WareHouse.
- Chapter 31, "Using Internet Information Server 4.0 to Manage Your Web Applications," demonstrates how to use the various features of Internet Information Server to help manage your sites and applications.
- Chapter 32, "Putting It All Together: Creating an N-Tier Online Catalog Application," demonstrates how to build ActiveX database components managed by the Microsoft Transaction Server to create an n-tier distributed catalog application for the Amazing DataWidget WareHouse site.

Part

III

Ch

16

Active Server Components

Implementing Existing Server-Side Components

One of the most powerful features of the Internet Information Server and Active Server Pages is the capability to tap into COM-based components. These server-side objects greatly extend the functionality of the Web server by providing a virtually limitless warehouse of programming functionality. Furthermore, the server-side components help transition traditional application developers into creating Web applications by enabling ActiveX components to be created in their native COM-based development environments, such as Visual C, C++, Visual Basic, Delphi, and PowerBuilder. This chapter demonstrates the various server-side components that are shipped and installed with the Internet Information Server and Active Server Pages. ■

The Browser Capability and Advertisement Rotator Components

Learn how to use the Browser Capability Component to determine requesting browsers' characteristics and how to use the Advertisement Rotator Component to dynamically generate scrolling advertisement bars.

The Counter Component and Page Counter Component

Investigate how the Counter Component is used to create incremental variables within your ASPs and how to use the Page Counter Component to track the number of times a page is requested.

The Content Rotator and Content Linking Components

Utilize the Content Rotator to change the content on a page every time the page is requested or refreshed and learn how to use the Content Linking Component to create a systematic Web page navigation technique for pages within a site.

The Active Messaging/SMTP Component and Tools Component

Discover how to tap in to the power of Microsoft Exchange and other e-mail–based systems using the Active Messaging/SMTP Component and how the Tools Component brings additional functionality to server-side processing.

The Ad Rotator Component

The Ad Rotator Component is designed to display and rotate different advertisements on Web pages. This rotating billboard approach is tailored to selling advertising space on commercial Web sites. The Rotator Component can display a new advertisement every time based on the frequency specified in a schedule file. The displayed banner can be programmed to route the browser to a destination site when the user clicks the banner, or can be used simply to display the banner without forwarding to another site. For example, the Ad Rotator Component is responsible for managing the banner display mechanisms for an ASP page, as shown in Figure 17.1.

FIG. 17.1

The Ad Rotator displays rotating banner images based on a scheduling file.

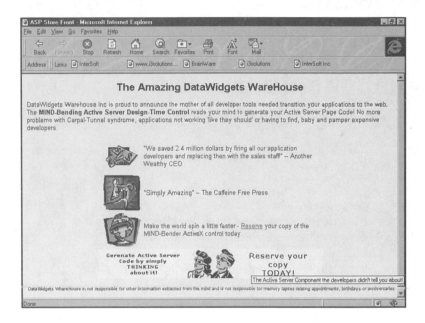

When the site is revisited or refreshed, the Ad Rotator can display another banner based on the frequency set in the scheduling file, as shown in Figure 17.2.

Let's take a closer look at how the Ad Rotator uses methods and properties to display the rotating banners.

The *GetAdvertisement* Method

To activate the Ad Rotator Component, the `Server.CreateObject` method is used to instantiate an instance of the Ad Rotator Component:

```
Set ad = Server.CreateObject("MSWC.AdRotator")
```

In this situation, the `Set` command is used in conjunction with the `Server.CreateObject` tag to create a reference to the `MSWC.AdRotator` object. The Ad Rotator Component ships with the Internet Information Server and is automatically registered on the Web server when IIS is installed. The Ad Rotator Component is created from an instantiated instance of the `Adrot.dll`.

Typically, the `Adrot.dll` file is installed in the `\WINNT\System32\InetSrv` directory on the NT Web server. The Ad Rotator has one method: the `GetAdvertisement` method. The `GetAdvertisement` method manages and retrieves information from the scheduling file. When the `GetAdvertisement` method is called from a new page request or a page refresh request, the `GetAdvertisement` method loops through the schedule file to display the next advertising banner. To use the `GetAdvertisement` method, use the following syntax:

```
GetAdvertisement(ScheduleFilePath)
```

where *ScheduleFilePath* is the virtual path to the schedule file.

FIG. 17.2
When the page is revisited or refreshed, the Ad Rotator Component displays a new banner image.

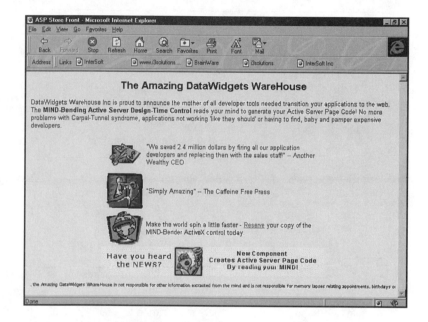

Part
IV

Ch

17

The Ad Rotator Component Required Files

As mentioned in the `GetAdvertisement` method, the Ad Rotator references other files to complete its tasks. The Ad Rotator Component requires two other files to complete its functionality, as shown in Table 17.1.

Table 17.1   The Ad Rotator File References

Name	Description
Rotation schedule file	Text file that manages the frequency or schedule of the displayed banner.
Redirection file	Redirects the requesting browser to the destination site for a given banner.

The Rotator Schedule File

The Rotator schedule file controls the frequency and the properties of the Ad Rotator Component. The schedule file determines the frequency or schedule of the advertisements, manages the properties of the advertisements, and is also used to set the various properties of the banner object. These properties are shown in Table 17.2.

Table 17.2   The Schedule File Properties

Name	Description	Scope
Redirect (URL)	Sets the default location to route the browser (optional).	All images in rotator schedule.
Width (imgWidth)	Sets the default pixel width of the banner image (optional).	All images in rotator schedule.
Height (imgHeight)	Sets the default pixel height of the banner image (optional).	All images in rotator schedule.
Border (imgBorder)	Sets the default border width of the banner image (optional).	All images in rotator schedule.
*	Separates the default values (shown above) from the individual banner detail specifications in the schedule file.	
AdURL	Sets the location to retrieve the image file.	Individual image in rotator schedule.
AdHomePageURL	Sets the location of the advertiser home page.	Individual image in rotator schedule.
Text	The textual display for text-based browsers or if displaying images are deactivated on the browser.	Individual image in rotator schedule.
Impressions	Sets the percentage of time that the image will be displayed.	Individual image in rotator schedule.

For example, Listing 17.1 demonstrates a sample scheduling file.

Listing 17.1   A sample rotation schedule file.

```
---DecemberInfo.TXT---
REDIRECT /scripts/adredir.asp                         '=== Sets redirect
➥location for logging
WIDTH 400                                             '=== Sets the default
➥width
HEIGHT 50                                             '=== Sets the default
➥height
BORDER 0                                              '=== Sets the default
➥border
*                                                     '=== Separator
http://myDataWidgets/DecemberSales/mywidget.gif       '=== First Advertisement
➥banner image
http://www.myDataWidgets.com/                         '=== Home page location
Free Demo of the new Data Widget Deluxe for ODBC      '=== Textual Content
20                                                    '=== Frequency displayed
http://DataCom/DataComObject.gif                      '=== Second
➥Advertisement banner
-                                                     '=== No Home page
➥location
It's Coming, DataCom Inc, the new way of doing business '=== Textual Content
80                                                    '=== Frequency Displayed
```

This scheduling file, named DecemberInfo.text, is used to display two advertisements. The first advertisement points to a company at www.myDataWidgets.com, and the advertisement is to be displayed 20 percent of the time. The second advertisement is used to display an image from the DataCom virtual directory. This image, however, does not have a home page location, so a dash (-) character is used. This image is activated 80 percent of the time when this site is refreshed.

The Redirection File

The *redirection file* is responsible for routing the browser to the destination site, as determined in the scheduling file. This redirecting approach is not directly needed to shift the user to the advertiser site when the banner is clicked. Simple HTTP can accomplish this. However, the redirection file is needed to keep track of the number of hits generated from an Ad Rotation banner. For example, in the aforementioned scheduling file, the redirection file /scripts/ adredir.asp is designated in the first line of the DecemberInfo.txt file. This redirection file is not only used to push the requesting client to the requested advertisement, but also to store a variety of information about the requesting client, such as the browser type or IP address. The following code demonstrates using the Response.Redirect method to guide the browser to the page specified in the banner scheduling file.

```
--- adredir.asp ---
<% Response.Redirect(Request.QueryString("myAdUrl")) %>
```

At this point, you can use various Web analysis logging tools or the Page Counter Component to determine the number of hits the redirection page received. The Page Counter Component is another built-in component that is discussed later in this chapter. For more information about the Response object, refer to Chapter 14, "Speaking to the Web Client: The Response Collection."

The Ad Rotator Properties

The Ad Rotator banner has three properties that control the Ad Rotator Component, as displayed in Table 17.3.

Table 17.3 The Ad Rotator Properties

Name	Description
Border	Sets the width of the border around the advertisement.
Clickable	Sets whether the rotator banner is a hyperlink or simply an image.
TargetFrame	Sets the name of the target frame to display the banner.

The properties of the Ad Rotator all follow the same syntax of requiring an object to act upon:

```
Object.Property
```

Table 17.4 illustrates a quick guide to the syntax for the Ad Rotator properties.

Table 17.4 The Ad Rotator Property Syntax

Property	Syntax
Border	Border (*size*)
Clickable	Clickable (*value*)
TargetFrame	TargetFrame (*frame*)

The Border property is used to set the size of the border around the banner image. To set the border size, use the following syntax:

```
Border (size)
```

where *size* is an integer specifying the thickness of the border. To display a banner with no border, similar to an image with no border, set the border size to 0, as shown in the following example:

```
ad.BorderSize(0)
```

In this code example, the border size of the Ad Rotator object named ad is set to 0. The result of setting the border width is shown in the following figures.

Figure 17.3 displays a banner with border size set to 2.

The Clickable property determines whether the displayed image acts as a hyperlink or simply acts as a random image generator. To set the Clickable property, use the following syntax:

```
Clickable (value)
```

where *value* is True or False. The values of the Clickable property are shown in Table 17.5.

FIG. 17.3

Adjusting the border size of the banner to size of 2.

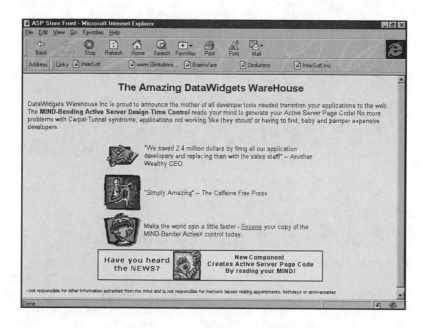

Table 17.5 The Ad Rotator's Property Values

Value	Description
True	Sets the displayed banner to act as a hyperlink.
False	Disables the hyperlink property of the banner.

If the value of the Clickable property is set to True, the display banner acts like a hyperlink. If the value is set to False, the Ad Rotator simply displays the banner and the hyperlink effect of the banner is disabled. To use this display-only banner effect, use the following code:

```
<% Set Ad = Server.CreateObject("MSWC.AdRotator")      '=== Create Ad Rotator
Object %>
<% Ad.Clickable(False)                                 '=== Disables the
hyperlink property of the banner %>
<%= Ad.GetAdvertisement("/ASPSamp/Samples/adrot.txt")  '=== Display a new banner
%>
```

This code would not just present rotating images on ASP pages. Because these images are not hyperlinks anymore, the default hyperlink border color will not surround the image and the standard image border is used. The TargetFrame property is used to indicate the name of the frame in which the Ad Rotator object is to be displayed. The TargetFrame property behaves similarly to the HTML TARGET tag, where you can name the destination location within a browser window for the results to be displayed. To use the TargetFrame property, use the following syntax:

```
TargetFrame (frame)
```

where *frame* is the name of an HTML frame. The name property supports all native HTML Frame tags, including _TOP, _NEW, _CHILD, _SELF, and _PARENT.

For example, to display the results of the Ad Rotator Component in a frame named AdWindow, use the following syntax:

```
<%
Set myAdObj = Server.CreateObject("MSWC.AdRotator")    '=== Create AdRotator
Object
FrName = "AdWindow"                                     '=== Set Frame Name
myAdObj.TargetFrame (FrName)                            '=== Set target frame
%>
<%= myAdObj.GetAdvertisement("/June/specials.txt")     '=== write the Ad to page
%>
```

The Browser Capabilities Component

The Browser Capabilities Component retrieves browser information from the requesting browser. The Browser Capabilities Component retrieves information from the USER Agent HTTP header string to determine the type and version number of the browser that is requesting the page. The Browser Capabilities Component then references an external file that stores additional information about the requesting browser.

To use the Browser Capabilities Component, use the following syntax:

```
Set BrowserType = Server.CreateObject("MSWC.BrowserType")
```

where *BrowserType* is the reference to the instantiated MSWC.BrowserType object from the BROWSCAP.DLL. Usually the BROWSCAP.DLL is located in the \WINNT\System32\InetSrv of the NT Web server.

The *BROWSCAP.INI* File

The Browser Capabilities Component uses a text file named BROWSCAP.INI to act as a reference card to store information about the capabilities of various browsers. The Browser Capabilities Component retrieves the User Agent Header string from the requesting browser and uses that value to look up additional features about the requesting browser in the BROWSCAP.INI file. If a match cannot be found, the default browser settings from the BROWSCAP.INI are used.

The BROWSCAP.INI file must be located in the same directory as the BROWSCAP.DLL file. The BROWSCAP.INI file is initially installed to the Web server when IIS is installed. The BROWSCAP.INI file can be created, edited, and maintained via any ANSI editor.

The BROWSCAP.INI structure is shown in Table 17.6.

Table 17.6 The *BROWSCAP.INI* File Structure

Symbol	Description
;;	Comments.
[header info]	Sets a key field defining a HTTP User Agent Header request.
property=value	Sets the various properties of the specific browser type.
[Default Browser Capability Settings]	Sets the default property settings.

Chapter 15, "Retrieving User Information: The Request Object," demonstrated how to use the Server variable to extract information from the HTTP header string. For example, the following Server variables extract browser information.

```
<% myBrowserType = Request.ServerVariables("HTTP_USER_AGENT") %>
```

If an America Online browser is making a request on your site, the variable myBrowserType would return the following string information:

```
Mozilla/2.0 (compatible; MSIE 3.0; AOL; Windows 95)
```

To determine the additional properties of this browser that are not located within the HTTP header string, reference the header string in the BROWSCAP.INI file. The header string must be included in the hard brackets ([ ]) within the BROWSCAP.INI file, as shown below:

```
;;AOL Browser           '=== Comment to help identify AOL browser
[Mozilla/2.0 (compatible; MSIE 3.0; AOL; Windows 95)]
parent=IE 3.0
version=3.01
minorver=01
platform=Win95
```

Now these additional features can be referenced by the Browser Capabilities Component to help identify characteristics of the specific browser type.

The interesting thing about the identification fields in the BROWSCAP.INI file is that you can include wildcard (*) placeholders to group common types of browsers. For example, to group all Internet Explorer-compatible browsers running on Windows 95, use the following code to identify the browser identification field in the BROWSCAP.INI file:

```
;;IE 3.01
[Mozilla/2.0 (compatible; MSIE 3.0;* Windows 95)]
parent = IE 3.0
version = 3.01
minorver = 01
platform = Win95
```

Part
IV

Ch
17

The addition of the wildcard in the identification field now groups the following browsers together:

```
[Mozilla/2.0 (compatible; MSIE 3.0; Windows 95)]
[Mozilla/2.0 (compatible; MSIE 3.0; AK; Windows 95)]
[Mozilla/2.0 (compatible; MSIE 3.0; SK; Windows 95)]
[Mozilla/2.0 (compatible; MSIE 3.0; AOL; Windows 95)]
```

You can further expand the different browser types within the BROWSCAP.INI file by using the parent tag within the browser identification tags. The parent tag enables inheritance from previous browser versions, which enables previous browser properties to be built on each other without having to maintain full property lists for every version of a browser that is released. If existing property values are detected, the new values overwrite existing values and new properties are appended to the existing property list.

Listing 17.2   A sample *BROWSCAP.INI* file.

```
;; IE 3.0                          '=== Internet Explorer 3.0 version
[IE 3.0]
browser = IE
Version = 3.0
Majorver = 3
Minorver = 0
Frames = TRUE
Vbscript = TRUE

;; IE 3.01                         '=== Internet Explorer 3.1 version
[Mozilla/2.0 (compatible; MSIE 3.01*; Windows 95)]
parent = IE 3.0                    '=== Inherit value from the IE 3.0
version = 3.01                     '=== Overwrites version info
minorver = 01                      '=== Overwrites minor version info
platform = Win95                   '=== Appends the platform property

; Default Browser
[Default Browser Capability Settings]
browser = Default
frames = FALSE
tables = TRUE
cookies = FALSE
backgroundsounds = FALSE
vbscript = FALSE
javascript = FALSE
```

In Listing 17.2, if an IE 3.01-compatible browser is detected by the Browser Capabilities Component, the parent tag of the IE 3.01 header refers to the IE3.0 version defined earlier in the INI file. In this situation, the version is overwritten now to 3.01, the minorver tag is now overwritten to 01, and the platform property of Win95 is appended to the property list.

The Browser Capabilities Component Properties

Once the Browser Capabilities Component has been created, information about the browser can be determined by examining its properties. By using the properties you can ensure that the requesting clients of your application and site meet specific criteria. The properties of the Browser Capabilities Component are illustrated in Table 17.7.

Table 17.7   The Browser Capabilities Component Properties

Property	Description
ActiveXControls	Specifies whether the browser supports ActiveX controls.
Backgroundsounds	Specifies whether the browser supports background sounds.
Beta	Specifies whether the browser is beta software.
Browser	Specifies the name of the browser.
Cookies	Specifies whether the browser supports cookies.
Frames	Specifies whether the browser supports frames.
JScript	Specifies whether the browser supports JScript.
Platform	Specifies the platform that the browser runs on.
Tables	Specifies whether the browser supports tables.
VBScript	Specifies whether the browser supports VBScript.
Version	Specifies the version number of the browser.

After the Browser Capabilities Component has been created, you can access these properties to ensure a specific browser functionality level. For example, Listing 17.3 displays information about a requesting browser:

Listing 17.3   Detecting and displaying information about the browser capabilities.

```
<%
Dim myBrowser
Set myBrowser = Server.CreateObject("MSWC.BrowserType") %>
<table border = 1 width = 100% CellPadding = 2 CellSpacing = 2>
<tr><td>Browser Type</td><td>  <%= myBrowser.browser  %>           '=== Writes
Browser Name
<tr><td>Version</td><td>  <%= myBrowser.version  %>  </td></TR>      '===
display Version
<tr>
<td>Frames</td>
```

Part

IV

Ch

17

continues

Listing 17.3   Continued

```
<td>
<%
if (myBrowser.frames = TRUE) then          '=== Test for Frames
     Response.Write("TRUE")
else
     Response.Write("False")
end if
%>
</td></TR>
<tr><td>VBScript</td>
<td>
<%
if (myBrowser.vbscript = TRUE) then        '=== Test for VBScript Support
     Response.Write("TRUE")
else
     Response.Write("False")
end if
%>
</td></TR>
<tr>
<td>ActiveX Controls</td>                   '=== Test for ActiveX support
<td>
<%
if (myBrowser.ActiveXControls = TRUE) then
     Response.Write("TRUE")
else
     Response.Write("False")
end if
%>
</td></TR>
</table>
```

Knowing information about the browser will help you control how your application behaves in various browsers. In real-world applications, you will need to build off the Browser Capabilities Component to test for capability and display issues. For example, the following code uses both the Browser Capabilities Component and the Request object to ensure that requesting browsers are either Internet Explorer 3.0 or Netscape Navigator 3.0 compatible.

```
<%
dim isBrowserOK
Set browserobj = Server.CreateObject("MSWC.BrowserType")       '=== Create
➥Browser Component
if Instr(Request.ServerVariables("HTTP_USER_AGENT"),"MSIE") then   '=== Check
➥for Browser info using '=== the Request Object
     if browserobj.MajorVer = 3 then             '=== Uses Browser Object to get
➥version number
          isBrowserOK = true
     else
          isBrowserOK = false
     end if
```

```
else
    if Instr(Request.ServerVariables("HTTP_USER_AGENT"),"Mozilla") then      '===
Check for Netscape
        isBrowserOK  = true
    end if
end if
%>
```

The previous example creates a variable named isBrowserOK to determine whether the requesting browser is either IE 3.0 or Netscape. If the requesting browser is either Netscape or Internet Explorer 3.0, the isBrowserOK variable is set to True. Now you can use this value to route the user to the appropriate location, as shown in the following code:

```
<% If browserOK Then %>
    '=== Proceed to next step in client validation
<% Else %>
    '=== Warn user to upgrade browser
<% End If %>
```

The Database Access Component

Active Server Pages can access databases through the use of the *Active Data Object* (ADO). *ADO* is an optimized database connection based off the Data Access Object (DAO) and Remote Data Object (RDO) used in traditional application development tools such as Visual Basic. The ADO provides critical features that are needed to transform existing client-server applications into Web-enabled applications. The ADO object supports various cursor types, batch updating, extended recordset management techniques, and advanced stored procedure support.

The details of the ADO object are fully described in Part V, "Database Management with Active Server Pages." Those seven chapters are dedicated to demonstrating how to manage your database connection in Active Server Pages.

The ADODB object is used to add a database connection to your ASP application. To create the ADO connection, use the following syntax:

```
Set myDataConn = Server.CreateObject("ADODB.Recordset")
```

where *myDataConn* is the instantiated reference to the ADODB object. Once the database connection object exists, a database connection can be made by using the Open method. The Open method can accept query strings or stored procedure names. For example, the following code uses the recordset object created in the previous example to store the result from the SQL statement Select * From CustomerInfo:

```
myDataConn.Open "SELECT * FROM CustomerInfo", "DATABASE = pubs;UID = sa;PWD=;DSN
= Publishers"
```

Now that the results have been stored in the myDataConn recordset object, the information can be written to the page by using a Do...While loop and checking for the beginning of file (BOF) and end of file (EOF) markers. If both BOF and EOF values are True, no records are returned. The following code example demonstrates this iterative technique to write information returned from the database onto an HTML page:

```
<%
Set myDataConn = CreateObject("ADODB.Recordset")        '=== Creation Connection
Object
myDataConn.Open "SELECT * CustomerInfo", "DATABASE = pubs;UID = sa;PWD=;DSN =
Publishers"
If myDataConn.EOF and myDataConn.BOF Then               '=== Check to see if data is
returned
        '=== No Results returned
Else
    Do While Not myDataConn.EOF           '=== Iterate through result set
            Response.Write (myDataConn("CustomerID") & "<BR>")  '=== write the
            customerID field                           ' ===
            and an HTML break to the page
    Loop                                   '=== End of While Loop
End If
%>
```

The Active Messaging/SMTP Component

The Active Messaging Component is an exciting component that opens the object model of various Simple Mail Transfer Protocol (SMTP) messaging systems. These messaging systems enable you to directly tap into the power of Internet-based mail and groupware software solutions such as Microsoft Exchange. Now you can not only create and manage e-mail messages, but also other resources such as discussion databases. The Active Messaging Component uses the Microsoft Exchange Server to store and access mail-based information. In this way, Exchange can be used as a gateway to other SMTP interfaces, as well as expose its calendar and scheduling features such as displayed Microsoft Outlook to any HTML client.

As with other programming models, the Messaging object model follows a hierarchical format that is used to manipulate its programmable objects. The Messaging/SMTP Messaging object model is shown in Figure 17.4.

FIG. 17.4
The Active Messaging object model exposes the functionality found in Microsoft Exchange and Outlook.

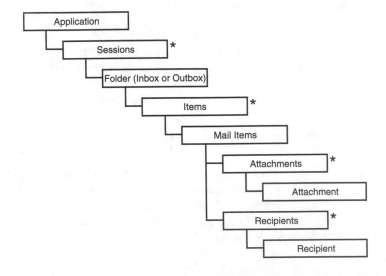

The SMTP interface enables you to manage your messaging system with relative ease by instantiating the `ACTMSG32.DLL` file. Similar to the other installed server components, the `ACTMSG32.DLL` file is typically installed in the `\WINNT\System32\InetSrv` directory on the NT Web server.

Although, I could dedicate a several chapters to discussing the details of the SMTP interface, this section only will briefly highlight the capabilities of the Active Messaging Component. For example, Listing 17.4 sends a mail message to `Information@myDomain.com` with the subject line of `MAPI Subject Line` and a textual message of `This message was generated via the Active Messaging Component`.

Listing 17.4   Send e-mail via ASP and the Active Messaging Component.

```
<%
Set myMAPISession = Server.CreateObject("MAPI.Session")            '=== Creates
➡MAPI Object
myServerProfile = "myServer"                                       '=== Creates
➡Login String
myMailboxProfile = "myUserProfile"
myMailProfile = myServerProfile + chr(10) + myMailboxProfile
myMAPISession.Logon "", "", False, True, 0, True, myMailProfile    '=== Session
➡Logon
Set myMessageObj = myMAPISession.Outbox.Messages.Add              '=== Open New
➡OutBox message
Set myDestinationObj = myMessageObj.Recipients.Add                '=== Address
➡new message
myDestinationObj.name = ("Information@myDomain.com")              '=== Send to
➡this user
myDestinationObj.Resolve                                          '=== Resolve
➡user name
myMessageObj.subject = "MAPI Subject Line"                        '=== Set the
➡Subject Line
strMsgText = "This message was generated "
strMsgText = strMsgText & "via the Active Messaging/SMTP component"
myMessageObj.Text = strMsgTxt                                     '=== Assigns
➡body  text
myMessageObj.Send showDialog = false                             '=== Send the
➡message
set myDestinationObj = Nothing                                    '=== Clean up
➡objects
set myMessageObj = Nothing
set myMAPISession = Nothing
%>
```

Part

IV

Ch

17

Once the previous code is run, Figure 17.5 verifies that the message was sent and received by checking the Inbox of the Microsoft Exchange HTML/ASP interface.

FIG. 17.5
The Active Server Code
generated this mail
message as viewed by
the Exchange HTML/ASP
interface.

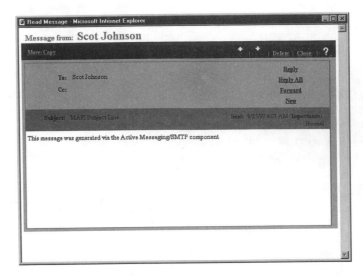

To check on the contents of the message, select the hyperlink under the From categories and view the detail of the message, as shown in Figure 17.6.

FIG. 17.6
The Exchange HTML
interface displays the
message generated
from the ASP code.

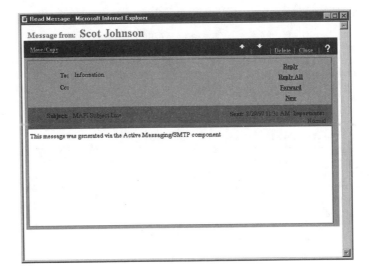

You can see where this automatic messaging system can be very useful and very straight-forward to implement. For example, a remote sales-force automation application can benefit from the automatic mailer system. The automatic e-mail notification can be used to trigger an action item at headquarters when a remote user updates information.

The Active Messaging HTML (AMHTML) object model is a very powerful interface responsible for exposing the native functionality found in Outlook into an HTML format.

In order to expose the AMHTML object model, the AMHTML Component must be instantiated, as shown in the following line of code:

```
Set myExchObj = Server.CreateObject("AMHTML.Application")
```

where *myExchObj* is the name of the object instantiated by the AMHTML application. In order for the different message items and views to be accessed, they must be translated or rendered into HTML. This rendering process is activated by calling the `CreateRenderer` method, as seen below:

```
Set myRenderingObj = myExchObj.CreateRenderer(arg)
```

where *myRederingObj* is the instantiated reference to the `CreateRenderer` tag and *arg* is the `CreateRenderer` argument. The exposed items can then be obtained by extracting information from the session Inbox or OutBox. When the specific view is called, the `Datasource` object is used to act as an index to retrieve specific properties from the selected item. To use the `Datasource` property, use the following code example:

```
myRenderingObj.DataSource = myMessageItem
```

Keep in mind that Exchange requires proper authorization every time you call any Active Messaging HTML (`AMHTML`) object. Therefore, session validation will be required when interfacing the `AMHTML` object on different ASP pages. The authorization can be verified by using the `Response` object, as covered in Chapter 14. To ensure that proper authorization is available, use the following code to trap the authentication method supported by the server:

```
<%
bAuthType = Request.ServerVariables("auth_type")
If InStr(1, "_basicNTLM", bAuthType, vbTextCompare) < 2 Then
     Response.Buffer = TRUE
     Response.Status = ("401 Authorized")
     Response.AddHeader "WWW.Authenticate", "Basic"
     Response.End
End If
%>
```

The previous code example extracts the authentication scheme from the `Request` object. Next, the VBScript `InStr` function checks to see whether the requested authentication scheme supports NTML authentication. If so, the `Response` object is used to prompt the user for a username and password by forcing a basic authentication dialog with the server. Basic authentication transmits the username and password between the browser and the Web server to provide login permissions to the Web server. NTML authentication also verifies user authentication but does not send the actual username and password between the browser and the Web server to prevent possible security violations. As a result of this ASP code, the user is presented with a authentication dialog box to log in to the system, as shown in Figure 17.7.

Table 17.8 gives a description of the available `AMHTML` objects that are available once the user is authenticated. These `AMHTML` object can be accessed via ASP create, read, send, and delete messages.

FIG. 17.7

The user is prompted for proper authorization to access the Active Messaging/SMTP objects.

Table 17.8 Active Message Component Objects

Object	Purpose
AddressEntry	Specifies address information for an individual messaging user.
Application	Acts as a top-level object for a messaging application.
Attachment	Associates an additional object with a mail item.
Attachment collection	Accesses all attachments on a mail item; creates new attachments.
Folder	Opens the default Inbox or Outbox folder in a message store.
Items collection	Accesses all mail items in a folder; creates new mail items.
MailItem	Composes, populates, sends, and receives e-mail documents.
Recipient	Specifies information for a messaging user intended to receive a mail item.
Recipients collection	Accesses all recipients of a mail item; creates new recipients.
Session	Establishes a connection between an application and a messaging system.
Sessions collection	Accesses all sessions for an application; creates new sessions.

The power of the AMHTML object can be easily seen in a simple ASP example that opens the Inbox view of an Exchange Server user profile view and reads the first message.

```
<%
Set myMapiObj = Server.CreateObject( "MAPI.Session" )        '=== Creates MAPI
➥Session
strProfile = "myExchangeServer" + vbLF + "myUserName"        '=== Creates Login
➥String
myMapiObj.Logon "", "", False, True, 0, True, strProfile     '=== Login the
➥MAPI Session
Set myInboxObj = myMapiObj.Inbox                             '=== Opens the
➥InBox
Set myMessageObj = myInboxObj.Messages.GetFirst             '=== Get the first
➥message
Set myRenderApp = Server.CreateObject("AMHTML.Application")  '=== Creates
➥AMHTML Object
```

```
Set myRendererObj = myRenderApp.CreateRenderer(2)          '=== Begin
➥translation
myRendererObj.DataSource = myMessageObj                     '=== Set the
➥datasource
%>
```

The previous code logs you into the Exchange mail session and retrieves the first mail message in the Inbox folder. When the code has finished processing the datasource, the current message position is located on the first message. Now ASP code be integrated with HTML code to extract the specific fields of the Exchange item, as shown in Listing 17.5.

Listing 17.5   Extracting information from an Exchange e-mail message.

```
<HTML>
<HEAD>
<TITLE>Read The First Exchange Inbox Message</TITLE>
</HEAD>
<BODY TEXT=000000 BGCOLOR=FFFFFF>
Message from:<% AddrType =
myRendererObj.RenderProperty(ActMsgPR_SENT_REPRESENTING_ADDRTYPE)
Address  =
myRendererObj.RenderProperty(ActMsgPR_SENT_REPRESENTING_EMAIL_ADDRESS)
myRendererObj.RenderProperty ActMsgPR_SENT_REPRESENTING_NAME, 0, Response %><BR>

To: <% myRendererObj.RenderProperty ActMsgPR_DISPLAY_TO, 0, Response %><BR>
Cc: <% myRendererObj.RenderProperty ActMsgPR_DISPLAY_CC, 0, Response %><BR>
Subject: <% myRendererObj.RenderProperty ActMsgPR_SUBJECT, 0, Response %>
Time: <% myRendererObj.RenderProperty ActMsgPR_CLIENT_SUBMIT_TIME, 0, Response
%><BR>
Message: <% myRendererObj.RenderProperty ActMsgPR_RTF_COMPRESSED, 0, Response %>
</Body>
</HTML>
```

Listing 17.5 assumes that the user has sufficient permissions to open the view and that a first record exists in the Exchange Inbox. This listing will generate the HTML interface, shown in Figure 17.8, which reads the message originally generated from the ASP code.

FIG. 17.8

The Active Messaging HTML Component exposes an SMTP interface that enables you to read, write, and manage your mail messages via ASP.

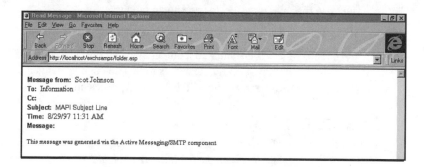

The Active Messaging/SMTP Components are robust object models that are not completely covered within this chapter. For complete information on the Active Messaging/SMTP object models, see your online documentation or download the Active Messaging SDK from www.microsoft.com.

The Tools Component

The Tools Component provides additional server-side processing mechanisms that add functionality to server-side processing. The Tools Component uses a total of five different methods, as shown in Table 17.9. Two of the five Tool Component methods, Owner and PluginExists, are only applicable to the Personal Web Server for the Macintosh.

Table 17.9   The Tools Component Methods

Method Name	Description
FileExists	Checks for the existence of a file.
Owner	Checks to see whether the current user is the site administrator (Macintosh only).
PluginExists	Checks the existence of a server plug-in (Macintosh only).
ProcessForm	Processes an HTML form.
Random	Generates a random integer.

The Tools Component can be created with either global scope or page-level scope. To create a Tools Component in the GLOBAL.ASA file, use the following syntax:

```
<OBJECT RUNAT = Server SCOPE = Session ID = Tools PROGID = "MSWC.Tools">
</OBJECT>
```

This OBJECT reference tag creates the Tools Component with session-level scope that can be accessed from any ASP page for a particular user. The session-level object will exist until the user Session object is destroyed. To create a page-level instance of the Tools Component in a ASP file, use the CreateObject tag as shown below:

```
Set myToolObj = Server.CreateObject("MSWC.Tools")
```

The myToolObj object is instantiated from an instance of the TOOLS.DLL, which is typically installed in the \WINNT\System\InetSrv directory. The page-level instance of the myToolObj object will be destroyed when the ASP is finished processing.

The *FileExists* Method

The FileExists method checks for the existence of a file within a virtual directory and returns whether the file exists. This is a particularly useful feature because it not only helps prevent broken HREF links to other pages, but it can also verify the existence of other files before these files are called or used. For example, you might want to use the FileExists method to verify that an image file, content scheduling file, or include file exists before trying to reference the desired file. This method is particularly useful when sites are moved from Web server to Web server to keep up with scaling and growth needs on your sites.

To use the `FileExists` method, the Tools Component requires the following syntax:

`myToolObj.FileExists(URL)`

where *myToolObj* represents the instantiated Tools Component and *URL* is the path to the request file.

The `FileExists` method returns either one of two values. The return value of -1 is used to symbolize that the file is found as designated within the URL. If the file cannot be found, the `FileExists` method returns a 0.

The `FileExists` method is also helpful when you want to ensure that a file exists before you reference the file. You can use the `FileExists` method to prevent runtime errors or broken link items. For example, to prevent a broken hyperlink, the `FileExists` method first checks for the existence of the calling page in the potential hyperlink, as shown below:

Part
IV
Ch
17

```
<% Set Tools = Server.CreateObject("MSWC.Tools")
If Tools.FileExists("=/OnLineLearningCenter/chapter2.asp") Then %>
        <p> <a href="/OnLineLearningCenter/chapter2.asp">chapter2.asp</a></p>
<% Else %>
    <p>File Not Found</p>
<% End If %>
```

In this code example, the `FileExists` method is used to determine whether the `/OnLineLearningCenter/chapter2.asp` page exists. If the file does exist, the code generates a valid link to that page. If the file does not exist, it prints a `File Not Found` message. Similarly, the same process can be used to validate whether image files exist, as shown below:

```
<% Set Tools = Server.CreateObject("MSWC.Tools")
If Tools.FileExists("corplogo.gif") Then %>
        <p> <a href="http://www.i3solutions.com/"><img src="corplogo.gif"
border=0></a><p>
<% Else %>
    <p><a href="http://www.i3solutions.com/">Use Link Instead</a></p>
<% End If %>
```

In this code example, if the requested image file `corplogo.gif` does not exist, a text hyperlink is generated to replace the missing image file.

In most situations, you will use the `FileExists` method in conjunction with other components that do not have built-in error trapping for files that cannot be located. For example, the following code checks to see if the `acolades.txt` exists before calling the Tools Component.

```
<%
Dim objTool
Set objTool = Server.CreateObject("MSWC.Tools")
If objTool.FileExists("acolades.txt") Then %>                '=== If the file
➥exists, use the component
    <TR><TD>
        <%
```

```
            Dim NextTip
            Set NextTip = Server.CreateObject("MSWC.ContentRotator")
            Response.Write NextTip.ChooseContent("acolades.txt")
            %>
        </TD></TR>
        <TR><TD>
            <% Response.Write NextTip.ChooseContent("acolades.txt")%>
        </TD></TR>
<%
Else                                '=== File does not exist, write a text version
%>
        <TR><TD>
            <FONT FACE="Arial">Make the world spin a little faster -
            <A HREF = "userprofile1.asp">Reserve</A> your
            copy of the MIND-Bender ActiveX control today.</FONT>
        </TD></TR>
<% End If %>
```

In this code example, the Tools Component is used to check that the acolades.txt file does exist before creating an instance of the Content Rotator control. If the Content Rotator control called the missing acolades.txt file, the control would generate a fatal runtime error. To prevent this situation from occurring, the Tools Component verifies whether the file exists. If the file does exist, the Content Rotator control generates content from the acolades.txt file. If the Tools Component does not find the acolades.txt file, a static message is displayed.

The *Owner* Method

The Owner method is specific to the Personal Web Server on the Macintosh computer. The Owner method checks to see whether the current user of the site has administrator privileges for the Web server. To use the Owner method, use the following syntax:

```
Tools.Owner
```

The Owners method returns–1 if the current user has administration privileges, and 0 if the current user does not have administration privileges. For example, the following code displays the administration menu for an application to the site administrator only.

```
<%
Set Tools = Server.CreateObject("MSWC.Tools")    '=== Creates Tools Object
If Tools.Owner Then                              '=== Checks Owner Method
     Response.Redirect "/menu/AdminMenu.asp"     '=== Redirect to Administration
➥Menu
Else
     Response.Redirect "/menu/RegularMenu.asp"   '=== Redirect to Normal Menu
End if
%>
```

The *PluginExists* Method

The PluginExists method is also a Macintosh Personal Web Server-specific method that verifies if server-side plug-ins have been installed. To use the PluginExists method, use the following syntax:

```
Tools.PluginExists(PluginName)
```

where *PluginName* is the name of the Web server plug-in. The `PluginExists` method also returns `True` or `False` to indicate whether the plug-in exists. If the specific plug-in does exist, the
method returns –1. Likewise, if the server-side plug-in is not found, the `PluginExists` method
returns 0. The following example performs a test to a plug-in named `myPlugin` on the
Macintosh PWS.

```
<%
If Tools.PluginExists(myPlugin) Then
     '=== Perform Plug-in methods
End If
%>
```

The *Random* Method

The `Random` method is used to generate a random integer between -32768 and 32767. To use
the `Random` method, use the following syntax:

```
Tools.Random
```

To display a random number, use the following code example:

```
<% Set Tools = Server.CreateObject("MSWC.Tools") %>
<% Response.Write Tools.Random %><BR>                <!--Writes a Random number to the
page -->
```

Keep in mind that you can use other arithmetic functions in conjunction with the random
method. For example, to limit the scope or range of the randomly generated numbers, use the
`MOD` and `ABS` statements:

```
<% = ( Abs( Tools.Random ) ) Mod 10 %>       <!--Generates a random number from 0
to 10 -->
```

This example generates random numbers between 0 and 10.

The Permission Checker Component

The Permission Checker Component is used to identify whether the requesting user has permission to access a file, which enables you to maintain strict security levels for files that are
tailored for both private and public viewing. The Permission Checker Component not only
gives you the ability to check access permissions after a request for a page has been made, but
also to control navigation flow. For example, you can first check permissions and, depending on
whether the user is authorized, display or hide navigation links. This capability to monitor
access is particularly important for permission-dependant applications and pages with intranet-,
extranet-, and Internet-based applications. For example, you can use the Permission Checker
Component to only give managers access to monthly payroll accounts that regular employees
should not see.

To use the Permission Checker Component, use the following syntax:

```
Set myPermissionObj = Server.CreateObject("MSWC.PermissionChecker")
```

Part

IV

Ch

17

where *myPermissionObj* is the name of the instantiated Permission Checker object. When using the Permission Checker Component, keep in mind that Internet Information Server supports three different authentication schemes. *Anonymous access* uses the NT Internet access account to control access to files within the Web Server domain. If anonymous access is selected for files, the Permission Checker Component has nothing to authenticate because the requesting browser already has access to the files within NT.

N O T E   For permission-dependent applications and pages, disable the anonymous access authentication to prevent it from overriding the Permission Checker Component.   ■

If anonymous access has been disabled, NT uses the basic or NTLM authentication method to monitor permissions. You can set individual or group permissions by using the Access Control List. Chapter 14 demonstrated how to force authentication by using the following script:

```
<%
If Request("LOGON_USER") = "" Then
    Response.Status = "401 Unauthorized"
End If
%>
```

However, the Permission Checker Component accomplishes the same task by using the HasAccess method, as shown in Table 17.12.

Table 17.12   The Permission Checker Component's Method

Method Name	Description
HasAccess	Verifies whether the requesting browser has access to a file.

The *HasAccess* Method

The HasAccess method is used to determine whether the requesting user has permission to read a file. To use the Permission Checker Component, the HasAccess method requires the following syntax:

HasAccess(*FilePath*)

where *FilePath* is the physical or virtual path to the requested file. The HasAccess method returns a True value if the user is successfully authorized and False if the authentication fails.

You can use the Boolean result from the HasAccess method to check access permissions. The following code displays the access permission for both a virtual and a physical file path.

```
<% Set myKeyObj = Server.CreateObject("MSWC.PermissionChecker") %>
Permissions: <BR>
Virtual Directory: <%= myKeyObj.HasAccess("c:\inetpub\wwwroot\default.asp")
%><BR>      <!-- Virtual -->
Physical Directory: <%= myKeyObj.HasAccess("/default.asp") %><BR>      <!--
Physical -->
Mis-spelling: <%= myKeyObj.HasAccess("/default.asp") %><BR>      <!-- Mis-spelled
-->
```

This code examines the `default.asp` file permissions and returns the results. Notice that the `HasAccess` method does not return an error if the file does not exist. If the file cannot be found, the `HasAccess` method returns a `False` value, as demonstrated below:

```
Permissions:
Virtual Directory: True
Physical Directory: True
Mis-spelling: False
```

The most common means of implementing the `HasAccess` method is to check the access permissions for a Web page or file and, if the user is authorized, allow access to a requested site or page. Typically, this is implemented by presenting a hyperlink pointing to the permission-dependent site. For example, Listing 17.6 demonstrates using the Permission Checker Component to check access rights to the `report1.asp`.

Listing 17.6   Using the Permission Checker to authorize access to information.

```
<%
dim vUserHasAccess
Set myKey = Server.CreateObject("MSWC.PermissionChecker")       '=== Creates
Permission Object
UserHasAccess = myKey.HasAccess("/private/report1.asp")         '=== Checks
permission of report1.asp
%>
<% If vUserHasAccess Then %>
     <A HREF = "/private/default.htm">Administrative Reporting!</A>       '=== If
Authorized, display this link
<% Else %>                                                      '=== Else warn off
the user
     Sorry, you are not authorized to access this report. Your IP Address has
been recorded.
<% End If %>
```

Keep in mind that you do not have to display a results page with a hyperlink to let the user know if he has the appropriate permissions. You can provide a seamless navigational flow directly to the requested page using the `Response.Redirect` method. The direct routing requires fewer steps for the user and prevents unnecessary requests from being processed by the server. The following example uses the `Response.Redirect` method to eliminate displaying the Web page that displays the *Administrative Reporting* hyperlink and to automatically route the browser to the `/private/default.htm` page:

```
<%
dim vUserHasAccess
Set myKey = Server.CreateObject("MSWC.PermissionChecker")       '=== Creates
➡Permission Object
vUserHasAccess = myKey.HasAccess("/private/report1.asp")        '=== Checks
➡permission of report1.asp
If vUserHasAccess Then
     Response.Redirect "/private/report1.asp"                   '=== If Authorized,
➡route user to this page
End If
%>
```

Part
IV

Ch

17

The Content Linking Component

The Content Linking Component is used to help manage and control links within a set of documents. The set of documents is usually clearly defined, such as a table of contents for a document, an online manual, or the required steps for a wizard. The Content Linking Component provides value by generating and maintaining the order of the files and tracking which item is active in this list.

To use the Content Linking Component, use the following syntax:

```
Set myNextLink = Server.CreateObject("MSWC.Nextlink")
```

where *myNextLink* is the reference to the instantiated MSWC.Nextlink object. The Content Linking Component is an instantiated instance of the Nextlink.DLL file, which is usually installed in the \WINNT\System\InetSrv directory.

The *NextLink* Files

The Content Linking object requires two files to properly function on the Web server, as shown in Table 17.13. The first is the NextLink.DLL filter, which is required for the creation and interpretation of the Content Linking object. The second file is the Content Linking list. The Content Linking list is responsible for managing the sequential list of files within a single text file, and managing the current location of the user in the schedule file list. Now groups of pages can be easily managed and maintained without having to update links on each page. This automatic update of the navigation links can be seen in Figures 17.9 and 17.10. Figure 17.9 illustrates displaying content with a next page link that points to the next URL.

FIG. 17.9

The Content Linking Component stores your relative position in a list of sequential URLs and automatically updates the navigation links with the appropriate links.

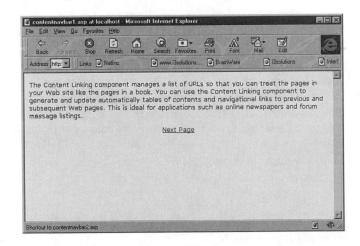

After clicking the Next Page link, the second page of content is displayed and the Content Linking Component creates a Previous Page link and updates another Next Page link, as shown in Figure 17.10. In this situation, the Previous Page link points to the first page of content and the Next Page link points to the third URL. If the Next Page link were activated, the same process of automatically updating the URL navigation link would be repeated.

FIG. 17.10
After moving to the second page, the Content Linking Component updates the URL locations for the navigation links with new URLs embedded in the Previous Page and Next Page hypertext.

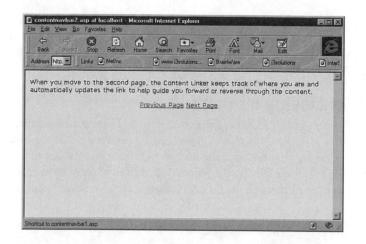

Part
IV

Ch
17

Table 17.13   The Content Linking Component Required Files

Name	Description
NextLink.DLL	Required to create the Content Linking object.
Content Linking list	A text file used to sequentially list the files to be viewed.

The Content Linking List

The Content Linking list serves as the master index for managing workflow and scheduling content on the Web. The Content Linking file stores the Web page location, textual information describing the location, and comments for the specified item. The Content Linking list uses the tab character to separate the URL field, the description field, and the comments field, as shown in the following syntax:

Page-URL[➡][text-description[➡][comment]]

where *Page-URL* is the destination of the text description field, *text-description* is the description of the URL, and *comment* is comments to help identify and track the pages.

N O T E The Content Linking file searches for the tab character to separate the fields and a hard return to create a new row. ■

The following code is an example of a Content Linking list that is used to consecutively manage and navigate three pages and their descriptions:

```
---------- MylinkText.txt ----------
Chapter1.asp     Chapter 1     First Chapter
Chapter2.asp     Chapter 2     Second Chapter
Chapter3.asp     Chapter 3     Third Chapter
```

In the previous example, the Content Linking list is named MylinkText. The Content Linking list contains three Web pages that are to be displayed in sequential order. The first page to be displayed is the Chapter1.asp file, with a description of Chapter 1. The comment First chapter is added just as a reference for the authors or administrators of the list file.

The Content Linking Methods

After the series of files has been designated in the Content Linking list, the Content Linking object uses methods to retrieve and navigate through the Content Linking list. The Content Linking Component uses eight methods to help manage your Content Linking list, as shown in Table 17.14. These methods are generally separated into the forward and reverse navigation (or up and down) through the list or are used to retrieve information about the link.

Table 17.14   The Content Linking Methods

Name	Description
GetListCount	Counts the number of items linked in the Content Linking list file.
GetNextURL	Gets the URL of the next page listed in the Content Linking list file.
GetPreviousDescription	Gets the description line of the previous page listed in the Content Linking list.
GetListIndex	Returns the index of the current page in the Content Linking list.
GetNthDescription	Gets the description of the Nth page listed in the Content Linking list.
GetPreviousURL	Gets the URL of the previous page listed in the Content Linking list.
GetNextDescription	Gets the description of the next page listed in the Content Linking list.
GetNthURL	Gets the URL of the Nth page listed in the Content Linking list.

The GetListCount and GetListIndex methods are used to refer to the number of items in the Content list and the current page. The GetNextURL, GetPreviousURL, and GetNthURL methods use the Content Linking Component to retrieve the URL locations from the Content Linking list. The GetNextDescription, GetPreviousDescription, and GetNthDescription methods complement the previous methods to extract description values from the Content Linking list.

GetListCount The Content Linking Component uses the `GetListCount` method to retrieve the total number of pages stored in the Content Linking list. The total number of pages stored in the list is important to help loop through the Content list. To use the `GetListCount` method, use the following syntax:

```
GetListCount(listURL)
```

where *listURL* is the virtual path to the Content Linking list. To determine the number of pages in the Content Linking list, use the following example:

```
<%
Set myLinkObj = Server.CreateObject("MSWC.NextLink")
iCount = myLinkObj.GetListCount("MylinkText.txt")
%>
```

In this situation, the `iCount` returns a value of 3. The `GetListCount` index is 1-based, meaning that it starts at 1 and contains integers greater than 1. However, if the Content Linking list `MylinkText.txt` is not found, the `GetListCount` method returns a zero value. If you try to perform subsequent methods on a Content Linking list that cannot be found, a runtime error will be generated. To prevent these runtime errors from occurring, trap the value of the `count` property, as shown below:

```
<%
Set myLinkObj = Server.CreateObject("MSWC.NextLink")
iCount = myLinkObj.GetListCount("MylinkText.txt")
Do While (iCount > 0)  %>
--- Do Something ---
Loop
%>
```

The `GetListCount` method is also useful in navigation management. For example, you may want to add special hyperlinks or closing messages when the last page is reached. You can accomplish this by using the `GetListCount` and `GetListIndex` methods. The `GetListCount` method returns the number of pages in the list and the `GetListIndex` determines the current page, as demonstrated in the following code:

```
<%
Set myNextLinkObj = Server.CreateObject ("MSWC.NextLink")       '=== Create
➥Content Linker
iCurrent = myNextLinkObj.GetListIndex ("/data/mylink.txt")      '=== Retrieves
➥current position
iMax = myNextLinkObj.GetListCount("/data/mylink.txt")           '=== Determines
➥maximum amount of links
If iCurrent = iMax Then                                         '=== Checks for
➥max condition
    Response.Write ("Thank you for registering for "&vClassTitle & "<BR>")
    Response.Write("<A HREF = 'top.menu.Reload(main)'>Main</A>)
End If
%>
```

In this example, if the user has successfully navigated to the last page of the registration wizard, that is, `iCurrent = iMax`, a thank you message is written to the page with a hyperlink that calls a function named `Reload`, which is located in the frame named `menu`.

GetListIndex   The `GetListIndex` method is used to return the list index of the current page in the Content Linking list. To use the `GetListIndex` method, use the following syntax:

```
GetListIndex(listURL)
```

where *listURL* is the virtual path to the Content Linking list. The `GetListIndex` method returns an integer result identifying the current position within the Context Linking list. To retrieve the current position within the content list, use the `GetListIndex` method, as shown in the following example:

```
<%
Set myNextLinkObj = Server.CreateObject ("MSWC.NextLink")
IcurrentLink = myNextLinkObj.GetListIndex ("/data/mylink.txt")
%>
```

In most situations, you will use the `GetListIndex` method to customize the display for the first page within the list. For example, if you only want have a single hyperlink to the second page, but have forward and reverse links on the remaining pages, you would trap the `GetListIndex` value for a return result of 1 and tailor the results accordingly.

```
<%
Set myNextLinkObj = Server.CreateObject ("MSWC.NextLink")
If (myNextLinkObj.GetListIndex ("/data/mylink.txt") > 1) Then
 '=== Display only the forward navigation toolbar on first page
Else
     '=== Display standard forward and reverse toolbar on remaining pages
End If
%>
```

GetNextURL   The next three methods, `GetNextURL`, `GetPreviousURL`, and `GetNthURL`, are used to retrieve the URL locations from the Content Linking list. The `GetNextURL` method is used to take the current position indicator and retrieve the next URL in the Content Linking list. To implement the `GetNextURL` method, use the following syntax:

```
GetNextURL(listURL)
```

where *listURL* is the virtual path to the Content Linking list. For example, to extract the next URL location, use the `GetNextURL` method as shown in the following example:

```
<%
Set myNextLinkObj = Server.CreateObject ("MSWC.NextLink") %>
<a href = "<%= myNextLinkObj.GetNextURL ("/data/mylink.txt") %>">Next Page</a>
```

This example retrieves the next URL in the Content Linking list and inserts the URL into the hyperlink ANCHOR tag, as you saw in Figure 17.9. When the user clicks the Next Page link, the next URL in the list will be viewed. For example, if the user is located on the second content page, `chapter2.asp`, the Next Page hyperlink will point to `chapter3.asp`.

N O T E   The `GetNextURL` will point to the first URL in the Content Linking list if the user is positioned on the last page in the list. ■

You can combine the `GetListIndex` method sample code with the previous `GetNextURL` sample code to only generate a Next Link hyperlink when the user is on the first page in the scheduling file.

```
<%
Set myNextLinkObj = Server.CreateObject ("MSWC.NextLink")
If (myNextLinkObj.GetListIndex ("/data/mylink.txt") > 1) Then %>
     <a href = "  <%= myNextLinkObj.GetNextURL ("/data/mylink.txt") %>">Next
➥Page</a>
<% Else %>
     '=== Display standard forward and reverse toolbar on remaining pages
<% End If %>
```

GetPreviousURL The `GetPreviousURL` tag complements the `GetNextURL` method by enabling reverse or descending navigation through the items in the content list. The `GetPreviousURL` method can be executed by using the following syntax:

```
GetPreviousURL(listURL)
```

where *listURL* is the virtual path to the Content Linking list. To navigate to the previous URL in the list, use the `GetPreviousURL` method, as shown in the following example:

Part

IV

Ch

17

```
<%
Set myNextLinkObj = Server.CreateObject ("MSWC.NextLink")
<a href = "<%= myNextLinkObj.GetPreviousURL ("/data/mylink.txt") %>">Previous
Page</a>
%>
```

Now you can combine the `GetPreviousURL` and the `GetNextURL` methods to provide page-by-page navigation through your content.

```
<% '============ Next Page Navigation HyperLink =================================
Set myNextLinkObj = Server.CreateObject ("MSWC.NextLink") %>
<a href = "<%= myNextLinkObj.GetNextURL ("/data/mylink.txt") %>">Next Page</a>
<% '=========================== Previous Page Navigation Hyper Link =========== %>
<a href = "<%= myNextLinkObj.GetPreviousURL ("/data/mylink.txt") %>">Previous
Page</a>
```

This code sample is what generates the browser navigation you saw in Figures 17.9 and 17.10.

GetNthURL The `GetNthURL` method rounds out the URL navigation methods by enabling the user to skip beyond the sequential navigation techniques demonstrated with the `GetPreviousURL` and `GetNextURL` navigation methods. Typically this specific index navigation is used when specific items are picked from a list, such as a table of contents or picking the starting alphabetical letter form an index ranging from A to Z. The `GetNthURL` provides the capability to navigate to any URL within the Content Linking list based on the index number. To implement the `GetNthURL` method, use the following syntax:

```
GetNthURL(listURL, iContent)
```

where *listURL* is the virtual path to the Content Linking list and *iContent* is the URL location specified in the Content Linking list. For example, to jump from any page within the content list and navigate to the `chapter2.asp` listing, set the *iContent* variable to `2`, as demonstrated in the following example:

```
<% Set myNextLinkObj = Server.CreateObject ("MSWC.NextLink") %>
<a href = "<%= NextLink.GetNthURL("/data/mylink.txt", 2)%>"> ">Chapter 2</a>
```

With ASP filename information, you can display the entire navigational list, as shown in the left frame in Figure 17.11.

FIG. 17.11
Use the `GetNthUrl` method to provide list or table of contents navigation.

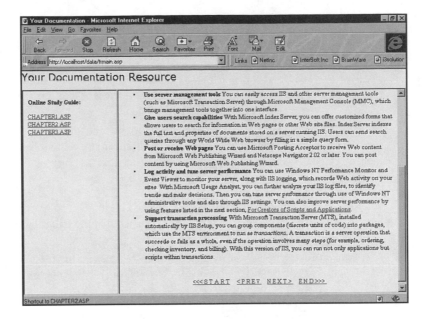

Now, with this ability to manipulate URL information, you can create a complete navigational toolbar with move-first, move-last, move-next, and move-previous navigation links. This functionality is implemented using the combination of the `GetNthURL`, `GetNextURL`, and `GetPreviousURL` methods (see Figure 17.12).

FIG. 17.12
Use the combination of the `GetNthUrl`, `GetPreviousUrl`, and `GetNextURL` methods to construct a complete navigational toolbar.

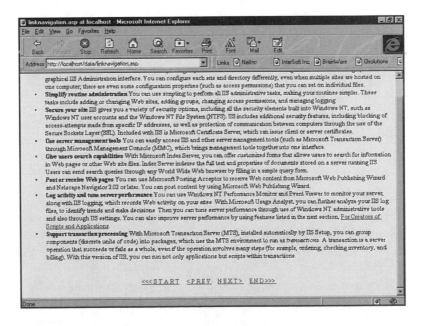

The navigation links displayed in Figure 17.12 were created by using the code shown in Listing 17.7.

Listing 17.7 Creating a content navigation toolbar using the Content Linking Component.

```
<%
Set myNextLinkObj = Server.CreateObject ("MSWC.NextLink")
iMaxLinks = myNextLinkObj.GetListCount("/data/mylink.txt")
iMinLink = 1              '=== Linking file is 1-based
%>
<Center>
<Table Cellpadding = 4 CellSpacing = 4 border = "0">
<TR align = center><TD>
    <a href = "<%= myNextLinkObj.GetNthURL("/data/mylink.txt", iMinLink)%>">
    <<<  S T A R T</a>
    </TD><TD>
      <a href = "<%= myNextLinkObj.GetPreviousURL ("/data/mylink.txt")  %>">
    <   P R E V </a>
    </TD><TD>
    <a href = "<%= myNextLinkObj.GetNextURL("/data/mylink.txt")%>">
     N E X T   > </a>
    </TD><TD>
    <a href = "<%= myNextLinkObj.GetNthURL("/data/mylink.txt", iMaxLinks)%>">
     E N D  >>>  </a>
    </TD></TR>
</Table>
</Center>
```

In Listing 17.7, the hyperlinks to the move-first, move-next, move-previous, and move-last links are embedded within an HTML table to ensure page layout. The iMaxLinks variable is used to set the total number of links contained within the Content Linking list.

Now you can combine the table of content view with the sequential page navigation methodology to enable complete navigation through your content (refer to Figure 17.11).

The table of contents view, shown in the left frame, is generated by looping through all the URL locations in the Content Linking list. In this situation, the direct ASP filename is being displayed as the hyperlink.

```
<% Set myNextLinkObj = Server.CreateObject("MSWC.NextLink") %>
<% count = myNextLinkObj.GetListCount("mylink1.txt") %>
<% I = 1 %>
<% Do While (I <= count)  %>
    <A Href = "<%= UCASE(myNextLinkObj.GetNthURL("mylink1.txt", I))%>">
    <% Response.Write UCASE(myNextLinkObj.GetNthURL("mylink1.txt", I))%></A><BR>
    <% I = (I + 1) %>
<% Loop %>
```

GetNextDescription   The remaining three methods, GetNextDescription, GetPreviousDescription, and GetNthDescription, mimic the functionality of the previously discussed URL navigation features, but instead retrieve the descriptions from the Content Linking file.

The GetNextDescription method is used to retrieve the description of the next content item in the Content Linking list. To use this method, the following syntax is required:

```
GetNextDescription(listURL)
```

where *listURL* is the virtual path to the Content Linking list. The GetNextDescription method provides a better description of the content file than just displaying the filename itself.

```
<% Set myNextLinkObj = Server.CreateObject("MSWC.NextLink") %>
<a href = "<%= myNextLinkObj.GetNextURL("/data/mylink1.txt")%>">
<%= myNextLinkObj.GetNextDescription ("/data/mylink1.txt")%></a>
```

In the previous code example, the next content page URL address is placed inside the anchor list using the GetNextURL method. But now the description of the page can also be extracted from the Content Linking list and used as the description within the hyperlink. For example, if the user is currently on the chapter1.asp page, which is the first item in the Content Linking list, the hyperlink would read Chapter 2 and the HTML anchor tag would point to chapter2.asp.

GetPreviousDescription

The GetPreviousDescription method complements the GetNextDescription method by supplying the capability to move to the previous description within the Content Linking list. To implement this feature, use the following syntax:

```
GetPreviousDescription(listURL)
```

where *listURL* is the virtual path to the Content Linking list. To provide a user-friendly message description to return to a previous file, use the GetPreviousDescription method, as shown in the following example:

```
<% Set myNextLinkObj = Server.CreateObject("MSWC.NextLink") %>
<a href = "<%= myNextLinkObj.GetPreviousURL("/data/mylink1.txt")%>">
<%= myNextLinkObj. GetPreviousDescription ("/data/mylink1.txt")%></a>
```

If the user has navigated to the second page within the Content Linking list, this sample code would create a hyperlink with the text of Chapter 1 and the HTML anchor tag of chapter1.asp.

GetNthDescription

The GetNthDescription method enables you to extract the URL description from any valid content index without using relative positions, as is the case with the GetNextDescripton and GetPreviousDescriptions methods. To implement this non-sequential description retrieval method, the Content Linking Component requires the following syntax:

```
GetNthDescription(ListUR, iURL)
```

where *ListURL* is the virtual path to the Content Linking list and *iURL* is the URL location specified in the Content Linking list. The GetNthDescription method complements the GetNthURL method to provide a user-friendly description of the URL. For example, an easier to read table of contents can be created by looping through the Content Looping file and using the GetNthDescription method to display the descriptions, *Chapter 1*, *Chapter 2*, and *Chapter 3*, as shown in Figure 17.13.

FIG. 17.13
The `GetNthDescription` method provides a useful description of the content pages.

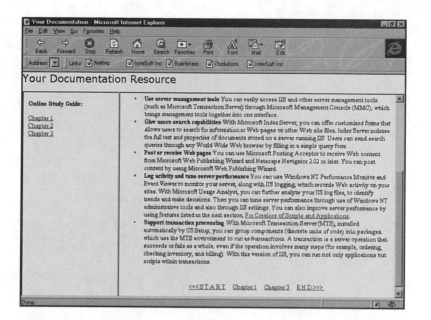

The code behind Figure 17.13 illustrates the various aspects of using the `GetListCount` method, looping through the Content file, and using the `GetNthDescription` and `GetNthURL` methods to provide navigation and description information.

```
<B>Online Study Guide:</B><BR><BR>
<% Set myNextLinkObj = Server.CreateObject("MSWC.NextLink") %>
<% count = myNextLinkObj.GetListCount("mylink.txt") %>
<% I = 1 %>
<% Do While (I <= count)  %>
    <A HREF = "<%= myNextLinkObj.GetNthURL("mylink.txt", I)%>">
    <%= myNextLinkObj.GetNthDescription ("mylink.txt", I)%></A><BR>
    <% I = (I + 1) %>
<% Loop %>
```

Keep in mind that you are not just limited to using hyperlinks for your page navigation. Figure 17.14 demonstrates using HTML buttons to provide a navigation methodology.

Furthermore, remember to exploit the description field within the Content Linking list. This description field is treated as a text field, and any values within this description field are translated into HTML. This means that you can embed HTML within the content location file, such as image files. Figure 17.15 illustrates the use of adding HTML tags with the `DESCRIPTION` tag of the Content Linking list.

Part
IV

Ch
17

FIG. 17.14
Use any workflow or navigation motif, such as images, buttons, or links, with the Content Linking Component.

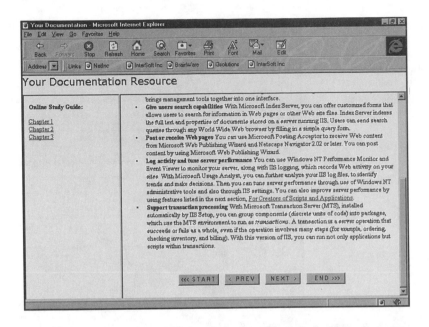

FIG. 17.15
HTML tags, such as the IMAGE tag, can be embedded within the description field of the Content Linking file.

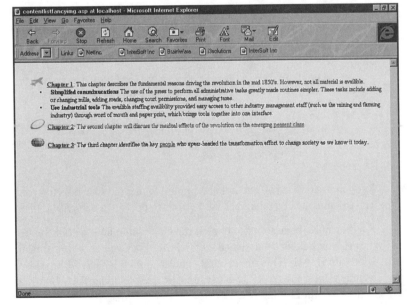

Figure 17.15 demonstrates the capability to embed various HTML tags within the description field of the Context Linking list. This entire HTML page, including the images, hyperlinks, anchors, and bulleted lists, exists within the description field. To ensure that the following code examples are easy to read, only the image attributes have been included in the following Content Linking list.

```
---------- myLink.txt with embedded HTML tags----------
chapter1.asp    <img src = "bplaney.gif" border=0 width=30 height=20><Font
Size=+1><B>Chapter 1</B></font></a>:    This chapter ...
chapter2.asp    <img src = "bswoop.gif" border=0 width=30 height=20><Font
Size=+1><B>Chapter 2</B></font></a>:    The second chapter will discuss the
residual effects of the revolution on the emerging <a href =
"peasants.htm">peasant class</a>.<BR><BR>
chapter3.asp    <img src = "bglobey.gif" border=0 width=30 height=20><Font
Size=+1><B>Chapter 3</B></font></a>:    The third chapter identifies the key ...
```

Remember that the Context Linking Component only looks for tabs to separate the URL, description, and comment fields when parsing through the Content Linking list. Therefore, you can embed HTML characters directly in the Context Linking list.

The Content Rotator Component

The Content Rotator Component is responsible for displaying and managing a schedule of how often content is displayed on a page. The role of the Content Rotator is similar to the Ad Rotator Component; however, instead of displaying an image banner, it delivers HTML content to the page. The Content Rotator expands this role by not only providing the capability to transfer content, but also providing the capability to embed HTML tags within the content string itself. This embedding feature enables you to provide HTML formatting, hyperlinks, and image tags.

To use the Content Rotator Component, the following syntax is required:

```
<% Set myObjVar = Server.CreateObject("MSWC.ContentRotator") %>
```

where *myObjVar* is the reference to the instantiated Content Rotator Component.

The Content Rotator requires two files, the `ContRot.dll` and the Content Schedule file, as shown in Table 17.15. The `ContRot.dll` file is the Dynamic Link Library needed to create the Content Rotator Component on the server.

Table 17.15   The Content Rotator Required Files

Name	Descriptions
ContRot.dll	Required DLL for the Content Rotator.
Content Schedule file	Text file that manages the content and the frequency with which it is displayed.

The Content Schedule File

The Content Schedule file has two responsibilities. The first responsibility is simply to house the different content items. The second responsibility is to set the frequency or weight with which the content is displayed. The Content Schedule file uses the following syntax:

```
%% [#Weight] [//Comments] ContentString
```

Part

IV

Ch

17

where the double percent symbols (%%) designate a new content item; #*Weight* is an optional value that specifies the relative weight, which determines how often the specific content item is displayed; *Comments* enables comments to be attached to the content item; and *ContentString* is the content string.

Listing 17.8 is an example of a Content Linking file.

Listing 17.8   A Sample Content Rotator file.

```
- - - - - - - - - - - -content.txt- - - - - - - - - - - - - - - - - - -
%% #1 // The DataSource Solutions Item
<body><FONT FACE = "ARIAL" SIZE = "2">
<IMG SRC = "barrow.gif">World-wide Intranet rollout <a href = "/DS/
Intro.ASP">saves $300k</a> per month
</FONT></BODY>

%% #1 // NetHouse AD
Download the newest <a href = "/NH/default.asp">IP packet tools</a> from
NetHouse Inc

%% #0 // Place ad once bill is paid
<Body BGCOLOR = "#CC9900">
New design tools from <H2>World Environmental Technologies Inc</H2> <A HREF =
"/wet.asp">(WETInc)</A> help simulation programs reduce vehicle emissions
</Body>
```

The weight of each content item acts as the relative weight compared to the other content items. The greater the relative weight of the content item, the greater the frequency with which content item will be displayed. The relative weight is determined by dividing the weight of the content item by the sum of the other items in the Content Schedule file, as viewed in the following formula:

```
Probability = Weight of Content Item / (Sum of all weights in Content File)
```

For example, in the listed Content Schedule, the first item is assigned a weight value of 1 and the second item is assigned the weight of 3. The probability that the first content item will be displayed is 25 percent. The second content item has 75 percent probability that it will be displayed. For example, the Amazing DataWidget WareHouse online catalog, as demonstrated in Chapter 19, "Putting It All Together: Creating an Online Registration System," uses this probability to determine the frequency with which product and related news information will be displayed on the site. To gain attention to a particular sale item or news event, increase the weight in the Content Schedule file.

By default, if no weight is assigned, the content is assigned a value of 1. If a content item is assigned a weight of 0, the content item will be ignored.

Notice that the content items can house HTML tags. For example, the third content link changes the background color of the page to #CC9900.

Remember that this content information is not being physically rotated in a circle on the HTML page. The Content Rotator simply determines what information will be loaded the next time the page is requested.

The Content Rotator Methods

The Content Rotator uses two methods to post and rotate content to a page (see Table 17.16). The ChooseContent method is used to retrieve a specific content item. The GetAllContent method retrieves all items from the Content Schedule file.

Table 17.16   The Content Rotator Methods

Name	Description
ChooseContent	Extracts a specific content item from the Content Schedule file.
GetAllContent	Extracts all the content items from the Content Schedule file.

The *ChooseContent* Method

The ChooseContent method extracts individual content items from the Content Linking list based on the item's relative weight each time the page is called. To retrieve content information, use the following syntax:

```
ChooseContent(ContentSchedule)
```

where *ContentSchedule* is the virtual path pointing to the Content Schedule file. For example, to extract the content items from the previous content file, use the following code:

```
<BODY bgcolor = "#FFFFFF"><center>
<%
Set myContentItem = Server.CreateObject("MSWC.ContentRotator") %>
<% Response.Write myContentItem.ChooseContent("/data/content.txt") %>
</Center></Body>
```

This example produces the rotating content in the bottom frame shown in Figures 17.16 and 17.17.

Once the page is revisited or refreshed, the Content Rotating Component automatically updates the page with new content from the Content Schedule file (see Figure 17.17).

Notice that the HTML BODY background tags in the calling ASP of white (#FFFFFF) are overwritten by the HTML contained within the Content Linking file.

FIG. 17.16
The Content Rotator pulls a content string from the scheduling file based on its weight or frequency setting.

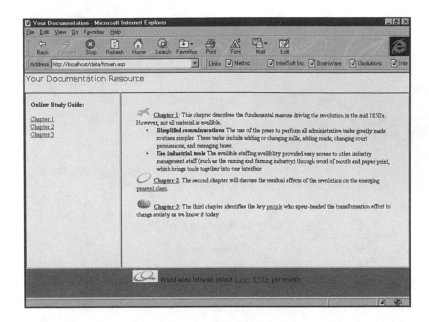

FIG. 17.17
The next time the page is refreshed, new content is retrieved from the schedule file.

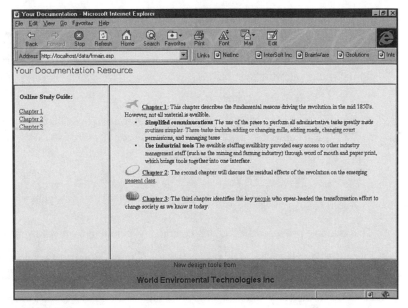

The *GetAllContent* Method

The GetAllContent method retrieves all the content in the Content Schedule file and displays the content items on the calling page separated by horizontal rule (<HR>) tags. To use the GetAllContent method, use the following syntax:

```
GetAllContent(ContentSchedule)
```

where *ContentSchedule* is the virtual path to the Content Schedule file. To display all the items within the Content Schedule file, use the GetAllContent method, as shown in the following example:

```
<HTML><BODY bgcolor = "#FFFFFF"><center>
<% Set Tip = Server.CreateObject("MSWC.ContentRotator") %>
<% = Tip.GetAllContent("/data/content.txt") %>
```

This code produces the output displayed in Figure 17.18.

FIG. 17.18
The GetAllContent method extracts all the content information from the Content Schedule file.

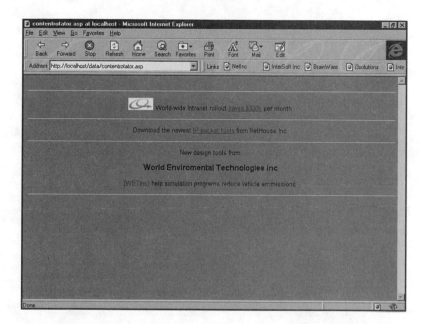

Notice that this example performs in a manner similar to the ChooseContent method in terms of overwriting the calling HTML tags. The HTML tags assigning white (#FFFFFF) as the background color are overwritten by the last calling instance of the HTML BODY tag in the Context Schedule file. In this situation, the HTML BGCOLOR tag is changed from #FFFFFF to #669900 in the first content item and to #CC9900 in the last content item.

The Page Counter Component

The Page Counter Component is used to keep track of how many times a specific page has been opened. The Page Counter Component temporarily stores in memory the number of times a page has been opened and then stores the counter information in a text file at regular intervals. This memory caching prevents excessive resources from being consumed with a large number of input/output and read/write requests to the hard drive. To use the Page Counter Component, the following syntax is required:

```
<% Set myObjVar = Server.CreateObject("MSWC.PageCounter") %>
```

Part
IV

Ch
17

The Page Counter Component requires the combination of two files, the PageCnt.DLL and the Hit Count Data file, as shown in Table 17.17.

Table 17.17 Required Page Counter Component Files

Name	Description
PageCnt.Dll	Dynamic Link Library needed to create the Page Count component
Hit Count Data file	The text file to which the Page Count Component writes the current hit count.

The PageCnt.DLL is the Dynamic Link Library needed to create the Page Count Component on the server. The Hit Count Data file is the text file that the Page Count Component writes the current page count to. The Page Count Data file acts as a storage area to store the number of times a page was opened. After a given number of hits, the page count that is stored in memory is written to a text file. The Registry settings are used to specify how often this storing to a text file occurs and stores the path location to the Hit Counter file. Table 17.18 summarizes the Registry file settings.

Table 17.18 The Page Counter Component Registry Settings

Registry Name	Description
File_Location	Specifies the location and filename of the counter file.
Save_Count	Specifies the increment at which the current page count is written to the Hit Count Data file (default is 25).

By default, the Hit Count Data file name is HitCnt.cnt in your Windows directory. If you follow the standard NT installation, the HitCnt.cnt file will be located in the \WINNT directory. The HitCnt.cnt file stores two pieces of information: the name of the page and the number of times that page was requested. An example of the HitCnt.cnt file is displayed in the following:

```
------------- HitCnt.cnt -------------
11025     /data/download/default.asp
43775     /data/default.asp
```

The Page Counter Component Methods

The Page Counter Component uses two methods, as shown in Table 17.19, to manage page count information.

Table 17.19   The Page Counter Component Methods

Method	Description
Hits	Returns the number of times a page has been opened.
Reset	Initializes the value of a page count to 0.

The *Hits* Method

The Hits method of the Page Counter Component returns the number of times an Active Server Page has been requested. The Hits method uses the following syntax:

```
Hits([pathInfo])
```

where *pathInfo* is the optional location for the requested page. If no path information is given, the current page is assumed. For example, to use the Page Counter Component to track and display the page counter information for the current page, use the following code example:

```
<% Set MyPageCounter = Server.CreateObject("MSWC.PageCounter") %>
This Web page has been viewed <%= MyPageCounter.Hits %> times.
```

Alternately, if you want to display information about the number of times that another page was requested, use the Hits method and specify the path to the desired page, as shown below:

```
<%
Set MyPageCounter = Server.CreateObject("MSWC.PageCounter")
vPageStr = "/data/download.asp"
%>
The Web page, '<% =vPageStr %>', has been viewed <%= MyPageCounter.Hits(vPageStr)
%> times.
```

This example looks at the page stored in the virtual path of /data/download.asp and extracts the page count for that page, as shown in the following results:

```
The Web page, '/data/download.asp', has been viewed 24750 times.
```

The *Reset* Method

The Reset method clears the current page count value and reinitializes the page count for the page to zero. To utilize this method, use the following syntax:

```
Reset([pathInfo])
```

where *pathInfo* is the virtual path to the requested ASP. The Reset method shares many similar characteristics with the Hits method. If no path information is specified, the Reset method assumes that it should be activated on the current page. The path information can also be applied to various other ASP files by specifying the path information to the desired file. For example, to reset the current ASP count to 0, use the following syntax:

```
<%
Set MyPageCounter = Server.CreateObject("MSWC.PageCounter")      '=== Create
➥Component Instance
```

```
MyPageCounter.Reset                                        '=== Resets the
➥current page
%>
```

Furthermore, use the Path statement to reset counter information in multiple files located in different directories. This use of the Path statement can be seen in the following example:

```
<%
Set MyPageCounter = Server.CreateObject("MSWC.PageCounter")    '=== Create
➥Counter Object
vPageStr = "/data/download.asp"          '=== Set File/Path Info
MyPageCounter.Reset(vPageStr)            '=== Reset counter for '/data/
➥download.asp'
MyPageCounter.Reset                      '=== Rest Counter for current page
%>
```

The Counter Component

The Counter Component plays a role similar to the Page Counter Component, except that the Counter Component operates not at the individual page level, but at the variable level. In addition, the Counter Component is used to manage one or multiple counter variables within ASPs. These variables can symbolize the frequency of any action you may want to keep track of, such as the number of times a user runs a specific script or has failed to correctly enter information on a page.

The Counter Component counter variables are different from the Page Counter Component objects because they do not automatically increment when a page is accessed. The Counter Component requires explicit actions to increment the individual or multiple counter variables.

You can see that this same functionality could be achieved by using application-level variables and writing an incremental variable to a text file for storage. However, the Counter Component has done all that work for you by grouping that functionality into one method.

The Counter Component variables can be updated from any ASP page in the application. For example, you can use the Counter Component to record the total number of errors that occur through an application by incrementing a variable, named iErrorCount, whenever an error occurs. If an error occurs on the login.asp page, the Counter Component can be used to increment the iErrorCount variable. Likewise, if the user fails to complete a specified application task, the Counter Component can be used to increment another variable, named iErrorLoanProcess.

To use the Counter Component, two files are needed, as illustrated in Table 17.20. The first file is the Dynamic Link Library itself that is needed to create the Counter Component functionality. The second file, the Counters.Txt file, is a simple text file that is used as the storage location for one or multiple counter variables. The following is an extract of the Counters.txt file:

```
-------------- Counters.txt --------------
iErrorCount:57
iTimeOut:3
iBadRequest:7
iDownLoads: 382
```

Table 17.20   The Counter Component Files

File Name	Description
Counters.Dll	Dynamic Link Library needed to create the counter object.
Counters.Txt	The text file used to store the integer values of the counter object.

To initialize the Counter Component, you have to create the Counter Component in the GLOBAL.ASA as shown below:

```
<OBJECT RUNAT = Server SCOPE = Application ID = Counter progID = "MSWC.Counters">
</OBJECT>
```

After the Counter Component has been created, its four methods, the Get, Increment, Set, and Remove methods, are used to manage the various counter values (see Table 17.21).

Table 17.21   The Counter Component Methods

Name	Description
Get	Returns the count property of the given counter name.
Increment	Increments the counter name by one.
Set	Assigns the counter name counter to a specific value.
Remove	Removes the counter name from the counter object.

The *Get* Method

The Counter Get method is used to retrieve the value of the counter variable. To extract this value, use the following syntax:

```
Counter.Get(CounterName)
```

where *CounterName* is the name of the variable that is to be retrieved. To retrieve the current value of a counter variable, use the Get method as shown in the following example:

```
<% Response.Write ("<Center>" & "Admin Summary:" & "</Center><BR>")%>
Timeout Errors: <% = myCounterObj.Get("iTimeOutCount") %>
Bad HTTP Request Errors: <% = myCounterObj.Get("iTimeOutCount") %>
```

Over the course of the ASP application, if five timeout errors and two bad HTTP request errors are produced, the previous code would produce the following results:

```
Admin Summary:
Timeout Errors: 5
Bad HTTP Request Errors: 2
```

If the counter variable does not exist, the variable is automatically created and assigned a value of 0.

Part

IV

Ch

17

Of course, the counter variables do not just have to deal with ASP applications. For example, you can return the results of a recent Web-based poll that asked a question about co-ed ice hockey:

```
Should Co-ed Ice Hockey continue?
94% No
2% Yes
4% Undecided
```

The *Increment* Method

The Increment method is used to automatically increment a counter variable. If the variable called by the Increment method does not exist, the variable is created, its value is set to 0, and then it is incremented. To implement this method, use the following syntax:

```
Counter.Increment(CounterName)
```

where *CounterName* is the variable to be incremented. This method is used to create a running total for a variable. For example, the following example instructs the user to seek professional guidance after failing to complete a task 10 times.

```
<%
Dim iMaxTries
iMaxTries = 10
Counter.Increment("UserError") %>
If Counter.Get("UserError") > iMaxTries Then
    Response.Write "Stop wasting bandwidth and call the help desk"
End If
%>
```

The *Set* Method

The Set method is used assign a specific integer value to a counter variable name. The Set method requires the following syntax:

```
Counter.Set(vCounterName, iCountValue)
```

where *vCounterName* is the name of the variable to be assigned a value, and *iCountValue* is the integer value that is assigned to the variable name. For example, if you want to send an e-mail to the webmaster after every tenth application error that occurs, the Set method can be used to reset the counter variable name.

```
<%
If (myCounterObj("iErrorCount") > 10) Then          '=== Checks how the value of
➥errors
    iReturn = SendMail("ASP Manager")               '=== Executes a SendMail
➥Function
    myCounterObj.Set(iErrorCount,0)                 '=== Resets error count to 0
End If
%>
```

The *Remove* Method

The Remove Method is used to remove a counter variable from the counter object and the Counters.txt files. The Remove method requires the following syntax:

```
Counter.Remove(CounterName)
```

where *CounterName* is the counter variable name. For example, to remove the iErrorCount variable from the Counter object and disregard its value, use the Remove method as shown in the following example.

```
<% Counter.Remove("iErrorCount") %>
```

From Here...

This chapter has demonstrated the installable ActiveX components that can be used by your ASP applications. These components represent significant server-side functionality that extends the reach and connectivity of the Internet Information Server that is not available in native ASP scripts. In particular, this chapter has covered how to use:

Part
IV

Ch
17

- The Advertisement Rotator Component to create dynamic image banners.
- The Browser Capabilities Component to determine browser characteristics.
- The Database Access Component to connect to any ODBC-compliant database.
- The Counter Component to create incremental counter variables.
- The Page Counter Component to track how many times a page is requested.
- The Content Rotator Component to automatically rotate or change content on a page.
- The Tools Component to access additional server-side administration features.
- The Content Linking Component to provide automatic page linking capabilities.
- The Permission Checker Component to manage user access permission for your site.

These components can be used individually or collected to add exciting functionality to your site. The next chapter will cover how to create your own ActiveX components. After you learn how to create your own components, Chapter 19 will demonstrate how to use the components covered in this chapter to create the fictitious DataWidget Warehouse Web site. For additional related information, see the following chapters:

- Chapter 18, "Creating Your Own Active Server Components," walks you through the tools and examples of how to create tailored functionality via custom-created components.
- Chapter 19, "Putting It All Together: Creating an Online Registration System," demonstrates how to use the components that ship with IIS 4.0 to build a sample Web site.

■ Chapter 20, "Database Access with ADO," teaches how to use the Data Access Component to connect to any ODBC-compliant database.

■ Chapter 31, "Using Internet Information Server 4.0 to Manage Your Web Applications," demonstrates how to use the various features of the Internet Information Server to help manage your sites and applications.

CHAPTER 18

Creating Your Own Active Server Components

In Chapter 17, "Implementing Existing Server-Side Components," you learned how to declare and use the Dynamic Link Libraries that ship with the Internet Information Server. While these components provide great functionality, there are times when no component that you can download or purchase will fit your needs exactly. In these cases, you will have to create your own component. Luckily, they are not difficult to create if you understand how to program in Visual Basic.

Creating your own components can greatly enhance your value as an Internet programmer. Components enable you to create classes that can do nearly anything that can be done on a computer, except create a user interface. Normally, programmers create objects in order to accomplish one of the following:

Create ActiveX Components

ActiveX components are the building blocks of server programs. They enable you to create functionality using Visual Basic and call it from your Active Server Pages.

Deal with Datatype Differences

The fact that ASP supports only the Variant datatype causes some problems that you must deal with.

Access the ASP Intrinsic Objects from within an ActiveX Component

You can access the ASP intrinsic objects from within Visual Basic.

Wrap Built-in Visual Basic Functions

If you need a VB function in your program, just wrap it in an ActiveX Server.

Encapsulate Complex Calculations

If your logic is complex, you may find it easier to program in VB than in ASP.

Speed Up Your ASP Program

Learn how to use ActiveX components to speed up your applications.

Port Existing Applications

If you have complex calculations already written in VB, don't port them, wrap them.

- Gain access to functions that are not supported by the dialect of VBScript that runs in the Active Server Pages.

- Create complex calculations that could potentially be reused in many Visual Basic, C++, and ASP applications. This removes the need to code a special version of the program for ASP.

- Speed up applications. If your application contains complex logic, you can move programming logic from the Active Server Pages to the component where it can be compiled.

- Port code to ASP. Many of the existing Visual Basic programs will be ported to Active Server Pages applications. Moving the code into components instead of into ASP files can alleviate much of the pain associated with this.

- Debug complex algorithms. Microsoft has promised improved debugging facilities for ASP in future releases of the Internet Information Server, but it will be some time before it can compete with the Visual Basic's heavy-weight champion debugger. ■

Creating ActiveX Components

ActiveX components are the next generation of what was previously known as OLE Automation Servers. They are created in the same fashion as the OLE Servers were in previous releases of Visual Basic and Visual C++.

In this section, you will create a simple ActiveX component using Visual Basic 5.0, although ActiveX components can be created using any COM-compliant language such as C++.

This example creates a component that multiplies two numbers and returns the result. The simplicity of this example will allow us to concentrate on the process of component creation. The examples that follow will be of increasing complexity.

First start Visual Basic 5.0. The first screen to appear is the New Project dialog box shown in Figure 18.1.

FIG. 18.1
The New Project dialog box gives you a choice of project types to create.

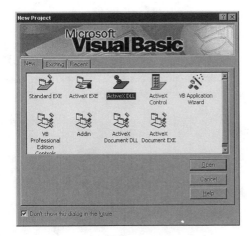

Choose the ActiveX DLL icon. (Visual Basic calls ActiveX components ActiveX DLLs because the file suffix is .DLL, which stands for Dynamic Link Library.) This action creates a new project called Project1, which contains a single class called Class1. Change these names to the following:

- Project—SimpleProj
- Class—SimpleClass

Next, save the project by choosing Save from the File menu. At this point, you are ready to add a function to the class, and thereby to your component. To do this, choose Code from the View menu. This will display the code window in the center region of your screen.

Listing 18.1   *SIMPLECLASS.CLS*—A simple function illustrating the use of ActiveX components.

```
Function Mult1(X As Variant, Y As Variant) As Variant
  Mult1 = X * Y
End Function
```

This function was chosen for its simplicity, and to maximize the chances that you will be able to get it to work on the first try. It is a good idea to test all ActiveX components in the Visual Basic debugger before using them in Active Server Pages. To perform this test, you need to add another project. To do this, choose Add Project from the File menu. When the New Project dialog box appears, choose the Standard EXE icon. This will add a second project to your IDE session. There is no need to rename this project or the form that it creates, as we are only using it to test our component.

Create a form that looks like the one shown in Figure 18.2.

FIG. 18.2

A test form is needed to verify that the component works properly.

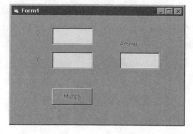

The following names are used in this example:

- txtX—Text box
- txtY—Text box
- txtAnswer—Text box
- cmdMultiply—Command button

In order to use the debugger, you must remove the component project by highlighting SimpleProj in the Project Window and choosing Remove Project from the File menu. You can immediately add it back by choosing Add Project from the file menu. Finally, choose the References entry from the Project menu and choose the SimpleProj entry. This makes the SimpleClass available to the test program. This odd procedure makes the project visible to the debugger.

At this point, you are ready to use the SimpleClass and its method. To do this, enter the code shown in Listing 18.2.

Listing 18.2   *TESTMULT.BAS*—The object must be created before its methods can be used.

```
Private Sub cmdMultiply_Click()
    'Create the Object
    Dim objSimple As New SimpleClass
    Dim Num1 As Variant
    Dim Num2 As Variant

    Num1 = txtX
    Num2 = txtY

    'Use the Object to call the Mult1 method
    txtAnswer = objSimple.Mult1(Num1, Num2)

End Sub
```

If you look at the code, you can see that I had to create an instance of the SimpleClass and assign the name objSimple to the new object. I then used the object's name to make a call to the method named Multi. I passed it two Variant variables and it returned the answer as advertised.

If you look at the SimpleClass in the Object Browser, you can see that it has the same kind of attributes as any other object, just not as many of them. This is due to the simplicity of the object rather than to its mode of creation. Choose Object Browser from the View menu to bring up the browser, as shown in Figure 18.3.

Now that you are armed with a working ActiveX component, it is time to use it in an Active Server Page. To do so, open WordPad or any other text editor and enter the code shown in Listing 18.3.

FIG. 18.3
The Object Browser can be used to examine the interface of an ActiveX component.

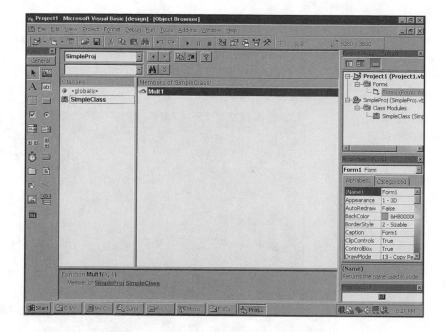

Listing 18.3 *TESTMULT.ASP*—ActiveX components can be called from Active Server Pages.

```
<HTML>
<HEAD>
<TITLE>
ASP calling an ActiveX Component
</TITLE>
</HEAD>
<H3>
<BODY>
<%
X = 10
Y = 15 %>

   The value of X: <% = X %> <BR>
   The value of Y: <% = Y %> <P>

<%
   Set tstObj = Server.CreateObject("SimpleProj.SimpleClass") %>

<%
   Amt = tstOBJ.Mult1(X,Y)
   Response.Write("The Answer is :" )
   Response.Write(Amt)
%>
</BODY>
</HTML>
```

Part
IV

Ch

18

Looking at the code, you can see that there are parallels between this code and that in the Visual Basic example above. In both cases, the object was created and given a name. In the ASP example, this was done using a method in the Server called `CreateObject`. This name was used to provide access to the `Mult1()` method. Instead of writing the output to a form, the ASP example used the `Response` object's `Write()` method to send the output to a browser.

FIG. 18.4
The result of the call to the `Mult1()` method is displayed in the browser.

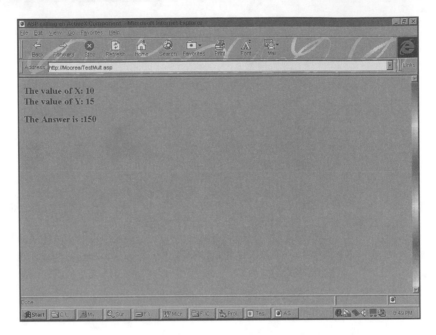

One of the complications of creating ActiveX components is changing them once they have been built. If you try to make `SimpleProj.DLL` again because you found and fixed a bug in it, you will likely receive an error message that states `"Permission Denied"`. This is happening because your Internet server has used this class and Visual Basic thinks that IIS has it "checked out." The way around that is to shut down the Internet Information Server. Visual Basic can then make the DLL.

Take a moment to let the significance of what you have seen demonstrated sink in. This example shows that you can create an arbitrary ActiveX component and call it from any Active Server Page. You can call an Active Server Page from any browser that has permission to access your server. You can create an ActiveX component that can do anything that a Visual Basic application can do, therefore you now have the power to create an application that can do anything that you want it to, and make it available to anyone in the world. This means that you can program for the Internet using native Visual Basic.

Dealing with Datatype Differences

One limiting factor that you saw in the preceding example was that the method received parameters that were of the `Variant` datatype. This is the easiest way to create an ActiveX component, but not the only way. Suppose that you have an existing application that accepts two parameters, one a `Single` and the other an `Integer` that returns a `Single`. In this case, you have two choices:

- Rewrite the ActiveX components to accept and return `Variants`.
- Find a way to call the ActiveX component as it is.

The first option is only available if the component is not being used by other non-Internet applications. Even then, the work required to recode and debug the server can be considerable. Clearly the second way is preferred.

It is possible to change the datatype of a parameter by casting its type using one of the functions shown in Table 18.1.

Table 18.1 The Data Conversion Functions

Function Name	Returns `Variant` Subtype
CBool	Boolean
CByte	Byte
CDate	Date
CDbl	Double
CInt	Integer
CLng	Long
CSng	Single
CStr	String

The return type of the function is handled automatically because the assignment is from its type to a variant in the ASP file. The following example shows how this is done.

Create an ActiveX component. Call the project `TypeCast` and the class `TypeCastClass`. Next, create a method called `AddThem()`. Add the code shown in Listing 18.4 to this method.

Listing 18.4 *TYPECASTCLASS.CLS*—This class is expecting to be passed a *Single*, an *Integer*, and returns a *Single*.

```
Function Mult2(X As Single, Y As Integer) As Integer
  Mult2 = X * Y
End Function
```

Next, you can run the ASP file in Listing 18.5 and see what happens.

Listing 18.5   *TESTTYPEMULT.ASP*—Trying to call a method with non-variant datatypes without type casting.

```
<HTML>
<HEAD>
<TITLE>
ASP calling an ActiveX Component
</TITLE>
<H1>The Data Type Example
</HEAD>
<H3>
<BODY>
<%
X = 10
Y = 15 %>
The value of X: <% = X %> <BR>
The value of Y: <% = Y %> <P>
<%
Set tstObj = Server.CreateObject("TypeCast.TypeCastClass") %>
<%
Amt = tstOBJ.Mult2(X,Y)
Response.Write("The Answer is :" )
Response.Write(Amt)
%>
</BODY>
</HTML>
```

Because the method `Mult2()` was written to accept a `Single` and an `Integer` parameter, I would not expect it to work in this example, and it doesn't, as shown in Figure 18.5.

There is, however, a simple fix to this problem. By type casting the ASP variables to be the right subtype, the ActiveX component will be able to accept them as shown in the corrected version of this example, shown in Listing 18.6.

Listing 18.6   *TESTTYPEMULT2.ASP*—Type casting is the solution to the Type Mismatch problem.

```
<HTML>
<HEAD>
<TITLE>
ASP calling an ActiveX Component
</TITLE>
<H1>The Data Type Example
</HEAD>
<H3>
<BODY>
<%
X = 10
```

```
Y = 15 %>
The value of X: <% = X %> <BR>
The value of Y: <% = Y %> <P>
<%
Set tstObj = Server.CreateObject("TypeCast.TypeCastClass") %>
<%
Amt = tstOBJ.Mult2(CSng(X),CInt(Y))
Response.Write("The Answer is :" )
Response.Write(Amt)
%>
</BODY>
</HTML>
```

FIG. 18.5

Mixing up datatypes is
a sure way to get this
error message.

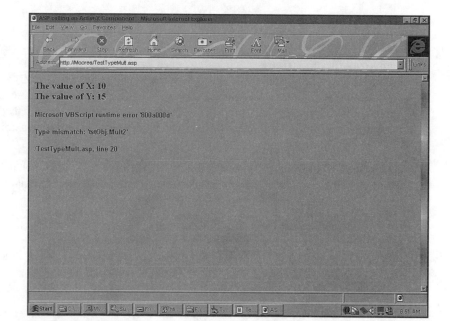

Notice in the 18th line that the parameters are being converted to the correct subtype before
being sent to the Mult2() method for processing. This is sufficient to solve the problem, and it
causes the correct answer to appear as was shown in Figure 18.4.

Now we have the ability to call ActiveX component methods regardless of the parameter types
that they expect. This opens up all the existing classes that you have written for use in Visual
Basic applications and makes them callable from within your ASP applications. From this point
forward, you can use ActiveX components to perform a number of useful functions in your
programs. I will not explicitly show the testing of these components in the Visual Basic IDE,
but I encourage you to apply the techniques demonstrated earlier in this chapter to verify the
correctness of your classes before deploying them in an ASP application.

Part
IV

Ch
18

N O T E   Any ActiveX components, including those created with Visual C++, can be used in Active
Server Pages. ■

Wrapping Built-In Visual Basic Functions

At this point, you know how to create ActiveX components from scratch, and how to overcome
datatype conflicts between ASP applications and components that expect parameters of types
other than Variant. Now you are in a position to do some really useful work with these components.

One of the addictions that all Visual Basic programmers share is to the built-in utility functions
that ship with the product. Some of the most common of these functions are made available to
ASP programmers by the Internet Information Server, but many useful ones are not. In order
to provide access to these functions, you must write an ActiveX component that provides an
interface to the ASP application. Because the ActiveX component is really a Visual Basic program, all built-in functions are available to it. The process of encapsulating functionality in this
manner is called *wrapping*, and the components that are produced are called *wrappers*. This
name is derived from the analogy of a piece of candy being wrapped in a protective covering
made of paper or cellophane.

Let's work an example to illustrate this approach. The Format() function in Visual Basic provides a number of useful conversions concerning time, dates, and format of data. If I want to
provide this capability to my programs, then I must wrap this function in an ActiveX component, as it is not available to ASP applications normally.

To create this wrapper, create an ActiveX DLL project exactly as you did above. Name the
project ConvertIt and the class Formats. Next, write code to add several methods to the class,
as shown in Listing 18.7.

Listing 18.7   *FORMATS.CLS*—The methods in this class wrap the *Format()*
function to provide its functionality to ASP applications.

```
'This method accepts time in AM and PM format then converts it to Military Time.
Public Function Militarytime(Intime As Variant) As Variant
    Militarytime = Format(Intime, "hh:mm:ss")
End Function

'This method accepts time in military format and converts it to AM and PM.
Public Function AMPM(Intime As Variant) As Variant
    AMPM = Format(Intime, "h:mm:ss AMPM")
End Function
'This method converts a terse date into a day of the week, month, day, year
➥format.
Public Function FullDate(InDate As Variant) As Variant
    FullDate = Format(InDate, "dddd,mmm d yyyy")
End Function
```

```
'This method capitalizes all letters in a string that it is passed
Public Function AllCaps(InString As Variant) As Variant
    AllCaps = Format(InString, ">")
End Function
```

The following methods make up this class:

- ■ `MilitaryTime()`—Accepts time in AM and PM format, and then converts it to military time.

- ■ `AMPM()`—Accepts time in military format and converts it to AM and PM.

- ■ `FullDate()`—Converts a terse date into a day of the week, month, day, year format.

- ■ `AllCaps()`—Capitalizes all letters in a string that it is passed.

These functions are contained in the same object because all of them are based on the `Format()` built-in function. Packaging of methods in ActiveX components is a trade-off between simplicity in coding and program size. If you put every function that you would ever need in one class, then every ASP application could just perform one `Server.CreateObject()` method and access everything that they would ever need. On the other hand, that would create a massive DLL that would have to be uploaded to every Web server that wanted to run the ASP application. In addition, the load size of the DLL could make the working set of the program very large and take resources away from other programs running on the same Web server. The DLL created here is tiny, so it is not a problem. Normally, this size problem will only have an impact when dozens of fairly large functions are created.

Using these methods is simply a matter of declaring the class and calling them from your ASP file, as shown in Listing 18.8.

Part

IV

Ch

18

Listing 18.8 *CONVERTITTEST1.ASP*—You can call the new utility functions by creating an object of that class type.

```
<HTML>
<H1> Testing the ConvertIT ActiveX Component
<H3>
<%
Set MyFormats = Server.CreateObject("ConvertIt.Formats")
OutTime1 = MyFormats.MilitaryTime("5:13:14 PM")
OutTime2 = MyFormats.AMPM("17:15")
OutDate = MyFormats.FullDate("7/3/97")
OutString = MyFormats.AllCaps("Hello,Planet")
%>
Input = 5:13:14 PM
Output =
<% = OutTime1 %><BR><BR>
Input = 17:15
Output =
<% = OutTime2 %><BR><BR>
Input = 7/3/97
```

continues

Listing 18.8 Continued

```
Output =
<% = OutDate %><BR><BR>
Input = Hello, Planet
Output =
<% = OutString %>
</HTML>
```

Running this file gives the results shown in Figure 18.6.

FIG. 18.6
All of the component's methods are now available to you inside the ASP file.

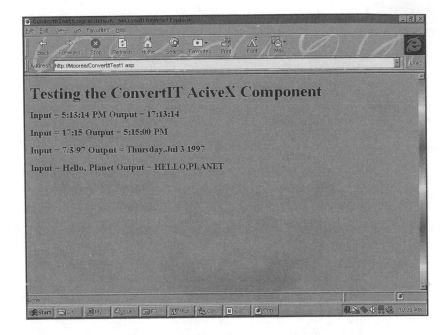

Proving that this technique works will open up more programming doors for you. Not only do you now have the entire library of built-in Visual Basic functions available to your program, you also have any other module available by this same technique.

Encapsulating Complex Calculations

There are times when you are performing complex calculations that require considerable debugging. In addition, these calculations are needed by non-ASP applications as well. In these cases, ActiveX components provide the dual-purpose capability that you need.

In addition, any calculation that has been placed in a DLL is compiled and might result in a performance advantage over calling the same function from within an ASP file. You cannot assume that this is so in all cases because of the overhead associated with calling a DLL versus calling a function in the same ASP file.

An example of this kind of calculation is the net present value calculation that is used to calculate the cost of breaking a lease early. This calculation takes into account the fact that many leases have a built-in formula for rent increases in future years. Additionally, it is customary for the lease to provide a discount allowing for the time value of money. This means that the company renting the building will be given a discount over the full value of all future rent to reflect the fact that they are paying off the lease all at once, instead of slowly over time.

To perform this calculation, create an ActiveX component called Financials and a class called Formulas. This class contains only one method, called CalcNPV(). This method will accept a maximum of three rent increases over term of the lease. Table 18.2 shows the input parameters for this method.

Table 18.2 The Inputs to the *CalcNPV* Function

Parameter	Datatype	Meaning
NowPayment	Variant	The current rent amount
LeaseExp	Variant	The date that the lease expires
YrPctInterest	Variant	The yearly interest rate for calculating the discount
ReDate1	Variant	The first date that the rent will go up
ReAmount1	Variant	The amount of the rent after the first date
ReDate2	Variant	The second date that the rent will go up
ReAmount2	Variant	The amount of the rent after the second date
ReDate3	Variant	The third date that the rent will go up
ReAmount3	Variant	The amount of the rent after the third date

Notice that all the parameters are of the Variant datatype. This allows us to avoid type conversions. The code for this calculation is shown in Listing 18.9.

Listing 18.9 *FORMULAS.CLS*—The net present value calculation method.

```
Public Function CalcNPV(NowPayment As Variant, LeaseExp As Variant,
➥YrPctInterest As Variant, ReDate1 As Variant, ReAmount1 As Variant, ReDate2 As
➥Variant, ReAmount2 As Variant, ReDate3 As Variant, ReAmount3 As Variant) As
➥Variant
    Dim Today
    Dim PmtArray()        ' Declare dynamic array.
    Dim Months
    Dim I
    Dim ThatMonth
    Dim pctInterest
    Dim TempValue
```

continues

Listing 18.9   Continued

```
      Today = Now()

'Find out how many months until the lease expires
      Months = DateDiff("m", Today, LeaseExp)
      If Months < 1 Then
       CalcNPV = 0
       Exit Function
      End If

'Deal with the fact that some leases have less than 3 rent increases
      If IsNull(ReDate1) Then
        ReDate1 = LeaseExp
      End If

      If IsNull(ReDate2) Then
        ReDate2 = LeaseExp
      End If

      If IsNull(ReDate3) Then
        ReDate3 = LeaseExp
      End If

      ReDim PmtArray(Months)      ' Allocate elements.
      ThatMonth = Today

    'fill in the pmtarray with the right rent for each month through lease exp.
    For I = 1 To Months
        Select Case ThatMonth

        Case Is < ReDate1 'first escalation date hasn't been reached
            PmtArray(I) = NowPayment 'today's fixed rent
        Case Is < ReDate2
            PmtArray(I) = ReAmount1
        Case Is < ReDate3
            PmtArray(I) = ReAmount2
        Case Else
            PmtArray(I) = ReAmount3
        End Select
      'ThatMonth is the month that is being represented in the array
      ThatMonth = DateAdd("m", 1, ThatMonth)
    Next I

    TempValue = 0
    pctInterest = YrPctInterest / 100 / 12

    'Apply the discount
    For I = 1 To Months
    TempValue = TempValue + (PmtArray(I) / (1 + pctInterest) ^ I)
    Next I
CalcNPV = TempValue
End Function
```

The calculation is somewhat complex due mainly to the rent increases. Once the rent that would normally be due is loaded into the PmtArray, the discount is applied to each payment. The payments that are far in the future are discounted more than the payments that are due sooner.

You can use this class and method from either a Visual Basic or an ASP application. Listing 18.10 shows this object being used to perform 1,000 calculations.

Listing 18.10   *TESTNPV.ASP*—Testing the execution speed of a calculation in a DLL.

```
<%@ LANGUAGE = VBScript %>
<HTML>
<HEAD>
<TITLE>PropertyWorks</TITLE>
</HEAD>
<H1> Testing the speed of Complex Calculations
<H3>
<%
'Create the Object
Set tstNPV = Server.CreateObject("Financials.Formulas")

'Assign some dummy values
 NowPayment = 1000
 LeaseExp = "12/31/2005"
 YrPctInterest = 12

 Redate1 = "1/1/2000"
 ReAmount1 = 1100
 Redate2 = "1/1/2002"
 ReAmount2 = 1200
 Redate3 = "1/1/2004"
 ReAmount3 = 1300

'Perform the call 1000 times to measure the speed
 For i=1 to 1000
    Response.Write(i& ",")
    NPVAmt = tstNPV.CalcNPV(NowPayment, LeaseExp, YrPctInterest, ReDate1,
➥ReAmount1, ReDate2, ReAmount2, ReDate3, ReAmount3 )
 Next

%>
<BR>
<%= FormatCurrency(NPVAmt) %>
</BODY>
</HTML>
```

Part
IV

Ch
18

Running this code shows the output in Figure 18.7 in approximately 38 seconds on my Pentium laptop.

FIG. 18.7
The ActiveX component version of this application ran in approximately 38 seconds.

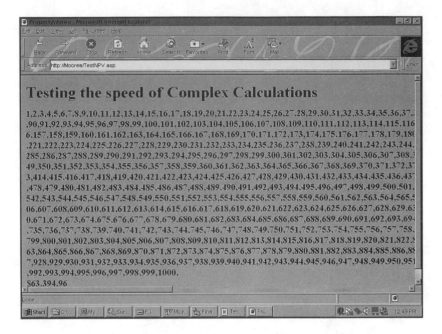

The question naturally arises as to whether this is slower or faster than running the same calculation from within the ASP file. In order to test this, the code was ported to the ASP file. In the following section I will port the code to ASP and test the execution speed.

Porting Existing Applications

It would be wonderful if the creators of VBScript and those of Visual Basic Professional Edition communicated so that any differences in the language would be intentional and based on the differing missions of the two products. Unfortunately, this is not the case. When porting from Visual Basic to VBScript, you will find more tiny differences in the capabilities and syntax of the languages than can be explained by common sense.

There are two kinds of changes that you have to make to port your code to VBScript and run it in an ASP file. The first kind makes sense and is based on the fact that all variables are Variant in ASP files. This means that all parameters accept no explicit typing, even as Variant, and the function return type is missing. It would be better if VBScript checked to see if the return type and parameter types were Variant before objecting to them, but life is not fair, so it doesn't. This means that you will have to remove them by hand.

The second type of change will have to be made for no reason other than the fact that your program won't run if you don't. These changes are the most annoying of all because they cause you to debug code that is already working. Listing 18.11 shows a version of the TestNPV.asp program called TestASPNPV.asp. It contains the CalcNPV routine that has been ported to be run as 100 percent VBScript.

Listing 18.11 *TESTASPNPV.ASP*—The *CalcNPV* calculation can be coded entirely in the ASP file.

```
<%@ LANGUAGE = VBScript %>
<HTML>
<HEAD>
<TITLE>PropertyWorks</TITLE>
</HEAD>
<H1> Testing the speed of ASP Calculations
<H3>
<%
Function CalcNPV(NowPayment, LeaseExp,YrPctInterest, ReDate1 , ReAmount1 ,
➥ReDate2, ReAmount2, ReDate3, ReAmount3)
    Dim Today
    Dim PmtArray()      ' Declare dynamic array.
    Dim Months
    Dim I
    Dim ThatMonth
    Dim pctInterest
    Dim TempValue

      Today = Now()

'Find out how many months until the lease expires
      Months = DateDiff("m", Today, LeaseExp)
      If Months < 1 Then
       CalcNPV = 0
       Exit Function
      End If

'Deal with the fact that some leases have less than 3 rent increases
      If IsNull(ReDate1) Then
        ReDate1 = LeaseExp
      End If

      If IsNull(ReDate2) Then
        ReDate2 = LeaseExp
      End If

      If IsNull(ReDate3) Then
        ReDate3 = LeaseExp
      End If

      ReDim PmtArray(Months)      ' Allocate elements.
      ThatMonth = Today

    'fill in the pmtarray with the right rent for each month through lease exp.
    For I = 1 To Months

        PmtArray(I) = ReAmount3
        If ThatMonth < ReDate3 Then
            PmtArray(I) = ReAmount2
        End If
```

continues

Listing 18.11 Continued

```
        If ThatMonth < ReDate2 Then
            PmtArray(I) = ReAmount1
        End If
        If ThatMonth < ReDate1 Then   'first escalation date hasn't been reached
            PmtArray(I) = NowPayment 'today's fixed rent
        End If

        ThatMonth = DateAdd("m", 1, ThatMonth)
    Next

    TempValue = 0
    pctInterest = YrPctInterest / 100 / 12

    'Apply the discount
    For I = 1 To Months
    TempValue = TempValue + (PmtArray(I) / (1 + pctInterest) ^ I)
    Next
CalcNPV = TempValue
End Function
 NowPayment = 1000
 LeaseExp = "12/31/2005"
 YrPctInterest = 12
 Redate1 = "1/1/2000"
 ReAmount1 = 1100
 Redate2 = "1/1/2002"
 ReAmount2 = 1200
 Redate3 = "1/1/2004"
 ReAmount3 = 1300
 For i=1 to 1000
    Response.Write(i& ",")
    NPVAmt = CalcNPV(NowPayment, LeaseExp, YrPctInterest, ReDate1, ReAmount1,
➡ReDate2, ReAmount2, ReDate3, ReAmount3 )
 Next
%>
<BR>
        <%= FormatCurrency(NPVAmt) %>
</BODY>
</HTML>
```

As you can see, the type declarations have been removed from the parameters and from the function itself. Next, the Select Case statement (around the 48th line) has been removed and replaced with a very strange set of If...Then...Else logic. This is because the ASP processor objected to both the Case statement and the equivalent If...Else If logic. In order to get this to work, that part of the algorithm had to be replaced. Finally, when it runs, it produces the output shown in Figure 18.8 below.

Notice that there is a $.03 difference between these two calculations. This can be attributed to the fact that the code in the ASP case was being processed by ASP.DLL, which is being run by IIS. The Visual Basic version was compiled by the VB compiler, which is not only a different piece of software, but also a different kind of software—a compiler. Clearly, the rounding algorithms are slightly different between the DLL and the compiler.

FIG. 18.8
The ASP version of the CalcNPV processing produced a slightly different answer.

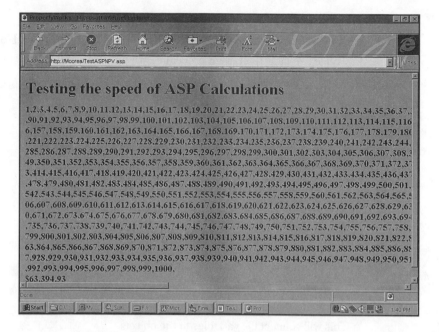

The speed of execution issue produced a mild surprise. The ASP version of the application only took 22 seconds to execute. This is probably because the overhead associated with making the call to the class was greater than the speed advantage gained by performing the calculation when compiled. The moral of the story has two parts:

■ Don't rush off to create all of your calculations in ActiveX components. They may be slower than the ASP version for processing up to a certain level of complexity.

■ Avoid porting existing Visual Basic code to ASP if possible. Make an ActiveX component out of it instead. The difficulty encountered in performing the port may outweigh any advantage gained.

For example, a debugged piece of code may not port as written. In this case, create an ActiveX component out of it. On the other hand, as shown above, performance improvement is not guaranteed.

Accessing the ASP Intrinsic Objects from Within an ActiveX Component

Another very intelligent feature of the Active Server Pages design is the fact that you can access the five intrinsic objects (Server, Request, Response, Application, and Session) from within an ActiveX component. This has the potential to improve the performance of your application by allowing you to perform almost any task for either the ASP file or the ActiveX component that it calls. The following process is used to accomplish this:

1. Create a new ActiveX DLL in Visual Basic 5.0.
2. Add a reference to the Microsoft Active Server Pages 1.0 Object Library.
3. Create two page-level event procedures within your component: `OnStartPage` and `OnEndPage`.
4. Add the following code to your component's general declaration section:

```
Dim rp as Response
Dim rq as Request
Dim ap as Application
Dim sr as Server
Dim sn as Session
```

This will give your program access to the objects through these variables.

5. Add the following code to the `OnStartPage()` event procedure:

```
Public Sub OnStartPage(mySC as ScriptingContext)
    Set rp as mySc.Response
    Set rq as mySc.Request
    Set ap as mySc.Application
    Set sr as mySc.Server
    Set sn as mySc.Session
End Sub
```

This will connect the variables to the objects.

6. Create your application and use the objects declared in the `OnStartPage()` event procedure.

In order to understand how this works, here's a simple example. Create a new ActiveX component; call the project `SCProj` and the class `SCClass`. Add the code shown in Listing 18.12 to the class.

Listing 18.12 *SCCLASS.CLS*—The SC class uses the scripting context to access the intrinsic object.

```
Dim rp as Response
Dim rq as Request
Dim ap as Application
Dim sr as Server
Dim sn as Session

'This routine is called when the component is used
Public Sub OnStartPage(mySC As ScriptingContext)
    Set rp as mySc.Response
    Set rq as mySc.Request
    Set as as mySc.Application
    Set sr as mySc.Server
    Set sn as mySc.Session
    rp.Write "<I> Been to StartPage</I><P>"
End Sub
```

```
'This routine runs when the application is done.
Public Sub OnEndPage()
    rp.Write "<P><I>Been to EndPage</I>"
    Set rp = Nothing
    Set rq = Nothing
End Sub

' This subroutine echoes back the user's input
Public Sub Echo()
    UserInput = rq.Form("AnyNumber")
    rp.Write "<H3>Visual Basic Echo Method Called<BR></H3>"
    rp.Write "<H3>You entered " & UserInput & "<BR></H3>"
End Sub
```

This component uses the Request object to find out what the user entered in the Input box on the form. It then uses the Response object to echo that number back to the browser along with several lines of code that trace the execution. The ASP file shown in Listing 18.13 is called from an HTML file.

Listing 18.13   *ECHO.ASP*—This ASP file calls the *Echo()* method.

```
<HTML>
<HEAD><TITLE>Echo Tester</TITLE></HEAD>
<BODY>
<%
Set MyCompute = Server.CreateObject("SCProj.SCClass")
MyCompute.Echo
%>
</BODY>
</HTML>
```

Notice that this code doesn't touch either the input or output at any time. It merely serves as a mechanism to call the Echo() method in the SCClass class.

The final piece of the puzzle is the HTML file (see Listing 18.14).

Listing 18.14   *TESTECHO.HTM*—This HTML gathers user input to be passed to the Echo ASP application

```
<HTML>
<HEAD><TITLE>Echo Tester</TITLE></HEAD>
<BODY>
Please provide a number to echo
<FORM METHOD=POST ACTION = http://default/echo.asp>
Your Number: <INPUT NAME=AnyNumber SIZE=25><P>
<HR><INPUT TYPE=SUBMIT><INPUT TYPE=RESET><P>
</FORM>
</BODY>
</HTML>
```

Running the TestEcho.htm file in the browser brings up the screen shown in Figure 18.9.

FIG. 18.9

The input from the screen will be passed to the ActiveX component by an ASP file.

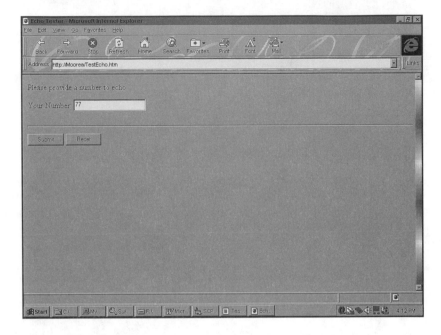

The result of running this program is shown in Figure 18.10.

FIG. 18.10

The Echo program displays the input back to the user in the browser.

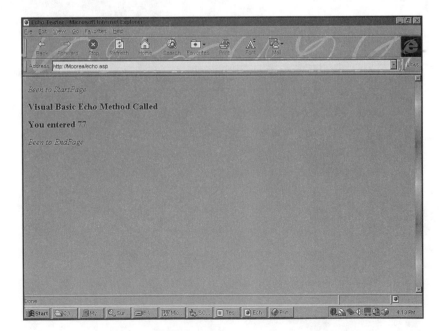

This technology allows you to use the Active Server Page in a sort of "pass thru," which allows an HTML file to call a Visual Basic program indirectly.

Speeding Up Your ASP Program

Let's see if you can use this access to intrinsic objects from within Visual Basic to speed up a program. To do this, you will measure the program running in its normal mode as an ASP application, and then convert it to an ActiveX component that uses the intrinsic objects. You will then measure the difference in wall clock time to execute.

The application that we will use retrieves records from the BIBLIO.MDB database (which ships with VB 5) using the ActiveX Data Object (ADO). This database is normally found in the c:\VB directory. It does some non-trivial formatting and writes its results to the browser. Listing 18.15 shows the ASP version of this application.

Listing 18.15 *DBASP.ASP*—Accessing a database from an ASP application.

```
<%@ LANGUAGE = VBScript %>
<HTML>
<HEAD>
<TITLE>Biblio Author Listing</TITLE>
</HEAD>
 Author Listing
<HR>
<%
    Set OBJdbConnection = Server.CreateObject("ADODB.Connection")
    OBJdbConnection.Open "Biblio"
    SQLQuery = "Select * From Authors Where Au ID < 500"
    Set RSAuthorList = OBJdbConnection.Execute(SQLQuery)
%>
<TABLE COLSPAN=8 CELLPADDING=5 BORDER=0>
<!-- BEGIN column header row -->
<TR>
<TD>
Author ID
</TD>
<TD>
Author Name
</TD>
<TD>
Year Born
</TD>
</TR>
<!-- Put the data in the table -->
<% Do While Not RSAuthorList.EOF %>
<TR>
  <TD>
      <%= RSAuthorList("Au_ID")%>
  </TD>
```

continues

Listing 18.15 Continued

```
   <TD>
      <%= RSAuthorList("Author")%>
   </TD>
   <TD>
      <%= RSAuthorList("Year Born")%>
   </TD>
</TR>
<!-- Next Row -->
<%
   RSAuthorList.MoveNext
   Loop
%>
</TABLE>
</BODY>
</HTML>
```

This application takes approximately 11 seconds to complete. It looks like Figure 18.11 below.

FIG. 18.11
The no-frills database example takes 11 seconds to complete.

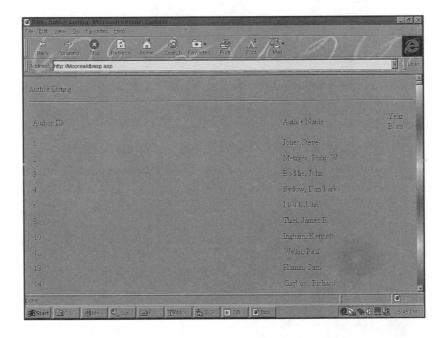

Now, let's look at an ActiveX component version of this same application. In order do this, create an ActiveX DLL in Visual Basic. Call the project ADOProj and the class ADOLookup. Next, create a method called LookUp and add the code shown in Listing 18.16 to it.

Listing 18.16 *ADOLOOKUP.CLS*—**This is an ActiveX component version of the DBASP.**

```
Dim rp As Response
Dim rq As Request

Public Sub OnStartPage(mySC As ScriptingContext)
    Set rp = mySC.Response
    Set rq = mySC.Request
End Sub

Public Sub OnEndPage()
    Set rp = Nothing
    Set rq = Nothing
End Sub

Public Sub Lookup()
    rp.Write " "
    rp.Write " "
    rp.Write "<HTML>"
    rp.Write "<HEAD>"
    rp.Write "<TITLE>Biblio Author Listing</TITLE>"
    rp.Write "</HEAD>"
    rp.Write "Author Listing"
    rp.Write "<HR>"

    Dim RSAuthorList As New ADODB.Recordset
    RSAuthorList.ActiveConnection = "DSN=Biblio"
    RSAuthorList.Open "Select * From Authors Where AU_ID < 500"
    rp.Write "<TABLE COLSPAN=8 CELLPADDING=5 BORDER=0>"
 ' BEGIN column header row
    rp.Write "<TR>"
    rp.Write "<TD>"
    rp.Write "Author ID"
    rp.Write "</TD>"
    rp.Write "<TD>"
    rp.Write "Author Name"
    rp.Write "</TD>"
    rp.Write "<TD>"
    rp.Write "Year Born"
    rp.Write "</TD>"
    rp.Write "</TR>"
    ' Put the data in the table
    Do While Not RSAuthorList.EOF
        rp.Write "<TR>"
        rp.Write "<TD>"
        rp.Write RSAuthorList("Au_ID")
        rp.Write "</TD>"
        rp.Write "<TD>"
        rp.Write RSAuthorList("Author")
        rp.Write "</TD>"
        rp.Write "<TD>"
```

continues

Listing 18.16   Continued

```
      rp.Write RSAuthorList("Year Born")
      rp.Write "</TD>"
      rp.Write "</TR>"
    ' Next Row
      RSAuthorList.MoveNext
  Loop
rp.Write "</TABLE>"
rp.Write "</BODY>"
rp.Write "</HTML>"
RSAuthorList.Close
End Sub
```

Running the application this way requires that you create a simple ASP file like that shown in Listing 18.17, even though all the work is done inside the ActiveX component.

Listing 18.17   *ADODBTEST.ASP*—An ASP file is required even if all of the work is done inside an ActiveX component.

```
<HTML>
<HEAD><TITLE>ADODB Tester</TITLE></HEAD>
<BODY>
<%
Set MyCompute = Server.CreateObject("ADOProj.ADOLookup")
MyCompute.Lookup
%>
</BODY>
</HTML>
```

This version of the application ran in nine seconds, which is slightly faster than the same application written entirely in VBScript. This will not be universally true, especially for small applications.

From Here...

In this chapter, you learned how to use ActiveX components to improve your programs. You saw how these servers can help in porting existing applications to the Internet. You also saw how ActiveX components can improve the speed of execution of your applications. The following chapters contain related topics:

- Chapter 19, "Putting It All Together: Creating an Online Registration System," demonstrates how to use the components that ship with IIS 4.0 in building a sample Web site.

- Chapter 20, "Database Access with ADO," teaches how to use the Data Access Component to connect to any ODBC-compliant database.

- Chapter 31, "Using Internet Information Server 4.0 to Manage Your Web Applications," demonstrates how to use the various features of the Internet Information Server to help manage your sites and applications.

Putting It All Together: Creating an Online Registration System

This chapter will use some of the installable components covered in Chapter 17, "Implementing Existing Server-Side Components," to build an online product registration wizard for a company Web site. In this sample application, a fictitious company called Amazing DataWidgets WareHouse Inc. has created a server-side ActiveX design-time control for Visual InterDev that is capable of generating Active Server Page code by reading your mind! To better market its product, the company is giving away free beta copies of the control from their site. This company wants to continuously change information that is delivered to the browser. To achieve this effect, the application automatically varies the product's accolades and the marketing information in different banners at the bottom of the page, as seen in Figure 19.1. ■

Using the Content Rotator and the Ad Rotator

Implement the Content Rotator to vary information displayed at your site and discover how to use the Ad Rotator to include a rotating image banner in your site.

Determining the Browser Type

Learn how to use the Browser Capability Component to identify and utilize different browser capabilities.

Tools Component and the Page Component

Prevent broken links and errors in application logic by using the Tools Component, and use the Page Component to display the number of times a page has been accessed.

Implementing the Content Linker Component

Use the Content Linker to create a programmatic application workflow process.

FIG. 19.1

This Amazing DataWidgets WareHouse Web site offers changing content as well as changing product banners.

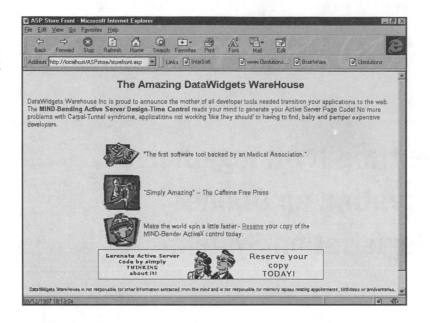

The site also uses scrolling effects to display a disclaimer across the bottom of the page that varies depending on the browser type. If the browser is the Internet Explorer, the Marquee control is used. If the browser is Netscape Navigator, a scrolling text box is used, as shown in Figure 19.2.

FIG. 19.2

This site also formats output for different browser types.

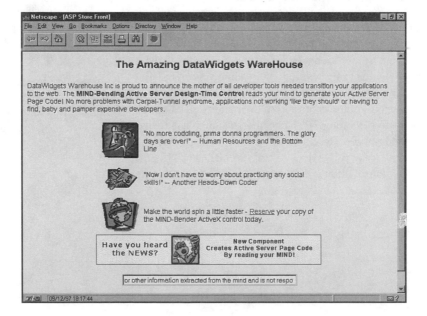

The site uses various components to make these features possible: The Browser Component is used to determine the type of browser that is accessing the site; the Ad Rotator Component is used to display product information at the bottom of the page; the Content Rotator Component is used to vary information that is displayed to the user; the Content Linker Component is used to create an online registration wizard; the Page Counter Component tracks the page access for the site; and the Tools Component is used to verify that files exist on the server before they are referenced. In addition, client-side JavaScript is implemented throughout the site to enhance the functionality delivered by the Active Server Page components.

Rotating the Content with the Content Rotator Component

One of the easiest ways to create the appearance of a dynamic site is to periodically change the information on the Web pages. However, this task of updating the Web site is no small job. One of the easiest ways to minimize the maintenance effort needed to maintain a dynamic site like this is to rotate the content. There are definite advantages and disadvantages to using the rotating approach when it comes to content. Although changing the content of your site makes it appear that you are always updating the information, the users must be able to navigate back to the site to find the information that they originally found at your site. If they can't, your site will lose it effectiveness and frustrate the users.

The Amazing DataWidgets WareHouse Web site features many different praises for their MIND-bender design-time control. To create a dynamic effect, the site will rotate these different accolades. In this situation, the first two items describing the product change every time you load the page, as shown in Figures 19.1 and 19.2. This capability to rotate the content is made possible by the Content Rotator Component. The Content Rotator Component reads content from a scheduling file, and the scheduling file determines the content that is displayed and the frequency in which it is displayed.

To begin this project, start your Active Server Page by creating the template for the first page. As discussed in Chapter 8, "Putting It All Together with VBScript," you can create and maintain your Active Server Pages by hand by using an ASCII editor, or you can use a development environment such as Visual InterDev. The easiest way to minimize the amount of time writing and testing HTML code is to use a GUI HTML editor, such as FrontPage or HotMetaL. Using these tools enables you to quickly generate visual templates for placement of information. This method also enables the new members of the Web development team, such as the graphic artists and content creators, to have direct input in sharing the workload. Use an HTML editor to create the title, opening paragraph, and a two-column, three-row border-less table, as shown in Figure 19.3.

FIG. 19.3
Use a GUI HTML editor
to generate a visual
template to place your
Active Server code.

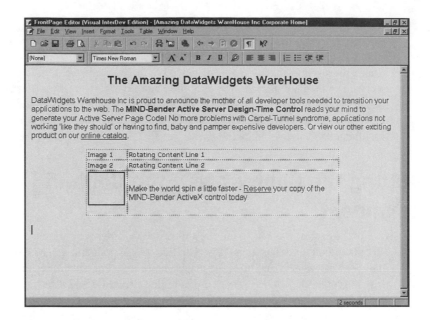

To help determine where to put your code modules when you are in an editor coding Active
Server Pages, place comments to yourself to help identify where the Active scripts should be
used. This example will use the second column of each row to display the rotating content. To
place a mental bookmarker where to add the code, type **Rotating Content Line 1**. Now, save
the ASP file, and re-open it in your editor of choice. Find the location of the text *Rotating Content Line 1* to determine where to write the first instance of the dynamic content.

The Content Rotator, as discussed in Chapter 17, "Implementing Existing Server-Side Components," extracts content and scheduling information from a text file. This text file can contain
HTML tags that are transported by the Content Rotator to the Web page. To create an instance
of the Content Rotator Component, use the `Server.CreateObject` statement and reference the
appropriate content scheduling file, as shown in Listing 19.1.

You can also separate the `CreateObject` tag so it is located outside of the table to make things
look neater, as shown in Listing 19.1. Remember, you want to batch process multiple lines of
Active Server scripts to improve performance.

Listing 19.1   Embedding the Content Rotator in an HTML table.

```
<%
Dim NextTip
Set NextTip = Server.CreateObject("MSWC.ContentRotator")
%>
<TABLE border="0" cellpadding="2" width="60%">
<TR>
    <%
```

```
     Response.Write NextTip.ChooseContent("acolades.txt")
     %>
</TR>
<TR>
     <%
     Response.Write NextTip.ChooseContent("acolades.txt")
     %>
</TR>
<TD align="center">
     <img src = "images/TN00605A.gif" width="77" height="69"></TD>
     <TD><FONT FACE="Arial">Make the world spin a little
     faster - </FONT><A Href = "userprofile1.asp"><FONT
FACE = "Arial">Reserve</font></A><FONT FACE = "Arial"> your
     copy of the MIND-Bender ActiveX control today.</FONT></TD>
     </TR>
</TABLE>
```

In this example, the Content Rotating object uses information from the content scheduling file named `acolades.txt` by using the `NextTip` method. The Content scheduling file enables you to specify the relative weight or frequency that the content item will be displayed and the content itself, as shown in Listing 19.2.

Listing 19.2   The Content Rotator scheduling file.

```
%% #1 // Money Bags CEO
<TD align="center"><font face="Arial">
<img src="/ASPstore/images/bs00044a.gif" width="67"
height="67"></font></TD><TD><font
face="Arial">&quot;We saved 2.4 million dollars by firing all our
application developers and replacing then with the sales
staff!&quot; -- Another Wealthy CEO</font></TD>

%% #1 // Java Quote
<TD align="center"><font face="Arial"><img
src="/ASPstore/images/PE03328A.gif" width="76"
height="73"> </font></TD>
<TD><font face="Arial">&quot;Simply Amazing&quot; -- The
Caffeine Free Press</font></TD>

%% #1 // Developer
<TD align="center"><font face="Arial">
<img src="/ASPstore/images/bs00044a.gif" width="67"
height="67"></font></TD><TD><font
face="Arial">&quot;Now I don't have to worry about practicing
any social skills!&quot; -- Another Heads-Down Coder</font></TD>
```

In this situation, all the weights are equal to provide an even level of content distribution to requesting browsers. When a browser requests the calling page, the text is translated directly to the server and is displayed to the client as if the page were generated entirely by hand. Also, notice that the scheduling file contains the table definition cells (<TD> and </TD>). As a result, the call to the `NextTip.ChooseContent` method is called from the table row (<TR>) definition.

Rotating the Banner with the Ad Rotator Component

The same concept used in the Content Rotator can be applied to rotating images on a Web page with the Ad Rotator Component. The Ad Rotator Component can be used to rotate images to promote your own products and services, sell advertising space, or simply to rotate and display images. The Ad Rotator Component also uses a scheduling file to determine the image that is going to be displayed and the frequency with which it will be displayed. The Ad Rotator Component uses the GetAdvertisement method to read the specified scheduling file, as shown in Listing 19.3.

Listing 19.3   Creating a rotating image banner.

```
<%
Dim ScheduleAD, adrot
ScheduleAD = "datawidgetswarehouse.txt"
Set adrot = Server.CreateObject("MSWC.AdRotator")
Response.Write adrot.GetAdvertisement(ScheduleAD)
%>
```

The Ad Rotator scheduling file enables you to set the properties of the displayed image (see Listing 19.4).

Listing 19.4   The Ad Rotator scheduling file.

```
REDIRECT GoTo.ASP
WIDTH 468
HEIGHT 60
BORDER 1
*
/aspstore/images/banner1.gif
/aspstore/userprofile1.asp
The Active Server Component the developers didn't tell you about!
50
/aspstore/images/banner2.gif
/aspstore/userprofile1.asp
Sign up for the Ultimate Design-Time Control
50
```

The REDIRECT options located on the first line in the Listing 19.4 specify a redirection file that is used to route the user to the proper destination. The redirection file is used as a counting mechanism to track the effectiveness of the banner. This file provides you the flexibility to keep track of your banners and the number of times that a banner is clicked. The redirection file, in this situation named GoTo.ASP, is an ASP file that you create to route the user to the appropriate URL parameter, as shown in the following code.

```
<%@ LANGUAGE="VBSCRIPT" %>
<% Response.Redirect (Request.QueryString("URL")) %>
```

This file uses the `Request.Redirect` method to redirect the browser to the designated URL. The round-about method of directing the user to the final destination is used to measure the effectiveness of an advertisement banner. Now you can build extensive logging capabilities into this ASP file that can be used to measure and record the amount of hits on the REDIRECT file.

Verifying that a File Exists with the Tools Component

In simple terms, the Web server is just a file server that sends files to the client's browser. The browser receives the files and translates the ASCII text into graphical output. When images cannot be found or links are broken, the Web server skips over the missing files and delivers the remaining information until it stops looking for the missing file. However, if required files are missing from server-side components, the Active Server scripting engine will produce a runtime error and terminate the processing of any more information on the page. For example, if you misspell the name of the Content Rotator file, the following runtime error is produced:

```
MSWC.ContentRotator.1 error '80070002'
The system cannot find the file specified.
/aspstore/storefrong.asp, line 86
```

The Tools Component can be used to help minimize these errors by using the `FileExists` method. The `FileExists` method provides server-side validation of any file within a virtual directory on the server. For example, the previous error could have been prevented if `FileExists` was applied to the Content Rotator file. In the Amazing DataWidgets WareHouse site, the Tools Component is used explicitly for this purpose. For instance, Listing 19.5 demonstrates not calling the Content Rotator Component if the Content Rotator scheduling file is not found.

Listing 19.5 Using the Tools Component to check on the existence of files on the Web server.

```
<TABLE border = "0" cellpadding = "2" width = "60%">
<%
Dim oDoesThe                                        '=== Variable Declaration
Set oDoesThe = Server.CreateObject("MSWC.Tools")    '=== Creates Tool Component
➥instance
If oDoesThe.FileExists("acolades.txt") Then         '=== If the file exist then
➥write table
%>
<TR>
    <%
    Dim NextTip
    Set NextTip = Server.CreateObject("MSWC.ContentRotator")
    Response.Write NextTip.ChooseContent("acolades.txt")   '=== Write content
    %>
    </TR>
    <TR>
    <%
```

continues

Listing 19.5   Continued

```
        Response.Write NextTip.ChooseContent("acolades.txt")
        %>
        </TR>
<%
End If            '=== File not found, start constructing default table
%>
<TR><TD>
        <TD align="center"><font face="Arial"><img
        src="/ASPstore/images/TN00605A.gif" width="77" height="69"> </font></TD>
        <TD><font face="Arial">Make the world spin a little
        faster - </font><a href="../ASPstore/UserProfile1.asp"><font
        face="Arial">Reserve</font></a><font face="Arial"> your
        copy of the MIND-Bender ActiveX control today.</font></TD>
    </TD></TR>
</TABLE>
```

If the Content schedule file acolades.txt is not found, only the last row of the table is generated (see Figure 19.4).

FIG. 19.4

The FileExists method of the Tools Component can validate whether the file is found on the Web server.

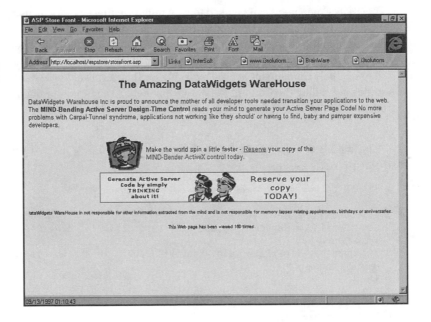

If the scheduling file is found, the Content Rotator is called to display the full table displayed in Figures 19.1 and 19.2. Keep in mind that this same principle can be applied not only to component-dependent files, but also to any file within the server's virtual root, such as GIF, JPG, text, and even ASP files themselves.

Detecting the Browser with the Browser Capabilities Component

The next step in building the Amazing Web site is to determine what type of browser is looking at the site. This is useful if you build a site that is designed to meet a specific HTML standard, or support advanced functionality of a specific browser without generating errors. Because this site deals specifically with product sales, you did not want to limit the user base, but at the same time you do want to give advanced browser functionality to newer browsers. For the Amazing DataWidgets WareHouse site, the CEO insists on not using any client-side ActiveX controls or Java applets, but at the same time wants to use a scrolling effect to display the disclaimer across the bottom of the page. To meet these needs, a marquee is displayed if the browser is Internet Explorer, as you saw in Figure 19.1. If Netscape Navigator is used, as pictured in Figure 19.2, an HTML text box uses JavaScript to scroll the text. If another browser is used, the disclaimer is simply displayed on the page.

To accomplish this, a server-side ASP script will initially detect and deliver HTML to the appropriate browser. If a Netscape browser is used, the server-side ASP will generate client-side JavaScript that scrolls the text in a text box and displays the time in the status bar of the browser. If Internet Explorer is used, the server-side VBScript code will generate the HTML tags for the marquee and generate the JavaScript for the status bar clock. If neither of these browsers is used, it won't generate any JavaScript or marquee tags.

To determine the requesting browser's display functionality, the combination of VBScript, the Active Server Request object, and the Browser Capabilities Component will be used. The Request object, as covered in Chapter 15, is used to extract information about the requesting browser. The Request object will retrieve information from the client's HTTP header request. The Request.ServerVariables property, as shown in Listing 19.6, is used to retrieve the HTTP_USER_AGENT server variable.

Part
IV

Ch
19

Listing 19.6   Determining the browser type using the *Request* object.

```
<%
If Instr(Request.ServerVariables("HTTP_USER_AGENT"),"MSIE") Then
    '=== This is an IE browser
Elseif Instr(Request.ServerVariables("HTTP_USER_AGENT"),"Mozilla") Then
    '=== This is a Netscape Browser
End If
%>
```

This server-side script uses the VBScript Instr function to search for a sub-string within a parent string. In this situation, VBScript is looking for the string MS IE within the HTTP_USER_AGENT server variable. If the string is found, the requesting browser is an Internet Explorer browser. If the browser is not Internet Explorer, then the same test can be applied to determine if the user is using a Netscape browser.

Now you need to extract more information about the specific capabilities of the requesting browser. The Browser Capabilities Component enables you to find out detailed information about the requesting browser by extracting the HTTP_USER_AGENT header and performing lookups against the BROWSAP.INI file. The BROWSCAP.INI file is a text file that contains browser definitions that define the capabilities of each browser. For the latest BROWSCAP.INI file, visit http://www.microsoft.com/iis/usingiis/developing/updates.htm. You can use the combination of the server variables and the Browser Capabilities Component to extract browser capabilities, as shown in Listing 19.7.

Listing 19.7 Extracting version information with the Browser Capabilities Component.

```
<%
Dim BrowserType, MinBrowser, isitIE
isitIE = Instr(Request.ServerVariables("HTTP_USER_AGENT"),"MSIE")
Set BrowserType = Server.CreateObject("MSWC.BrowserType")
If isitIE Then                                      '=== Drill down on
➥specifics
     If BrowserType.MajorVer = "3" Then             '=== Test version
➥using component
          MinBrowser = True
     Else
          MinBrowser = False
     End If
Else                                                '=== Its not IE
     If Instr(Request.ServerVariables("HTTP_USER_AGENT"),"Mozilla") Then
          MinBrowser = True
     End If
End If
%>
```

This code example is used to set to variables that will be used throughout the remaining code: the isitIE and the MinBrowser. For example, when the page is loaded into the browser, the ONLOAD event of the HTML <BODY> tag is used to trigger different JavaScript functions (see Listing 19.8).

Listing 19.8 Triggering different JavaScript functions on the *ONLOAD* event of an HTML page.

```
<% IF isitIE Then %>
   <body bgcolor="#FFFFCC" onload="loadclock()">
<% Elseif MinBrowser Then%>
   <body bgcolor="#FFFFCC" onload="loadinit()">
<% Else %>
   <body bgcolor="#FFFFCC">
<% End If %>
```

Likewise, you can use this same approach to determine whether you are going to display the marquee, the JavaScript scrolling text box, or the standard text disclaimer, as shown in Listing 19.9.

Listing 19.9   Determining display options with the Browser Capabilities Component.

```
<%
Dim strDisclaimer
strDisclaimer = "*Note, the Amazing DataWidgets WareHouse in not responsible for
other information extracted from the mind and is not responsible for memory
lapses relating to appointments, birthdays or anniversaries."
%>
<%If isitIE Then %>
    <p><font size="1" face="Arial"><marquee scrollamount="2"
    scrolldelay="50"><% Response.Write strDisclaimer %></marquee></font></p>
<% ElseIf MinBrowser Then %>
    <form name="frmmsg">
    <p align="center"><Font face="Arial" color="#FFFFFF" size="2"><input
type="text" size="50"    name="txtmsg"></font></p>
    </form>
<% Else %>
    <% Response.Write strDisclaimer %>
<% End If %>
```

Determining Page Hits with the Page Counter Component

The Page Counter Component is used to keep track of how many times a page has been requested. The Page Counter Component stores the count in memory until it writes the amount to a text file. The value is written to the file at a regular intervals to prevent grossly inaccurate numbers as a result of failure. To change this value from the default value of 25, change the Save_Count Registry setting. The Amazing DataWidgets WareHouse site uses the Page Counter to display how many times the site has been requested (see Listing 19.10).

Listing 19.10   Creating a page counter with the Page Counter Component.

```
<%
Dim oPageCount
Set oPageCount = Server.CreateObject("MSWC.PageCounter")
%>
<font face="Arial" size="1">This Web page has been viewed <%= oPageCount.Hits %>
➥times.</font>
```

The Page Counter Component tracks only the amount of requests for a page, not the total amount of hits per page. The distinction between the two is important to understand. Because HTTP must make individual connections and requests for every item contained on a Web page, a Web page that has five images would generate at least six hits, one for the initial page request for the page and five separate requests for each image on the page.

Build a Web Registration with the Content Linker

At this point, the main page for the Amazing DataWidgets WareHouse is finished. However, you need to build a registration wizard to help download the new design-time control. This registration wizard enables you to sign up for the component, designate the shipping information, and then assign billing information. The Content Linker Component is used to provide an automatic page linking and navigation builder that enables the links to pages to be automatically updated. Consider the situation if you build an application that requires four screens and you have to add a new form into page position two. As a result of the insert, the remaining links have to be updated by hand to reflect the new changes. However, the Content Linker Component eliminates hand-coding navigation issues by providing the automatic page linking and relative positioning between pages.

The Content Linker uses a file to create and maintain the navigation list. The navigation list acts as a table of contents specifying what files to access. This table-of-contents method enables you to access files from anywhere in the navigation list at any time. The Amazing DataWidgets WareHouse uses the combination of the Content Linker Component and client-side JavaScript to help provide navigation through the beta wizard. By having the Content Linker automatically update links to determine what page is next and previous, you are effectively letting the Content Linker control the order of the pages in the registration wizard. The Content Linker controls page navigation by reading values from a Content Linking List. This text file controls the order and descriptions of the Web pages. For example, the Content Linking List, named userwizard.txt for the Amazing DataWidgets WareHouse, is shown in Listing 19.11.

Listing 19.11   The Content Linking List File for the DataWidgets site.

```
storefront.asp     Main Page
userprofile1.asp   Setup user
userprofile2.asp   Billing Info
userprofile3.asp   Shipping Info
summary.asp        Summary Page
```

In this situation, the Content Linking List File provides sequential navigation and is used to determine relative positioning within this list. The Content Linker uses this list to keep track of what page the user is currently viewing to help determine what page is next and what page is previous. In this situation, if the user is currently browsing the userprofile2.asp page, the Content Linker provides a pointer to the previous page, userprofile1.asp, and to the page after the current page, userprofile3.asp. For example, Listing 19.12 determines the total amount of files in the Content Linking File by using the GetListCount method.

Listing 19.12 Using the *GetListCount* method to determine the number of files in the Content Linking File.

```
<%
dim NextLink, MaxPage, CurrentPage, LinkingFile
LinkingFile = "userwizard.txt"
Set NextLink = Server.CreateObject ("MSWC.NextLink")
MaxPage = NextLink.getlistcount(LinkingFile)
CurrentPage = NextLink.GetListIndex (LinkingFile)
%>
```

This example also extracts the index of the current page the user is browsing with by using the GetListIndex method.

In Chapter 17, "Implementing Existing Server-Side Components," you saw examples of using the Content Linking Component to create hypertext links to navigate among the files in the content list. This is fairly straightforward when you just need to provide a navigation technique though textual documents, such as an online reference guide or newspaper. However, passing information from page to page becomes a little more difficult. For the Amazing DataWidgets WareHouse site, buttons were chosen as the navigation motif, as shown in Figures 19.5, 19.6, and 19.7.

FIG. 19.5

The registration wizard guides the user through requested information.

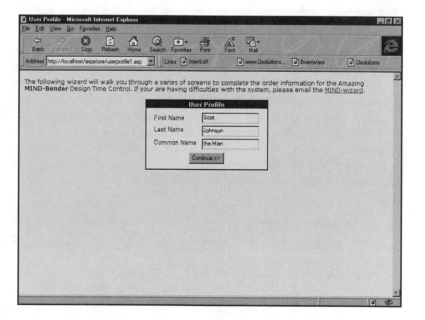

The purpose of the registration wizard is to gather information from the user and submit the collected information. You only have two ways to pass information from page to page in HTML. The first method passes information in the URL string by concatenating variable names and values onto the posted URL string. This method is typically used when you use hyperlinks as the navigation method. The requested page can then extract this information from the URL and use it as needed.

The second method passes the HTML form information by using the POST method. The POST method transfers HTML form values to the calling page specified in the ACTION method of the Form tag. Because the Form tag can only have one direction for controlling programming flow, the difficulty arises when you want to give the user the ability to navigate in different directions. There are two means to work around the limitation of only one Action item per form. The first method uses the button's OnClick event to trigger the page to browse to a new location by setting the location.href property. To the user, using the OnClick event of a button causes the page to react like a hyperlink and sends the browser to the designated page. However, the location.href property does not automatically submit or pass the form information to the Web server. If you want to pass information onto the next page, the variable and values must be posted to the server.

The second away around these issues is to use a non-visual Active Server Page that processes different application logic depending on the value of the button submitted to the Active Server Page. Once the value of the button is sent to an ASP on the Web server, the Web server can direct the browser to the appropriate page. An example of posting values to different locations using a single Form is demonstrated in Chapter 16, "Putting It All Together: Building an Online Catalog."

However, in this example, the approach demonstrated in Chapter 16 is not used because you are relying on the Content Linker to manage consecutive visual Active Server Pages. For the Amazing DataWidgets WareHouse site, combinations of the HREF and POST methods are used to control navigation. For forward navigation, the Form POST method is used to transfer information to the next page designated by the Content Linking File. For reverse navigation, the locations.href event is executed to return to the previous page designated in the Content Schedule File. Both of these events are activated using two client-side JavaScript functions: the LoadNextPage and LoadPrevPage functions. Listing 19.13 displays the Active Server VBScript that generates the client-side JavaScript. JavaScript is used on the client to ensure the largest potential browser community.

Listing 19.13   Creating client-side JavaScript navigation techniques using the Content Linker Component, Submit, and *Href* HTML attribute.

```
<%
Response.Write "<Script language='JavaScript'>"
Response.Write "function loadnextpage(form) {"
Response.Write "Form.Submit()"
Response.Write "}"

Response.Write "function LoadPrevPage() {"
Response.Write "location.href= '" &NextLink.GetPreviousURL("userwizard.txt")
&"'"
Response.Write "}"
Response.Write "</Script>"
%>
```

The `LoadNextPage` function triggers the `Form.Submit` event for the specific form. When this event is executed, the form information is passed to the page specified in the `Action` event of the form. To transfer information to the next page in the Content Linking File, the `GetNextURL` method is used, as shown in the following example:

```
<form method = "POST" name = "frmuser" Action = "<%
=NextLink.GetNextURL("userwizard.txt") %>">
```

The `LoadPrevPage` JavaScript uses the `location.href` event to navigate to the previous page in the Content Linking File. These two generic functions can be used to uniformly control navigation throughout all pages on the registration wizard.

The next phase needed to finish the registration wizard is to create the individual buttons on the appropriate pages. The first page of the registration wizard, as shown in Figure 19.5, will only have one button that enables the user to only navigate to the second page. The remaining pages in the wizard will enable forward and reverse navigation. For example, Figure 19.6 demonstrates the billing information page that uses the Content Linking File to create the Previous and Continue buttons.

FIG. 19.6

The registration wizard uses the Content Linking Component to aid in navigation.

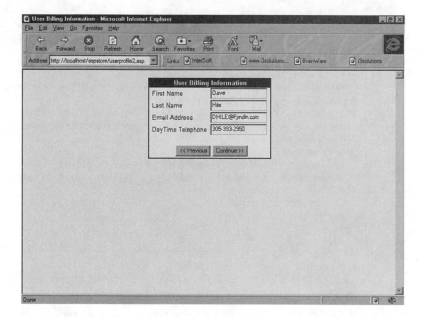

Of course, you want to create a generic function to automatically create the buttons when new pages are added to the wizard. To accomplish this feat, an Active Server Page VBScript function is written to automatically create the correct navigational buttons throughout the online wizard. The self-sustaining code, as shown in Listing 19.14, will retain complete control over the links within the online wizard and does not require significant coding effort when new pages are added to the wizard.

Part
IV

Ch
19

Listing 19.14   Creating forward and reverse navigation buttons.

```
<%
dim nextlink, maxpage, nextpage, currentpage, str, LinkingFile
LinkingFile = "userwizard.txt"
Set NextLink = Server.CreateObject ("MSWC.NextLink")
Maxpage = Nextlink.getlistcount(LinkingFile)
Currentpage = NextLink.GetListIndex (LinkingFile)
Sub CreateNavButtons()
If (currentpage > 2) and (currentpage < maxpage) Then
    '============================ Display forward and next buttons============
    '=== Prev Page ====
    str ="<TR><TD><input type='button' name='btnprev' value=' << Previous' "
    str = str & "language='JavaScript' onclick='loadprevpage()'></TD>"
    Response.Write str
    '============================== Next Page button =========================
    str ="<TD><input type='button' name='btnnext' value='Continue >>' "
    str = str & "language='JavaScript' onclick='loadnextpage(this.form)'></
TD></TR>"
    Response.Write str
Elseif currentpage = 2 Then
    '============================= only display next page ====================
    str ="<TR><TD><input type='button' name='btnnext' value='Continue >>' "
    str = str & "language='JavaScript' onclick='loadnextpage(this.form)'></
TD><TR>"
    Response.Write str
Elseif currentpage=maxpage-1 Then
    '============================== display previous and finish buttons =======
    '=== display previous button ===
    str ="<TR><TD><input type='button' name='btnprev' value='<< Previous' "
    str = str & "language='JavaScript' onclick='loadprevpage()'></TD>"
    Response.Write str
    '=== display finish button
    str ="<TR><TD><input type='button' name='btnnext' value='Order Now!' "
    str = str & "language='JavaScript' onclick='loadnextpage(this.form)'></
TD><TR>"
    Response.Write str
End If
End Sub
%>
```

This function tests for three conditions to determine what buttons are to be created on the page. If the current page is the last page of the wizard, that is, page 3 in the Content Linking File, two buttons will be created that are labeled << Previous and Order Now!, as shown in Figure 19.7.

To implement this function, call the CreateNavButtons function where you need the button to be added.

FIG. 19.7
Form navigation information is made possible by using the Content Linker, JavaScript, and HTML POST and HREF commands.

User Shipping Information	
First Name	Susan
Last Name	Adams
Email Address	Suzad@Kiva.Com
DayTime Telephone	703 756-6533

<< Previous   Order Now!

```
<TABLE border="0" cellpadding="2" cellspacing="0">
<% CreateNavButtons %>
</TABLE>
```

The final result of the wizard displays the information that was collected on various pages on the summary page, as shown in Figure 19.8.

FIG. 19.8
The registration wizard displays the summary information.

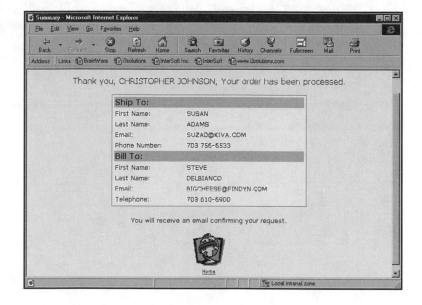

From Here...

In this chapter, you have seen the combination of several installable components that ship with Active Server Pages. Specifically, the Browser Capability Component, in conjunction with server variables, was used to demonstrate how to identify different browsers to tailor output to their specific viewing capabilities. The Ad Rotator and Content Rotator Components were used to illustrate how to rotate images and content on your site. The Content Linker was used to create an automatic navigational method between pages based on files listed in the Content

Linking file. The Tools Component was used to demonstrate extra server-side administration tools to help prevent broken links or errors from missing required files. Finally, the Page Component was used to display the number of times a page has been accessed.

For related information, please refer to the following chapters:

- Chapter 18, "Creating Your Own Active Server Components," walks you through the tools and examples on how to create tailored functionality via custom created components.

- Chapter 20, "Database Access with ADO," teaches how to use the Data Access Component to connect to any ODBC-compliant database.

- Chapter 26, "Putting It All Together: Creating a Dynamic Database Application," illustrates how to use the `Application` object to store information extracted from a database to provide database interaction for the Amazing DataWidget WareHouse.

- Chapter 31, "Using Internet Information Server 4.0 to Manage Your Web Applications," demonstrates how to use the various feature of the Internet Information Server to help manage your sites and applications.

Database Management with Active Server Pages

CHAPTER 20

Database Access with ADO

So far, you have seen how ASP can help you create a rich interactive environment for your Web site. The `Session` and `Application` objects enable you to create Web sites that "remember" users. The powerful scripting allowed by VBScript further extends what you can put on your Web page.

Now, you will examine *ActiveX Database Objects (ADO)*. ADO is a collection of objects that enable ASP developers to connect to databases. Database access can be the difference between a Web application that is a toy and a full-powered, enterprise-level application.

Many of your ASP applications will rely on some sort of database connectivity. While you can build ASP pages that aren't data driven, there are many more useful (and fun!) applications that you can build by using a database behind the scenes. For instance, you can create a simple Web-based telephone directory for your company's employees very quickly and easily with ADO.

This chapter will introduce you to ADO and its objects, collections, and methods. Later chapters examine each object and its methods in more detail. Feel free to play with the example code in the text as you work through each chapter. ■

Learn the History of ADO

Why is ADO so significant? How does it relate to other data access methods like DAO, RDO, and ODBC?

Examine the ADO Object Model

Learn how and when you should exploit ADO for maximum efficiency.

Discover ADO's Transaction and Rollback Processing Capabilities

ADO enables you to maintain your applications data integrity with easy-to-use transaction processing.

See Why the Advanced Data Connector Can Save You Hours of Development Time

A firm understanding of the fundamentals of the Advanced Data Connector can save you hours of development time.

Build a Working Example of a Database-Driven Application

Build a drill-down application that finds a fellow employee's phone number in a database using ASP with ADO.

Understanding ADO

If you have ever used data objects before, ADO will seem very familiar. And while there are some differences you will need to be aware of, you should be able to start coding with it very quickly.

Unlike DAO and RDO, there is no complicated hierarchy to be navigated in order to create a recordset. Sometimes you just want to get to your data. ADO enables developers to create a recordset quickly.

Accessing versus Creating

This would be a good time to explain the difference between *accessing* and *creating* a recordset. The basic difference is one of usage. You *create* a recordset. That recordset is then used to *access* the data.

An example in the real world would be telephoning a friend. By dialing (creating the recordset) you can talk to (access the underlying data) your friend.

At first I thought that Microsoft was just renaming DAO to make it fit the ActiveX marketing plan. But I soon discovered I was wrong: ADO is built on an entirely different foundation than DAO, or RDO for that matter. ADO is part of OLE DB (Object Linking and Embedding for Databases), an exciting new way to access and manipulate data that Microsoft has developed.

OLE DB

OLE DB is an object-oriented specification that enables you to access data. It is an Application Programming Interface (API) based on the Component Object Model (COM). ODBC, for instance, is an API based on C. However, don't think that ODBC has been replaced by OLE DB; ODBC is a subset of OLE DB and it is still a great way to interact with SQL-based databases. Figure 20.1 shows how OLE DB fits into the access paradigm.

OLE DB versus ODBC

So, when do you use OLE DB? When should you think about using ODBC? In reality, it isn't really a question of one versus the other, but more of an understanding which technology is more appropriate to apply to the problem at hand.

OEL DB is a specification that is a superset of ODBC. However, OLE DB enables developers to access data from more than just the row-based databases that ODBC was designed for.

ODBC is a specific API that gives developers access to SQL-compliant databases. Both OLE DB and ODBC give developers low-level access to databases.

But OLE DB is better because it is based on component architecture. Data is in a tabular format, but is not reliant on SQL. This means that regardless of what type of datasource you are accessing—for instance, an e-mail store—you can still use the same components you would with a SQL server database. With OLE DB, you have data providers and data consumers, which are components that enable this encapsulation.

FIG. 20.1
OLE DB offers a better approach to accessing your data.

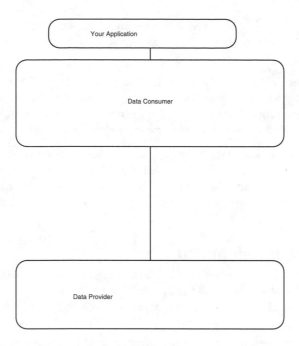

OLE DB is going to be a big deal in the near future, and ADO is a great way to start understanding and using OLE DB. Understanding OLE DB will put you ahead of the pack. But that's the future. Now, in the present, by using ADO, you can simplify and speed up your development. You can use its simplified, data-centric architecture to create robust Web-based applications now.

> **N O T E** You can learn more about OLE DB, along with other information about Microsoft's data access strategy, at **www.microsoft.com/Data**. ■

Web Application Development

Developing Web-based applications can be very different from other types of programming. Unlike normal client/server applications, Web pages are *stateless*, which means that you call the page, it grabs the data it needs, and then it sends your document to you. Once a Web server sends you a page, it forgets about it. In other words, the server does not know if this is the fortieth time you have accessed a page or the first.

In traditional client/server development, a client application maintains a connection with its server component. Besides requesting and sending data, the client queries the server periodically to make sure the connection is still alive. If the server goes down, it will sense this and take the appropriate measures such as sending an error to the user and exiting.

As a Web application developer, you not only have to deal with the short-lived memory of Web servers, you also have to deal with the Internet being a connectionless network. When a browser requests a page, it is served up and sent out. That's it. The server is not going to check and see whether the page and all of its components (graphics, sounds, and so on) made it to the browser.

But don't despair. ASP and ADO are significant steps in dealing with these issues. An Active Server doesn't forget the way an old-fashioned server does; it has a memory. Think of an ASP server as a loyal machine that can remember its friends and past dealings. When you are dealing with millions of hits a month, this feature will become a lifesaver.

Of course, this new functionality comes at a cost. An Active Server needs more RAM than a server that doesn't offer the capability to "remember" users. And if you use databases to store information about users that span across multiple visits (as opposed to using the Session object to remember information per visit), you will need more hard disk space to hold the information your database contains.

Products for Web Development

Some of you might be familiar with IDC/HTX, and you may wonder whether Microsoft has abandoned IDC. Not exactly, it still works with IIS 3.0. But don't expect to see any improvements in version 4. However, Microsoft is offering a tool to help port your existing IDC projects into ADO.

You might also be a Web developer who has used a really great product from Allaire called Cold Fusion. Cold Fusion works much like IDC/HTX. It enables you to connect to an ODBC datasource, and embed its data in your HTML pages. Basically, it's a better version of IDC/ HTX (with a larger price tag as well!).

Cold Fusion is very easy to learn and it still has a definite place in your toolkit. ASP works best when it is used for larger, more complex programs that need the robustness a scripting language can offer. Cold Fusion is a great choice for simple data-driven programs.

N O T E   Allaire's Web site, **www.allaire.com**, is always a great place to check out the latest information on Cold Fusion. Updates, new releases, and great examples of Cold Fusion products can be found there. ■

The ADO Object Model

The ADO object model provides developers a quick, yet powerful, method of accessing a datasource. Like DAO, you have Recordset objects. The Connection object is new and provides a similar functionality that DAO's Workspace object gives.

- Connection
- Error
- Command
- Parameter

■ `Recordset`

■ `Field`

The list above comprises all the objects that make an ADO hierarchy. There are three major objects in ADO that provide an interface to your data: the `Connection`, `Command`, and `Recordset` objects. Think of the `Connection` interface as the road to the datasource. Without it, you can't get there. It also contains the `Error` object, where errors from the datasource are logged. The `Command` interface provides a way to send parameters to stored procedures when opening a recordset. The `Command` interface is optional, but still very important. Finally, the `Recordset` interface is the workhorse of ADO. It is the object that you will use to interact with your data. `Recordset` uses the `Field` object.

Objects, Collections, and Interfaces

In many texts on ADO and other object models, authors use the words collection, object, and interface. But they rarely explain what they mean by these words (if anything!).

An *object* has both properties and methods. For instance, a phone has a dialer (a property) and speed dial (a method). Other properties of a phone object might include its color, location, and whether it is a pulse or rotary dialer. However, some of these properties, such as color, might not be publicly accessible. To change the phone's color, you might need to invoke a method called ChangeColor, and send that method the color you want to change the phone to. Other properties, however, might be publicly accessible, allowing you to change them without having to call a certain method.

The set of properties and methods in an object that are publicly accessible are collectively referred to as the *interface* of the object. In practice, however, interface and object hold the same meaning. So, when I say "the `Collection` object" or "the `Collection` interface," it will be easiest to equate these as speaking of the same thing.

(Most authors, including myself, will switch between the two quite frequently. Why? To alleviate the boredom of writing—and reading—the same word 20 times on a page.)

However, collection *is* different. A *collection* is just a collection of objects. Sometimes, you don't have just one object; you have several of them grouped together. This group of objects is referred to as a collection.

For instance, in ADO, there is the `Error` object. But, generally, I will refer to the `Errors` collection— meaning the set of `Error` objects. Collections in ADO often have their own properties and methods that are separate form the properties and methods of the individual object.

Properties and Methods of ADO Objects

ADO object's properties and methods are fairly easy to understand and use. They offer developers a non-complicated way to access and manipulate data. If you are at all familiar with the hierarchical model imposed on developers from DAO, ADO will seem like a breath of fresh air with its capability to quickly access data without having to navigate through an extensive hierarchy of objects first.

Like all good objects, ADOs have both methods and properties that are publicly accessible. Many of these properties and objects offer very similar functionality. For instance, the Connection, Command, and Recordset objects all offer a way to specify a datasource that will be the active connection.

The *Connection* Object   The Connection object provides a connection to the datasource. Because it is the connection to the datasource, it also contains the Error collection for any errors that the datasource may return. You can learn more about the Connection object in Chapter 21, "Working with ADO's Connection Object."

Table 20.1 lists the various properties of the Connection object. These properties cover a wide variety of functionality, and give developers quite a bit of control over the connection to the datasource.

Listing 20.1 shows an example of how easy it can be to create and configure a Connection object, and then use it to connect to a datasource.

Listing 20.1   *20ASP1.ASP*—Creating a *Connection* object can be easy!

```
Dim dataConn
dataConn = Server.CreateObject("ADODB.Connection")
dataConn.ConnectionString = "SampleDSN"
dataConn.open
```

Table 20.1   The *Connection* Object's Properties

Property	Description
Attribute	Specifies whether a new transaction will be started after a transaction rollback or commit.
CommandTimeout	How long to wait for a command to process. Default is 30 seconds. Setting this value to 0 will make the wait indefinite.
ConnectionString	The DSN, provider, username and password, and other information necessary to connect to the database.
ConnectionTimeout	How long to wait to connect to the datasource. Default is 15 seconds. Set to 0 to wait indefinitely.
DefaultDatabase	If the datasource you are connecting to enables multiple databases, this property enables you to specify which one is the default.
Isolation	The isolation level of the connection.
Mode	Used to set the permissions on a connection, such as read-only or read-write.

Property	Description
Provider	The provider of a connection.
Version	The version of ADO being used.

Table 20.2 lists the methods of the Connection object. There are relatively few methods used with the Connection object. Generally, the properties of the Connection object are used to configure the connection, and then either the Execute or Open method is called.

Table 20.2 The *Connection* Object's Methods

Method	Description
BeginTrans	Begins a transaction.
ComitTrans	Commits the transaction to disk.
RollBackTrans	Rolls back the transaction.
Close	Closes the connection.
Execute	Executes a command on the datasource, returning a recordset.
Open	Opens the connection.

The *Error* Collection and *Error* Object The Error collection is part of the Connection object. When the datasource generates and returns an error (or errors), this is where they will be found. Sometimes, these errors are actually just warnings. More about the Error object and Errors collection can be found in Chapter 21.

Listing 20.2 shows an example of working with the Error collection. In this example, after opening a connection, the Errors collection is checked to see if any errors were generated by this opening.

Listing 20.2   *20ASP1.ASP*—Checking the *Error* collection.

```
Dim dataConn
dataConn = Server.CreateObject("ADODB.Connection")
dataConn.ConnectionString = "SampleDSN"
dataConn.open

If dataConn.Errors.Count > 0 Then
     'We know errors occurred, so we can
     'investigate those errors, or (as in this case)
     'we can print them out
     for each error in dataConn.Errors
          Response.Write(Error.Number & ":" & Error.Description)
     Next
End if
```

Table 20.3 lists the properties of the Error object. These properties can be used to uncover such information as the type of error that occurred, what its source was, and a description of the error.

Table 20.3   The *Error* Object's Properties

Property	Description
Description	This is the description of the error.
HelpContext	The help topic in the help file that contains more information on the error.
HelpFile	The filename of the help file that has more information on the error.
NativeError	This is a provider-specific error code.
Number	A unique ID to distinguish this Error object form others in the Error collection.
Source	The name of the application (or object) that returned the error.
SQLState	The five-digit SQL error code.

Table 20.4 shows the properties of the Errors collection. These properties are helpful in understanding the number of errors that have been raised, and in accessing these errors individually.

Table 20.4   The *Error* Collection's Properties

Property	Description
Count	The number of Error objects in the collection.
Item	Returns a specific Error object by name or number.

Table 20.5 lists the methods found in the Errors collection. Many of the methods of one collection will work with another, but understanding what is different about each collection can be very helpful.

Table 20.5   The *Error* Collection's Methods

Method	Description
Clear	Removes all the objects in the collection.

The *Command* Object   The Command object is a specific command executed against the datasource, and it returns a recordset. The Command object is optional, but is particularly valuable when dealing with stored procedures. You can learn more about the Command object in Chapter 22, "Using Command Objects."

N O T E   What is a command? A *command* is a series of instructions executed by a database that return a recordset.

Commands are most often represented as SQL, which stands for Structured Query Language. You can learn more about SQL in Chapter 24, "Managing Your Database." ▨

Listing 20.3 shows an example of the Command object at work. Here, you are creating a Command object, setting its ActiveConnection property to the name of your DSN, and setting its CommandText to a SQL command. You then invoke the Execute method of the Command object.

Listing 20.3   *20ASP1.ASP*—Creating a *Command* object.

```
Dim dataCmd
Set dataCmd = Server.CreateObject("ADODB.Command")

dataCmd.ActiveConnection = "SampleDSN"
dataCmd.CommandText = "SELECT * FROM tblStuff"

set rs = dataCmd.execute (, , adCmdTxt)
```

In Table 20.6, the properties of the Command object are listed. These properties can be used to configure the Command object, including setting its data connection, and the command that it contains, along with many other valuable settings.

Table 20.6   The *Command* Object's Properties

Property	Description
ActiveConnection	Specifies the Connection object the Command object belongs to.
CommandText	A text string that indicates the command to run against the datasource.
CommandTimeout	Specifies how long to wait for a command to execute. Default is 30.
CommandType	The type of command.
Prepared	Tells the provider to prepare, or compile, the command before execution.

Part
V

Ch
20

Table 20.7 shows the methods of the Command object. The methods of the Command object are used to create new parameter objects and execute the command.

Table 20.7   The *Command* Object's Methods

Method	Description
CreateObject	Creates a new Parameter object.
Execute	Executes the command stored in the CommandText property.

The *Parameter* Object and Collection   The Parameter object is used to store parameters that will be passed to a stored procedure. *Parameters* are variables that you can send to the database that will be needed for the execution of certain queries and stored procedures. You can learn more about the Parameter object in Chapter 22.

Some commands are already stored in the database in a special form called a *stored procedure* (or query, depending on the database). Some of the queries need a parameter (or parameters) sent to it to execute.

For instance, there might be a stored procedure in your database for returning the row that contains a customer's phone number. This procedure will need the customer's name to look up the phone number. In this case, the customer's name is the parameter.

In Listing 20.4, a parameter is created and appended to the Parameter collection.

Listing 20.4   *20ASP1.ASP*—Creating a *Parameter* object.

```
StrName = "customerName"
StrValue = "Jones"
intType = adChar
intSize = 50
intDirection = adParamInput
dataParam = DataConn.CreateParameter(strName, intType, intDirection, intSize,
➥strValue)
DataConn.Append DataParameter
```

Table 20.8 lists and explains the properties of the Parameter object. These properties are used to configure the Parameter before it is appended to the Parameter collection and sent to the database. For instance, in the case of sending the customer name to find the phone number, you need to configure the parameter as an input parameter, meaning that it will be used as input to the query.

Table 20.8   The *Parameter* Object's Properties

Property	Description
Attributes	Indicates what type of data the parameter accepts.
Direction	Indicates whether the parameter is an input or output parameter, or both.
Name	The parameter's name.
NumericScale	For numeric parameter values, indicates the number of digits to the right of the decimal point that it will be resolved to.
Precision	For numeric parameter values, indicates the number of digits that will be used.
Size	The maximum size, in bytes, of the Parameter object.
Type	The data type of the parameter.
Value	The value of the parameter.

Table 20.9 lists the methods of the Parameter object. Basically, the only method you will ever use with the Parameter object is that of appending a chunk of data to it.

Table 20.9   The *Parameter* Object's Methods

Method	Description
AppendChunk	Appends a large amount of data to a Parameter object.

Table 20.10 lists the properties of the Parameter collection. Like the properties of most collections, these deal with accessing a particular parameter by number and counting the number of parameters.

Table 20.10   The *Parameter* Collection's Properties

Property	Description
Count	The number of Parameter objects in the collection.
Item	A specific parameter in the collection.

Part
V

Ch
20

Once you have created a Parameter object, it needs to be appended to the Parameter collection. Why have a collection of parameters? Some stored procedures take more than one parameter. For instance, in the procedure you looked at earlier that returns a customer's phone number, you would probably send the first and last names as separate parameters—thus, the need for a collection. Table 20.11 lists the methods of the Parameter collection.

Table 20.11 The *Parameter* Collection's Methods

Method	Description
Append	Adds a new parameter to the collection.
Delete	Deletes a parameter from the collection.
Refresh	Retrieves information from the provider on the parameters in the stored procedure specified in the CommandText property.

The *Recordset* Object   The Recordset object is the workhorse of ADO. It is the object you most often use to manipulate the data in your database. Using the Field collection of the Recordset interface, you can access individual fields of the recordset and change, delete, and update them. You can find out more about the Recordset object in Chapter 23, "Working with ADO's Recordset Object."

In Table 20.12, the properties of the Recordset object are listed and described. These properties are most often used to find out various status-type information about the recordset, such as the number of records or the current position of the record pointer.

Table 20.12 The *Recordset* Object's Properties

Property	Description
AbsolutePage	Which page the current record is on.
AbsolutePosition	The place in the recordset the current record is on.
ActiveConection	The current connection the recordset is using.
BOF,EOF	Beginning of file, end of file.
Bookmark	A unique reference in a recordset set.
CacheSize	The number of records stored in memory of the client machine.
CursorType	The type of cursor to open the recordset with.
EditMode	Indicates whether the current record is being edited or added.
Filter	Filters a recordset.
LockType	The type of locking the recordset will enforce.
MaxRecords	The maximum number of records the recordset will return.
PageCount	The number of pages in the recordset.
PageSize	The number of records a page will have.
RecordCount	The number of records in the recordset.
Source	The source of the recordset (that is, a table or query).
Status	The status of a record.

Table 20.13 shows the methods of the Recordset object. Use these methods to manipulate the set of data as a whole, and to navigate through the recordset.

Table 20.13　The *Recordset* Object's Methods

Method	Description
AddNew	Creates a new record.
CancelBatch	Cancels a pending batch update.
CancelUpdate	Cancels the changes made to a recordset.
Clone	Creates a new recordset with the records in the current recordset.
Close	Closes the recordset.
Delete	Deletes the current record.
GetRows	Copies the specified records into an array.
Move	Moves to a specific record.
MoveFirst, MoveLast, MoveNext, MovePrevious	Moves to the record specified in the name.
NextRecordset	Closes the current recordset and opens the next one.
Open	Opens a recordset.
Requery	Reruns the query and updates the recordset.
Resync	Syncs up with the database. Updates any locally cached records.
Supports	Indicates whether certain functions will be present in the datasource.
Update	Saves the changes made to the current record.
UpdateBatch	Saves the changes from the batch update.

The *Field* Object and Collection　The Field object is the interface to a specific field in the current record. The collection is the group of fields that make up the current record.

Table 20.14 shows the various properties of the Field object. Use these properties to discover information about the underlying nature of that particular field in the database. For instance, if you need to know the maximum size in bytes the field can be, look at its DefinedSize property.

Table 20.14   The *Field* Object's Properties

Property	Description
ActualSize	The actual length of the data.
Attribute	This is data for the field.
DefinedSize	The maximum size of the field.
Name	The name of the field.
NumericScale	For numeric field values, indicates the number of digits to the right of the decimal point that it will be resolved to.
OriginalValue	The value of the field before it was changed.
Precision	For numeric field values, indicates the number of digits that the field will be resolved to.
Type	The type of data.
UnderlyingValue	The current value of the field in the database.
Value	The actual value of the field.

In Table 20.15, the methods of the Field object are listed. These methods are used to append and retrieve chunks of information from the field when that information is very large.

Table 20.15   The *Field* Object's Methods

Method	Description
AppendChunk	Appends data to a field.
GetChunk	Gets data from a field.

Table 20.16 lists the properties of the Field collection. This collection is used to access a particular field by number or to find out how many fields are in the collection.

Table 20.16   The *Field* Collection's Properties

Property	Description
Count	The number of fields in the collection.
Item	The specific field in the collection.

Table 20.17 lists the lone method of the Field collection. This method doesn't really do anything, but is included for the sake of consistency.

Table 20.17   The *Field* Collection's Methods

Method	Description
Refresh	This really doesn't do anything. You will need to use the recordset's `Requery` method to refresh a field collection.

ADO in Action

The best way to understand how these objects work together to provide access to your datasource is to see them in action (see Listings 20.5 and 20.6).

Listing 20.5   *CHAP20.ASP*—Opening a recordset can take two lines...

```
Set rs_main = Server.CreateObject("ADODB.Recordset")
rs_main.Open "Select * from tbl_stuff", "DSN=stuff"
```

In Listing 20.5, I created a recordset with just two lines of code. However, this recordset is severely limited in the functionality it provides. In Listing 20.6, you can see an example of a more functional recordset, one that took eight lines of code to create.

Listing 20.6   *CHAPTER20.ASP*—...or eight.

```
Set DataConn = Server.CreateObject("ADODB.Connection")
DataConn.Open "DSN=Stuff"
Set DataCmd = Server.CreateObject("ADODB.Command")
DataCmd.CommandText = "SELECT * FROM tbl_stuff"
DataCmd.CommandType = adCmdTxt
Set DataCmd.ActiveConnection = DataConn
Set rs_main = Server.CreateObject("ADODB.Recordset")
rs_main.Open DataCmd
```

The code above utilizes, in turn, a `Connection` object and then a `Command` object to get to a `Recordset` object, which the developer can then use to access data. The `Recordset` is the interface that you will use to access and manipulate your data. The `Connection` and `Command` interfaces are just the roads that enable you to get to the `Recordset`.

Although they have a more limited role than that of the `Recordset` object, the `Command` and `Connection` objects still have very important roles to play. The `Connection` object enables the developer to control many details of the actual connection to the datasource. The `Command` object gives the developer the ability to manage the commands that will be executed by the datasource (see Figure 20.2).

The `Connection` object is always present. If you don't explicitly create one, ADO will implicitly create one for you. The `Connection` object represents the connection to your datasource. It has various properties that enable it to be configured before you actually open anything with it. In Listing 20.5, I implicitly created a connection when I opened the recordset rs_main. In Listing 20.6, I explicitly created a `Connection` object, DataConn.

FIG. 20.2
The Connection and Command interfaces are for creation of a recordset.

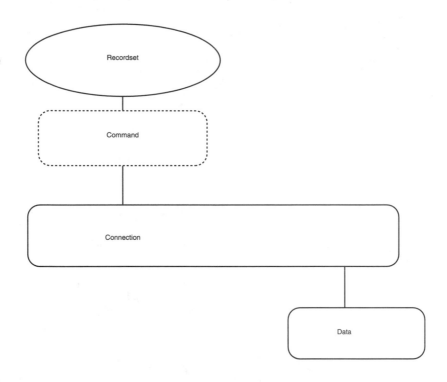

Naming Conventions

What should you name your ADODB variables? Naming conventions can become a heated debate. Everyone has their preferred names for variables and methods. I suggest that when you are developing with Visual Interdev—especially if you will be using any wizards—that you stick to InterDev's names.

For instance, DataConn is what the Data Range Wizard names the Connection object it creates. I like that name, so I use it in my own code. I further decided to name my Command object DataCmd.

What really matters, however, is that you use names that will be descriptive. Choose a convention that will allow you to automatically know what kind of variable you are looking at and you'll be fine. This means including in each variable name a couple letters that represent what type of variable it is. For example: Conn for a Connection Object, Cmd for Command, and rs for Recordset.

After you create the Connection object, create a Command object, DataCmd. The Command object contains a command (in this case, a SQL statement) that the datasource can execute. It also allows for passing parameters, with the Parameters property.

In Listing 20.7, a recordset is created with the Command object. A Connection object is still being created, but implicitly.

Listing 20.7   *CHAP20.ASP*—**Opening a recordset with the *Command* object.**

```
Set DataCmd = Server.CreateObject("ADODB.Command")
Set rs_main = Server.CreateObject("ADODB.Recordset")
DataCmd.ActiveConnection = "phone_numbers"
DataCmd.CommandText="qry_list_numbers"
Set rs_main = dataCmd.Execute
```

Benefits of Coding with the ADO Object Model

I know what you're thinking: "If I can create a recordset with two lines of code, why take eight?" Or, to put it another way: "Why explicitly use the Connection or Command objects?" There are actually some very good reasons to explicitly create those objects whenever possible.

N O T E The Command object is definitely optional. As a matter of fact, not all of your datasources will even support it. But it still has a definite use. ∎

To see the benefits of coding with the object model in mind, let's start by doing just the opposite. The code in Listing 20.8 creates two recordsets, rs_people and rs_places. Both are created with a SQL statement: one on a table, and one on a query.

Listing 20.8   *CHAPTER20.ASP*—**Creating recordsets the wrong way.**

```
Set rs_people = Server.CreateObject("ADODB.Recordset")
Set rs_places = Server.CreateObject("ADODB.Recordset")
rs_people.Open "Select * from tbl_people", "DSN=PeopleAndPlaces"
rs_places.Open "Select * from qry_places", "DSN=PeopleAndPlaces"
```

What is so bad about the above code? For starters, two Connection objects are being created. There is only need for one. So resources are being wasted. Second, the Command object could be used to manage the opening of these recordsets, which would result in improved performance.

Listing 20.9 is another code snippet (which should look pretty familiar by now) opening these same recordsets in a more appropriate manner.

Listing 20.9   *CHAPTER20.ASP*—**Creating a recordset the better way.**

```
Set DataConn = Server.CreateObject("ADODB.Connection")
DataConn.Open "DSN= PeopleAndPlaces"
Set DataCmd = Server.CreateObject("ADODB.Command")
DataCmd.CommandText = "tbl_people"
DataCmd.CommandType = adCmdTbl
Set DataCmd.ActiveConnection = DataConn
Set rs_people = Server.CreateObject("ADODB.Recordset")
rs_people.Open DataCmd
DataCmd.CommandText = "qry_places"
DataCmd.CommandType = adCmdStoredProc
Set rs_places = Server.CreateObject("ADODB.Recordset")
rs_places.Open DataCmd
```

In the code above, there is only one `Connection` object. Because both recordsets are accessing data from the same datasource, this makes sense. Just as you don't build a separate road for every car, you don't need to create a new `Connection` object for every recordset. The same goes for the `Command` object.

Also, notice how `DataCmd`'s `CommandText` is not a SQL statement. In both cases, instead of writing `"Select *"`, the `CommandText` property is the name of the table or query. This can give you increased performance primarily because `CommandType` is also set to what you are asking for. This primes the pump, so to speak, and readies the connection.

This doesn't mean that every time you create a recordset you should have first created a connection and command interface for it. Some data providers don't allow a `Command` object. And if all you are writing is a quick-and-dirty page, it might be overkill to create the `Connection` object. That having been said, I would still always do it, at least at first. Better to overcode than undercode, especially in the learning phase.

Now that you have looked at some benefits to coding with the ADO object model in mind, let's look at another great benefit of ADO: transaction processing.

Transaction and Rollback Processing

ADO makes transaction processing incredibly easy. You can increase the reliability of your data and the speed of your application with only a few lines of code. It's really that simple. But what is transaction processing?

Imagine for a moment that you have created a program to manage bank accounts. Customers have asked for a way to transfer funds from one account to another. You write the code, and everything works great. It takes the money out of the first account, and puts it into the second account. But one day there is a power outage and the money is taken out, but never put back in anywhere.

How can you avoid this error in the future? Transaction processing. Instead of subtracting the money first, and then adding it to the next account, you can do both inside a transaction. If something goes wrong, the transaction won't be written out to the database.

Listing 20.10 shows how easy it can be to include transaction processing in your code.

Listing 20.10   *CHAPTER20.ASP*—**Transaction processing at work.**

```
DataConn.BeginTrans

    ' Insert your code here

If DataConn.Errors.Count = 0 Then
    DataConn.CommitTrans
Else
    DataConn.RollbackTrans
End If
```

Whatever data handling you insert into this code will now only execute and write to the database if there are no errors. If the datasource returns an error, the transaction will be rolled back. In other words, it will be as if it never happened.

As wonderful as data integrity is, there is an even better reason to get excited about transaction processing: increased performance. By waiting before it writes out to disk, your application can see a marked increase in speed. This is because everything is happening in RAM until CommitTrans is called. Then it is written out to disk. The actual amount of difference you will see will depends mostly on the size of your database and the tables involved.

 TIP Take the above code and start wrapping it around any code you now have that may need it. You will be amazed at the increased performance you will see.

Remote Data Services

So far, you have seen how to access data that can be put into a page any browser can understand. That is the beauty of ASP—its browser independence. But this does present a drawback. What if you want to create a fat client? The browser can be a rich environment, and there are times (especially on an intranet) where you will want to enable the browser far more control than you would in a more Internet-like environment.

This is where the Advanced Data Connector (ADC) and Remote Data Services (RDS) come in. RDS enables developers to create rich, interactive experiences. However, it requires an ActiveX-enabled browser, such as Microsoft's Internet Explorer 4. You can learn more about the Advanced Data Connector and Remote Data Services in Chapter 25, "Accessing Databases with Remote Data Services."

N O T E You can also check out Microsoft's Web site on Remote Data Services and the Advanced Data Connector at **www.microsoft.com/data/adc**. ■

In a page that utilizes the ADC, an invisible ActiveX control called AdvancedDataControl is embedded. A visual control, like a data grid, is then added to the page and bound to the AdvancedDataControl. Finally, client-side VBScript can be used to extend the functionality of the page.

Part

V

Ch

20

Visual Controls and Data Grids

What are visual controls? If you are a developer who doesn't have a VB background, this question may be in your mind right now. That's okay. Visual controls are easy to understand. And rest assured that developing ASP does not require a VB background, though it can help.

Visual controls are visual components of a Windows program that have certain functionality and code bound with them. For instance, a data grid control consists of several text fields that represent different fields in a database, along with buttons for moving through the data.

Creating a Simple Data-Driven ASP Program

Listing 20.11 is rather simple. It is a drill-down to find an employee's phone number. On the first page, search.asp, the user enters the last name of the employee. At Results.asp, a recordset is created that displays all the employees with that last name. Also displayed are their first names and phone numbers. From this list the user can choose the employee he wants and dial their number.

Listing 20.11 *SEARCH.ASP*—A simple page that takes an employee's last name from the user.

```
<HTML>
<HEAD>
<TITLE>
    Search for a phone number
</TITLE>
</HEAD>
<BODY>
<CENTER>
    <H1>
    Search for a phone number
    </H1>
    <P>
    <FORM ACTION="results.asp"method="post">
    Enter Employees last name:
        <INPUT TYPE="text" NAME="Last_Name">
        <BR>
        <INPUT TYPE="submit" Value="Submit">
    </FORM>
</CENTER>
</BODY>
</HTML>
```

In Listing 20.12, you search the database for a matching employee. This is done by first creating a Connection object and setting its connection to the DSN that is your database. Next, you create a Command object that contains a SQL statement that is executed against the datasource to return the correct employee. Finally, you open a connection to the datasource and have a recordset returned that contains the right employee.

Listing 20.12 *RESULTS.ASP*—The results page lists all employees with the last name entered.

```
<%@ LANGUAGE="VBSCRIPT" %>

<HTML>
<HEAD>
<TITLE>
Document Title
</TITLE>
</HEAD>
<BODY>
```

```
<%
Set DataConn = Server.CreateObject("ADODB.Connection")
DataConn.Open "DSN=Employees"
Set DataCmd = Server.CreateObject("ADODB.Command")
DataCmd.CommandText = "SELECT * FROM tbl_employees WHERE LastName = '" &
Request.Form("Last_Name") & "'"
Set DataCmd.ActiveConnection = DataConn
Set rs_main = Server.CreateObject("ADODB.Recordset")
set rs_main =  DataCmd.execute
%>

<TABLE>
     <TR>
     <TD>First Name</TD>
     <TD>Last Name</TD>
     <TD>Phone</TD>
     </TR>

<%
     do While not rs_main.EOF
          Response.write("<TD>")
          Response.write(rs_main("FirstName"))
          Response.write("</TD>")
          Response.write("<TD>")
          Response.write(rs_main("LastName"))
          Response.write("</TD>")
          Response.write("<TD>")
          Response.write(rs_main("Phone"))
          Response.write("</TD>")
          Rs_main.moveNext
     loop
%>
</TABLE>
</BODY>
</HTML>
```

The above sample code might seem pretty simplistic. However, it does illustrate several points from the chapter. For instance, notice how the recordset rs_main is created. It is created through both a Connection and a Command object. In later chapters, when you extend the functionality of this application, you will see further reasons why coding even simple apps to the ADO object model is always a good idea.

From Here...

In this chapter, you have been introduced to ActiveX Data Objects, also known as ADO. ADO is an amazing new way to access a database inside of an Active Server Page. It is an implementation of OLE DB, which is a huge step forward in database connectivity. By learning about ADO and OLE DB now, you are setting yourself up for huge returns in the future.

This chapter has prepared you to begin leveraging ADO in your development efforts by introducing you to its fundamental building blocks. You've seen how each of the major objects interrelate, the benefits to coding with the ADO object model in mind, and how ADO's transaction processing capabilities can help you with your data integrity and application performance. You've also seen how the Advanced Data Connector can simplify your development efforts.

There are three major objects you use with ADO: Connection, Command, and Recordset. Each of these is discussed in the chapters ahead.

- Chapter 21, "Working with ADO's Connection Object," will help you to further understand how to use this interface in your code.

- Chapter 22, "Using Command Objects," will show you how and when to use this object for better performance and ease of development.

- Chapter 23, "Working with ADO's Recordset Object," will cover how to use the workhorse of ADO, the recordset.

Working with ADO's *Connection* Object

The previous chapter introduced you to ActiveX Database Objects (ADO). With the exception of the Session object, ADO is, perhaps, ASP's greatest feature. Previously, database access within Web pages either relied on tools that were too simple to create very robust applications, or too clumsy to expand. ASP enables thousands of VB programmers to start leveraging their knowledge to create working applications immediately. Furthering the idea that database access shouldn't be difficult, ADO enables developers to create data-driven applications quickly.

Now that you have had a chance to look at some of the exciting features of ADO in Chapter 20, "Database Access with ADO," you are probably anxious to examine in more detail the three objects that you will use with ADO: the Connection, Command, and Recordset objects. The Command and Recordset objects will be looked at in more detail in the next two chapters. This chapter will examine the Connection object.

The Connection object represents the connection to your data. It is the road to your data—in other words, it is the way in which you will connect to your databases. By using the Session and Application objects, you can implement connection pooling with the Connection object. ■

▬ **Linking to Your Database with the *Connection* Object**

Connecting to a database can be easy with the *Connection* object. Creating it is the first step in database access.

▬ **Configuring the *Connection* Object and Its Properties**

Configure the *Connection* object for maximum efficiency. Learn how to optimize for the type of application you are creating.

▬ **Controlling the *Connection* Object**

See when to use the methods of the *Connection* object in your application.

▬ **The *Error* and *Command* Objects**

Learn when to use the *Error* collection for better error handling.

In addition, you can execute SQL statements directly against your datasource. The Connection object also contains the Error object, which you use for error handling. And best of all, the Connection object allows for transaction processing.

Properties and Methods of the *Connection* Object

The Connection object contains a rich set of properties and methods for creating, maintaining, and configuring itself. While some properties and methods (like Version) may not have many uses, others will totally change how you create data-driven applications.

For instance, using the ConnectionString property, you can set up the string that contains the connection information, and then send this information to the Session object for use throughout the application. This allows you to develop your applications even more quickly.

Here are the properties and methods of the Connection object, along with a brief description.

Connection Object Properties

Attribute specifies whether a new transaction will be started after a transaction rollback or commit. There are two values: adXactCommitRetaining, which specifies to automatically start a new transaction after CommitTrans is called; and adXactAbortRetaining, which starts a new transaction after RollbackTrans is called. Not all data providers will support this property, though Microsoft's Transaction Server will.

CommandTimeout determines how long to wait for a command to process (the default is 30 seconds). Setting this value to 0 makes the wait indefinite. This is a global value that applies to all commands that are issued through the connection.

ConnectionString is a string that contains the information necessary to create the connection. This string will contain information on the connection such as the DSN, provider, username, password, and filename. When the connection is open, this is a read-only property.

ConnectionTimeout determines how long to wait to connect to the datasource (the default is 15 seconds). Set to 0 to wait indefinitely.

If the provider you are connecting to enables multiple databases, DefaultDatabase enables you to specify which one is the default. This means that SQL commands issued to the provider will have to specify which database to run the statement against if it is not the default.

IsolationLevel is the isolation level of the connection. This property applies after BeginTrans is called. Use it to specify whether other transactions will be able to see your transactions effects and when (see Table 21.1).

Table 21.1   Isolation Levels

Value	Description
adXactUnspecified	Isolation level of provider is unknown.
adXactChaos	This value means that you cannot overwrite changes from more highly isolated transactions.
adXactBrowse	This means that you cannot view uncommited changes from other transactions.
adXactReadUncommitted	Same as above.
adXactCursorStability	This value indicates that you can view changes from other transactions after they have been committed.
adXactReadCommitted	Same as above.
adXactRepeatableRead	This value indicates that you can bring in a new recordset by requerying.
adXactIsolated	This value indicates that the transactions will be competely isolated from one another.
adXactSerializable	Same as above.

Mode is used to set the permissions on a connection, such as read-only or read-write. This property can also be set to deny access to others.

Provider is the provider of a connection.

Version is the version of ADO being used.

Connection Object Methods

The methods of the Connection object give the developer quite a bit of power and freedom. For instance, with the Execute method, you can execute a SQL statement against the datasource without having to create a Command object.

BeginTrans begins a new transaction.

CommitTrans saves any changes and ends the current transaction. It may also start a new transaction if the Attributes property is set for this.

RollBackTrans rolls back the transaction; in other words, it cancels it. It, too, may start a new transaction if the Attributes property is set for this. The following snippet of code shows an example of using all three of the preceding methods together.

```
DataConn.beginTrans     'DataConn is our connection object
Rs.AddNew
    Rs("name") = Keith
    Rs("phone") = "555-1212"
```

Part

V

Ch

21

```
Rs.Update
If DataConn.Errors = 0 then
     DataConn.CommitTrans
Else
     DataConn.RollbackTrans
End if
```

`Close` closes the connection. This method also closes any recordsets associated with the object. Invoking this method looks like the following code.

```
DataConn.Close
```

`Execute` executes a command on the datasource and returns a recordset. This method can also be used to find out how many records were effected by the command. This method can take three optional parameters: `CommandText`, `RecordsAffected`, and `Options`. An example of this method is seen in the following snippet.

```
myRecordset = dataConn.Execute("SELECT * FROM tblMoney", intNumRecs, adCmdTxt)
```

Now that you have called `Execute`, you can look at `intNumRecs` and see how many records were returned. If you do pass a command text (such as the `SELECT` statement in this example), you should also send the appropiate `Options` parameter telling the provider what type of command this is.

`Open` opens the connection. This method is fairly simple to use. It can be sent three optional parameters: `ConnectionString`, `UserID`, and `Password`. `UserID` and `Password` are just as they say. `ConnectionString` is a more complicated parameter.

A `ConnectionString` is a string of name value pairs separated by semi-colons. The possible names that can be set here are `Provider`, `Datasource`, `User`, `Password`, and `FileName`. The following is an example of calling this method.

```
Set dataConn = Server.CreateObject("ADODB.Connection")
DataConn.Open "DSN=myDataSource"
```

Linking to Your Data with the *Connection* Object

There are three basic uses for the `Connection` object: creating and maintaining a link to your datasource, creating recordsets, and error handling. Later in this chapter, you will see how to implement error handling and create recordsets. Now, let's examine how to create a `Connection` object.

In Listing 21.1, a `Connection` object is created with the `CreateObject` method of the `Server` object. This object is then set to a variable named `DataConn`.

Listing 21.1   *21code01.ASP*—Creating a *Connection* object.

```
Set DataConn = Server.CreateObject("ADODB.Connection")
```

> **N O T E** You will see the same line with slight modifications for the creation of the `Command` and `Recordset` objects. If you're like this author, you will tend to cut and paste similar lines from one part of your code to another. Watch out that you don't end up creating a second `Connection` object instead of a `Recordset`. ■

In Listing 21.1, a `Connection` object is created with the `Server` object's `CreateObject`. Once you have created a `Connection` object, you will probably want to assign it to the `Session` object. Listing 21.2 does just that (again, in one line!).

Listing 21.2   *21code02.ASP*—Setting the *Session* property *ConnObject*.

```
Set Session("ConnObj") = DataConn
```

Later, in Chapter 24, "Managing Your Database," you will see a better connection pooling than what ODBC 3.0 gives. For now, this enables you to scope the `Connection` object across multiple pages. You could even set this as an `Application` object property and scope it across all the sessions.

CAUTION

Sometimes you will create code that sets a `Connection` object to the `Session`. Don't do this! In reality, you will always want to use connection pooling as provided by ODBC 3.0 and above.

A Note from the Author

This author's very first programming language was a spaghetti code version of BASIC found on the Commodore Vic 20 computer. With this version of BASIC, all variables were global. This, of course, would cause massive problems with debugging, and made creating interesting and useful application almost impossible.

Next came C. With C, I learned to scope variables. (And learned the reason why my old BASIC programs were so tough to decipher!) However, temptation would often lead to ignoring this feature in C and still relying on variables of global scope. Of course, this soon lead to many of the same problems I had before: programs too hard to maintain.

Around the time I learned C++, I also read Steve McConnell's text *Code Complete*. Now, finally, I understood why scoping was so important in the creation of programs that would stand the test of time.

How does this relate to ASP development? Well, it can be very easy to set an `Application` or `Session` property, just as it can be very easy to set a global variable in a C++ program. And sometimes, there are very good reasons to do so. But most of the time, it will pay off in the long run to scope your variables as small reasonable.

Configuring the *Connection* Object

Now that you have created a `Connection` object and set it to a `Session` property, you need to configure it before you actually open the connection. There are several properties that you can use to configure it. In this section, you will examine the `ConnectionString`, `Mode`, and `ConnectionTimeOut` properties in terms of how they relate to configuring your connection before opening it.

The *ConnectionString* Property   From the list of `Connection` object properties, you may remember the property `ConnectionString`. The `ConnectionString` is a string that contains information on the data provider that is needed to connect to it. This string contains a set of name value pairs delimited by semicolons. These name value pairs are optional.

A connection string generally will look something like Listing 21.3.

Listing 21.3   *21code03.ASP*—Setting the *ConnectionString* property.

```
Set DataConn.ConnectionString = "DSN=Customers;User=sa;Password=elmoisgod"
```

The above code tells the `Connection` object that the DSN it will connect to is called `Customers`. The data provider will look for a user ID and password, so those are also set. As you can see, the syntax when setting the `ConnectionString` property is *argument = value*. The following is a list of the arguments you can set with the `ConnectionString` property:

- Provider
- User
- Password
- Filename

CAUTION

Set either the `provider` or `datasource` arguments, not both. They both provide similar functionality. If you pass both to the `ConnectionString` property, your application may not work.

N O T E   The `ConnectionString` property can be overridden with the `Open` method of the `Connection` object. When you examine this method later, you will see this for yourself. For now, just remember that you are not tied down to what is set with this property. ■

The *Mode* Property   The `Mode` property is used to set the permissions for a connection. You can also use it to find out what the permissions are. When the `Connection` object is closed, you can set the permissions. When it is open, you can only read what the permissions are.

The most popular uses of Mode are those involving an application- or session-wide Connection object. You may find it necessary in some parts of your application to set the permissions on the connection to, say, read-only (for instance, when an administrative section of the application is opened).

N O T E   Mode can only be set while the connection is closed. When the connection is open, Mode is read-only. ■

Table 21.2 summarizes the most popular modes of Mode.

Table 21.2   Mode Values

Value	Description
adModeUnknown	This value means that the Mode is unknown.
adModeRead	This sets read-only permissions.
adModeWrite	This sets write-only permissions.
adModeReadWrite	This sets read and write permission for the connection.

ConnectionTimeout

The ConnectionTimeout property has a very simple job: to set the amount of time the connection object should wait to connect to the provider. However, knowing what value to set this property to can be anything but simple. Listing 21.4 sets the property's value.

Listing 21.4   *21code04.ASP*—Setting the *ConnectionTimeout* property.

```
Set DataConn.ConnectionTimeout = 30
```

The code above sets the ConnectionTimeout property to 30 seconds. This means that the Connection object, DataConn, will wait 30 seconds before returning an error when it tries to connect to a provider.

N O T E   The ConnectionTimeout property's default value is 15 seconds. ■

Generally, you do not need to change this value. However, you may design applications that reside on a server that has a slow pipe to the client. (For instance, your corporate presence server may reside on a 128KB ISDN line.) In cases like these, you may want to bump up the value of the ConnectionTimeout property to 30 seconds, or even a minute.

Part
V

Ch
21

TIP Occasionally, you may even want to have the `Connection` object wait forever for the connection to work out. If this is the case, set the `ConnectionTimeout` property to 0. However, if you do this, you better be `very` sure your connection will eventually appear. Otherwise, your user will eventually get tired of waiting for the page to appear. (Or you will get a script timeout, unless that, too, is set to wait forever, which I really don't recommend.)

The *DefaultDatabase* Property This interesting property sets the default database for a connection. This can be confusing. Most developers are used to the idea of one datasource (or provider), meaning one database. However, some providers may contain multiple databases. When this is the case, you need to specify the database in all of your SQL statements. When no database is specified, the default database is used.

TIP If you are dealing with a provider that uses multiple databases, I still recommend specifying the database in your SQL string. Why? It will produce self-documenting code.

For instance, imagine you have a database called `inventory` and one called `salesmen`. You could set your default database to `inventory`. Then, when you are selecting the number of some item, your SQL statement would look something like this: `SELECT numberFruit FROM tblFruit`. Instead, you could specify the database with `SELECT numberFruit from inventory.tblFruit`. This way, someone else new to your code will know instantly which database `tblFruit` is part of.

The *IsolationLevel* Property This property is used to set the level of isolation in the connection. It is fairly easy to use, as Listing 21.5 shows.

Listing 21.5 *21code05.ASP*—Setting the *IsolationLevel*.

```
Set DataConn.IsolationLevel = adXactIsolated
```

Listing 21.5 sets the isolation level very high. With this level of isolation, all transactions take place completely separate from other transactions.

`IsolationLevel` is the degree to which transactions are isolated from one another. A transaction can be completely isolated from other transactions, or it can be set to some of the other transactions also taking place. Table 21.3 summarizes some of the values the `IsolationLevel` property can be set to.

Table 21.3 *IsolationLevel* Property Values

Value	Description
`adXactUnspecified`	This value means that it is impossible to determine the level of isolation.
`adXactChaos`	This value means that you cannot overwrite changes pending from other transactions.

Value	Description
adXactBrowse	With this value, you cannot browse values from pending transactions.
adXactIsolated	Complete isolation for your transactions.

Controlling the Connection

Now that you have configured the Connection object by setting its various properties, you can open and close the connection. You can also execute a SQL statement against the data provider and set a recordset. And most importantly, you can set up transaction processing with the Connection object's methods.

Open* and *Close   Opening the connection is very simple. Closing it is even simpler. Listings 21.6 and 21.7 show just how easy these methods can be to use.

Listing 21.6   *21code06.ASP*—Opening the connection...

```
DataConn.Open
```

Listing 21.7   *21code07.ASP*—...and closing it.

```
DataConn.Close
Set DataConn = nothing
```

 TIP   Notice how I have set the Connection object, DataConn, to nothing after closing it. Although not strictly necessary, taking this additional step may help with troubleshooting later. Setting the object to nothing releases the memory used for it; closing it does not.

However, don't think there is nothing to these methods. The Open method provides developers with many options in terms of setting properties for the connection right as it is opened, as opposed to before. Listing 21.8 shows how you can configure and open a connection with the Open method.

Listing 21.8   *21code08.ASP*—Using *Open* to configure the *Connection* object.

```
DataConn.Open "DSN=customers", "sa", "password"
```

Part
V

Ch
21

In Listing 21.8, the Open method is being used to not only open to connection, but to also configure the ConnectionString, User, and Password properties.

Even though there are no additional ways to use it, with Close, there are several issues to keep in mind. First and foremost is that Close does not eliminate the Connection object you have created from memory. It is still there, ready to be re-opened should the need arise. Second, any recordsets that were associated with the connection will be closed. Finally, any Command objects associated with the connection will be cleared of any parameters, along with their ActiveConnection property.

> **CAUTION**
>
> Also, be sure to note that if a connection is closed during a transaction, the transaction will be cancelled.

Executing the Connection   Using the Execute method of the Connection object, you can create a recordset that is ready to go. Using Execute is easy; Listings 21.9 and 21.10 show two different ways you can use it in your code.

Listing 21.9   *21code09.ASP*—Using *Execute.*

```
Set rs_main = DataConn.Execute "Select * from tbl_phoneNumbers"
```

In Listing 21.9, a SQL statement is executed against the provider. This SQL statement returns a recordset, which the recordset, rs_main, is then set to. This is a great way to set up a recordset with some data, and will probably be how you set a recordset most of the time.

Listing 21.10   *21code10.ASP*—Further uses of *Execute.*

```
DataConn.Execute "Delete * from tbl_phoneNumbers", intRecs, adCmdTezt
```

In Listing 21.10, there is no recordset being set. This is because the SQL statement used this time is a Delete, which returns an empty recordset. However, as developer, you may want to know how many records were deleted. That is where the integer intRecs comes into play. You could later use this number to tell the user how many records were deleted. For instance, you might want to delete all the records for a particular product which you no longer carry. But if you note how many records were deleted, you could then return that information to the user as follows:

```
Number of records deleted = <%=intNumRecs%>
```

By passing intRecs to the Execute method, I can later test how many records were affected by the command (affected in this case meaning deleted). Finally, to optimize the speed of execution of the command, I sent the value adCmdTxt as the Option parameter of the Execute method. The Option parameter tells the provider what kind of command you are executing, and allows the provider to save time by not having to figure it out itself.

TIP Whenever possible, send a value for the Option parameter! It can substantially increase the performance of your applications.

Table 21.4 summarizes the various values you can send in the Option parameter.

Table 21.4   Values for the *Option* Parameter

Value	Description
adCmdText	This tells the provider that the CommandText will be a SQL string.
adCmdTable	This tells the provider that the CommandText is a table.
adCmdStoredProc	This value enables the parameter to prepare for a stored procedure.
adCmdUnknown	This says that the CommandText is unknown. Don't use this value.

Transaction Processing with the *Connection* Object   As you saw in Chapter 20, transaction processing with the ADO is easy. All it takes are three simple steps:

1. Call the BeginTrans method to begin the transaction.
2. Do whatever data processing you need to.
3. Check for errors and then call either CommitTrans or RollbackTrans based on whether there were any errors.

A Transaction Processing Example   When should you use transaction processing? At the very least, you should employ it when you are faced with creating applications that rely on mission critical data. A popular and easy to understand example of this would be the banking software example you saw in Chapter 20. Let's examine this example in a little more detail, and see how to code this transaction.

Imagine the portion of a banking application that deals with the transfer of funds from one account to another. This program would need to delete the funds from the first account and then add them to the second. But what if the power goes out after the delete? The funds would never be accredited to the second account, and there would be no real way to find out what went wrong.

With transaction processing, both the delete and the adding of the funds have to be completed before the transaction is committed to disk. This means that if the lights go out, the whole shebang is rolled back. The money is left in the first account, where it can be tried again later.

In Listing 21.11, you can see this process in action. The recordset used in this example has two records, the first record is the account to take the money out of, the second is the account to deposit the money into.

Listing 21.11   *21code11.ASP*—Transaction processing in action.

```
Set intAmount = 200   ' the amount to be transferred is $200
DataConn.BeginTrans
'delete the money from the first account
Set tmpAmount = rs_main("Balance") - intAmount
Rs_main.AddNew
     Rs_main("Balance") = tmpAmount
Rs_main.update

'move the recordpointer to the account to add the funds to
rs_main.movenext
Set tmpAmount = rs_main("Balance") + intAmount
Rs_main.AddNew      Rs_main("Balance") = tmpAmount
Rs_main.update
'Check for errors, rollback if there are any, otherwise commit
If DataConn.Errors.Count = 0 Then
     DataConn.CommitTrans
Else
     DataConn.RollbackTrans
End If
```

Transaction Processing with the* `Attributes` *Property   `BeginTrans`, `CommitTrans`, and `RollbakcTrans` are easy to use. But what if you want to automatically start a new transaction after each transaction ends? You use the `Attributes` property.

By setting the `Attributes` property to `adXactCommitRetaining`, you will start a new transaction right after a `CommitTrans` is called. If you set it to `adXactAbortRetaining`, a new transaction will start after `RollbackTrans` is called. If you are going to use transaction processing with all of your database activity, I would recommend setting the `Attributes` property to both of these values.

Other Benefits to Transaction Processing   Besides the obvious benefit of helping to keep data from being corrupted, transaction processing offers another significant reason for its use: better performance. When you wrap your data processing around the code listing found in Chapter 20, you can see some pretty hefty speed increases in your application. Why?

By keeping the transaction completely in memory, transaction processing only writes to disk when `CommitTrans` is called. Because RAM is much faster than the hard drive, this enables optimized disk writes only when needed. When they aren't needed, they don't happen (that is, the transaction is rolled back), and when a disk write happens, it writes all the data out at once, also saving time due to less movement by the hard disk head going out and finding the correct spot to write the data several times.

Error Handling with ADO

Although ASP's error-handling capabilities are rather sparse at this time, ADO provides its own error handling through the Errors collection and Error object. The Error collection belongs to the Connection object. It is further made up of none to many Error objects, one object for each error.

Why is the Error collection part of the Connection object? Because the errors that are captured and stored in the Error collection are those errors that the data provider sends out.

The Properties and Methods of the *Error* Collection

While the Errors collection doesn't offer many properties or methods, it does enable the developer to discover how many Error objects there are, and to specify any particular one. In addition, by using the Clear method you can clear the Errors collection of all Error objects currently in it.

- Item—This property returns a specific Error object by number or name.
- Count—This property holds an integer that is the number of Error objects (and thus errors) in the collection.
- Clear—This method clears the collection of all objects. An example of this method would be:

```
dataConn.Errors.Clear
```

where dataConn is your Connection object, and Errors is how you refer to the collection. It is a good idea to call this method before calling any transaction methods or the Filter method of the Recordset object. This enables you to accurately determine the number of errors those calls generate.

The Properties of the *Error* Object

The Error object holds information about a specific error that was generated. The Error object has no methods, and has only a few properties that are used to gain more information about the error raised.

- Description—The text of the error.
- Number—A number that corresponds to a unique error condition.
- Source—The object that raised the error.
- HelpFile and HelpContext—If they exist, these properties hold the help file and topic that contain more info on the error.
- SQLState and NativeError—These provide ANSI SQL codes that further describe the error.

So, how do you use the Errors collection and Error object to intelligently handle errors? Listing 21.12 shows a small example.

Listing 21.12 *21ASP12.ASP*—**Error handling with ASP.**

```
MyRecordset.AddNew
     MyRecordset("firstName") = "Heather"
     MyRecordset("lastName") = "Urschel"
MyRecordset.Update

If dataConn.Errors.Count > 0 then
     Response.Write("The following errors occurred:<BR>")
     For each Error in dataConn.Errors
          Response.Write("Error #: " & Error.Number & "<BR>")
          Response.Write("Error Description: " & Error.Description & "<BR>")
     Next
Else
     Response.write("Update Successful!")
```

Table 21.5 provides a list of the error codes and what they mean. Use it to intelligently program your error-handling routines to react based on what errors they receive.

Table 21.5   Error Types

Error	Description
adErrInvalidArgument	The arguments are of the wrong type or are out of range.
adErrNoCurrentRecord	There is no current record. In other words, BOF or EOF is true.
adErrIllegalOperation	The operation requested is not allowed.
adErrInTransaction	You are trying to close a connection during a transaction.
adErrFeatureNotAvailable	The operation is not featured by the provider.
adErrItemNotFound	The item you specified was not found.
adErrObjectNotSet	The reference you are using no longer points to an object.
adErrDataConversion	You are using the wrong datatype.
adErrObjectClosed	The object is closed, so the operation is not allowed.
adErrObjectOpen	Same as above, only now the operation is not allowed because the object is open.
adErrBoundToCommand	This error is generated if the ActiveConnection of a recordset attempts to change when the recordset was created with a Command object.

Error	Description
adErrInvalidParamInfo	The parameter wasn't defined correctly.
adErrInvalidConnection	The operation requested won't work, because there is no connection, or the connection doesn't allow it.
adErrProviderNotFound	The provider specified was not found.

As you can see, the Error object and the Error collection have quite a few properties that can help with error handling. If you remember from Listing 21.11, a simple error-handling routine was in place to help with the transaction processing. This error handling could be beefed up to examine any errors if they were created and try to find a way to re-execute the transaction correctly the next time.

The *Command* Object and the *Connection* Object

The Command object can be optional. It isn't needed to create a connection, nor to open a recordset. It really has a fairly specialized purpose in comparison to its two sister objects, the Connection and Recordset objects. It is used to pass parameters to stored procedures.

This means that the Command object can be used to create a recordset. And, it is also closely tied to the Connection object. Listing 21.13 illustrates this close relationship.

> **Listing 21.13   *21code12.ASP*—The *Command* object.**
>
> ```
> Set DataCmd = Server.CreateObject("ADODB.Command")
> Set rs_tmp = Server.CreateObject("ADODB.Recordset")
> DataCmd.CommandType = adCmdText
> Set DataCmd.ActiveConnection = DataConn
> Rs_tmp.Open DataCmd, , 0, 1
> ```

In Listing 21.13, the Command object's property ActiveConnection is set to the Connection object DataConn. Then the recordset rs_tmp is opened with one of the parameters being the Command object. Both the Command and Recordset objects are created and utilized through the Connection object DataConn.

Revisiting the Employee Phone Application

Now let's revisit the phone application you created in Chapter 20. You can probably see several places where you can improve the code. Using your newly found knowledge of the Connection object, examine this new and improved version of results.asp (see Listing 21.14).

The changes to this file from the code in Chapter 20 have been made bold. As you can see, the big change is that you are now more closely tuning the Connection object's properties to match your situation (in this case the higher than usual traffic that our site will be getting) instead of relying on defaults.

Part
V

Ch
21

Listing 21.14   *21code13.ASP*—A new and improved *results.asp*.

```
<%@ LANGUAGE="VBSCRIPT" %>
<HTML>
<HEAD>
<TITLE>
Search For Employee - By Last Name
</TITLE>
</HEAD>
<BODY>

<%
Set DataConn = Server.CreateObject("ADODB.Connection")

'Set our connection and command timeouts higher, due
'to all the heavy traffic we will be getting
DataConn.ConnectionTimeout = 60
DataConn.CommandTimeout = 60

DataConn.Open "DSN=Employees;User=Keith;Password=HiElizabeth"
Set DataCmd = Server.CreateObject("ADODB.Command")
DataCmd.CommandText = "SELECT * FROM tbl_employees WHERE LastName = '" &
Request.Form("Last_Name") & "'"
Set DataCmd.ActiveConnection = DataConn
Set rs_main = Server.CreateObject("ADODB.Recordset")
set rs_main =  DataCmd.execute
%>

<TABLE>
    <TR>
    <TD>First Name</TD>
    <TD>Last Name</TD>
    <TD>Phone</TD>
    </TR>

<%
    do While not rs_main.EOF
        Response.write("<TD>")
        Response.write(rs_main("FirstName"))
        Response.write("</TD>")
        Response.write("<TD>")
        Response.write(rs_main("LastName"))
        Response.write("</TD>")
        Response.write("<TD>")
        Response.write(rs_main("Phone"))
        Response.write("</TD>")
        Rs_main.moveNext
    loop
%>
</TABLE>


</BODY>
</HTML>
```

The `connectionTimeout` value has been raised to enable the heavy traffic we know this application will take. The connection closes itself at the end of the code.

From Here...

In this chapter, you have learned how to use the `Connection` object to connect to your databases. You are now ready to begin implementing the basics of error handling with the `Error` collections. Further, you have explored the many properties and methods of the `Connection` object and how to use them in your applications. Using the `Session` and `Application` objects in conjunction with the `Connection` object, you have learned how to implement connection pooling in your applications.

- Chapter 22, "Using `Command` Objects," will show you how and when to use this object for better performance and ease of development.
- Chapter 23, "Working with ADO's `Recordset` Object," will cover how to use the workhorse of ADO—the recordset.

Using *Command* Objects

Chapter 21, "Working with ADO's Connection Object," showed you how to create an active connection to your data with the Connection object. Using the Session and Application objects and connection pooling, you saw how to optimize the link to your data and keep traffic down. Further, you saw how to execute a SQL statement against the datasource with the Connection object.

In Chapter 23, "Working with ADO's Recordset Object," you will learn how to manipulate the recordset objects you have been creating in these last two chapters. There, you will find the true richness and usefulness of ADO and ASP.

In this chapter, you will learn how to execute commands against your datasource in an even more controlled and optimal fashion. You will create a collection of parameters that can be fed to a stored procedure in your database. You will also see how we can bypass creating a Connection object and implicitly create one with the Command object.

What is the Command object? It is the ADO object that represents a command you want to execute against your database. With it, you can create recordsets quickly and easily—whether that recordset is based on a table, a SQL statement, or a stored procedure. ■

The *Command* Object

There is one ADO object that your program wouldn't ever *have* to use: the Command object. The Command object has a slightly more specialized use than the Connection and Recordset objects. Its best use (and what it was designed for) is sending parameters to stored procedures and queries in your database.

You can create and use the Command object in several different ways. In this section, I examine in greater detail the properties and methods of the Command object, and how they can help you.

Creating a *Command* Object

There are two major ways to create a Command object. The first is to explicitly create a Connection object. The second is to implicitly create a Connection object. When you explicitly create a Connection object, you use the Server.CreateObject method, and set a variable to its return. From then on, you can manipulate the connection via that variable. When you implicitly create a Connection object, there is no call to Server.CreateObject, and you do not have the ability to manipulate your connection (due to the fact that you have no variable to use).

Listing 22.1 shows the creation of a Command object, without first creating a Connection object.

> **Listing 22.1   *22code01.ASP*—Creating a *Command* Object without the *Connection* object.**
>
> ```
> Set DataCmd = Server.CreateObject("ADODB.Command")
>
> 'Customers is the DSN
> DataCmd.ActiveConnection = "Customers"
> DataCmd.CommandText = "qryListAllCustomers"
>
> Set rs_tmp = Server.CreateObject("ADODB.Recordset")
> rs_main = DataCmd.Execute
> ```

Listing 22.2 shows the creation of a Command object using a predefined Connection object.

> **Listing 22.2   *22code02.ASP*—Creating a *Command* object with a *Connection* Object.**
>
> ```
> Set DataConn = Server.CreateObject("ADODB.Connection")
> DataConn.Open "DSN=Employees"
>
> DataCmd.ActiveConnection = DataConn
> DataCmd.CommandText = "qryListAllCustomers"
>
> Set rs_tmp = Server.CreateObject("ADODB.Recordset")
> Set rs_main = DataCmd.Execute
> ```

In Listing 22.1, after creating the Command object, the ActiveConnection property is set to a Datasource(DSN) called Customers. Then, its CommandText property is set to a query in the database called qryListAll. This query lists all the customers in the database, and sorts them by region. The recordset rs_main is then set to the results of that query.

N O T E Don't think that there wasn't a Connection object created in Listing 22.1. One was created; it was created implicitly, which means you have no real way to access it for things such as error handling. ■

T I P There is really no reason to not first create a Connection object before creating a Command object. If you don't, you won't have access to the Error collection, or be able to optimize and configure the Connection object that is implicitly created.

In Listing 22.2, a Command object is created. Its ActiveConnection property is then set to the Connection object DataConn, which was created earlier. After that, it is very similar to the other listing; a query is run that results in the recordset rs_main.

Properties and Methods of the *Command* Object

Table 22.1 lists the properties and methods you can use to configure the Command object.

Table 22.1 *Command* Object Methods and Properties

Method/Property	Description
ActiveConnection	Used to set which connection the Command object is part of.
CommandText	Used to specify the command the Command object will use.
CommandTimeout	This property specifies how long to wait before timing out a command.
CommandType	This property tells the provider what type of command is stored in CommandText.
Prepared	Used to tell the provider to create a compiled version of the command for later use.

ActiveConnection This property indicates the Connection object that the Command object will be a part of. The string that this property is set to can be either a Connection object, or the definition of a connection.

Listing 22.3 demonstrates setting the ActiveConnection property to an already existing Connection object.

Listing 22.3   *22code03.ASP*—Setting the *ActiveConnection* to a *Connection* object.

```
Set dataConn = Server.CreateObject("ADODB.Connection")
DataConn.Open = "myDSN"
DataCmd.ActiveConnection = DataConn
```

Listing 22.4 shows setting a Command object's ActiveConnection property with a connection string.

Listing 22.4   *22code04.ASP*—Setting the *ActiveConnection* with a connection string.

```
DataCmd.ActiveConnection = "DSN=Customers;User=sa;password=bob"
```

Notice in Listing 22.3 that the ActiveConnection property is set to the Connection object DataConn. In Listing 22.4, a connection string is used. This connection string should look familiar to you. It accepts the same arguments as the Connection object's ConnectionString property. This string is passed to the ConnectionString property of the Connection object that is implicitly created.

Usually, you will want to set your Command object's active connection property to an already existing connection. Not doing this should be the rare exception.

TIP   Here's a neat tip for you: Imagine you are setting up an ASP application on a remote machine, and you don't have a way to create an ODBC datasource on the machine. You can set the ConnectionString to the following to create on-the-fly in your code:

```
"DRIVER={Microsoft Access Driver (*.mdb)}; DBQ=c:\path\database.mdb"
```

Here, you specify the driver needed for the database—and you also tell the system the location of the database file itself.

CommandText   CommandText is a string value that represents the command you want to execute against the provider. It can be a SQL statement, the name of a table, or the name of a stored procedure.

In Listing 22.5, you can see an example of setting the CommandText property to a SQL statement.

Listing 22.5   *22code05.ASP*—Setting the *CommandText* property to a SQL statement.

```
DataCmd.CommandText = "SELECT * FROM tbl_customers"
```

In Listing 22.6, you can see an example of setting the CommandText property to a table name.

Listing 22.6 *22code06.ASP*—**Setting the *CommandText* property to a table name.**

```
DataCmd.CommandText = "tbl_customers"
```

In Listing 22.7, I set the CommandText property to the name of an Access query called qryCustomers.

Listing 22.7 *22code07.ASP*—**Setting the *CommandText* property to a query.**

```
DataCmd.CommandText = "qryCustomers"
```

Each of the above listings does the same thing. Each creates a recordset based on the records in the table named tbl_customers. Later, when you examine the Prepared property, you will see how you can have ADO compile the CommandText for you.

When would you use a stored procedure? When do you use a table name? And, when is it a good idea to use SQL text? In general, try not to use table names. This can result in way too much information being transported around.

The big choice is between stored procedure and SQL statement. Stored procedures on database servers such as SQL Server can execute more quickly. SQL statements, however, are more readable. Then again, you can always comment your code.

CommandType Now that you have set the CommandText property to either a SQL statement, stored procedure, or table name, you need to set the CommandType property. This property tells the provider what type of command is being set. This allows for a faster execution time when the provider executes the command.

N O T E If the CommandType does not accurately reflect the command held in CommandText, an error will be returned when the Execute method is called.

Why? Knowing what type of command is coming down the pike means that the provider won't have to spend any time trying to figure it out. In Listing 22.8, you can see what to set the CommandType to if the CommandText property is a SQL statement. ■

Listing 22.8 *22code08.ASP*—**Setting the *CommandType* property.**

```
DataCmd.CommandType = adCmdText
```

Table 22.2 lists the possible values that CommandType can take. You should always use these values, as opposed to their numeric equivalent, because the integer they represent may change.

Table 22.2   Values for the *CommandType* Property

Value	Description
AdCmdText	This tells the provider that the CommandText will be a SQL string.
AdCmdTable	This tells the provider that the CommandText is a table.
AdCmdStoredProc	This value enables the parameter to prepare for a stored procedure.
adCmdUnknown	This says that the CommandText is unknown. Don't use this value.

CommandTimeout   The property CommandTimeout specifies the amount of time to wait for the command to execute. This property is fairly straightforward. Often, you will not need to change it; however, there may be circumstances where you will need to set it to something other than its default. Listing 22.9 sets the property's value.

Listing 22.9   *22code09.ASP*—Setting the *ConnectionTimeout* property.

```
Set DataCmd.CommandTimeout = 30
```

In Listing 22.9, the CommandTimeout property is set to 30 seconds. The application will now wait 30 seconds for the command to execute before it times out.

N O T E   The CommandTimeout property's default value is 15 seconds. ■

If your application is residing on a Web server that is running slowly (perhaps from the millions of hits you are receiving), it might be worth your while to increase this property's value to 30 seconds. Generally, however, you will want to keep this value set to its default.

 Occasionally, you may even want to have the Command object wait forever for the connection to work out. If this is the case, set the ConnectionTimeout property to 0. However, I would highly recommend against doing this.

Prepared   This is a Boolean value that tells the provider to prepare a compiled version of the command. This will slow down the command the first time it is run, but after that, the provider will execute the command more quickly. Listing 22.10 shows how to set this property.

Listing 22.10   *22code10.ASP*—Using the *Prepared* property.

```
DataCmd.Prepared = True
```

N O T E   Notice that not all providers will be able to create a compiled version of the command. If the provider doesn't support that functionality, it will ignore any attempts to set this property. In that case, if queried, the Prepared property will return a value of False. ■

Execute This is the method that actually executes the command contained in `CommandText`. It returns a recordset. If the command is an update or some other command that isn't supposed to return any records, a null recordset will be returned. Listing 22.11 is an example of how to call `Execute`.

Listing 22.11 *22code11.ASP*—Executing the command.

```
Dim inNumRecs
Set Rs_main = DataCmd.Execute intNumRecs, , adCmdTExt
```

Listing 22.11 sets the recordset `rs_main` to the results of the command. In addition, the variable `intNumRecs` is set to the number of records affected by the command. You can later examine it and see how many records were deleted (for instance, assuming that was the command sent). The last value, `adCmdText`, tells the provider what kind of command is coming. This is the same value you set the `CommandType` to.

The general format used when you call `Execute` is:

```
command.Execute RecordsAffected, Parameters, Options
```

where *RecordsAffected* is a variable you can later query to find the number of records involved in your command, `Parameters` is a set of parameters to feed the command, and `Options` tells the provider what type of command will be executed.

Using the *Command* Object to Access Data

Now that you have examined some of the properties and methods of the `Command` object, you are now ready to use it to create recordsets. Listing 22.12 is an example of how to set a recordset with a `Command` object.

Listing 22.12 *22code12.ASP*—Accessing data with the *Command* object.

```
Set DataConn = Server.CreateObject("ADODB.Connection")
DataConn.Open "DSN=Employees"

DataCmd.ActiveConnection = DataConn
DataCmd.CommandText = "SELECT * FROM tbl_employees where fname = Joe"

Set rs_main = Server.CreateObject("ADODB.Recordset")
Set rs_main = DataCmd.Execute intRecs, , adCmdTxt
```

In Listing 22.12, all employees with the first name Joe are put into a recordset called `rs_main`. Now, when the `Execute` method is called, it includes the arguments `intrRecs` and `adCmdTxt`. The argument `intRecs` can be queried later to find out how many records are in the newly created recordset, and `adCmdTxt` told the provider that it was being sent a SQL string to execute.

The *Parameters* Collection and the *Parameter* Object

The Command object is best used for sending parameters to stored procedures or queries of the providers. To provide this functionality, the Command object includes a collection of Parameter objects. Using the CreateParameter method, you can very easily take advantage of stored procedures for faster performance.

A *stored procedure* (or *query*) is a command that has been compiled by the data provider and stored in the database. There are two types of stored procedures: parameterized and non-parameterized queries.

A *parameterized query* is a stored procedure that is expecting arguments. For example, the procedure could list all the doctors in the table tbl_doctors from a specific region. The parameter in this case would be the region.

Methods and Properties of the *Parameters* Collection

The Parameters collection contains several methods and properties that you can use to add and delete new parameters. Some of these, like Item, are common to all collections in ADO (see Fields collection in Chapter 23 for an example), whereas others are very specific to the Parameters collection, such as CreateParameter (see Table 22.3).

Table 22.3   *Parameters* Collection Methods and Properties

Method/Property	Description
Item	This property returns the parameter specified.
Count	This property returns the number of parameters.
CreateParameter	This method is used to create new parameters.
Append	This method is used to add a new parameter to the collection.
Delete	This method is used to delete a parameter from the collection.
Refresh	This method is used to refresh the collection.

Item   This property returns a specific Parameter object by number or name.

Count   This property holds an integer that is the number of Parameter objects in the collection.

CreateParameter   This method creates a Parameter object. You can set most of the attributes of the object with this method or you can choose to set them later, before you append it to the collection. The syntax for this method is

```
Set parameter = command.CreateParameter(Name, Type, Direction, Size, Value)
```

Notice how this method takes five different values. These values are the *Name* of the parameter, the *Type* of the parameter, the *Direction* of the parameter (input or output), the *Size* of the parameter, and the *Value*.

> **CAUTION**
>
> If the datatype can be of variable length, you must set the Size attribute also. If you don't, an error will occur.

Append This method is used to insert the parameter in the collection after you have created the parameter with the CreateParameter method. You must specify a type for the parameter before you append it, or you will receive an error. The following is the form the Append method should take:

```
dataCmd.Append myNewParameterObject
```

Delete The Delete method is used to remove a parameter from the collection. You must refer to the parameter by name when using this method:

```
DataCmd.Delete NewParameterObject
```

Refresh This method queries the provider for information on the parameters the stored procedure in the CommandText property will take. If you try accessing the Parameters collection before calling this method, it will be called for you. The following code shows an example of calling this method:

```
DataCmd.Refresh
```

> **CAUTION**
>
> When Refresh populates with variable length parameters, you should still explicitly set the size value.

Methods and Properties of the *Parameter* Object

The methods and properties of the Parameter object enable you to configure to a great degree of detail the parameter you will send. For instance, you can set the direction of the parameter, and even the size in bytes of the parameter's value (see Table 22.4).

Table 22.4 *Parameter* Object's Methods and Properties

Method/Property	Description
Attributes	This property sets what type of values the parameter will accept.
Direction	This property specifies in which direction the parameter is.
Name	This property is the parameter's name.
NumericScale	This property sets the how many decimal points the parameter may contain.
Precision	This property specifies how many digits the parameter may be.
Size	This property specifies how big the parameter may be.

continues

Table 22.4   Continued

Method/Property	Description
Type	This property is used to set the data type of the parameter.
Value	This property is used to set the value of the parameter.
AppendChunk	This method is used to append a chunk of bytes to the parameter.

Attributes   This property sets what kind of parameter attributes the parameter has. It takes a ParameterAttributesEnum value, of which the following are possible values. Table 22.5 lists the various possible values.

Table 22.5   Values for the *Attributes* Property

Value	Description
AdParamSigned	This is the default value. It indicates that the parameter accepts signed values.
AdParamNullable	This indicates that the parameter will accept NULL values.
AdParamLong	This value indicates that the parameter will accept long binary data.

Direction   This property indicates whether the parameter is an input, output, or return value. It can take any of the values listed in Table 22.6.

Table 22.6   Values for the *Direction* Property

Value	Description
AdParamInput	This value indicates that the parameter is an input parameter.
AdParamOutput	This indicates that the parameter is an output parameter.
adParamInputOutput	This value indicates that the parameter is both an input and an output parameter.
adParamReturnValue	This value indicates that the parameter is a return value from the stored procedure.

Name   This is the name of the parameter. Before you append the parameter, this value is read-write. Once you have appended it, it is read-only.

Numeric Scale   The value of the Numeric Scale property sets how many points to the right of the decimal place the parameter will be resolved to. So, for instance, let's say it is pi, which goes on forever to the right of the decimal place. By setting this value to 2, you would get back 3.14.

Precision The `Precision` property works much like the `Numeric Scale` property. However, `Precision` determines the total number of digits. In the previous example, if the `Precision` property were set to 2, the value for the parameter would be 3.1.

Size This property sets the maximum size of the parameter. This value will be an integer that represents the size in bytes or in characters, as the case may be.

Type This value for this property is the type of data the parameter is. Table 22.7 summarizes the various types of values this property can be set to.

Table 22.7 Values for the *Type* Property

Value	Description
adBigInt	An 8-byte signed integer.
adBinary	A binary value.
adBoolean	A Boolean value.
adBSTR	A null-terminated character string.
adChar	A string value.
AdCurrency	A currency value.
adDate	A date value.
adDBDate	A date value in the format yyyymmdd.
adDBTime	A time value.
adDBTimeStamp	A date-time stamp.
adDecimal	An exact numeric value.
adDouble	A double-precision floating-point value.
adEmpty	No value was specified.
adError	A 32-bit error code.
adGUID	A globally unique identifier.
adIDispatch	A pointer to an `IDispatch` interface on an OLE object.
adInteger	A 4-byte signed integer.
AdIUnknown	A pointer to an `IUnknown` interface on an OLE object.
adLongVarBinary	A long binary value.
adLongVarChar	A long string value.
AdLongVarWChar	A long null-terminated string value.
adNumeric	An exact numeric value.

continues

Table 22.7 Continued

Value	Description
adSingle	A single-precision floating-point value.
adSmallInt	A 2-byte signed integer.
adTinyInt	A 1-byte signed integer.
adUnsignedBigInt	An 8-byte unsigned integer.
adUnsignedInt	A 4-byte unsigned integer.
adUnsignedSmallInt	A 2-byte unsigned integer.
adUnsignedTinyInt	A 1-byte unsigned integer.
adUserDefined	A user-defined variable.
adVarBinary	A binary value.
adVarChar	A String value.
adVariant	An OLE Automation Variant.
adVarWChar	A null-terminated Unicode character string.

Parameters in Action

Now that you have covered the properties and methods of the Parameter object and collection, let's look at an example of implementing the great functionality this object gives us. Listing 22.13 creates a Parameter object and then appends it to the collection.

Listing 22.13   *22Code13.ASP*—A new and improved *results.asp*.

```
'setting the name and value of the parameter
StrName = "last_name"
StrValue = "Jones "

'setting the type, direction, and size
intType = adChar
intSize = 50
intDirection = adParamInput

'creating the parameter object
dataParam = DataConn.CreateParameter(strName, intType, intDirection, intSize,
strValue)

'appending the parameter to the collection
DataConn.Append DataParameter
Set rs = DataConn.Execute(,,adCmdStoredProc
```

As you can see, I created a `Parameter` object by using the `CreateParameter` method of the `Command` object. I then appended this to the `Parameters` collection. After this, I call the `Execute` method of my `Command` object, which returns a recordset that I call `rs`. Now, I can use this recordset as I would any other recordset.

Revisiting the Phone Application

Let's see how to apply your new and improved knowledge of the `Command` object to the employee phone database from the previous two chapters. So far, this application has been relying on SQL statements to create the recordset `rs_main`. Now, try using a parameterized query, passing the parameters as part of the `Parameters` collection.

In Listing 22.14, you have the new and revised results page of your phone-book application. This time around, you are using the `Parameter` object to speed up your development time and your program's execution.

Listing 22.14   22Code14.ASP—A new and improved *results.asp*.

```
<%@ LANGUAGE="VBSCRIPT" %>

<HTML>
<HEAD>
<TITLE>
Search For Employee - By Last Name
</TITLE>
</HEAD>
<BODY>

<!-- #include file="adovbs.inc" -->

<%
Set DataConn = Server.CreateObject("ADODB.Connection")

'Set our connection and command timeouts higher, due
'to all the heavy traffic we will getting
DataConn.ConnectionTimeout = 60
DataConn.CommandTimeout = 60

DataConn.Open "DSN=Employees;User=Keith;Password=HiElizabeth"
Set DataCmd = Server.CreateObject("ADODB.Command")
Set DataCmd.ActiveConnection = DataConn

'setting the name and value of the parameter
StrName = "last_name"
StrValue = Request.Form("last_name")

'setting the type, direction, and size
intType = adChar
intSize = 50
intDirection = adParamInput
```

continues

Listing 22.14 Continued

```
'creating the parameter object
set dataParam = dataCmd.CreateParameter(strName, intType, intDirection, intSize,
strValue)

'appending the parameter to the collection
dataCmd.Parameters.Append dataParam
dataCmd.CommandText = "qryLastName"
Set rs_main = Server.CreateObject("ADODB.Recordset")
Set rs_main = DataCmd.execute
%>

<TABLE>
    <TR>
    <TD>First Name</TD>
    <TD>Last Name</TD>
    <TD>Phone</TD>
    </TR>

<%
    do While not rs_main.EOF
        Response.write("<TD>")
        Response.write(rs_main("FirstName"))
        Response.write("</TD>")
        Response.write("<TD>")
        Response.write(rs_main("LastName"))
        Response.write("</TD>")
        Response.write("<TD>")
        Response.write(rs_main("Phone"))
        Response.write("</TD>")
        Rs_main.moveNext
    loop
%>
</TABLE>


</BODY>
```

The above code will perform even faster than it did before. Why? When you use a query that is part of the data provider, the time it takes to gather the data drops significantly.

From Here...

In this chapter, you delved further into the *Command* object. With it, you can directly link to data providers, instead of having to explicitly create a *Connection* object. You can even connect to a provider that hasn't been set up as an ODBC datasource.

With the *Parameters* collection, you have seen how to take advantage of your data provider's stored procedures and queries. This little object can speed up your applications quite impressively.

In the following chapter, you will examine the Recordset object. This object will be the one you work with most of the time. Its powerful methods and properties will allow you to manipulate your data with greater ease than you have ever experienced.

Later chapters will discuss how to optimize your datasources, and use the Advanced Data Connector and Microsoft's Transaction Server in your applications.

- Chapter 23, "Working with ADO's Recordset Object," will prepare you to use this object in your applications.

- In Chapter 24, "Managing Your Database," you will examine how to optimize your database with Microsoft's Transaction Server, ODBC 3.0, and look at other issues related to databases.

Working with ADO's *Recordset* Object

In the past two chapters, you have examined the Connection and Command objects. These objects exist for one reason: to create a Recordset object that you will manipulate and navigate through.

Now, you *can* manipulate your data with the Connection and Command objects, but there is only so much you can do. Inserting data is often easy with Parameter collection, but when you need to display lots of data and then manipulate several records, the Recordset object is really the interface to use.

This chapter will introduce you to the methods and properties of the Recordset object. As you read through the next few pages, keep in mind that ADO was designed for many different and disparate types of data—not just the tabular data many of us are use to. ■

Retrieving Data

Examine the issues that surround creation of a *Recordset* object.

***Recordset* Properties**

Learn the properties of the *Recordset* object.

Navigating the *Recordset*

See how to swim through your data. The *Recordset* object contains some great methods for accessing the data you need.

Manipulating Your Database

Discover the methods to manage and manipulate your data.

Retrieving Data into a Recordset

There are several issues that should be examined before creating a recordset. Basically, it is a battle between performance and integrity. You, as the developer, need to find a happy medium for the applications you develop.

When developing for an Internet site that will be hit by thousands (or even hundreds of thousands) of people every day, speed will probably be much more of an issue than it is when developing for a small intranet. By understanding how your database works and how ADO retrieves data, you can save yourself major headaches.

Integrity versus Performance

When examining the issue of data integrity versus application performance, there is one overwhelming thought that always comes to mind (of course, this is just my opinion): If your data isn't protected and becomes corrupt, it is useless. And computers get faster all the time.

In other words, choose integrity over performance, because you can always find faster hardware, but you can't always retrieve corrupt data.

On the other hand (and this is where it gets sticky), if your application is too slow, no one will use it. Happily, ADO enables developers to strike a happy, nice medium.

To help you in this task, I will examine isolation of data and cursor types. Isolation is how much you insulate your data connections from each other. The type of cursor you choose to create will be the major way in which you decide the performance versus integrity battle.

Isolation

ADO's `Connection` object includes a property called `IsolationLevel` that is used to specify exactly how much isolation a transaction will have and give. Table 23.1 summarizes the various values this property can be set to.

As you may remember, isolation is an attribute of transactions. When a transaction is completely isolated, it cannot see what other transactions are doing, and other transactions cannot see it.

For instance, in the midst of transaction #1, you may change the number of widgets on hand from 100 to 99. In transaction #2, you may ask for the number of widgets on hand. If the transactions are both completely isolated, then transaction #2 will think there are 100 widgets still. This example seems to portray isolation as a bad thing, but there are times when you will want your transactions isolated from one another.

Table 23.1 Popular *IsolationLevel* Values

Value	Description
AdXactUnspecified	This value means that it was impossible to determine the level of isolation.
AdXactChaos	This value means that you cannot overwrite changes pending from other transactions.
AdXactBrowse	With this value, you cannot browse values from pending transactions.
AdXactIsolated	Complete isolation for your transactions.

By choosing the appropriate level of isolation, you can avoid dirty reads and phantom records. *Phantom records* are records that used to exist that have been deleted by other transactions. *Dirty reads* occur when you read a value that has been changed by another transaction.

Locking

Locking is where the developer specifies how much and to what level the data in the database will be locked up and inaccessible by other recordsets. Why should you care about locking? Probably the best way to answer this question is to examine the various types of locks you can apply.

To begin with, you create a lock when you open up the recordset. One of the arguments in the Open command is the type of locking you want to employ. The following snippet of code creates an optimistic lock (don't worry, I will explain what that is in a moment).

```
RsMaim.Open DataCmd, DataConn, adOpenForwardOnly, adLockOptimistic
```

Here's an example of how to correctly apply locking. Suppose you are editing the number of widgets in your factory from 100 to 99 because someone just bought one. You will probably want to lock the record that contains the number of widgets before you actually reduce the number, and then unlock it once you are done.

If you didn't do this, you might first read in the number currently available (100) and then reduce it by one and write that new number (99) back to the database. But what if in between that time, someone else bought a widget and they reduced the number from 100 to 99 already? Then you would write 99 again, and the count would be off by one! Instead, you lock the record before getting the number currently available, and keep it locked until you have written the new number. *Then*, the next transaction can do the same thing, this time reducing 99 to 98. Thus everything remains accurate.

Identifying Cursor Types

There are four types of cursors in ADO. By using a combination of IsolationLevel and the appropriate cursor type, a developer can exert a great level of control over the access and manipulation of his data. Table 23.2 lists these cursor types.

Table 23.2 Cursor Types for Recordsets	
Value	**Description**
Forward-Only	This is the default type of cursor. It provides for forward-only and read-only movement through the recordset. It is also the quickest cursor type.
KeySet	This cursor is read- and write-enable. It also enables movement both ways through the recordset. It is unlike a dynamic cursor in that you cannot see deletions and additions of other recordsets.
Dynamic	Like the KeySet cursor, this cursor is read-and write-enabled. Unlike the KeySet, it can see the deletions, additions, and changes of other recordsets. Using a dynamic cursor exacts the highest overhead.
Static	A static cursor is read and write-enabled. It can also move throughout the recordset set in either direction. However, additions and deletions by other users are not visible to this cursor type.

Let's examine each of these in a little more detail and see how to create each type of cursor. I hope a more detailed examination will also help you see when to employ each type of cursor.

Forward-Only Cursor   The forward-only cursor is the default. When you create recordsets with the `Connection` or `Command` objects, it is this type of cursor that you received back. In the line of code below, a recordset with this type of cursor is opened:

```
RsMaim.Open DataCmd, DataConn, adOpenForwardOnly
```

Creating any type of cursor is just as easy. Great, you now know how to create a forward-only cursor. But when and why would you use one?

The forward-only cursor is often referred to as the firehose cursor. If all you want to do is display some data for read-only access, this is the cursor for you. For example, imagine you have an Internet site that displays the closest regional office to its location based on the ZIP code the Web surfer enters. This information is just for display. The surfer is not going to edit it in any way. The fastest and easiest cursor to use in this situation would be the forward-only cursor.

Static Cursor   The static cursor is created in almost the exact same manner as the forward-only cursor. The only difference is, instead of the `adOpenForwardOnly`, you supply `adOpenStatic`. Besides the slight difference in creation, a static cursor is much like a forward-only in use.

The major difference is that a static cursor can move both forward and backward in the recordset. When is this of value? Suppose you want to create a report on the sales the midwest section of the business did in the month of August. This report might include totals, along with breakdowns by product, salesman, and week.

Instead of using a forward-only cursor and having to run from the beginning to the end of the recordset while gathering each type of data, the static cursor enables you to move forward and backward to look for the correct data. At the same time, you will not incur the additional over-head of a read-and-write cursor type such as KeySet.

KeySet Cursor   The KeySet cursor is a read-write cursor type that can move throughout a recordset. Its largest limitation is its inability to see the additional records that are created. You still see changes and deletions, but additional records are a no-no.

The KeySet cursor is created in the same manner as the previous two cursors, with the value `adOpenKeySet` for the `cursorType` argument.

You want to use the KeySet cursor for applications where users will be modifying and deleting data, such as a customer service phone agent application. The typical scenario in this type of application is that the customer has called and wants to change his address. The phone agent would then bring up his record and enter the change.

There would be no reason to see additional records (customers) created during this session, because all you care about in this model is the data on one particular customer. The adding of others customers or new information on other customers by other users will not affect how you program this type of application.

Dynamic Cursor   The dynamic cursor is the heavyweight of cursor types. It is the most pow-erful. But this power comes at the cost of slower performance. Basically, use the dynamic cursor when no other cursor type will work.

The value to send to the open command for this cursor is `adOpenDynamic`.

Using the dynamic cursor, you can move both forward and backward in the recordset. You can also see the deletions and additions made by other recordsets.

For instance, you may have a recordset use this cursor when moving through a recordset based on all the employees in a table with the last name "Smith." If another recordset adds a new Smith before you are done, you will be able to see this new record and display it also.

Recordset **Properties**

Now that you have created your `Recordset` object and set its cursor, you are ready to examine some of the other properties of the `Recordset` object that you will use in your development.

BOF/EOF

When running through a recordset looking for data, you need a way to check for the end of the recordset. Slightly less popular, but still very useful, is the capability to check for the beginning of the recordset. Both of these conditions can be tested for with the BOF and EOF properties.

BOF stands for Beginning Of File. EOF stands for End Of File. This property is used to find whether the current record position is before the first record or after the last record. If the property returns a value of True, then it is before or after the recordset. The following code shows a test for EOF.

```
If rs_main.EOF then
     We are at end of the recordset
else
     do something
end if
```

What is meant by the current record position? The following figures show a recordset and what is meant by the position of the current record. In Figure 23.1, the pointer is before the first record; in Figure 23.2, the pointer is after the last record. In other words, it is impossible to continue forward in the recordset.

FIG. 23.1

At the beginning of the recordset object...

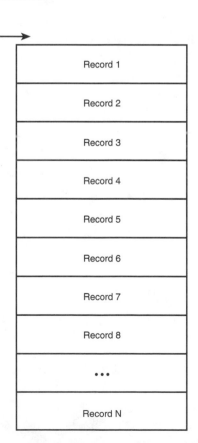

Current Record

| Record 1 |
| Record 2 |
| Record 3 |
| Record 4 |
| Record 5 |
| Record 6 |
| Record 7 |
| Record 8 |
| ••• |
| Record N |

FIG. 23.2
...and at the end.

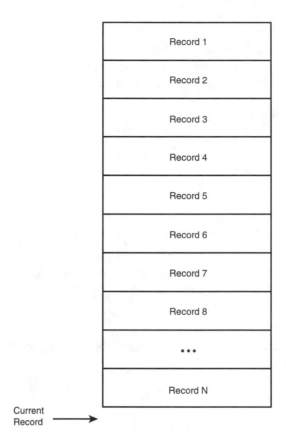

Part
V

Ch
23

RecordCount

This `property` returns the number of records in the recordset. There are many uses for this property, but one of the best is for looping through the recordset without having to check for EOF. The following code loops through a recordset.

```
IntNumRecs = rs_main.RecordCount
Do While I < intNumRecs
      ...something interesting
Loop
```

> **CAUTION**
>
> Be cautious about using the RecordCount property. If your recordset contains 500,000 records, imagine how long it will take for the server to return the number of records if you also have 500,000 surfers!
>
> A better way to set up your loops would be to check for EOF or BOF as you move through the recordset.

AbsolutePosition

The AbsolutePosition property enables the developer to designate exactly which record to set the current pointer to. If the current record is the first in the recordset, it is equal to 1. The following line of code sets the absolute property to the fifth record.

```
Rs_main.AbsolutePosition = 5
```

Figure 23.3 shows where the current record pointer would now reside.

FIG. 23.3

Setting the current
record with
AbsolutePosition.

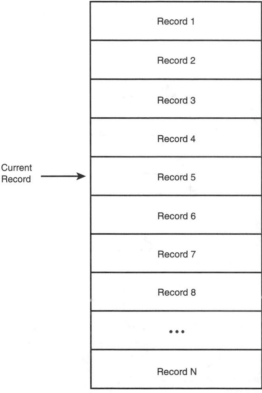

 TIP Some of the records in a recordset are cached in memory. (The size of this cache is set with the CacheSize property.) When you set the AbsolutePosition property, all the records in the cache are reloaded, even if the record you are setting up to point to was in the cache.

AbsolutePage

There is a way to group records in a recordset that is called *pages*. By setting the PageSize property, you can set (for instance) four records per page. You can then use the AbsolutePage property in much the same manner as AbsolutePosition. Figure 23.4 shows this grouping.

FIG. 23.4
Pages simplify data management.

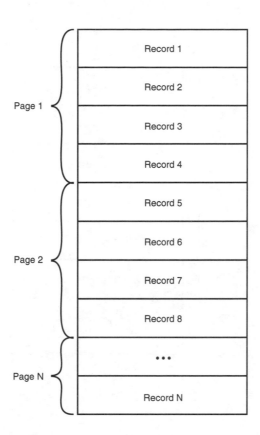

Part
V

Ch
23

In the following code, I set the page size to 4 and the AbsolutePage property to 3.

```
Rs_main.PageSize = 4
Rs_main.AbsolutePage = 3
```

Figure 23.5 shows the results of setting these properties.

Filter

Perhaps the most interesting of all the recordset properties is Filter. This property sets the current record pointer to the first record that satisfies its conditions. For example, if you want to filter the recordset and look just at the records where the last name is Smith, the code would look like the following (assume the field name for last name is Last_name).

```
Rs_main.Filter "Last_Name = 'smith'"
```

The current record pointer would now be set at the first record that satisfies this condition, namely, that has the last name field matching "smith." Moving through the recordset would now take you to the next record that satisfies the filter.

What if you want to turn off the filter and run the recordset in the normal manner again? The following code does just that.

```
Rs_main.filter = adFilterNone
```

FIG. 23.5
Setting the current
record pointer to a new
position.

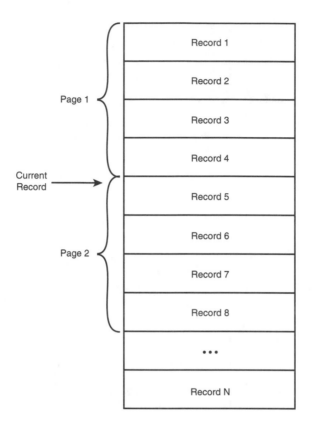

Besides enabling navigation based on criteria for fields, `Filter` also has some interesting presets, as summarized in Table 23.3.

Table 23.3 *Filter* **Settings**

Name	Description
AdFilterNone	Removes the filter.
AdFilterPendingRecords	This enables a view of the records that have been changed but not sent to the server.
AdFilterAffectedRecords	This shows the records affected by the last ReSync, Delete, UpdateBatch, or CancelBatch.
AdFilterFetchedRecords	This shows you the records in the cache.

 While `Filter` is a great tool, be wary. If you know that your recordset only needs people with the last name Smith to begin with, don't pull everyone into the recordset and then filter. Moving that much data, especially on a well-surfed Internet site, will put a huge load on the server.

Instead, try to narrow down your recordset with a SELECT statement. For instance, SELECT * FROM tbl_people WHERE last_name = "smith".

Navigating the Recordset

Now that you have studied some of the properties you can set with the Recordset object, it's time to learn how to *move* through the recordset. You have already seen how to move to certain recordsets with the AbsolutePosition and AbsolutePage properties, but you will generally want to move in more conventional manners. Figure 23.6 shows a recordset with five records that you will navigate through as I talk about MoveFirst, MoveLast, MoveNext, and MovePrevious.

FIG. 23.6
This recordset contains five records.

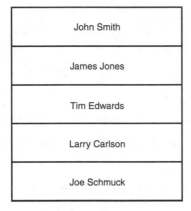

| John Smith |
| James Jones |
| Tim Edwards |
| Larry Carlson |
| Joe Schmuck |

MoveFirst

This method moves the current record pointer to the first record. In this position, BOF would return a value of True. When you first create the recordset, you won't need to use this method, because the current record pointer will already be set to the first record.

However, there may be times when you will want to reuse code, so it is good practice to begin using this method before you start moving though the recordset.

The following line of code moves to the first record in the recordset:

```
Rs_main.MoveFirst
```

Figure 23.7 shows the result of this line of code, with the record pointer set at the first record.

MoveLast

This method acts much like MoveFirst. MoveLast, however, moves beyond the last record. So, EOF would return True after running this method.

FIG. 23.7

At the first record, ready to go.

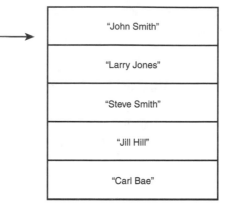

Current
Record
Pointer

"John Smith"

"Larry Jones"

"Steve Smith"

"Jill Hill"

"Carl Bae"

 TIP You won't really use `MoveLast` much except to append records onto the end of the recordset. So it is a good idea to make sure that you have a cursor type (like KeySet or dynamic) that supports changing the recordset.

The code below sets the record pointer to `EOF`.

```
Rs_main.MoveLast
```

Figure 23.8 shows the results of this line of code, with the record pointer now set beyond the fifth (and last) record.

FIG. 23.8

At the end of the recordset.

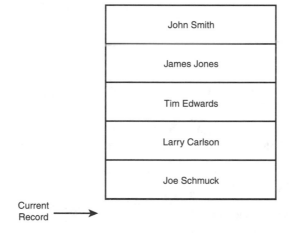

John Smith

James Jones

Tim Edwards

Larry Carlson

Joe Schmuck

Current
Record

MoveNext

`MoveNext` is probably the most executed method in ADO. It is also one of the easiest to use. When you run this method, all you are doing is moving the record pointer one record forward. The following line of code does just that:

```
Rs_main.MoveNext
```

Assuming that the record pointer was BOF before you ran this method, the record pointer would now look like Figure 23.9.

FIG. 23.9
At the second record.

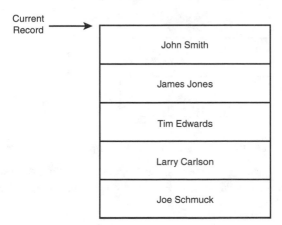

Current
Record

| John Smith |
| James Jones |
| Tim Edwards |
| Larry Carlson |
| Joe Schmuck |

Part
V

Ch
23

> **CAUTION**
> Always be sure to check for end of file when using MoveNext. If you attempt to move forward when at EOF, an error will be generated.

MovePrevious

MovePrevious works just like MoveNext, only backward. It moves the current record pointer back one record. So, if you just moved to the second record as in seen in Figure 23.9, this line of code

```
Rs_main.MovePrevious
```

would result in the recordset looking like Figure 23.10.

FIG. 23.10
At the begining of the recordset, again.

Current
Record

| John Smith |
| James Jones |
| Tim Edwards |
| Larry Carlson |
| Joe Schmuck |

> **CAUTION**
>
> The same caution about checking for EOF before executing MoveNext also applies to MovePrevious. Only, now, you should check for BOF. In the example above, running MovePrevious again would result in an error that you have tried to beyond BOF, so always check for BOF first.

Manipulating the Recordset

Moving through a recordset can be a lot of fun. If your application only needs to see information, it is also all you need to do. But often you will want to edit or manipulate the information in your recordset. For those times, ADO includes some great methods for doing just that. The methods enable the developer to easily add, delete, and change values in the database.

Basically, there will be three actions you will want to perform on a recordset:

- Update an existing record.
- Add a new record.
- Delete an existing record.

Update

This method is used to update an existing record in the recordset. Using this method is as easy as ABC. The code below updates the phone field to a new phone number.

```
NewPhone = "555-1212"
Rs_main.Update phone, newPhone
```

In Figure 23.11 you can see an example of a recordset before the update.

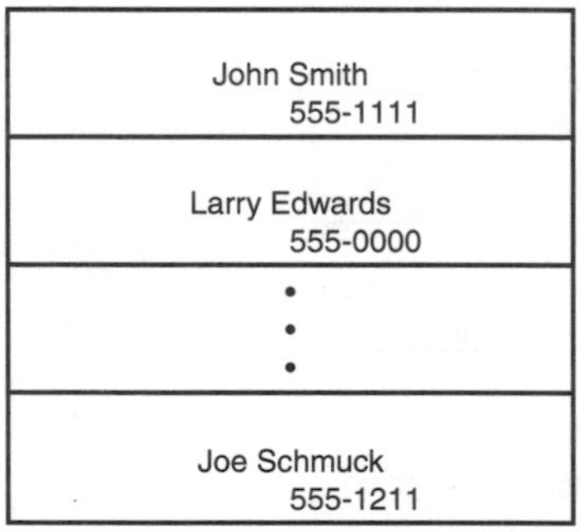

FIG. 23.11

Before an update.

John Smith 555-1111
Larry Edwards 555-0000
• • •
Joe Schmuck 555-1211

In Figure 23.12, you see the recordset after we have updated the values.

The parameters that Update can take can be a single field in the database or several fields. Generally, you will set several fields to their new values all at once, and then call the Update method.

FIG. 23.12
After an update.

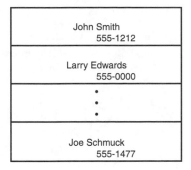

John Smith 555-1212
Larry Edwards 555-0000
•   •   •
Joe Schmuck 555-1477

AddNew

AddNew is used to add a new record to the recordset. The following code adds a new record for Jim Smith, 555-1121.

```
Rs_main.AddNew
     Rs_main("firstName") = "Jim"
     Rs_main("lastName") = "Smith"
     Rs_Main("phone") = "555-1121"
Rs_main.update
```

After you create a new record with AddNew, you need to call Update to post the information to the database. Until Update is called, the current record will be the one you added. Additionally, the record won't exist in the database until you call Update.

Figure 23.13 shows the recordset from Figure 23.12 after I have added a new employee.

FIG. 23.13
Adding a new employee
with AddNew.

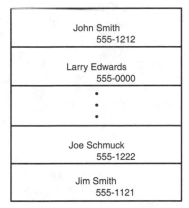

John Smith 555-1212
Larry Edwards 555-0000
•   •   •
Joe Schmuck 555-1222
Jim Smith 555-1121

 Many people (including those at Microsoft) will say that you should use the Supports method first to make sure your recordset is writeable and that you can, in fact, add a new record. In reality, a good programmer should know what type of recordset he has created. I would consider calling Supports pretty redundant in most situations.

Part
V

Ch
23

Delete

Delete removes the current record from the recordset. Of course, the recordset must support deletions (in other words, it can't be read-only) or an error will be generated. Delete can also delete all records that satisfy the filter with an optional tag. The following code shows both examples.

```
Rs_main.Delete  'This deletes the current record
Rs_main.Delete adAffectGroup  ' this deletes all records in the recordset that
satisfy the filter
```

Supports

The Supports method is used to determine whether the recordset supports a particular action or not. You call it and send it a CursorOption, which represents the activity you want to try. It then will return a Boolean value indicating whether it will work. The following code shows an example of the Supports method in action:

```
If rs_Main.Supports(adAddNew) then
    'we can add a new record!
    Rs_main.AddNew
    Rs_main("firstName") = "Jim"
    Rs_main("lastName") = "Smith"
    Rs_Main("phone") = "555-1212"
    Rs_main.update
End if
```

The Recordset in Action

Now that you have examined the properties and methods of the recordset, let's look at the employee drill-down application you have been developing in the last two chapters and try to enhance it with your new found knowledge and skill.

First, let's look at the form you will use to gather the last name to search on (see Listing 23.1).

Listing 23.1   Entering the last name to search on.

```
<%@ LANGUAGE="VBSCRIPT" %>

<HTML>
<HEAD>
<META NAME="GENERATOR" Content="Microsoft Visual InterDev 1.0">
<META HTTP-EQUIV="Content-Type" content="text/html; charset=iso-8859-1">
<TITLE>Employee Search</TITLE>
</HEAD>
<BODY>

<H1> Employee Search </H1><BR>
* Required
<FORM NAME="searchForm" Action="results.asp">

    <TABLE>
    <TR>
```

```
                <TD>
                    Last Name:
                </TD>
                <TD>
                    <INPUT TYPE="text" NAME="lastName">*
                </TD>
        </TR>
        <TR>
                <TD>
                    First Name:
                </TD>
                <TD>
                    <INPUT TYPE="text" NAME="firstName">
                </TD>
        </TR>
        <TR>
                <TD>
                    <INPUT TYPE="submit">
        </TABLE>

    </FORM>

    </BODY>
    </HTML>
```

The form in Listing 23.1 asks for the last name and, optionally, the first name of the employee to search on. You could add a simple VBScript or JavaScript on the page to check for this field before submiting, if you want.

Listing 23.2 checks the variable submitted by the form and opens a recordset of those records that satisfy the condition.

Listing 23.2   Displaying the first five records.

```
<%@ LANGUAGE="VBSCRIPT" %>

<HTML>
<HEAD>
<TITLE>
Search For Employee - By Last Name
</TITLE>
</HEAD>
<BODY>

<!-- #include file="adovbs.inc" -->

<%
Dim i
i=0

Set DataConn = Server.CreateObject("ADODB.Connection")
```

continues

Listing 23.2 Continued

```
'Set our connection and command timeouts higher, due
'to all the heavy traffic we will getting
DataConn.ConnectionTimeout = 60
DataConn.CommandTimeout = 60

DataConn.Open "DSN=Employees;User=Keith;Password=HiElizabeth"
Set DataCmd = Server.CreateObject("ADODB.Command")
Set DataCmd.ActiveConnection = DataConn

'setting the name and value of the parameter
StrName = "last_name"
StrValue = Request.Form("last_name")

'setting the type, direction, and size
intType = adChar
intSize = 50
intDirection = adParamInput

'creating the parameter object
set dataParam = dataCmd.CreateParameter(strName, intType, intDirection, intSize,
strValue)

'appending the parameter to the collection
dataCmd.Parameters.Append dataParam
dataCmd.CommandText = "qryLastName"
Set rs_main = Server.CreateObject("ADODB.Recordset")
Set rs_main = DataCmd.execute
%>

<TABLE>
    <TR>
    <TD>First Name</TD>
    <TD>Last Name</TD>
    <TD>Phone</TD>
    </TR>

<%
    do while i < 5 AND not rs_main.EOF
        Response.write("<TR>")
        Response.write("<TD>")
        Response.write(rs_main("FirstName"))
        Response.write("</TD>")
        Response.write("<TD>")
        Response.write(rs_main("LastName"))
        Response.write("</TD>")
        Response.write("<TD>")
        Response.write(rs_main("Phone"))
        Response.write("</TD>")
        Response.write("</TR>")
        Rs_main.moveNext
         i = i +1
    loop
%>
<TR>
```

```
        <TD>
            <form action="next.asp">
                <input type="submit" name="next" value="next">
            </form>
        </TD>
    </TR>
    </TABLE>

<% set Session("rs") = rs_main %>
</BODY>
</HTML>
```

As you can see, after you open up the connection, you create a SQL command to select the records that satisfy the search criteria. Then, you open up a recordset based on that Command object. Notice how I have optimized the code by hard coding what type of command (text, in this case) this will be. Once you have created the recordset, you then loop through and display the first five records. If the user wants to see the next five records, he presses the Next button, which will take him to this same page, with the next five records displayed. This is possible because you have set the Recordset object rs_main to the Session.

When the user presses the Next button, the next page is called, which pulls the recordset out of the session, and then displays the next five. Listing 23.3 shows this page.

Listing 23.3 Displaying the next five records.

```
<%@ LANGUAGE="VBSCRIPT" %>

<HTML>
<HEAD>
<META NAME="GENERATOR" Content="Microsoft Visual InterDev 1.0">
<META HTTP-EQUIV="Content-Type" content="text/html; charset=iso-8859-1">
<TITLE>Search Employees</TITLE>
</HEAD>
<BODY>

<%  set rs_main = Session("rs")
    dim i
    i = 0
%>

<TABLE>
    <TR>
    <TD>First Name</TD>
    <TD>Last Name</TD>
    <TD>Phone</TD>
    </TR>

<%
    do while i < 5 AND not rs_main.eof
        Response.write("<TR>")
```

continues

Listing 23.3   Continued

```
    Response.write("<TD>")
        Response.write(rs_main("FirstName"))
        Response.write("</TD>")
        Response.write("<TD>")
        Response.write(rs_main("LastName"))
        Response.write("</TD>")
        Response.write("<TD>")
        Response.write(rs_main("Phone"))
        Response.write("</TD>")
            Response.write("</TR>")
        Rs_main.moveNext
                i = i +1
    loop
%>
<TR>
    <TD>
        <form action="next.asp">
            <input type="submit" name="next" value="next">
        </form>
    </TD>
</TR>
</TABLE>

<% set Session("rs") = rs_main %>
</BODY>
</HTML>

</BODY>
</HTML>
```

From Here...

Now that you have seen the simple, yet powerful, ways in which you can use the Recordset object, you have everything you need to create some really great Web-based applications.

You have seen how to navigate and manipulate your data with the Recordset methods. You have also examined the issues revolving around creation of Recordset objects. Hopefully, you are as excited as I was when I finally understood ADO and the Recordset object.

The following chapters will now probably be of interest to you:

- Chapter 24, "Managing Your Database," will delve deeper into database issues such as ODBC 3.0, Transaction Server, and concurrency.

- Chapter 25, "Accessing Databases with Remote Data Services," will show you how to create data-driven applications that use these ActiveX objects on the client.

- Chapter 26, "Putting It All Together: Creating a Dynamic Database Application," will show you how to put this disparate information together. You will see how to create a powerful and functional Web-based application.

CHAPTER 24

Managing Your Database

Now that you have examined how to integrate your ASP applications with your data, it's time to examine in more detail how to manage your database. Database management is not database administration. Database management is the tools and techniques you employ to design and secure a robust and well-behaved database.

When developing application access to a database, two very large problems loom over developers. The first is *transactions*. The second is *concurrency*.

Transactions are the idea of grouping actions against the database to enable faster and more robust execution. Without transactions, you cannot guarantee the reliability of your database.

By definition, a Web-based application is one that will have multiple users. With multiple users, however, comes the idea of concurrency. How do you protect the integrity of your data when several (perhaps thousands of) users are accessing it at once? In this chapter, you will look at some of the issues surrounding concurrency, and how to best protect your application depending on how you need to use it.

Understanding Databases

Examine database basics.

Transaction Processing with Microsoft Transaction Server

See how to implement robust data-driven applications with MS Transaction Server.

Concurrency Issues

Examine the issues surrounding concurrency and database applications.

ODBC 3.0

Find out what's new with ODBC 3.0, and how it can help you develop more robust and portable code.

Designing and Configuring Databases

Learn guidelines for designing and configuring your Web databases.

This chapter will also discuss issues surrounding the design of your database. A well-designed data model can mean a much more efficient and higher-performing application. In reality, creating a robust data model can be quite simple, as long as you follow some simple guidelines. ■

Understanding Databases

In the most simple terms, a database is the permanent storage of data. However, how you store your information is anything but simple. Databases must be able to support thousands, if not millions, of records. At the same time, there must be ways to quickly access and manipulate this information.

Another issue that arises is the capability to quickly port your applications from one database to another. This means that there needs to be a standard upon which databases are built.

Finally, modern business applications need to enable multiple users to access the same database over a network. This type of application development is called *client/server development*. You can save yourself many headaches in the future by designing applications that take into consideration a client/server architecture from the start.

Types of Databases

Many different types of data storage solutions have been created over the years, including network, hierarchical, and flat databases. Each of these has pretty much had its day, and due to one imperfection or another, has been replaced with far more effective solutions. Today, most serious database work is done with either relational database systems or with object-oriented database systems.

Object-Oriented Databases   *Object-oriented databases* (ODBMS) are fairly new to mainstream database application development. With an object-based database, there is one-to-one mapping of the objects found in the application (and the real world) with the objects stored in the database. In relational databases, there is a "flattening" of real-world data to make it fit that database structure. With ODBMS, a more natural structure of data is achieved.

Object-oriented databases implement an object model. A popular object model is the ODMG object model, which was developed by the Object Database Management Group. This object model provides for the implementation of such concepts as the following:

- *Attributes and properties of database objects*. This means you can specify in more detail what type of data the various objects hold.
- *Object methods and exceptions*. You can create methods for your data objects to use.
- *Multiple inheritance for objects*. You can inherit a Toyota data object from a general car object.
- *Object lifetimes*. This means you can control how long a data object lives in the database.
- *Concurrency control and object locking*. You can have even greater control over the locking and control of the data.

Relational Databases   *Relational databases* are the world standard for database architecture. With a relational database, data is stored in sets of two-dimensional arrays called tables. Columns in the table contain properties. Rows are the individual records in the database. Figure 24.1 shows an example table from such a database.

FIG. 24.1

An example table.

Emp #	first name	last name	phone
101	Ted	Smith	555-1212
102	John	Johnson	555-1211
201	Sara	Scott	555-1111
202	Michael	Wilson	555-1110
300	Lara	Cooper	555-1010

Where relational databases become interesting is the idea of having multiple tables that link to each other. For example, one table might list all of the employees in a business. It might contain columns for employee number, name, title, and department. Another separate table may contain a daily summary of hours worked by each employee. It might contain columns for employee number, date, and hours worked. Figure 24.2 shows a graphical representation of how this might look.

FIG. 24.2

Two linked tables.

first name	last name	phone	Emp #		Emp #	Date	Hours
Ted	Smith	555-1212	100		100	9-1-97	8
John	Johnson	555-1211	101		100	9-2-97	7.5
Sara	Scott	555-1111	200		101	9-1-97	8
Michael	Wilson	555-1110	201		200	9-1-97	10
Lara	Cooper	555-1010	300		⋮	⋮	⋮
Dan	Edgar	555-0000	301				
Alex	Mundlin	555-1000	302		302	10-4-97	7

SQL

A major goal of application development is *portability*. This is the notion of creating an application that can be easily ported to various other environments with its behavior remaining the same. When applied to databases, portability means that your applications should behave the same regardless of which database they hook up to.

If each database vendor created its own proprietary method of accessing data in the database, then this goal of portability would be very difficult. This is where the *Structured Query Language* (SQL) comes into play.

SQL is a language designed for accessing and manipulating data. There are many different dialects of SQL, but most SQL implementations support the most common SQL statements. The list below summarizes the major SQL keywords and their uses.

SELECT—This keyword is used to select data from the database.

UPDATE—This keyword is used to update existing records.

INSERT—This keyword is used to add new records to the database.

DELETE—This keyword is used to delete records from the database.

To quickly illustrate each of these keywords, I will create a small table containing a list of employees in my building. This table contains a bare set of information: employee ID, name, and phone number. The Figure 24.3 shows this table graphically.

FIG. 24.3

A table of employees.

	empID	First_Name	Last_Name	Phone
	1 John		Golby	555-1212
	2 Dan		Edgar	555-1000
	3 Lara		Cooper	555-2929
	4 Alex		Mundlin	555-1234
	5 John		Richardson	555-0098
	6 John		Hart	555-9775
	7 Susie		Harris	555-0927
*	(AutoNumber)			

Suppose you want to look at, and possibly manipulate, the records in this table where the employees' first names are "John." The select statement to do this would be:

```
SELECT employeeID, firstName, lastName, phone FROM tblEmployees WHERE firstName =
➥"John"
```

The results of this statement can be seen in Figure 24.4.

FIG. 24.4

SELECTing all records with the first name of John.

	empID	First_Name	Last_Name	Phone
▶	1 John		Golby	555-1212
	5 John		Richardson	555-0098
	6 John		Hart	555-9775
*	(AutoNumber)			

Record: ⏮ ◀ | 1 ▶ ⏭ ▶* of 3

Now imagine that you want to delete every record that begins with John. That SQL statement would look like the following:

```
DELETE * FROM tblEmployees where firstName = "John"
```

After executing this statement, the table looks like Figure 24.5.

FIG. 24.5

DELETEing all the Johns.

	empID	First_Name	Last_Name	Phone
	2 Dan		Edgar	555-1000
	3 Lara		Cooper	555-2929
▶	4 Alex		Mundlin	555-1234
	7 Susie		Harris	555-0927
*	(AutoNumber)			

Now suppose you want to update a person's record. Imagine that your employee Susie Harris was married and her last name is now "Smith." The SQL statement to update this record would be the following:

```
UPDATE tblEmployees SET lastName = "Smith" WHERE firstName = "Susie" and lastName
= "Harris"
```

The results of this operation would look like Figure 24.6.

FIG. 24.6

Susie, with her new last name.

empID	First_Name	Last_Name	Phone
2 Dan	Edgar	555-1000
3 Lara	Cooper	555-2929
4 Alex	Mundlin	555-1234
7 Susie	Smith	555-0927
(AutoNumber)		

Finally, suppose that a new employee is hired to fill the shoes of all the Johns that were deleted. The INSERT statement to handle this is

```
INSERT INTO tblEmployees (firstName, lastName, phone) VALUES ("Elizabeth",
➥"Ballinger", "555-8765")
```

This statement results in the table shown in Figure 24.7.

FIG. 24.7

Adding a new employee.

empID	First_Name	Last_Name	Phone
2 Dan	Edgar	555-1000
3 Lara	Cooper	555-2929
4 Alex	Mundlin	555-1234
7 Susie	Smith	555-0927
8 Elizabeth	Ballinger	555-8765
(AutoNumber)		

Part

V

Ch

24

Client/Server Development

When developing a database-driven application, it will be a very rare case where many users do not access the database at once over a network or the Internet. This type of application is called *client/server*, and it refers to a system in which there is a client program that handles some tasks, and a server program that handles others. The Web is an example of a client/server application. The Web server handles certain tasks, such as finding the appropriate page, and the browser displays the page contents. With client/server database programming, there is, at the very least, a server where the database resides, and several client machines on which a client program is used to access the database server. Figure 24.8 shows this type of two-tier setup.

When developing client/server systems, you must consider which tasks and processes are performed by the server, and which ones the client should handle. The very best applications are a marriage of tasks between these two components.

FIG. 24.8
A simple client/server
setup.

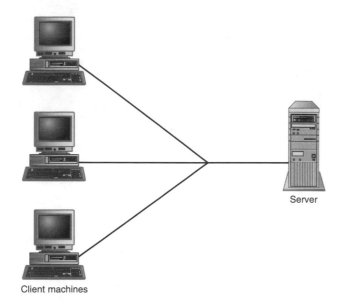

Server

Client machines

Some of the tasks best suited for the client include the following:

- Display of result sets from the database
- Simple data validation
- Gathering data before querying the database
- Formatting and filtering result sets from the database

Meanwhile, the server is often best used for these tasks:

- Complex data validation
- Indexing data
- Finding and returning result sets to the client
- Maintaining database integrity
- Managing transactions

Transaction Processing with Transaction Server

Microsoft Transaction Server is an exciting product that can reduce application development
by up to 40 percent. It enables developers to concentrate on developing the business logic of
their applications, and not worry about object brokering, transaction processing, and other
issues such as connection management.

For more information on these subjects, please see Chapter 28, "Working with the Microsoft
Transaction Server."

Transactions

Before I go into more detail on how Transaction Server can help ease development and increase the security of your system, let's examine transactions themselves in a little more detail. You cannot write a database application without considering transactions.

Imagine the Bank of Mongolia has hired you to create an intranet-based teller application. One of the main functions of this application will be to transfer money (right after deposit and withdrawal of funds).

First, the teller enters the account to take the money out of your account. Then, he enters the account to deposit the funds into (Account 2), along with the amount, and then submits/confirms the changes. Behind the scenes, the application is going to first withdraw the money from Account 1. Then, after ensuring that it has done this successfully, it will need to deposit the funds into Account 2. But what happens if there is a system failure between the first step (taking the money out of Account 1) and the second (deposit into Account 2)?

To prevent this from happening, developers have created what is called *transaction processing*, which enables you to specify certain tasks to be completed together. If any task fails, then they all fail.

There is a more formal, specific definition of transactions called the ACID test. *ACID* is an acronym that stands for Atomicity, Consistency, Isolation, and Durability. Figure 24.9 illustrates this concept.

FIG. 24.9
ACID.

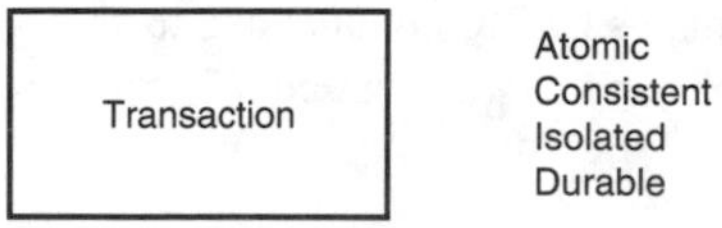

Transaction	Atomic Consistent Isolated Durable

Atomicity means that no matter how many objects or procedures are called, the transaction is treated as a single unit. If any piece of the transaction fails, the transaction as a whole fails. If everything succeeds, then the transaction as whole succeeds.

Consistency means that the transaction will work the same way every time. It also means that it won't change aspects of the system that should be invariant.

Isolation means that nothing external to the transaction should affect its execution. At least, no other transaction should. Transactions are totally isolated from one another, and have no knowledge of each other's successes or failures.

Durability means that that the results of the transaction will be durable and lasting, even if the system the database is on is shut off.

Inside Transaction Server

Transaction Server is a complex system made up of many different components. There are four key elements that are especially important: the Transaction Server executable, resource managers, resource dispensers, and the Distributed Transaction Coordinator.

Part
V

Ch
24

The Transaction Server executable is a service that provides for the context and thread management of business objects that are registered with Transaction Server. It can be thought of as the "brain" of Transaction Server.

The Microsoft *Distributed Transaction Coordinator* (DTC) actually precedes Transaction Server (it first showed up in Microsoft SQL Server). DTC is used to manage transactions that take place on several servers, as opposed to all transactions occuring on just one machine.

To explain further, think back to the bank example. Imagine that you have a separate database on a different server that is used to log all transfers and the information about them, such as the people involved, the time, the teller, and so on. With DTC, you can be assured that, if the transaction fails to write to either the database that contains the funds information or the new activity database, the transaction as a whole will fail.

Resource managers provide the data that is durable to the transaction. By using resource managers, such as SQL Server, the transaction can be guaranteed to be isolated and atomic. There are two phases to a transaction: the prepare phase and the commit. The prepare phase is where the provider *prepares* for the transaction. The commit phase is where it actually executes the transaction. The resource manager helps to ensure that if there is an error, it will roll back any changes.

Resource dispensers are similar to resource managers. The basic difference is that with a dispenser, you don't have the guarantee of durability. There are two major resource dispensers right now: the ODBC resource dispenser and the shared property resource dispenser.

The ODBC resource dispenser manages ODBC connections to your various datasources. By using the ODBC resource dispenser, your system can benefit from connection pooling that this dispenser employs.

Concurrency Issues

Now return to the example from the last section, the bank teller application. But now, think about happens when you have 100 bank tellers all accessing the database at once.

Suppose the bank teller transfers funds from your account into your mom's. At the same time, Mom is at her local branch trying to close her account. If the money is deposited before she finishes closing the account, but after they have tallied up how much money she has left, your poor mother will be out the several hundreds of dollars you were sending her.

To deal with these problems of concurrency, or multiple users accessing the same data, several different techniques have been developed. Most of these involve locking the database, or a section of it, during a transaction. Let's look at some of these techniques, particularly locking.

When developing a multi-user database application, you should strive to develop an application that behaves exactly the same as if it were a single-user application. To help to this end, databases provide a feature called *locking*. Locking is the means to prevent all but the lock-issuing process access to the data that has been locked.

There are two major types of locks: *shared locks* and *exclusive locks* (Figures 24.10 and 24.11 show these types of locks). A shared lock is one that can be shared by several processes at once. For instance, if all you and your mother want to do is see how much money is in her account, both of the processes that have this information would be able to share a lock. This type of lock only works for read-only connections.

FIG. 24.10
Locks can be shared...

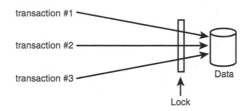

Processes that are going to update, insert, or add information to the database issue exclusive locks. In the case of the funds transfer, each process would create an exclusive lock for mom's account.

Besides the classification of locks into exclusive or shared, there is also the issue of just how much data to lock. Most databases enable several levels of granularity in terms of what data can be locked. These range from locking the entire database to locking a single row.

FIG. 24.11
...or exclusive.

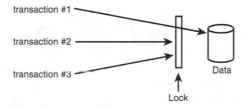

Part
V
Ch
24

ODBC 3.0

The Open Database Connectivity 3.0 standard is the most popular way to connect to a database in the Windows world. By using ODBC, developers need not concern themselves with the particular database they are hooking up to. Instead, by using ODBC, you can deal with a level of abstraction above the particular database.

Specifically, ODBC is an API for accessing, manipulating, and creating databases. It is based on the X/Open Call-level Interface and uses SQL.

As a Web developer, you don't need to know the exact API for ODBC. However, a good understanding of ODBC will do you a world of good.

When you access a database through ODBC, that database must be registered as an ODBC datasource. By registering the database as a datasource, the application only needs to know its datasource name. The location of the database makes no difference, nor even what type of database it is.

There are three types of datasources you can create: System, User, and File. Figure 24.12 shows how to access any of these from the ODBC control panel.

FIG. 24.12

Datasources can be system wide, user specific, or located in a file.

A *system datasource* is one that is available to any user of the system. (Of course, the database itself could be password protected.) A *user datasource* is one that is only available to that user. Finally, a *file datasource* is a description of the database. It can be used to hook up to the database without having to register the database itself with the system.

Generally, with Web applications you want to create system datasources. Only rarely would you use a file or user datasource. But if you do find the need, they are available to you.

Designing and Configuring Databases

Relational databases enable very powerful functionality. For instance, Oracle databases can store millions of records. Even with tools such as Access, anyone can develop a database to hold his or her information. Using ASP with ADO, you can publish that information to the Web quickly and easily. However, it is very easy to start running into problems with your database.

There are two aspects of database design that I will look at here. The first is data modeling; the second is data access. If done wrong, each can have its own difficulties, ultimately rendering a program useless. If done right, your application will run more efficiently and more quickly.

Data Modeling

The goal of a good data model is to avoid duplicate data. Also high on the list is creating a model that is understandable and easy to develop for. Another very important piece of the data modeling puzzle is a database structure that won't slow down the application.

Another name for a database that doesn't repeat data is a *normalized* database. The opposite of a normalized database is one that is flat, or non-relational. The best way to learn how to design is to see a design in action.

Imagine that you are building an application to store the client companies for a fictional company, along with any key contacts at the company. Now, you don't really know how many contacts you will record for each client; some might have one, while others have 10. You could guess, and build a database structure that will hold up to 10 contacts per client. In that case, the database would look something like that shown in Figure 24.13.

FIG. 24.13

A flat database structure.

This type of database structure is a compromise. It is not flexible, and it requires writing code to figure out how many contacts for each salesman have been written to see what slots are still available. Additionally, every client record that doesn't have 10 contacts would be wasting space. This is a classic example of a flat database.

A relational design, on the other hand, would enable you to have as many contacts, or as few, as the business client has. That would not only mirror real life more, it would also be easier to code.

To implement this, you need to create one more table. This table will be called tblContact, and it will link each record in the contact table with a record in tblClient. You link tables together through the use of keys. A key is a unique identifier for each record in a table. Figure 24.14 shows the new and improved database structure.

FIG. 24.14

Relationships can exist between tables in a database.

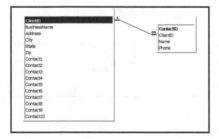

Notice in Figure 24.14 that there is a line drawn between clientID in the table tblClient, and the clientID field in tblContact. This line has a "1" on one end, and the sign for infinity on the other. This denotes a one-to-many relationship. In other words, for every one record in tblClient, there are (or can be) many records in tblContact. This more closely mirrors what you have in real life. For each one client your company has, there can be many contacts.

Another situation you will run up against is the possibility of adding salesmen to the database. You will probably want to link your salesmen to the accounts they are in charge of. However, you may have several salesmen attached to a single client. And, most salesmen will have several clients.

To handle this, add two new tables. The first will contain information about the salesmen. The second will be a link between salesmen and clients. Figure 24.15 shows this structure.

FIG. 24.15
Salesmen and their clients.

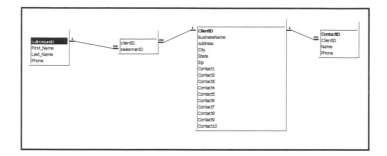

This design enables you to have as many salesmen per client as you need, and salesmen can also have as many clients as you want to assign them.

This idea of normalized databases can be measured through what are called levels of normalization. Generally, third-level normalization is the goal to shoot for. It provides the best compromise between data redundancy and development ease.

The following is a list of the various levels of normalization you should care about.

- Not at all
- First-level
- Second-level
- Third-level

A database that is not normalized at all is shown in Figure 24.16.

FIG. 24.16
A non-normalized database.

Department	Employees	Department Phone
Marketing	Brittany Black, Jeff Smith, Earl Wayne	55624
Sales	Lara Ballinger, John Goalby	23222
Development	Alex Mundlin, Keith Ballinger, Daniel Edgar	23232

This database contains a list of employees, but all the employees for a certain department are found in a single column, which is a very awkward way to store this information. It would better to give each employee his own record, and record their location in another column for that row. Figure 24.17 shows a revised version of this table. This is the first level of normalization.

FIG. 24.17
First-level normalization.

Department	Employee	Phone
Marketing	Brittany Black	55824
Sales	Lara Ballinger	23222
Development	Alex Mundlin	23232
Marketing	Jeff Smith	23232
Marketing	Earl Wayne	23232
Sales	John Goalby	55624
Development	Keith Ballinger	55624
Development	Daniel Edgar	55624

To achieve second-level normalization, you need to give each record a unique identifier. This can be done by adding a new column for employee number. Figure 24.18 shows this added change.

FIG. 24.18
Second-level normalization.

employeeID	Department	Employee	Phone
1 Marketing		Brittany Black	55824
2 Sales		Lara Ballinger	23222
3 Development		Alex Mundlin	23232
4 Marketing		Jeff Smith	23232
5 Marketing		Earl Wayne	23232
6 Sales		John Goalby	55824
7 Development		Keith Ballinger	55824
8 Development		Daniel Edgar	55824
(AutoNumber)			

To achieve full third-level normalization, you need to eliminate the data redundancy of naming the department that each employee is in by keeping departments in their own table with their own unique record identifier. You can then refer to this identifier in the employee table. If something changes within your department, such as location, you only need to update the record in the department table. Making this change gives us third-level normalization, as shown in Figure 24.19.

FIG. 24.19
Third-level normalization.

employeeID	Department	Employee	Phone
1 1		Brittany Black	55824
2 2		Lara Ballinger	23222
3 3		Alex Mundlin	23232
4 1		Jeff Smith	23232
5 1		Earl Wayne	23232
6 2		John Goalby	55824
7 3		Keith Ballinger	55824
8 3		Daniel Edgar	55824
(AutoNumber)			

Keys and Indexes

There are two different unique identifiers in the last example: one for the employee table (employee number) and one for the department table (department number). In each of these tables, this column is called the *key*. In the employee table, you also have the department number. Because this a key in another table, it is called a *foreign key*.

By using keys, you can group data together in a logical manner. Departments have their own table. Employees have their own table. You can add other parts of the business, such as clients, and give that set of data its own table. By linking these keys together, you create relationships.

Using SQL statements across multiple tables, you can quickly pull a result set of data that groups this information together for the user. For instance, the following SQL statement:

```
SELECT tblEmp.employeeName, tblDept.location WHERE tblEmp.deptNum =
➥tblDept.deptNum
```

creates a result set that looks like the one shown in the Figure 24.20.

Indexes are used in some databases to speed up access to data. Instead of having to scan every record in a table, if the table has an index, that index can be used to quickly narrow down which records to select. With SQL Server, you can have multiple columns be used as indexes. For instance, you can index both zip code and last name of a table that includes customer information.

FIG. 24.20

A result set from two different tables.

Employee	location
Lara Ballinger	South Wing
John Goalby	South Wing
Lara Ballinger	North Hall
John Goalby	North Hall
Lara Ballinger	Valhalla
John Goalby	Valhalla

Indexes can be quite helpful, and can improve performance dramatically. However, they take up additional space in the database. So before implementing indexes, it is always a good idea to understand the use of the table involved. Is the customer database searched often? If so, what are the usual search criteria? Do users search by zip code? If they do, create an index based on the zip code.

But what if last name or phone is used to search far more often? In that case, creating a zip code index would probably be a waste of time and space. A better choice would be an index based on those criteria.

Data Access

The other major issue to consider besides how you design your data is to think about how you access it. This discussion will deal with SQL statements. Basically, there are two issues to consider when designing your SQL statements.

The first issue deals with the amount of information that you move. When dealing with lots of hits, you need to be aware of the huge amount of data that might be shuffled around by your processes. For instance, in the database that you designed in the last section, you might want to pull out a list of all customers. All this statement needs to do is display a list of names. Here is one way to grab that list:

```
SELECT *
FROM tblClients
```

This statement will return all the fields in the table `tblClients` (see Figure 24.21).

FIG. 24.21

Selecting too much information.

ClientID	BusinessName	Address	City	State	Zip	Contact1	C
1	Rob's Hambuugers	100 Main	Hillsboro	OR	97124		
2	Roy's Hotdogs	110 Main	Beaverton	OR	97124		
3	Jen's Veggy	120 Main	hillsboro	OR	97124		
4	Ken's HairShop	200 Main	Hillsboro	OR	97124		
(AutoNumber)							

As you can see, for as simple a request as client name, you are grabbing way too much information. For an application that isn't used a lot, this isn't a big problem. But imagine the implications of this SQL statement being hit thousands of times an hour, and you can see the problem.

It is good coding practice to always specify the exact fields you want in a SQL statement. This will avoid the problem of grabbing too much information. The following statement does just that:

```
SELECT clientName
FROM tblClients;
```

This statement results in Figure 24.22, which is much more economic.

FIG. 24.22

Only pull as much information as you need.

businessName
Rob's Hambuugers
Roy's Hotdogs
Jen's Veggy
Ken's HairShop

Database Security

One of the major facets of developing Web-based databases that you must consider is data security. A secure database is a must. If just anyone is allowed to access, delete, and manipulate your data, it can become useless. Many databases enable you to set up permissions for various levels of access to the database.

In particular, Microsoft's SQL Server gives the database administrator and developer a high level of control over who can access what information. If you have seen connection string arguments that specify usernames and passwords, it is probably because the database being accessed is a database that requires user logins, such as Microsoft SQL Server or Sybase SQL Server.

To configure a new login and its access privileges, follow these steps:

1. Start SQL Server Enterprise Manager.
2. Select the server you want to configure.
3. Type in the login and password of the user.
4. Choose which database operations this user is allowed to perform.
5. Click the Add button.

By carefully considering which permissions to give each type of user, you can secure your database from allowing just any user to manipulate it. In an ASP application distributed over the Internet, this may be anyone on the earth with a browser and Internet connection. You don't want unauthorized users typing in your database, or possibly even deleting sensitive and important information from it.

From Here...

In this chapter, you examined some of the basics of databases. You learned the differences between relational and object-oriented databases, and you saw how SQL can help you develop portable, database-driven applications.

Further, you have seen how Microsoft's Transaction Server can help you implement transaction processing in your applications. With this powerful new application, you can have your transactions span multiple servers, which enables distributed processing.

You have also seen how concurrency, or multiple users accessing your application simultaneously, can lead to the loss of data integrity. You have seen how locking can help alleviate this situation, and what amount of locking to apply, based on the situation.

You have further examined ODBC 3.0. This standard of database access enables developers to forget about the exact nature of the database they are accessing, and instead spend their development time on the business logic of the application.

Finally, you have seen some guidelines for data modeling and data access that will help you to develop your applications faster, and to develop faster applications. For related information, please see the following chapters:

- Chapter 26, "Putting It All Together: Creating a Dynamic Database Application," will show you how to create a sample application with ASP and ADO.
- Chapter 28, "Working with the Microsoft Transaction Server," will give you more in-depth information on this powerful new product from Microsoft.

CHAPTER 25

Accessing Databases with Remote Data Services

Formerly named the Advanced Data Connector, Remote Data Services enable you, the developer, to create Web pages that are bound to a data source on the Web server. This exciting technology is integrated with IE 4, but can also be used with IE 3.

Using this technology, you can bind data to your Web pages and then cache it on the client browser, which releases the browser from having to make unnecessary trips to the server. This means that you can create full-blown, database-driven programs that run from within the browser. You can do this because Remote Data Services utilize existing technologies that you are already familiar with: ActiveX Data Objects, OLE DB, VBScript, and more. ■

Remote Data Services Overview

An overview of how the Remote Data Services can help you create powerful applications more quickly.

Using the RDS Components

Examine the components that make up Remote Data Services.

Limitations of the Remote Data Services

When Remote Data Services are not enough.

Extending the Phone Book

See how the simple phone book application from earlier chapters can be written for RDS.

Understanding Remote Data Services

Using the Remote Data Services, developers can now create powerful applications using the familiar three-tier approach. By embedding components like drop-down and list boxes, you can turn a Web page into a full-featured application. Figure 25.1 shows a graphical example of traditional three-tier architecture.

FIG. 25.1

Traditional three-tier architecture.

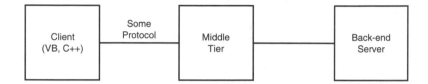

Figure 25.2 shows three-tier architecture with RDS. Notice that the browser technology creates a stateless and connectionless environment for the application, which is substantially different from traditional client/server architecture.

FIG. 25.2

Three-tier architecture with RDS.

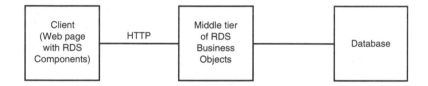

With a Web page, updates are easy. Change the page, and next time your users visit, it will be different. At the same time, the downside of Web pages—their static nature—is avoided with client-side data caching. This means that the browser won't have to make trip after trip to the server for more data. It can be sent once, manipulated and navigated, and then finally, any changes can be sent back to the server at the end of the transaction.

Of course, this isn't always the best way to handle data. There will be times when you will need to query the server for data, and then requery often before your user is done with his transaction. In particular, a very active application that is used by multiple people will probably need to check for data changes more often than a single user or less-used application.

There are three key objects that are used in most RDS applications:

- AdvancedDataControl
- AdvancedDataSpace
- AdvancedDataFactory

AdvancedDataControl is a non-visual ActiveX control that is used to bind data to other visual controls on a Web page. It is scriptable to enable navigation and data manipulation with an already familiar language such as VBScript.

NOTE What is a non-visual ActiveX control? As you know, an ActiveX control is a control that you embed in an HTML page that delivers more functionality than what HTML alone can deliver. Most ActiveX controls are visual elements like enhanced tree views of Web sites and the like.

However, not all ActiveX controls have to be visual. For instance, there is a control that can be used as a timer on a Web page. This control fires off an event at some specified time, as set up by the page author. This control doesn't actually appear on the page—it is non-visual. The `AdvancedDataControl` is the same way. ■

The `AdvancedDataSpace` object is a constructor used to create DCOM marshaling proxies, HTTP proxies, and Automation objects.

The `AdvancedDataFactory` object is the default middle tier in RDS applications. It is used to send SQL queries and updates to the back-end ODBC-compliant datasource.

Creating Business Objects

Business objects are components that encapsulate application logic and business rules. By componentizing the logic and rules of the application, you can more quickly and efficiently develop and deliver Web-based applications.

For example, you may have an application that is used in online ordering. A business object in that application might be a set of code that is used to validate credit cards and make sure they have enough money in available credit. This set of code is a business object.

Business objects can be created with any tool that can create ActiveX objects. Generally, the business components of RDS will be created with either Visual C++ or Visual Basic. By using this model, many benefits can be realized. The biggest of these (in my opinion) is that business objects are, for the most part, independent of the interface and database. The logic of these components can be deployed in a variety of situations, enabling for faster development of future versions of the application.

In creating an RDS application, the following principles apply well:

Part
V

Ch

25

- Use the client for user interface and most data validation. This means that the focus during the development of the client should be on a usable interface, not on the internal logic of the program. (By simple data validation, I mean such functions as checking for illegal characters [such as $, %, #, and so on] in a name field, or for only numbers in an area code.)

- Encapsulate business logic into components using a black-box approach, where you can later change the component and the program still works. This means true encapsulation and data hiding. The server-side components should be independent of the front-end. Changing either the server-side objects or the client browser shouldn't impact the program.

Understanding IE 4 and Dynamic HTML

Internet Explorer 4.0 includes a new feature called *Dynamic HTML*. With Dynamic HTML, Web pages can respond and interact with users in complex manners previously only seen in stand-alone applications. There is even a version of the classic arcade game Asteroids written completely in JavaScript and Dynamic HTML (DHTML).

What exactly is meant by Dynamic HTML, and what does it have to do with Remote Data Services? With IE 4, Microsoft has made every element of a Web page scriptable, which means that using JavaScript or VBScript, a page author can manipulate the letters and words on a page—changing them dynamically.

Using a combination of Remote Data Services and DHTML, you can create a Web page that displays, for instance, a list of employees in your department. Next, you can filter and sort the list by clicking on the column you want to sort by. This is possible through two new tags that Microsoft has introduced with DHTML: DATASRC and DATAFLD.

Active Server Pages and RDS

ASP and RDS go together for two reasons. The first is that, as an ASP developer, you are already familiar with ADO, which is used on the client for navigation and manipulation through the recordset bound to the AdvancedDataControl.

The second is the capability to dynamically create the appropriate page based on information the user has previously entered. For instance, the user may enter a login password that enables him both read and write access to the database, while others may only be allowed read access. This can be achieved by checking the password on the server with ASP, and then writing a page based on the permissions of that login. Later in this chapter, you will see an example of this.

Using the RDS Components

You have already briefly looked at the major objects that are used with the Remote Data Service in the previous section, "Understanding Remote Data Services." Now, let's look more in detail at these and the other components that you will utilize in your RDS development.

Advanced Data Virtual Table Manager

The Virtual Table Manager (VTM) takes care of caching data that is sent to the client, and also manages the updates to that data. The VTM is a set of data structures that are used to buffer information on table structure along with that actual information in the table.

To be able to manage the caching and updating of data that the VTM does, it has the capability to create and delete temporary tables. It also can provide schema information such as base tables and key columns.

One of the best features of the Virtual Table Manager is its capability to send only the records that have been updated. This means that unnecessary traffic to and from the browser can be greatly reduced when using RDS.

How does the VTM marshal (transfer) the data it sends? It uses *tablegrams*. Tablegrams are a special MIME type that was designed for transporting table-based information over HTTP. One of the nicest features of tablegrams is their capability to normalize the information they send. This means that if there are certain rows of information that are repeated throughout a table, they will send the actual information only once; thereby saving bandwidth once again.

AdvancedDataControl Object

The AdvancedDataControl object is a non-visible ActiveX control that binds data from a recordset (which is, itself, the result of a query such as a Select statement) to various text fields and other visible ActiveX controls on the Web page.

How do you use the AdvanceDataControl in a Web page? Basically, you embed it in the same way as any other ActiveX control, and give it a Width and Height of 1 to avoid losing any space to it. The code below shows an example of how to do this.

```
<OBJECT CLASSID="clsid: 9381D8F2-0288-11d0-9501-00AA00B911A5"
  ID="ADC1">
    <PARAM NAME="Bindings" VALUE="SGrid;">
    <PARAM NAME="SQL" VALUE="SELECT * FROM tbl_phone">
    <PARAM NAME="Connect" VALUE="DSN=EmployeeDB;">
    <PARAM NAME="Server" VALUE="http://hr-www; ">
</OBJECT>
```

 TIP When using the Sheridan grid control with RDS, make sure to create the AdvancedDataControl last on the page. There is a known bug that will cause your application to act weird otherwise.

The code above should look very familiar. It is the standard method in which ActiveX controls are embedded into a Web page. There are four major parameters that you will set when using this control (see Table 25.1).

Table 25.1 Parameters of the *AdvancedDataControl*

Parameter	Description
Binding	Specifies which controls to display the recordset with on the page. Can range from a single data grid that handles all of the columns of data to several controls that each handle a column of data.
SQL	This specifies the SQL statement to use in the creation of the recordset.
Connect	This property specifies the DataSource to use. This parameter can also take a user name and password if the database requires one.
Server	This specifies the IIS sever and protocol used to connect to the server-side objects.

Part
V

Ch
25

N O T E If you will be binding your data to single-threaded ActiveX controls, you should use a ClassID of 259381D8F2-0288-11D0-9501-00AA00B911A5 for the AdvancedDataControl. If you are using apartment-threaded controls, you should use a ClassID of C5C18AE2-4D6E-11D0-9823-00C04FC29E30. ∎

AdvancedDataSpace Object

This object is used as a proxy between the client and server-side business objects by using the CreateObject method of the AdvancedDataSpace object to create these proxies. When using this method, send the URL and ProgID of the business object. The URL is of the server that contains the business object.

The CreateObject method returns a pointer to the server-side business object. The proxy created is then responsible for packaging and marshaling (transporting) the data to the business object. The following code shows an example of how to use the AdvancedDataSpace object.

```
<OBJECT CLASSID="clsid: 99586D40-DB60-11cf-9D87-00AA00B91181"
 ID="AdvancedDataSpace"
</OBJECT>
Set rsBusinessObject = AdvancedDataSpace.CreateObject("AdvancedDataFactory",
➥"http://hr-www;")
```

Notice how two pieces of information were sent with the CreateObject method. The first was the ProgID of the business object—in this case the AdvancedDataFactory. The second was the URL of the server where this object is located.

AdvancedDataFactory Object

The AdvancedDataFactory is the default server-side object in RDS. It provides for read and write access to the database. By default, this is the object that the AdvancedDataControl uses to gather and send data to and from the server.

The following code shows an example of the AdvancedDataFactory at work.

```
<OBJECT CLASSID="clsid:9381D8F5-0288-11d0-9501-00AA00B911A5"
ID=AdvancedDataFactory1 HEIGHT=1 WIDTH=1>
</OBJECT>
dim rs_temp
set AdvancedDataFactory1 = ADS1.CreateObject("AdvancedDataFactory", "http://hr-
➥www")
set rs_temp = AdvancedDataFactory1.Query("DSN=Employees;", "SELECT * FROM
tbl_employees")
ADC1.Recordset = rs_temp
```

Notice how the preceding code uses both the AdvancedDataControl (or, more properly put, the instantiation of it—ADC1) and AdvancedDataSpace. By default, most of this work can be done in the instantiation of the AdvancedDataControl.

Replacing the *AdvancedDataFactory*

One of the first things you will notice when reading through the Remote Data Service documentation, or any materials from Microsoft on RDS, is how often Microsoft mentions that the AdvancedDataFactory is generic and can be replaced with a custom object that can also contain various business rules.

While the AdvancedDataFactory is actually a nice piece of work, and works just fine, I would take Microsoft's advice if you at all have the resources. Why?

The business rules of your application have to exist somewhere. If they don't exist in the server-side component, they will most probably exist on your client (browser) in the form of scripting. For simple applications, this approach is fine. But if you are creating an anti-brevatious application, it would be better to handle complex business logic in a compiled form running on the server as opposed to an unmanageable amount of client-side scripts.

In other words, if you have 3,000 lines of code per Web page, it's going to be a nightmare to update. And no one will.

Understanding the Limitations of RDS

The biggest limitation with the Remote Data Service is its lack of browser independence. The only browser that can use RDS with no problem is Microsoft's Internet Explorer 4.0. Netscape won't be of any help, because it has no support for ActiveX, which is the cornerstone technology of RDS.

The next big limitation of RDS is the absence of third-party server-side components for use with RDS. Of course, this can also be thought of as an opportunity. Instead of using the AdvancedDataFactory or creating your own business object, wouldn't it be nice if there were a set of other objects for such things as user registration and bug tracking?

Extending the Phone Book Application

Now, let's create a real-live application by applying some of this newfound knowledge. Let's return to our phone book application of earlier chapters. Only now, let's use Remote Data Services to deliver the data to our users.

This example will run on an IE 4 client with IIS 3.0 for the server. First, I'll create a read-only version of the application for anyone to use. Then, I'll introduce some ASP into the application to enable for creating pages based on a login the user will provide. After all, someone has to delete, modify, and add people to the phone database, right?

There are several steps involved in creating this application.

1. Create the grid that will display the data, and the AdvancedDataControl object that it will bind to.
2. Add HTML buttons and text fields.

3. Add code for searching through the recordset.

4. Add code for navigating through the recordset.

Actually, before adding the code for the grid and `AdvancedDataControl`, you need to make sure there is a datasource named `Employees` on the server. This can be done by opening the ODBC Control Panel on the server and adding a new datasource, as shown in Figure 25.3 and Figure 25.4.

FIG. 25.3

Adding a datasource.

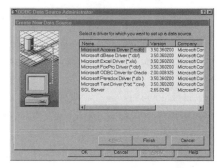

To check your datasource, follow these steps:

1. Click the Start button, and choose Control Panel.

2. Double-click the ODBC32 icon.

3. Click the System DSN tab.

4. Under the System DSN tab, you should find the datasource you need. If not, go ahead and click the Add button.

FIG. 25.4

Adding a datasource.

Now, let's look at the code necessary to add the grid and `AdvancedDataControl`. As you may remember, adding the `AdvancedDataControl` is easy. Listing 25.1 shows how.

Listing 25.1 *25code01.ASP*—Adding the *AdvancedDataControl*.

```
<OBJECT classid="clsid:BD96C556-65A3-11D0-983A-00C04FC29E33"
ID="AdvancedDataControl1" HEIGHT=1 WIDTH=1>
</OBJECT>
```

Notice how the HEIGHT and WIDTH of the control is set to 1. This in effect enables the control to take up no space. It is already invisible, but you don't want it to take up any room, either.

Next you can add the datagrid that the data will be bound to. In this example, you will use the Sheridan Data Grid. Listing 25.2 shows how to embed it into the application.

Listing 25.2   25code02.ASP—Adding the data grid.

```
<OBJECT CLASSID="AC05DC80-7DF1-11D0-839E-00A024A94B3A"
ID="DataGrid" HEIGHT="200" WIDTH="600"
CODEBASE="http://hr-www/apps/phonebook/sheridan.cab"
DATASRC="#AdvancedDataControl1">
     <PARAM NAME="_Verson" VALUE="131072">
     <PARAM NAME="BackColor" VALUE="-2147483643">
     <PARAM NAME="BackColorOdd" VALUE="-2147483643">
     <PARAM NAME="BackColorEven" VALUE="0">
</OBJECT>
```

This object is bound to the data that the AdvancedDataControl will gather. You bind the two together with the DATASRC tag of the grid. DATASRC is one of two new HTML tags in DHTML. So this tag could actually be used in a table.

Now that you have added the grid, add some HTML buttons that will enable you to navigate through the recordset (see Listing 25.3).

Listing 25.3   25code03.ASP—Buttons.

```
<INPUT TYPE="button" NAME="First" VALUE="First" onClick="MoveFirst">
<INPUT TYPE="button" NAME="Last" VALUE="Last" onClick="MoveLast">
<INPUT TYPE="button" NAME="Next" VALUE="Next" onClick="MoveNext">
<INPUT TYPE="button" NAME="Prev" VALUE="Prev" onClick="MovePrev">
```

Now that you have the buttons, you need to write the code that will run when the user clicks on the buttons, along with some initialization code to run when the page loads up (see Listing 25.4).

Listing 25.4   25code04.ASP—Code to navigate through the data.

```
Sub Init
     Server.Value = "http://hr-www"
     Connect.Value = "DSN="Employees"
     SQL.Value = "SELECT * FROM tbl_employees"
     AdvancedDataControl1.Server = Server.Value
     AdvancedDataControl1.Connect = Connect.Value
     AdvancedDataControl1.SQL = SQL.Value
End Sub
Sub MoveFirst
     AdvancedDataControl1.MoveFirst
End Sub
```

continued

Part

V

Ch

25

Listing 25.4   Continued

```
Sub MoveLast
     AdvancedDataControl1.MoveLast
End Sub
Sub MoveNext
    On Error Resume Next
    AdvancedDataControl1.MoveNext
    If ERR.Number <> 0 Then
        AdvancedDataControl.MoveLast
    End If
End Sub
Sub MovePrev
    On Error Resume Next
    AdvancedDataControl1.MovePrevious
    If ERR.Number <> 0 Then
        AdvancedDataControl.MoveFirst
    End If
End Sub
```

Now you can combine all of this code into one ASP page and give it a name. Listing 25.5 shows the entire page, Y.asp.

Listing 25.5   *25code05.ASP*—The phone book.

```
<HTML>
<HEAD>
    <TITLE>
        Phone Book Application
    </TITLE>
<SCRIPT LANGUAGE="VBSCRIPT">
     Sub Init
    Server.Value = "http://hr-www"
    Connect.Value = "DSN="Employees"
    SQL.Value = "SELECT * FROM tbl_employees"
    AdvancedDataControl1.Server = Server.Value
    AdvancedDataControl1.Connect = Connect.Value
    AdvancedDataControl1.SQL = SQL.Value
    End Sub
    Sub MoveFirst
AdvancedDataControl1.MoveFirst
    End Sub
    Sub MoveLast
AdvancedDataControl1.MoveLast
    End Sub
    Sub MoveNext
On Error Resume Next
AdvancedDataControl1.MoveNext
If ERR.Number <> 0 Then
        AdvancedDataControl.MoveLast
    End If
    End Sub
    Sub MovePrev
```

```
            On Error Resume Next
            AdvancedDataControl1.MovePrevious
            If ERR.Number <> 0 Then
                AdvancedDataControl.MoveFirst
            End If
            End Sub
    </SCRIPT>
    </HEAD>
    <BODY BGCOLOR="white">
        <OBJECT CLASSID="AC05DC80-7DF1-11D0-839E-00A024A94B3A"
          ID="DataGrid" HEIGHT="200" WIDTH="600"
          CODEBASE="http://hr-www/apps/phonebook/sheridan.cab"
          DATASRC="#AdvancedDataControl1">
            <PARAM NAME="_Verson" VALUE="131072">
            <PARAM NAME="BackColor" VALUE="-2147483643">
            <PARAM NAME="BackColorOdd" VALUE="-2147483643">
            <PARAM NAME="BackColorEven" VALUE="0">
        </OBJECT>
        <BR>
        <INPUT TYPE="button" NAME="First" VALUE="First" onClick="MoveFirst">
        <INPUT TYPE="button" NAME="Last" VALUE="Last" onClick="MoveLast">
        <INPUT TYPE="button" NAME="Next" VALUE="Next" onClick="MoveNext">
        <INPUT TYPE="button" NAME="Prev" VALUE="Prev" onClick="MovePrev">
        <BR>
        <OBJECT classid="clsid:BD96C556-65A3-11D0-983A-00C04FC29E33"
          ID="AdvancedDataControl1" HEIGHT=1 WIDTH=1>
        </OBJECT>
    </BODY>
    </HTML>
```

Part
V

Ch
25

Figure 25.5 shows what the phone book page should now look like.

FIG. 25.5

The phone book
application.

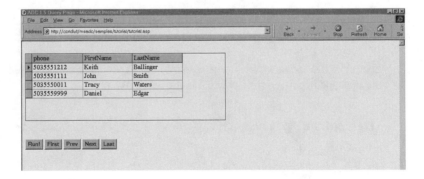

Now let's create a login page for the phone book. This page will ask just for a login name. It will then check this login to see if it is the administrator of the phone book. If it is, it will enable the user to make changes to the phone book and update the database accordingly.

Listing 25.6 shows the ASP page that asks for the user login.

Listing 25.6   *25code06.ASP*—Getting the user login.

```
<HTML>
<HEAD>
        <TITLE>
                Phone Book Login
        </TITLE>
</HEAD>
<BODY BGCOLOR="white">
        <FORM ACTION="y.asp" METHOD="POST">
                Phone Book Login:
                <INPUT TYPE="text" NAME="login">
                <BR>
                <INPUT TYPE="submit" NAME="Submit">
        </FORM>
</BODY>
</HTML>
```

What code do you have to add to enable updating the database? Actually, very little. The data grid is already designed to enable edits to the fields. So all you really need to do is add a button called Update and a function that actually does it (see Listing 25.7). These buttons will fire off the built-in methods of the AdvancedDataControl, SubmitChanges, and Refresh.

Listing 25.7   *25code07.ASP*—Update: The button and the function.

```
Sub Update
    AdvancedDataControl1.SubmitChanges
    AdvancedDataControl1.Refresh
End Sub
.
.
.
<INPUT TYPE="Button" Name="Submit" VALUE="Submit Changes" OnClick="Update">
```

Listing 25.8 is the new code integrated into the phone book application, and Figure 25.6 shows the new and improved page when it is the admin login.

Listing 25.8   *25code08.ASP*—New and improved phone book.

```
<HTML>
<HEAD>
    <TITLE>
        Phone Book Application
    </TITLE>
<SCRIPT LANGUAGE="VBSCRIPT">
Sub Init
    Server.Value = "http://hr-www"
    Connect.Value = "DSN=Employees"
    SQL.Value = "SELECT * FROM tbl_employees"
    AdvancedDataControl1.Server = Server.Value
    AdvancedDataControl1.Connect = Connect.Value
```

```
        AdvancedDataControl1.SQL = SQL.Value
          End Sub

        <% IF Request.Form("Login") = "Admin" Then %>
              Sub Update
        AdvancedDataControl1.SubmitChanges
        AdvancedDataControl1.Refresh
              End Sub
          <%End IF%>
          Sub MoveFirst
        AdvancedDataControl1.MoveFirst
          End Sub
          Sub MoveLast
        AdvancedDataControl1.MoveLast
          End Sub
          Sub MoveNext
        On Error Resume Next
        AdvancedDataControl1.MoveNext
        If ERR.Number <> 0 Then
            AdvancedDataControl.MoveLast
        End IF
          End Sub
          Sub MovePrev
        On Error Resume Next
        AdvancedDataControl1.MovePrevious
        If ERR.Number <> 0 Then
            AdvancedDataControl.MoveFirst
        End If
          End Sub
</SCRIPT>
</HEAD>
<BODY BGCOLOR="white">
    <OBJECT CLASSID="AC05DC80-7DF1-11D0-839E-00A024A94B3A"
      ID="DataGrid" HEIGHT="200" WIDTH="600"
      CODEBASE="http://hr-www/apps/phonebook/sheridan.cab"
      DATASRC="#AdvancedDataControl1">
        <PARAM NAME="_Verson" VALUE="131072">
        <PARAM NAME="BackColor" VALUE="-2147483643">
        <PARAM NAME="BackColorOdd" VALUE="-2147483643">
        <PARAM NAME="BackColorEven" VALUE="0">
      </OBJECT>
      <BR>
      <INPUT TYPE="button" NAME="First" VALUE="First" onClick="MoveFirst">
      <INPUT TYPE="button" NAME="Last" VALUE="Last" onClick="MoveLast">
      <INPUT TYPE="button" NAME="Next" VALUE="Next" onClick="MoveNext">
      <INPUT TYPE="button" NAME="Prev" VALUE="Prev" onClick="MovePrev">
      <% IF Request.Form("Login") = "Admin" Then %>
            <INPUT TYPE="Button" Name="Submit" VALUE="Submit Changes"
➥OnClick="Update">
      <%End If%>
      <BR>
      <OBJECT classid="clsid:BD96C556-65A3-11D0-983A-00C04FC29E33"
      ID="AdvancedDataControl1" HEIGHT=1 WIDTH=1>
      </OBJECT>
</BODY>
</HTML>
```

FIG. 25.6
The phone book with
the update.

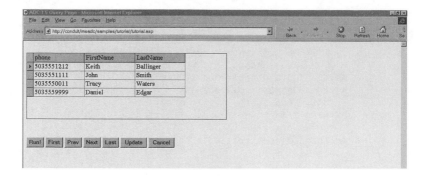

Of course, this example doesn't have any real security, as anyone who knows to log in as
Admin can make changes to the database. A more secure example would have both a login and
a password. You could also have a password on the database itself, and send that information
when setting up the connection to the database.

From Here...

In this chapter, you have examined the Remote Data Services and seen how RDS can help you
create data-bound Web pages. Leveraging your knowledge of ADO, you have seen how to
utilize RDS even further. The applications you can create are endless.

You have also seen some of the limitations of Remote Data Services, most significant of these
being the lack of browser independence. If you use RDS, you are playing in the realm of
Internet Explorer.

However, Remote Data Services offer developers a new level of freedom in building Web pages
driven by data. Using this technology, combined with ASP and Dynamic HTML, there is, literally, very little you cannot have your Web site do.

For related information, please see the following chapters:

- Chapter 24, "Managing Your Database," for more information on database development
  and management.
- Chapter 30, "Application Development for the Corporate Intranet/Extranet," to uncover
  the major issues involved in creating Web-based applications for these two arenas.

Putting It All Together: Creating a Dynamic Database Application

Use the ADO object to Load and update Database Information

Learn how to implement the different ADO objects to connect and extract information from the database and how to use the ADO object to update information in the DataWidget database.

Implement Visual InterDev's Data Control and Data Form Wizard

Utilize the design-time data control to visually create the database connections and create ASPs to administer database information.

Configure Web Site and Application Security Settings

Discover how to control and manage who can access your Web site.

In this chapter, you will convert the Amazing DataWidgets WareHouse Web site from a static Web site into a database-driven Web site. Specifically, you will use the Active Data Object (ADO) to load the DataWidgets product into application-level variables to be used throughout the online catalog system. Database code will be developed to add and remove items from the current inventory. This chapter will also demonstrate how to use Visual InterDev to generate an administration HTML interface that enables new products to be added to the Products table. In addition, I will demonstrate how to control access to the HTML administration interface to control access permissions to the HTML administration interface. ■

Loading the Products Table

The Amazing DataWidget WareHouse Web site provides an online catalog and order entry system. This catalog system was demonstrated in Chapter 19, "Putting It All Together: Creating an Online Registration System." That chapter demonstrated how the catalog information was originally loaded from variables stored in Active Server Pages into application-level variables. If new products needed to be added to the site or product name, description or pricing information changed, the changes would have to be made directly in the ASP code. Now you are going to expand the Web site's functionality by retrieving the information from a database when the application starts. From the user perspective, the site will not change appearance when viewed by a browser. However, the changes will be evident to the Web administrators who are responsible for the site's upkeep and maintenance.

Create the ActiveX Data Object Connection

The first step in retrieving product information from the Amazing DataWidgets database is to establish the ODBC connection to the database. The ActiveX Data Object (ADO) is responsible for establishing the database connection. The ADO object provides a programmable communication mechanism to manage and manipulate database information through the RecordSet object. The RecordSet object gives the programmer the ability to utilize multiple database connections, support stored procedures and triggers, and implement advanced data control and management through multiple cursor types and cache management to support scaleable, distributed Web-based applications.

To use the ADO object, you will create an ASP function called LoadProductsTable. The LoadProductsTable function actually performs two roles. The first role is to retrieve the available catalog information. This information will be used to write what products are currently available for sale on the Web page. Second, the same RecordSet object is going to be used to create a temporary, empty shopping basket for each individual user visiting the site. The session-level variables are needed to enable the ASP code to be modified according to the users' actions. The application-level product listing is needed to remain constant throughout the entire application. This dual approach provides the capability to load application- and session-level variables with just one connection to the database.

To tap into this functionality for DataWidget's Web site, first create the ADO Connection object. Use the CreateObject method to reference the ADO object, as shown in the following example.

```
Set DataConn = Server.CreateObject("ADODB.Connection")
DataConn.Open strODBC
```

This code example creates an object named DataConn to reference an instantiated ADO connection using the CreateObject method. After the connection object is created, the ADO opens the ODBC datasource name represented by the variable strODBC. The Connection object represents a direct interface with a specific datasource to the DataWidgets database. For more information on using the CreateObject method, please see Chapter 12, "Controlling the Server with the Server Object and Using Transaction Processing with the ObjectContext Object."

Next, create `Command` and `Recordset` objects to send commands to the database and store the returned information, as shown in the following snippet:

```
Set cmdConn = Server.CreateObject("ADODB.Command")
Set cmdRS = Server.CreateObject("ADODB.Recordset")
```

The `Command` object is used to provide database command strings that are executed against a datasource. The `Recordset` object is used as a container to store the results of the `Command` object.

Note that the `Recordset` object does not need explicitly defined `Connection` and `Command` objects to retrieve information from the database, as shown above. The `Recordset` object automatically creates a new `Connection` object for every request sent by the `Recordset` object, even if the same connection string is used to establish the database connection. Therefore, in order to maximize your connection resources, the `Connection` object should be used to minimize the amount of database connections created throughout the application.

The `Command` object enables you to explicitly control the ADO object. For example, the following code example creates a SQL statement that selects specific fields from the `Products` table and explicitly defines that the `Command` object is a text-based SQL statement.

```
cmdConn.CommandText = "SELECT ProductName, Description, UnitPrice FROM Products"
cmdConn.CommandType = 1          '=== Evaluates CommandText as a textual
➥definition of a command.
```

After the command string has been set, the following code sets the active datasource connection and opens the instantiated `Recordset` to contain the results of the command string.

```
Set cmdConn.ActiveConnection = DataConn
cmdRS.Open cmdConn, , 0, 1      '=== Constants: adOpenForwardOnly, adLockReadOnly
```

This code generates a forward-only, read-only `Recordset` object.

Note that in order to call the ADO constants by name, the `Adovbs.inc` must be included in the ASP. You can reference the file by using a server-side `include`:

```
<!--#INCLUDE FILE = "adovbs.inc"-->
```

After the `Recordset` is created, you have to test to see if any records have been returned into the `Recordset`. If no records have been returned, the record's `BOF` and `EOF` (begin of file and end of file) properties are `True`, as shown in the following `If...Then` statement.

```
If cmdRS.EOF And cmdRS.BOF Then
     '=== no records
Else
     '=== records found
End if
```

If results are returned into the `Recordset`, the script iterates through the recordset creates a customized user array. The array extracts the `ProductName`, `Description`, and `UnitPrice` fields from the `Recordset` and creates a fourth array item. This last item will represent the amount of each product item the user has ordered.

```
Do While Not cmdRS.EOF
    i = i + 1
    aProductArray(i, 1) = cmdRS("ProductName")
    aProductArray(i, 2) = cmdRS("Description")
    aProductArray(i, 3) = cmdRS("UnitPrice")
    aProductArray(i, 4) = 0
    cmdRS.MoveNext
  Loop
```

After the array is populated, the RecordSet and Connection objects are closed and the entire local array is passed as a variable back to the calling statement:

```
cmdRS.Close
dataconn.Close
LoadProductsTable = aProductArray
```

The entire LoadProductsTable function is displayed in Listing 26.1.

Listing 26.1   Returning a customized *Recordset* via an array.

```
Function LoadProductsTable(strODBC)

    '=== Loads the ProductName, Description and Price Fields from the Product
table
    Set DataConn = Server.CreateObject("ADODB.Connection")
    DataConn.Open strODBC
    Set cmdConn = Server.CreateObject("ADODB.Command")
    Set cmdRS = Server.CreateObject("ADODB.Recordset")
    cmdConn.CommandText = "SELECT ProductName, Description, UnitPrice,
UnitsInStock FROM Products"
    cmdConn.CommandType = 1
    Set cmdConn.ActiveConnection = DataConn
    cmdRS.Open cmdConn, , 0, 1

    If cmdRS.EOF And cmdRS.BOF Then
        '=== no records
    Else
        Dim icount
        cmdRS.MoveFirst
        Do While Not cmdRS.EOF
          icount = icount + 1
          cmdRS.MoveNext
        Loop
        cmdRS.MoveFirst
        ReDim aProductArray(icount, 4)

        Do While Not cmdRS.EOF
          i = i + 1
          aProductArray(i, 1) = cmdRS("ProductName")
          aProductArray(i, 2) = cmdRS("Description")
          aProductArray(i, 3) = cmdRS("UnitPrice")
          aProductArray(i, 4) = 0
          cmdRS.MoveNext
        Loop
```

```
        End If
        cmdRS.Close
        Dataconn.Close
        LoadProductsTable = aProductArray

End Function
```

Now that the `LoadProductsTable` function extracts the customized `RecordSet` variable from the DataWidget's database, you will develop the script to call the function. To implement this new function, call the `LoadProductsTable` function as shown below:

```
Application("aSoftware") = LoadProductsTable(Application("strODBC"))
```

This code creates an application-variable named `aSoftware` and assigns it the array value returned by `LoadProductsTable`. However, you have to trap whether the `LoadProductsTable` function returns an empty recordset. To eliminate the possibility that an empty string will be assigned to the `catalog` array, use the `IsArray` VBScript function to determine the results of the `LoadProductTable` function:

```
Dim aTestArray
aTestArray = LoadProductsTable(Application("strODBC"))
If IsArray(aTestArray) Then
     Application("aSoftware") = aTestArray
     Set aTestArray = Nothing      '=== Destroys array
Else
     Err.Raise (1)                 '=== Generate an error
End if
```

Next, trap any errors that may occur to prevent additional errors from filtering throughout the site. In this situation, you have already created an `error.asp` that accepts various arguments to display errors messages to the user.

```
If Err Then
     page = Request.ServerVariables("SCRIPT_NAME")
     errortype = "Critical"
     errormsg = "A Critical Error has occurred on page " &page &". <BR>Please
contact the System Administrator"
     urlstr="error.asp?errortype=" &Server.URLEncode(errortype) &"&errormsg="
&Server.URLEncode(errormsg)
     Response.Redirect urlstr
End If
```

Now all this logic can be applied together to form the script shown in Listing 26.2.

Listing 26.2   Loading the Recordset values into application- and session-level variables.

```
<%@ LANGUAGE="VBSCRIPT" %>
<% On Error Resume Next
'===================== Procedures =========================
Sub LoadInitValues()
```

continues

Part

V

Ch

26

Listing 26.2   Continued

```
      '=== Load Catalog Values by hand
      Dim aCatalog(2,2)
      aCatalog(1,1) = "Software Components"
      aCatalog(1,2) = "SoftwareCatalog.asp"
      aCatalog(2,1) = "Hardware Components"
      aCatalog(2,2) = "HardwareCatalog.asp"

      '=== Set General variables
      Application("aCatalog") = aCatalog
      Application("strODBC") = "DataWidget"
      Application("iTimeOut") = 30
End Sub

'===================== Begin Application Code =================

Application.Lock
Application("aSoftware") = LoadProductsTable(Application("strODBC"))

If Err Then
      page = Request.ServerVariables("SCRIPT_NAME")
      errortype = "Critical"
      errormsg = "A Critical Error has occurred on page " &page &". <BR>Please
contact the System Administrator"
      urlstr="error.asp?errortype=" &Server.URLEncode(errortype) &"&errormsg="
&Server.URLEncode(errormsg)
      Response.Redirect urlstr
End If

Application.UnLock
'=== Now load the users empty basket
Session("basket")=Application("aSoftware")    '=== Create user's new, but empty
basket
Response.Redirect "main.asp"
%>
```

The application-level variables are used to produce the catalog listing shown in Figure 26.1.

Modifying the Inventory Database

Now it's time to create the database capabilities to handle when a user places an order for a product. You will create two functions to add and delete items from the Inventory table.

Deleting Items from the Inventory

To delete items from the current Inventory table in the DataWidgets database, a DeleteProductInventory function is created to remove the ordered amount from inventory. The DeleteProductInventory function accepts the ODBC connection name, the product name to be deleted, and the amount of items to be deleted. You will build the function using the same Connection, Command, and Recordset objects used in the LoadProductsTable example.

FIG. 26.1

The catalog list is extracted from the ActiveX Data Object.

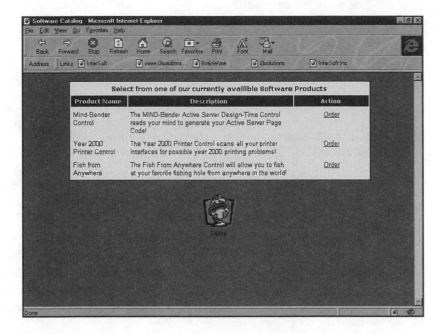

However, there are a couple of differences to be pointed out with this new function. First is obviously the SQL statement. The UPDATE statement is used to find the current value of an existing field and modify the value. In this situation, the UnitsInStock field is being updated for the specific product name:

```
sql = "UPDATE Products Set UnitsInStock = UnitsInStock -"
sql = sql & iAmount & " WHERE ProductName = '" & strProductName & "'"
```

Furthermore, because the RecordSet object does not return any information from the query, the provider automatically closes the recordset. Therefore, the cmdRS.Close command is not needed. The DelteProductInventory function is illustrated in Listing 26.3.

Part

V

Ch

26

Listing 26.3   Deleting products from inventory.

```
Function DeleteProductInventory(strODBC, strProductName, iAmount)
'=== This function delete inventory once an item is ordered
    Set DataConn = Server.CreateObject("ADODB.Connection")
    DataConn.Open strODBC
    Set cmdConn = Server.CreateObject("ADODB.Command")
    Set cmdRS = Server.CreateObject("ADODB.Recordset")
    sql = "UPDATE Products Set UnitsInStock = UnitsInStock -"
    sql = sql & iAmount & " WHERE ProductName = '" & strProductName & "'"
    cmdConn.CommandText = sql
    cmdConn.CommandType = 1
    Set cmdConn.ActiveConnection = DataConn
    cmdRS.Open cmdConn, , 0, 1
    Dataconn.Close
```

continues

Listing 26.3 Continued

```
        If Not Err Then
            ret = True
        End If
        DeleteProductInventory = ret
End Function
```

This listing demonstrates the DeleteProductInventory function that accepts the ODBC string name, the name of the product that is ordered, and how many of that item is ordered. With that information, the function creates a new database connection and deletes the amount of product from the inventory when a user orders an item. It is important to reemphasize that you want to create and release the database connections as needed in the calling code. Your Web sites and applications could possibly have thousands of concurrent users. Let ODBC 3.0 and the Microsoft Transaction Server (demonstrated in Chapter 32, "Putting It All Together: Creating an N-Tier Online Catalog Application") handle the connection pooling for you.

You may be tempted to create a subroutine to perform this inventory functionality because no information is being returned via the Recordset object. However, you actually do want to return whether the function was executed successfully. To call function from the client ASP, use the following code:

```
ret = DeleteProductInventory(Application("strODBC"), strProductName,
iUnitQuantity)
```

To examine the return value, you can check the value of the return value or examine the function inline, as shown below:

```
If DeleteProductInventory(Application("strODBC"), strProductName, iUnitQuantity)
then
    '=== Record is deleted
End If
```

Adding Records to the Database

The AddProductInventory function is used to complement the DeleteProductInventory functionality, but is responsible for adding items to the Inventory database. The AddProductInventory, as shown in Listing 26.4, uses the UPDATE statement to create a query string that adds the amount an amount of an item to the Products table.

Listing 26.4 Creating a function to add inventory via the ADO connection.

```
Function AddProductInventory(strODBC, strProductName, iAmount)
'=== This function adds inventory to the database
    Set DataConn = Server.CreateObject("ADODB.Connection")
    DataConn.Open strODBC
    Set cmdConn = Server.CreateObject("ADODB.Command")
    Set cmdRS = Server.CreateObject("ADODB.Recordset")
```

```
sql = "UPDATE Products Set UnitsInStock=UnitsInStock + "
sql = sql & iAmount & " WHERE ProductName = '" & strProductName & "'"
cmdConn.CommandText =sql
cmdConn.CommandType = 1
Set cmdConn.ActiveConnection = DataConn
cmdRS.Open cmdConn, , 0, 1
Dataconn.Close
If Not Err Then
    ret = True
End If
AddProductInventory = ret

End Function
```

Likewise, the AddProductInventory function can be called using the following code:

```
ret = AddProductInventory(Application("strODBC"), strProductName, iUnitQuantity)
```

To examine the return value, you can check the value of the return value or examine the function inline, as shown below:

```
If AddProductInventory(Application("strODBC"), strProductName, iUnitQuantity)
then
    '=== Record has been added
End If
```

Using Visual InterDev to Access the Data

As you can see, the ADO provides a fully programmable interface to tailor database access to your application needs. However, to speed up development time to create the database access, you can use the visual database tools found in Visual InterDev.

Using Visual InterDev's Design Data Control to Retrieve Records

Visual InterDev uses ActiveX design-time controls to help speed up the development of Active Server code. The database connection features are directly controlled by the Data Command control. To start generating the database code, start a new Web project in Visual InterDev. To start using the design-time controls, a database connection to the current project is needed. This connection is used at runtime to provide a real-time connection to the datasource at design time. This design-time capability enables a direct interface to test and debug your database applications. You will use the Data Command control to generate a function to retrieve the current amount of in-stock items for a particular product.

To add a database connection, right-click the Visual InterDev project folder and select Add Database Connection. A dialog box will appear that enables you to select from an existing file or machine data source or create a new datasource, as shown in Figure 26.2.

Part
V

Ch
26

FIG. 26.2

The Visual InterDev Connection wizard enables you to create a new datasource name or select from an existing database connection.

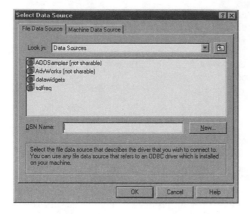

After selecting the DataWidgets datasource, the Connection wizard prompts for information about the data connection. Figure 26.3 illustrates the interface to set the database connection properties, such as the connection and command timeout properties.

FIG. 26.3

The Data Connection dialog box is used to set general properties of the database connection.

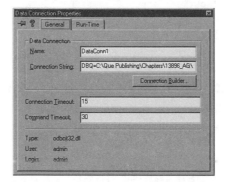

The Run-Time tab of the Data Connection dialog box is used to set the runtime properties of the database connection, as shown in Figure 26.4. The runtime connection properties are used to set and monitor access to the datasource. This information is stored on the Web server and is transmitted to the database source when the data connection is embedded. This is actually an important architecture aspect of access information from the Web server. By enabling the Web server to keep and maintain runtime connection information, the intercepting of database username and permissions is minimized because you don't have to continuously transmit this information over the Internet.

After you enter the connection information, the Connection wizard inserts the database connection information into the Session_OnStart event of the GLOBAL.ASA file, as shown in Figure 26.5.

FIG. 26.4

The Run-Time tab sets the runtime database permissions needed to access the datasource.

FIG. 26.5

The Connection wizard creates the database connection information in the Session_OnStart event of the GLOBAL.ASA file.

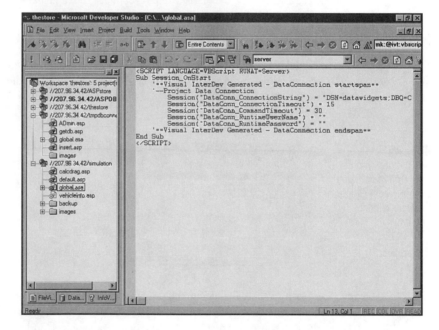

N O T E   Keep in mind that Session objects are only applicable with cookie-compliant browsers and networks. You might want to convert this database connection information into a non-visual ASP file and track information using hidden HTML fields to enable non-cookie-supporting environments to properly access the Web site. ∎

For more information on using the Session object and cookies, please refer to Chapter 13, "Managing the User Session: The Session Object." Listing 26.5 is the listing of using the Session_OnStart event in the GLOBAL.ASA file to set the database connection properties.

Listing 26.5 Setting database connection properties in the *Session_OnStart* event.

```
<SCRIPT LANGUAGE = VBScript RUNAT = Server>
Sub Session_OnStart
    '==Visual InterDev Generated - DataConnection startspan==
    '--Project Data Connection
    Session("DataConn_ConnectionString") = "DSN=datawidgets;DriverId=25;FIL=MS
Access;MaxBufferSize=512;PageTimeout=5;"
    Session("DataConn_ConnectionTimeout") = 15
    Session("DataConn_CommandTimeout") = 30
    Session("DataConn_RuntimeUserName") = ""
    Session("DataConn_RuntimePassword") = ""
    '==Visual InterDev Generated - DataConnection endspan==
End Sub
</SCRIPT>
```

Now that the database connection is created, you can use the design-time Data Control to create ADO connections to the database. To use the Data Command control, right-click an ASP and select Insert ActiveX Control. From the Design-Time tab control, select the Data Command control, as shown in Figure 26.6.

FIG. 26.6

Use the design-time Data Command control to create connections to the Data Widget database.

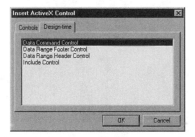

The Data Command Properties dialog box provides a visual interface to set the properties of the data connection. The Control tab, as shown in Figure 26.7, enables you to set the name of the connection, the datasource connection, the type of Command object, and the command string.

You can then use the SQL Builder button illustrated in Figure 26.7 to open Visual InterDev's Query Builder. The Query Builder provides a visual development environment to create and test your database queries. Because you want to generate a query that selects the current amount in inventory, a simple query can be created to extract this information, as shown in the Figure 26.8.

After successfully testing and saving the query, the Data Control wizard generates the Active server Page code, as shown in Listing 26.6, to retrieve the database information from the query created in the Query Designer.

FIG. 26.7
The Data Connection Properties dialog box displays a visual interface to set the properties of the Command object.

FIG. 26.8
The Query Designer provides a visual query building and testing interface.

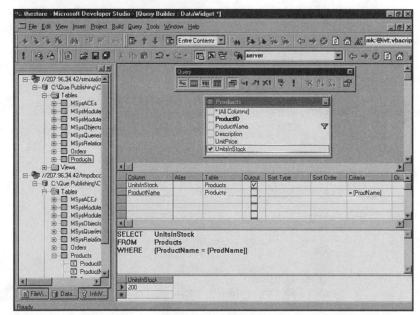

Listing 26.6 Creating ASP code to retrieve database information using the Query Designer.

```
<%
Set DataConn = Server.CreateObject("ADODB.Connection")
DataConn.ConnectionTimeout = Session("DataConn_ConnectionTimeout")
DataConn.CommandTimeout = Session("DataConn_CommandTimeout")
DataConn.Open Session("DataConn_ConnectionString"),
```

continues

Listing 26.6 Continued

```
Session("DataConn_RuntimeUserName"), Session("DataConn_RuntimePassword")
Set cmdTemp = Server.CreateObject("ADODB.Command")
Set DataWidget = Server.CreateObject("ADODB.Recordset")
cmdTemp.CommandText = "SELECT UnitsInStock FROM Products WHERE (ProductName = "
& ProdName & ")"
cmdTemp.CommandType = 1
Set cmdTemp.ActiveConnection = DataConn
DataWidget.Open cmdTemp, , 0, 1
%>
```

Now, you can modify this generated code to create the GetProductInventory function shown in Listing 26.7.

Listing 26.7 Creating a function from the ASP code generated by the Query Designer.

```
Function GetProductInventory(strODBC, strProductName)
'=== This function retrieve that current inventory for a product
    Set DataConn = Server.CreateObject("ADODB.Connection")
    DataConn.Open strODBC
    Set cmdTemp = Server.CreateObject("ADODB.Command")
    Set cmdRS = Server.CreateObject("ADODB.Recordset")
    sql = "SELECT UnitsInStock FROM Products where ProductName= '" &
strProductName & "'"
    cmdTemp.CommandText =sql
    cmdTemp.CommandType = 1
    Set cmdTemp.ActiveConnection = DataConn
    cmdRS.Open cmdTemp, , 0, 1
    If cmdRS.EOF And cmdRS.BOF Then
       ret = 0
    Else
       ret = cmdRS("UnitsInStock")
    End If
    cmdRS.Close
    Dataconn.Close
    GetProductInventory = ret
End Function
```

This GetProductInventory function returns the amount of items in the current inventory. Now, with the previously created AddProductInventory and DeleteProductInventory functions, you can add and remove items from the user's shopping basket and remove the appropriate items from inventory, as shown in Listing 26.8.

Listing 26.8 Adding and removing items from the shopping basket and inventory.

```
Call SetSessionVariables()                          '=== Set session
variables
If ValidateNumber(Session("UserAccountNumber")) Then  '=== Is it a valid
```

```
account number
    aUsersBasket=Session("basket")              '=== Create a local copy of the
users shopping basket
    iProductsOrdered = UBound(aUsersBasket,1)   '=== How many items are there?
    For iCounter = 1 to iProductsOrdered        '=== Start looping through
basket
        iUnitQuantity=clng(aUsersBasket(iCounter,4))    '=== How many items are
ordered?
            If iUnitQuantity > 0 Then
                strProductName = aUsersBasket(iCounter,1)      '=== Get name of
ordered item
                If GetProductInventory("datawidgets", "Mind-Bender Control") > 15
Then   '=== Restock inventory?
                    '=== Everything is fine, remove inventory
                    ret = DeleteProductInventory(Application("strODBC"),
strProductName, iUnitQuantity)
                Else
                    '=== Add more items to inventory
                    ret = AddProductInventory(Application("strODBC"),
strProductName, 25)        '=== Restock items
                    ret = DeleteProductInventory(Application("strODBC"),
strProductName, iUnitQuantity)
                End If
            End If
    Next
    Response.Redirect "summary.asp"              '=== Order is successful print
receipt
Else                                             '=== Invalid Account number
    dim errortype, returnpage, fieldname, urlstr
    errortype="Retry"
    returnpage ="customer.asp"
    fieldname ="Account Number"
    urlstr="error.asp?errortype=" &Server.URLEncode(errortype) & "&returnpage="
&Server.URLEncode(returnpage) & "&fieldname=" &Server.URLEncode(fieldname)
    Response.Redirect urlstr
End If
```

Listing 26.8 first checks to ensure that the account number passes verification. If the account number is correct, the script determines the amount of items in the user's shopping basket. Next, the amount of existing inventory for that product is determined to ensure that enough items are in stock to fill the order. If the in-stock inventory is greater than a minimum threshold value, the products are removed from the inventory. If not enough inventory is available, the AddProductInventory function restocks the inventory and then the items are processed. If the user enters an invalid account number, the error function is used to prompt the user for valid information, as shown in Figure 26.9.

If the account number is valid, the script continues to process all the items in the shopping basket and generates a virtual receipt for the order, as shown in Figure 26.10.

FIG. 26.9
The order is not processed if an invalid account number is entered.

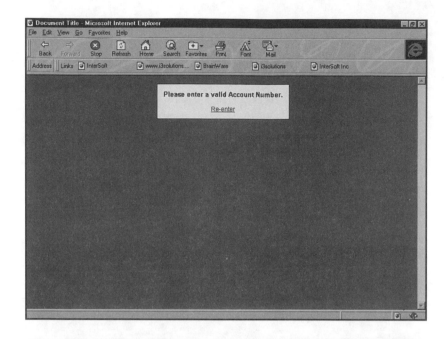

FIG. 26.10
The inventory items are adjusted and the virtual receipt is generated.

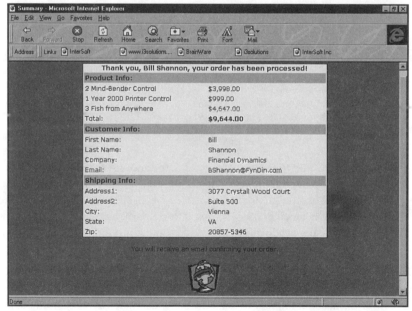

Using the Visual InterDev Forms Wizard to Create the Product Administration Interface

Now that the user interface and ordering processing sections are complete, you are going to create the HTML administration utilities to update the product information. This information can then be updated from any browser, depending on proper authorization. To accomplish this, you will use the Visual InterDev Forms wizard to quickly create Active Server Pages to provide insert, update, and delete capabilities to the Products table.

To create the Web-based administration interface, create a new Visual InterDev project and add the database connection, as described earlier in the chapter. To start the Forms wizard, select New from the File menu. Now select the Data Form Wizard from the File Wizards tab. After naming the file, the first page in the Data Form wizard appears, as shown in Figure 26.11. This page of the wizard prompts for the appropriate datasource connection and for the title that appears on the top of each page.

FIG. 26.11

The Data Form wizard is used to collect the information for the database connection and title of the HTML page.

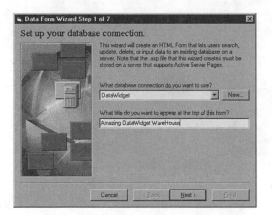

After selecting the DataWidget datasource and entering *Amazing DataWidget WareHouse* for the page titles, the second page of the wizard requests the source type of the housed information. Because you want to provide administration access to the Products table, select Table. After selecting Next, the third page of the Form wizard enables you to select which fields to display on the page, as shown in Figure 26.12.

Page four of the wizard enables you to decide whether the user has the ability to insert, update, or delete the displayed data, or is just allowed to view the data. After selecting the appropriate permissions, the fifth page in the wizard prompts you to decide how the database information will be viewed, as shown in Figure 26.13.

FIG. 26.12
The Forms wizard enables you to select and control the heading names for the displayed fields.

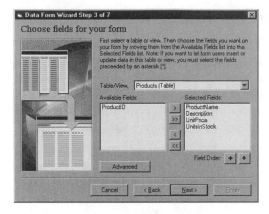

FIG. 26.13
The Data Form wizard enables you to decide whether the table information is going to be displayed in a List view or a Form view.

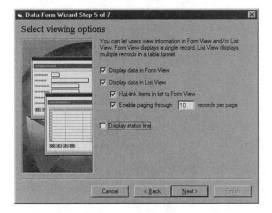

The List view provides a sequential list of records to be displayed on a Web page extracted from a database table. The Form view provides a forms-based view of the individual records.

Finally, the last page of the wizard provides the capability to select a theme. Themes are implemented by using Cascading style sheets (CSSs) to control the look and feel of your site. Keep in mind that all browsers do not support CSS. After you select the theme, the Form Wizard generates three Active Server Pages that are used to display the data.

The List view page, which is shown in Figure 26.14, displays the sequential listing of records in the Product table. From this page, you can systematically navigate through all the records in the Products table.

The List view page, as seen in Figure 26.14, enables you to drill down into the details of a database record by selecting the product number. The drill-down capability enables the user to edit the individual fields in the Form view page, as shown in Figure 26.15. Not only can you edit and update records, but you can also delete, create, and provide filters on the existing data.

FIG. 26.14
The List view provides the capability to sequentially list and filter information.

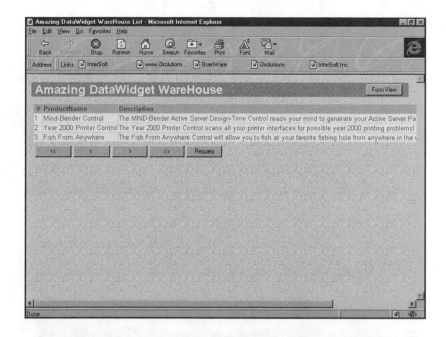

FIG. 26.15
The Form view provides the capability to edit the individual fields in the specific record.

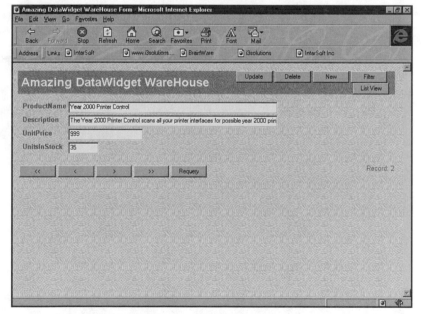

For example, the Amazing DataWidget WareHouse has created a new design-time control that is available for market. The site administrator, as shown in Figure 26.16, uses the Form view to enter the new information. In this example, the CoffeeX ActiveX control is added to the database via the HTML administration page.

If you navigate back to the List view, you will notice that the new item is now displayed in the product list, as shown in Figure 26.17.

FIG. 26.16
The Form view enables new product information to be added to the database.

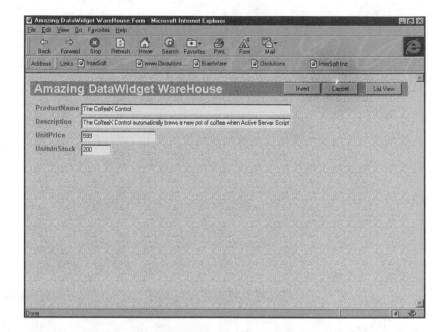

FIG. 26.17
The List view displays the new product information.

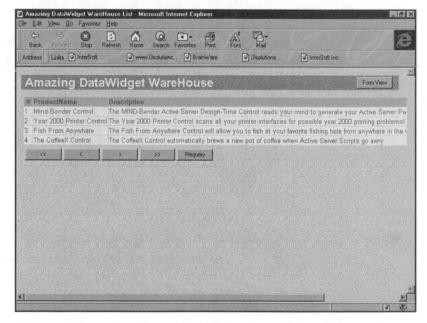

As a result, when new users browse the catalog application, the new CoffeeX control product is displayed in the online catalog and is available for sale. Figure 26.18 displays the new product as it appears in the catalog listing.

FIG. 26.18
The product information is now automatically displayed to new users that browse the site!

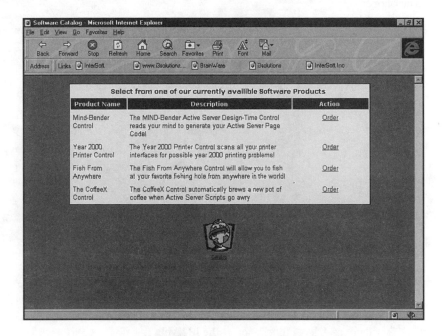

Now the users can seamlessly order the new components without you, the developer, having to change any ASP code on the Web site. Figure 26.19 illustrates two orders for the new CoffeeX control.

If you try to view the List page generated by the Data Form wizard and the following OLE DB error occurs, make sure that a hard coded path statement is not defined in the database connection string.

```
Microsoft OLE DB Provider for ODBC Drivers error '80004005'
[Microsoft][ODBC Microsoft Access 97 Driver] '(unknown)' isn't a valid path.
Make sure that the path name is spelled correctly and that you are connected to
the server on which the file resides.
/ASPDBstoreAdmin/Product AdminList.asp, line 266
```

Controlling Access to the Site

Although the capability to control the information in the Product table provides remote HTML administration from any browser in the world, deciding who has access to change this information is paramount. Likewise, for many intranet sites that need extranet capabilities, the capability to grant and restrict access to their sites is critical to maintaining control over sensitive information. As you saw in Chapter 10, "The Composition of an Active Server Application," there are two ways to provide access to your Web sites: at the Web server level and at the file level.

FIG. 26.19
Active Server Pages place Web site maintenance back into the hands of the content providers.

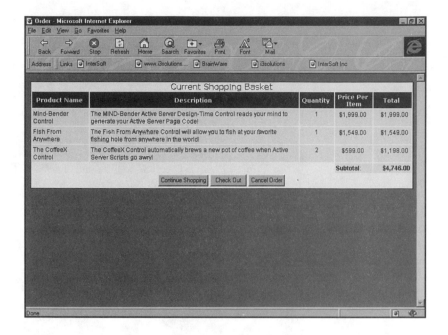

The first layer of control is established through TCP/IP packet filtering at the Web server level. Because you want to enable the database administration site to be maintained from defined IP packets from within the DataWidgets domain and from any external IP addresses, you will not restrict authorization at the IP level.

However, the second layer of control is to regulate the permission of the site at the file level. Typically, when you set up the Internet Information Server, a user name IUSR_machinename is created to represent the Internet guest account. When an anonymous user requests pages from your public site, NT uses this security setting to verify access for the requested files. Therefore, to restrict access to only authorized users or groups, use the NT file permission to administer create and delete user rights. Use the Security tab, as illustrated in Figure 26.20, to remove Internet Guest Account and add the proper group rights for the DataWidget HTML administration site.

Now that the Internet guest account has been removed, when the Internet Information server tries to access this file, the user will be prompted for proper identification. This technique was applied to the Amazing DataWidget WareHouse administration Web site to only enable members of the DataWidgets Operator's group to have access to this site. Now, when any page on the administration Web site is requested, the user is prompted with an authorization dialog box, as shown in Figure 26.21.

FIG. 26.20
Remove the Internet Guest Account to eliminate anonymous access to your site.

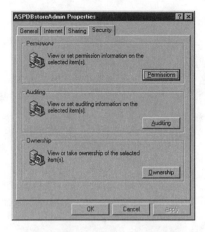

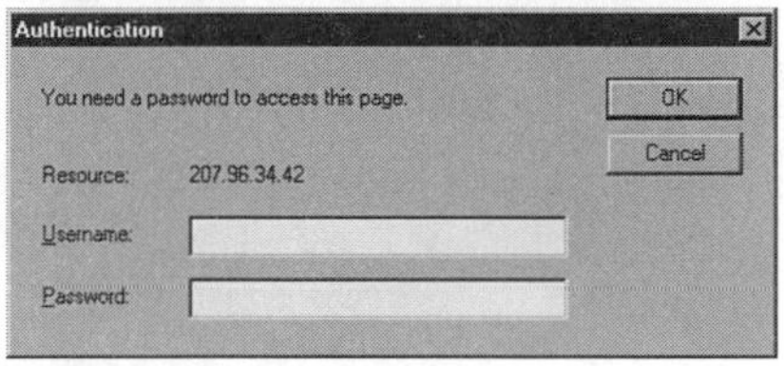

FIG. 26.21
With anonymous access permission removed, the Amazing DataWidgets WareHouse administration site is only accessible to defined users.

Keep in mind that the username and password are being passed in non-encrypted form from the Web browser to the Web server. A potential hacker could intercept the packet and retrieve the NT username and password. To prevent this situation from occurring, only transmit usernames and passwords over a Secure Socket Layer or other encrypted channels. Use the HTTPS server environment variables to ensure information is being transmitted over a secure channel. For more information the server variables, please refer to Chapter 15, "Retrieving User Information: The Request Object."

From Here...

In this chapter, you learned how the ActiveX Data Object is used to add database-driven information on the Amazing DataWidgets WareHouse site. The ADO's Connection object, the Command object, and RecordSet object all work together to provide a robust, light-weight, fully programmable interface to any ODBC-compliant database. In addition to coding the ADO objects by hand, Visual InterDev's design-time Data Command control was used to demonstrate how to use the design-time control to generate Active Server ADO script. Finally, setting access permissions to the Data Widgets administration site was also demonstrated by controlling the user permission at the file level.

Part
V

Ch
26

For related information, please see the following chapters:

- Chapter 28, "Working with the Microsoft Transaction Server," illustrates the use of the Transaction Server to manage components within your ASP applications.

- Chapter 30, "Application Development for the Corporate Intranet/Extranet," demonstrates how to properly use your network topology to create intranet and extranet applications.

- Chapter 31, "Using Internet Information Server 4.0 to Manage Your Web Applications," demonstrates how to use the various features of the Internet Information Server to help manage your sites and applications.

- Chapter 32, "Putting It All Together: Creating an N-Tier Online Catalog Application," demonstrates how to build ActiveX components to create an n-tier distributed application for the Amazing DataWidget WareHouse Catalog.

Active Server Pages and the Enterprise Solution

CHAPTER 27

Visual InterDev: The Active Server Pages Integrated Development Environment

Using Visual InterDev

Visual InterDev provides an integrated development environment for creating, developing, managing, and deploying Active Server Page-based applications.

Interfacing with the Databases

Learn how to use the visual database tools integrated into Visual InterDev to provide both design-time and runtime connections to any ODBC database.

Increase Productivity with Design-Time Controls and Wizards

Expedite development time for your Active Server Page applications by using ActiveX design-time controls and wizards to generate ASP code.

Visual InterDev provides the first integrated development environment for creating Active Server Page applications. Visual InterDev provides a single development environment to help you create your Active Server Page applications and manage the content, various file types needed, database connections, and source control features. This integrated development environment provides the first opportunity for Rapid Application Development (RAD) for Active Server Page applications. This chapter presents an overview of Visual InterDev, so for a more detailed discussion I recommend *Special Edition Using Visual InterDev* from Que. ∎

A Development Environment for Active Server Pages

The joys of tapping into the power and extensibility of Active Server Pages can be quickly doused when you consider that the only Active Server Page development environment is any ASCII-based editor. Although using an ASCII editor enables developers to create pages on a variety of platforms, developers that are accustomed to advanced development environments such as Visual Basic, C++, Delphi, and PowerBuilder find this unacceptable. To prevent the powerful functionality of Active Server Pages from going to waste, Microsoft created Visual InterDev as the Active Server Page development environment.

An Introduction to Visual InterDev

Visual InterDev is actually categorized into two components: the client- and server-side components, as shown in Figure 27.1. The client component is further separated into four modules: The Visual InterDev Client, the Image Composer, the Music Producer, and the Media Manager. The Visual InterDev IDE is the actual development environment used to create Active Server Pages, and it also includes the HTML layout editor, which assists in placing and layering Active controls. The Image Composer, Music Producer, and Media Manager are utilities that help you create your own multimedia aspects to integrate with your Web sites.

FIG. 27.1
The Visual InterDev client and server components.

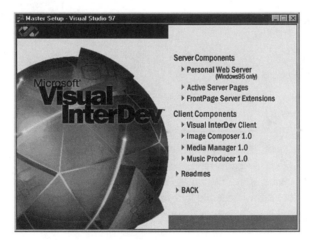

The second component of Visual InterDev is the collection of server-side components. The server-side components consist of the Personal Web Server, Active Server Pages, and the FrontPage extensions. The Personal Web Server enables developers to install an HTTP server on any Windows 95 machine, which gives you the ability to create and test your ASP pages on any machine without having to rely on having the NT Server installed. The Active Server Pages component installs the Active Server engine, which is responsible for processing Active Server scripts on the HTTP server. The FrontPage extensions are used to establish the communication link between the requesting client development tools and the Web server. This communication link is needed to enable both FrontPage developers and Visual InterDev developers to manage the same project files, directories, and permissions on the server over the stateless HTTP protocol.

FIG. 27.2
The Visual InterDev integrated development enviroment.

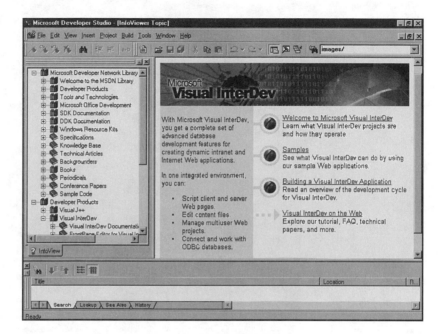

Keep in mind that in most situations, content creators such as the marketing and human resources departments will use a GUI-centered HTML creation tool such as FrontPage. Application developers will create ASP scripts in a more code-centric development tool such as Visual InterDev to add the logic needed for the ASP application. Even though these two tools are tailored to meet the demands of two different groups, the projects created in FrontPage and Visual InterDev are completely interchangeable, as shown in Figure 27.3. A Visual InterDev project is a FrontPage web and, conversely, a FrontPage web is a Visual InterDev project.

Creating Projects and Workspaces

Visual InterDev uses two different motifs to manage projects. Visual InterDev and Active Server Pages identify *projects* as individual applications on the Web server that reside in a virtual directory. A Visual InterDev project consists of creating the virtual directories of Active Server projects on both the Web server and the client development workstation. These Active Server projects are the same format as, and can be accessed by, FrontPage clients. A Visual InterDev *workspace* is created on the client machine to help house and manage multiple ASP projects within one environment, as shown in Figure 27.4.

FIG. 27.3
A Visual InterDev project can access a FrontPage web and vice versa.

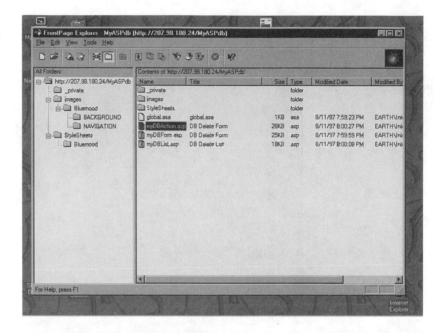

FIG. 27.4
Visual InterDev can manage multiple projects from one developer workspace on the client's machine.

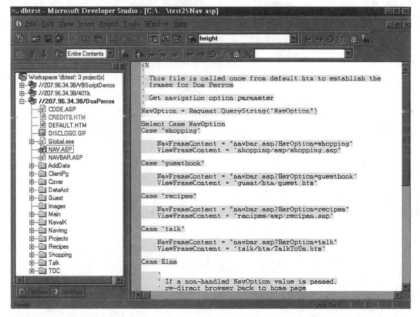

This capability to have multiple projects open at the same time is not just limited to Active Server Page or FrontPage projects; it can also accommodate Visual C++ and Visual J++ projects in the same workspace. This multiple-project development environment enables you to work on your Java applets and COM components without having different development environments open. Figure 27.5 shows an Active Server project and a Java project open in Visual InterDev.

FIG. 27.5
Visual InterDev can manage and house various projects within the same IDE.

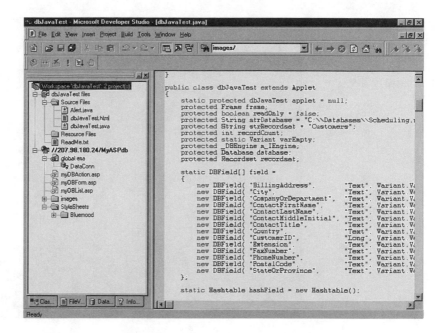

To create a Visual InterDev project, select File | New from the Visual InterDev toolbar. From this menu, most of the productivity features can be accessed for all Visual Studio projects. Remember, Visual Studio is the collection of all the Microsoft Visual Development tools, whereas Visual InterDev is part of the Visual Studio collection that is used to create Active Server Page applications. The New dialog box that appears enables you to select the different options available: New Files, New File Wizards, New Projects, New Workspaces, and New Other Documents. Each category consists of subcatogies that enable you to drill down into detailed items. For example, to create a new ASP Web project, select the Web Project Wizard from the Projects tab, as shown in Figure 27.6.

The Visual InterDev Environment

Visual InterDev is comprised of different panes, as illustrated in Figure 27.7. Each pane has a specific purpose. The Project window is responsible for representing a hierarchical navigation display of source code files, help files, and database objects. The Project window is comprised of three views: the Info View, the Data View, and the File View. The Info View displays the available help document for any Visual Studio tool installed on the desktop. The Data View displays the live, design-time ODBC connections. The File View represents the physical file structure of the current Web project.

Part
VI

Ch
27

FIG. 27.6
Visual InterDev uses wizards to reduce redundant coding and help speed development.

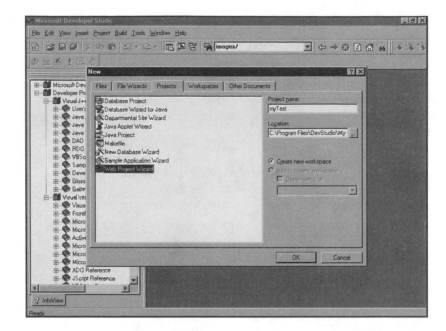

FIG. 27.7
The Project window, the Document window, and the Output window provide different interfaces to the Visual Studio project.

Project window

Document window

Output window

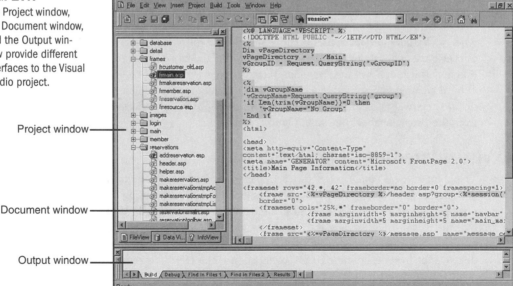

The Document window is basically an enhanced version of Notepad. The Document window supports color highlighting to help differentiate between standard HTML and ASP script. By default, ASP script is highlighted in yellow.

The Project window provides a familiar Explorer organization model of the various project items needed for the Web application. The Project window is comprised of three views: the File View, the Data View, and the Info View. The File View, as shown in Figure 27.8, represents the physical file structure of the current project and is the default tab when a new project is opened. The File View uses folders to create logical storage locations to help manage the project files.

FIG. 27.8
The File View organizes the physical file systems for your Visual Studio projects.

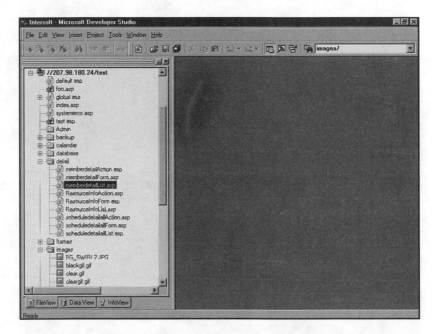

The Data View window also provides a hierarchical organization of database objects. Not only does Visual InterDev provide database access at runtime, but the Data View window also provides design-time access to any heterogeneous datasource via ODBC. This interface provides direct design-time access to any ODBC data storage unit without relying on external native database interfaces to access the data store, as shown in Figure 27.9.

The exciting feature of the Data View is that the listed objects are a *live* connection to the datasource. This real-time connection enables you to have direct access to the structure and actual data within the database. For example, Figure 27.10 illustrates executing a query from an Access database and directly viewing the results.

FIG. 27.9

The Data View provides a design-time connection to any ODBC database.

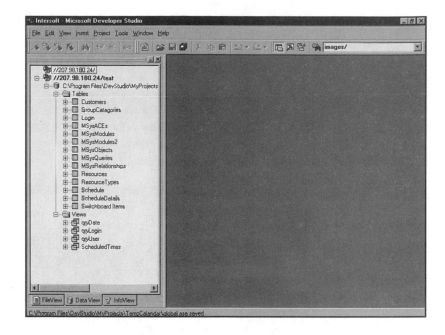

FIG. 27.10

The Data View provides real-time access to the information and structure of the data source.

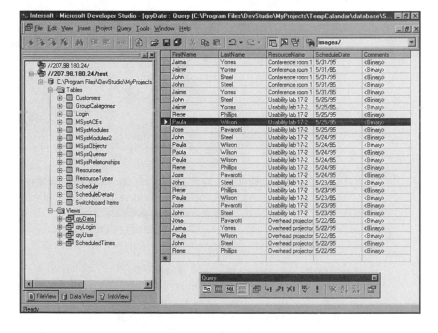

The Info View tab displays the Visual Studio documentation, as shown in Figure 27.11. The Info View tab is the default view when you open Visual InterDev. This view is a convenient storage location for the multiple help files that are needed when you create Internet-based applications. It is also a warehouse for all Visual Studio help files.

FIG. 27.11
The Info View provides a central location for storing reference files for the multitude of technologies needed for Web-based applications.

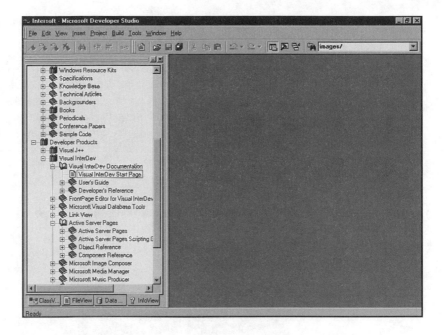

Visual Database Tools

Although Visual InterDev does a good job of managing and organizing the multitude of different files needed for Web-based applications, its real power is captured in the integration of the visual database tools. Visual InterDev provides a rich set of database management tools that come integrated as a part of Visual Studio.

The shared database tools provide a common interface point for data access. Furthermore, they prevent developers from installing the native database administration tools on the workstations. This direct database interface is centered on the Data View tab of the Project window. The Data View, as shown in Figure 27.10, provides real-time information about database objects and properties. Not only is the Data View good for displaying information about the database and its objects, but it is also integrated with the Query Designer and the Database Designer. The Query Designer enables you to graphically build and test queries on the database. The Database Designer provides a visual interface for performing sophisticated database development, management, and administration. The combination of these tools provides a powerful developer interface for managing connections to any ODBC-compliant database.

The Integrated Data View

The Data View is created in the Project window after a database connection is created for the application. The Data View provides a visual representation of the active database objects for the project. Notice that the visual interface is similar to the graphical user interface found in Microsoft Access or SQL Server Enterprise Manager. Through this interface, you can visually design and test queries; directly insert, update, or delete data (permission depending); and display relationships between tables to any ODBC-compliant datasource.

To create the Data View tab, insert a database connection into the Web project by selecting New Database Item from the Insert menu. Visual InterDev will prompt for a datasource name. The datasource name (DSN) provides parameters to the ODBC driver manager to establish a connection to a database. The DSN is stored in one of two connections. If the information is stored in a file, the DSN is a File Data Source. If the datasource is stored within the Registry, the DSN is a Machine Data Source. The File Data Source generates a DSN-free connection, enabling greater flexibility for developers with the same drivers installed on their machines to access the same database. The Machine Data Source connection must be physically configured on the calling system. Figure 27.12 shows this configuration.

FIG. 27.12

Use a File or Machine Data Source to insert a data connection in an Active Server Page.

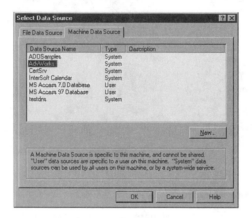

After you establish a live connection to a database, the Data View can be used to explore all database objects in your database connection. This enables you to not only drill down through the database structures and view the database properties, but also to view and manipulate data directly by opening views or tables or executing queries. Right-clicking on an object exposes its shortcut menu to enable further manipulation of an object. For example, right-clicking the Tables folder exposes the available table options, such as Open, Design, New Trigger, New Table, Copy, Delete, Docking View, Hide, and Properties.

The Query Designer

One of the most exciting aspects of Visual Studio and Visual InterDev is the integration of the Visual Database tools. The Visual InterDev database tools establish a live, design-time connection to any ODBC-compliant database. The Query Designer enables you to design, execute, and save queries using a graphical format similar to that found in Microsoft Access, as shown in Figure 27.13. Because the database connection established is a live database connection, you can directly edit, insert, and delete information in a database.

Furthermore, Visual InterDev enables you to directly create, edit, and modify database objects, such as tables, triggers, and stored procedures, at design time. When you make changes to the existing database schema, a temporary schema is created. This temporary schema enables you to test a new database scheme before you actually change the real database schema. Alternatively, you have the option to save the changed scripts that create the new database structure. This is particularly useful if you do not have the proper permission to change the structure of the database.

FIG. 27.13
The Query Designer provides drag-and-drop query creation techniques to any OBDC-compliant database.

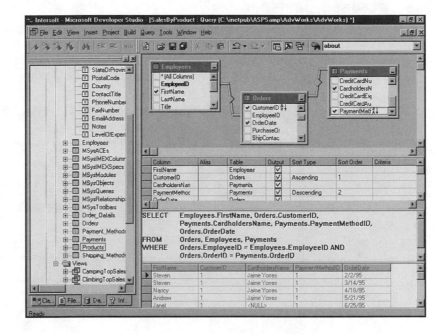

The Query Designer consists of four panes: the Diagram pane, the Grid pane, the SQL pane, and the Results pane. The Diagram pane is used to display the tables in your database. You can use the Query Designer to manipulate database tables by dragging the table from the Data View onto the Diagram pane.

After the table is placed in the Diagram pane, the table's fields are available database field names. Once the items are selected, these fields are returned from the executed query. The Diagram pane also enables you to create relationships between tables. Following this similar drag-and-drop metaphor, joins can be created by dragging the fields from one table onto the fields in another table. The Grid pane is used to display the selected or output fields in a columnar format. The SQL pane displays the SQL statement in SQL format. After you run and test the query, the Results pane displays the results of the executed query in a spreadsheet-like display.

The interesting point about the Query Designer is that because these four panes are synchronized, you are not limited to using one particular query creation pane to create SQL statements. The synchronized panes update automatically to reflect any changes in another pane. For example, if you build a query by selecting columns in the Diagram pane, the SQL window

Part
VI

Ch
27

automatically constructs the resulting SQL statement. If the field name from the SQL string is deleted in the SQL pane, the Diagram and Grid panes automatically remove the same field from their panes.

The Database Designer

The third component of the Visual Database tools is the Database Designer. The Database Designer enables you to directly create, edit, and delete SQL Server 6.5 database components using *database diagrams*. The database diagrams provide a method to visually represent tables, columns, and relations for the whole or part of a database, as illustrated in Figure 27.14.

FIG. 27.14

The Database Designer enables SQL Server database structures to be directly manipulated and modified.

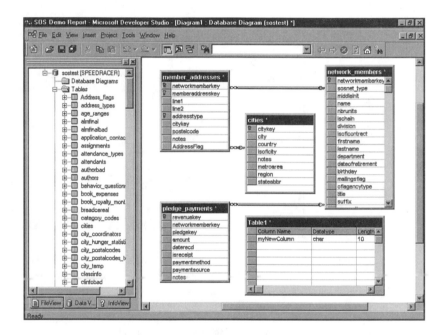

This visual representation provides developers with two main database development features without having to leave the Visual InterDev development environment. The first feature of the database diagrams is the capability to create a visual understanding of the database schema without having to reverse-engineer a schema using external tools such as ErWin or S-PowerDesigner. The second and often overlooked advantage of using database diagrams is the capability to temporarily change the structure of the database and experiment with the altered database without modifying the actual database structure.

For example, if the Database Designer is used to modify the structure of the database, the changes are not made to the underlying database until the database diagram is closed and saved. This temporary database diagram enables you to develop and optimize various database schemas according to your development needs. The Database Designer provides further flexibility to change the database diagram by presenting three options to the developer: save the changes to the underlying database, disregard the proposed changes, or save the

Transact-SQL code. The generation of the Transact-SQL code is of particular importance in a team development environment.

Typically, the application developers do not have the database rights to change the structure of the database. The generation of the Transact-SQL code provides a convenient means to save the change script and pass it along to the database administrator. Remember, the previous two tools, the Data View and Query Designer, are designed to connect with any ODBC-compliant databases. The Database Designer, however, is focused specifically on creating and administering a SQL Server 6.5 database.

Data Form Wizards

The Data Form Wizard reproduces the data-binding concept of attaching a database field to a client-side object, such as a text box, multi-line edit box, or combo box. However, remember that this data binding is not a consistent connection as in traditional applications. The Data Form Wizard simply associates an HTML text box with a given field in a database and updates that field only on a Submit event in the HTML. The Data Form Wizard creates a total of three Active Server Pages that provide the add, edit, delete, and filter functionality that is needed for most basic database applications. The Data Form Wizard accomplishes this by generating a List page, a Form page, and a Filter page after requiring the developer to complete a series of steps, as shown in Figure 27.15.

FIG. 27.15
The Data Form Wizard generates ASP to provide edit, update, insert, and delete functionality.

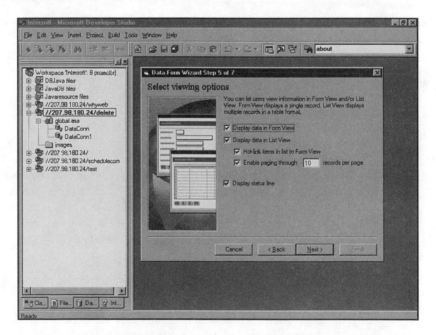

The List page displays the results of a database query in a list form on an HTML page. The List page enables the user to drill down to the Form page to view the details of a selected record. The Filter page enables the user to tailor his list according to customized input. The real usefulness of Visual InterDev is that it not only creates the Active Server Pages for database access and application workflow, but it also enables you to modify the wizard-generated Active Server code to further tailor and customize your application. Furthermore, the Visual InterDev Wizard Software Developer's Kit (SDK) can be used to design your own wizards to meet your company- or technology-specific development needs. The Wizard SDK is available at the Microsoft Web site at www.microsoft.com/VInterDev.

Database Design-Time Controls

In addition to providing an environment for inserting and manipulating client-side ActiveX controls into a HTML page, Visual InterDev provides controls that are specifically tailored to be used at design time. A design-time ActiveX control represents a code object that creates Active Server code based on a wizard-like approach. Design-time controls are analogous to wizards because they provide a visual interface for generating ASP code. But unlike wizards, design-time controls do not require a sequential navigation of steps to complete the intended task. The design-time controls are also different from the wizards because a design-time control focuses on creating code for a particular section of a Web page, whereas the wizards often focus on creating one or more related pages, as demonstrated with the Data Form Wizard.

The three database design-time controls that ship with InterDev are the Data Command, Data Range Header, and Data Range Footer, as shown in Figure 27.16.

FIG. 27.16
Design-time controls
create specific code
modules within an
Active Server Page.

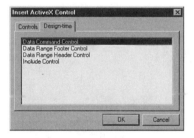

The Data Command control writes the Active Server script that creates a RecordSet object based on the Active Data Object (ADO) on the Microsoft Internet Information Server. The ADO is a logical combination of the RDO and DAO object models that have been shipping with Visual Basic for some time. The ADO object model has been specifically optimized for database access over the Web and provides an object model developers can program against to meet the specific needs of their application.

The Data Range Header creates an ADO RecordSet object and begins a loop method to move through the record in the result set.

The Data Range Footer is used with the Data Range Header to complete the loop method started by the Data Range Header control to cycle through the recordset. Visual InterDev extends its versatility by enabling third-party vendors to develop and distribute their own ActiveX design-time controls. Any tool that can create ActiveX controls, such as Visual Basic 5.0, Visual C++, or Borland's Delphi, can create the design-time controls.

To insert a design-time ActiveX control, right-click an ASP file and click Insert ActiveX Control. At this point you can either insert an ActiveX control onto the Web page that will get downloaded to the client browser, or you can insert a design-time ActiveX control that will be used only at design time to automatically create a server-side script. Because all the design-time controls center on the Data Command control, choose it from the Design-Time Control tab. The Object Editor then displays the Design window and a property sheet to set the properties of the control, such as the Name, Data Connection, Command Type, Command Text, and SQL Builder, as shown in Figure 27.17.

FIG. 27.17
Design-time controls generate ASP code using the Query Designer interface.

After a data connection is established, you can use the Query Builder, as mentioned above, to create and test a query. After closing the Query Builder window, the Data Command control creates the Active Server script that creates the database connection and cycles through the result set based on your query. The important thing to remember is that no ActiveX runtime component is needed to display the results of the database query. The Active Server processes the database request and sends only HTML to the client, thus eliminating any platform or browser dependence.

Productivity Features

The Visual Database tools provide a direct interface for manipulating database objects that was missing from traditional application development tools. Visual InterDev provides several productivity features to extend its functionality for creating database-driven Web applications. Developers can use existing wizards or components, or build their own authoring wizards and components using tools such as Visual Basic to develop applications with unique or business-specific needs.

An Active Server script can be added to a page in one of three ways. The first way to add a script onto the page is to simply type the Active Server script in the Document window. The second way to add an Active Server script to a page is through the use of design-time controls. Design-time controls are ActiveX controls that are run at design-time, instead of runtime. From a functional aspect, design-time controls are analogous to wizards, except that design-time controls are focused on generating smaller sections of Active Server script within a page instead of complete pages. The third method to add an Active Server script to your Web application is to use a wizard. Wizards display a series of panels that solicit information from the developer. When finished, the wizard generates one or more complete Active Server Pages.

Visual InterDev ships with seven wizards that minimize the development time that must be focused on setting up sites, projects, and databases. The Web Project Wizard creates and manages a Visual InterDev project on a server. The Template Page Wizard creates a page based on a template or theme and adds the page to the current project. You can create custom themes according to your own corporate standards. A *theme* is the visual combination of images, layout, bullets, and line treatment that gives a site a particular look and feel.

The Template Site Wizard creates a site based on the selected templates and themes. The Department Site Wizard creates a customized site at the department level within your organization. The New Database Wizard creates and administers a SQL Server database and inserts a data connection into your InterDev project. The Input Wizard creates Active Server Pages that are specifically designed to enable users to insert information into your database application. The Data Range Builder Wizard creates Active Server Pages that enable users to search, update, insert, or delete records in any ODBC-compliant database (see Figure 27.18).

FIG. 27.18
The Data Range Builder
Wizard generates Active
Server code to display
records returned from a
database query.

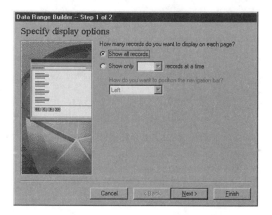

The Script Wizard

The Script Wizard provides a visual interface for generating client- and server-side VBScript and JavaScript. The Script Wizard examines all the objects on an HTML page and determines the objects' properties, methods, and events. These objects can then be tied into the HTML object model to become an integrated part of the HTML page. For example, the text in HTML intrinsic text boxes can be set to a specific value every time a page loads by using the Window.OnLoad event. To activate the Script Wizard, right-click an open Active Server Page in the Visual InterDev editor. Alternatively, selecting the Script Wizard option from the Visual InterDev View menu also starts the Script Wizard (see Figure 27.19).

This Script Wizard is the same Script Wizard that comes with the ActiveX Control Pad and FrontPage editors.

FIG. 27.19
The Script Wizard can be used to produce client and server VBScript and JavaScript.

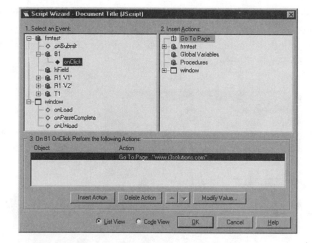

The Visual InterDev Editor

The Visual InterDev default editor (see Figure 27.20) provides a text-based interface to code the application logic into your Active Server applications. This text-based editor provides an equivalent to an intelligent Notepad interface, similar to the source code editor found in FrontPage. The Visual InterDev Editor provides color-coding to help you easily separate ASP scripts from standard HTML tags. The Visual InterDev Editor is also able to read the HTML tags to provide shortcut menus when you right-click over code items such as design-time ActiveX controls.

FIG. 27.20
The Visual InterDev Editor provides access to HTML and ASP script in an ASCII-based environment.

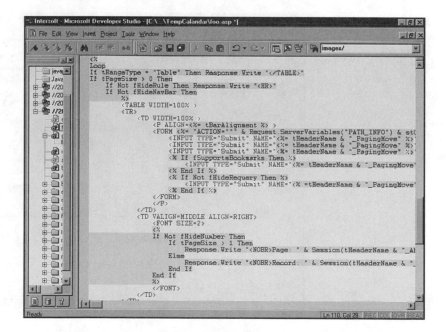

Part
VI
Ch
27

The Visual InterDev Editor is not the only editor available to create Active Server Pages. Visual InterDev enables you to create and edit HTML or ASP code from any editor. You can import existing code from other locations and activate any editor of your choice by using the Open With option, as shown in Figure 27.21.

FIG. 27.21
Visual InterDev enables you to use the editor of your choice to create and edit your content.

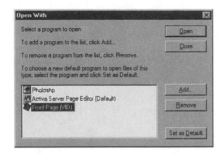

HTML Layout Control Editor

Visual InterDev also integrates the Layout Control Editor into the Visual InterDev IDE. The Layout Control Editor provides a drag-and-drop interface for adding ActiveX controls to a page, and a forms-based motif for controlling properties, methods, and events of an object within the page. Furthermore, the Layout Control Editor provides the familiar look and feel environment that developers are used to in Visual Basic, as you can in Figure 27.22. However, it requires either the Internet Explorer browser or an ActiveX plug-in when viewed with other browsers.

FIG. 27.22
Visual InterDev incorporates the Layout Control Editor for managing ActiveX controls on a page.

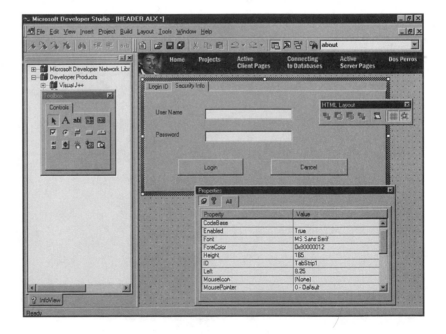

Integrated File Management   Visual InterDev provides excellent file management capabilities by providing hooks into any source code control mechanism, such as Visual SourceSafe or PVCS. The "check-in" and "check-out" capabilities are mandatory for team-based development and are particularly useful in Web-based application development. Because Web development is a file-based delivery system, tighter permissions and controls on file management are critical. This capability to roll back changes to previous file versions or prevent files from being overwritten is especially important when you consider the new format of the Web application development team. The new Web development team is more than the traditional project managers, application developers, and network engineers, but now includes content creators, graphic artists, and multimedia specialists.

To regulate file management, Visual InterDev uses the combination of the FrontPage Server extensions and HTTP to create and maintain file permissions on file transfer capabilities to the Web server. The FrontPage Server extensions are installed on the Internet Information Server to enable Visual InterDev and FrontPage clients to create a connection to the Web server. The FrontPage extensions are used to provide administration features needed to manage Web projects. For example, the FrontPage Server extensions are used to track who has the most recent working copy of a document. Visual InterDev uses HTTP to transfer information between the Visual InterDev client and the server. Visual InterDev also enables you to use SSL to encrypt your Active Server Pages as you post changes to the Web server.

When you create a Web project in Visual InterDev, you are creating a virtual directory on the Internet Information Server. This virtual directory represents an Active Server Page application. Not only are you creating a directory structure on the hosting Web server, but you are also mimicking that directory structure on your local machine. The local directory structure is used as a temporary cache to hold the files and reduce download times. This local caching feature is different from the way a FrontPage client interfaces with the Web server. When a FrontPage client interacts with the Web server, the FrontPage client only loads the page into memory on the FrontPage client.

A FrontPage project can be opened by a Visual InterDev client and a Visual InterDev project can be opened by a FrontPage client. This multi-product editing capability is needed to provide access to the same information between the content creators and application developers. FrontPage, as shown in Figure 27.23, is targeted at the content creators and Visual InterDev is targeted at application developers.

Visual InterDev provides full drag-and-drop functionality to help maintain and organize the files on your site. You can also import or add files or entire folders into Visual InterDev projects. One of the design features of Visual InterDev is the capability to house multiple project types within the same workspace. This means your Web project can consist of Java applets and entire Visual J++ and Visual C++ applications. This feature is a direct result of the fact that Visual InterDev is part of Visual Studio, Microsoft's suite of visual design tools. This capability to house different projects within the same IDE enables you to develop your COM-based components, Java applets, and Active Server Pages without opening three different development environments.

FIG. 27.23
FrontPage is tailored for
content creators,
whereas Visual InterDev
is targeted for
application developers.

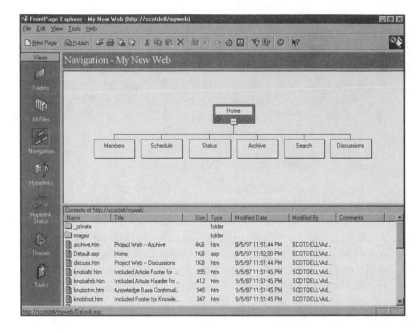

FIG. 27.23
FrontPage is tailored for
content creators,
whereas Visual InterDev
is targeted for
application developers.

The Link View Furthermore, once all your files have been imported to the project, use the
Link View tools to display the valid and broken links from a page. For example, Figure 27.24
illustrates the Link View of the Intel Web site.

FIG. 27.24
The Link View tools
analyze the site for
broken HTML links.

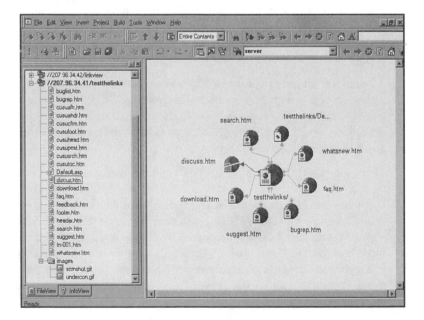

After you save the files, you can view the pages in a variety of ways. The files can be viewed directly within the Project window as the Document window is transformed into the Internet Explorer viewer. Alternatively, Visual InterDev enables you to browse the page from outside Visual InterDev by using the Browse With Preview option. You can configure Visual InterDev to launch any HTML browser to view your content.

Microsoft Image Composer

The Microsoft Image Composer provides a fully featured image editor that enables you to create and manipulate graphics. The Image Composer, shown in Figure 27.25, provides a straightforward approach to image design that is found in traditional imaging tools. The Image Composer is based on a technology called *sprites*. Sprite technology treats each image within an image as its own separate object that has transparency information built in. This transparency feature enables images to be easily combined and merged to form a collective picture without having to understand the details of channels or layering found in many editing tools.

FIG. 27.25

The Image Composer enables you to create exciting images tailored for Web-site designs.

The Microsoft Image Composer is loaded with a wide variety of imaging tools and utilities that are essential for delivering high-quality images. These tools provide a full range of image manipulation capabilities that enable you to arrange images or spites with ease. Additional functionality is found in the built-in art effects, which enable you to generate exciting images that catch the user's eye by providing features such as embossing, charcoal, stained glass, and chrome effects. Furthermore, the Image Composer enables you to use many of the third-party imaging plug-ins that exist for Adobe Photoshop to add extract functionality not found natively in the Image Composer.

However, the reason the Image Composer ships with Visual InterDev is that it is tailored to meet many of the requirements needed for creating images for the Web. The Image Composer saves the spites in JPG and GIF (interlaced and transparent) formats and displays the created image exactly how it would be displayed on the Web page.

Microsoft Music Producer

The Microsoft Music Producer, shown in Figure 27.26, is a client tool that is shipped with Visual InterDev. It enables you to compose your own music score for Web sites or other multimedia interfaces. The Music Producer enables you to combine different music themes to meet the custom nature of your Web site or presentation by enabling you to control the different themes, keys, personalities, and instruments that make up your composition. Not only can you change the feel of the music, but you can also mix the instrumentation as desired. This mixing enables you to control the effects of your composition. For example, not only can you control the volume of your composition, but you can also control the strength of each instrument within the composition.

FIG. 27.26

The Music Producer enables custom-created music based on different themes, instruments, and mixing capabilities.

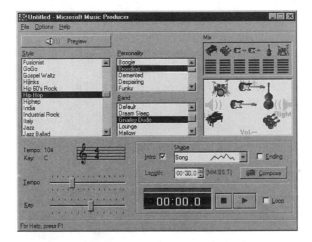

Microsoft Media Manager

The Microsoft Media Manager provides a centralized storage and indexing location for various media files and other data files. In addition, the Media Manager enables you to create annotations for the media files. These annotations are used to help maintain comments and organize and catalog the media. Once the Media Manager is installed, the Media Manager creates an annotation database that stores the user-defined image properties. The Media Manager is directly integrated into the Window Explorer to provide thumbnail images of the files and the ability to simply right-click the media file to expose its annotations. These annotations also stay with the image even if the image is moved or renamed.

From Here...

This chapter quickly pointed out many of the developer specifics of Visual InterDev. One of the most exciting aspects of Visual InterDev is the Visual Database tools. Clearly, as applications are transitioned to the Web, the tight integration with database development tools is essential for minimizing development time. The Data View within Visual InterDev is primarily responsible for managing the database connections. The Data View is complemented by the addition of the Query Designer. The Query Designer provides a graphic interface to create, edit, and test queries. Furthermore, design-time ActiveX controls and wizards help speed development time by generating Active Server script.

For related information, please see the following chapters:

- Chapter 28, "Working with the Microsoft Transaction Server," illustrates the use of the Transaction server to manage components within your ASP applications.
- Chapter 30, "Application Development for the Corporate Intranet/Extranet," demonstrates how to properly use your network topology to create intranet and extranet applications.
- Chapter 31, "Using Internet Information Server 4.0 to Manage Your Web Applications," walks you through the new features of Internet Information Server 4.0.

Working with the Microsoft Transaction Server

There has been a lot of discussion in the client/server industry over the past few years about "second generation" and "three-tier" architectures. These are two different terms for the same application infrastructure. This is an architecture in which the application's processing is not divided into the traditional two parts, the front-end user interface and the back-end database, but into at least three

Distributed Transaction Processing

Distributed transaction processing involves spreading the logical and business rule processing over multiple computers. This chapter shows you how this works, and how it requires you to design your applications differently from traditional client/server applications.

Microsoft's Transaction Server

Microsoft recently released its own Transaction Server for use in building distributed transaction architectures. I'll dig in to how Transaction Server works, and how it uses Microsoft's Distributed Common Object Model (DCOM) technology to provide a transparent platform for building distributed applications.

Active Server Pages and Transaction Server

One of the key advantages offered by Microsoft's Transaction Server is the capability to build modules using Visual Basic (along with Microsoft's other development languages, including Visual C++ and Visual J++) that can be easily called from Active Server Pages. This enables you to distribute some of the processing required for your ASP application onto other servers within your organization. I'll look at what is involved in integrating Active Server Pages with Transaction Server.

separate and distinct parts. There are several reasons given for why this application architecture is superior to the original client/server model, such as:

- *Scalability.* The capability of an application architecture to scale up to hundreds of simultaneous users.

- *Manageability.* The ease with which problems can be isolated, updates distributed, and configurations managed.

- *Transparency.* The capability to switch server processing from one particular computer to another, as dictated by scheduled or unexpected system outages.

One of the key differences between traditional, two-tier client/server models and second generation, three-tier (also known as *n*-tier, where *n* is any number greater than two) client/server architectures is in the use of what is known as *middleware*. Some of the most popular kinds of middleware are *transaction monitors* and *object request brokers* (ORB). Microsoft's Transaction Server is a combination of these two technologies, providing you with a flexible and powerful middleware component that can be used to build very large-scale distributed-processing applications with minimal coding and configuration effort on your part.

N O T E   A transaction monitor is used to manage database access and to control transactional consistency for data-entry type applications. An object request broker manages services that are distributed across one or more computers, providing applications with a single service to connect to, which then provides the applications with access to other services in a transparent manner. This frees the application from the constraint of having to know where within the network each service it needs to use is located. Both of these technologies will be explained in further detail later in the chapter. ■

N O T E   The typical three-tier architecture is composed of the following three tiers:

- The *presentation tier*, which consists primarily of the user interface running on the desktop computer. This tier would typically be built using languages designed for creating user interfaces, such as Visual Basic, PowerBuilder, and Delphi.

- The *business-logic tier*, which consists of shared application processing logic modules running on one or more application servers. Each of these application servers is connected to multiple desktop computers. In the past, modules in this tier would typically be built using Visual C++, working with either an object request broker or a transaction monitor. Now, with tools like Microsoft's Transaction Server, components in this tier can easily be built with languages such as Visual Basic and Delphi.

- The *data server tier*, also known as the database server. There is usually one database server serving multiple application servers. If there are multiple database servers, they are normally spread out over a large geographical area with the common data replicated between them. This would typically be an enterprise-scale database server such as SQL Server, Oracle, Sybase, or Informix. ■

This chapter takes an in-depth look at Transaction Server, how it works, and how you can use it in building applications. I'll also discuss what's involved in using Transaction Server with Active Server Pages, and what considerations need to be taken into account when building Visual Basic objects that can be integrated into Transaction Server for use with Active Server Pages to provide a large, distributed application. In addition, I'll look at how Transaction Server can be integrated into a Web site to provide the capability to build an integrated enterprise-wide application system that stretches far beyond what most Web sites currently are capable of.

Understanding Distributed Transaction Processing

Imagine that your company has several independent database systems: one for maintaining the current inventory in the company warehouse; one for maintaining all items that have been requisitioned and should be arriving on the receiving dock; and a third database for maintaining customer orders and shipping information, such as that shown in Figure 28.1. In this company, when an order comes in, the order is entered into the order entry system, which produces a shipping order. This order is then taken to the warehouse, where each item in the order is removed and taken to the shipping dock to be packaged up and sent to the customer. At the warehouse, the employee filling the order finds that one or two items are out of stock. The employee then takes the order to the requisition department and has the missing items back ordered for later shipping. At each of these points, the individual systems have to be updated so that they are up to date. Even the shipping dock system has to be updated in order to produce an accurate shipping bill-of-lading, which correctly reflects the back-ordered items.

FIG. 28.1
A typical catalog company has systems to track current inventory, requisitioned or back-ordered items, and shipping orders.

Order Entry

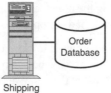
Order Database

Shipping

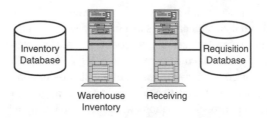
Inventory Database — Warehouse Inventory — Receiving — Requisition Database

Part

VI

Ch

28

This seems like a lot of wasted and duplicated effort. Wouldn't it make a lot more sense to connect all of these systems together so that they could all exchange the necessary information to perform most of these tasks themselves? If you put a network in place and connect all of these systems to the network, as shown in Figure 28.2, the potential for these systems to exchange the appropriate information can be realized.

FIG. 28.2

A network could be used to connect all of the company systems, so that they could exchange information with each other.

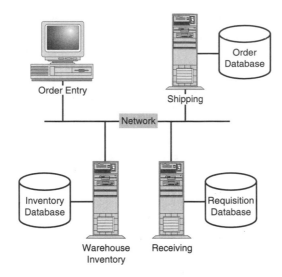

Unfortunately, as anyone who has attempted to connect separate systems together in this way knows, once you have all the systems on a network, the work is just beginning. The work of enabling all of these systems to work together is part of what middleware is all about.

Another function of middleware is to reduce the processing load on the desktop, enabling business-rule logic, which is likely to be updated and revised on a frequent basis, to be located on central servers. This configuration makes the process of updating business-logic modules a simple task of replacing the affected modules on a few servers, instead of updating the software sitting on hundreds of desktops.

A third function of middleware is to place data-processing logic close to the database server in order to minimize network traffic between the database server and the client applications running on the desktop. Most of the same network traffic is still created on the network segment between the database server and the data processing modules (unless they are located on the same computer). This still isolates the network traffic and congestion to that specific network segment, and keeps most of it off the rest of the corporate network.

Typically, client/server types of applications don't scale well to large numbers of users using a two-tier architecture. Even if an application is using only a single database, if the application is being used by more than a couple dozen users at once, it is advisable to use some sort of middleware and a three-tier architecture to maintain reasonable application performance. In the past, this usually required extensive redesign on most two-tier applications. With the latest set of tools, the process of converting a two-tier application to a three-tier application is getting much easier. However, there are still situations where the two-tier application was originally designed such that extensive modifications are required to make the transition.

Transaction Monitors

The original idea behind the client/server computing model was to split the application processing between two computers. This split was normally made so that the database processing was all performed on the server, while all application processing was performed on the client, as shown in Figure 28.3. This model worked reasonably well except for the fact that it was fairly easy to overload the client system with data, if the application allowed the database to return more data than the client computer could handle (remember that this was when the standard desktop computer was a 386 with 4MG of RAM, and a 486 was a high-end workstation).

FIG. 28.3

The original idea behind client/server computing was to split the application processing between the client and the database server.

Client

Database Server

As the number of active users of these early client/server systems increased, the workload on the database would increase. A normal application would maintain an open connection to the database server for the entire time the application was running (see Figure 28.4). This required the database server to have additional processing power in order to service all of those open connections, even if they were sitting idle. This also increased the cost associated with the database itself, as most traditional enterprise database license prices are based on the number of users that can be connected to the database simultaneously.

N O T E The practice of maintaining open database connections was developed for two primary reasons. First, it made the development of database applications easier if the database connections were maintained throughout the life of the application, instead of constantly having to close and reopen the connection (not to mention having to keep track of whether the connection is open or closed). The second reason was to avoid the overhead involved in opening and closing the database connection. This overhead can add a couple of seconds (on a congested network, or to a busy database server) to the time the application requires to perform certain actions. Users are typically willing to wait through delays like this during the startup and shutdown of applications, but not during the midst of the application. ■

As the number of databases that an application needs to interact with increases, the number of open connections that the application must maintain also increases. This adds to the processing load on the client computer, as well as the network management and configuration. The total number of connections that must be maintained can be calculated as the number of clients times the number of database servers to which the client connects, as shown in Figure 28.5.

FIG. 28.4
As the number of users increase, the number of active connections that must be serviced by the database increases.

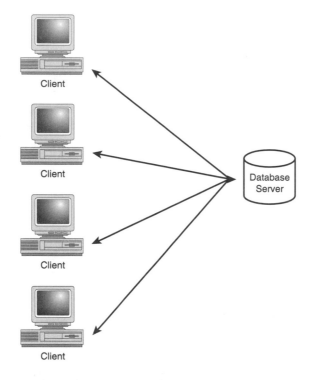

FIG. 28.5
The total number of open connections that must be maintained can be calculated as the number of clients times the number of servers.

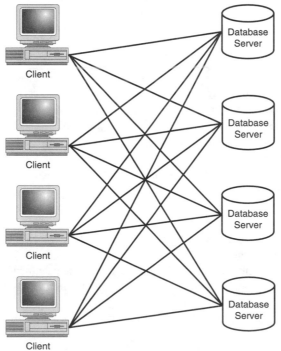

This is a lot of configuration information that has to be maintained for each client computer. If one of the databases that an application uses has to be taken offline, and the backup database brought online, the configuration of each and every client that connects to the database has to be updated to reflect the new database server (with care taken not to update the wrong database server information).

This is one of the primary problems that transaction monitors were designed to solve. A *transaction monitor* goes between the client systems and the database servers, as in you can see in Figure 28.6. Each of the clients maintains a single connection to the transaction monitor instead of the database servers. Likewise, the transaction monitor maintains connections to each of the database servers. This enables the transaction monitor to act as a traffic cop, passing each database query or update to the appropriate database, and to maintain only as many open database connections as are currently required, which enables the database servers to run more efficiently.

FIG. 28.6
A transaction monitor reduces the number of open connections to the number of clients plus the number of database servers.

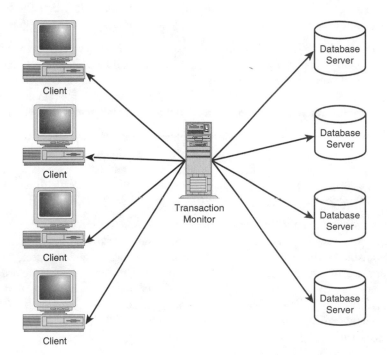

Object Request Brokers

Object request brokers (ORBs) fall into a different category of middleware than transaction monitors. ORBs provide *location transparency* to application modules and services, which means that when an application needs to interact with a server process, the application does not need to know where that specific server process is located on the network. The only process that the application knows the location of is the ORB client stub located on the same machine as the application.

Part
VI

Ch
28

The ORB knows where all server processes are running, or on which machines the server processes may be run. If a particular server process is not running when an application requests access to it, the ORB will start the server process on one of the machines for which the process is configured to run. The client application does not know on which server the requested process is running or if the server process is even running. The ORB keeps track of all server processes for the client applications. The ORB may even perform load balancing between two or more servers running the same process, so that each of the servers is servicing around the same number of requests.

Returning to the catalog sales company example, it is reasonable to expect that the order entry system would make use of various services that could be located on a series of servers on the company network. One of these services could be a sales tax engine, which calculates the tax for each of the customer orders. It would make sense to keep this set of calculations on a server, as tax laws have a tendency to change. By keeping this processing module on the server, it will be a lot easier to update in this one location every time the tax laws change, as opposed to having to update every order entry workstation in the company.

Another service that each of the order entry systems would be likely to take advantage of is a credit check application. By having all the credit authorization requests go through a single server, it would be easy for that one server to maintain an open connection to the credit clearinghouse, as compared to outfitting each workstation with a modem and the software to call up the credit authority (not to mention all of the additional phone lines this would require).

A third service that each of the order entry systems could use might be the business rules engine. This would be the system that calculates shipping costs based on the quantity or weight of the ordered items or enforces minimum purchase rules. By keeping this module on one or two servers, you would once again be able to easily update the module as the powers-that-be within the company change the business rules that this module has to enforce.

Considering that the functions provided by these server modules are critical to the core business of our catalog sales company, it's important to make sure that these modules are always available for the order entry systems. In order to make sure that these systems have high availability, they are probably loaded onto more than one system. If the order entry application made direct accesses to these services, each copy of the application would have to know which machines each of these services are running on at all times. By using an ORB, the individual copies of the order entry application don't know and don't care what servers any of these services are running on; the ORB takes care of making the connections and passing the results back to the order entry application, as seen in Figure 28.7.

Introducing Microsoft Transaction Server

Microsoft's Transaction Server is somewhat of a cross between a transaction monitor and an ORB, although it tends to lean more toward the ORB set of functionality. If you are running an application on a Windows NT system that has Transaction Server installed, and you are using ODBC to access a database, Transaction Server transparently inserts itself between your application and the database to manage that connection (as well as all of the other open connections to the same database). Transaction Server also enables application functionality to be built as a series of ActiveX DLLs and distributed across a network to run on any number of servers running on the corporate network.

FIG. 28.7
The ORB relieves the client application from having to know which server computer each of the services is running on.

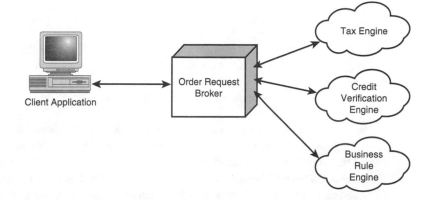

Managing Database Connections

When an application is using the ODBC interface to access a database, Transaction Server takes control of the database connection to provide more consistent access, quicker connection, and transaction control. By placing itself between the application and the database, Transaction Server is able to open its own connection to the database, thereby providing the application with a connection to Transaction Server instead of the database. This enables Transaction Server to limit the actual number of database connections to only as many as are necessary to service all the application requests, as seen in Figure 28.8. This relieves the work of maintaining all those connections from the database, enabling the database to perform better and be more responsive.

FIG. 28.8
By inserting itself between the applications and the database, Transaction Server is able to limit the number of active connections that the database has to service.

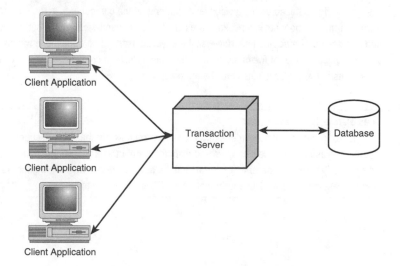

Part
VI

Ch
28

N O T E Transaction Server performs this resource allocation through the Microsoft Distributed Transaction Coordinator (DTC). The DTC performs resource allocation by communicating with a resource manager (such as a database server) through the OLE-Transaction protocol. Not all databases support this protocol, and many require the use of an additional transaction monitor that supports the X/Open XA protocol, which can interact with the DTC through the OLE-Transaction/XA translator. ▪

N O T E Transaction Server is required to be running on each server on which there are components that it needs to run, or that call components that run within Transaction Server. This means that a minimal installation of Transaction Server needs to be on every client computer, even if all of the components being called reside on other computers within the organization. ▪

When an application closes its connection to the database, Transaction Server maintains the open database connection so that the connection can be reused either by the application that closed the connection, or by another application (or client) that needs the same connection to the database. This enables application modules to be written in such a way that they only maintain open connections to a database for those periods of time that the application really needs to have the connection open. The performance penalty for closing and re-opening a database connection is removed, making it more attractive to write applications that release the associated resources while they are not needed.

N O T E Transaction packages are configurable for how long the components within the package are kept open and maintained in memory. The default length of time is three minutes, but this can be set to any number of minutes, or set to keep the components open constantly. When Transaction Server closes the open components, because they have been idle for the specified time, it also releases any database connections associated with those components by letting the resource manager know that the connection is going to an inactive state and may not be needed for awhile. ▪

The setting controlling how long Transaction Server maintains components in memory within a certain package should be based on the typical usage patterns of the components in the package. For instance, if the components in a package are called very frequently, leaving the setting at the default three minutes may be appropriate. However, if the typical usage of an application will have the components sitting idle for five or six minutes between calls, then configuring the package to keep the components active for 10 minutes may be more appropriate. ▪

Resource Management

The management and allocation of shared resources such as database connections is performed through the use of resource managers and resource distributors. The resource managers are usually part of the database management system, and the resource distributors are built into Transaction Server. These two systems interact through the OLE Transaction protocol.

Managing Distributed Objects

Transaction Server provides a facility for building distributed applications by enabling you to build functionality into a series of ActiveX server DLLs and distribute them across your network. Transaction Server keeps track of where each of these DLLs is located, and performs all the communications between them and your application. This enables you to move your functionality modules to the most suitable computer on your network based on the processing load that each module will be requiring in order to service all the requests from applications needing the services of the module. You can even double up and place the same module on multiple computers and enable Transaction Server to load balance between the copies. This provides you with the flexibility to take a complex processing module that might take several minutes to perform its tasks and place it on several computers. This way, if the copy on one computer was sitting idle while the copy on another computer was servicing two or three requests, if a new request came in, Transaction Server could direct the request to the idle copy of the module instead of the copy that was already busy.

Transaction Server also provides you the capability to easily mix and match modules of functionality that are built in a number of different programming languages. Any language that can be used to build ActiveX server DLLs can be used to build modules to be used with Transaction Server. This includes not just Microsoft's Visual Basic, Visual C++, and Visual J++, but also Borland's Delphi, Symantec's Café, and Sybase's PowerBuilder. This enables you to pull together functional modules together into a large distributed application, regardless of what language was used to build the individual modules, as shown in Figure 28.9. This capability of Transaction Server enables you to build an extensive application using "best-of-breed" modules and components.

FIG. 28.9

Using Transaction Server, you can use functional modules that were built using many different languages in a single application.

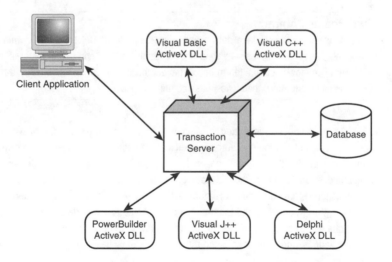

Part

VI

Ch

28

Transaction Coordination

One of the many beneficial features of Transaction Server is the way it provides coordinated transaction control through many objects and over multiple databases. Transaction Server accomplishes this by using the Microsoft Distributed Transaction Coordinator (DTC). The DTC was first released as part of SQL Server 6.5, and is included with Transaction Server. It provides a low-level infrastructure for distributed transactions, controlling and guaranteeing the outcome (either commit or rollback) across multiple databases and database connections. The DTC uses a two-phase commit protocol to ensure the outcome of these transactions.

An example of how this works is if you were running a bank and had two separate databases for savings and checking accounts. With most transactions, only one database would be involved, as most customers place money into or take money out of either their checking or savings account. However, whenever a customer transferred money from his checking account to his savings account, or vice versa, then both databases would need to be involved. This transaction would require debiting the amount of money transferred from the account on one database, and crediting the same amount on the other database. If either of these two actions fails, for whatever reason, the entire transaction needs to fail, rolling back both databases to their pre-transaction state. This is the task that the DTC handles. The DTC controls the transactions for both databases, making sure that either both databases commit the transaction, or both databases rollback the transaction. The DTC does not enable one of the two databases to commit the transaction while the other is rolling back the same transaction, as this would leave the databases in an inconsistent state (not to mention that it would likely result in a very happy, or a very upset customer). This coordination of the transactions of two or more databases is called *two-phase commit*.

Two-Phase Commit

A two-phase commit is where a data change (insert, update, or delete) to two or more databases absolutely has to be successful in all or unsuccessful in all. If the situation dictates that the changes to the data cannot be committed in one of the databases without being committed in the others, then this is the situation where two-phase commit is necessary.

N O T E   The Microsoft Distributed Transaction Coordinator provides the flexibility to extend transactions to non-database resources. The Transaction Server SDK provides the tools and documentation to build resource managers for any resource you might want to be part of a transaction. For instance, if you need to perform certain manipulations on a file, or send an e-mail message as part of the transaction, you could build your own resource manager using Visual C++ and the Transaction Server SDK, which could be used to control and coordinate your non-database tasks as part of the transactions being controlled by Transaction Server. This would enable you to commit or roll back your file manipulations, and send or not send the e-mail message based on the success of the transaction. ■

Integrating Active Server Pages with Transaction Server

Integrating Transaction Server into an Active Server Page application is very similar to integrating custom components into an Active Server Page application, with a few differences. First, any components that you will be calling through Transaction Server must be registered. Next, the components are instantiated slightly differently from custom components. From this point on, the differences are hard to spot.

There are some differences in how custom components need to be built in order to work within Transaction Server, but I'll get to that later in this chapter. First, I'll look at using Transaction Server components from the perspective of Active Server Pages.

I'll cover how to integrate Active Server Pages with Transaction Server by using a simple bank account maintenance application included with Transaction Server. This example enables the user to credit or debit small amounts to either of two accounts, as well as transfer funds between the two accounts. This example will require that you adapt the Visual Basic user interface provided as the user interface for this sample application to work as an Active Server Page application. You'll also have to make some minor changes to the Visual Basic components so that they work with Active Server Pages.

N O T E This example is limited to using two specific account numbers, 1 and 2, and small amounts of money by some of the constraints coded into the sample application. The application only performs updates to the database, except if the account table does not yet exist in the database. If the table does not exist, then the sample application creates the table and inserts two records for accounts 1 and 2. From this point on, all SQL statements issued to the database are either selects or updates. For the sample application to enable other account numbers, you will need to modify the sample code to recognize that the account specified doesn't exist in the database, and to insert a new record for the new account.

Because we are using a sample application that is provided with Transaction Server, the code for the Transaction Server components used in this chapter is not included with the source code on the CD in the back of the book. However, any modifications necessary to get these components to work with Active Server Pages are documented in this chapter so that you should be able to make the appropriate changes yourself with a copy of Visual Basic 5. ■

Registering Components with Transaction Server

Before you can register a custom component with Transaction Server, the component has to be built as an in-process, ActiveX server DLL. After you have built your component as an ActiveX DLL, you need to register it with Transaction Server before it can be used. You do this through the Transaction Server Explorer. When you have started up the Transaction Server Explorer, you need to make sure that the Distributed Transaction Coordinator (DTC) is running. You

Part
VI

Ch
28

can tell if the DTC is running by looking at the color of the screen in the computer icon for your computer. When the DTC is running, the screen on the computer icon is green, and when the DTC is not running, the screen on the computer icon is black. If the DTC is not running, click the computer icon for your computer, and then select Tools|MS DTC|Start.

N O T E   The DTC can be easily configured to start automatically when the NT system boots up. The Transaction Server installation routine will default to configuring the DTC for starting automatically. However, if you are installing Transaction Server on a development workstation, you might want to configure the DTC for manual starting if you need to have control over whether the DTC is running. ▪

Creating Packages   Before you can start registering components in Transaction Server, you must have a package into which you are going to install the components. *Packages* are logical groupings of objects that are generally used as a unit. As a general rule, you want to create one package for every set of applications that will be making use of Transaction Server. A package is an organizational grouping of components within Transaction Server. These are typically a set of components that are to be used in a certain suite of applications (or a single application). Because security and how long components are kept in memory once they become idle are configured on a package level, these aspects will need to be taken into account when planning packages for use with Transaction Server. You can create a package by following these steps:

1. Select the Packages Installed folder.
2. Choose File | New from the main menu.
3. On the first screen of the Package Wizard, choose Create An Empty Package (see Figure 28.10).

FIG. 28.10

To register components that you have built, you need to create an empty package into which the components will be installed.

4. Type a name for the package, as shown in Figure 28.11. For the catalog sales company package, call it **Bank**. Click the Next button.

FIG. 28.11

Provide the package with a name that reflects the functionality, or family of applications, that the components in the package will be providing.

5. If the objects in the package need to run under a specific login account, select the This User radio button and provide the user name and password. Otherwise, leave the default radio button selected, as shown in Figure 28.12. The default choice runs all of the objects in the package under the account of the user using the application that `call these objects` (this could effect the availability of resources for the process components, depending on how the access privileges are configured in the system security).

N O T E A package can be configured so that all of the components within it run using a specific user account. This will enable you to configure the security settings of resources needed by the components so that the resources will always be available. The default setting, however, is for the components in the package to run using the user account of the application that calls them. This means that if the calling application is running under a user account that has limited access to resources, some of the components called by the user may not have full access to any resources needed by the components. ■

6. Click the Finish button to complete the process.

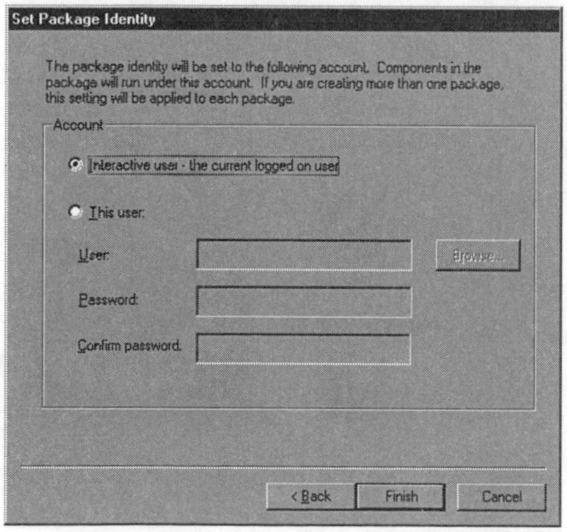

FIG. 28.12

If you need the components in the package to execute as a specific user login for resource access purposes, you need to specify the user login and password.

Installing Components Once you have a package, you can install components into it. This is where you register the ActiveX DLLs that you have and will be creating. You can register your components by following these steps:

NOTE In the following section, I use the terms "install" and "register" interchangeably. Installing components into Transaction Server and registering components with Transaction Server are two ways of referring to the same process. ■

1. Select the Components folder in the package into which you want to install the components (in this case, it's the Bank package that we just created), as shown in Figure 28.13. Then select File|New from the menu.

FIG. 28.13
Select the Components folder in the package that you have created to install components into the package.

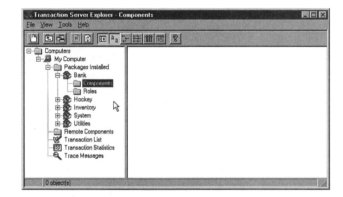

2. Click the Install New Component(s) button, as seen in Figure 28.14.

FIG. 28.14
If you are installing components that you have built, you need to select the Install new components option.

3. Click the Add Files button, and then select the ActiveX DLL that you want to register, as shown in Figure 28.15.

FIG. 28.15

You need to select the DLL containing the components that you are installing.

4. When you return to the Install Components screen, the upper list box should show the DLL that you are installing, and the lower box should show all the classes within the DLL (see Figure 28.16).

FIG. 28.16

The Install Components dialog displays all the components found in the specified DLL.

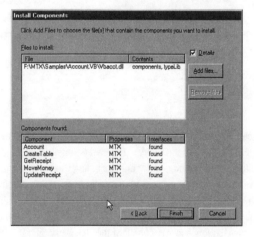

5. Click the Finish button, and the components will be installed in Transaction Server, as shown in Figure 28.17.

6. Select the components you just installed, one at a time, and right-click the mouse. Select Properties from the pop-up menu. On the Component Properties editor, select the Transaction tab, and select the transaction attribute desired for the currently selected component, as shown in Figure 28.18.

I'll take a closer look at the Banking example included with Transaction Server later in this chapter, as you begin to build the functionality you need for your ASP application.

Part
VI

Ch
28

FIG. 28.17

After you install the components, they will show up in the Transaction Server Explorer.

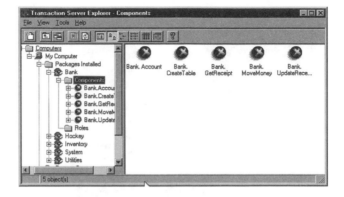

FIG. 28.18

You need to open the Properties dialog for the installed component in order to specify the transaction attribute setting.

N O T E Whenever you recompile any ActiveX DLL built in Visual Basic, you need to refresh the component information in Transaction Server. This can be easily done by deleting the component from the Transaction Server Explorer, and then reinstalling the component by following the same steps as you followed to install the component originally. Another way of refreshing the component information in Transaction Server is to choose Tools | Refresh All Components. The reason that the component has to be re-registered with Transaction Server is because Visual Basic generates a new CLSID (globally unique Class ID) for each component in the DLL every time the DLL is compiled. This is not the case for most other development languages. ■

CAUTION

In working with Transaction Server 1.0, the Refresh All Components menu option often scrambled the component names in the package that I was working with. I would end up with what would look like two or three copies of the same component in the package, and some components would appear to be missing. I did not notice any problems when attempting to run the applications that used these components, but I usually ended up deleting all the components from the package and reinstalling them.

In version 1.1, the refresh does work better, but Visual Basic components must still be dropped and reregistered. However, once the components have been recompiled on the same system with Transaction Server, attempting to delete the components from Transaction Server without refreshing them first will cause you to be subjected to several confusing error messages, all due in part to the Class ID of the components having changed with the recompile. The class is changing confuses Transaction Server, and the refresh helps unconfuse it.

Creating Transaction Server Components

Creating Transaction Server components for use within an Active Server Page is similar to creating any other custom component for use within an Active Server Page. The biggest difference is that you do not use the Server object when you create your objects. You still have to call the CreateObject() function, but not as a member of the Server object. For instance, you can create an instance of the Bank.Account component from the sample application by using the following VBScript:

```
Dim objMTX      'The Transaction Server Component

'Create the Transaction Server Component
Set objMTX = CreateObject("Bank.Account")
If objMTX is nothing Then
   'Perform error handling here
Else
   'Call component methods here
End if
```

N O T E The code above contradicts all documentation from Microsoft on how to instantiate Transaction Server components. According to all Microsoft documentation, the third line of code should read:

```
Set objMTX = Server.CreateObject("Bank.Account")
```

However, I have not been able to successfully instantiate any Transaction Server components using the Server object. You do need to be aware of this situation, as Microsoft could correct this functionality in new versions of either ASP or Transaction Server, making the documented method for creating Transaction Server objects in an ASP application work correctly. ■

Once you have successfully created the component, you will be able to see the component begin spinning the Transaction Server Explorer, as you can in Figure 28.19. After you access a component once or twice, the component may be activated and deactivated so quickly that the Transaction Server Explorer doesn't have time to update its display. As a result, you may not see the components spin, even though they are active and working correctly.

FIG. 28.19

The components that are visible in the Transaction Server Explorer spin when they are active.

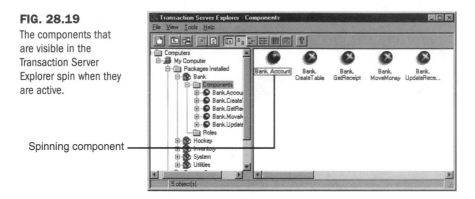

Spinning component

Calling Component Methods

After you create an instance of a Transaction Server component, you can call the component's methods much like you would call the methods of any other component. By referencing the component methods via the component itself, you can call any of the methods that have been exposed on the component that meet the requirements for use with Active Server Pages. For instance, you can call the Post method of the Bank.Account component like this:

```
lRetnVal = objMTX.Post(lPrimeAcct, (lAmount * Multiplier), RtnMsg)
```

Something to keep in mind when designing your Active Server Page application is that well-designed Transaction Server components do not maintain any state information. Because of this, Transaction Server component methods should require that all information the method needs must be passed as parameters to the method. There should be nothing for the component to maintain between method calls. In a sense, working with Transaction Server components is much like building a Web application, where the server is not maintaining any state information between calls.

Returning Data from Components

The best way to return information from Transaction Server components is through the use of parameters to the component method. The standard return value of the method will be a success code to inform you whether the method was successful or not. This means that all data that needs to be returned to the calling routine needs to be returned in parameters that were passed to the method.

For instance, if you needed to call a component method called DoThis and you need to be returned a textual message to display for the user, your calling code would look something like this:

```
Dim lstrMsg As String

'Call the DoThis method of the object
obj.DoThis(lstrMsg)
'Display the message returned by the component
MsgBox(lstrMsg)
```

Meanwhile, the component's code for this same method would look like this:

```
Public Sub DoThis(astrMsg As String)
   'Set the message to the string passed in as a parameter
   astrMsg = "This is what I'm doing"
End Sub
```

You can get your first experience integrating Active Server Pages with Transaction Server components by using the Bank Account Maintenance application that is provided with Transaction Server. This example has a simple Visual Basic front end, as shown in Figure 28.20. This simple application provides the user with the ability to specify:

- An account number
- The amount to credit or debit
- A second account number (if performing a transfer)
- The transaction type
- The number of iterations to perform (we'll be leaving this option out of our ASP version)
- Which component to call (we'll only provide the first two of these)
- Which language version to call: Visual Basic, Visual C++, or Visual J++ (we'll limit our ASP version to calling only the Visual Basic version of the components)

N O T E The sample application has three different versions of the component code, developed in Visual Basic, Visual C++, and Visual J++. In the user interface for the sample application, the user has a choice of which version to call. For our purposes here, we'll only use the Visual Basic version, although you can easily make the necessary modifications yourself to include all three versions in the ASP adaptation of this sample application. ■

This application also displays the response time statistics and the result of each transaction for the user.

FIG. 28.20
The Visual Basic application that calls the Bank Account Maintenance components will be fairly easy to implement as an Active Server Page application.

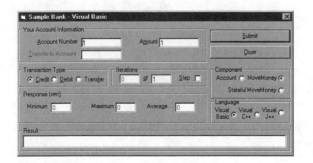

The Account Components

The Bank Account Maintenance application that is provided as an example with Transaction Server consists of five classes. These classes, and their functionality, are listed in Table 28.1. They can be used to credit and debit either of two accounts, or to transfer funds from one account to the other. Along with this functionality, these classes also create the required tables in SQL Server, if they don't already exist, generate sequential receipt numbers, and maintain blocks of receipt numbers in the database.

Table 28.1   Bank Account Example Classes

Class	Description
Bank.Account	This class performs the credit and debit actions on a specified account, returning the resulting balance. It may be called directly to perform simple credits and debits, or be called through the Bank.MoveMoney class to perform more sophisticated actions.
Bank.MoveMoney	This class acts somewhat like a traffic cop, calling all the other classes to perform complex actions. This class calls the Bank.Account class to perform credits and debits on a single account by making two calls to transfer funds between two accounts. This class also calls the Bank.GetReceipt class to generate a receipt number that is returned to the calling application.
Bank.GetReceipt	This class generates sequential receipt numbers using the shared resource facilities of Transaction Server. Whenever a block of receipt numbers has been used up, it calls the Bank.UpdateReceipt class to allocate the next block of receipt numbers.
Bank.UpdateReceipt	This class maintains the starting number of the next block of receipt numbers in the database. By only updating the database once for each block of receipt numbers generated, the number of database transactions is minimized, thereby improving performance.
Bank.CreateTable	This class is called by the Bank.Account and Bank.UpdateReceipt classes to create the necessary tables in SQL Server if the tables don't already exist. This class also inserts starting records for accounts 1 and 2. No records are inserted for any other account numbers, thus limiting the functionality of this example to those two accounts.

Calling the Account Components from ASP

Before you can call the Bank Account Maintenance components through Transaction Server, you need to re-create the front-end application as an HTML form. A simple version of this form can be seen in Figure 28.21 (the HTML document is located on the CD accompanying this book). This form contains the field names specified in Table 28.2.

FIG. 28.21
You can easily build an HTML form that closely matches the Visual Basic user interface in functionality.

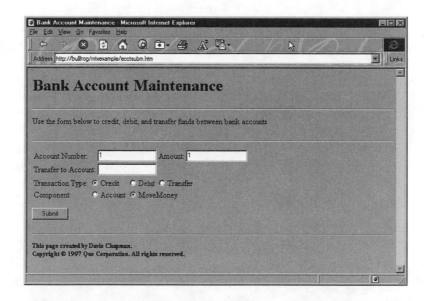

Table 28.2   The HTML Form Element Names

Element Prompt	Element Name
Account Number	PrimeAcct
Amount	Amount
Transfer to Account	SecondAcct
Transaction Type	TransType
Component	Component

The transaction type radio buttons have the following values:

- Credit
- Debit
- Transfer

and the component radio buttons have these values:

- Account
- MoveMoney

Once you have converted the Visual Basic code to VBScript, handling the submitted data elements and leaving out the code dealing with the unnecessary elements that we have eliminated from our ASP version, you have the code listed in Listing 28.1.

Part
VI

Ch
28

Listing 28.1   *ACCTRUN.ASP*—Capturing the submitted data elements in VBScript, we can create and call the Bank Account components through Transaction Server.

```
Dim ProgID        'Transaction Server Component to call
Dim RtnMsg        'A Return Message to be displayed to the user
Dim TransType     'The Transaction Type to run
Dim Multiplier    'A multiplier to automatically credit or debit an account
Dim lPrimeAcct    'The primary account
Dim lSecondAcct   'The second account into which to transfer funds
Dim lAmount       'The amount to be credited, debited, or transferred
Dim objMTX        'The Transaction Server Component
Dim lRetnVal      'The Return Value

RtnMsg = ""
'Decide which component to use
If (Request.Form("Component") = "Account") Then
    ProgID = "Bank.Account"
Else
    ProgID = "Bank.MoveMoney"
End if

'Decide the transaction type
If (Request.Form("TransType") = "Debit") Then
    TransType = "Debit"
    Multiplier = "-1"
Elseif (Request.Form("TransType") = "Credit") Then
    TransType = "Credit"
    Multiplier = "1"
Else
    If (ProgID = "Bank.Account") then
        RtnMsg = "Error. You must select the MoveMoney component to transfer
➡funds."
    Elseif (Request.Form("SecondAcct") = "") Then
        RtnMsg = "Error. You must provide a second account number to transfer
➡funds into."
    Else
        TransType = "Transfer"
        Multiplier = "1"
        lSecondAcct = Request.Form("SecondAcct")
    End if
End if

'Check for values
If (Request.Form("PrimeAcct") = "") Then
    TransType = ""
    RtnMsg = "Error. You must provide the account number to be credited or
➡debited."
Else
    lPrimeAcct = Request.Form("PrimeAcct")
End if
```

```
If (Request.Form("Amount") = "") Then
   TransType = ""
   RtnMsg = "Error. You must provide the amount to be credited or debited."
Else
   lAmount = Request.Form("Amount")
End if

If (TransType <> "") Then
   'Create the Transaction Server Component
   Set objMTX = CreateObject(ProgID)
   If objMTX is nothing Then
      TransType = ""
      RtnMsg = "Error. Could not create Transaction Server Object."
   End if
End if

'Call the Transaction Server Component
If (TransType <> "") Then
   If (Request.Form("Component") = "Account") Then
      lRetnVal = objMTX.Post(CLng(lPrimeAcct), (CLng(lAmount) *
➥CLng(Multiplier)), RtnMsg)
   Else
      lRetnVal = objMTX.Perform(CLng(lPrimeAcct), CLng(lSecondAcct),
➥CLng(lAmount), TransType, RtnMsg)
   End if
End if
```

After you perform this script, you can build virtually the same HTML document, including the response message returned from the Transaction Server components, and populate the HTML elements with the values the user submitted, as shown in Figure 28.22. For the complete HTML and ASP listings, you can find the full documents on the CD enclosed with this book.

FIG. 28.22
The same HTML form can be used for the response from the Transaction Server components by adding the result message above the form.

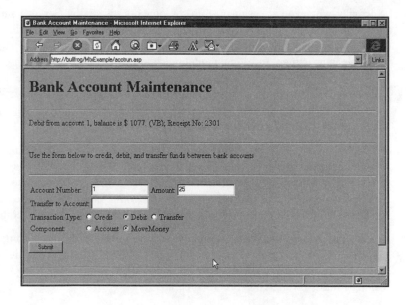

A Note from the Author

If you have been following along with this example, loading the Bank component into Transaction Server and building the Active Server Page application using the above code (or by pulling the code off the CD), you have probably found that it doesn't work. Instead of working the way that this text leads you to believe that it should, you receive an error message. The reason for this problem is that you still need to make modifications to the Banking sample application that accompanies Transaction Server in order to be able to use it with Active Server Pages. The VBScript in our ASP page is passing all parameters to the Transaction Server components as `Variant` datatypes, while the components are expecting `string` and `long` datatypes. You need to modify the VB components to expect all method parameters to be `Variant` before these components will work with our ASP version. The next section explores how components need to be designed for use with Transaction Server and Active Server Pages.

Building Transaction Server Components for Use with Active Server Pages

When designing and building custom components for use with Transaction Server and Active Server Pages, there are a few design constraints that you need to keep in mind. These constraints include how the component methods need to be designed to work with the Transaction Server threading, and how this will affect the way the component is used within ASP applications. Also affected are how parameters need to be declared for all public methods that might be called from an ASP application.

Threading and Transaction Server Components

Normally, when you are using custom components with Active Server Page applications, the component threading is controlled by the ASP executable so that a single ASP page has a dedicated component thread for the duration of the ASP processing for that page. With components that use an apartment threading model (such as those used with components built using Visual Basic), this means that your ASP application can set variables within the component and make subsequent calls to the component, knowing that the variables that you have set in the component are still there. The state of the component is consistent until the page has completed all of its processing and the component thread has been ended.

With components in Transaction Server, Transaction Server is controlling the threading of components, not the ASP engine. Once Transaction Server has activated a component and has it running in a thread, Transaction Server can share that single component thread among multiple processes. This means that you cannot count on the state of the component to stay as you have left it until the next call you make to one of the component's methods.

Because of the way that Transaction Server controls the threading of components, each component method call needs to be self-contained. The method should receive all necessary data and variables through parameters to the method, and should return any results back to the calling routine through other method parameters.

N O T E   It is possible to design and develop components for use with Transaction Server that do maintain state between method calls. However, it is not advisable to do this, as they incur a significant amount of additional overhead and don't perform or scale as well as stateless components. State-full components are also more prone to cause errors in processing because as soon as a component signals to Transaction Server that it has successfully completed its actions, Transaction Server commits the transaction and resets the component. This wipes out all state information that was being maintained in the component.

An alternative to state-full components is the use of the shared objects within Transaction Server. This is a facility within Transaction Server where it maintains a set of data values, and controls access to them so that only one process thread may reference or update them at any point in time. These shared objects are just what the name implies; they are shared between all process threads running within Transaction Server, and may be altered by any of the running process threads. ■

Parameter Passing with Active Server Pages

Because all variables in VBScript are Variant, you need to make all of the parameters in the public component methods to be Variant, also. Once you are within the component method, the parameters can be converted into whatever datatype they need to be for the proper functioning of the component itself.

For example, the Post method of the Account component in the Transaction Server banking example was declared as follows:

```
Public Function Post(lngAccountNo As Long, lngAmount As Long, _
                ByRef strResult As String) As Long
```

Because none of the parameters for this method are Variant, the method call fails when made from an ASP application. In order to get this method to work with an ASP application, the first line of the method was converted to the following code, where all variables are passed in as Variant, and then converted to variables of the original datatypes.

```
Public Function Post(alngAccountNo As Variant, _
                alngAmount As Variant,
                ByRef astrResult As Variant) As Long

    Dim lngAccountNo As Long
    Dim lngAmount As Long
    Dim strResult As String

    lngAccountNo = CLng(alngAccountNo)
    lngAmount = CLng(alngAmount)
```

Just before returning from this method, the result string is copied to the Variant version.

```
astrResult = strResult
```

After these changes have been made to the Post method in the Account class and the equivalent changes made to the Perform method in the MoveMoney class, you need to recompile the ActiveX DLL in which these components are encapsulated. Next, you need to delete the components from

Part

VI

Ch

28

Transaction Server, and re-register the new version. After you have done all of this, you should be able to get the example ASP application to work with Transaction Server.

From Here...

In this chapter, you have learned about Microsoft's Transaction Server: what it is, how it works, and how to use it with Active Server Pages. You've learned how Microsoft designed Transaction Server to be a combination of a transaction monitor and an object request broker. You've seen how using Transaction Server enables you to build your applications as a series of small, single-purpose modules that use Transaction Server to glue them all together. Transaction Server also enables you to build large, distributed applications that are scaled across several servers, with relative ease.

The biggest shortcoming with Transaction Server is that all processing that you can perform with it is synchronous in nature. This means that everything in the processing chain has to wait until everything else in the chain is complete before processing control can be returned to the calling application. If your application needs to perform some time-consuming actions that the calling application does not need to wait for, you will have trouble creating this capability by using Transaction Server alone. However, if you also incorporate Microsoft's Message Queue Server into your application architecture, you can use it to provide you with the capability to spawn off asynchronous processes to perform these time-consuming tasks.

From here you might want to check out some of these other chapters on related subjects:

- To gain an understanding of messaging between application processes and systems, and how this can be used in an Active Server Page application, read Chapter 29, "Working with the Message Queue Server."

- To learn what's involved in building a corporate intranet or extranet application, check out Chapter 30, "Application Development for the Corporate Intranet/Extranet."

- To see how you can integrate all of these technologies together to build a large-scale Active Server Page application, see Chapter 32, "Putting It All Together: Creating an N-Tier Online Catalog Application."

CHAPTER 29

Working with the Message Queue Server

When you build enterprise Web applications, you often need to pass information to other applications within your organization. Usually, this information is either passed in a synchronous manner, where the Web application waits until the other application has the information, or in some sort of asynchronous manner, often by writing the information to a file that is then picked up by another process. Neither of these standard approaches are an ideal approach to the problem of passing this information along. A better solution would be to send the information directly to the other application—whether it was located on the same computer as your Web server, or on another computer within your corporate network—without having to wait for the other application to receive the information from you. It would be even better if the receiving application doesn't even have to be running or reachable when you send the information. This would enable your Web application to continue working even when the other application was unavailable, your internal network was having problems, and so on.

Message Queuing in a Distributed Environment

In most large, distributed enterprise environments, there are several computer systems that need to pass information back and forth. Most of this information does not need to be passed in an interactive manner, but can make use of message queues instead.

Microsoft's Message Queue Server

Microsoft's new Message Queue Server, part of its Windows NT Server, Enterprise Edition, enables you to build large, distributed messaging applications.

Integrating Active Server Pages with Message Queue Server

You can use Active Server Pages to create and send messages to other applications in your environment. This provides you with the capability to spawn separate processes from your ASP application that do not need to be located on the same computer as your Web server.

This is all possible through the use of what is known as *message queuing systems* (also knows as *message-oriented middleware*, or MOM for short). These systems enable you to send a message containing the information you need to pass to another application, in whatever form you need to send the information in (text, binary, and so on), without waiting for the receiving application to get the information. If the other application isn't running or isn't reachable, the message is maintained in the queue until the other application is available and can retrieve the message. One of the newest products in this category is Microsoft's Message Queue Server.

Not all the functionality of Microsoft's Message Queue Server is available or practical for use in Active Server Page applications. There is, however, a core set of functions that are not only available, but are very practical for use in your ASP applications. Anywhere you need to pass information to another process and your ASP application does not need to receive any results from the other process, Message Queue Server might be a potential, if not the most practical, solution for use in your implementation. ■

What Is Message Queuing?

If you haven't heard about message queuing systems, it is currently one of the quickest growing areas of enterprise software systems. It enables application developers to build systems that easily pass information to other systems that are running on the same computer, on another computer in the local area network (LAN), or on another computer that is far away over the companies' wide area network (WAN), or possibly even over the Internet.

In a sense, message queuing can be thought of as e-mail for applications. When you send someone an e-mail message, you don't know (or care) if the message recipient is logged into the e-mail system at the time. You don't even care if the recipient's computer is turned on. You do know that, if you have addressed the message correctly, your message will eventually get to the recipient. Now imagine that the sending and receiving people are applications instead. If the sending application needs to pass information to another application, but doesn't need to wait for the receiving application to act on the information, then why should the sending application need to make sure that the receiving application is up and running?

The message queuing system handles getting the message from the sending system to the receiving system, regardless of what network protocols are being used, and performs whatever translations are necessary to convert the message to the format needed by the receiving system (ASCII to EBCDIC, Little Endian to Big Endian, and so on). The message queuing system also maintains the message when one or more of the systems involved in the message delivery are down or unreachable due to network problems.

In a sense, message queuing systems can be thought of as e-mail for applications. As you can probably guess from the previous list of functions that the message queuing systems perform, they provide much more than just mail delivery. Some of the functionality provided by message queuing systems include:

- Guaranteed message delivery.
- Store and forward capabilities.

- Queue browsing capabilities for the receiving application.
- Message prioritization and aging for controlling the delivery and storage of messages.
- Transactional messages.
- Journal and dead-letter queues for auditing and administrative purposes.

Guaranteed Message Delivery

Message queuing systems provide guaranteed message delivery from the sending application to the receiving application by maintaining the message queue on the disk drive of every computer involved in the message delivery. If the sending application is on one computer and the receiving application is on another, the message is first written to the queue on the disk of the sending computer. The message is then sent to the queue on the disk of the receiving computer. Only after the message has successfully made it into the disk queue on the second computer is it removed from the disk queue on the first computer. The message is maintained in the queue on the disk of the receiving computer until it is retrieved by the receiving application, as shown in Figure 29.1.

FIG. 29.1

Message queuing systems guarantee message delivery by maintaining the message queues on the disk drives of both the sending and receiving computers.

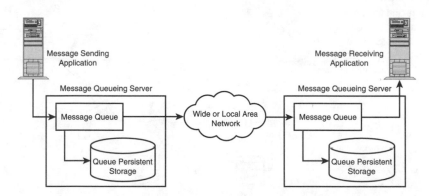

N O T E Although the message queuing systems do guarantee message delivery, there is still the possibility of losing messages in the event of a catastrophic disk failure. In this case, if the disk is not mirrored or some other means of providing a fault-tolerant disk drive system, then messages in the queue could be lost. ▪

With most message queuing systems, it is also possible to send messages that are maintained in memory only for faster delivery to the destination system (often called express delivery). When messages are sent in this way, if the computer holding the message crashes for some reason before being able to pass the message on to the next process or computer in line, then the message will be lost. This mode of message delivery is usually designated as an unrecoverable method of message delivery.

For instance, if you are building a virtual store front, and you want to automate as much as possible, you would want to pass every order placed by your customers to your order fulfillment system. If the order fulfillment system were currently offline (performing maintenance or daily batch processing), you would not want to risk losing the customer's order in the event that your Web server crashes before the order fulfillment system could come back online. For this very reason, you would want to specify that the order message was recoverable when you placed it into the queue to be passed to the order fulfillment system.

Store and Forward

Store and forward functionality enables message queues to be defined and configured so that they take several hops between the sending and receiving systems. With each hop, the message is maintained on the next intermediate computer until such time that the message can be passed along to the next computer in the chain. This is a desirable configuration in situations where the computers are very far apart geographically and communications between any two points may be out of service at any point in time. It is also a useful configuration to use when the means of communication is diverse, with a mixture of networking technologies in use, as shown in Figure 29.2.

FIG. 29.2

Store and forward functionality is desirable in situations where multiple communication technologies are in use.

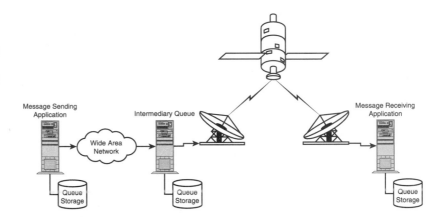

The primary benefit of the store and forward model is that each hop a message takes from one computer to the next can be kept down to a reasonable length with a fairly high level of availability. By using this model over a world-wide network, an efficient message queuing system could be designed, configured, and made operational with only a moderate amount of effort.

For instance, if your virtual store made use of numerous shipping outlets scattered around the world, you would want to pass the order information to the shipping outlet closest to the customer. Because of time differences, the servers at all of your shipping outlets are not likely to be up and running at the same time. Another factor to take into consideration is the reliability of the network. If there is a realistic chance that network connections between any two servers may not be operational at all times, then you might want to design a series of queues through which the order messages may pass when traveling from your Web server to the destination shipping outlet. By configuring your network with numerous short hops that a message will take between the origination and destination, the reliability that the message will reach its destination is greatly increased. For this type of configuration, you would want to make extensive use of store and forward functionality in your message queuing system.

Queue Browsing

Normally, when the receiving application retrieves a message from the queue, the message is removed from the queue. However, there are times when you don't want the message to be removed from the queue. For these situations, most message queuing systems enable the receiving application to browse the queue instead. By browsing the queue, the receiving application can retrieve the contents of the messages in the queue without removing it from the queue.

One way in which this capability can be used is if you have an application that needs to use the data in the queue messages to perform some task that is dependent on another system. If that other system isn't available, you don't want the message to be removed from the queue because your application needs to maintain the data until the other system is available for performing the necessary task. In this case, the receiving application could browse the queue for the incoming message, and then attempt to perform the task with the other system. If the application is successful in performing its task, it can retrieve the message from the queue, thereby removing it from the queue. If the application is unsuccessful in performing its task because the other system is unavailable, the message can be left in the queue. Then, after a suitable amount of time had passed (depending on the situation and the needs of the application, this could be a short as 5-10 seconds to several hours), the application could browse the queue and attempt its task again, repeating this pattern until the other system is available and the application is able to successfully complete its tasks. If this application were taking data updates from a message queue and making the appropriate changes to a database server, the process would look something like Figure 29.3.

FIG. 29.3
An application could browse a message queue for data updates to be run against a database server. If the database is unavailable, the messages can be left in the queue.

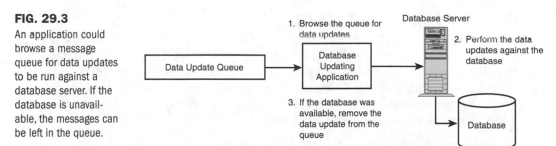

Message Prioritizing and Aging

Message sending applications can assign a priority to a message to control the delivery and where in the destination queue the message is placed. A higher priority message will be delivered to the destination queue in a quicker manner, and will likely be placed into the queue closer to the front than messages with lower priority. The priority does not affect how the messages are retrieved from the queue, and cannot force the receiving application to retrieve the message from the queue any faster than it would a message with a lower priority. The receiving application can only retrieve the messages from the destination queue in the order in which they were placed in the queue. The receiving application does not have the capability to bypass lower priority messages in the queue to retrieve higher priority messages first.

N O T E   The primary benefit of sending a message with a high priority is that the message is delivered to the destination queue faster than messages with a lower priority. This will make a difference in situations where a large number of messages are being placed into the queue with a mix of priorities. If the situation has few messages being placed in the queue on an infrequent basis, then there will be little benefit with setting a high priority for specific messages. ■

When sending a message, the sending application can specify a length of time for the message to remain in the queue. If this time expires and the message has not been retrieved from the queue by the receiving application, the message is automatically removed from the queue. The message is removed from the queue even if it has not reached the destination queue, but is somewhere in the process of being delivered. This is a feature that is useful when dealing with data that is time sensitive and must be acted on within a certain amount of time. However, this should only be used with data that, if not acted on within the specified time frame, is better off not being acted on at all.

Transactional Messages

Most message queuing systems enable the sending and receiving of transactional messages. These are messages that make use of a transaction coordinator, such as Microsoft's Distributed Transaction Coordinator (DTC), to control the sending and receiving of the message. If anything goes wrong in the entire process and the receiving application is not successful in retrieving the message, the entire transaction is rolled back and the sending application is notified of the failure along with what caused the transaction to fail.

Journal and Dead-Letter Queues

Most message queuing systems provide at least two administrative message queues, known as the *journal* and *dead-letter queues*. These two queues perform two different functions for the purpose of auditing and error recovery. The journal queues are used to record every message that passes through the queue with which the journal queue is associated. These queues can be used to perform audit-trail analysis of where and how a message passed on its way from the sending application to the receiving application.

Dead-letter queues store messages that could not be delivered. If a message was being directed from an origination queue on one machine to a nonexistent destination queue on another machine, that message would be undeliverable. As a result, the message would be moved into the dead-letter queue for later examination by the system administrator in order to determine what problem the message had. The dead-letter queue also often acts as an overflow queue, where if a destination computer is unavailable and more messages are being sent to that destination than can be held in the origination queue, the excess messages may be redirected to the dead-letter queue. If this is the case, the messages in the dead-letter queue will not be delivered once the destination computer becomes available and begins receiving messages. Instead, an administrator will have to manually resend the messages to the appropriate destination queue.

N O T E The sender will not automatically be notified if the message ends up in the dead-letter queue unless the application is specifically designed and built to perform this type of automatic notification. ■

Microsoft's Message Queue Server

One of Microsoft's newest products is Message Queue Server, Microsoft's entry into the message queuing system market. This is a very impressive product that is easy to use, both as a developer and an administrator. In this section, you will examine Message Queue Server from the perspective of understanding what is possible and realistic in Active Server Pages applications. There is a lot more functionality in Message Queue Server than will be covered in this section, but most of it is beyond the scope of this chapter and this book.

One of the things that sets Message Queue Server apart from the competition is the capability to automatically trigger events in the receiving application when a message has arrived at the destination queue. This enables the receiving application to be completely event driven, while other products require the receiving application to perform some sort of polling to check for arriving messages. This can be accomplished through the use of call-back functions (where Message Queue Server calls an exposed function in your application), or by passing a window event to your application.

N O T E Some competing products, such as IBM's MQSeries, provide a separate application that can signal the receiving application that a message has arrived in the destination queue. This can be done by triggering an event in the receiving application, or by starting the receiving application. While accomplishing the same end result, this approach is not integral to the product and results in additional processing overhead not present in Microsoft's Message Queue Server. ■

Because Active Server Pages lend themselves more toward using the ActiveX components of Message Queue Server than the API, the next section looks at Message Queue Server from the perspective of the components. In examining these components, you'll look at the properties with which you need to be familiar and how to use them. You'll also look at the various methods involved that enable you to find and open message queues, send and receive messages from the queues, and close and delete the queues, all from within an Active Server Page application (although some of these functions are better left to other processes, I'll still cover how you can perform them using Active Server Pages). Because of the nature of Active Server Page applications, I will not be looking at Message Queue Server events and how to take advantage of them in applications that lend themselves to using them.

ActiveX Components

Message Queue Server comes with a series of ActiveX components that can be used to perform various functions. These components are listed in Table 29.1.

Table 29.1 Message Queue Server ActiveX Components

Component	Description
MSMQQuery	This component can be used to locate a collection of existing queues.
MSMQQueueInfos	This is a collection of queues located using the MSMQQuery component.
MSMQQueueInfo	This component contains the information needed to create or open a queue.
MSMQQueue	This component represents an actual message queue, and provides functionality to receive and send messages.
MSMQMessage	This component represents a message that is to be sent or received.
MSMQEvent	This component contains all of the event handling for Message Queue Server. It can be used to trigger application events when messages arrive in a destination queue. We will not be looking at this component in this chapter.
MSMQTransactionDispenser	This component is used to create a transaction object.
MSMQTransaction	This component is used to commit and abort transactions.

I'll examine each of the components in detail as you look at each of the basic functions that you will need to perform in working with Message Queue Server. These functions are:

- Creating a new queue.
- Locating an existing queue.
- Opening a queue for sending or receiving.
- Sending messages to a queue.
- Receiving messages from a queue.
- Closing an open queue.
- Deleting an existing queue.

Creating Queues

Creating a queue is done through the use of the MSMQQueueInfo component. This component has several properties, which are listed in Table 29.2. Only two of them have to be provided with any data.

Table 29.2   Properties of the *MSMQQueueInfo* Component

Property	Description
dateCreateTime	Indicates when the queue was created. This is a read-only property and cannot be set.
dateModifyTime	Indicates when the queue's properties were last modified. This is a read-only property and cannot be set.
guidQueue	This is a unique ID for the queue that is created by Message Queue Server when the queue is created. This is a read-only property and cannot be set.
guidServiceType	This is a GUID that identifies the queue type. A queue type ID can be generated by using the uuidgen.exe application. This is an optional property that can be used to locate the queue. This property must be specified before creating the queue.
isTransactional	This is a boolean value that specifies whether the queue is transactional or not. This is a read-only property and cannot be set.
lAuthenticate	This property specifies whether the queue will accept nonauthenticated messages.
lBaseProperty	This property defines the default priority of all messages submitted to this queue.
lJournal	This property defines whether messages retrieved from the queue should have a copy written to the journal queue.
lJournalQuota	This property specifies the maximum size of the journal queue.
lPrivLevel	This property specifies the privacy level of the queue, and whether the queue will accept unencrypted messages.
lQuota	This property specifies the maximum size of the queue.
strFormatName	This property specifies the format name of the queue. This property must be filled in before the queue can be opened. However, this does not have to be provided to create the queue, in which case Message Queue Server creates a value from the strPathName property.
strLabel	This is a string label that describes the queue. This property should be filled in before creating a new queue, as this is one of the most common properties that you will use in searching for an existing queue. The maximum length of this string is 124 characters.
strPathname	This is the only property that is required for creating a new queue. This specifies the computer name, whether the queue is public or private, and the name of the queue. The maximum length of this property is 124 characters.

To create a new queue, all you really have to specify is the queue path, which consists of the computer name, whether the queue is private, and the queue name separated by slashes. The computer name may have a single period substituted for it to specify the local computer. If a queue is to be a private queue, which means that it will only be accessible to applications running on the same computer as the queue, the middle portion of the path name should be Private$. Queue path names are formatted as follows:

```
<Computer name>/[Private$/]<Queue name>
```

So, to create a queue on a computer named Bullfrog, with a queue name of MyQueue, you would format the queue path name as follows:

```
Bullfrog/MyQueue
```

To create that same queue as a private queue, it would be:

```
Bullfrog/Private$/MyQueue
```

And to create the queue on the local computer, you could use this form instead:

```
./MyQueue
```

After you have specified the path name and the label for your queue, you can create the queue using the Create method of the MSMQQueueInfo component. You can create a new queue using the following VBScript code:

```
Dim qinfoMyQueue
Set qinfoMyQueue = Server.CreateObject(MSMQ.MSMQQueueInfo")
qinfoMyQueue.strPathName = "./MyQueue"
qinfoMyQueue.strLabel = "My Queue"
qinfoMyQueue.Create
```

At this point, you have a queue that you can open and begin sending and receiving messages through.

> **CAUTION**
>
> In the beta version of Message Queue Server that I am working with to write this chapter, I cannot advise that you create queues within an Active Server Page application. The queues that I create in an ASP application cannot be opened for receiving messages in any other application or programming language. I could open the queue for sending messages in anything else, but I could not receive messages. I could open the queue in any mode and perform any action from within an ASP application. If I create the queue using another application, I still have full functionality within my ASP application, as well as within any other application or programming tool.

Locating Queues

To locate an existing queue, you use a combination of the MSMQQuery and the MSMQQueueInfos components. First, you create an instance of the MSMQQuery component and run its LookupQueue method, which returns a MSMQQueueInfos component instance. The LookupQueue method takes a number of parameters, all of which are optional. The parameters are listed, in the order in which they are passed to the LookupQueue method, in Table 29.3.

Table 29.3 Parameters for the *MSMQQuery.LookupQueue* Method

Parameter	Description
guidQueue	The ID of the queue to be located.
guidServiceType	The service type of the queue to be located.
strLabel	The label of the queue to be located.
dateCreateTime	The creation time of the queue to be located.
dateModifyTime	The modification time of the queue to be located.
relServiceType	Relationship parameter for the service type parameter.
relLabel	Relationship parameter for the label parameter.
relCreateTime	Relationship parameter for the creation time parameter.
relModifyTime	Relationship parameter for the modification time parameter.

The relationship parameters default to a test for equality on the values supplied for the corresponding parameters. Any of the parameters that are left out are not used in locating matching queues. The relationship parameters can be any of the values listed in Table 29.4.

Table 29.4 *LookupQueue* Relationship Parameter Values

Label	Value	Description
REL_EQ	1	Equal
REL_NEQ	2	Not equal
REL_LT	3	Less than
REL_GT	4	Greater than
REL_LE	5	Less than or equal
REL_GE	6	Greater than or equal
REL_NOP	0	Ignore this parameter

The MSMQQuery.LookupQueue method returns a MSMQQueueInfos component, which is a collection of queue information components (MSMQQueueInfo). This component has two methods, both of which you use in navigating through the collection of queues. The first method, Reset, places you at the beginning of the collection of queues. You use the Next method to navigate to the first queue in the collection, as well as to the remaining queues in the collection. The Next method returns an instance of the MSMQQueueInfo component.

By using these two components, you can locate the queue that you created earlier by using the following VBScript code:

```
Dim query
Dim qinfos
Dim qinfoMyQueue
Set query = Server.CreateObject("MSMQ.MSMQQuery")
Set qinfos = query.LookupQueue(,,"My Queue")
qinfos.Reset
Set qinfoMyQueue = qinfos.Next
```

Notice in the LookupQueue method that you must supply two commas to indicate that you are supplying the third parameter, and to use the default for all of the rest of the parameters. If you had been using Visual Basic, you could have just specified the parameter name and let VB determine which parameter you were supplying.

At this point, you should have a queue description object, assuming that the queue was located. You can check to make sure that the lookup was successful by checking to see if the queue descriptor is "nothing." If the queue is "nothing," then the queue was not located and may need to be created. Otherwise, you can continue by opening the queue.

Opening Queues

To open the queue, you have to use the Open method of the MSMQQueueInfo component. This method takes two parameters, the access mode and the sharing mode. The available access modes are listed in Table 29.5.

Table 29.5 Queue Open Access Mode Parameter Values

Label	Value	Description
MQ_PEEK_ACCESS	32	The application will only be able to peek at messages in the queue without removing any messages.
MQ_RECEIVE_ACCESS	1	The application will be able to retrieve messages, thereby removing them from the queue. If the queue is opened using this access mode, the application will also be able to peek at the messages without removing them from the queue.
MQ_SEND_ACCESS	2	The application will be able to send messages to the queue.

The sharing mode of the queue must be one of the values listed in Table 29.6.

Table 29.6 Queue Sharing Mode Parameter Values

Label	Value	Description
MQ_DENY_NONE	0	This is the default value and must be used if opening the queue to peek at or send messages. This sharing mode enables other applications to open the same queue.
MQ_DENY_RECEIVE_SHARE	1	This value should only be used if opening the queue for receiving messages. This value will prevent any other applications from opening the same queue for receiving messages.

This method returns a MSMQQueue component instance. After you have either located a queue or created a new queue, you can open the queue for sending messages with the following code.

```
Dim qMyQueue
Set qMyQueue = qinfoMyQueue.Open(2, 0)
```

At this point, you can begin sending messages to the queue.

N O T E In VBScript, you must use the values for the open access mode and sharing mode, as the ASP application does not understand the textual representations of these values. ■

Sending Messages

In order to send a message, you have to use an instance of the MSMQMessage component. After you have the message object, you need to set several of its properties, including the message label and body properties. The properties of the message component are listed in Table 29.7.

Table 29.7 *MSMQMessage* Component Properties

Property	Description
body	This is the actual message that is being sent. This can be any datatype, structure, binary data, or even an ActiveX object.
binSenderCert	The digital security certificate of the sender. This is for use in sending and receiving encrypted messages.
binSenderID	This is an identifier of the application that sent the message. This is a read-only property that is set by Message Queue Server.
dateArrivedTime	This property contains the time that the message arrived in the destination queue. This is a read-only property that is automatically set by Message Queue Server.

continues

Table 29.7 Continued

Property	Description
dateSentTime	This property contains the time that the message was sent. This is a read-only property that is automatically set by Message Queue Server.
quidSrcMachine	This is the GUID (Globally Unique Identifier) of the machine that sent the message. This is a read-only property that is automatically set by Message Queue Server.
id	This is a unique message identifier that is generated by Message Queue Server. This is a read-only property.
idCorrelation	This is the ID of an original message, if this message is a response or acknowledgment of another message.
isAuthenticated	This is a Boolean value that specifies whether the message has been authenticated by Message Queue Server. This is a read-only property that is automatically set by Message Queue Server.
lAck	This property specifies what sort of acknowledgment should be placed in to the journal queue when the message is received from each queue.
lAppSpecific	This property can be used for an application-specific index that can be used for sorting messages.
lAuthLevel	This property specifies whether the message needs to be authenticated when it reaches the target queue.
lClass	This property specifies the message type. This can be a normal message, a positive or negative acknowledgment, or a report message. This is a read-only property that is automatically set by Message Queue Server.
lDelivery	This property specifies the method of delivery. The default value for this property is MQMSG_DELIVERY_EXPRESS, which keeps the message in memory where it is not recoverable in case of a system crash. The other possible setting for this property is MQMSG_DELIVERY_RECOVERABLE, which keeps the message stored on the disk drive of every computer in the delivery chain, so that the message can be recovered and delivered in the event of a system crash.
lEncryptAlg	This property specifies the encryption algorithm to be used for encrypting the message.
lHashAlg	This property specifies the hash algorithm to be used for authenticating the message.
lJournal	This property specifies whether to log this message in the journal queue when it is retrieved, or to store it in the dead-letter queue if the delivery time expires.

Property	Description
lPriority	This property specifies the priority of the message. This is a value from 0 (lowest) to 7 (highest), with a default value of 3. This value is used to determine how the message is routed across the network to its destination queue.
lPrivLevel	This property specifies whether the message is private and should be encrypted.
lMaxTimeToReachQueue	This property specifies in seconds the maximum time for the message to reach the destination queue. If the time specified expires before the message has reached its destination queue, the message is deleted or stored in the dead-letter queue. The default value for this is LONG_LIVED, which is an administratively controlled time that has a default value of 90 days.
lMaxTimeToReceive	This property specifies in seconds the maximum time for the message to be retrieved from the destination queue. If the time specified expires before the message has been retrieved, the message is deleted or stored in the dead-letter queue. The default value for this is LONG_LIVED, which is an administratively controlled time that has a default value of 90 days. This value should always be equal to or greater than the lMaxTimeToReachQueue property.
lSecurityContext	This property specifies the security information needed to authenticate messages.
lSenderIDType	This property specifies the type of sender sending the message.
lTrace	This property specifies whether the message should produce a tracing report, which specifies the queue manager, message ID, time to next hop, and so on.
lenBody	This property specifies the length of the message body. This is a read-only property that is automatically set by Message Queue Server.
queueinfoAdmin	This property specifies the queue to be used to send acknowledgment messages.
queueinfoDest	This property specifies the destination queue for the message. This is a read-only property that is automatically set by Message Queue Server.
queueinfoResponse	This property specifies a response queue for sending response messages.
strLabel	This property specifies a descriptive label for the message.

Part

VI

Ch

29

N O T E The types of encryption that are available with Message Queue Server are RC2 and RC4, two standard encryption algorithms that fall under the RSA banner using a Public/Private Key methodology. Message Queue Server does provide the hooks so that you can plug in different encryption algorithms if you so desire. ■

After you create an instance of the MSMQMessage component, you can set various properties, and then send the message using the Send method, specifying the open queue to be used. The properties that you will probably want to set include the lAck, lDelivery, strLabel, and body. Other common properties that you might want to set are lMaxTimeToReceive and lPriority. Using the queue that you opened in the previous section, you could send a message using the following VBScript:

```
Dim MyMsg
Set MyMsg - Server.CreateObject("MSMQ.MSMQMessage")
MyMsg.strLabel = "My message"
MyMsg.body = "This is my message, which I am sending through the queue."
MyMsg.lAck = MQMSG_ACKNOWLEDGMENT_NONE
MyMsg.lDelivery = MQMSG_DELIVERY_RECOVERABLE
MyMsg.Send qMyQueue
```

Receiving Messages

Receiving messages is even simpler than sending messages. After you have a queue open for receiving, you can create the MSMQMessage object by calling the MSMQQueue.Receive method as in the following code:

```
Dim RecvdMsg
Set RecvdMsg = qMyQueue.Receive
```

Once you have a message object, you can look at the message properties to read the message label and body, as well as the various other message properties.

Closing Queues

When you finish sending all the messages you need to send or receiving the messages you need to receive, you can close the queue by using the MSMQQueue component's Close method, as follows:

```
qMyQueue.Close
```

Once you have closed the queue, you cannot send or receive any more messages without re-opening the queue.

Deleting Queues

When you have completely finished using a queue, you can always delete it using the MSMQQueueInfo component's Delete method, as in the following VBScript:

```
qinfoMyQueue.Delete
```

Deleting the queue does not delete the queue information object that you used to delete the queue. It can be reused to create a new queue with the appropriate properties reset as necessary. Once a queue has been deleted, it cannot be opened for sending or receiving and all messages currently in the queue are lost.

Message Queue Server and Active Server Pages

Because the logical use of an Active Server Page application with Message Queue Server is in the generation of messages that are to be received by another application, that is where you will be putting your focus in building a working example application. You'll make use of the API test application that is included with Message Queue Server as one of the example applications to perform all the tasks that you don't want to include in your ASP application. You could perform all of these tasks in the ASP application, and I encourage you to try it using the example code provided above with each of the examples.

In your application, you will perform the following tasks:

1. Use the MQ API test application to create your message queue.
2. Locate, open, and send a message to the queue using ASP and VBScript.
3. Receive the message from the queue using the MQ API test application.
4. Delete the queue using the MQ API test application.

Once you have this system up and running, you might want to repeat steps 2 and 3 several times, performing step 2 several times before performing step 3 for each step 2 you performed.

Creating a Message Queue

If you pull up the Message Queue Server Explorer, you should see all the existing queues on your system in either the Sites or the Enterprise Server folders. If you haven't created any queues, Explorer should look like Figure 29.4.

If you open the MQ API test example application (located in the \Msmq\Sdk\Samples\Bin directory, and may also be installed on the Start menu in the samples folder within the Message Queue Server folder), which is included with Message Queue Server, you can create a queue for use in this example (I'll include the code to create the queue if it is not found in the ASP application, but everything will work better if you create the queue here). If you choose Api | MQCreateQueue from the application menu, you will be presented with a dialog box asking for the path name and the queue label. This first part of the path name should already be filled in with the computer name on which you are running. Fill in the remaining portion with the path name for the queue you are creating. Next, fill in a label for the queue, which you will be using to locate the queue in you ASP application. In this case, you can fill in the path name as **ASPExampQueue** and the label as **ASP Example Queue**, as shown in Figure 29.5. When you click the OK button, you'll be presented with a confirmation in the main API test window, as shown in Figure 29.6.

FIG. 29.4

Upon opening the Message Queue Server Explorer, you will be presented with all of the existing queues on the computers in your enterprise configuration.

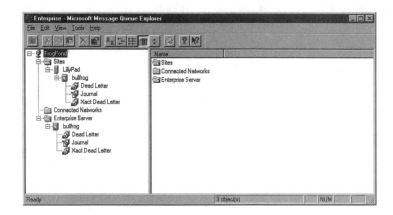

FIG. 29.5

Using the API test application, you can create a new queue by providing just the path name and label.

FIG. 29.6

The API test application displays a message confirming that the queue was created successfully.

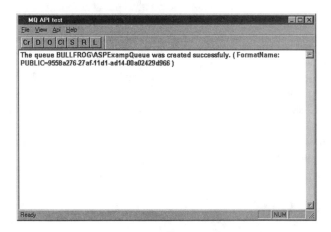

After you create the queue, go back to the Message Queue Server Explorer, choose View | Refresh from the main menu, and see the queue you just created appear in your server (see Figure 29.7).

FIG. 29.7

After creating a new queue, you can see the new queue in the Message Queue Server Explorer by refreshing the display.

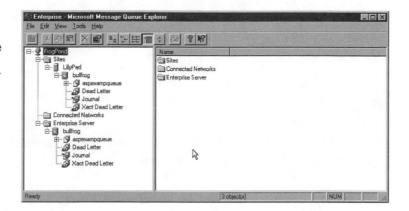

Sending a Message to the Queue

To be able to submit messages to the queue that you just created, you first need to have an HTML form that you can use for sending messages to the Web server. For this example, use a simple form like the one shown in Figure 29.8, which prompts the user for the message label and textual contents. (The HTML form used in this example, MSMQExample.htm, is available on the CD that accompanies this book.)

FIG. 29.8

You can use a simple HTML form to submit a message label and text for submitting to your message queue.

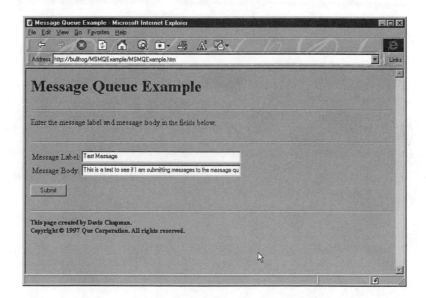

On the receiving end of your Web server, you need to write a little VBScript in your ASP document that is receiving the data submitted by your HTML form, and pass the data along to the message queue. In this ASP page, you will perform the following steps:

1. Try to locate the queue that you created.

2. If you are unable to locate the queue, create a new queue.

3. Open the queue for sending the message.

4. Create a `MSMQMessage` object, and populate it with the data values submitted by the form.

5. Send the message to your queue.

6. Close the queue.

You can perform all of these steps using the code in Listing 29.1.

Listing 29.1 *SUBMSG.ASP*—**You can capture the data submitted by the user and place it into the queue as a message.**

```
Dim query
Dim qinfos
Dim qinfoDest
Dim qDest
Dim msgSent
Dim msgBody
'Find or create the ASP Example Queue
Set query = Server.CreateObject("MSMQ.MSMQQuery")
Set qinfos = query.LookupQueue(,,"ASP Example Queue")
qinfos.Reset
Set qinfoDest = qinfos.Next
If qinfoDest Is Nothing Then
    Set qinfoDest = Server.CreateObject("MSMQ.MSMQQueueInfo")
    qinfoDest.strPathName = ".\ASPExampQueue"
    qinfoDest.strLabel = "ASP Example Queue"
    qinfoDest.Create
End If
'Open the Queue
Set qDest = qinfoDest.Open(2, 0)
'Send the Message
Set msgSent = Server.CreateObject("MSMQ.MSMQMessage")
msgSent.strLabel = Request.Form("MsgLabel")
msgBody = Request.Form("MsgBody")
msgSent.body = msgBody
msgSent.lAck = MQMSG_ACKNOWLEDGMENT_NONE
msgSent.lDelivery = MQMSG_DELIVERY_RECOVERABLE
msgSent.lMaxTimeToReceive = -1
msgSent.Send qDest
qDest.Close
```

N O T E Notice in Listing 29.1 that you did not set the message body directly to the value submitted by the user. It would seem like it would be easier to just do the following:

```
msgSent.body = Request.Form("MsgBody")
```

However, when you attempt this, you will receive an error message stating that the object cannot be automated. Instead, you need to place the value of the message body into a temporary holding variable, and then set the message body to the variable. I can't explain why this object cannot be automated, and it may be fixed in a future version of ASP and/or MSMQ. ■

After you submit the message to the queue using the ASP page containing the code listed previously (the entire ASP document can be found on the CD accompanying this book), you can pull up the Message Queue Server Explorer to see whether the message was submitted into the queue. If you select the queue you created, right-click the mouse, select Properties, and then select the Status tab, you can see how many messages are currently in the message queue (see Figure 29.9). You can also choose View | Refresh from the main menu with your queue selected to see the messages in the queue in the main Explorer window, as shown in Figure 29.10. Double-clicking the message brings up a Message Properties dialog box, which you can use to examine the contents of the message by choosing the Body tab, as shown in Figure 29.11.

FIG. 29.9

You can browse the current status of your queue through the Message Queue Server Explorer.

FIG. 29.10

You can visually display the message in the queue by refreshing the Explorer view of the queue.

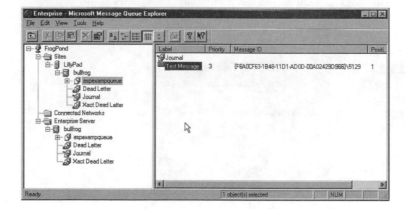

FIG. 29.11

From the Explorer window, you can examine the contents of messages in the queue.

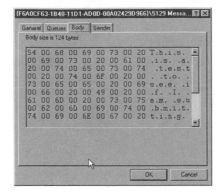

Receiving the Message from the Queue

Now that you have submitted a message to the queue, you can try and retrieve the message from the queue. You can build the code to do this into an ASP application, although that is not a very practical means of retrieving the message as it is unlikely that you would do this in a real application situation. Your other options are to build a custom application, or use the API test example application. For this example, use the API test application.

Before you can retrieve any messages, you need to open the message queue for receiving messages. You can do this by choosing Api | MQOpenQueue from the main menu of the API test application. This will bring up a dialog box that you can use to choose which queue to open. (If you closed the API test application since you created the queue, you need to locate the queue first.) Select the check box to indicate that you are opening the queue for receiving messages, as shown in Figure 29.12, and then click OK. If you are able to open the queue, the main window of the API test application will show that the queue was opened successfully (see Figure 29.13).

FIG. 29.12

When opening the message queue for receiving messages, you need to specify the access mode for receiving.

FIG. 29.13

The API test application will inform you whether the queue was opened successfully.

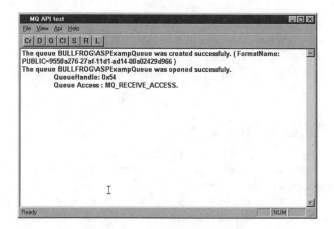

When you have the queue open, you can choose Api | MQReceiveMessage to retrieve the message from the queue. Once again you will be presented with a dialog box for you to specify the open queue and the timeout value (how long to wait before returning if there is no waiting message already in the queue), as shown in Figure 29.14. If you click OK, the message will be retrieved and its contents will be displayed in the main window of the API test application, along with information about the message, such as the sending user, the message priority, and whether the message was encrypted or authenticated (see Figure 29.15).

FIG. 29.14

The API test application will ask you to verify the queue and the timeout period before receiving a message.

FIG. 29.15

The received message contents will be added to the display in the API test main window.

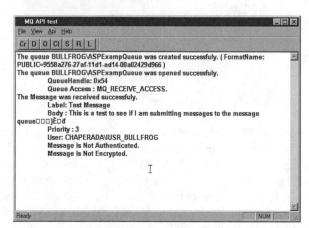

> **N O T E** In the beta version of Message Queue Server that I am using to write this, the API test application is adding additional garbage to the end of the message text in the display. This is being added by the API test application, and is not actually part of the message. If you check the contents of the message through the Explorer, you will find that this garbage is not included in the message. ▨

Closing and Deleting the Queue

When you finish sending and receiving all the messages from this application, you need to close the queue in the API test application. You can do this by choosing Api | MQCloseQueue from the main menu. You will then see a dialog box to verify which open queue you want to close, as shown in Figure 29.16. Clicking OK will close the queue and add a message to the API test application main window stating that the queue has been closed (see Figure 29.17).

FIG. 29.16

The API test application will ask you to select which open queue to close.

FIG. 29.17

The API test application will inform you if there is any problem closing the queue.

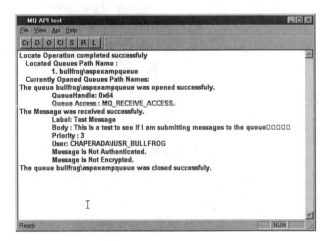

Once you have completely finished with this queue, you can delete it, thereby removing it from your Message Queue Server configuration. The queue must be closed before you can delete it in the API test application. Choose Api | MQDeleteQueue from the main menu. You will be presented, once again, with a dialog box asking you to select which queue is to be deleted (see Figure 29.18). Clicking the OK button will delete the queue, with the confirmation message being added to the main window display of the API test application (see Figure 29.19). If you pull up the Message Queue Server Explorer and refresh the computer, you will see that the queue is gone.

FIG. 29.18
When you delete a queue, the API test application will ask you to specify which queue to delete.

FIG. 29.19
Once you have chosen the queue to be deleted, the API test application will display whether the queue was successfully deleted.

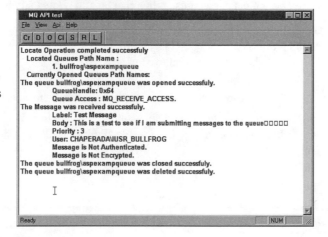

At this point, if you submit a new message using the ASP application, the ASP application will create a new version of the queue, which you may have to modify the ASP code to receive all messages from and to delete once you are done.

> **N O T E** To gain a better understanding of Message Queue Server, you might want to build your own version of the API Test sample application using Visual Basic and the Message Queue Server ActiveX components (the same ActiveX components we used in our ASP application.) You can also build the MSMQ API Test application using Visual C++ or Delphi by using either the ActiveX components or writing directly to the MSMQ API. The API Test sample application is supplied with MSMQ complete with source code for Visual C++, which you can examine and modify yourself. ■

From Here...

In this chapter, you have learned what message queuing systems are and how they work. You've also taken a look at Microsoft's new Message Queue Server, and seen how it can be used with an Active Server Page application to submit messages to another process that would need to act on the information provided. This could be used in any context where you need to trigger another process from input provided to an ASP application, in which you do not need to provide the user with the immediate results of the process.

From here, you might want to perform some experiments with Message Queue Server to see what kind of custom applications you can build to receive the messages, and what you can have those applications do with the information you have passed to them. You can also dig into the administration and configuration of Message Queue Server, configuring queues that take information from one server to another, where the sending ASP application is on one computer and the receiving application is located on another. Unfortunately, the administration and configuration issues involved in performing this are beyond the scope of the chapter and this book.

You might want to check out some of these other chapters on related subjects:

- To learn how to use Microsoft's Transaction Server with Active Server Pages to off-load synchronous processing to other servers in your enterprise environment, read Chapter 28, "Working with the Microsoft Transaction Server."
- To learn what's involved in building a corporate intranet or extranet application, check out Chapter 30, "Application Development for the Corporate Intranet/Extranet."
- To see how you can integrate all of these technologies together to build a large-scale Active Server Page application, see Chapter 32, "Putting It All Together: Creating an N-Tier Online Catalog Application."

Application Development for the Corporate Intranet/ Extranet

Developing Applications for an Intranet

See how to increase productivity right away with little investment.

Building an Extranet

Understanding this marriage of the intranet and Internet can mean creating cutting-edge applications.

When most people think of Web-based applications, the examples that spring to mind are of the interactive sites seen at **www.intel.com** or **www.microsoft.com**. But, in reality, most of the application development you will probably end up doing with ASP will be on an intranet server somewhere.

Many recent surveys have found that nearly 100 percent of all companies will be implementing intranets in the coming months and years. As an ASP developer, this is great news. There are literally thousands of stand-alone applications for everything from bookkeeping to customer support that will be ported to an internal Web server, if they aren't already.

Extranets are Web-based applications that contain both an intranet and Internet part. By burrowing through the firewall to query a database that is populated internally, you can securely provide information to those who need it. ■

Developing Intranet Applications

If you counted all the Internet sites in the world, you would get a pretty big number. But if you counted all the intranet sites in the world, you would have a huge number. Many companies have an intranet site for every department. Others have taken a more structured approach. Still, there will always be far more intranet Web sites than those on the Internet.

As a Web developer, this means that you will probably spend most of your time developing applications for one of these intranet sites. In a recent poll, nearly every company asked stated their intention to start porting their existing non-Web based applications to a version that will run on a browser.

This means that most of the time, you won't have to worry about having the greatest looking graphics and the most eloquent prose accompanying your application. Instead, you can concentrate on functionality.

When building an intranet application, there are a couple big differences to be aware of: larger bandwidth and standardized browsers. In reality, these differences enable you to develop more complex applications more quickly.

Leveraging Bandwidth

The vast majority of Internet surfers are browsing the Web on a modem. And while modems have grown faster and faster in speed, they come nowhere near the speed of a modern internal network.

This means that you can expect the users of your intranet application to be surfing at a minimum of 10MB a second. Generally, when developing for the Internet, you have to keep page size small for fear of bogging down someone's browser with a long download.

So what do you do with this larger than usual bandwidth? The figures below illustrate the trade offs involved in creating any client/server application. Figure 30.1 shows an example of a thin client, and Figure 30.2 shows fat-client browsers.

When developing an Internet-based application, you want to send as little information as possible, while simultaneously putting as much of the processing as possible onto the browser.

When building an intranet application, you don't need to worry nearly as much about the amount of information being sent. And, except for special cases, you also don't have to worry about excessive processor load on your server.

FIG. 30.1
Web browsers can be thin clients...

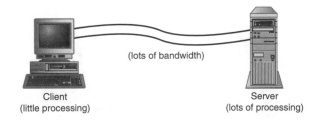

Client
(little processing)

(lots of bandwidth)

Server
(lots of processing)

FIG. 30.2
...or fat clients.

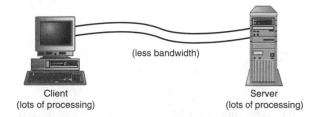

(less bandwidth)

Client
(lots of processing)

Server
(lots of processing)

> **CAUTION**
>
> Don't take this to mean that you don't ever need to worry about excessive processor load. If you are running a heavy-duty app that is going to be hit by thousands of employees every day (or even every hour), you will indeed need to start thinking about the load on the server.
>
> As a matter of fact, when it comes to very large corporate intranets, it is almost better to think of the site as an Internet site.
>
> Another point to consider is the amount of telecommuters that will be using your applications. These users will be surfing to you on modem lines. If you expect a large number of these mobile users, it is also good to think in terms of an Internet site.

A lot of development time is spent working around the limitations of the Internet and World Wide Web. With an intranet, most of these problems go away. Instead, as a developer, you can focus on creating a useful application.

Another nice advantage that you receive with increased bandwith is the capability to incorporate multimedia into your Web pages. On the Internet, graphics, sounds, and movies have to be carefully manipulated to make sure they don't require the user to wait for them to download. With your intranet, you can incorporate a large AVI and not have to sweat about it being too large.

So, imagine you are creating a training Web page. This Web page may be based on an existing CD-ROM. There will probably be many movie-type tutorials on the CD-ROM. You can convert these to some browser-enabled format and go. The bandwidth you will receive on your corporate intranet gives you this freedom.

When You Know What Browser They Have...

...then write for that browser.

If all of your users are going to be using Netscape Navigator, then it doesn't make a lot of sense to utilize client-side ActiveX controls. Conversely, if your client base is Internet Explorer, you can include ActiveX controls in your layout.

When building Web-based applications, many developers prefer to use client-side scripting for their data validation. JavaScript and VBScript can both be used to catch a multitude of errors. The following list shows some examples of validation that client scripting works great for.

- Multiple spaces
- Null values
- Illegal characters
- Characters that must be present (such as the @ in e-mail)
- Proper length

Of course, some types of validation are either very cumbersome or impossible with client-side validation. The following is a list of validation that should probably take place on the server:

- Duplicates in database
- Validating address fields like ZIP code and country
- Data integrity

On the Internet, if you want to use client-side scripting, you have several choices. You can detect which type of browser the user has. Once you know that, you can then use either VBScript for Internet Explorer and JavaScript for Navigator clients. However, taking this kind of approach requires a lot more work because you have to develop the validation in both scripting languages.

Another alternative is to write your client-side scripting using the subset of JavaScript that both browsers support. (Both Internet Explorer and Navigator support JavaScript to one degree or another.) However, you have to be careful to only use those features of JavaScript that you are sure the various browsers that will be visiting your site will be using.

When developing for the corporate intranet, these worries evaporate to a very large degree. Most companies have defined a standard browser for their users. If you know which browser your users will be using, you can save development time when developing your client scripting.

Below is a list of some of the features you can expect to be able to utilize if your standard browser is Internet Explorer.

- VBScript
- JScript (Microsoft's version of JavaScript)
- ActiveX controls
- ActiveX Documents
- Java
- Dynamic HTML (version 4)

Here are the major features you can use if your user's browser is Netscape Navigator:

- Java
- JavaScript
- Internet Foundation Classes

- LiveWire
- Dynamic HTML (version 4)

As you can see from the preceding lists, there are some similarities, but also some vast differences in the two major browsers. So, knowing which browser you are developing for can greatly enhance your development effort.

Sample Applications for the Intranet

On the Web, certain applications are seen over and over again: user registration, online ordering, and so forth. With intranets, other types of applications can be found on almost every site. In this section, you will examine some of the major applications that you will (or already have) developed and build a simple framework for them.

Project Management Tool

One of the major uses of an intranet is as a project management tool. This is an application that enables project teams to record tasks for various team members, record meeting notes, and other activities related to tracking a project from start to finish.

There will be four major components to this application: 1) a page to create a new project, 2) a page to add, delete, or modify a member of the project team, 3) a page to record, view, and modify tasks that are assigned to team members, and 4) a page to view and record meeting notes.

In this section, you will learn how to create pages that enable you to create a project, add members to a project, and assign tasks to team members. The other features, such as modifying members and tasks, will be left as an exercise for the reader.

One of the first design features you need to decide on is which technologies to leverage. To a very large degree, this will be based on what type of browser is on the network. In this case, let's assume it is Internet Explorer 3.02. So, you have a choice between VBScript and JScript for browser validation. You know what the browser is, so you don't have to worry about Navigator browsers. In this case, let's use VBScript for the client-side data validation.

Next, you need to decide what scripting language to use for your ASP pages. Again, the choice is between VBScript and Jscript. For consistency sake, let's again go with VBScript. One of the most compelling reasons for using VBScript in ASP pages is the wealth of documentation and examples in VBScript for ASP, although there are more and more JScript examples coming out.

Finally, you can leverage the increased bandwidth of your intranet by including some gratuitous graphics and sounds for users to use to personalize the application. This feature doesn't really benefit application performance, but it is easy to implement, and makes using the application more fun and easy for the user.

Listing 30.1 shows the ASP code to create a new project.

Listing 30.1   Adding a new project.

```
<html>
    <head>
        <meta http-equiv="Content-Type"
        content="text/html; charset=iso-8859-1">
        <meta name="GENERATOR"
        content="Microsoft FrontPage (Visual InterDev Edition) 2.0">
        <title>Add New Project</title>
    </head>

    <body bgcolor="#FFFFFF">
        <form name="form1" method="POST">
            <p align="center"><font size="6">Add New Project</font></p>

            <p align="center">Project Name
            <input type="text" size="20" name="projectName"></p>
            <p> </p>

            <p align="center">Project Lead ID
            <input type="text" size="20" name="projectLead"
            <%    if Session("projectLead") <> "" then
                      Response.Write("value=" & Session("projectLead"))
                  end if%>>
            <A HREF="empLookup.asp">Click here</A> to find your ID number</p>

            <p align="center">Project Description
            <input type="text" size="20" name="projectDescription"></p>
            <p> </p>

            <p align="center">
            <input type="submit" name="Submit" value="Submit"></p>
        </form>
    </body>
</html>
```

Notice how the code asks for the ID of the employee in charge of the project. The user creating this project might not have any idea what that ID is. So, you are proving them a simple lookup page where they can find their ID.

This is another example of the great power of the intranet. On the Internet, you would probably not allow this type of functionality. Imagine you write an Internet-based widget ordering system. You might give people a page they can visit to look up the status of their order. However, you will probably not give them the capability to look up their order.

First of all, this would be a security hole, enabling intruders to find out the status of orders that are not theirs. The second reason to not enable this is the strain on your server. With Internet sites, you must assume that the server load could grow exponentially. Allowing a status order lookup might bring your server over the edge. Listing 30.2 shows the code to add a new employee.

Listing 30.2 Adding a new employee.

```html
<html>
    <head>
        <meta http-equiv="Content-Type"
        content="text/html; charset=iso-8859-1">
        <meta name="GENERATOR"
        content="Microsoft FrontPage (Visual InterDev Edition) 2.0">
        <title>Add New Employee</title>
    </head>

    <body bgcolor="#FFFFFF">

    <% if Request.Form("name") = "" then %>
        <form name="form1" method="POST">
            <p align="center"><font size="6">Add Employee</font></p>

            <p align="center">Employee Name
            <input type="text" size="20" name="name"></p>
            <p> </p>

            <p align="center">Phone
            <input type="text" size="20" name="phone"></p>
            <p> </p>

            <p align="center">
            <input type="submit" name="Submit" value="Submit"></p>
        </form>
    <% else
        Dim name
        Dim phone
        name = request.form("name")
        phone = request.form("phone")

        set objConn = Server.CreateObject("ADODB.Connection")
        objConn.Open "DSN=ProjectTool;DriverId=25;FIL=MS
Access;MaxBufferSize=512;PageTimeout=5;"

        set objRst = Server.CreateObject("ADODB.Recordset")
        objRst.ActiveConnection = objConn
        objRst.LockType = adLockOptimistic
        objRst.Source = "tblEmp"
        objRst.CursorType = adOpenKeyset
        objRst.Open

        objRst.AddNew
                objRst("empName") = name
                objRst("empPhone") = phone
        objRst.Update

        'set the empID in the session not a variable
        Session("empID") = objRst("empID")
        objRst.Close
    %>
```

continues

Part

VI

Ch

30

Listing 30.2   Continued

```
        The following employee was added:
        <pre>
            <%=name%>
            <%=phone%>
            ID #: <%=Session("empID")%>
    <%end if%>
    </body>
</html>
```

In Listing 30.2, you are adding new employees to the database. Because this system resides on an intranet, you can also add some interesting functionality. If there exists in the images directory of the Web server a JPEG called *firstNameLastName*.jpg, you can display that employee's photo whenever you look at his information.

On the Internet, giving each employee a photo might become a huge bandwidth burden. But on an intranet, it can give you huge benefits. Imagine you are a new employee assigned to a project. You surf to the page that contains a list of the other employees in the project. By going to that page, you can see what the other employees you will be working with look like. Listing 30.3 shows the code to add a new task for an employee.

Listing 30.3   Adding a new task.

```
<html>
    <head>
        <meta http-equiv="Content-Type"
        content="text/html; charset=iso-8859-1">
        <meta name="GENERATOR"
        content="Microsoft FrontPage (Visual InterDev Edition) 2.0">
        <title>Add New Task</title>
    </head>

<body bgcolor="#FFFFFF">

<% if Request.Form("task") = "" then %>
    <form name="form1" method="POST">
            <p align="center"><font size="6">Add Task</font></p>

            <p align="center">Task
            <input type="text" size="20" name="name"></p>
            <p> </p>

            <p align="center">Status
            <input type="text" size="20" name="phone"></p>
            <p> </p>

            <p align="center">Project ID - <A href="projectlookup.asp">click
here</A> to look up
            <input type="text" size="20" name="phone"></p>
            <p> </p>
```

```
                        <p align="center">Employee ID - <A href="emplookup.asp">click
here</A> to look up
                        <input type="text" size="20" name="phone"></p>
                        <p> </p>

                        <p align="center">
                        <input type="submit" name="Submit" value="Submit"></p>
                </form>
        <% else
            Dim task
            Dim status
            Dim empID
            Dim projectID
            task = request.form("task")
            status = request.form("status")
            empID = request.form("empID")
            projectID = request.form("projectID")

            set objConn = Server.CreateObject("ADODB.Connection")
            objConn.Open "DSN=ProjectTool;DriverId=25;FIL=MS
Access;MaxBufferSize=512;PageTimeout=5;"

            set objRst = Server.CreateObject("ADODB.Recordset")
            objRst.ActiveConnection = objConn
            objRst.LockType = adLockOptimistic
            objRst.Source = "tbltasks"
            objRst.CursorType = adOpenKeyset
            objRst.Open

            objRst.AddNew
                        objRst("task") = task
                        objRst("status") = status
                        objRst("empID") = empID
                        objRst("projectID") = projectID
            objRst.Update
            objRst.Close
        %>

            The following task was added:
            <pre>
                <%=task%><BR>
                <%=status%>
        <%end if%>
        </body>
</html>
```

Part VI Ch 30

In the figures below, you can see what these three pages look like.

In Figure 30.3 you can see the HTML page as it exists to add a new project. Notice that although the layout is simple, there is quite a bit that will need to happen in the background.

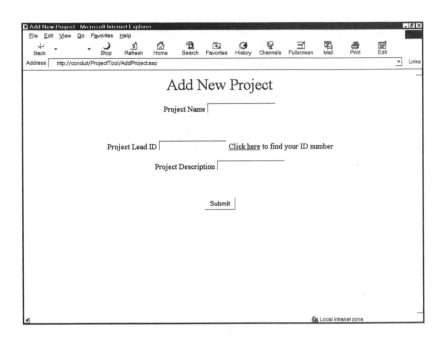

In Figure 30.4, you can see the page that adds a new employee.

Next, check out Figure 30.5 to see what the page looks like to add a new task.

FIG. 30.5
Adding a new task.

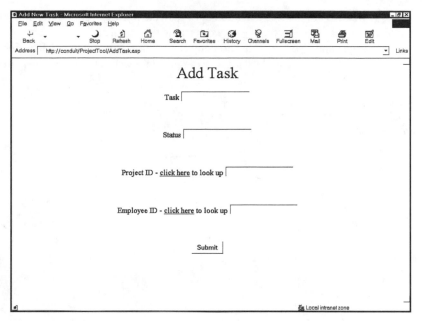

Another interesting idea you can implement with an intranet-based project tool is to enable the project leader to create an AVI discussing the project. Management, the project team, and other employees could browse this AVI. It would give them a nice multimedia presentation of what that project is all about.

Building an Extranet

An *extranet* is an application that contains both an intranet component and an external Internet component. The reasons for building this type of application are obvious; most of them revolve around communicating to customers' information that usually requires more expensive mediums, such as mail and freight, or selling materials online, such as wine, books, or what have you.

However, extranets can be very difficult to develop because of the added level of security that is necessary. If your extranet is compromised by unscrupulous sorts, you can open yourself up to lawsuits and lost customers.

Securing Your Extranet from Intruders

There are a number of ways in which to secure your site against intruders. The most popular are firewalls and dual-homed gateways. Each of these two devices can help to prevent intruders from breaking into your site by carefully managing the traffic that is allowed in and out at a very low level.

Firewalls are devices that sit in between your Web server and the outside world. They can be configured to enable only network traffic that is harmless to communicate with your Web server, and also to enable and deny access based on criteria such as destination address and protocol. See Figure 30.6 for an example of firewalls preventing unwanted access.

FIG. 30.6
Firewalls can prevent unwanted access.

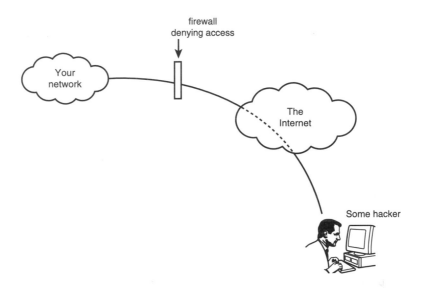

While this device can be a very powerful mechanism for preventing unwanted access, it is not fool-proof. By using techniques such as spoofing, intruders can still find ways to break past firewalls and access your data. However, if used correctly, they can provide powerful protection for your extranet application.

Dual-homed gateways are computers that contain two network cards and sit on two different networks. Because of the increased intelligence present with a dual-homed host, you can completely shut down traffic from the outside world except for communication from specifically designed machines.

Dual-homed hosts give you a huge amount of flexibility, while securing you better than any other form of protection (next to taking out the network cable). However, they can cause the traffic between networks to crawl. As with all things, it is a trade off of performance/development time versus security.

Confidential Information

The other major aspect of securing your extranet is to make sure that the communication link between the browser and the server is free from prying eyes while confidential information is being passed.

The primary technique to secure communications is through encryption. Encryption is an old-fashioned technology. There are several different ways in which you can encrypt the communication between your Web server and your user's browser. The most popular is Secure Sockets, an encryption method that Netscape developed.

Secure Sockets are based on public key encryption, in which you can encrypt your data from prying eyes. The way it works is fairly simple.

You have what is called a *key pair*. With this pair, there is a private key and a public key. Everyone has access to your public key. With this key, they can encrypt a message they are sending to you. However, only you have your private key, which is necessary to decrypt the message. The public key is one way—prying eyes cannot use it to decrypt messages sent to you.

Conversely, you can encrypt a message with your private key, and the only way to decrypt it is to use your public key. At first, this may not seem useful, but in reality, it is a really great way for someone to authenticate that the data is truly from you, otherwise, it would decrypt to garbage.

The technology to generate these key pairs can vary, but most key pairs are generated using the RSA public key cryptography. This cryptography is available from RSA Data Security, Inc., and Netscape has licensed this cryptography specifically for encryption.

Secure Sockets are easy to set up and they don't require any additional programming on the developer's part. The server and browser take care of everything.

It is simple to implement Secure Sockets on your Web server. The following are the steps involved:

1. Generate a key pair and a request file.
2. Get a certificate from a certificate authority.
3. Install your certificate on your server.
4. Turn on SSL security on those folders.

From Here...

In this chapter you have examined some of the concepts involved in creating applications for corporate intranets. You have also seen what an extranet is, and how it can be used to create powerful and lucrative online solutions.

You have learned how to best take advantage of the increased bandwidth of the intranet. You have also seen how knowing what browser your users will be using can lower development time.

Further, you have learned the issues of building a secure extranet application. Understanding security can mean the prevention of huge headaches later. I encourage you to delve further into the topic of security as a developer. Too much information has never hurt a programmer, and knowing too little about security can bite you in the end.

For related information, please see Chapter 31, "Using Internet Information Server 4.0 to Manage Your Web Applications," which will explore this great new Web server from Microsoft and show you how it will ease your Web application development time and costs! ∎

Part

VI

Ch

30

Using Internet Information Server 4.0 to Manage Your Web Applications

The Microsoft Management Console

Learn how to use the Microsoft Management Console to administer your ASP applications and other network services.

Increase Active Server Page Functionality

Review how IIS 4.0 expands the functionality of Active Server Pages with transactional-based scripts, process isolation, and new ASP components.

Internet Information Server 4.0 consolidates the Microsoft Transaction Server, Active Server Pages, HTTP, FTP, and Gopher servers, the Certificate server, the News and Mails servers, and advanced Web site management into one manageable interface. Of course, with no bias, one of the most exciting aspects of IIS 4.0 is the increased real-world functionality needed for Active Server Pages. IIS includes transactional-based scripts, the capability to run ASP applications in their own memory space, and the capability to activate client- and server-side script debugging capabilities, which finally provides a well-rounded framework needed to build mission-critical applications. ■

The Microsoft Management Console

IIS 4.0 provides a centralized network management tool called the *Microsoft Management Console* (*MMC*). From the Management Console, you can manage and configure the HTTP, FTP, and Gopher servers, the Transaction Server, the Certificate server, and the News and Mails servers.

Network Service Management

The Microsoft Management Console is a new administration interface that is designed to act as the common denominator for various network administration needs. The MMC interface is used to manage network components through "snap-in" technology. A *snap-in* is an in-process OLE server that is responsible for managing a specific network interface. At the time of this writing, the MMC supports a centralized control mechanism over the HTTP, FTP, Gopher, News, and SMTP Mail servers and the Transaction Server, as shown in Figure 31.1.

FIG. 31.1
The Microsoft Management Console uses snap-in technology to manage various network interfaces.

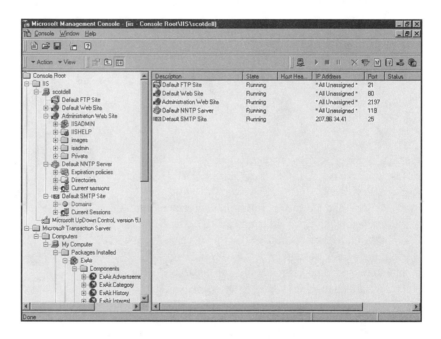

The MMC is divided into two panes. The left pane displays a hierarchical tree-view of snap-in items, or *namespaces*. The namespace items can act as objects, containers, or tasks representing the highest level of the snap-in component. These namespaces enable you to add objects such as URL links and ActiveX monitoring tools directly into the MMC. The individual items within the namespaces are called *nodes*. The detailed information of each node is displayed in the right pane, or the result pane.

The real power of MMC technology is that you are able to create your own MMCs. These customized MMCs can be tailored to your own specific administration needs, without risking the stability of an entire mission-critical system. You can use MMC to disperse administration tasks throughout your organization without giving complete control or full administrator rights to "network–impaired" users. For example, you can create customized MMCs for different levels of administration experience for a staff help desk application. As the level of experience grows, the staff can be given access to advanced MMCs with more powerful administration and security features. Less experienced users would use MMCs that minimize the potential of a catastrophic failure from a simple mistake. Figure 31.2 shows a selection of snap-ins you can choose from.

FIG. 31.2

Use snap-in technology to build and customize MMCs to disperse network administration.

The portability of the MMC is twofold. The MMC files themselves can be transferred to any machine on which the MMC is installed. By moving the MMC files between machines, administration tasks can be easily distributed throughout the organization. Second, the MMC can connect to any other machine where the MMC has been installed to access, control, and manage remote namespaces. Of course, the capability to remotely manage an MMC is dependent on NT security settings defined for your domains.

Besides providing a direct interface to network components, MMCs also provide direct access to the native NT administration tools, such as the Key Manager, Performance Monitor, Event Viewer, Server Manager, and User Manager. These tools can be readily accessed when you need them for the desired service, as shown in Figure 31.3.

The MMC uses property sheets to configure the various services. By right-clicking the service and selecting the Property item, you can access the settings for the service. For example, Figure 31.4 demonstrates accessing News Server property settings via the MMC. You can use these configuration settings in conjunction with the various network management tools, such as the Performance Monitor, to help troubleshoot and optimize your services. A practical situation that combines these tools might be if users are complaining that they cannot connect to the News server. You can use the MMC to activate Performance Monitor to see whether the maximum number of users for that News server is being reached. From the same MMC interface, you can use the Property tag of the News namespace item to increase the amount of connections allowed.

FIG. 31.3
The MMC provides quick access to networking administrative tools such as the Performance Monitor.

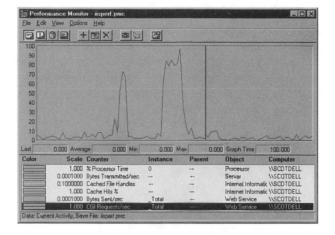

FIG. 31.4
The MMC provides easy access to the Add-ins administration tools and properties.

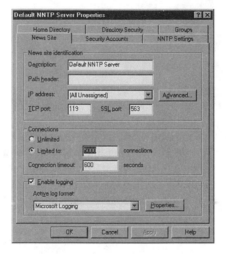

Web Site Management

The direct control over the networking components can also be applied to creating and administering your Web sites. Unlike previous versions of the Internet Information Server, IIS 4.0 enables multiple sites within the same HTTP server. With the previous version of IIS, you were limited to hosting only one site per IP address. Now you can create multiple sites bound to the same IP address, as you can see in Figure 31.5.

For example, assume that you create two Web sites on one IIS server bound to the same IP address and name the sites engineering and customer support. You can access the engineering site by using HTTP://engineering as the URL. To access the customer support site, use HTTP://customer support.

Part

VI

Ch

31

FIG. 31.5

IIS 4.0 enables
multiple sites bound to
a single IP address.

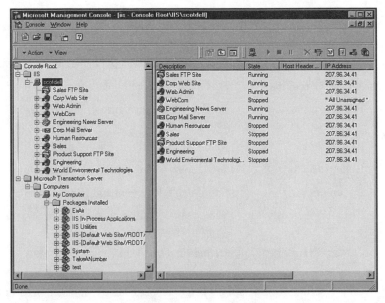

In addition to the capability to create multiple virtual sites within one HTTP server, each individual site can have its own unique settings. These settings are independent from other sites hosted by the same HTTP server. To configure the settings for a particular site, right-click the Web or FTP site. When you select the Property tag, a tabbed dialog box appears displaying the current configuration settings for the site, as shown in Figure 31.6.

FIG. 31.6

IIS 4.0 enables each
site on the server to
have its own configura-
tion settings.

The Web Site Property dialog box uses nine tabs to set the configurations of that site. These settings enable you to control the Web site, security accounts, performance, ISAPI filter, home directory, documents, HTTP Headers, and custom error settings, as you can see in Table 31.1.

Table 31.1   The Web Site Configuration Tabs

Tab Name	Description
Web Site	Sets the IP address and port connections and login capabilities.
Security Accounts	Sets the user permissions and remote operator permission.
Performance	Establishes performance tuning, bandwidth, and connection configurations.
ISAPI Filters	Manages ISAPI filters for the sites.
Home Directory	Sets access permissions and application configurations.
Documents	Sets default document and footer information.
Directory Security	Sets password authentication, secure communication, and TCP/IP restrictions.
Custom Errors	Defines and sets HTTP error messages.

Of these settings, three tabs pertain to configuring the application settings for your Web-based applications: the Home Directory, Directory Security, and the ISAPI Filter tabs.

Home Directory   The Home Directory tab, as shown in Figure 31.7, is used to set the application settings of the site. From this location, you can activate the site to run in its own process space, set the application permission for the site, and create, configure, or remove and unload the application from memory.

FIG. 31.7
The Home Directory tab controls the Web application settings for a specific Web site.

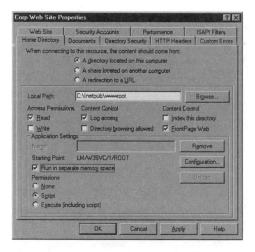

If you want to configure your site or virtual directory to run as an application, click the Create button. When you transform your site or virtual directory to an application that runs within its own memory space, IIS treats your site as a component and automatically registers the site object within the Transaction Server, as shown in Figure 31.8.

FIG. 31.8
IIS 4.0 treats your site or virtual directory as a component and uses the Microsoft Transaction Server to manage the application.

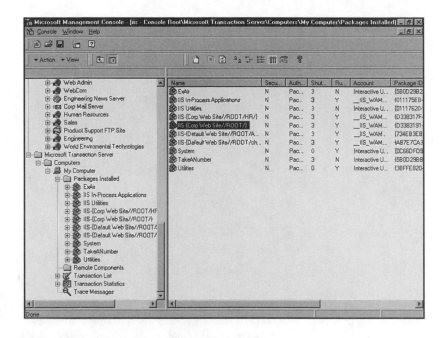

Directory Security The Directory Security tab, as shown in Figure 31.9, is used to control password authentication, secure communication, and TCP/IP access control.

FIG. 31.9
The Directory Security tab is used to set or view authentication methods, access control permissions, and secure data transfer methods for your applications.

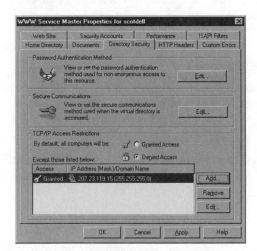

Authentication methods specify how the users will be identified when they access the site. The Authentication Methods dialog box, as shown in Figure 31.10, enables four different authentication methods to access the NT file system (NTFS):

- Allow Anonymous Access
- Basic Authentication

■ Windows NT Challenge/Response

■ Enable SSL Client Authentication

FIG. 31.10

IIS 4.0 supports four different authentication methods to help identify users of HTTP connections.

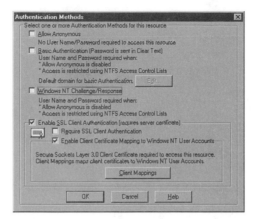

In order for any HTTP request to be processed, NT checks to see whether the request is being made by a valid user account with appropriate permissions. To enable anonymous access to your site, IIS creates a user account named IUSER_*computername* with Log On Locally user rights. In most situations, anonymous access is used for general information-sharing situations.

Basic authentication is used when information is limited only to a specific user community based on NT user accounts. Basic authentication will prompt the user for a valid username and password. However, keep in mind that the username and password are being passed in clear text or unencrypted form. This information could be extracted from a variety of network packet analyzers and cause possible security infractions.

To protect against this possible security violation, Microsoft developed an authentication method named Windows NT Challenge/Response. The authentication scheme provides an encrypted data exchange between the Internet Explorer browser and the IIS Web server to valid NT user accounts.

However, because the Windows NT Challenge/Response is limited to the Internet Explorer browser, using Secure Socket Layer provides the capability to send username and password from any browser to the hosting Web server.

In Enable SSL Client Authentication, you have the two options to control permissions to your site. The SSL Client Certificate Required To Access Resource option requires that the requesting browser has a digital certificate. Digital certificates are issued to validate the authenticity of users. These certificates can be issued from a trusted third party or from your own certificate server from within your Intranet. The option Mapping a Certificate to an NT User Account will take the information from the client certificate to find a valid NT user account. This enables you to control different levels of permissions within the site through NT without having to change or reissue user certificates.

From the Directory Security tab, you can also choose the Secure Communication option to create a secure channel between the Web server and SSL-complaint browsers. You can further control access to your sites based on the requesting browser's IP address. Although limiting the IP address is not generally used on public Web sites, it is particularly useful for intranet and extranet applications where business groups are organized by their IP address. For example, you can regulate permissions to the accounting Web site by accepting only requests from the account IP sub-mask.

ISAPI Filters   The ISAPI Filters tab, as shown in Figure 31.11, is used to add, edit, and remove ISAPI filters for your site. Remember that the filters can be applied to a specific site within the HTTP server. In previous versions of IIS, ISAPI filters could only be applied to the HTTP service level and not targeted to a specific site.

FIG. 31.11
The ISAPI Filters tab enables ISAPI applications to be applied to a specific Web site.

Part
VI

Ch
31

Configuring Active Server Application Settings

To drill down into the specific configurations of your Active Server Page application, use the Create or Configuration buttons that were shown in Figure 31.7. From this interface, you can set the application settings for the site or virtual directory. In particular, you can control the application mappings, Active Server Pages, Active Server Page debugging, and CGI script timeout values, as shown in Figure 31.12.

The Application Mappings tab shown in Figure 31.12 enables you to set what application will be used to process files according to its file extension. For example, files ending with .ASP extensions (Active Server Pages) will be processed by the asp.dll located in the c:\winnt\system32\inetsrv directory. The Cache ISAPI Application option enables you to cache the API DLLs. Therefore, when additional .ASPs are called, this path mapping to the DLL is not necessary. By default, this option is selected.

FIG. 31.12

IIS 4.0 enables you to configure and manage the settings of your application.

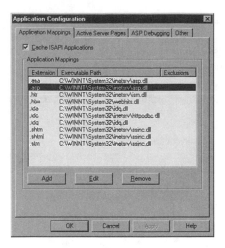

The Active Server Pages tab is used to set the default properties of Active Server Pages when the server-side scripts are processed. The Active Server Page tab enables you to manage application configurations and script file caching (see Figure 31.13).

FIG. 31.13

The default settings for Active Server Pages can be configured in this tab.

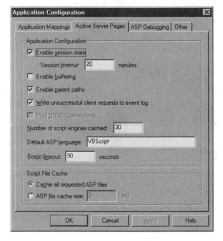

The Application configuration section enables you to set the default properties of Active Server Pages, as shown in Table 31.2.

Table 31.2 Configuring Active Server Page Properties

Property	Description	Page-Level Override Variable
Enable Session State	Creates a new Session object to track user variables.	EnableSessionState

Property	Description	Page-Level Override Variable
Session timeout	Sets the timeout value that destroys the user Session object.	Session.TimeOut
Enable buffering	Determines whether the entire page is completely generated on the server before sending the page to the browser.	Response.Buffer
Enable Parent Path	Sets whether the browser can navigate up the directory structure using the parent directory (..).	N/A
Write unsuccessful requests to log	Used to write unsuccessful HTTP page requests to the NT event log.	N/A
Number of script engines cached	Sets the maximum number of Active scripting languages to be cached in memory.	N/A
Default ASP language	Sets the default Active Server Page scripting language.	Language
Script Timeout	Sets the amount of time in seconds a script will process before terminating.	Server.ScriptTimeout

Part
VI

Ch
31

You can also use this tab to set ASP caching options. When an ASP file is cached, the .ASP source file is cached, not the results of a processed ASP. Also, you can see performance increases by specifying more memory for caching. To cache all .ASP files, select the Cache All Requested ASP radio button. To limit the size of cached ASPs in memory, set the desired amount of memory in megabytes to be assigned for caching. The optimal cache setting depends on the nature of your ASP application. Use the NT Performance Monitor to monitor your Web server resources to find the optimal settings for your ASP applications.

N O T E Keep in mind that most of these variables can be overwritten at the page level when the script is processed. ■

You can override these default ASP settings at the page level to ensure that your scripts are properly executed if the default settings are changed for the site, or if your application is moved to another server.

The ASP Debugging tab of the Application Configuration dialog box, as shown in Figure 31.14, enables you to manage the debugging and script errors messaging of the Internet Information Server. IIS 4.0 can utilize client and server debugging capabilities using Microsoft's Script Debugger. To enable ASP server or client debugging, select the appropriate check box. This tab also enables you to control the error messages sent to the client. The error messages can consist of either displaying the detailed message generated by the server or can be a generic error message that you specify. In most situations, displaying the detailed ASP error message is recommended as this information can be helpful in identifying the source of the scripting error.

FIG. 31.14
Use the MMC to activate client- and server-side ASP debugging.

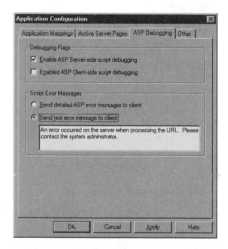

The fourth tab of the Application Configuration dialog box, shown in Figure 31.15, enables you to set the timeout value for Common Gateway Interface (CGI) scripts to expire. The CGI timeout value is expressed in seconds.

Setting Security Accounts

Another great aspect of the MMC and IIS 4.0 are the remote administration features. As more and more sites are integrating scripts and application logic, the centralized administration tasks of network administrators and webmasters have grown exponentially. Because of this growth, meeting the various configuration needs is often the bottleneck to delivering applications. To prevent the bottleneck from occurring, the Security Accounts tab, as shown in Figure 31.16, provides the capability to disperse administration features to other remote operators.

FIG. 31.15
Common Gateway
Interface timeout values
are also set in the
Application Configura-
tion dialog box.

FIG. 31.16
IIS 4.0 offloads administration tasks to remote users.

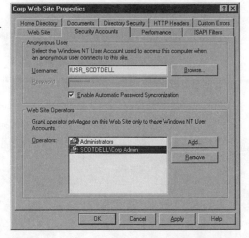

Now the specified remote users, as designated by NT user accounts, can control the properties
of a site—without having to contact the webmaster—via HTML. This process still enables
network administrators and webmasters to manage sites at a higher level, but it allocates the
administration specifics of a minor site to localized developers or project managers. Figure
31.17 illustrates a remote user using the HTML interface to manage his site.

These remote management capacities are not only exciting for application developers, but can
also be directly applied to Internet service providers. Now Internet service providers can initially set up a site for a user and enable the user to maintain and manage the specifics of the
site. For example, Figure 31.18 illustrates a remote user applying security settings to his site.

Part
VI

Ch
31

FIG. 31.17
Remote users can completely manage their site via HTML.

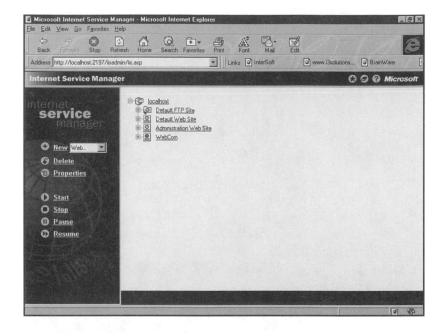

FIG. 31.18
Webmasters can deploy the HTML interface to manage all the sites on a server at a higher level, leaving the detailed site management up to localized site users.

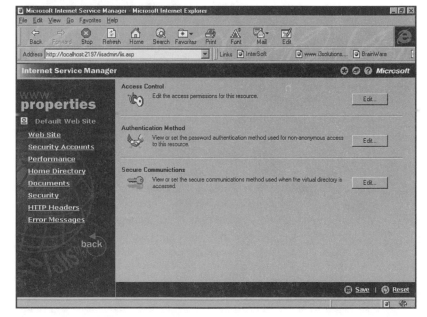

Creating New Sites and Virtual Directories

The MMC provides wizards to help set up new Web and FTP sites and virtual directories. The Setup Wizard asks a series of questions that create a site or directory based on information you provide. To create a new Web or FTP site, right-click the machine you want to create the new site on and select Create New. Alternatively, you can choose the Action and Create New options from the MMC menu. After choosing a new Web or FTP site, the Setup Wizard will guide you through the site setup, as shown in Figure 31.19.

FIG. 31.19
Creation of Web sites, FTP sites, and virtual directories is facilitated by the use of wizards.

The Web Site Creation Wizard will ask for the IP address and port number of the Web server, the path of the *home* directory, permit anonymous access, and select script permission levels.

When you create a new virtual directory, the Configuration dialog window will be slightly different from the Web site configuration window. Because a virtual directory does not need HTTP service specifications, such as performance configuration, IP address, ISAPI filter, and remote configuration issues, these options are eliminated from the virtual directory dialog box. The remaining tags essentially remain the same as the Web site configuration window. This difference is illustrated in Figure 31.20.

FIG. 31.20
Setting Virtual Directories directory options.

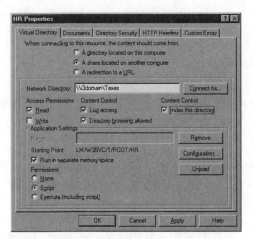

Changing the Default Site Values

The use of wizards may help you to create individual sites, but they do not necessarily enable you to set all the properties needed to run a site. The purpose of any wizard is to provide a simple interface to gather information that varies from user to user. The wizard does not need to prompt for values that are considered constant. These assumed constants are stored in a master template. You can also change the default settings for the master template for the specific machine. To change the default settings, select the machine name hosting the HTTP or FTP service in the MMC. Then select the Edit button under the Master Properties section, as shown in Figure 31.21.

FIG. 31.21
The default settings for Web sites and FTP sites are stored in a master template file for each hosting machine.

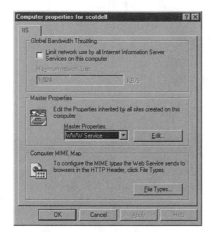

New Active Server Pages Functionality

With the new release of the Internet Information Server 4.0 comes the advanced functionality of Active Server Pages. This extended functionality is based on advances in the programming functionality, development, and debugging environments and new components. Because the information covered in this section has already been covered in detail in various chapters, this section will provide a summary of the new features with Active Server Pages.

The Script Debugger

Before IIS 4.0, debugging your Active Server Page code was a very tedious and frustrating job. With the release of IIS 4.0, Microsoft Script Debugger provides a debugging environment for both client- and server-side VBScript and JScript. The Script Debugger replicates most of the functionality found in Visual Basic. This environment, as shown in Figure 31.22, enables you to set breakpoints, retrieve and set property and object values, and provide different stepping mechanisms to step through the scripting code. For a closer view at the Script Debugger, see Chapter 9, "Using the Script Debugger."

Transactional Scripts, Microsoft Transaction Server, and Isolated ASP Applications

One of the most significant advances for developing Internet-based applications made possible with the release of the Internet Information Server 4.0 is the capability to create transaction-based scripts. Because processing ASP scripts is what really controls the application workflow and component's functionality, the capability to wrap transaction processing around components at the ASP script level is critical.

FIG. 31.22

IIS 4.0 integrates a Script Debugger to set, analyze, and step through client- and server-side code.

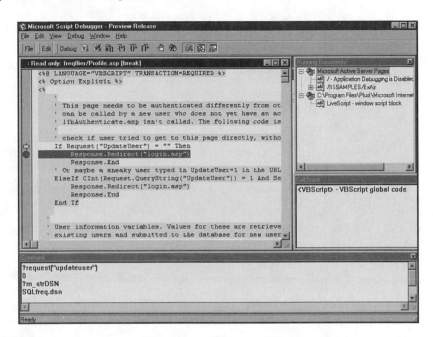

By separating your applications into components, you benefit from code reuse, a centralized location for software updates, and the capability to distribute your applications across machine boundaries to address scalability issues that might plague your applications. Now you can directly use these components within transactional-based scripts. These components are then managed by the Transaction Server using the `ObjectContext` object. The `ObjectContext` object enables you to either commit or abort a processed transaction.

The Transaction Server enables you to isolate individual components, as well as entire ASP applications, to be executed in their own memory space. The creation of individual runtime environments protects other Web applications from failing as a result of another component's failure. This is particularly valuable in preventing the entire Web server from shutting down as a result of a single individual Web application suffering catastrophic failure. Furthermore, process isolation enables you to stop an application and unload its components by stopping and restarting the Web server.

The Transaction Server is now implemented as a Microsoft Management Console (MMC) snap-in. The MMC provides a centralized administration point to various network interfaces, such as the HTTP, FTP, News, Mail, and Transaction Servers. Through the Transaction Server Explorer, you can completely manage component interaction by viewing the status of various packages and components, managing individual and groups of objects, setting the startup

Part

VI

Ch

31

options, and shutting down individual server processes. For more information on using transactions in your ASP scripts, refer to Chapter 12, "Controlling the Server with the `Server` Object and Using Transaction Processing with the `ObjectContext` Object."

New ASP Components

ASP provides new base components that add to the native scripting functional of the Internet Information Server. Table 31.3 provides a summary of the installable components.

Table 31.3   The Active Server Page Components

Component Name	Description
Browser Capabilities Component	Determines the requesting browser's characteristics.
Advertisement Rotator Component	Generates scrolling advertisement bars.
Counter Component	Creates incremental variables.
Page Counter Component	Keeps track the amount of times a page is requested.
Content Rotator	Dynamically changes the content on a page every time the page is requested or refreshed.
Content Linking Component	Creates a systematic Web page navigation system.
Active Messaging/SMTP Component	Creates an interface into Microsoft Exchange and other e-mail–based systems.
Tools Component	Provides additional programming functionality for server-side processing.
Permission Checker Component	Checks the user access permissions for files.
Database Access Component (Active Data Object)	Creates a database connection to an ODBC-compliant database.

For more information on these components, see Chapter 17, "Implementing Existing Server-Side Components."

Utilizing New HTTP 1.1 Support

The Internet Information Server 4.0 benefits from four new features of the HTTP 1.1 specification. These new features focus on connection functionality and HTTP file management. The four features can be summarized as shown in Table 31.4.

Table 31.4   HTTP 1.1 Features

Feature	Description
Persistent Connection	Keeps the TCP connection between the client and server alive.
Pipelining	Enables multiple requests to be made on a connection before receiving any response from the host.
HTTP PUT	Provides update functionality on the Web server.
HTTP DELETE	Provides delete functionality on the Web server.

The persistent connection and pipelining features transform the stateless nature of the Web into a connection-oriented system. Traditionally, HTTP dictated that after a Web server was finished servicing your request, the connection between the browser and the server was released. The connection is then established with another user and then dropped after the Web server finishes delivered information. However, the constant process of establishing and releasing TPC connections requires a significant amount of resources.

HTTP 1.1 helps to solve the need to establish multiple connections by establishing and maintaining a connection between the browser and the Web server. The capability to maintain a constant connection is refered to as *persistent connection*.

Second, HTTP 1.1 also supports pipelining. *Pipelining* enables multiple requests to be transmitted over the same connection before receiving any responses from the host.

The remaining two features of HTTP 1.1 deliver value to Web server by enabling publishing and managing files via HTTP. HTTP 1.1 supports HTTP PUT and HTTP DELETE commands. The HTTP PUT command enables information to be uploaded to a server. The HTTP DELETE command provides the capability to remove content from the Web server.

The HTTP 1.1 specification was designed to be backward compatible, but in order to use the new features of HTTP 1.1, both the browser client and Web server must support HTTP 1.1. If the requesting browser is not HTTP 1.1 compatible, the IIS 4.0 Web server will generate HTTP 1.0 responses. The IIS Web server accomplishes this by scanning the header information sent from the requesting browser. The Header information identifies the HTTP level of the requesting client. If the browser is HTTP 1.1-compliant, the IIS server responds by sending HTTP 1.1 responses. If the browser is 1.0-compliant, the Web server uses HTTP 1.0 to respond to the client.

From Here...

In this chapter, you can see that the Internet Information Server and Active Server Pages work in conjunction with the Transaction Server to provide a transactional-based application deployment mechanism over the Web. The Internet Information Server 4.0 is managed as a snap-in interface to the Microsoft Management Console. The MMC provides a centralized administration tool to various network interfaces, such as IIS, FTP News, Mail, and Transaction Servers.

Part

VI

Ch

31

The consolidated interface provides property sheets to quickly administer and configure the network services. The MMC enables you to easily configure your Web site to run as its own application within its own memory space. The capability to capitalize on process isolation prevents the site from being influenced by other applications and prevents your components from affecting other applications. Furthermore, the MMC also provides a centralized location to manage the access permission of your site and well as enable you to tailor the Active Server Pages runtime environments.

- Chapter 12, "Controlling the Server with the `Server` Object and Using Transaction Processing with the `ObjectContext` Object."

- Chapter 13, "Managing the User Session: The `Session` Object," illustrates the nuances of tracking a user through an ASP application.

- Chapter 15, "Retrieving User Information: The `Request` Object," demonstrates how to collect information from the user using forms, hidden fields, and cookies.

- Chapter 18, "Creating Your Own Active Server Components," will teach how to create your own ActiveX components to meet the needs of your applications.

- Chapter 28, "Working with the Microsoft Transaction Server," illustrates the use of the Transaction Server to manage components within your ASP applications.

- Chapter 32, "Putting It All Together: Creating an N-Tier Online Catalog Application," will demonstrate how to use the various features of Active Server Pages to build a multi-tier Web-based application.

Putting It All Together: Creating an N-Tier Online Catalog Application

This chapter represents the beginning steps in transforming your Web-based application into a distributed, component-based Web system. This chapter demonstrates this approach for the Amazing DataWidget WareHouse online catalog. Specifically, this chapter will demonstrate how to convert the database application logic and embedded business rules demonstrated in Chapter 26 and convert them into ActiveX components managed by the Microsoft Transaction Server. These ActiveX components can then be processed on the Web server or can be distributed onto remote application servers. In addition, the middle-tier components can be accessed by Active Server Pages and by any COM-compliant Windows application.

The new components will be created to contain the database access logic that was once embedded in existing Active Server scripts. These scripts will perform the database access and compile into ActiveX Dynamic Link Libraries (DLLs).

Building Database Components

Learn how to create ActiveX database components to take advantage of transaction processing for your database resources from Active Server Pages.

Creating Business Rule Servers

Create business rules and ActiveX components in Visual Basic that can be distributed across your organization to form the foundation of your applications.

Register and Distribute Your Components

Learn how to register your components using the Microsoft Transaction Server to manage and distribute your COM components on local and remote machines.

Deploying ASP and Win32 Clients Using the New Components

Learn how Active Server Pages and Win32 clients can both access the same functionality from the middle tier components and how Visual Basic can be used to test and debug Active components.

These database components will be responsible for loading the initial products into the application, determining the current inventory of an item, and adding and deleting items from inventory. Furthermore, you will take embedded Active Server application logic to create another business rules server to validate account numbers before placing an order. After building these various layers, the components will be installed or registered to use their functionality regardless of machine boundaries and network protocol. In addition, this chapter will demonstrate how these middle-tier business servers can be accessed from any Web browser or any Win32 client. ■

Create the Application Initialization Component

In the previous "Putting It All Together" chapters, the Amazing DataWidgets WareHouse Web site has demonstrated various coding methods to present the online catalog material to the potential customers. Chapter 16, "Putting It All Together: Building an Online Catalog," demonstrated loading the catalog product listing from values entered directly in ASP, and Chapter 26, "Putting It All Together: Creating a Dynamic Database Application," demonstrated extracting the catalog information from a database. In both situations, you have loaded the variables that are used throughout the site into application-level variables when the Web application is first started. This one-time data-load enables all users of the application to have access to the same data without wasting resources on establishing and maintaining connections to external systems throughout the application. This loading sequence used the Application_OnStart event of the GLOBAL.ASA file to load variables and variable arrays into application-level variables.

The fundamental reason for using the one-time data load is to maximize performance by minimizing input/output from the IIS server to other systems, such as database or messaging systems. This approach provides three advantages in delivering and deploying applications. First, minimizing I/O through the application reduces system resources that can be better used for your application. Second, by designing closed looped systems, your applications won't be associated with or dependent on poor performance from external systems. Minimizing data access points provides a more centralized data filter or control mechanism at both design time and runtime. Providing defined locations in the application where external information can access data helps maintain strict data-flow, minimize data corruption from incomplete transaction processes, and enables you to better scale software concerns.

Reducing the I/O is considerably more important in a Web-based architecture. Not only are you sharing the same resources to deliver HTML documents to the browser, but you are also sharing the same I/O resources the Web server has access to. Therefore, at any one time, your Internet applications could possibly have tens of thousands concurrent users, all of which are trying to access a variety of back-end systems. This is why an optimized Input/Output approach, as shown in Figure 32.1, can have significant effects on your Web-based applications.

With this in mind, in this chapter you will create two ActiveX components using Visual Basic 5.0. These components will be compiled as DLLs to run as in-process, non-visual application servers that will perform specific tasks. The first custom-built ActiveX component, the Datawidget.dll, will be used to house several database functions needed for the order processing section of the Web site. This component is used to provide insert, update, and delete methods to the Amazing DataWidgets inventory database. The second ActiveX component, the `DataWidgetProcessing.dll`, is responsible for processing and verifying correct account numbers. This component does not include any database functionality and is simply used to process account validation rules.

FIG. 32.1
Optimized I/O systems can have significant performance effects on your Web-based systems.

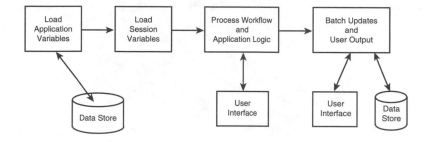

(An optimized system)

Creating the Customized Database Access Component

When a user first enters an application, the application-level variables are loaded into memory using the `Application_OnStart` event. In the original catalog application, the variables are loaded via VBScript using Active Server Pages. To take advantage of database connection pooling, the initial load sequence will be transferred into the Database Object Component, which will be created using Visual Basic 5. The database component will contain a variety of database functionality needed for this application. A specific unit of functionality can be implemented from external objects using a *method*. Methods are used to trigger embedded functionality of an object.

N O T E Keep in mind that you can build the components with any COM-compliant application development tool, such as Visual Basic, Visual C, Delphi, or PowerBuilder. ■

To begin creating the ActiveX database component, open Visual Basic 5.0. Choose ActiveX DLL from the New tabbed dialog box when Visual Basic is opened, as shown in Figure 32.2.

If this menu has been disabled, you can create a new ActiveX component by selecting New from the File menu to display the available Visual Basic templates, as shown in Figure 32.3.

Part
VI

Ch
32

FIG. 32.2
Visual Basic 5.0 can be used to create in-process Dynamic Link Libraries to house your application logic.

FIG. 32.3
Use Visual Basic project templates to create ActiveX DLLs.

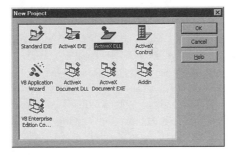

After the class module has been created, Visual Basic uses different windows to organize and manage projects. Use the Properties window, or press F4, to name the new class module `clsDBinfo`. Likewise, name the project `DataWidgets`. These two names are used to identify the `Application.Class` object reference needed by Active Server Pages to use `Server.CreateObject(Application.Class)` method.

Visual Basic uses functions and subroutines to create ActiveX DLL methods, which methods expose an object's internal functionality. Other COM-compliant objects can then call this functionality. To create a method that returns the information in the Products table, create a public function called `LoadProductsTable`. This function will return an array that extracts information from the Products table. The Products table contains the currently available product information from the Amazing DataWidgets WareHouse.

To create the new function, either directly type the syntax on the page, or select Add Procedure from the Tools menu to display the Add Procedure dialog box (see Figure 32.4).

This dialog box will create the following Visual Basic code:

```
Public Function LoadProductsTable()

End Function
```

FIG. 32.4

Create your component's methods using functions and subroutines in Visual Basic.

Now, you want to expand the functionality of the procedure by adding an input variable to identify an ODBC name. Furthermore, because you know that you will be returning the results to Active Server Pages, the function results should be returned as a Variant. These accommodations can be met by changing the function as shown in the following:

```
Function LoadProductsTable (strODBC) As Variant

End Function
```

Now you can add the desired application logic to the function. In this situation, you are going to mimic the Active Server script in the previous version of the Amazing DataWidgets WareHouse site. Listing 32.1 selects all records in the Products table and transfers selected members of the recordset into an array that is passed back to the calling page.

Part
VI

Ch
32

Listing 32.1 Loading the available product listings with the
***LoadProductTable* method.**

```
Function LoadProductsTable(strODBC) As Variant
'=== Load the catalog information from the specified data source
  Set dataconn = CreateObject("ADODB.Connection")
  dataconn.Open strODBC
  Set cmdRS = CreateObject("ADODB.RecordSet")
  sql = "SELECT ProductName, Description, UnitPrice, UnitsInStock FROM Products"
  cmdRS.Open sql, dataconn, adOpenKeyset, adLockBatchOptimistic
  If cmdRS.EOF And cmdRS.BOF Then
      '=== no records
  Else
      Dim icount As Integer
      cmdRS.MoveFirst
      Do While Not cmdRS.EOF
        icount = icount + 1
        cmdRS.MoveNext
      Loop
      cmdRS.MoveFirst
      ReDim aProductArray(icount, 4)
      Do While Not cmdRS.EOF
        i = i + 1
        aProductArray(i, 1) = cmdRS("ProductName")
        aProductArray(i, 2) = cmdRS("Description")
        aProductArray(i, 3) = cmdRS("UnitPrice")
        aProductArray(i, 4) = 0
        cmdRS.MoveNext
```

continues

Listing 32.1 Continued

```
        Loop
    End If
    cmdRS.Close
    dataconn.Close
    LoadProductsTable = aProductArray
End Function
```

After the function is finished, the class module needs to be compiled as a DLL. But before you do so, the Data Object Library must be referenced in the project to create the database connection. The reference can be added to the project by selecting Reference from the Project menu. A dialog box displaying the currently installed object libraries will be displayed. Select the Microsoft ActiveX Data Objects 1.5 Library. Now that component has been coded, it is ready to be compiled. To do this, select Make Datawidget.dll from the File menu and save the new DLL.

Registering the Component

In order for other COM-based programs to use the new DLL, the component DLL must be registered with the machine that will call the DLL. The DLL itself can be physically located on the same machine or located on a remote machine. These components can be installed and registered it two ways. The first and recommended method is to install the components in a transaction monitor, such as the Microsoft Transaction Server (MTS). The Microsoft Transaction Server provides, as covered in Chapter 28, "Working with the Microsoft Transaction Server," straightforward component registration, administration, and configuration features with runtime resource management features. The second method to register your component is to use the Regsrv32 and DCOMCNF utilities. The Regsrv32 utility gives you the capability to register the component on a local or remote machine. The DCOMCNF utility provides the administration utility to configure the installed components. Note that using the Regsrv32 and DCOMCNF methods does not supply the runtime resource management of the components that is supplied when using the Transaction Server. The Regsrv32 and DCOMCNF utilities rely on the individual components to manage their own runtime resources.

Installing Components on the Microsoft Transaction Server

To optimize the performance and scalability of the Amazing DataWidget WareHouse online ordering system, the validation and database processing components will be installed in the Microsoft Transaction Server. The Transaction Server automatically registers the component when the components are installed on the Transaction Server.

To install the components in MTS, use the Microsoft Management Console to open the Transaction Explorer view. The Transaction Explorer provides a hierarchical navigation formation to manage local and remote components, as shown in Figure 32.5.

FIG. 32.5

The Transaction Explorer provides a hierarchical administration utility to manage components.

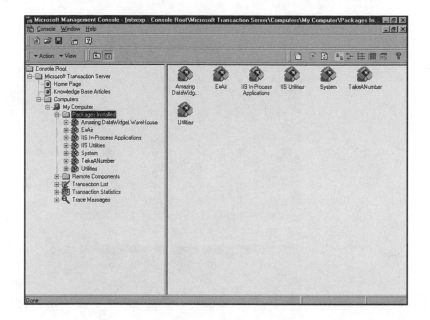

To install your components, a transaction package must be created first. A *package* is used to group common components together to provide a central administration utility for the installed components. To create a package for your component, highlight the Packages Installed folder and either select New from the Action menu or right-click the folder and select New. The Transaction Server will prompt you to install a pre-built package or create a blank package. After selecting the Create Blank Package option, name the package "Amazing DataWidget WareHouse." Next, the Package wizard will prompt you for information about what NT user account to run the packages under. For demonstration purposes, assume you have the proper rights to run the components, select the Interactive User – The Current Logged On User option. Click the Finish button, and the Package Wizard will create the new package and display the package in the Transaction Explorer view.

After the new package is created, two folders are created under the Package folder. The Components folder is used to house the individual components, and the Roles folder is used to set permission and security settings. To install the two components, right-click the Components folder and select New to activate the Component Wizard, as shown in Figure 32.6.

The Component Wizard will prompt you to install components that are already registered on the system or to install a new component. After selecting the Install New Component(s) option, click the Add Files button to select the location of the DLLs, as shown in Figure 32.7.

FIG. 32.6

Installing the compo-
nents in the Transaction
Server with the
Component Wizard.

FIG. 32.7

Multiple components
can be simultaneously
installed with the
Component Wizard.

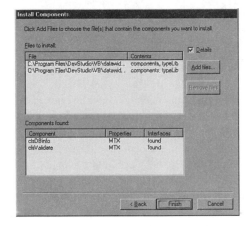

After you click the Finish button, the Component Wizard installs the components, returns you
to the Transaction Explorer view, and displays the newly installed components, as shown in
Figure 32.8.

After the components are installed, the Explorer view provides different display formats to
access the properties of the components and packages installed in the MTS. For example, you
can expose a component's properties or methods by right-clicking the item, as shown in Figure 32.9.

Now that the components have been installed on the Transaction Server, the Transaction
Server will handle all resource management for the components. The Transaction Server
combines the installation and registration of components with the capability to manage the
runtime component resources. However, you do not have to use the Transaction Server to
remotely install and configure your components. The following section demonstrates how to
register your components without installing the components in the Transaction Server.

FIG. 32.8

The installed components can now be administered within the Transaction Server.

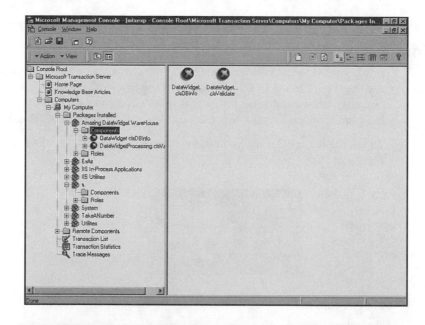

FIG. 32.9

Viewing and administering the package, components, and methods properties is accomplished by right-clicking the item.

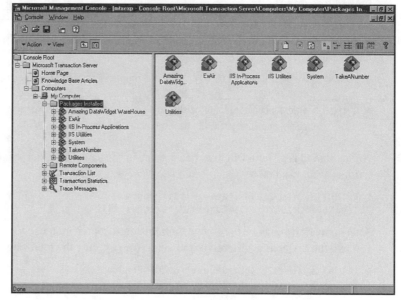

Using the Regsrv32 and DCOMCFG Utilities for Component Configuration

An alternative to installing and configuring the component with the Transaction Server is to use the Regsrv32 and DCOMCFG utilities. The Regsvr32.exe utility, found in your system directory, is used to register the local or remote component. The DCOMCFG utility provides the administration interface to set and configure the component settings.

To use the Regsrv32 utility, you can use the command prompt or the Run window, as shown in Figure 32.10.

FIG. 32.10

Use the Regsrv32 command to register components on local or remote machines.

For example, the following code registers the new `datawidget.dll` on the current machine:

```
C:\WINNT\system32\regsvr32.exe C:\WINNT\system32\datawidget.dll
```

To register a component located on a remote machine, specify the path to the host machine. For example, the following code registers a DLL located on a machine named `CompaqAppServer`:

```
C:\WINNT\system32\regsvr32.exe \\CompaqAppServer\system32\datawidget.dll
```

N O T E   In order for components to be shared on remote machines, DCOM must be installed, enabled, and configured with the appropriate NT security settings. ■

Notice that to register a DLL that has a space in the path, you must wrap the DLL path in quotations, as shown below:

```
C:\WINNT\system32\regsvr32.exe "C:\Program
Files\DevStudio\VB\datawidgets\datawidget.dll"
```

Alternatively, if you need to remove the registered component, use the –u flag. For example, to remove the previous registered `datawidget.dll`, execute the following line of code:

```
C:\WINNT\system32\regsvr32.exe –u "C:\Program
Files\DevStudio\VB\datawidgets\datawidget.dll"
```

This capability to activate remote components is made possible through Distributed COM (DCOM). Of course, you just can't start distributing your process loads onto other machines without proper security and configuration rights. To enable and configure this distributed processing capability, use the DCOMCNFG utility, as shown in Figure 32.11.

FIG. 32.11

Use DCOMCNFG to administer distributed component properties.

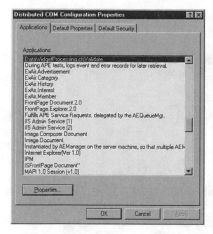

To start the DCOMCNFG utility, type **DCOMCNFG** from any command window or select Run from the Start menu to initiate the Run dialog box. Use the Default Properties tab of the DCOM Configuration dialog box to set whether DCOM is enabled on the current machine, as shown in Figure 32.12. Make sure that the option to Enable Distributed COM on This Computer is checked.

FIG. 32.12

Use the Default Properties tab of DCOMCNFG to enable DCOM.

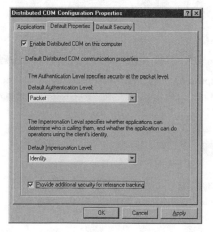

Finally, DCOMCFG enables you to administer DCOM permissions using the Default Security tab. From here, you can set the general access, launch, and configuration DCOM settings shown in Figure 32.13.

FIG. 32.13
The Default Security tab is used to administer access, launch, and configuration permissions of DCOM.

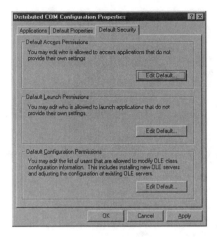

Integrating the New ActiveX Components into the ASPs

Once the new component has been created and registered, the Active Server scripts have to be modified to use the component's methods. After the components have been integrated into the ASP, you will add error trapping to ensure that the components did establish their proper connections.

Calling the Component from the Active Server Page

Now that the new ActiveX component is properly mapped, the Active Server Pages have to be modified to call the methods of the new components. You could simply replace the code modules that used to exist in the GLOBAL.ASA file with references to the new Data Widget's database component. However, the Amazing DataWidget WareHouse Web developers want the flexibility to update the application variables whenever new product information changes in the database without having to restart the Web server or Web site.

To accomplish real-time updates to application variables, a new initialization Active Server Page is created to update the Products information stored in the application variables. This page gives the Web developer the flexibility to update the application level without relying on the Application_OnStart event. The requesting users can be automatically routed to this page when they enter the Web site. Web developers can simply include this non-visual initialization page directly in the user workflow to automatically update the application-level variables. For example, the default site can use redirection methods to call this page automatically when the root directory is accessed. Alternatively, you can place security settings on this file to only give the administrators access to this page. Therefore, when the data needs to be refreshed, all the administrator has to do is browse to the page to load the new application-level variables.

Regardless of how or where the page is called, the new component is called the same way. You can create an instance by naming the application and class name. Once the object is instantiated, you can reference any of its methods. For example, the following ASP code returns the Product table information into a local array called aProductArray by calling the LoadProductsTable method of the DataWidgets datasource.

```
<%
Application("strODBC") = "DataWidgets"
Dim aProductArray
Set myDBObject = Server.CreateObject("datawidget.clsDBinfo")
aProductArray = myDBObject.LoadProductsTable(Application("strODBC"))
%>
```

Notice that the ODBC name has been added as an application variable.

Creating the Generic Error Form

Now that your custom-created component can be called from Active Server Pages, you want to be able to trap invalid user input as well as possible component failure. This user and component failure is integrated into the Amazing DataWidget WareHouse Web site with the addition of server-side error trapping. This error screen, as shown in Figure 32.14, is generated by sending values to an Active Server Page that displays different error types depending on the values passed to it.

FIG. 32.14
Create generic error screens to accept a variety of processing errors.

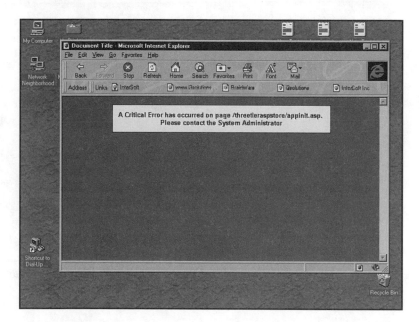

Now you will implement some of the error trapping logic that was covered in Chapter 10, "The Compostition of an Active Server Application." Error trapping can be enabled by using the `On Error` statement. The `On Error` statement enables you to control how the script will react to an error. Listing 32.2 demonstrates the use of the `Resume Next` statement to trap for possible errors.

Listing 32.2   Using ASP error trapping to ensure the component has been properly referenced.

```
<%
Application.Lock
dim aProductArray
Set myDBObject = server.CreateObject("datawidget.clsDBinfo")
aProductArray = myDBObject.LoadProductsTable(Application("strODBC"))

On Error Resume Next
If Err Then
     page = Request.ServerVariables("SCRIPT_NAME")
     errormsg = "A Critical Error has occurred on page " &page &". <BR>Please
contact the System Administrator"
     urlstr = "error.asp?errortype=" &Server.URLEncode(errortype) & "&errormsg="
&Server.URLEncode(errormsg)
     Response.Redirect urlstr
Else
     Application("aSoftware") = aProductArray
     set atemp = nothing
End If
Application.UnLock

'=== initial user's session to be an empty basket
session("basket")=Application("aSoftware")

Response.Redirect "main.asp"
%>
```

In Listing 32.2, the script checks to see whether the `Err` object exists. When an error occurs, Visual Basic script creates an `Err` object. If an error does exist, the user is automatically routed to an error template Active Server Page. Depending on the input, the error box presents itself in different ways. In this case, the call to the `DataWidget` component failed and presents a `Critical` error message to the user.

If an error does not occur, the application variable `aSoftware` is transferred to a user's session variable named `basket`. This transfer is used to enable individuals to modify their own orders without affecting application variables.

Creating the Validation Server

In order to help distribute the processing load away from the Web server, a validation ActiveX Server is going to be created to process account information. The Amazing DataWidget

WareHouse has pre-defined algorithms to help identify and validate accounts. In this situation, the validation server will validate any nine-digit number beginning with 200 and ending with 16.

Because this validation server is going to be distributed onto another machine that has been designated as an application server, a completely separate DLL needs to be created. Create a new ActiveX DLL project following the same steps as described in the preceding example. Name the project DataWidgetProcessing and the new class module clsValidate. Next, create a function named ValidateNumber that accepts an account number to process, as shown in Figure 32.15.

FIG. 32.15
Use Visual Basic to create an account validation server to transfer processing power from the Web server onto remote machines.

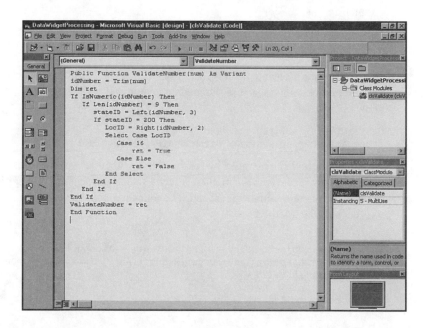

Next, create the code to match the required processing logic. Listing 32.3 demonstrates the simple validation routine that accepts only nine-digit numbers beginning with 200 and ending with 16.

Listing 32.3 Creating an account validation method.

```
Public Function ValidateNumber(num) As Variant
'=== Performs a validation process on the account number
   idNumber = Trim(num)
   Dim ret
   If IsNumeric(idNumber) Then
      If Len(idNumber) = 9 Then
         stateID = Left(idNumber, 3)
         If stateID = 200 Then
```

continues

Part VI
Ch 32

Listing 32.3 Continued

```
            LocID = Right(idNumber, 2)
            Select Case LocID
                Case 16
                    '=== The pre-approved mailing IDs
                    ret = True
                Case Else
                    ret = False
            End Select
        End If
    End If
End If
ValidateNumber = ret
End Function
```

After successfully saving the new DLL, place the new DLL on the application server. To register the remote component, use the machine name and path with the `regsrv32` command, as shown below:

```
C:\WINNT\system32\regsvr32.exe
\\CompaqAppServer\system32\DataWidgetProcessing.dll
```

Now, this method can be called by referencing an instance of the `DataWidgetProcessing` component. The `ValidateNumber` method returns `True` if the account number is valid and returns `False` if the account number is invalid. The following code example demonstrates using the `ValidateNumber` method.

```
<%
Set myAccountObject = Server.CreateObject("datawidgetprocessing.clsvalidate")
If myAccountObject.validateNumber(Request.Form("txtaccountnumber")) Then
'=== Account is Valid
Else
'=== Account failed
End If
%>
```

Creating the Order Processing and Inventory Control Database Component

The next part of the Amazing DataWidget WareHouse application demonstrates the use of the database access components created earlier in this chapter to place an order. The program uses three methods to retrieve, add, and delete items from the inventory database.

Creating the *GetProductInventory* Method

The `GetProductInventory` method is used to determine how many items of a specific type are available in inventory. The amount of inventory in stock is needed to trigger an automatic warehouse ordering process if the inventory gets below a specific threshold. To create this method, reopen the DataWidget Visual Basic project. To add additional methods the existing component, simply create additional functions. For example, to create the `GetProductInventory` function, add the following function to the class module as shown in Listing 32.4.

Listing 32.4   Creating the *GetProductInventory* method.

```
Public Function GetProductInventory(strODBC, strProductName) As Variant
'=== Retrieves the amount of items in the inventory for a specific item
   Set dataconn = CreateObject("ADODB.Connection")
   dataconn.Open strODBC
   Set cmdTmp = CreateObject("ADODB.Command")
   sql = "SELECT UnitsInStock FROM Products where ProductName= '" &
strProductName & "'"
   Set cmdRS = CreateObject("ADODB.RecordSet")
   Set cmdTmp.ActiveConnection = dataconn
   cmdRS.Open sql, dataconn, adOpenKeyset, adLockBatchOptimistic
   If cmdRS.EOF And cmdRS.BOF Then
       ret = 0
   Else
       ret = cmdRS("UnitsInStock")
   End If
   cmdRS.Close
   dataconn.Close
   GetProductInventory = ret
End Function
```

This listing retrieves how many of the specific product is in stock. To implement the `GetProductInventory` method from a client, reference the `GetProductInventory` method after an instance of the component has been created:

```
Set myObject = CreateObject("datawidget.clsDBinfo")
txtInventory.Text = myObject.GetProductInventory("datawidgets", "Mind-Bender
Control")
```

Creating the *AddProductInventory* Method

The `AddProductInventory` method is used to add an amount of a specific product to the inventory table (see Listing 32.5).

Listing 32.5   Creating the *AddProductInventory* method.

```
Public Function AddProductInventory(strODBC, strProductName, iAmount) As Variant
'=== Adds an amount of a specific inventory item
   Set dataconn = CreateObject("ADODB.Connection")
   dataconn.Open strODBC
   Set cmdTmp = CreateObject("ADODB.Command")
   sql = "UPDATE Products Set UnitsInStock=UnitsInStock+"
   sql = sql & iAmount & " WHERE ProductName = '" & strProductName & "'"
```

continues

Part

VI

Ch

32

Listing 32.5   Continued

```
    Set cmdRS = CreateObject("ADODB.RecordSet")
    Set cmdTmp.ActiveConnection = dataconn
    cmdRS.Open sql, dataconn, adOpenKeyset, adLockBatchOptimistic
    dataconn.Close
    If Not Err Then
        ret = True
    End If
    AddProductInventory = ret
End Function
```

The AddProductInventory method is used to add more inventory for a specific product when items in the warehouse are restocked. The AddProductInventory method can be called by using the following code:

```
Set myObject = CreateObject("datawidget.clsDBinfo")
ret = myObject.AddProductInventory("datawidgets", "Mind-Bender Control", 5)
```

Creating the *DeleteProductInventory* Method

The DeleteProductInventory method is called when a user places an order and the amount of items ordered is removed from inventory. This method can be implemented using Listing 32.6.

Listing 32.6   Creating the *DeleteProductInventory* method.

```
Public Function DeleteProductInventory(strODBC, strProductName, iAmount) As
Variant
'=== Remove a specific amount of product from inventory
  Set dataconn = CreateObject("ADODB.Connection")
  dataconn.Open strODBC
  Set cmdTmp = CreateObject("ADODB.Command")
  sql = "UPDATE Products Set UnitsInStock=UnitsInStock-"
  sql = sql & iAmount & " WHERE ProductName = '" & strProductName & "'"
  Set cmdRS = CreateObject("ADODB.RecordSet")
  Set cmdTmp.ActiveConnection = dataconn
  cmdRS.Open sql, dataconn, 0, 1
  dataconn.Close
  If Not Err Then
      ret = True
  End If
  DeleteProductInventory = ret
End Function
```

This method can be accessed after creating a reference to the DataWidget component using the following code:

```
Set myObject = CreateObject("datawidget.clsDBinfo")
ret = myObject.DeleteProductInventory("datawidgets", "Mind-Bender Control", 3)
```

Building and Testing Components

After you create the new class module, one of the best ways to test your new DLL is through another Visual Basic application. To accomplish this, add a new project to the current Visual Basic workspace by selecting File, Add Project, and then Standard Exe. Visual Basic 5.0 enables you to open multiple projects within one instance of Visual Basic, as shown in Figure 32.16. Notice the Project Group Window in the upper-right corner of Figure 32.16 displays having a class module project and a forms project open within the same environment.

FIG. 32.16
Visual Basic enables you to host multiple projects within one development environment.

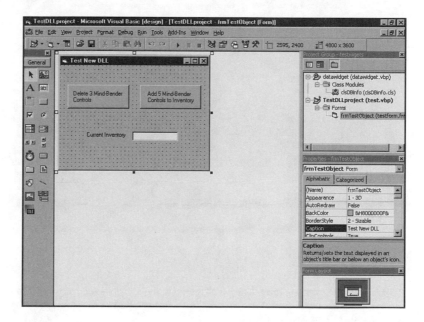

At first, this capability to house multiple projects may just seem like a convenience. But the real power of this feature is that it enables you to provide inline-debugging capabilities to your new component. Now you can place breakpoints within the DataWidget class module to provide inline component debugging after the client calls the specific method. This debugging capability is illustrated in Figure 32.17.

To start testing the new component, add two command buttons and a text box to the form. These command buttons are going to be used to test the AddProductInventory and DeleteProductInventory methods. After naming the command buttons, create an instance of the DataWidget component using the CreateObject syntax. Now any of the instantiated object's methods can be referenced. Listing 32.7 demonstrates using different form events to trigger the three new methods.

Part
VI

Ch
32

FIG. 32.17

Visual Basic provides inline-debugging capabilities for your components.

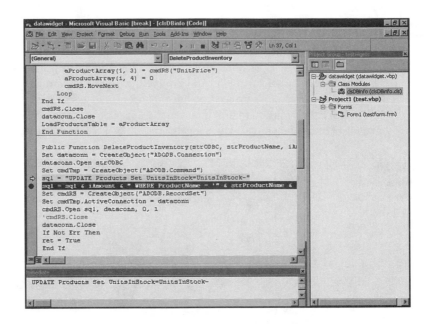

Listing 32.7   Creating method calls to the new component in a native Visual Basic form.

```
Private Sub btnAdd_Click()
    Dim myObject As Object
    Set myObject = CreateObject("datawidget.clsDBinfo")
    ret = myObject.AddProductInventory("datawidgets", "Mind-Bender Control", 5)
    txtInventory.Text = myObject.GetProductInventory("datawidgets", "Mind-
Bender Control")
    Set myObject = Nothing
End Sub

Private Sub btnDelete_Click()
    Dim myObject As Object
    Set myObject = CreateObject("datawidget.clsDBinfo")
    ret = myObject.DeleteProductInventory("datawidgets", "Mind-Bender Control",
3)
    txtInventory.Text = myObject.GetProductInventory("datawidgets", "Mind-
Bender Control")
    ret = LoadProductsTable("datawidgets")
    Set myObject = Nothing
End Sub

Private Sub Form_Load()
    Dim myObject As Object
    Set myObject = CreateObject("datawidget.clsDBinfo")
    txtInventory.Text = myObject.GetProductInventory("datawidgets", "Mind-
Bender Control")
    Set myObject = Nothing
End Sub
```

To run the form application to test your new component, right-click the new project and choose Select As Startup. When you run the application, the standard EXE project will execute to display the form you created to test the DataWidget DLL, as shown in Figure 32.18.

FIG. 32.18
Use native VB forms to test your middle-tier components.

This Visual Basic application can now access the Datawidget's methods that you created. This Visual Basic form accesses the same non-visual, middle-tier component that the ASP and the IIS server will hit against.

Putting It All Together: Filling the Order

Now that you have created the various components to perform account validation and database manipulation, you can integrate the components together into a logical unit of work. When the order is placed, the user's account number is the first item to be processed. If the account number is not valid, the error page instructs the user to enter a correct account number, as shown in Figure 32.19.

Part
VI
Ch
32

FIG. 32.19
The error page template displays the invalid field name and prompts the user to retry.

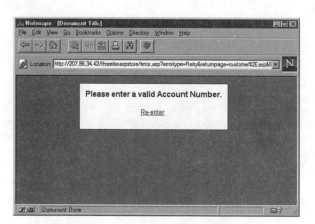

The second stage starts to iterate through the user's basket looking for any items that have been ordered. When an item is found, the database checks the current amount of that item in inventory. If the inventory amount is greater than 15, the requested order amount is deducted from inventory. If the inventory amount is below 15, more items are added to the inventory and then the requested amount to the product item is deducted from inventory. After all the ordered items are processed, the user is routed to the summary page where information about their order is displayed. Listing 32.8 demonstrates this capability.

Listing 32.8   Placing the order: Integrating the database and validation components together into one ASP.

```
<%
Set myAccountObject = Server.CreateObject("datawidgetprocessing.clsvalidate")
If myAccountObject.validateNumber(Request.Form("txtaccountnumber")) Then
   Set myOrderingObject = server.CreateObject("datawidget.clsDBinfo")
   aUsersBasket=Session("basket")
   iProductsOrdered = UBound(aUsersBasket,1)
   For iCounter = 1 to iProductsOrdered
      iUnitQuantity=clng(aUsersBasket(iCounter,4))
      If iUnitQuantity > 0 Then
         strProductName = aUsersBasket(iCounter,1)
         '=== reserve items
   iCurrentProductInventory=myOrderingObject.GetProductInventory(Application("strODBC"),
strProductName)
         If iCurrentProductInventory > 15 Then
            '=== Everything is fine
             ret = myOrderingObject.DeleteProductInventory
(Application("strODBC"), strProductName, iUnitQuantity)
         Else
            '=== Add more items
             ret = myOrderingObject.AddProductInventory(Application("strODBC"),
strProductName, 25)
             ret = myOrderingObject.DeleteProductInventory (Application("strODBC"),
strProductName, iUnitQuantity)
         End If
      End If
   Next
   Response.Redirect "summary.asp"
Else
   dim errortype, returnpage, fieldname, urlstr
   errortype="Retry"
   returnpage ="customer.asp"
   fieldname ="Account Number"
   urlstr="error.asp?errortype=" &Server.URLEncode(errortype) & "&returnpage="
&Server.URLEncode(returnpage) & "&fieldname=" &Server.URLEncode(fieldname)
   Response.Redirect urlstr
End If
%>
```

Listing 32.8 first checks to ensure that the account number passes verification using the DataWidgetProcessing component. If the account number is valid, the script determines the amount of items in the user's shopping basket. Next, the amount of existing inventory for that product is determined to ensure that enough items are in stock to fill the order using the DataWidget component. If the in-stock inventory is greater than a minimum re-order value, the products are removed from the inventory using DeleteProductInventory. If not enough inventory is available, the AddProductInventory method restocks the inventory and then the items are processed.

Finally, if everything is successful, the summary page is displayed to the user (see Figure 32.20).

FIG. 32.20
A successful order generates a virtual receipt.

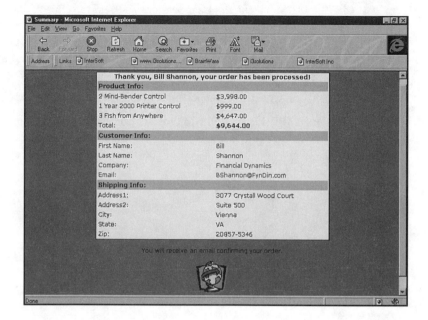

If the user enters an invalid account number, the `error` function is used to prompt the user for valid information, as shown in Figure 32.15.

From Here...

This chapter demonstrated how to create a database access component and an account number verification ActiveX server. The ActiveX servers are compiled as in-process DLLs and can run within the same application process space of the Web site or processed on remote machines. This chapter also illustrated that the same business logic embedded in the ActiveX components can be accessed by any HTML browser client via Active Server Pages as well as native Win32 applications. The dual role of component architecture enables a diverse user community to access your pages while allowing advanced functionality of native GUI development tools available to in-house staff to access the same application logic.

The goal of this chapter is to demonstrate the techniques so that you can build and implement your own Web-based solutions. At this point, you should be able to look back on the evolution of the Amazing DataWidget's WareHouse online catalog system and apply the same model to fit your specific application and development needs. With the IIS and Active Server Pages, the potential for developing, deploying, and managing applications over the Web is an exciting reality.

- Chapter 12, "Controlling the Server with the Server Object and Using Transaction Processing with the ObjectContext Object."

- Chapter 13, "Managing the User Session: The Session Object," illustrates the nuances of tracking a user through an ASP application.

- Chapter 15, "Retrieving User Information: The Request Object," demonstrates how to collect information from the user using forms, hidden fields, and cookies.

- Chapter 18, "Creating Your Own Active Server Components," will teach you how to create your own ActiveX components to meet the needs of your applications.

- Chapter 28, "Working with the Microsoft Transaction Server," illustrates the use of the Transaction Server to manage components within your ASP applications.

Appendixes

VBScript 2.0 Reference

VBScript 2.0 is a light-weight scripting language that provides both server-side and client-side scripting functionality. VBScript is the default scripting language of the Internet Information Server, and is used to provide advanced server-side processing that extends the power and reach of your Web server. VBScript can be run on the Web server to process application logic and is used to generate the standard HTML. As a result of only delivering standard HTML to the clients, no browsers, user groups, or operating systems are restricted from receiving information from your Web site or Web-enabled applications. ■

Scripting Active Server Pages

Dynamically generating HTML based on server-side scripts is made possible by the Active Server scripting engine. The Internet Information Server provides native scripting support for VBScript and JScript. To ensure that the proper scripting engine interprets your script, specify the scripting language for the Active Server Page using the LANGUAGE directive. The LANGUAGE tag must be made on the first line of code on the Active Server Page, as shown below:

```
<%@ LANGUAGE="VBSCRIPT" %>
```

This example sets VBScript as the page scripting language responsible for interpreting the script nested within the inline ASP delimiters <% %>. VBScript can be embedded within these delimiters and directly integrated within the HTML on a page, as shown in the following code:

```
<%@ LANGUAGE="VBSCRIPT" %>
<HTML>
<BODY>
<% If session("NewUser") Then %>
      <P>Hello, Welcome to the online community news letter</P>
<% Else %>
      <P>Welcome back, <% Session("UserName") %>! </P>
<% End If%>
</BODY>
</HTML>
```

VBScript procedures can be implemented in two ways on the Internet Information Server: either within the ASP delimiters, <% and %>, or by explicitly using the <SCRIPT> tag. To embed procedures within your ASP delimiters, define the subroutine or procedure as shown below:

```
<%
Sub CalcNewBalanceRef(ByRef Balance)
      Balance = (FormatCurrency(Balance+Balance*22.5/100/12))
      Response.Write Balance
End sub
%>
```

The previous code example creates a subroutine called CalcNewBalance and accepts an argument named Balance. The procedure can then be accessed from the script by using the Call statement, as shown in the following example:

```
<%@ LANGUAGE="VBSCRIPT" %>
<HTML>
<BODY>
<% '=== Begin Sub ===
Sub CalcNewBalanceRef(Balance)
      Balance = (FormatCurrency(Balance+Balance*22.5/100/12))
      Response.Write Balance
End Sub
%>
'==== Begin Body ===
Dim myAcctBalance
myAcctBalance = 3250
Call CalcNewBalanceRef(myAcctBalance)
%>
</BODY>
</HTML>
```

You can also create individual procedure calls with the `<SCRIPT>` tag. However, if this script is going to run on the server, you need to include the RUNAT attribute to specify where the script should be executed.

```
<SCRIPT RUNAT = Server LANGUAGE = "VBScript">
<!--
    Function TrapNull(vDBText)
        Dim Ret
        If ISNULL(vDBText) Then
            Ret = ""
        Else
            Ret = Trim(vDBText)
        End if
        TrapNull = Ret
End Function
. -->
</SCRIPT>
```

In this example, a function called `TrapNull` removes null characters by using the `IsNull` function. If the data is null, a zero-length string is returned to the calling function. If the value is not null, the `Trim` function will eliminate any leading or trailing spaces from the string and return the value to the calling parent code. For example, the previous example could be called as shown in the following code:

```
<TR><TD Align = "Left"><% Response.Write TrapNull(tbl_user_name) %></TD></TR>
```

You can also use multiple scripting languages within ASP, as shown below:

```
<%@ LANGUAGE="VBSCRIPT" %>
<HTML>
<SCRIPT LANGUAGE = "JScript" RUNAT = SERVER>
function WriteJavaScript(str){
    Response.Write(str);
    }
</SCRIPT>
<SCRIPT LANGUAGE="VBScript" RUNAT=SERVER>
Function WriteVBScript(str)
    Response.Write(str)
End Function
</SCRIPT>

<BODY>

<%
str = "Hello, Welcome to the online community news letter<BR>"
WriteJavaScript(str)
str = "Today's top news stories are:<BR>"
WriteVBScript(str)
%>

</BODY>
</HTML>
```

This previous example demonstrated using the LANGUAGE tag to assign the default scripting languages that translate the script embedded between the `<%    %>` delimeters and also demonstrates how to add VBScript and JavaScript functions to the same ASP page. This script will produce the following results:

```
Hello, Welcome to the online community news letter
Today's top news stories are:
```

VBScript can also be implemented as a client-side scripting vehicle, but only for the Internet Explorer browser. To use VBScript on the client, use the <SCRIPT> tag:

```
<SCRIPT LANGUAGE="VBScript">
<!--
Sub loadAbortRetryIgnor()
    dim strMsg, iButton, strTitle, indexid
    strMsg = "Could Not Access Database"                    '=== Set the
➥message string
    iButton = vbAbortRetryIgnore + vbQuestion + vbDefaultButton2
    strTitle = "VBScript Abort, Ignore and Retry Message Box"   '=== Set the
➥title bar text
    indexid = MsgBox(strMsg, iButton, strTitle)             '=== Trap the
➥results
End Sub
-->
</SCRIPT>
```

VBScript only has one datatype: the Variant datatype. The Variant is used because of its flexibility with all datatypes. The Variant datatype is unique in the sense that the Variant actually changes behavior depending on the type of data it is storing. The Variant does use subtypes to help provide some optimization and datatype-specific functionality. The subtype information is shown in Table A.1.

Table A.1   The Variant Subtypes

Subtype	Description
Empty	Variant is un-initialized.
NULL	Variant intentionally contains no valid data.
Boolean	Contains either True or False.
Byte	Contains integer in the range 0 to 255.
Integer	Contains integer in the range -32,768 to 32,767.
Currency	-922,337,203,685,477.5808 to 922,337,203,685,477.5807.
Long	Contains integer in the range -2,147,483,648 to 2,147,483,647.
Single	Contains a single-precision, floating-point number in the range -3.402823E38 to -1.401298E-45 for negative values; 1.401298E-45 to 3.402823E38 for positive values.
Double	Contains a double-precision, floating-point number in the range -1.79769313486232E308 to -4.94065645841247E-324 for negative values; 4.94065645841247E-324 to 1.79769313486232E308 for positive values.

Subtype	Description
Date (Time)	Contains a number that represents a date between January 1, 100, and December 31, 9999.
String	Contains a variable-length string that can be up to approximately 2 billion characters in length.
Object	Contains an object.
Error	Contains an error number.

If the variant subtype is identified as Empty, the variable's value is 0 for numeric variables or a zero-length string ("") for string variables.

Operators

VBScript has a wide range of built-in operators that are used to manipulate, control, and compare variables. The VBScript operators are listed in Table A.2.

Table A.2   Operators

Name	Symbol	Description
Addition Operator	+	Sums two numbers.
And Operator	&	Performs a logical conjunction on two expressions.
Concatenation Operator	&	Forces string concatenation of two expressions.
Division Operator	/	Divides two numbers.
Eqv Operator	EQV	Performs a logical equivalence on two expressions.
Exponentiation Operator	^	Raises a number to the power of an exponent.
Imp Operator	IMP	Performs a logical implication on two expressions.
Integer Division Operator	\	Divides two numbers and returns an integer result.
Is Operator	IS	Compares two object reference variables.
Mod Operator	MOD	Divides two numbers and returns only the remainder.
Multiplication Operator	*	Multiplies two numbers.

continues

Table A.2   Continued

Name	Symbol	Description
Negation Operator	-	Finds the difference between two numbers or sets the negative value of a number.
Not Operator	NOT	Performs logical negation on an expression.
Or Operator	OR	Performs a logical disjunction on two expressions.
Subtraction Operator	-	Finds the difference between two numbers or sets the negative value of a number.
Xor Operator	XOR	Used to perform a logical exclusion on two expressions.

Statements and Conditional Statements

VBScript uses statements to define and help organize coding structures. Conditional statements are used to control application flow and program execution. Table A.3 displays the declaration statements and conditional statements found in VBScript 2.0.

Table A.3   Statements

Name	Description
Call	Transfers program execution to a subroutine or function.
Const	Declares a constant's value to use in place of literal values.
Dim	Declares variables and allocates storage space.
Do...Loop	Repeats a block of statements while a condition returns True.
Erase	De-allocates dynamic array storage space.
Exit	Exits a procedure or conditional statement.
For...Next	Repeats a group of code statements a specified number of times.
For Each...Next	Repeats a group of code statements for each element in an array or collection.
Function	Declares a function procedure.
If...Then...Else	Conditionally executes a group of statements.

Name	Description
On Error	Enables error-handling.
Option Explicit	Forces explicit declaration of all variables.
Private	Used to declare and allocate storage space for private variables.
Public	Used to declare and allocate storage space for public variables.
Randomize	Initializes the random-number generator.
ReDim	Declares dynamic array variables and allocates or reallocates storage space.
Rem	Used to add comments or remarks within the code.
Select Case	Executes one of several groups of statements, depending on the value of an expression.
Set	Assigns an object reference to a variable or property.
Sub	Declares subroutine procedure.
While...Wend	Executes a series of statements as long as a given condition is True.

Intrinsic Functions

VBScript provides access to compiled application logic built into the VBScript programming language by the use of functions. These functions usually accept information, process the information, and return the results of the function to the calling line of code. Table A.4 can be used to help identify a function name depending on its functionality.

Table A.4   VBScript 2.0 Function Categories

Category or Topic	Function Name
Array handling	Array, IsArray, Erase, LBound, UBound
Conversions	Abs, Asc, Chr, CBool, Cbyte, CCur, Cdate, CDbl, Cint, CLng, Sng, CStr, DateSerial, DateValue, Hex, Oct, Fix, Int, Sgn, TimeSerial, TimeValue
Dates/times	Date, Time, DateAdd, DateDiff, DatePart, DateSerial, DateValue, Day, Month, MonthName, Weekday, WeekdayName, Year, Hour, Minute, Second, Now, TimeSerial, TimeValue
Formatting strings	FormatCurrency, FormatDateTime, FormatNumber, FormatPercent

continues

Table A.4   Continued

Category or Topic	Function Name
Input/output	InputBox, LoadPicture, MsgBox
Math	Atn, Cos, Sin, Tan, Exp, Log, Sqr, Rnd
Script engine ID	ScriptEngine, ScriptEngineBuildVersion, ScriptEngineMajorVersion, ScriptEngineMinorVersion
Strings processing	Asc, Chr, Filter, Instr, InstrRev, Join, Len, LCase, Ucase, Left, Mid, Right, Replace, Space, Split, StrComp, String, StrReverse, LTrim, RTrim, Trim
Variants processing	IsArray, IsDate, IsEmpty, IsNull, IsNumeric, IsObject, TypeName, VarType

For a complete alphabetical listing of VBScript functions and their descriptions, see Table A.5.

Table A.5   Alphabetical Listing of VBScript 2.0 Functions

Function Name	Description
Abs	Returns the absolute value of a number.
Array	Returns a Variant containing an array.
Asc	Returns the ANSI character code of a string.
Atn	Returns the arctangent of a number.
CBool	Returns an expression that has been converted to a Boolean subtype.
CByte	Returns an expression that has been converted to a Byte subtype.
CCur	Returns an expression that has been converted to a Currency subtype.
CDate	Returns an expression that has been converted to a Date subtype.
CDbl	Returns an expression that has been converted to a Double subtype.
Chr	Returns the character associated with the specified ANSI character code.
CInt	Returns an expression that has been converted to an Integer subtype.
CLng	Returns an expression that has been converted to a Long subtype.

Function Name	Description
Cos	Returns the cosine of an angle.
CreateObject	Creates and returns a reference to an Automation object.
CSng	Returns an expression that has been converted to a Single subtype.
CStr	Returns an expression that has been converted to a String subtype.
Date	Returns the current system date.
DateAdd	Returns a date to which a specified time interval has been added.
DateDiff	Returns the number of intervals between two dates.
DatePart	Returns the specified part of a given date.
DateSerial	Returns a Variant of subtype Date for a specified year, month, and day.
DateValue	Returns a Variant of subtype Date.
Day	Returns a whole number between 1 and 31, inclusive, representing the day of the month.
Exp	Returns e (the base of natural logarithms) raised to a power.
Filter	Returns a zero-based array containing a subset of a string array.
Fix	Returns the integer portion of a number.
FormatCurrency	Returns an expression formatted as a currency value.
FormatDateTime	Returns an expression formatted as a date or time.
FormatNumber	Returns an expression formatted as a number.
FormatPercent	Returns an expression formatted as a percent value with a trailing percent (%) symbol.
Hex	Returns a string representing the hexadecimal value of a number.
Hour	Returns a whole number representing the hour of the day between 0 and 23.
InputBox	Displays a prompt for an input dialog box.
InStr	Returns the numeric position of the first occurrence of one string within another.
InStrRev	Returns the numeric position of one string within another string from the end of string.

App

A

continues

Table A.5 Continued

Function Name	Description
Int	Returns the integer portion of a number.
IsArray	Returns a Boolean value indicating if a variable is an array.
IsDate	Returns a Boolean value indicating if an expression can be converted to a date.
IsEmpty	Returns a Boolean value indicating whether a variable has been initialized.
IsNull	Returns a Boolean value that indicates whether an expression contains no valid datatypes.
IsNumeric	Returns a Boolean value indicating whether an expression can be evaluated as a number.
IsObject	Returns a Boolean value indicating whether an expression refers to an Automation object.
Join	Returns a string created by joining strings stored in an array.
LBound	Returns the base index value for a dimension of an array.
LCase	Returns a string that has been converted to lowercase.
Left	Returns the specified number of characters from the left side of a string.
Len	Returns the number of characters in a string.
LoadPicture	Returns a reference to a picture object.
Log	Returns the natural logarithm of a number.
LTrim	Returns a copy of a string without leading spaces.
Mid	Returns a specified number of characters from a string.
Minute	Returns the amount of the minutes in the current system's time.
Month	Returns the month of the year.
MonthName	Returns a string identifying the specified month.
MsgBox	Displays a message in a dialog box.
Now	Returns the current system date and time.
Oct	Returns a string representing the octal value of a number.
Replace	Returns a string in which a specified sub-string has been replaced with another sub-string a specified number of times.
Right	Returns a specified number of characters from the right side of a string.

Function Name	Description
Rnd	Returns a random number.
Round	Returns a number rounded to a specified number of decimal places.
RTrim	Returns a copy of a string without trailing spaces.
ScriptEngine	Returns the scripting language in use.
ScriptEngine BuildVersion	Returns the build version number of the script engine in use.
ScriptEngine MajorVersion	Returns the major version number of the script engine in use.
ScriptEngine MinorVersion	Returns the minor version number of the scripting language in use.
Second	Returns the seconds value of the current system time.
Sgn	Returns an integer indicating whether a number is positive, negative, or zero.
Sin	Returns the sine of an angle.
Space	Returns a string consisting of the specified number of spaces.
Split	Returns a zero-based, one-dimensional array containing a specified number of sub-strings.
Sqr	Returns the square root of a number.
StrComp	Returns a value indicating the result of a string comparison.
StrReverse	Returns a string in which the character order of a specified string is reversed.
String	Returns a repeating character string of the length specified.
Tan	Returns the tangent of an angle.
Time	Returns the current system time.
TimeSerial	Returns the time for a specific hour, minute, and second.
TimeValue	Returns the current time.
Trim	Returns a copy of a string without leading and trailing spaces.
TypeName	Returns subtype information about a variable.
UBound	Returns the largest available subscript for a dimension of an array.
UCase	Returns a string that has been converted to uppercase.
VarType	Returns the subtype of a variable.

continues

Table A.5   Continued

Function Name	Description
Weekday	Returns a whole number representing the day of the week.
WeekdayName	Returns the specified day of the week.
Year	Returns the current year.

The following section demonstrates how to use each function by exposing the syntax of the VBScript 2.0 intrinsic functions.

The *Abs()* Function

Description: Returns the absolute value of a number.

Syntax: Abs(*number*)

Arguments: *number* is any numeric expression.

The *Array()* Function

Description: Returns a Variant containing an array.

Syntax: Array(*clist*)

Arguments: *clist* is a comma-delimited list of values to add to the array.

The *Asc()* Function

Description: Returns the ANSI character code of a string.

Syntax: Asc(*string*)

Arguments: *string* is any valid string expression.

The *Atn()* Function

Description: Returns the arctangent of a number.

Syntax: Atn(*number*)

Arguments: *number* is any valid numeric expression.

The *CBool()* Function

Description: Returns an expression that has been converted to a Boolean subtype.

Syntax: CBool(*expression*)

Arguments: *expression* is any valid expression.

The *CByte()* Function

Description: Returns an expression that has been converted to a Byte subtype.

Syntax: CByte(*expression*)

Arguments: *expression* is any valid expression.

The *CCur()* Function

Description: Returns an expression that has been converted to a Currency subtype.

Syntax: CCur(*expression*)

Arguments: *expression* is any valid expression.

The *CDate()* Function

Description: Returns an expression that has been converted to a Date subtype.

Syntax: Cdate(*expression*)

Arguments: *expression* is any valid date expression.

The *CDbl()* Function

Description: Returns an expression that has been converted to a Double subtype.

Syntax: CDbl(*expression*)

Arguments: *expression* is any valid expression.

The *Chr()* Function

Description: Returns the character specified by the ANSI character code.

Syntax: Chr(*ansicode*)

Arguments: *ansicode* is the ANSI character code.

The *CInt()* Function

Description: Returns an expression that has been converted to an Integer subtype.

Syntax: CInt(*expression*)

Arguments: *expression* is any valid expression.

The *CLng()* Function

Description: Returns an expression that has been converted to a Long subtype.

Syntax: CLng(*expression*)

Arguments: *expression* is any valid expression.

The *Cos()* Function

Description: Returns the cosine of an angle.

Syntax: Cos(*number*)

Arguments: *number* is any valid numeric expression.

The *CreateObject()* Function

Description: Creates and returns a reference to ActiveX Automation object.

Syntax: CreateObject(*objname*)

Arguments: *objname* is any valid ActiveX Automation object.

The *CSng()* Function

Description: Returns an expression that has been converted to a Variant of subtype Single.

Syntax: CSng(*expression*)

Arguments: *expression* is any valid expression.

The *CStr()* Function

Description: Returns an expression that has been converted to a Variant of subtype String.

Syntax: CSng(*expression*)

Arguments: *expression* is any valid expression.

The *Date()* Function

Description: Returns the current system date.

Syntax: Date()

Arguments: none

The *DateAdd()* Function

Description: Returns a date to which a specified time interval has been added.

Syntax: DateAdd(*timeinterval*, *number*, *date*)

Arguments: *timeinterval* is the time interval to add (as specified in Table A.6); *number* is amount of time intervals to add; and *date* is the starting date.

Table A.6   Time Intervals

Setting	Description
YYYY	Year
Q	Quarter
M	Month
D	Day
W	Weekday
WW	Week
H	Hour
M	Minute
S	Second

The *DateDiff()* Function

Description: Returns the number of intervals between two dates.

Syntax: DateDiff(*timeinterval*, *date1*, *date2* [,*firstdayofweek*[, *firstweekofyear*]])

Arguments: *timeinterval* is the time interval to add (as specified in Table A.6); *date1* and *date2* are valid date expressions to be evaluated; and firstdayofweek and firstweekofyear are optional values to specify the first day of the week and first week of the year.

The *DatePart()* Function

Description: Returns the specified part of a given date.

Syntax: DatePart(*timeinterval*, *date*[, *firstdayofweek*[, *firstweekofyear*]])

Arguments: *timeinterval* is the time interval to add (as specified in Table A.6); date is a valid date expression; firstdayofweek and firstweekofyear are optional values to specify the first day of the week and first week of the year.

The *DateSerial()* Function

Description: Returns a Date subtype for a specified year, month, and day.

Syntax: DateSerial(*year*, *month*, *day*)

Arguments: *year* is the numeric expression representing the year; *month* is the numeric expression representing the month; *day* is the numeric expression representing the day.

The *DateValue()* Function

Description: Returns a Date subtype.

Syntax: DateValue(*date*)

Arguments: *date* is any valid date expression.

The *Day()* Function

Description: Returns a whole number representing the day of the month.

Syntax: Day(*date*)

Arguments: *date* is any valid date expression.

The *Exp()* Function

Description: Returns e, the base of natural logarithms, raised to a power.

Syntax: Exp(*number*)

Arguments: *number* is any valid numeric expression.

The *Filter()* Function

Description: Returns a zero-based array containing subset of a string array.

Syntax: Filter(*InputStrings*, *Value*[, bInclude[, Compare]])

Arguments: *InputStrings* is a one-dimension string array; *Value* is the value being searched; bInclude (optional) can be True or False. If set to True, the return array contains values found. False returns an array containing elements not matching the search. Compare is an optional value indicating a comparison constant.

The *Fix()* Function

Description: Returns the first negative integer greater than or equal to *number*.

Syntax: Fix(*number*)

Arguments: *number* is any valid numeric expression.

The *FormatCurrency()* Function

Description: Returns an expression formatted as a currency value.

Syntax: FormatCurrency(*Expression*[,iDigits [,bLeadingDigit [,bParen [,bGroupDigits]]]])

Arguments: *Expression* is a valid numeric expression; iDigits is an optional numeric value used to indicate number of digits to the right of the decimal point; bLeadingDigit is an optional

App

A

tristate value used to display a leading zero; bParen is an optional tristate value used to display parentheses around negative values; and bGroupDigits is an optional tristate value used to display a number as specified in the group delimiter settings of the Control Panel's regional settings. The Tristate values are displayed in Table A.16

The *FormatDateTime()* Function

Description: Returns an expression formatted as a date or time.

Syntax: FormatDateTime(*Date*[,NamedFormat])

Arguments: *Date* is any valid date expression, and NamedFormat is an optional date/time constant in Table A.10

The *FormatNumber()* Function

Description: Returns an expression formatted as a number.

Syntax: FormatNumber(*Expression*[,iDigits [,bLeadingDigit [,bParen [,bGroupDigits]]]])

Arguments: *Expression* is a valid numeric expression; iDigits is an optional numeric value used to indicate the number of digits to the right of the decimal point; bLeadingDigit is an optional tristate value used to display a leading zero; bParen is an optional tristate value used to display parenthesis around negative values; and bGroupDigits is an optional tristate value used to display a number as specified in the regional settings of the Control Panel.

The *FormatPercent()* Function

Description: Returns an expression formatted as a percent value with a trailing percent (%) symbol.

Syntax: FormatPercent(*Expression*[,iDigits [,bLeadingDigit [,bParen [,bGroupDigits]]]])

Arguments: *Expression* is a valid numeric expression; iDigits is an optional numeric value used to indicate the number of digits to the right of the decimal point; bLeadingDigit is an optional tristate value used to display a leading zero; bParen is an optional tristate value used to display parentheses around negative values; and bGroupDigits is an optional tristate value used to display numbers as specified in the group delimiter settings of the Control Panel's regional settings.

The *Hex()* Function

Description: Returns a string representing the hexadecimal value of a number.

Syntax: Hex(*number*)

Arguments: *number* is any valid numeric expression.

The *Hour()* Function

Description: Returns a whole number representing the hour of the day between 0 and 23.

Syntax: Hour(*time*)

Arguments: *time* is any valid date/time expression.

The *InputBox()* Function

Description: Displays a prompt for an input dialog box.

Syntax: InputBox(*promptmsg*[, *title*][, *default*][, *xpos*][, *ypos*][, *helpfile*, *context*])

Arguments: *promptmsg* is the message string to be displayed in the dialog box; *title* (optional) is the string expression displayed in the title of the dialog box; *default* (optional) is the string expression displayed in the text box of the dialog box; *xpos* (optional) is number of twips from the left side of the dialog box to the left of the screen; *ypos* (optional) is the number of twips from the top of the dialog box to the top of the screen; *helpfile* (optional) specifies the location of a help file; and *context* (optional) specifies the help context number in *helpfile*. Twips is a graphical constant used to set the ScaleMode property of an object

The *InStr()* Function

Description: Returns the numeric position of the first instance of one string within another.

Syntax: InStr([*start*,]*strSearchme*, *strsearchfor*[, *compare*])

Arguments: *start* (optional) is the numeric position to start the string search; *strSearchme* is the string expression to be searched; *strsearchfor* is the string expression search value; and *compare* (optional) is the value indicating the comparison constant, as described in Table A.8.

The *InStrRev()* Function

Description: Returns the numeric position of one string within another starting from the end of the string.

Syntax: InStrRev(*strSearchme*, *strsearchfor* [, *start*[, *compare*]])

Arguments: *strSearchme* is the string expression to be searched; *strsearchfor* is the string expression search value; *start* (optional) is the numeric position to start the string search; and *compare* (optional) is the value indicating the comparison constant, as described in Table A.8.

The *Int()* Function

Description: Returns the integer portion of a number.

Syntax: Int(*number*)

Arguments: *number* is any valid numeric expression.

The *IsArray()* Function

Description: Returns a Boolean value indicating whether a variable is an array.

Syntax: `IsArray(vName)`

Arguments: `vName` is the name of the variable to be determined.

The *IsDate()* Function

Description: Returns a Boolean value indicating whether the expression can be converted to a date.

Syntax: `IsDate(expression)`

Arguments: `expression` is any valid expression.

The *IsEmpty()* Function

Description: Returns a Boolean value indicating whether a variable has been initialized.

Syntax: `IsEmpty(expression)`

Arguments: `expression` is any valid expression.

The *IsNull()* Function

Description: Returns a Boolean value that indicates whether an expression contains no valid datatype.

Syntax: `IsNull(expression)`

Arguments: `expression` is any valid expression.

The *IsNumeric()* Function

Description: Returns a Boolean value indicating whether an expression can be evaluated as a number.

Syntax: `IsNumeric(expression)`

Arguments: `expression` is any valid expression.

The *IsObject()* Function

Description: Returns a Boolean value indicating whether an expression refers to an `Automation` object.

Syntax: `IsObject(expression)`

Arguments: `expression` is any valid expression.

The *Join()* Function

Description: Returns a string created by joining strings stored in an array.

Syntax: `Join(alist[, delimiter])`

Arguments: `aList` is the name of a one-dimensional array, and `delimiter` (optional) is the string delimiters used to separate the elements within the string. The default value is the space (`""`) character.

The *LBound()* Function

Description: Returns the base index value for a dimension of an array.

Syntax: `LBound(arrayname[, dimension])`

Arguments: `arrayname` is the name of any array, and `dimension` (optional) is a number indicating the dimension to find the lower bound.

The *LCase()* Function

Description: Returns a string that has been converted into lowercase characters.

Syntax: `LCase(string)`

Arguments: `string` is any valid string expression.

The *Left()* Function

Description: Returns the number of characters from the left side of a string.

Syntax: `Left(string, length)`

Arguments: `string` is any valid string expression, and `length` is the number of characters to return.

The *Len()* Function

Description: Returns the number of characters in a string or the number of bytes required to store a variable.

Syntax: `Len(string ¦ varname)`

Arguments: `string` is any valid string expression; `varname` is any valid variable name.

The *LoadPicture()* Function

Description: Returns a reference to a picture object.

Syntax: `LoadPicture(picturename)`

Arguments: `picturename` is the name of the picture filename.

The *Log()* Function

Description: Returns the natural logarithm of a number.

Syntax: Log(*number*)

Arguments: *number* is any valid numeric expression greater than 0.

The *LTrim()* Function

Description: Returns a string without leading spaces.

Syntax: LTrim(*string*)

Arguments: *string* is any valid string expression.

The *Mid()* Function

Description: Returns a specified number of characters from a string.

Syntax: Mid(*string*, *start*[, *length*])

Arguments: *string* is any valid string expression; *start* is a numeric character position to begin extraction from; and *length* (optional) is the number of characters to return.

The *Minute()* Function

Description: Returns the number of the minutes in current system time.

Syntax: Minute(*time*)

Arguments: *time* is any valid time expression.

The *Month()* Function

Description: Returns the number of the month of the year.

Syntax: Month(*date*)

Arguments: *date* is any valid date expression.

The *MonthName()* Function

Description: Returns a string identifying the specified month.

Syntax: MonthName(*month*[, bAbbreviate])

Arguments: *month* is the numeric representation for a given month; bAbbreviate (optional) is a Boolean value used to display month abbreviations. True will display the abbreviated month name, and False (default) will not show the abbreviation.

The *MsgBox()* Function

Description: Displays a message in a dialog box.

Syntax: MsgBox(*prompt*[, *buttons*][, *title*][, *helpfile*, *context*])

Arguments: *buttons* is an optional numeric expression indicating button style to display (see Table A.13 for messagebox constants); *title* (optional) is a string expression that is displayed in the title bar of the message box; *helpfile* (optional) specifies the location of the help file; and *context* (optional) specifies the help context number in the help file.

The *Now()* Function

Description: Returns the current system date and time.

Syntax: Now()

Arguments: None

The *Oct()* Function

Description: Returns a string representing the octal value of a number.

Syntax: Oct(*number*)

Arguments: *number* is any valid numeric expression.

The *Replace()* Function

Description: Returns a string in which a specified sub-string has been replaced with another substring a specified number of times.

Syntax: Replace(*strSearchMe*, *strSearchFor*, *strReplaceWith* [, *start*[, *count*[, *compare*]]])

Arguments: *strSearchMe* is a string expression containing a sub-string to be replaced; *StrSearchFor* is the string expression to search for within *strSearchMe*; *strReplaceWith* is the string expression to replace sub-string *strSearchFor*; *start* (optional) is the numeric character position to begin search; *count* (optional) is the numeric amount of time to replace values; and *compare* (optional) is a value indicating the comparison constant.

The *Right()* Function

Description: Returns a specified number of characters from the right side of a string.

Syntax: Right(*string*, *length*)

Arguments: *string* is any valid string expression, and *length* is any valid numeric expression representing the number of characters to return.

The *Rnd()* Function

Description: Returns a random number.

Syntax: Rnd[(*number*)]

Arguments: *number* is any valid numeric expression.

The *Round()* Function

Description: Returns a number rounded to a specified number of decimal places.

Syntax: Round(*expression*[, *numRight*])

Arguments: *expression* is any valid numeric expression to be rounded, and *NumRight* (optional) is any numeric expression use to indicate the number of digits to the right of the decimal point.

The *RTrim()* Function

Description: Returns a copy of a string without trailing spaces.

Syntax: RTrim(*string*)

Arguments: *string* is any valid string expression.

The *ScriptEngine()* Function

Description: Returns the scripting language in use.

Syntax: ScriptEngine()

Arguments: None.

The *ScriptEngineBuildVersion()* Function

Description: Returns the build version number of the script engine in use.

Syntax: ScriptEngineBuildVersion()

Arguments: None.

The *ScriptEngineMajorVersion()* Function

Description: Returns the major version number of the script engine in use.

Syntax: ScriptEngineMajorVersion()

Arguments: None.

The *ScriptEngineMinorVersion()* Function

Description: Returns the minor version number of the scripting language in use.

Syntax: `ScriptEngineMinorVersion()`

Arguments: None.

The *Second()* Function

Description: Returns the current seconds value of the current system time.

Syntax: `Second(time)`

Arguments: `time` is any valid time expression.

The *Sgn()* Function

Description: Returns an integer indicating the sign of a number.

Syntax: `Sgn(number)`

Arguments: `number` is any valid numeric expression.

The *Sin()* Function

Description: Returns the sine of an angle.

Syntax: `Sin(number)`

Arguments: `number` is any valid numeric expression that can express an angle in radians.

The *Space()* Function

Description: Returns a string expression consisting of the number of defined spaces.

Syntax: `Space(number)`

Arguments: `number` is any valid numeric expression.

The *Split()* Function

Description: Returns a zero-based, one-dimensional array containing elements constructed from a string expression.

Syntax: `Split(expression[, delimiter[, count[, compare]]])`

Arguments: `expression` is a string expression to build the one-dimensional array; `delimiter` (optional) is the string delimiter used to separate elements; `count` (optional) is the number of elements to return; and `compare` (optional) is the value indicating the comparison constant, as described in Table A.8.

The *Sqr()* Function

Description: Returns the square root of a number.

Syntax: Sqr(*number*)

Arguments: *number* is any valid numeric expression greater than or equal to zero.

The *StrComp()* Function

Description: Returns a value indicating the result of a string comparison.

Syntax: StrComp(*string1*, *string2*[, *compare*])

Arguments: *string1* and *string2* are any valid string expressions to be compared, and *compare* (optional) is the value indicating the comparison constant, as described in Table A.8.

The *StrReverse()* Function

Description: Returns a string where the character order has been reversed.

Syntax: StrReverse(*string*)

Arguments: *string* is any valid string expression.

The *String()* Function

Description: Returns a repeating character string of the length specified.

Syntax: String(*number*, *character*)

Arguments: *number* is any valid numeric expression greater than zero, and *character* is the ANSI character code used to build the string.

The *Tan()* Function

Description: Returns the tangent of an angle.

Syntax: Tan(*number*)

Arguments: *number* is any valid numeric expression that can express an angle in radians.

The *Time()* Function

Description: Returns the current system time.

Syntax: Time()

Arguments: None.

The *TimeSerial()* Function

Description: Returns the time for a specific hour, minute, and second.

Syntax: `TimeSerial(hour, minute, second)`

Arguments: *hour* is any numeric expression between 0 and 23; *minute* is any numeric expression between 0 and 59; and *second* is any numeric expression between 0 and 59.

The *TimeValue()* Function

Description: Returns the current time.

Syntax: `TimeValue(time)`

Arguments: *time* is any valid time expression.

The *Trim()* Function

Description: Returns a string without leading and trailing spaces.

Syntax: `Trim(string)`

Arguments: *string* is any valid string expression.

The *TypeName()* Function

Description: Returns subtype information about a variable.

Syntax: `TypeName(varName)`

Arguments: *varName* is the required variable name.

The *UBound()* Function

Description: Returns the largest available subscript for a dimension of an array.

Syntax: `UBound(arrayname[, dimension])`

Arguments: *arrayname* is the name of a valid array, and *dimension* (optional) is a number indicating the dimension to find the upper bound.

The *UCase()* Function

Description: Returns a string that has been converted to uppercase characters.

Syntax: `UCase(string)`

Arguments: *string* is any valid string expression.

The *VarType()* Function

Description: Returns the subtype of a variable.

Syntax: `VarType(varName)`

Arguments: `varName` is the required variable name.

The *Weekday()* Function

Description: Returns a whole number representing the day of the week.

Syntax: `Weekday(date, [firstdayofweek])`

Arguments: `date` is any valid date expression, and `firstdayofweek` is an optional date constant to assign the first day of week, as seen in Table A.9.

The *WeekdayName()* Function

Description: Returns the specified day of the week.

Syntax: `WeekdayName(weekday, [abbreviate, [firstdayofweek]])`

Arguments: `weekday` is the numeric representation for the day of the week; `abbreviate` is an optional Boolean value (if set to `True`, the weekday name will be abbreviated; if set to `False`, the full weekday name is displayed); and `firstdayofweek` is an optional date constant to assign the first day of week, as seen in Table A.9.

The *Year()* Function

Description: Returns the current year.

Syntax: `Year(date)`

Arguments: `date` is any valid date expression.

Constants

VBScript gives developers the ability to use constants to replace unmemorable or difficult-to-read numeric or string values. These intrinsic constants can be referenced by either their names or their values.

Color Constants

VBScript gives you the ability to use color constants within your scripts. These constants, as shown in Table A.7, can be referenced directly in your scripts.

Table A.7   Color Constants

Constant	Value	Description
vbBlack	&h00	Black
vbRed	&hFF	Red
vbGreen	&hFF00	Green
vbYellow	&hFFFF	Yellow
vbBlue	&hFF0000	Blue
vbMagenta	&hFF00FF	Magenta
vbCyan	&hFFFF00	Cyan
vbWhite	&hFFFFFF	White

Comparison Constants

Many intrinsic VBScript functions perform comparisons to complete a task. These give you the ability to explicitly define the comparison method by using the comparison constants shown in Table A.8.

Table A.8   Comparison Constants

Constant	Value	Description
VbBinaryCompare	0	Performs a binary comparison.
VbTextCompare	1	Performs a textual comparison.
VbDatabaseCompare	2	Performs a comparison based on information extracted in the database where the comparison is to be performed.

The Date/Time Constants

VBScript 2.0 provides new date/time functions that help speed scripting development and eliminate excessive coding that would otherwise have to be done by hand. Many of the new functions utilize the date/time constants to help customize the functions (see Table A.9).

Table A.9   Date/Time Constants

Constant	Value	Description
vbSunday	1	Sunday.
vbMonday	2	Monday.
vbTuesday	3	Tuesday.

Constant	Value	Description
vbWednesday	4	Wednesday.
vbThursday	5	Thursday.
vbFriday	6	Friday.
vbSaturday	7	Saturday.
vbFirstJan1	1	Uses the week in which January 1 occurs (default).
VbFirstFourDays	2	Uses the first week that has at least four days in the new year.
VbFirstFullWeek	3	Uses the first full week of the year.
VbUseSystem	0	Uses the date format contained in the regional settings on the host computer.
VbUseSystemDayOfWeek	0	Uses the day of the week specified in your system settings for the first day of the week.

Date Format Constants

In addition to the new date/time functionality, VBScript 2.0 also introduces new date format functions that can use the constants shown in Table A.10.

Table A.10   Date Format Constants

Constant	Value	Description
VbGeneralDate	0	Displays a date and/or time.
VbLongDate	1	Displays a date using the long date format.
VbShortDate	2	Displays a date using the short date format.
VbLongTime	3	Displays a time using the long time format.
VbShortTime	4	Displays a time using the short time format.

Notice that date and time settings are controlled within your regional settings found in the Control Panel. Consider the following script:

```
<%
Response.Write FormatDateTime(now,VbGeneralDate) &"<BR>"
Response.Write FormatDateTime(now,VbLongDate) &"<BR>"
Response.Write FormatDateTime(now,VbShortDate) &"<BR>"
Response.Write FormatDateTime(now,VbLongTime) &"<BR>"
Response.Write FormatDateTime(now,VbShortTime) &"<BR>"
%>
```

The previous script will produce the following results:

```
10/12/97 3:47:05 PM
Sunday, October 12, 1997
10/12/97
3:47:05 PM
15:47
```

File Input/Output Constants

The file input/output constants are used to tap into the functionality of the FileSystemObject. The FileSystemObject provides access to files on the server. The FileSystemObject can open a file with three different permission levels. The constants enabling read-only, write-new, and file-append modes are shown in Table A.11.

Table A.11   File Input/Output Constants

Constant	Value	Description
ForReading	1	Opens a file for read-only access.
ForWriting	2	Opens a file for write access. If the file exists, the previous content is overwritten.
ForAppending	8	Opens a file and appends the data stream to the end of the file.

Miscellaneous Constant

VBScript uses the constant shown in Table A.12 to represent an error returned from an ActiveX Automation object.

Table A.12   Miscellaneous Constant

Constant	Value	Description
VbObjectError	&h80040000	Error message from an Automation Object

The *MsgBox* Constants

The message box uses two sets of constants. The display constants, as displayed in Table A.13, are used to create the look and feel of the message box. The message box result constants, shown in Table A.15, are used to determine user response to the displayed message box.

Table A.13 Message Box Display Constants

Constant	Value	Description
vbOKOnly	0	Displays OK button only.
vbOKCancel	1	Displays OK and Cancel buttons.
vbAbortRetryIgnore	2	Displays Abort, Retry, and Ignore buttons.
vbYesNoCancel	3	Displays Yes, No, and Cancel buttons.
vbYesNo	4	Displays Yes and No buttons.
vbRetryCancel	5	Displays Retry and Cancel buttons.
vbCritical	16	Displays Critical Message icon.
vbQuestion	32	Displays Warning Query icon.
vbExclamation	48	Displays Warning Message icon.
vbInformation	64	Displays Information Message icon.
vbDefaultButton1	0	First button is set as the default button.
vbDefaultButton2	256	Second button is set as the default button.
vbDefaultButton3	512	Third button is set as the default button.
vbDefaultButton4	768	Fourth button is set as the default button.
vbApplicationModal	0	The user must respond to the message box before continuing work in the current application.
VbSystemModal	4096	System modal. All applications are suspended until the user responds to the message box.

App
A

You can trap the user response by the return values of the message box. The constants shown in Table A.14 are used to identify which button the user selected in the message box.

Table A.14 Message Box Results Constants

Constant	Value	Description
vbOK	1	OK button was clicked.
vbCancel	2	Cancel button was clicked.
vbAbort	3	Abort button was clicked.
vbRetry	4	Retry button was clicked.

continues

Table A.14   Continued

Constant	Value	Description
vbIgnore	5	Ignore button was clicked.
vbYes	6	Yes button was clicked.
vbNo	7	No button was clicked.

String Constants

VBScript can use string constants to help control output to the current page or file, as shown in Table A.15.

Table A.15   String Constants

Constant	Value	Description
vbCr	Chr(13)	Carriage return
vbCrLf	Chr(13) & Chr(10)	Carriage return–line feed combination
vbFormFeed	Chr(12)	Form feed; not useful in Microsoft Windows
vbLf	Chr(10)	Line feed
vbNewLine	Chr(13) & Chr(10) Chr(10)	Platform-specific new line character or whatever is appropriate for the platform
vbNullChar	Chr(0)	Character having the value 0
vbNullString	String having value 0	Not the same as a zero-length string (" "); used for calling external procedures
vbTab	Chr(9)	Horizontal tab
vbVerticalTab	Chr(11)	Vertical tab; not useful in Microsoft Windows

Tristate Constants

VBScript combines Boolean functionality with the capability to use the default values of a function into one set of constants called *tristate constants*. The tristate constants are shown in Table A.16. Typically, the default settings are extracted from the computer's region settings as found in the Control Panel.

Table A.16   Tristate Constants

Constant	Value	Description
TristateTrue	-1	True
TristateFalse	0	False
TristateUseDefault	-2	Use default setting of calling function

VarType Constants

VBScript enables you to determine the Variant subtype a variable is stored as by using the Vartype function. The Vartype function returns the subtype values shown in Table A.17.

Table A.17   VarType Constants

Constant	Value	Description
vbEmpty	0	Un-initialized (default)
vbNull	1	Contains no valid data
vbInteger	2	Integer subtype
vbLong	3	Long subtype
vbSingle	4	Single subtype
vbDouble	5	Double subtype
vbCurrency	6	Currency subtype
vbDate	7	Date subtype
vbString	8	String subtype
vbObject	9	Object
vbError	10	Error subtype
vbBoolean	11	Boolean subtype
vbVariant	12	Variant
vbDataObject	13	Data access object
vbDecimal	14	Decimal subtype
vbByte	17	Byte subtype
vbArray	8192	Array

VBScript Objects

VBScript provides access to four built-in objects (see Table A.18). These objects are used to encapsulate a specific area of code functionality. The objects use methods, shown in Table A.19, to perform an action, and have properties, shown in Table A.20, to describe the object.

Table A.18   VBScript Objects

Name	Description
Dictionary	Object that stores data key and item pairs.
Err	Contains runtime error information.
FileSystemObject	Provides access to a computer's file system.
TextStream	Provides sequential file access.

VBScript Object Methods

VBScript uses methods to perform an action on or to control an object. Table A.19 provides a quick guide to the VBScript 2.0 methods.

Table A.19   VBScript 2.0 Methods

Method	Description
Add	Adds a key and item pair to a Dictionary object.
Clear	Clears all settings of the Err object.
Close	Closes an open TextStream file.
CreateTextFile	Creates a specified filename and returns a TextStream object.
Exists	Returns whether a specified key exists in the Dictionary object.
Items	Returns an array containing all items in a Dictionary object.
Keys	Returns an array containing all existing keys in a Dictionary object.
OpenTextFile	Opens a specified file and returns a TextStream object.
Raise	Generates a runtime error.
Read	Reads characters from a TextStream file.
ReadAll	Reads an entire TextStream file.
ReadLine	Reads an entire line from a TextStream file.

Method	Description
Remove	Removes a specific key and item pair from a Dictionary object.
RemoveAll	Removes all key and item pairs from a Dictionary object.
Skip	Skips a specified number of characters when reading a TextStream file.
SkipLine	Skips the next line when reading a TextStream file.
Write	Writes a specified string to a TextStream file.
WriteBlankLines	Writes a specified number of newline characters to a TextStream file.
WriteLine	Writes a specified string and newline character to a TextStream file.

VBScript Object Properties

Properties of an object are used to describe specific information about an object. The properties of VBScript objects are shown in Table A.20.

Table A.20   Properties

Name	Description
AtEndOfLine	Returns whether the file pointer is positioned immediately on the end-of-line marker in a TextStream file.
AtEndOfStream	Returns whether the file pointer is positioned at the end of a TextStream file.
Column	Returns the column number of the character position in a TextStream file.
CompareMode	Sets or returns the comparison mode for comparing string keys in a Dictionary object.
Count	Returns the number of items in a Dictionary object.
Description	Returns or sets a descriptive string associated with an error.
HelpContext	Sets or returns a context ID for a topic in a help file.
HelpFile	Sets or returns a path to a Help File.
Item	Sets or returns an item for a specified key in a Dictionary object.
Key	Sets a key in a Dictionary object.

continues

Table A.20   Continued

Name	Description
Line	Returns the current line number in a TextStream file.
Number	Sets or returns a numeric value specifying an error.
Source	Sets or returns the name of the object that generated the error.

Active Server Object Reference

Active Server Pages derives its rich functionality from the use of six inherent objects. These six objects do have to be explicitly instantiated but are directly built into Active Server Pages. These objects have their own predefined roles and each has its own properties, methods, and events. These objects form the foundation of ASP development and consequently have their own chapters dedicated to fully describe them. The following provides a brief overview of each object's functionality. ■

Controlling the *Application* Object

The Application object is used to manage all information in the ASP application. The information can be accessed and passed between different users in the application. The Application object has two events, the Application_OnStart and Application_OnEnd events, as shown in Table B.1. The Application object is created by the Active Server to represent the instantiation of an Active Server application. The Application object is created when a user requests any page in the ASP application's virtual directory. Once the Application object is started, all subsequent users can reference its objects and variables.

Table B.1   The *Application* Object's Events

Event	Description
Application_OnStart	Initiated when the ASP application is first started.
Application_OnEnd	Initiated when the ASP application is terminated.

These individual application events are found in the GLOBAL.ASA file and are executed in a manner similar to any subroutine or function.

```
<SCRIPT LANGUAGE="VBScript" RUNAT = "Server">

Sub Application_OnStart              '=== Defines Application Object's OnStart Event
     Application("strMessage")= "Welcome to Active Server Pages"
End Sub
Sub Application_OnEnd

End Sub


</SCRIPT>
```

However, if an event is called and no event procedure is defined, a runtime error will occur because a reference is being made to an event that does not exist.

Declaring Application-Level Variables

Application-level variables are accessible by all users of the application. Application-level variables can be defined as needed in any .ASP file, not just in the Application_OnStart and Application_OnEnd events of the GLOBAL.ASA file.

To declare an application variable, use the following syntax:

```
Application(varName)
```

***Application_OnStart* Event**   The Application_OnStart event requires the following syntax within the GLOBAL.ASA file:

```
<SCRIPT LANGUAGE=ScriptLanguage RUNAT=Server>
Sub Application_OnStart
. . .
End Sub </SCRIPT>
```

The Application_OnStart event is executed before any user or session event is triggered. Any attempts to call a Session, Response, or Request object will generate a fatal runtime error because these objects have not been created at this point. However, you are able to reference the Server object.

Application_OnEnd Event   The Application_OnEnd event requires the following syntax within the GLOBAL.ASA file:

```
<SCRIPT LANGUAGE=ScriptLanguage RUNAT=Server>
Sub Application_OnEnd
    '=== Your Script Here
End Sub

</SCRIPT>
```

The Application_OnEnd event occurs when the Web server is shut down. As a result, the Application object is destroyed. The shutting down of the Web server can occur with the termination of the HTTP service or when the GLOBAL.ASA file needs to be recompiled and reloaded into memory.

Controlling Application-Level Variables with Methods

The Application object has two methods designed to control variable access: the Lock and UnLock methods. These methods help to prevent multiple users from changing application-level variables at the same time (see Table B.2).

Table B.2   The *Application* Object's Methods

Name	Description
Lock	Prevents other clients from changing Application object properties.
UnLock	Enables other clients to modify the Application object's properties.

Lock Method   The Lock method is to control the Application object's properties by preventing concurrent users from modifying the same application-level variable at the same time. The Lock method is implemented by using the following syntax:

```
Application.Lock
```

UnLock Method   The Application.UnLock method releases control of the application variables. The UnLock method is implemented using the following syntax:

```
Application.UnLock
```

The Application.UnLock method is implicitly called when the processing of a page is complete and the UnLock method has not been called or when the script processing times out. The default page-level script timeout value is 90 seconds.

Instantiating Application-Level Objects

You can create a reference to an application-level object's automation object by embedding the unique class identifier either by the ProgID or the ClassID within the object tag. The ProgID represents the registered name of the object. The ClassID refers to the registered class number of the object. To create a server-side object, use the following syntax:

```
<OBJECT RUNAT=Server SCOPE = Application ID=Identifier
{PROGID="progID"|CLASSID="ClassID"}>
</OBJECT>
```

where *Scope* identifies the object's lifetime and *ID* identifies the object's instantiated name.

The <OBJECT> tag must be placed outside the <SCRIPT> and </SCRIPT> tags used to define the GLOBAL.ASA file. If an <OBJECT> tag or any other tag is found between the <SCRIPT> tags, the script interpreter will try to process the <OBJECT> tags and generate an error. This <SCRIPT> and <OBJECT> tag layout is illustrated in the following code:

```
<SCRIPT LANGUAGE="VBScript" RUNAT="Server">
Sub Application_OnStart
'=== Application Level events and object placed here
End Sub

Application_OnStart
</SCRIPT>

<OBJECT RUNAT=Server SCOPE=Application ID=MyDataConn
PROGID="RemoteConn.DataConn">
</OBJECT>
```

The application-level object can now be accessed from any ASP file in the application by using the ID name of the object.

Controlling the *Server* Object

The Server object is an ASP object used to control administrative features of the IIS Web server and actions that deal with the HTTP service. The Server object represents a control interface to the HTTP service. The Server object is referenced using the following syntax:

```
Server.Method/Property
```

where Server is the Active Server object.

The Server object has four methods that are used to control various aspects of the Web server, as shown in Table B.3.

Table B.3   The *Server* Object's Methods

Method	Description
CreateObject	Creates a Server instance of an object.
HTMLEncode	Utilizes HTML encoding to deliver text to browser.

Method	Description
MapPath	Translates the virtual Web server path to the physical path on the server.
URLEncode	Utilizes URL encoding techniques.

The *CreateObject* Method

Perhaps one of the most exciting aspects of Active Server Pages is the capability to create an instance of an ActiveX object. This capability to tap into ActiveX objects provides a virtually endless number of ways to deliver information to any Web client that were once only available to propriety client software or dedicated network connections. The Server object acts as a translator between the in-house data and logic stores and virtually any HTML-compliant browser. The CreateObject method uses the following syntax:

```
Server.CreateObject(progID)
```

where *progID* is the class or type of object to be instantiated. The progID also requires the following special format:

```
appname.objecttype
```

where *appname* is the application name hosting the object and *objecttype* is the class or type of the object to create. All COM-based objects are required to have one class type per application name.

The CreateObject method only creates objects that have page-level scope. If you need to access the same component multiple times, in most situations you would benefit from using an application- or session-level object.

The *MapPath* Method

The Server object uses the MapPath method to track and manage path information on the server. The MapPath method requires the following syntax:

```
Server.MapPath( path )
```

where Server is the Active Server object and *path* is a physical or virtual directory. There are two basic rules to remember with the path variables.

- Path arguments that start with a backslash (\) or a forwardslash (/) are used to represent virtual directories.
- Path arguments that do not start with the backslash or forward slash represent relative directories.

The *ScriptTimeOut* Property

The ScriptTimeOut property is a property of the Server object that prevents a process from running endlessly. The ScriptTimeOut value requires the following syntax:

```
Server.ScriptTimeout = Seconds
```

where *Seconds* indicates the number of seconds allotted for page-level scripting to process. After this amount of time has been reached, the Server object terminates the process and writes an event to the event log.

Using Server Encoding Techniques

All Web technology is based on the transfer of simple text across the Internet or an intranet via the TCP/IP protocol and the translation of that text into content within the Web browser. Because the browser only interprets text, embedded non-ASCII characters are misinterpreted as text or simply are not available from the keyboard. The Server object uses the URLEncode and HTMLEncode methods to ensure the proper character translation between the Web server and browser.

The *URLEncode* Method

The URLEncode method of the Server object is used to deliver explicit information from the Web server to the client via the URL. To ensure that all the characters entered by the user are properly passed to the server, the characters must be scanned to ensure that only known characters are being sent. To use the URL encoding methods, follow this syntax:

```
Server.URLEncode(string)
```

where Server is the Server object and *string* is the string to apply the URL encoding rules.

The URLEncode method performs the following processes to the data:

- Spaces are transformed into plus (+) symbols.
- Fields are left unencoded.
- An unencoded equal sign assigns an unencoded field name with the data value.
- Non-ASCII characters are transformed into escape codes.

Using the *HTMLEncode* Method

The HTMLEncode method is used by the server to explicitly define the characters to be displayed on a page. To use the HTMLEncode feature, use the following syntax:

```
Server.HTMLEncode(string)
```

where Server is the Server object and *string* is the string to encode. The HTMLEncode method is important to ensure that the proper characters are displayed on the page and not processed by the server.

The *ObjectContext* Object: Interacting with the Transaction Server

With the Internet Information Server 4.0, Active Server Pages have a direct interface to controlling components in the Microsoft Transaction Server. This interface is made possible through the ObjectContext object. When the scripting engine processes this directive, the Active Server Page is executed as a transaction on the Transaction Server. To initiate the transaction processing of the ObjectContext object, use the following directive syntax:

```
<%@ Transaction = Required %>
```

ObjectContext uses two methods to control the objects managed by the Microsoft Transaction Server, as shown in Table B.4.

Table B.4   The *ObjectContext* Object's Methods

Method	Description
SetComplete	Sets the work of an object as a success and permanently accepts the changes to the resource.
SetAbort	Sets the work of an object as a failure and returns the resource to its original state, neglecting any changes made to the resource.

The *SetComplete* Method

The SetComplete method is used to commit an MTS object's transaction as a success. The changes made by the object method on a resource are permanently committed. To accept changes made by object, use the following syntax:

```
ObjectContext.SetComplete
```

After the SetComplete method is executed, the OnTransactionCommit event is triggered.

The *SetAbort* Method

The SetAbort method is used to roll back changes made by an object managed by the MTS. When the SetAbort method is called, the object has completed its work and is returned to its original state. To reject changes made by the MTS object, use the following syntax:

```
ObjectContext.SetAbort
```

After the SetAbort method is executed, the OnTransactionAbort event is triggered.

Trapping the *ObjectContext's* Events

ObjectContext has two events that are triggered after the ObjectContext's methods are executed, as shown in Table B.5.

Table B.5   The *ObjectContext* Events

Event	Description
OnTransactionCommit	Event triggered after the ObjectContext.SetComplete method is executed.
OnTransactionAbort	Event triggered after the ObjectContext.SetAbort method is executed.

The *OnTransactionCommit* Event

The OnTransactionCommit event is triggered by the ObjectContext object SetComplete method. When the SetComplete method is processed, the script will process the OnTransactionCommit subroutine.

```
Sub OnTransactionCommit()
    Response.Redirect "CreateVirutalReceipt.ASP"
End Sub
```

The relationship between OnTransactionCommit event and ObjectContext.SetComplete method is demonstrated in the following example:

```
<%@TRANSACTION = Required %>
<%
Sub OnTransactionCommit()
    Dim strMessage
    strMessage ="This was generated by executing the SetComplete method "
    strMessage = strMessage & "to trigger the OnTransactionCommit event"
    Response.Write strMessage
End Sub
%>
<HTML>
<HEAD>
<TITLE>Set Complete</TITLE>
</HEAD>
<BODY>

<%
ObjectContext.SetComplete
%>

</BODY>
</HTML>
```

The code example initiates transaction processing using the TRANSACTION = Required directive and executes the SetComplete method to trigger the OnTransactionCommit() event. In this example, the OnTransactionCommit subroutine, writes the following text to the page:

```
This text message was generated by executing the SetComplete method to trigger
the OnTransactionCommit event
```

OnTransactionAbort Event

Similar to its counterpart, the OnTransactionAbort event is triggered when the ObjectContext object SetAbort event is executed. When the SetAbort method is processed, the script will process the OnTransactionCommit event.

```
Sub OnTransactionAbort()
    Response.Redirect "InsufficientFunds.ASP"
End Sub
```

You can apply the same example shown in the OnTransactionCommit to OnTransactionAbort, as shown in the following example:

```
<%@TRANSACTION = Required %>
<%
Sub OnTransactionAbort()
    Dim strMessage
    strMessage ="This text message was generated by executing the SetAbort
    ➥method "
    strMessage = strMessage & "to trigger the OnTransactionAbort event"
    Response.Write strMessage
End Sub
%>
<HTML>
<HEAD>
<TITLE>Set Abort</TITLE>
</HEAD>
<BODY>

<%
ObjectContext.SetAbort
%>

</BODY>
</HTML>
```

The example initiates transaction processing using the TRANSACTION = Required directive and executes the SetAbort method to trigger the OnTransactionAbort() event. In this example, the OnTransactionAbort subroutine writes the following text to the page:

```
This text message was generated by executing the SetAbort method to trigger the
OnTransactionAbort event.
```

Communicating with Web Client: The *Response* Object

The Active Server uses the Response object to control and manage the data sent to the browser. The Response object is responsible for controlling the delivery of data, writing HTTP header information, writing text, HTML, scripting variables, and non-textual information, and controlling cookies on the client browser.

The *Response* Collection

The Response object uses the Cookie collection to manage and control both cookie files and the data stored within the cookies. The Cookie collection enables single or multiple variables to be stored and manipulated in temporary text files on the client's browser. The Response collection is shown in Table B.6.

Table B.6   The *Response* Collection

Collection Name	Description
Cookies	Sets cookies values.

The *Cookies* Collection

The Cookies collection enables single or multiple variables to be stored and manipulated in temporary text files on the client's browser. The Cookies collection requires the following syntax:

```
Response.Cookies(Cookie)[(key)¦.attribute] = value
```

where Response is the built-in Response object, Cookie is the name of the cookie file, key identifies a dictionary element, attribute is a specific characteristic of the cookie, and value is the value being assigned to the cookie.

Notice that you do not have to manually trap and replace non-ANSCI characters, that is, encode the string data that will be transferred to the cookie. The encoding process automatically filters out any non-ANSCI characters.

The Cookies collection also uses attributes to help manage cookies on the browser. Table B.7 displays the cookie attributes that can be set by the Response collection.

Table B.7   The Attributes of the *Response Cookie* Collection

Name	Description
Expires	Sets the date when the cookie will expire.
Domain	Specifies cookie delivery to only members specified by this domain.
Path	Determines the delivery path information.
Secure	Specifies whether the cookie is secure.
HasKey	Returns whether the cookie contains keys.

The *Response* Object's Properties

The Response object has various properties that can be used to set characteristics of information delivered by the server. Table B.8 illustrates the Response object's properties.

Table B.8   The Response Properties

Property Name	Description
Buffer	Sets whether or not page output is buffered.
Charset	Appends the name of the character set to the content-type header.
Expires	Sets the amount of time before the page cached on the browser expires.
ExpiresAbsolute	Sets the date and time a page cached on a browser expires.
IsClientConnected	Determines whether the browser has disconnected from the server.
Status	Indicates the status line returned by the server.
PICS	Adds the value of a PICS label to the PICS-label field of the response header.

The *Buffer* Property   The Buffer property is used to control and regulate when information is sent to the requesting browser. The Web server can either stream information to the user as the server is processing the script, or it can wait to release all the data after the entire script is finished processing. The output buffering uses the following syntax:

```
Response.Buffer [= flag]
```

where Response is the Response object and *flag* can be set to either True or False. If True, the server buffering is cached until the entire ASP page has completed processing or until the Flush or End methods have been called. If the flag is set to False, server buffering is disabled.

The *CacheControl* Property   The Response object uses the CacheControl property to enable a proxy server to cache output from Active Server Pages. The CacheControl requires the following syntax:

```
Response.CacheControl [= True/False ]
```

The *CharSet* Property   The CharSet property of the Response object is used to set the character set of the ContentType to be displayed on the requesting browser. The CharSet property controls the ContentType by using the following syntax:

```
Response.Charset(CharSetName)
```

where *CharSetName* is the character set designated for a particular page.

The *ContentType* Property   The ContentType Response object property enables you to specifically control the HTTP content-type that is sent to the browser. The browser uses the content-type information to determine how it should interpret the information, such as treating the information as text, HTML, or as an image file. The ContentType functionality is implemented using the following syntax:

```
Response.ContentType [= ContentType ]
```

where *ContentType* is the browser specific MIME Content type.

The *Expires* Property   The Expires property is an interesting feature that enables you to specify the amount of time in minutes before the page is expired from the browser cache. The Expires property uses the following syntax:

```
Response.Expires [= number]
```

where *number* is the number of minutes the page will remain active in the cache. Once this time has expired, the browser will be forced to retrieve information from the hosting site.

The *ExpiresAbsolute* Property   ExpiresAbsolute is an extension of the Expires property. The ExpiresAbsolute property enables you to specify the exact time and date a page will expire in the browser's cache. The ExpiresAbsolute property requires the following syntax:

```
Response.ExpiresAbsolute [= [date] [time]]
```

where *date* is the date on which the page will expire and *time* indicates the time the page will expire. However, note that the expiration date and time is converted to Greenwich Mean Time.

The *PICS* Property   The PICS property of the Response object enables you to control rating values of the PICS-label field in the response header. This functionality can be controlled by implementing the following syntax:

```
Response.PICS(Picslabel)
```

where *PicsLabel* is the formatted PICS label.

The *Status* Property   The Response object uses the Status property to control the status line returned by the Web server. The status line is used to determine the results of the Web server request and is specified by HTTP specifications. To implement this functionality, use the following syntax:

```
Response.Status = StatusDescription
```

where *StatusDescription* is the status code and status code description. The following is a list of common HTTP status lines that can be returned by the Web server:

400	Bad Request
410	Unauthorized - Login Failed
404	Not Found
406	Not Acceptable
412	Precondition Failed
414	Request-URL Too Long

500   Internal Server Error

501   Not Implemented

502   Bad Gateway

One of the most common uses of the Status property is to check or authenticate the rights of the requesting user. For example, to force user validation for a page, use the following code to prompt the user for a username and password dialog box:

```
<% Response.Status = "401 Unauthorized" %>
```

The *IsClientConnected* Property   IsClientConnected tracks whether the requesting browser has disconnected from the server since the last time the server issued a Response.Write command. The IsClientConnected property requires the following syntax:

```
Response.IsClientConnected()
```

The IsClientConnected property provides an extension of the Session.Timeout capability by enabling the requesting browser to exceed the session timeout variable without losing server connection and is often implemented before processing script. The following example tests the Response object to see whether the connection is valid before calling a function to transfer data.

```
If Response.IsClientConnected Then
        vTransfer = TranferInfo("AcctRetail", "AcctWholeSale")
Else
        VTransfer = ReConnect("UserName", "Department")
End If
```

Sending Output to the Browser: The *Response* Methods

The Response methods are used to explicitly control information flow from the server to the browser. Table B.9 lists the available Response methods.

Table B.9   The *Response* Methods

Method Name	Description
Write	Writes a string to the current HTTP output.
BinaryWrite	Writes information to the current HTTP output without any character conversion.
Clear	Erases any buffered HTML output.
End	Stops the Web server from processing the script and returns the current result.
Flush	Bypasses buffering and sends output immediately to client.
Redirect	Attempts to automatically route the browser to a URL.

continues

Table B.9   Continued

Method Name	Description
AddHeader	Writes a string to the HTML header.
AppendToLog	Writes a string to the end of the Web server log entry.

The *Write* Method

The Write method of the Response object is used to send output to the browser. The Write method requires the following syntax:

```
Response.Write variant
```

where *variant* is any Variant datatype supported by the Visual Basic scripting engine.

When using the Response.Write method, the Variant datatype to be delivered to the client cannot contain the string %>. This string is interpreted by the scripting engine as an end script delimiter. Instead, use the string %\> to write the closing script delimiter tag.

The Write method uses the Variant datatype to send information to the browser. The Variant datatype, although the most versatile of datatypes, does have its limitations. The Variant datatype itself can contain only 1,022 bytes of information. If you try to use a variable that is larger than 1,022 bytes, a runtime error will occur.

The *AddHeader* Method

The AddHeader method enables you to add header information to the existing HTTP header. To use the AddHeader method, use the following syntax:

```
Response.AddHeader name, value
```

where *name* is the name of the new header variable and *value* is the value assigned to the new header variable.

The AddHeader method must be called before any content is sent to the browser. Failure to do so will generate a runtime error because the HTTP protocol first sends header information to the browser.

The *AppendToLog* Method

The AppendToLog method of the Response object enables you to append information directly to the Web server log file. To use this functionality, use the following syntax:

```
Response.AppendToLog string
```

where Response is the built-in Response object and *string* is an 80-byte character string.

The *BinaryWrite* Method

The BinaryWrite method enables direct non-formatted output to be displayed to the requesting browser. This direct output is useful when displaying non-string information, such as various image formats. To use the BinaryWrite method, use the following syntax:

```
Response.BinaryWrite data
```

where *data* is information that will be sent to the browser without any character conversion.

The *Clear* Method

The Clear method is used to erase any HTML that has been buffered on the server. The Clear property uses the following syntax:

App

B

```
Response.Clear
```

where Response is the built-in Response object and Clear is the Clear method.

The *End* Method

The End method also is used to manage the buffered server output. The End method returns the current buffered output up to the point where the End method is called. To use the End method, use the following syntax:

```
Response.End
```

where Response is the built-in Response object and End activates the End method.

The *Flush* Method

The Flush method is used by the Response object to immediately send any buffered output to the browser. The syntax for the Flush method is as follows:

```
Response.Flush
```

where Response is the built-in Response object and Flush calls the Flush method. The Flush method can only be used if buffering has been activated.

The *Redirect* Method

The Redirect method is used to route the browser to another Web page. The Redirect method is implemented by using the following syntax:

```
Response.Redirect URL
```

where Response is the built-in Response object and *URL* is the Uniform Resource Locator that indicates where the browser is to be routed.

Retrieving Information Using the *Request* Object

The Request object is responsible for retrieving information from the Web browser. The Request object uses collections, properties, and methods to retrieve information from the user.

Accepting User Information Using the *Request* Collections

The Request object uses separate objects that can be grouped together to interface with the calling client (see Table B.10).

Table B.10   The *Request* Collection

Collection Name	Description
ClientCertificate	Retrieves the certification fields issued by the Web browser.
Cookies	Retrieves the values of the cookies sent in an HTTP request.
Form	Retrieves the values of form elements posted to the HTTP request.
QueryString	Retrieves the values of the variables in the HTTP query string.
ServerVariables	Retrieves the values of predetermined environment variables.

The *ClientCertificate* Collection   The Request object's ClientCertificate collection is used to provide proper security identification across unsecured environments. The ClientCertificate keys are shown in Table B.11.

Table B.11   The *ClientCertificate* Certification Fields

Key	Description
Subject	Returns a list of subfield values that contain information about the subject of the certificate.
Issuer	Contains a list of subfield values containing information about the issuer of the certificate.
ValidForm	Returns when the certificate becomes valid.
ValidUntil	Specifies when the certificate expires.
SerialNumber	Returns the certification serial number as an ASCII representation of hexadecimal bytes.
Certificate	Returns the binary stream of the entire certificate content in ASN.1 format.

The use of subfields enables specific information to be retrieved from the Subject and Issuer key fields mentioned above. Table B.12 presents the available subfields for the ClientCertificate collection.

Table B.12   The *ClientCertificate* Collection Subfields

Value	Description
C	Specifies the name of the country of origin.
O	Specifies the company or organization name.
OU	Specifies the name of the organizational unit.
CN	Specifies the common name of the user.
L	Specifies a locality.
S	Specifies a state or province.
T	Specifies the title of the person or organization.
GN	Specifies a given name.
I	Specifies a set of initials.

If no certificate is sent, the ClientCertificate collection returns EMPTY.

The *Cookies* Collection   The Cookies collection is used by the Request object to retrieve values stored in text files on the client's machine.

The Cookies collection requires the following syntax:

```
Request.Cookies(cookie)[(key)¦.attribute]
```

Its properties are summarized in Table B.13.

Table B.13   *Cookies* Collection Properties

Property	Description
HasKeys	Returns if the cookie contains keys.

The *Form* Collection   The Form collection helps to extract data from information submitted via the HTTP Post method. The Forms collection requires the following syntax:

```
Request.Form(parameter)[(index)¦.Count]
```

where *parameter* is the name of the Form collection, *index* is the specific form element, and *Count* identifies the number of elements that exist on a form.

For example, the following creates an ASP variable name vUserName by extracting values entered in HTML forms fields named txtUserFirstName and txtUserLastName:

```
<%
vUserName = Request.Form("txtUserFirstName") & " " &
Request.Form("txtUserLastName")
%>
```

The *QueryString* Collection   The QueryString collection is used by the Request object to extract variables from the HTTP query string. The query string is textual content that occurs after the question mark character (?) in the URL string:

```
Request.QueryString(variable)[(index)¦.Count]
```

where Request is the Request object, *variable* is the name of the variable name in the query string, *index* is the element index, and *Count* specifies the number of variables in the query string.

For example, to populate an ASP variable named myDBDrilldown from a QueryString variable named myDatabaseStr, use the following syntax:

```
<% myDBDrillDown = Request.QueryString("myDatabaseStr ") %>
```

If the URL http:/ASPapp/loadDB.asp?myDatabaseStr=AcctNumber was submitted to the server, the text AcctNumber would be assigned to the ASP variable.

The *ServerVariables* Collection   The ServerVariables collection is used to obtain server environmental variables. To use these features, the ServerVariables collection requires the following syntax:

```
Request.ServerVariables (ServerVariable)
```

where *ServerVariable* is the name of the server variable. Table B.14 displays a list of common server variables.

Table B.14   The Server Variables

Variable Name	Description
*ALL_HTTP	Displays all HTTP headers sent by the client.
*ALL_RAW	Retrieves all headers as they are sent by the client.
*APPL_MD_PATH	Retrieves the metabase path for the ISAPI DLL.
*APPL_PHYSICAL_PATH	Retrieves the physical path corresponding to the Metabase.
AUTH_TYPE	Displays the authentication method used by the server.
*AUTH_USER	Retrieves the authenticated user name in Raw format.
AUTH_PASSWORD	Displays the value entered in the client's authentication dialog using BASIC authentication security.
*CERT_COOKIE	Returns the unique ID for client certificate.

Variable Name	Description
*CERT_FLAGS	Displays whether the client certificate is valid.
*CERT_ISSUER	Displays Issuer field of the client certificate.
CERT_KEYSIZE	Returns the number of bits in Secure Sockets Layer connection key size.
*CERT_SERIALNUMBER	Displays the client certificate Serial number field.
*CERT_SERVER_ISSUER	Displays the server certificate Issuer field.
*CERT_SERVER_SUBJECT	Displays the server certificate Subject field.
*CERT_SUBJECT	Displays the client certificate Subject field.
CONTENT_LENGTH	Returns the length of the content.
CONTENT_TYPE	Returns the data type of the content.
GATEWAY_INTERFACE	Returns the version of the CGI specifications used on the server.
HTTP_<HeaderName>	Returns the information in the *HeaderName*.
*HTTPS	Returns whether or not the request came in through secure channel (SSL).
*HTTPS_KEYSIZE	Returns the number of bits in Secure Sockets Layer connection key size.
*HTTPS_SECRETKEYSIZE	Returns the number of bits in server certificate private key.
*HTTPS_SERVER_ISSUER	Returns the server certificate Issuer field.
*HTTPS_SERVER_SUBJECT	Displays the server certificate Subject field.
*INSTANCE_ID	Returns the ID for the IIS instance.
*INSTANCE_META_PATH	Returns the metabase path for the instance of IIS that responds to the request.
LOGON_USER	Displays the NT login account the request is made from.
PATH_INFO	Displays the server path information.
PATH_TRANSLATED	Returns the translated version of the PATH_INFO.
QUERY_STRING	Returns the query string in the URL.
REMOTE_ADDR	Displays the IP address of the requesting machine.
REMOTE_HOST	Displays the name of the requesting host.
REQUEST_METHOD	Returns the method that initiated the request.
SCRIPT_NAME	Displays the virtual path to the executing script.

App

B

continues

Table B.14   Continued

Variable Name	Description
SERVER_NAME	Returns the server's host name, DNS alias, or IP address.
SERVER_PORT	Returns the server port number the request is made on.
SERVER_PORT_SECURE	Returns a 1 if request is made on a secure port, 0 if unsecured.
SERVER_PROTOCOL	Returns the name and version of the requesting protocol.
SERVER_SOFTWARE	Returns the name and version of HTTP server.
URL	Returns the base portion of the URL.

*Where * indicates the new IIS 4.0 Server variables.*

The *Request* Properties and Methods

The Request object has one property and one method. The TotalBytes property dictates the total amount of bytes sent in the request. The BinaryRead method is used to accept and store data sent from a browser.

The *TotalBytes* Property   The TotalBytes property is used to return the number of bytes sent by the client and requires the following syntax:

```
Request.TotalBytes
```

The *BinaryRead* Method   The BinaryRead method is used to read binary information that is sent to the server from a POST request. To use the BinaryRead method, use the following syntax:

```
myBinArray = Request.BinaryRead(count)
```

where *count* is the number of bytes to place into an array named myBinArray.

Managing the *Session* Object

The Session object is responsible for managing information for a specific user session. These variables are not accessible by other user sessions, but they can be passed from page to page within the ASP application. The Session object is created when a new user enters an application. The termination of the application or the application's timeout threshold destroys the Session object for the user.

The *Session* Object: A Cookie-Dependent System

The Session object is based on using cookies to store and transfer a unique user ID between the browser client and the Web server. This session ID is used to create and reference Server objects specific to a particular user. If cookies are not permitted on the client browser (because of firewall issues, browser incompatibility, or desktop/network security concerns), the Session object is rendered useless. If cookies are not permitted, ASP applications can still be developed and deployed. However, most of the state tracking will have to be done through more cumbersome methods, such as using HTML hidden fields and passing information via the URL.

When a user enters the application, the server first checks to see whether the requesting user has a valid SessionID. If the SessionID is found in the HTTP header, the user is identified as an active user and is able to continue in the application. If no SessionID is found in the header, the server generates an identifier and sends it to the browser's cookie. This identifier is needed to create a unique Session object that represents the specific user session. The purpose of the identifier is to generate an exclusive identification to tie the actions of the browser client to corresponding objects on the Web server. Each time a browser request is made, this unique token is passed to identify the appropriate request.

> **CAUTION**
>
> Session objects are only supported on Web browsers that support cookies.

In a cookie-compliant browser world, the Session object greatly helps manage the user in the application. However, when dealing with a non-secure cookie-compliant browser, it is not possible to safely track user information via the Session object. Typically, this is of importance where client impersonation might occur. The counterfeiting of a user can occur in two situations. The first is if the session ID is captured while the data is in transit between the client and server. The second possible security violation occurs when the cookie file itself is copied from the user machine to another machine. With two valid session cookies, the user is able to temporary clone himself onto another machine.

Implementing *Session* Variables and Properties

The Session object is responsible for managing user information. The user can create and manipulate the Session object's methods and properties using the following syntax:

```
Session.property¦method
```

where Session is the Session object. The Session object has four properties, as listed in Table B.15.

Table B.15   The *Session* Object's Properties

Property	Description
SessionID	Returns the unique user session identifier.
TimeOut	Returns or sets the user timeout value in minutes.
CodePage	Sets the language attribute for the deployed pages.
LCID	Sets the local identifier used to set local date, currency, and time formats.

Declaring Session Variables

To create or reference a session variable, use the Session object and the name of the variable using the following syntax:

```
ObjectLevel(varName)
```

where *ObjectLevel* is the Session object and *varName* is the name of the variable.

Notice that you do not have to use the Dim, Redim, Public, Private, or Const declared statements that are found in VBScript to create variables.

Because the session variables are only available to the specific user session, no Lock and UnLock methods are needed to prevent simultaneous updates to the same variable. However, great care should be taken to ensure the correct spelling of session- and application-level variables. If a session or application variable is misspelled, a new variable with that misspelling is created.

The *SessionID* Property   The Session object uses the SessionID to keep track of user information from page to page within the ASP application. The server generates the SessionID when a new session is started. The SessionID is available using the following syntax:

```
Session.SessionID
```

The *TimeOut* Property   The TimeOut property sets or returns the amount of time, in minutes, that the Session object can remain inactive before the user's Session object is destroyed. To set the TimeOut property, use the following syntax:

```
Session.Timeout [ = nMinutes]
```

where Session is the Session object and *nMinutes* is the timeout value specified in minutes.

The *LCID* Property   The LCID property is used to set the local identifier properties for an ASP. The local identifier is used to control the display formatting that is specific to a localized location or region. The LCID property requires the following syntax:

```
Session.LCID(=LCIDcode)
```

where *LCIDcode* is the valid local identifier. The LCID is standard abbreviation that identifies localized formatting issues such as time, date, and currency formats.

The *CodePage* Property The CodePage property of the Session object is used to assign the system code page for an ASP. To implement this feature, use the following syntax:

```
Session.CodePage = CodePage
```

where *CodePage* is valid code page for the scripting engine.

Trapping Session Events

The Session object uses two events, shown in Table B.16, to help monitor when a user enters and exits the ASP application. A new Session object is created by the Active Server to represent when a new user has entered the ASP application. Once the Session object is started, information pertaining to that user's session can be stored on the Web server.

Table B.16   The *Session* Object's Events

Event	Description
Session_OnStart	Triggered when a new user enters ASP application.
Session_OnEnd	Initiated when the ASP Session Object is terminated.

The *Session_OnStart* Event To trap the start of the Session object, you must use the GLOBAL.ASA file. The Session_OnStart event requires a layout similar to the following GLOBAL.ASA syntax:

```
<SCRIPT LANGUAGE = ScriptLanguage RUNAT=Server>

Sub Session_OnStart
                    '=== The Code to be executed when a new user enters the
➥app
End Sub

Session_OnStart        '=== Calls the procedure Session_OnStart

</SCRIPT>
```

Session events can reference any other ASP object in the OnStart and OnEnd events.

The *Session_OnEnd* Event The Session_OnEnd event, which is located in the optional GLOBAL.ASA file, is triggered when the current Session objects are closed. The Session_OnEnd event requires the following syntax:

```
<SCRIPT LANGUAGE=ScriptLanguage RUNAT=Server>

Sub Session_OnEnd
    '=== Closing code here
End Sub

</SCRIPT>
```

where *ScriptLanguage* is any script-compliant language. The Session_OnEnd event is triggered when the Session object is abandoned or times out. During this pre-shutdown of the Session object, all interaction with the client browser is prohibited while the existing requests in the queue are processed.

Any ASP code requests to the Response or Request objects in the Session_OnEnd event will generate an error. References to all objects internal to the Web server, such as the Server, Application, or Session objects, are still valid. However, reference to the Server.MapPath method will cause a type mismatch error to occur. Table B.17 illustrates the valid object calls for the Session_OnEnd event.

Table B.17   *Session_OnEnd* Object Calls

Valid Objects	Invalid Object Calls
Server	Request
Session	Response
Application	

Controlling User Session Resources

The Abandon method is used to destroy and release the resources consumed by inactive Session objects. The termination of the Session object is called using the following syntax:

Session.Abandon

where Session is the current Session object. In most situations, the Abandon method will be executed implicitly when the Session.Timeout value has passed.

The Session.Abandon method has some special scoping characteristics that are important to remember. First, when the Session.Abandon method is called, the Web server continues to process the remaining ASP code on the page. This is unlike the Server.TimeOut event and the Response.Redirect method, where code execution on that page is instantly terminated.

The second scoping issue of the Session object is that all object properties that were created before the Session.Abandon method will be unavailable after the Abandon method is called. The Abandon method destroys the properties of the Session object without destroying the Session object itself.

Third, because the Session object is not yet destroyed, the Session object can be used to store user properties. Only after the page has completely finished processing is the current Session object placed in the queue for destruction.

Using Session-Level Objects

Session-level objects can be categorized into two classes based on how the item is declared, as shown in Table B.18. Objects can be declared with or without the <OBJECT> tag. If the session-level object is declared as an object using the <OBJECT> tag, the object is managed by the StaticObject collection. If the object is not declared using the <OBJECT> tag, the session-level item is managed by the Contents collection.

Table B.18 The *Session* Collection

Name	Description
Contents	Contains all session-level items that have not been created with the <OBJECT> tag.
StaticObject	Contains all session-level objects declared with the <OBJECT> tag.

The *Contents* Collection   The Contents collection is used to contain all items that have been created during a session that have not been declared with the <OBJECT> tag. The Contents collection requires the following syntax:

```
Session.Contents(Key)
```

where *Key* is the name of the property to retrieve.

The *StaticObject* Collection   The StaticObject collection is similar to the Contents collection, but StaticObject is used to manage all session-level objects that have been declared with the <OBJECT> tag. The StaticObject collection uses the following syntax:

```
Session.StaticObjects(Key)
```

where *Key* is the property to retrieve. StaticCollection can also be used to reference a single session variable or multiple session variables.

ADO Reference

This reference summarizes the various objects and collections of ActiveX Data Objects. Along with these collections and objects, this reference also lists the various properties and methods of these objects and collections. ■

Connection Object

The `Connection` object represents a connection to an OLE DB datasource.

Properties

Attributes

Used to set when and if to start a new transaction after a `RollbackTrans` or `CommitTrans` is called. It can be set to either of the following `XactAttributeEnum` values, or the sum of both:

adXactCommitRetaining	Starts a new transaction after a `CommitTrans` is called.
AdXactAbortRetaining	Starts a new transaction after a `RollbackTrans` is called.

CommandTimeout

Specifies how long to wait in seconds for a command to execute before giving up and returning an error. The default is 30. When set to 0, the wait is infinite.

ConnectionString

A string that contains the information necessary to connect to the datasource. This string is made up of up to five optional name-value pairs, or a single datasource name (DSN). All other name-value pairs are passed on directly to the provider.

Provider	The name of the provider to use for the connection.
DSN	The name of the ODBC datasource name to connect to.
User	The username to connect with.
Password	The password to log into the datasource with.
File	The name of a file that contains connection-specific information.

ConnectionTimeout

Specifies how long to wait in seconds when trying to establish a connection before giving up and returning an error. The default is 15. When set to 0, the wait is infinite.

DefaultDatabase

Specifies the default database for the connection. This is used when there are multiple databases for a provider. When you set this value, SQL statements will not have to specify a database.

IsolationLevel

Specifies the level of isolation to apply to transactions in the connection. Can be set to any of the following `IsolationLevelEnum` values:

adXactUnspecified	This value is returned when ADO can't determine the `IsolationLevel` present in the provider.
adXactChaos	Specifies that transactions can't overwrite pending values of more isolated transactions.

adXactBrowse	Specifies that transactions can view uncommitted changes in other transactions.
adXactReadUncommitted	This value is the same as adXactBrowse.
adXactCursorStability	The default value. Specifies that changes in other transactions are readable only after they have been committed.
adXactReadCommitted	This value is the same as adXactCursorStability.
adXactRepeatableRead	Specifies that changes from other transactions are not viewable until after commits. However, re-querying will result in new recordsets.
adXactIsolated	Indicates that all transactions are isolated from each other.
adXactSerializable	This value is the same as adXactIsolated.

Mode

This property sets the permissions for changing, deleting, and adding data through the connection. It can be any of the following ConnectModeEnum values.

adModeUnknown	Indicates that the permissions cannot be determined.
adModeRead	Indicates read-only permissions.
AdModeWrite	Indicates write-only permissions.
AdModeReadWrite	Indicates read and write permissions.
AdModeShareDenyRead	Prevents others from opening the connection with read permissions.
AdModeShareDenyWrite	Prevents others from opening the connection with write permissions.
AdModeShareExclusive	Prevents others from opening the connection with read and write permissions.

Provider

This property indicates the OLE DB provider to use for the connection. The default is MSDASQL, which is the ODBC provider for OLE DB.

Version

This property returns the version of ADO in use.

Methods

BeginTrans

Syntax:

```
intTransactionLevel = dataConn.BeginTrans
```

Used to start a new transaction. While the transaction is under way (until `CommitTrans` or `RollBackTrans` is called), no changes can be written to the database. This method returns an integer that indicates the transaction's level, if the provider supports nested transactions.

Close

Syntax:

`dataConn.Close`

Closes the open connection, and releases all resources associated with the connection. This method also closes any recordsets of the connection.

CommitTrans

Syntax:

`dataConn.CommitTrans`

Commits the transaction's changes to the database.

Execute

Syntax:

`Set rs = dataConn.Execute(CommandText, RecordsAffected, Options)`

Executes a SQL statement, query, or stored procedure. This method returns a recordset. It can be sent the following optional parameters:

CommandText	A string that is the name of the query, stored procedure, or SQL statement to execute.
RecordsAffected	An integer that represents the number of records affected by the operation.
Options	Specifies what the `CommandText` parameter is. This value is a `CommandTypeEnum`.

Open

Syntax:

`dataConn.Open ConnectionString, UserID, Password`

Opens the connection. Can be sent any of the following optional parameters:

ConnectionString	A string containing connection information.
UserID	The username to use when opening the connection.
Password	The password to use when opening the connection.

RollbackTrans

Syntax:

`dataConn.RollbackTrans`

Reverses any changes made during the transaction.

Errors Collection and Object

The `Errors` collection is part of the `Connection` object. The collection is a group of all the error objects generated while connected to the datasource. An `Error` object represents an error.

Properties

Description

A short description of the error generated by either the provider or ADO.

HelpContext

Specifies the Context ID in a Microsoft help file that contains information on the error. Used in connection with the `HelpFile` property.

HelpFile

Specifies the Microsoft help file that contains more information on the error.

NativeError

Returns a provider-specific error code.

Number

Returns a unique identification number for that error.

Source

Specifies the object or application that originally generated the error.

SQLState

Returns the ANSI SQL state error code for the error.

Command Object

This object is used to create and store a specific command to be executed on the datasource.

Properties

ActiveConnection

Specifies the connection object to use for the `Command` object. This also can be a valid connection string, in which case a connection object is created implicity.

CommandText

A string that is the command to be executed against the provider. This can be a SQL statement, table name, or the name of a stored procedure.

CommandTimeout

Specifies how long to wait in seconds for the command to execute before timing out and generating an error. The default is 30. If set to 0, the wait is infinite.

CommandType

Specifies the type of command that is contained in the CommandText property. Can be any of the following CommandTypeEnum values:

adCmdText	Indicates a SQL statement.
adCmdTable	Indicates a table name.
adStoredProc	Indicates a stored procedure.
adCmdUnknown	Indicates that CommandText has an unknown type.

Prepared

Specifies whether ADO should create a compiled version of the CommandText before executing it.

Methods

CreateParameter

Syntax:

```
Set paramObj = dataCmd.CreateParameter(Name, [Type, Direction, Size, Value])
```

Used to create a new parameter object for the parameter collection. It can be sent five fields, all of which are optional, except for name. The other values are

Type	Indicates the datatype of the parameter.
Direction	Specifies whether the parameter is an input, output, or both.
Size	Specifies the maximum size in bytes the parameter can be.
Value	The value of the parameter.

Execute

Syntax:

```
Set dataRS = dataCmd.Execute([RecordsAffected, Parameters, Options])
```

Similar to the connection object's Execute method, this method executes the command found in the CommandText property against the data provider. It can be sent the following optional parameters:

RecordsAffected	An integer that returns the number of records affected by the command.
Parameters	An array of parameters to be sent along with the command.

Options   Specifies the type of command found in `CommandText`. See
                           the `CommandType` property for specifics of values.

Parameters Collection and Objects

The `Parameters` collection is a set of `Parameter` objects. `Parameter` objects represent parameters to be sent to a data provider for parameterized queries.

Properties

Attributes

Specifies what type of data the parameter accepts. Can be any combination of the following `ParameterAttributesEnums`:

adParamSigned	Specifies whether the parameter accepts signed values.
adParamNullable	Specifies whether the parameter accepts null values.
adParamLong	Specifies whether the parameter accepts long values.

Direction

Specifies if the parameter is an input, output, or both. Can be any of the following `ParameterDirectionEnum` values:

adParamInput	Input only.
adParamOutput	Output only.
adParamInputOutput	Both input and output.
adParamReturnValue	Return value.

Name

Specifies the name of the parameter.

NumericScale

Indicates the number of decimal places the parameter can contain.

Precision

Specifies the maximum number of digits the parameter can contain.

Size

Specifies the maximum size in bytes the parameter may be.

Type

Specifies the datatype of the parameter.

Value

Specifies the value of the parameter.

Methods

AppendChunk

Syntax:

```
paramObj.AppendChunk Data
```

This method is used to append a chunk of binary data to the parameter.

Append

Syntax:

```
dataCmd.Append ParamObj
```

This method is used to append a new `Parameter` object to the `Parameters` collection of the `Command` object.

Delete

Syntax:

```
dataCmd.Delete Index
```

Used to delete a specific parameter from the `Parameters` collection. `Index` is the index of the parameter object.

Recordset Object

The `Recordset` object is the set of all records returned from an executed command.

Properties

AbsolutePage

Specifies which page to move the current record pointer to.

AbsolutePosition

Specifies which record to move the current record pointer to.

ActiveConnection

Specifies which connection object the recordset is part of.

BOF

Specifies that the current record pointer is at the beginning of the recordset.

Bookmark

Specifies the bookmark for the record that has been bookmarked.

CacheSize

Specifies the number of records from the recordset that are cached.

CursorType

Specifies the type of cursor to use in the recordset. Can be any of the following `CursorTypeEnum` values:

adOpenForwardOnly	Forward-only, read-only cursor.
adOpenKeyset	Like the dynamic cursor, except that records added by others are inaccessible.
adOpenDynamic	A fully scrollable read-write cursor capable of seeing the changes made by other users.
adOpenStatic	This cursor retrieves a copy of the recordset. Changes made by others are inaccessible.

EditMode

Returns the editing status of the recordset. Can be any of the following `editModeEnum` values:

adEditNone	Indicates no editing is taking place.
adEditInProgress	Indicates a change has been made in the current record, but it hasn't been saved to disk yet.
adEditAdd	Indicates the `AddNew` method is currently taking place.

EOF

Specifies that the current record pointer is past the last record in the recordset.

Filter

Specifies a filter to apply to the recordset. Can be a string of `AND` clauses, an array of bookmarks, or any of the following `FilterGroupEnum` values:

adFilterNone	Removes the current filter.
adFilterPendingRecords	Shows all records that have changed but have not yet been written to disk.
adFilterAffectedRecords	Shows all records affected by the last `Delete`, `CancelBatch`, `UpdateBatch`, or `Resync`.
adFilterFetchedRecords	Shows the records currently in the cache.

LockType

Specifies the type of locking to apply to the recordset when it is open. Can be any of the following `LockTypeEnum` values:

adLockReadOnly	A read-only recordset
adLockPessimistic	Each record is locked as it becomes the current record.

App

C

| adLockOptimistic | Each record is locked only when the Update method is called. |
| adLockBatchOptimistic | A batch of records that are locked only when the BatchUpdate method is called. |

MaxRecords

Specifies the maximum number of records the recordset may contain.

PageCount

Returns the number of pages in the recordset.

PageSize

Specifies the number of records that a single page contains.

RecordCount

Returns the number of records in the recordset.

Source

Specifies the source (SQL statement, stored procedure, or table name) from which the records came.

Status

Returns the status of the recordset.

Methods

AddNew

Syntax:

rs.AddNew Fields, Values

Adds a new record with the values specified.

CancelBatch

Syntax:

rs.CancelBatch recordsAffected

Cancels a batch update. Can return the number of recordsAffected by the cancel.

CancelUpdate

Syntax:

rs.CancelUpdate

Cancels the update.

Clone

Syntax:

```
Set newRS = oldRS.Clone
```

Returns a copy of the original recordset.

Close

Syntax:

```
rs.Close
```

Closes the recordset.

Delete

Syntax:

```
rs.Delete recordsAffected
```

Deletes the current record.

GetRows

Syntax:

```
Set myArray = rs.GetRows(rows, start, fields)
```

Sets an array with a series of records from the recordset.

Move

Syntax:

```
rs.Move NumRecs, start
```

This method moves the current record pointer to the number of records specified.

MoveFirst

Syntax:

```
rs.MoveFirst
```

Moves the current record pointer to the first record within the recordset.

MoveLast

Syntax:

```
rs.MoveLast
```

Moves the current record pointer to the last record in the recordset.

MoveNext

Syntax:

```
rs.MoveNext
```

App

C

Moves the current record pointer to the next record within the recordset.

NextRecordset

Syntax:

```
set newRs = oldrs.NextRecordset(recordsAffected)
```

Moves to the next recordset. This method can also return the *recordsAffected* by the move.

Open

Syntax:

```
rs.Open [Source, ActiveConnection, CursorType, LockType, Options]
```

Opens the recordset. This method can be passed the following optional parameters: Source, ActiveConnection, CursorType, LockType, and Options.

Requery

Syntax:

```
rs.Requery
```

Requires the database and updates the recordset.

Resync

Syntax:

```
rs.Resync recordsAffected
```

Refreshes the recordset by re-syncing it with the database. This method can be passed a recordsAffected parameter that will return the number of records affected by this method.

Supports

Syntax:

```
set bool = rs.Supports(cursorOption)
```

Used to determine what functionality the recordset supports. This method is passed a variable cursorOption that is the option you wish to see if the provider supports it.

Update

Syntax:

```
rs.Update Fields, Values
```

Used to update the current record with the values specified for the fields specified.

UpdateBatch

Syntax:

```
rs.UpdateBatch recordsAffected
```

Used to write a batch update to disk. Can return the number of recordsAffected.

Fields Collection and Objects

A field is a specific column of data in a recordset. The `Fields` collection is the set of all field objects in the recordset.

Properties

ActualSize

Returns the actual length of the field's value.

Attributes

Specifies the attributes of the field.

DefinedSize

Returns the defined size for the field.

Name

Returns the field's name.

NumericScale

Specifies the number of decimal points the field may contain.

OriginalValue

Returns the original value of the field's value before it was updated.

Precision

Returns the number of digits the field's value may contain.

Type

Returns the datatype of the field.

UnderlyingValue

Returns the value of the field in the database.

Value

Specifies the value of the field.

Methods

AppendChunk

Syntax:

`field.AppendChunk data`

Used to append a chunk of binary data to the field's value.

App

C

GetChunk

Syntax:

`field.GetChunk(NumberOfBytes)`

Used to retrieve a chunk of binary data from the field.

Active Server
Component Reference

Ad Rotator Component

Syntax:

```
Set ad = Server.CreateObject("MSWC.AdRotator")
```

The Ad Rotator component is used to rotate advertisements on a page.

Properties

Border

Syntax:

```
ad.Border(size)
```

Specifies the border size of the ad.

Clickable

Syntax:

```
ad.Clickable(bool)
```

Specifies whether the ad is clickable.

TargetFrame

Syntax:

```
ad.TargetFrame(frame)
```

Specifies the target frame for the ad link to be loaded in.

Methods

GetAdvertisement

Syntax:

```
ad.GetAdvertisement(pathAndFile)
```

This method retrieves the ad to be displayed from the list of ads in the file specified.

Files

Redirection File

This is a file the developer creates to capture which ads are being clicked, and then redirect to the appropriate link.

Rotator Schedule File

Syntax:

```
Redirect URL
Width     intWidth
Height intHeight
```

```
Border intBorder
*
adImageURL
adHomePageURL
Text
impressions
```

This file is used to set the properties of the various ads to be displayed. It has two sections: The first section contains properties that pertain to all ads; the second section contains ad-specific information.

Browser Capabilities Component

Syntax:

```
Set Browser = Server.CreateObject("MSWC.BrowserType")
```

This component is used to test whether the Web surfer's browser supports certain functionality. The following are some of the possible properties that can be tested for:

- ActiveX controls
- Beta
- Browser
- Cookies
- Frames
- JavaScript
- Tables
- VBScript
- VBScript version

Each of these can become properties of this object. To see if the browser supports JavaScript, you simply ask for that property's value.

Files

BROWSCAP.INI

This file contains information on browsers. It is used to determine their capabilities.

Syntax:

```
; comments
HTTPUserAgentHeader
parent = browserDefinition
propertyX = valueX
```

Comments are any line that begins with a semi-colon (;). *HTTPUserAgentHeader* is the header for any specific browser, and it is used to identify the browser. *BrowserDefinition* is used to specify a parent browser that will inherit its functionality. For each *property* there is a corresponding *value* (such as JavaScript = False.)

App
D

Content Linking Component

Syntax:

```
Set NextURL = Server.CreateObject("MSWC.NextURL")
```

This component is used to link URLs together in a like pages in a book or magazine.

Methods

GetListCount

Syntax:

```
NextURL.GetListCount(listFile)
```

Returns a count of all the URLs in the *listFile*.

GetNextURL

Syntax:

```
NextURL.GetNextURL(listFile)
```

Returns the next URL in the list in the *listFile*.

GetPreviousDescription

Syntax:

```
NextURL.GetPreviousDescription(listFile)
```

Returns a description of the previous URL in the *listFile*.

GetListIndex

Syntax:

```
NextURL.GetListIndex(listFile)
```

Returns the indexed position of the current page as found in the *listFile*.

GetNthDescription

Syntax:

```
NextURL.GetNthDescription(listFile, index)
```

Returns the description of the URL in the *listFile* at the position specified with the *index* variable.

GetPreviousURL

Syntax:

```
NextURL.GerPreviousURL(listFile)
```

Returns the previous URL in the *listFile*.

...in http:// or \\), and the

App
D

...m and TextStream.

```
Set filesys = CreateObject( ...)
```

This object is used to gain access to the file system. It can access existing files and create new ones.

Properties

Drives

Lists the drives on the local system available to the object. You can iterate through this property with the For...Each...Next construct.

Methods

CreateTextFile

Syntax:

```
filesys.CreateTextFile(filename, [overwrite, unicode])
```

This method is used to create a file. It is passed one required parameter, *filename*, and two optional parameters: overwrite, which is a bool value on whether to overwrite an existing file if it exists, and unicode, another bool, which, if True, writes the files as unicode.

OpenTextFile

Syntax:

```
filesys.OpenTextFile (filename, [iomode, create, format])
```

This method is used to open a file. It returns a TextStream object. It requires the *filename* parameter, which indicates which file to open. Optional parameters are iomode, which specifies whether the file is being opened ForReading or ForAppending; create, which is bool that indicates whether or not to create the file if it doesn't exist; and *format*, which indicates whether to open the file as unicode, or ascii, or use the system default.

TextStream

Syntax:

```
texts = filesys.CreateTextFile("c:\somefile.txt", True)
```

TextStream is the object used to actually write and read from a file.

Properties

AtEndOfLine

This property returns a value of True if the file pointer is at the end of a line.

AtEndOfStream

This property returns True if the file pointer is at the end of the file.

Column

This property returns the column that the file pointer is currently on.

Line

This property returns the current line that the file pointer is on.

Methods

Close

Syntax:

```
Texts.Close
```

This method closes the file.

Read

Syntax:

```
Texts.Read(intNumChars)
```

This method reads in the number of characters specified in *intNumChars* from the current file pointer.

ReadAll

Syntax:

`Texts.ReadAll`

This method reads in the entire file and returns it as a string.

ReadLine

Syntax:

`texts.RealLine`

This method reads in the entire line and returns it as a string.

Skip

Syntax:

`texts.Skip(intNumChars)`

This method moves the current file pointer forward the number of characters specified in the *intNumChars* variable.

SkipLine

Syntax:

`texts.SkipLine`

This method moves the current file pointer to the next line in the file.

Write

Syntax:

`texts.Write(string)`

This method writes out the *string* to the file at the position of the current file pointer.

WriteLine

Syntax:

`texts.WriteLine(string)`

This method writes out the *string* with a newline character added at the end. If *string* is omitted, the newline character is written out alone.

WriteBlankLines

Syntax:

`texts.WriteBlankLine(intNumLines)`

This method writes out the number of blank lines specified in the intNumLines parameter.

App

D

Index

Complete and Return this Card for a *FREE* Computer Book Catalog

Thank you for purchasing this book! You have purchased a superior computer book written expressly for your needs. To continue to provide the kind of up-to-date, pertinent coverage you've come to expect from us, we need to hear from you. Please take a minute to complete and return this self-addressed, postage-paid form. In return, we'll send you a free catalog of all our computer books on topics ranging from word processing to programming and the internet.

Mr. ☐   Mrs. ☐   Ms. ☐   Dr. ☐

Name (first) ☐☐☐☐☐☐☐☐☐☐   (M.I.) ☐   (last) ☐☐☐☐☐☐☐☐☐☐☐☐☐☐☐☐☐☐

Address ☐☐☐☐☐☐☐☐☐☐☐☐☐☐☐☐☐☐☐☐☐☐☐☐☐☐☐☐☐☐☐☐☐

☐☐☐☐☐☐☐☐☐☐☐☐☐☐☐☐☐☐☐☐☐☐☐☐☐☐☐☐☐☐☐☐☐

City ☐☐☐☐☐☐☐☐☐☐☐☐☐☐☐   State ☐☐   Zip ☐☐☐☐☐   ☐☐☐☐

Phone ☐☐☐ ☐☐☐ ☐☐☐☐   Fax ☐☐☐ ☐☐☐ ☐☐☐☐

Company Name ☐☐☐☐☐☐☐☐☐☐☐☐☐☐☐☐☐☐☐☐☐☐☐☐☐☐☐☐☐☐

E-mail address ☐☐☐☐☐☐☐☐☐☐☐☐☐☐☐☐☐☐☐☐☐☐☐☐☐☐☐☐☐☐

1. Please check at least (3) influencing factors for purchasing this book.

Front or back cover information on book .... ☐
Special approach to the content .... ☐
Completeness of content .... ☐
Author's reputation .... ☐
Publisher's reputation .... ☐
Book cover design or layout .... ☐
Index or table of contents of book .... ☐
Price of book .... ☐
Special effects, graphics, illustrations .... ☐
Other (Please specify): _____ ☐

2. How did you first learn about this book?

Saw in Macmillan Computer Publishing catalog .... ☐
Recommended by store personnel .... ☐
Saw the book on bookshelf at store .... ☐
Recommended by a friend .... ☐
Received advertisement in the mail .... ☐
Saw an advertisement in: _____ ☐
Read book review in: _____ ☐
Other (Please specify): _____ ☐

3. How many computer books have you purchased in the last six months?

This book only .... ☐   3 to 5 books .... ☐
2 books .... ☐   More than 5 .... ☐

4. Where did you purchase this book?

Bookstore .... ☐
Computer Store .... ☐
Consumer Electronics Store .... ☐
Department Store .... ☐
Office Club .... ☐
Warehouse Club .... ☐
Mail Order .... ☐
Direct from Publisher .... ☐
Internet site .... ☐
Other (Please specify): _____ ☐

5. How long have you been using a computer?

☐ Less than 6 months   ☐ 6 months to a year
☐ 1 to 3 years   ☐ More than 3 years

6. What is your level of experience with personal computers and with the subject of this book?

	With PCs	With subject of book
New	☐	☐
Casual	☐	☐
Accomplished	☐	☐
Expert	☐	☐

Source Code ISBN: 0-0000-0000-0

7. Which of the following best describes your job title?

Administrative Assistant .... ☐
Coordinator .... ☐
Manager/Supervisor .... ☐
Director .... ☐
Vice President .... ☐
President/CEO/COO .... ☐
Lawyer/Doctor/Medical Professional .... ☐
Teacher/Educator/Trainer .... ☐
Engineer/Technician .... ☐
Consultant .... ☐
Not employed/Student/Retired .... ☐
Other (Please specify): _____ ☐

8. Which of the following best describes the area of the company your job title falls under?

Accounting .... ☐
Engineering .... ☐
Manufacturing .... ☐
Operations .... ☐
Marketing .... ☐
Sales .... ☐
Other (Please specify): _____ ☐

9. What is your age?

Under 20 .... ☐
21-29 .... ☐
30-39 .... ☐
40-49 .... ☐
50-59 .... ☐
60-over .... ☐

10. Are you:

Male .... ☐
Female .... ☐

11. Which computer publications do you read regularly? (Please list)

_____
_____
_____
_____
_____
_____
_____
_____
_____
_____

Comments: _____
_____
_____

Fold here and scotch-tape to mail.

Check out Que® Books on the World Wide Web
http://www.quecorp.com

As the biggest software release in computer history, Windows 95 continues to redefine the computer industry. Click here for the latest info on our Windows 95 books

Examine the latest releases in word processing, spreadsheets, operating systems, and suites

Find out about new additions to our site, new bestsellers and hot topics

Make computing quick and easy with these products designed exclusively for new and casual users

The Internet, The World Wide Web, CompuServe®, America Online®, Prodigy® —it's a world of ever-changing information. Don't get left behind!

In-depth information on high-end topics: find the best reference books for databases, programming, networking, and client/server technologies

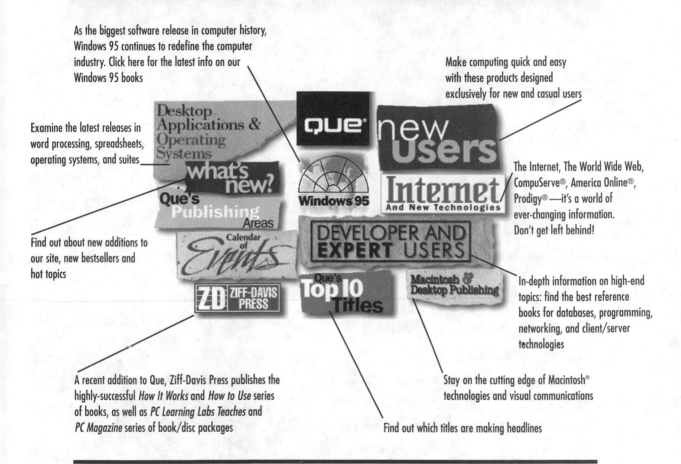

A recent addition to Que, Ziff-Davis Press publishes the highly-successful *How It Works* and *How to Use* series of books, as well as *PC Learning Labs Teaches* and *PC Magazine* series of book/disc packages

Find out which titles are making headlines

Stay on the cutting edge of Macintosh® technologies and visual communications

With 6 separate publishing groups, Que develops products for many specific market segments and areas of computer technology. Explore our Web Site and you'll find information on best-selling titles, newly published titles, upcoming products, authors, and much more.

- Stay informed on the latest industry trends and products available
- Visit our online bookstore for the latest information and editions
- Download software from Que's library of the best shareware and freeware